MAZARIN

MAZARIN

The Crisis of Absolutism in France

Geoffrey Treasure

London and New York

First published 1995
by Routledge
11 New Fetter Lane, London EC4P 4EE

Simultaneously published in the USA and Canada
by Routledge
29 West 35th Street, New York, NY 10001

Phototypeset in Baskerville by
Intype, London

Printed and Bound in Great Britain by
TJ Press (Padstow) Ltd, Padstow, Cornwall

British Library Cataloguing in Publication Data

A catalogue record for this book is available from the British Library

Library of Congress Cataloguing in Publication Data

A catalogue record for this book has been requested

ISBN 0–415–014573

To Magdalen

CONTENTS

CONTENTS

CONTENTS

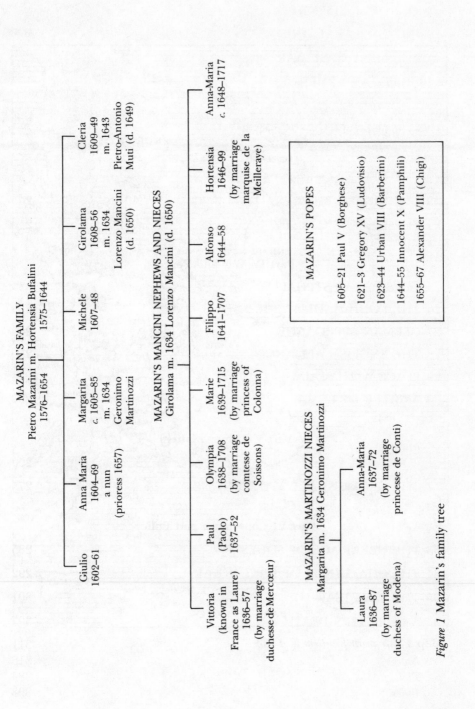

MAZARIN'S FAMILY
Pietro Mazarini m. Hortensia Bufalini
1576–1654   1575–1644

Giulio 1602–61	Anna Maria 1604–69 a nun (prioress 1657)	Margarita c. 1605–85 m. 1634 Geronimo Martinozzi	Michele 1607–48	Girolama 1608–56 m. 1634 Lorenzo Mancini (d. 1650)	Cleria 1609–49 m. 1643 Pietro-Antonio Muti (d. 1649)

MAZARIN'S MANCINI NEPHEWS AND NIECES
Girolama m. 1634 Lorenzo Mancini (d. 1650)

Vittoria (known in France as Laure) 1636–57 (by marriage duchesse de Mercœur)

Paul (Paolo) 1637–52

Olympia 1638–1708 (by marriage comtesse de Soissons)

Marie 1639–1715 (by marriage princess of Colonna)

Filippo 1641–1707

Alfonso 1644–58

Hortensia 1646–99 (by marriage marquise de la Meilleraye)

Anna-Maria c. 1648–1717

MAZARIN'S MARTINOZZI NIECES
Margarita m. 1634 Geronimo Martinozzi

Laura 1636–87 (by marriage duchess of Modena)

Anna-Maria 1637–72 (by marriage princesse de Conti)

MAZARIN'S POPES

1605–21 Paul V (Borghese)
1621–3 Gregory XV (Ludovisio)
1623–44 Urban VIII (Barberini)
1644–55 Innocent X (Pamphili)
1655–67 Alexander VIII (Chigi)

Figure 1 Mazarin's family tree

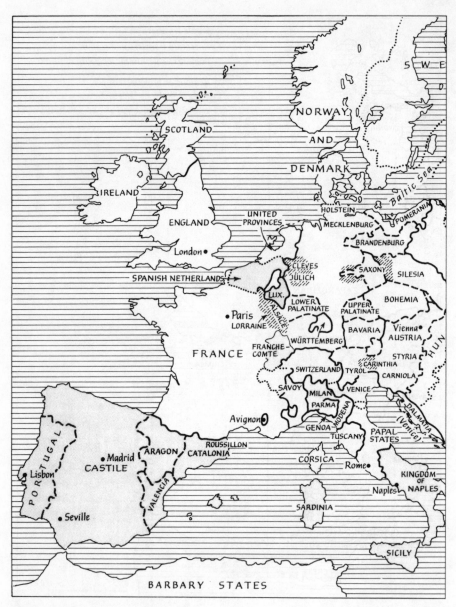

Map 1 *European frontiers in 1640*

DEN

ESTONIA

INGRIA

LIVONIA

E. PRUSSIA

LITHUANIA

POLAND

GARY

SLAVONIA

BOSNIA

SERBIA

ALBANIA

Ragusa

Stable frontiers
Uncertain frontiers and regions of conflict
Boundaries within larger political units
Regions of broken frontiers and 'islands' of territory
Spanish possessions

Moscow •

RUSSIA

KALMUKS

DON COSSACKS

ZAPAROZHIAN COSSACKS

JEDISAN

MOLDAVIA

TRANSYLVANIA

WALLACHIA

KHANATE OF THE CRIMEA

Black Sea

ARMENIA

Caspian Sea

BULGARIA

Constantinople

OTTOMAN

EMPIRE

TREBIZOND

KURDISTAN

ANATOLIA

MOREA

CYPRUS

CRETE

0   400 km

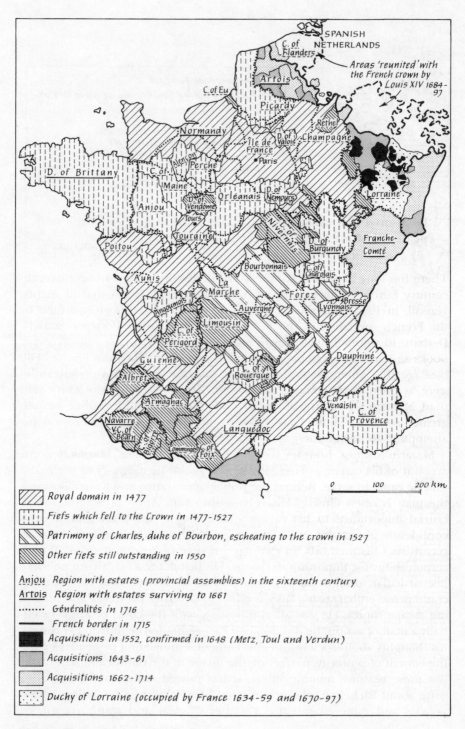

SPANISH
NETHERLANDS

C. of
Flanders

Areas 'reunited' with
the French crown by
Louis XIV 1684-
97

Artois

C. of Eu

Picardy

Rethel

Normandy

D. of
Valois

Île de
France

Champagne

Paris

C. of
Alençon

Perche

D. of
Nemours

Lorraine

D. of Brittany

C. of
Maine

Orléanais

Anjou

D. of
Vendôme
Tours

Franche-
Comté

Touraine

C. of
Nivernais

D. of Burgundy

Poitou

Aunis

Bourbonnais

C. of
Charolais

La
Marche

Forez

Bresse

Angoumois

Auvergne

Lyonnais

Limousin

C. of
Périgord

Dauphiné

Guienne

C. of
Rouergue

Albret

Armagnac

C. of
Venaisin

Navarre
V.C. of
Béarn

C. of
Bigorre

C. of
Provence

Languedoc

Comminges

C. of
Foix

0   100   200 km

/// Royal domain in 1477

||| Fiefs which fell to the Crown in 1477-1527

\\\ Patrimony of Charles, duke of Bourbon, escheating to the crown in 1527

▨ Other fiefs still outstanding in 1550

Anjou Region with estates (provincial assemblies) in the sixteenth century

Artois Region with estates surviving to 1661

...... Généralités in 1716

—— French border in 1715

■ Acquisitions in 1552, confirmed in 1648 (Metz, Toul and Verdun)

▒ Acquisitions 1643-61

░ Acquisitions 1662-1714

∷ Duchy of Lorraine (occupied by France 1634-59 and 1670-97)

Map 2 *The* ancien régime *in France*

PREFACE

'Be assured that, whatever misfortune befalls me, History will only speak well of me, if it wants to tell the truth.'

Cardinal Mazarin

There has long been a striking gap in the historiography of seventeenth-century Europe. The last life of Mazarin in English was that of Arthur Hassall, in 1903. Materials for bridging the gap have been provided by the French specialists in the field, notably M. Laurain-Portemer and G. Dethan, to whom I am specially indebted, and by the wealth of recent books and articles on so many aspects of seventeenth-century France. The message that emerges most clearly is that the difficulties of governing were as great as its rewards were high. No minister showed more skill than Mazarin in coming to terms with those difficulties; none reaped greater rewards. Those facts alone would be sufficient justification for attempting to bridge the gap.

Mazarin cannot however be an easy subject for a biographer. An account of his career as First Minister must also be a history of the realm that he came to serve. Behind the public appearance and formal business the man is often elusive. His relationship with Anne of Austria was of crucial importance to his career – and yet the historian cannot write confidently about the exact nature of that relationship. It is hard to reconstruct his methods, to envisage his style of government, to allocate responsibility for important decisions. His instinct was for 'alcove politics'; his particular strength lay in personal dealings. Where overt commitment could prove embarrassing he was adept at covering his tracks and providing escape routes. He was often travelling, with the court or army. Essentially a man of action, he did not, like Richelieu, devote time to expressing his thoughts about society and government, enunciating principles or, for the benefit of posterity, perfecting the image of the omniscient statesman. For these reasons, among others, it has proved easier for historians to write about Richelieu, about ministers, like Colbert or Le Tellier, whose policies and achievements are a matter of clear and ample record, or

xiii

notable personalities like Retz, who provided the chronicler with ample and self-revelatory material. By the same token, Mazarin has been vulnerable, in historians' assessments, as he was among contemporaries, to attitudes ranging from the patronising to the crudely xenophobic. His reputation has always, of course, tended to suffer by the inevitable comparison with Richelieu, 'the great Cardinal'. The cumulative effect of the *Mazarinades*, the strength of the *dévôt* tradition and the reputation of Fénelon helped to ensure that the 'Machiavellian' aspect which the latter deplored in his *Dialogues des Morts* would become one of the clichés of history.

There can be no doubting Mazarin's importance. He belongs to a very small group of statesmen who have succeeded in their main objectives and affected the course of history. To have followed Richelieu as First Minister and, like him, to have died in office after eighteen years; to have survived the Fronde with all that it brought, in political upheaval and personal onslaughts, was much. To have seen monarchy emerge from the ordeal, stronger in effectiveness and esteem, was more. To have been responsible, through arduous negotiations, for a series of treaties which extended the boundaries of France, provided a degree of security for the future, unprecedented influence for her king, together with the distinct possibility of a great inheritance to come – that was more still. There was good fortune along the way, not least in the declining power of Spain. But there was audacity, subtlety, courage and sheer, sustained toil. It was no accident that the young Louis who, of all men, appreciated what Mazarin had done, was able, after his mentor's death, to assume personal rule, the best trained and most competent of sovereigns. Nor that he had exceptionally capable ministers – Lionne, Le Tellier and Colbert – who had learned their trade in service with the Cardinal.

Mazarin died, as for months he had lived, in great pain, but with a Christian resignation and peace of mind to which many could attest. He regretted that he had had so little time to enjoy his paintings, sculptures, books, the great collections which now largely, in the Institut de France, the Bibliothèque National and the Louvre, belong to France. It is as he would have wished. He had never ceased to be concerned, like a good Italian, for his family and friends. His appetite for the artistic world's most desirable objects had grown with feeding. For all that, the mainspring of his life had come to be his passionate loyalty to the French crown, in the person of Louis XIV. Mazarin's greatness, was to be that of his adopted country.

Writing this book, as in all my work on seventeenth-century France, I have owed so much, in knowledge, understanding and sometimes in inspiration, to the labours of others, that it seems invidious to select a few. But there are special debts: to Joseph Bergin and Orest Ranum who read my manuscript and gave encouragement and helpful criticisms; to my friend Lloyd Moote, whose fine work on the Fronde first directed my thoughts to the study of Mazarin and whose enthusiasm and critical acumen came to my aid at that low point in authorship when one is unsure of the worth of what one has done. I am very grateful to Routledge who have had to wait a long time for my manuscript and there especially to Claire L'Enfant and my editors, Heather McCallum and Catherine Turnbull: indeed what a difference it makes, as in that friendly pile in New Fetter Lane, where efficiency is matched by humour and sympathetic understanding of the travails of authorship. As ever, my wife Melisa has been my constant ally, supporter and skilful first copy-editor, with the keenest eye for mistakes and infelicities of writing.

With thankfulness and pride I dedicate this book to our daughter Magdalen.

Kington, Herefordshire
Candlemas, 1995

Part I

GIULIO MAZARINI, PAPAL DIPLOMAT

'Don't think too much of rest or of remaining still.'
Francesco Barberini

1

THE YOUNG ROMAN

One day in 1915 the peace of the mountains and wooded valleys of the Abruzzi was shattered by an earthquake which killed more than 30,000 people. Among the ancient villages of the worst affected area was Pescina: among the houses reduced to rubble was one that had once belonged to the Bufalini family. There, on Saint Bonaventura's day, 14 July 1602, Hortensia Mazarini, born Bufalini, gave birth to her eldest son. Giulio Mazarini was destined to become an eminent statesman in the service of France and to play a significant part in re-aligning the map of Europe. Again it was 14 July, in 1789, when another kind of earthquake shook Paris as the Bastille fell to a revolutionary mob, demonstrating to the world the collapse of the old absolutist regime. To the early shaping of that regime no one had contributed more than Giulio Mazarini's predecessor, Cardinal Richelieu: to its preservation during the crisis of the Fronde, no one more than Mazarini himself.

The career of the Italian who became First Minister of France does not stand out in bold profile like that of Richelieu. Comparisons with Richelieu have tended to stress the lack, in Mazarini, of those heroic and ruthless traits that made the Frenchman the object of profound respect, tinged often with a certain awe. Mazarini could not have accomplished what he did without the exertions and example of Richelieu. With the opportunities bequeathed by the master in 1642 went, however, grave dangers. When Mazarini died, in 1661, France had been enlarged by two great treaties, her king was loved and generally obeyed: the regime looked secure. Even when allowance has been made for a generous measure of good fortune, it can be argued that Mazarini was as important in his way as the man whom the French have always called 'the great Cardinal' – and no less worthy of study.

Hortensia Mazarini had retreated to the family estate for her first confinement, seeking relief from Rome's torrid summer in the calm and fresh air of the hills. Her family was noble, originally from Umbria. One of her brothers was a Knight of Malta[1] who had written a treatise on duelling: a witness to nobility and to noble concerns. Her godfather was the Constable of Naples, Filipo Colonna,[2] and her marriage had been arranged to reward Pietro Mazarini for services to the Colonna family, one of the oldest and grandest in Italy. It brought her five more children after Giulio, severe suffering in their births and, subsequently, much disquiet and domestic turmoil; there was little harm to her reputation for beauty and goodness, but little happiness either, at least, it seems, until later years and her virtual separation from her husband. She was to live long enough however (till 1644) to hear of Giulio's becoming First Minister of France. His remarkable career, bringing vicarious glory to the *casa*, may have done something latterly to palliate the vexatious experience of a life on the fringe of grandeur, living in a series of houses too big to be adequately maintained.

La casa! recurring constantly through the family correspondence, the word signifies both house and family. Its history, during the years when the favoured son was rising to fame, was one of constant moves: three in one year, 1629, between houses in the fashionable Trevi quarter of the city, in the heart of Papal Rome, where, in 1640, he was to buy his own *palazzo*. The poverty of the Mazarinis was relative, but real enough, in the form of unpaid bills and the chronic dependence on a patron's whims; these are recorded in Pietro's letters and must have figured largely in the conversation of the household. The uneasy life of a nobleman's client, in which there was more of makeshift than of achievement, more of promises than of rewards, would not have been what Pietro would have expected when he came from his native Sicily to take up the post of major-domo to Colonna. It had been secured for him by his brother, Giulio Mazarini, a Jesuit,[3] renowned beyond Italy for his sermons which appeared in a French edition in 1612. He was the first member of the family to have attracted public notice, and he surely eased the path of his namesake. Giulio could perhaps have done more for Pietro if the latter had been more competent. The post was in itself neither demeaning nor undemanding. Having a leading position in the Constable's clientele. Pietro was responsible at different times for the administration of estates and the collection of taxes. He complained however that he was under-valued and under-paid. He was much praised by the Colonnas, he wrote in a letter of 1629, but 'I never see any fruits of this good will'.[4] His grievances can only have sharpened his son's ambition to excel.

As the family grew faster than his means, Pietro came to fix his hopes on Giulio, the prize pupil, popular companion of young nobles, favoured client of grandees and rising star of Papal diplomacy. There is indeed some pathos in the garrulous father's eagerness for his son's fame, besides his share in any pickings that came the young man's way. So opportunistic a view of his son's career is not surprising, for Pietro's difficulties were compounded by the needs of his other children. Besides the younger son Michele[5] there were four daughters for whom husband or convent had to be found. Giulio was apparently a devoted son; he was certainly a good brother. He was required to find various finances – Michele for education with the Dominicans at Bologna, then promotion: the four girls for board and teaching at convents, then for sufficient dowries to make suitable marriages, or, in the case of Anna Maria,[6] her permanent place at the convent of Santa di Campo Marzo in Rome – all depended on Giulio's ability to raise funds and secure an influential patron. With the exception of Anna Maria, unless indeed she wanted to remain in the convent of which she eventually became prioress, they were not disappointed. For several children of the next generation, Giulio's nieces, there was to be a future beyond the dreams of any of his sisters.

An eldest son's duty to maintain the *casa* was complemented by the prompting of Giulio's own ambition and sustained by a robust physique, pleasing looks and a fine instinct for exploiting any favourable opportunity. In one respect, to the discomfiture of historians, he failed lamentably to respond to his father's chiding: 'watch your handwriting'.[7] More significant traits of the mature statesman can also be detected in early Roman days, inspiring affection in those who enjoyed his companionship and zest for life, but a certain wariness perhaps too in those who thought that they might suffer from his ambition, or wondered what lay behind the relaxed and agreeable manner. Of one thing they could be sure: he was clever.

Giulio was taught, from the customary starting age of seven, at the Roman college of the Jesuits, a vast building designed to house nearly two thousand pupils. Already acknowledged leaders of reformed, militant Roman Catholicism, renowned for their schools, favoured instruments of Papal power, strong in discipline but flexible in methods as in theology, the Society of Jesus offered exciting prospects for those wanting to serve Christ, yet remain in the world. Giulio was one of their most talented pupils excelling in the Latin, theology, logic, geometry and rhetoric of their rigorous curriculum. Charmed by 'his fine spirit, capacity and gracious manners' they strove to win him for the Society. Indeed what a Jesuit he would have made!

So much of the character of this age is illuminated by the ideals and style of the Jesuits. They were faithful to the stern precepts and vaulting ambition of their founder, the Basque soldier and visionary Ignatius Loyola.[8] They worked eagerly on the frontiers of missionary enterprise, from the forests of Canada to the court of the Chinese Emperor, courting, sometimes receiving martyrdom for Christ. They did not frown however upon elegant manners nor assume that a wordly style detracted from a spirit of devotion. So Giulio remained *persona grata* to the fathers of the Colegio Romana. He was chosen to play the part of Ignatius in a pageant of 1622 to celebrate the canonisation of the founder and he performed to great acclaim. But his learning and expertise were soon to be put to other uses.

The *galantuomo*[9] moved with assurance in the *palazzi* of wealthier friends, a favourite at their card tables, displaying a talent for friendship that reflected good nature and a willingness to take trouble that went beyond the claims of self-interest. It was surely those qualities that evoked in Giulio's patrons an interest in his career that they would not have shown to a mere toady. It was as well – for he would not have relished the discipline required of Jesuit novices: for such committed souls there were no short-cuts to eminence: but, for a privileged few of those who sought preferment in the hierarchy of the church, there were. This secular-minded young Roman would in future keep his distance from the Jesuits and he would never have a Jesuit confessor; he would become a Cardinal without ever being ordained priest and would serve the church in ways that suited his gifts. Diplomacy would be his *métier.*

Idolised son and brother, clever place-hunter from impoverished *casa*, impressionable but wary pupil of the Jesuits: the clues to Giulio's person-ality are assembling, but they do not reveal enough. The setting is all-important. He was the child of Baroque Rome, in the efflorescence of the style that was making the Holy City a place of such exhilarating beauty. The Baroque[10] has been seen as an essentially theatrical style: to please the masses at a time of growing tension in overcrowded cities, subordinating accepted canons of taste to the search for the spectacular; again, as a mechanism employed by absolutist rulers to condition the masses to accept a hierarchical society; again as the spontaneous product of a society suffering from insecurity and chronic pessimism. The reader may be challenged by such theories; it is unlikely that the young Mazarini would delve far below the surface of the art and architecture that was transforming the face of Rome. Yet the physical setting of life is important: in this case it enables us to envisage the Roman world that could nurture and inspire an ambitious young cleric, and to come to terms with the mentality of such a man.

At its best there is a satisfying balance in Baroque art between the power of the architectural form and the drama that belongs to what was special about the style, the expression of movement in complex patterns and daring artifice. The artist may have aimed at illusion but the message was plain enough. In Carlo Maderna's glorious nave of St Peter's or in the masterpiece of Vignola and Della Porta,[11] their exuberant church of the Gesù, fortunate Romans could not fail to see an optimistic spirit. Behind the startling impact of plastic imagery, the brilliance of colour and the riotous vitality of the whole design, there was an unmistakable strength derived from the artists' confidence in what they were doing to please their patrons. They sought not merely to attract but to astonish the pilgrim; to induce a mood appropriate to the claims of a reformed

Papacy still imperial in aspiration and to express through their art the sense of the Tridentine decrees which had confirmed and defined traditional teaching.[12] The inherent conflict of humanist values and theocentric dogma had been resolved. In the citadel of the church, which saw the burning of the humanist Giordano Bruno and was soon to see the censure of Galilei Galileo,[13] there were clear limits to what man could be allowed to think. In figures of the saints, in sumptuous reliquaries and vaulting *baldacchinos* the artists of the Baroque witnessed to the feats, not of the unfettered individual, *l'uomo universale*, of Renaissance aspiration but of the servant of God, mindful only of His call: for his edification they celebrated the efficacy of prayers for the dead, the mediation of saints, the grace and power of Our Lady, the mystery of transubstantiation and the recurring miracle of the Mass.

The city to which Claude Lorrain and Poussin came from France to perfect their craft was gripped by a frenzy of building. Rome was full of artisans, stucco workers, masons, marblers, modellers. Among them, when Mazarini was studying with the Jesuits, was the young craftsman who had run away with his architect father and taken humble employment as a mason. Francesco Borromini: another was the Neapolitan, Giovanni Bernini.[14] These two artists were rivals in architecture as in career: together they did more than anyone to give to Rome its exalted character as capital of the Baroque. Every quarter had its cupola, St Peter's being only the grandest amongst the cluster of domes that make the distinctive Roman view. The Romans were busy adapting classical Rome to the needs of the new spiritual imperialism. They moved columns and obelisks to suit their grandiose plans; they crowned them with crosses to mark the triumph of the church over old pagan and new humanist alike.

Nor was the activity confined to churches. Ornate *palazzi*, fine streets and squares witnessed to the wealth of patrons for whom the Eternal City was the cynosure of the artistic world. Rome provided both a true perspective and, as presented in some of the devices of its characteristic art, a false one. There was abundant wealth and an incorrigibly extravagant mood with it. There were benefits for all. The beautiful fountains were fed by new aqueducts, providing the most abundant water supply, 180,000 litres a day, of any great city. In some respects though, with its rapidly expanding population, of 50,000 nearly doubled by mid-century, it was a parasitic growth. Leading Romans preferred living on interest from the *monti*, the bills with which the Papacy financed much of its work, to any commercial or manufacturing venture; many of the people were lazy, living off charity; some paupers, some brigands, many poor. Rome had no monopoly of urban squalor, or of the criminality remarked in the stormy life of the low-born Caravaggio,[15] but they were highlighted by the grandeur of its patrician class and the lofty assumptions of those who served the heir of St Peter at the summit. All went to provide the kind of contrast which Caravaggio, master of light and shade, evokes in works like the *Madonna of Loretto*, painted in the Jubilee year of 1600. Two old men, pilgrims, kneel before the Virgin: radiating faith and awe they well represent the ordinary men for whom, as well as for their patrons, the artists worked.

In the city of the seven hills it was still possible, among the thronging pilgrims, to luxuriate in the sense of being at the heart of the civilised world. If, however, it proved that real power lay elsewhere, in the burgeoning courts and chanceries of Madrid, Paris, Vienna, London, now even Amsterdam and Stockholm, was there not, in all this magnificence, an element of pretence? If so it was surely reinforced in Giulio's experience, by his domestic life – his father's clinging to the coat-tails of the mighty, whose *palazzi* of marble and stucco were financed by the rents of a depressed peasantry and the contributions of the faithful. Even in cultural life there was a hint of decadence in the reckless buying, commissioning and entertaining, characteristics of a pampered plutocracy.

2

THE POLITICS OF ROME[1]

The Pope from 1623 to 1644 was Maffeo Barberini, Urban VIII.[1] His elder nephew Francesco enjoyed the largest share of his patronage with the post of vice-chancellor and the control of four abbeys as the basis of a large fortune. Such endowment appeared to flout Tridentine prohibitions of pluralism and nepotism. But Cardinal Francesco Barberini, erudite, a discerning patron of the artists who employed their talents to serve the faith, somewhat given to melancholy, was a hard-working, if maladroit politician of blameless private life. His younger brother, Antonio, by contrast, Cardinal at the age of twenty, another grand pluralist, was, for all his charm and generosity, an embarrassment to his father and brother. Though he would eventually bestir himself to lead the Papal army in an unfortunate war against Parma (1642–4) he was disinclined to serious business. Contemporaries might shrug their shoulders at stories of his infatuation with Leonora Baroni, the celebrated singer. Posterity should not complain that he had a major hand in the building of the *palazzo* Barberini. He fostered the growth of opera and encouraged experiments in production which his client was later to introduce to the French. But the influence which this engaging aesthete could exert on Papal policy, soon to be exploited by Mazarini, who was to find in him a more manageable patron than Francesco, illustrates the critical flaw in the Papacy at this time.

A twentieth-century Pope described the Vatican in words which would not have displeased Urban VIII. 'The Vatican is not only a visible entity. The realisation of an idea, a design, its intention is to unite mankind . . . Over the centuries it has spoken of the everlasting rather than [that] which is fleeting . . . In contrast to the repeated faultiness of human institutions, an indelible rule holds sway here . . .' Mazarini's Roman upbringing gave him the criteria, the claim to spiritual hegemony, the mission of peace, on which to base his policies. It is likely too, however, that it disabused him of any idealised view of Papal politics, conditioned as they were by the besetting need to keep on terms with Spain, the paramount Catholic power, a major presence in Italy, after 1580 incorpor-

9

ating Portugal: the willing sword of Counter-Reformation and of Christendom against the Turks. Popes had to pay a high cost for maintaining the Rome-Madrid axis. The Spanish church which dealt so effectively with heresy was Catholic on its own terms: the crown controlled appointments. The Pope could not afford to contest its claims as he did in France, where the existence of powerful *dévôt*, ultramontane elements, helped maintain a balance which French kings were bound to respect.[2] Worldwide in aspiration, the Papacy remained essentially Italian in character and commitments; at the same time, it was generally Spanish in policy. Only during the Thirty Years War, with the emergence of Richelieu's France as a strong rival to Spain, did the possibility arise of a more open policy, conducive to the role of arbiter: it was the great challenge that faced Urban VIII. How he responded and how his policies affected the career of Giulio Mazarini will become clear. So will the difference between rhetoric and reality as revealed in the geography and government of the Papal states.

The role of Supreme Pontiff, having authority over the Catholic church world-wide, co-existed uneasily with that of ruler of the Papal states in Italy. Reaching from the Adriatic to the Mediterranean, from Bologna and Ravenna to within a hundred kilometres of Naples, producing revenue, mainly from a uniform direct tax, that amounted to around three-quarters of all Papal income, the states were too large to be insignificant, but not large enough to dominate Italy, let alone influence states outside the peninsula. The Apostolic Chamber was the training ground for the principal state officials who went out to manage the domains and represented, in their extensive powers, the absolutist side of Papal government. The state's bankers were highly reputed; there were funds available for the construction of modern fortresses and effective measures were taken against the pirates of the Adriatic. The aspiring Papal official was given a sound training in government. There was also plenty to prepare Mazarini for what he was to find in France, in the way of surviving urban and regional privileges, quasi-independent fiefs which Popes had created for their political clients and allies, autonomous cities, like Bologna and Orvieto, and, throughout, venality and nepotism. Here, as in other states, absolutism was in thrall to aristocracy. There was always potential conflict between the Curia and great families, and it was normally resolved by patrimonial preference: most senior posts were recruited from noble families, whose interest usually came before that of the state. Not surprisingly, the Papal states were slower than most others to implement the Papacy's own Tridentine reforms.

As in the previous century Rome was embroiled in dynastic conflicts, notably those of Bourbon and Habsburg. Consistency of policy, honest and sound government, required continuity. That is exactly what the Papal system did not provide, as each Pope came to serve towards the end of a life devoted probably to diplomacy or administration, Urban VIII enjoyed an unusually long reign; there were twelve Popes altogether in the seventeenth century. Each election brought unsavoury bargaining in the struggle for supremacy between the interested Catholic powers. For better or for worse the Papacy exhibited the characteristics, from intensive lobbying to open bribery, of elective government.

The Curia was the nerve centre of a vast enterprise of mission and propaganda: the headquarters of much that was brave, exalted and devout ought not to be viewed merely in political terms; but again the politics cannot be discounted. To study, for example, the disputes between the religious orders, notably the Jesuits and the Dominicans,[3] or the unceasing competition for ascendancy in the college of Cardinals, more specifically the protracted process undergone before Giulio Mazarini could become a Cardinal, is to enter a world of partisan politics, of patron-client relationships so close that they had as much of family as of faction about them, of incessant wheeling and dealing. It was Mazarini's world: the young diplomat would rightly be assumed to represent some political interest. The Pope who emerged from the arcane mysteries of the elective process sought inevitably to survive without yielding too much, either to rulers who wanted above all to control the church in their lands, or to doctrinal pressure groups, like the Jansenists,[4] who sought his support for their cause. All the time the Papacy's political influence was waning – though it might not have been apparent when Giulio Mazarini first served the Barberinis.

The pontificate of Urban VIII saw Papal power in retreat towards the margin of the international power struggle, though not without some spirited attempts to assert traditional authority. He and his family were principal creators of *Roma triumphans*, the spirit epitomised by his inauguration of the completed St Peter's in 1626. He was also a classical scholar and poet who composed sonnets in Latin and Greek and re-wrote hymns in the Roman breviary. Intransigent though he might be under the shadow of the political threat to the church, rigorous in his rules for the canonisation of saints, he was also open to new ideas, not only in architecture. He commissioned the draining of the malaria-infested Pontine marshes. After long audiences with Galileo he could not bring himself to sign the document condemning the astronomer's defiance of the teaching of the church. Yet, more than any Pope of the Counter-Reformation period, which can be said to have ended with him, Urban envisaged the church in mediaeval, crusading terms. His college of the *Propaganda Fidei* is one memorial to his enthusiasm for holy war. Another was the disastrous Parma war which exhausted the money collected for the crusade. The last years were poignant, for he was a good man according to his lights, fated to see Europe engulfed in wars in which religious zeal was deflected by secular aims. His influence on the young diplomat

11

can hardly be over-estimated. The achievements, paradoxes and ultimate débâcle of his pontificate provide an essential commentary on Mazarini's work.

A career in Papal diplomacy, so tempting to a spirited young man, could have proved enervating and, in the end, thwarting to a man of talent. It was fortunate for Giulio, first that he could make himself useful to the Colonna family, whose interests were not primarily ecclesiastical, second that it suited the Colonnas to support the Barberini faction in the Papal election of 1623. From the start it might have seemed that the alert young man, who might have served as a model for Castiglione's courtier,[5] was one of fortune's favourites. Yet there are gaps in our knowledge of his career at this time which reflect paucity of records; also perhaps, on his part, an inclination to hang around, with clear ideas only about what he did not want to be, an ecclesiastic or a lawyer; but with it an underlying self-assurance: he would, in his own good time, find his *métier*. Meanwhile a penchant towards gambling could have prevented his making the most of his advantages and it was to steady him up, as much as to further his interest with the Colonnas, that his father secured his appointment as tutor and companion to Girolamo Colonna.

The study of law at the University of Alcala provided the reason for their visit but did not monopolise their time and energy. Giulio acquired the fluency in Castilian that was later to recommend him to the Spanish-born queen of France. He admitted to being smitten by the beauty of Spanish women. Twenty-five years later, hostile French pamphleteers, digging for scandal and evidence of Spanish proclivities, were to make more than evidence warranted of his escapades. Not that the young Mazarini attempted to disguise his attachment to Spain, which was generally perceived, in the period of his stay, 1620–2,[6] after the renewal, under hopeful auspices, of war against the Dutch,[7] to be Rome's right arm: Spain was enjoying her *época de triumfo*, her armies still invincible, her resources apparently sufficient to sustain them. It is unlikely that he had serious misgivings at this stage. There had been nothing in the management of affairs in France, since Henry IV's death in 1610, to suggest a serious challenge from that quarter, or to cast doubt on the compatibility of Habsburg and Papal interests, Mazarini returned from his mission to find that his stock was as high with Filippo Colonna as it had evidently been with his son; indeed his good nature ensured that his friendships rarely suffered, as friendships can, from long exposure. He knew how to please, even bend, without abasing himself.

The Constable was delighted with Girolamo's development. The studious young man was now ready for the promotion expected of a Roman with his high connections. Aged twenty-three, he became a cardinal. His sister Anna married Urban's nephew, Taddeo, future prefect of Rome, sealing what Colonna hoped would be an alliance of mutual advantage.

Mazarini meanwhile attended the classes of the celebrated master Cosimo Fideli, securing without difficulty the doctorates in civil and canon law which would serve him well in diplomacy. Not a man to be satisfied with academic pursuits, he seems, during this period, to have been casting around; there was much to enjoy in the life of fashionable Rome, but that too would not be enough for him. He was much in the Colonna household, plainly looking for another opportunity to extend his experience. It came with the offer of a captain's commission in the regiment raised by the prince of Palestrina, Colonna's cousin; he was also entrusted with the care of Colonna's fourth son, Carlo, who had joined the Spanish army in Lombardy.

Palestrina's brief was to join in the defence of the Val Telline. This Alpine valley, north of Lake Como, had long been the scene of cantonal feuds embittered by religious differences. Its importance lay in its alignment, providing the vital link in the Habsburg line of communication leading from Milan to the Tyrol and South Germany, thence through family, or friendly lands, to Flanders. Count Feria, governor of Milan, was in no doubt about the importance of the Val Telline, to abandon which was 'to suffer this little piece of earth to stick in the windpipe of monarchy'. It figured prominently in Richelieu's calculations: one of his first acts, on coming to power in 1624, was to send in French troops.[8] Their withdrawal in 1626 left little opportunity for military distinction for the young captain and his regiment was disbanded in 1627. By all accounts he had been an excellent officer, punctilious and enterprising; but the regiment, raised to give substance to the Pope's claim to mediate, had been inactive. The experience was not however entirely fruitless. His superior officer, Torquato Contini, had sent Mazarini to negotiate the liaison of the Papal force and the Spanish under Gonsalvo de Cordoba. In January 1627, he had his first testing diplomatic encounter when he secured Cordoba's assent to the disbanding of the Papal force. He bearded the Spaniard in the middle of the night, stood up to his rage and gained what his Roman masters wanted. They were impressed.

On garrison duty at Milan Mazarini had also encountered Gian-Francesco Saccheti, apostolic commissioner to the Papal army. Now Papal nuncio, Saccheti appointed Mazarini his secretary. As at other times in his career, the timing was happy. It was not however entirely fortuitous for he was remarkably adept at building connections out of chance encounters and making use of them to serve his career. The friendship of the four Saccheti brothers,[9] members of an old Florentine family who had moved with the Florentine Pope into influential positions, was crucial at this stage, for even the Colonnas were unable to do much to help Mazarini against the Habsburg partisans in the curia. Gian-Francesco was working for the restoration of peace in Italy and, with it, the repair of the increasingly strained relations between Urban VIII and the Habsburgs.

He set out to train Mazarini in diplomacy. He sought too, to direct him towards a career in the church, and obtained a canonry for him, with a pension; for the first time Mazarini knew financial security but he did not seek ordination and let preferment make no difference to his style. He was still the elegant cavalier, five foot six, 'dressed always in lay habit', with thick, flowing locks of dark chestnut colour, large lustrous eyes, a long moustache twirling upwards at the ends and a beard of precise narrow cut. It is the fashionable style that can be seen perfectly in Van Dyck's portrait of Carlo Colonna.[10] Mazarini's duties were not onerous. He was later to reflect: 'I made myself important at that time more through my handling of affairs than by my actual post, which consisted only of informing my patrons of what was happening in Lombardy'.

Patience and discretion were among the virtues urged by Saccheti, who thought sufficiently highly of his protégé to entrust him with direction of the legation when he returned to Rome in 1629. Mazarini was given full powers to deal with the Spanish and French commanders, Spinola[11] and Créqui[12] respectively, and with Savoy. At the end of that year, a younger Saccheti, Giulio, cardinal and legate to Ferrara, heard that Louis XIII had called Mazarini to Lyons and wrote suggesting the way in which the Pope might go, and the part that Mazarini might play: considering the opportunity thus presented to cooperate 'in directing negotiations towards universal peace', he was sure that the results would 'correspond with our desires, inasmuch as that will depend on you, and I hope that the world will soon be able to rejoice at the greatness which France intends, and which the Roman court wishes, and which is what you merit'. Rome evidently appreciated that the intervention of France in the Mantuan affair had created a new situation and demanded a new policy. Spanish impetuosity had made a French presence seem more desirable than in 1624 after Richelieu's venture into the Val Telline. Mazarini's stock had risen fast. But what exactly was it that he was required to do for his masters in Rome?

To answer this question it is necessary first to look beyond the Mantuan crisis, to events in Europe since the Bohemian revolt of 1618 had provoked a conflict which, merging with others of separate origin, had evolved into the general mêlée which was to last until 1648.[13] The war which brought death, destruction and misery to so many brought also, to a fortunate few, opportunity and fame. Of no man was this to be more true than of the Papal diplomat who first attracted attention outside Italy by his dramatic role in the Mantuan affair, and who was later to be a leading architect of the peace which brought the general war to an end.

3

MANTUA: CRISIS AND OPPORTUNITY

Not only for Mazarini was the Mantuan Succession War to prove crucial. Until 1628, after early mishaps occasioned by the revolt in Bohemia and the Calvinist conspiracy which sought to exploit it, the Habsburgs had carried all before them. The fervently Catholic king of Bohemia, Ferdinand of Styria, so rudely deposed in 1618, was elected Emperor in the following year.[1] Habsburg Spain and Austria worked together. The Spanish were especially interested in defeating the Dutch, against whom they resumed the war, a year before the Twelve Year truce was due to expire, and in maintaining their grip over Northern Italy. Their common interest lay in restoring Catholicism where it had been rejected during or since the Reformation. Religion knew no frontiers.

The suppression of the Bohemian rebels which followed the battle of Bila Hora (November 1620): the valuable alliance of Maximilian of Bavaria,[2] who coveted Palatinate lands and the Electoral title and whose general, Tilly, won that battle; the relentless grinding down of Dutch resistance and successive defeats of Protestant armies, were all related parts of a single pattern. When there was also a unified strategy, as in 1620, as again in 1634, then the Habsburg cousins' alliance was truly formidable. It was a development which the Catholic Louis XIII[3] of France might watch as uneasily as the Lutheran king of Sweden, Gustavus Adolphus, who was locked in war with Poland.[4] The advance of Catholicism was also the promotion of Habsburg power; more effective in Bohemia than it had ever been before; most presumptuous in Germany, where the recovery by the church of lands secularised since the treaty of Augsburg (1555) normally meant their transfer to a Habsburg or Wittelsbach prince. After 1626[5] there was no significant Protestant army in the field. Also in March of that year Richelieu had to conclude the treaty of Monçon which confirmed the independence of the Grisons: the Spanish could again move freely from North Italy to the Netherlands.

The epic siege of La Rochelle ended in October 1628 with the triumph of the French royal army and was followed by a treaty at Alés,[6] in 1629, which ensured that the Huguenots would no longer be dangerous and that Richelieu could, for a second time, embark upon a foreign expedition. He moved fast, and with that unswerving aim which won the respect even of his enemies. By December the main body of the royal army was moving through deep snow over the Monte Geneva, then down to the valley where a line of forts guarded Turin. Fearful for his capital Charles Emmanuel of Savoy,[7] who had been Spain's ally, was compelled to sign a treaty which allowed the French army to cross his lands to Montferrate, in which he renounced his claim to that desirable territory. Cordoba withdrew from his siege of Casale and Olivarez,[8] *privado* of Philip IV, was left to assess the consequences of an earlier fateful decision. Was he now to persevere and attempt to secure Mantua, or accept the loss of face, with all the material consequences? The question leads back to others. How had it come about that Richelieu had been allowed to seize the initiative? Why was Cordoba in Mantua in the first place?

In December 1627, Vincenzo II, the last male Gonzaga, duke of Mantua and marquis of Montferrate, had died without a direct heir. For the succession there were only two serious candidates, the duke of Guastalla, a distant cousin and Spanish puppet, and the duc de Nevers,[9] a nearer cousin. Nevers, Italian by birth, but French in his principal estates and interests, was a *dévôt*, who had given years of his life and his great wealth to creating a fleet for a projected crusade against the Turks; his was the stronger claim and not only by blood relationship. When his son, the duke of Rethel, was married to the dying Vincenzo's daughter Maria Gonzaga, Richelieu's envoy had used the occasion to talk him into executing a will in favour of Nevers. The Pope took Richelieu's view. Neither could look favourably on the prospect of the Spanish domination of Mantua. Nor could it suit them that Charles Emmanuel, coaxed by Cordoba, should now be claiming Montferrate for his grand-daughter Marguerite, Vincenzo's niece. Urban had been impressed by the decisive way in which the Huguenots had been crushed. Richelieu had been criticised by the *dévôts* for not following up his victory by measures to restrict Huguenot freedom of worship, but he had yet to break decisively with them. Urban understood however that the stronger the Habsburgs grew, the more tempted Richelieu would be to find Protestant allies. Mantua was yet another Papal exercise in the precarious business of holding the balance. That is what Saccheti and Mazarini were trying to achieve in the face of Spanish belligerence and Savoyard opportunism.

The Pope did not however have sole right to Solomon's mantle. The Emperor claimed the right to arbitrate since Mantua was an Imperial fief. He was therefore dismayed when Cordoba marched into Montferrate and laid seige to its capital Casale, whose fortress dominated the upper Po valley and the arterial road from Milan to Genoa (March 1628). Philip IV, by allowing Cordoba to do precisely what, in the case of Nevers, was alleged to be an act of treason, would alarm the German princes. Meanwhile in Germany Wallenstein's huge army and apparently boundless ambition were raising uncomfortable questions about his master's intentions. The answer would come with the Edict of Restitution in 1629.[10] Meanwhile, in the summer of 1628, Wallenstein laid siege to Stralsund. The 'Admiralty plan', optimistically conceived in Madrid, envisaged the establishment of a naval base on the Baltic and the subsequent conquest of the United Provinces by combined naval and military operations.

It is not surprising therefore that the Emperor was embarrassed by Cordoba's precipitate move. When in the summer of 1629 Mazarini had prolonged talks with Cordoba, who by then had been forced to give up his siege of Casale, he found the Spaniard arrogant and narrow-minded. 'The entire world is nothing to Gonzales', he wrote, 'before the power of Austria'. Of course the frustrated Cordoba was taking a soldier's view of his own front and perhaps cared little about the intricate pattern of Habsburg policy. He had only acted as he did on the authority of the Spanish minister – although the latter assumed that the general had already invaded when he sent the crucial order to proceed. Olivarez' design was to remove Nevers in order to maintain military rule and political stability in Lombardy. It was a limited design to protect an essential link in the chain of Austro-Spanish power. If the French were to establish themselves in North Italy, not only Milan, but also Flanders and Germany would be affected.

The Spanish could claim that their dominance had been beneficial to Italians, providing peace and stability. They believed that they could rely on Savoy. In 1625 the duke had flirted with a French *entente*, only to see the French evacuate and make terms. He claimed to be fighting on behalf of the Italian princes when he joined in Cordoba's game, but of course he scented easy prey. It is not surprising that Olivarez failed to anticipate Richelieu's swift winter campaign, undertaken as it was only after anxious debate in council. It was after this episode that he came to be obsessed by Richelieu and to see the conflict of irreconcilable interests of state in the light of a duel, with personal antipathy sharpened to the point at which every move was suspect. Meanwhile he had to hope that the Frenchman would be overthrown by the combination of rivals and enemies at home. With ample opportunity to judge the issues and motives of the combatants, Mazarini was receiving invaluable lessons in power politics.

Was the Papal diplomat also looking behind the action, at the balance of strength? There were cogent domestic reasons for the Spanish invasion. The Austrian alliance was proving expensive: between 1618 and 1628 350,000 *ducats* a year went across the Alps to Tilly's and Wallenstein's armies. That palls however beside the cost of the Netherlands operation: around three million *ducats* a year. High taxation, soaring prices and declining manufactures had made Olivarez' government unpopular in

17

Castile. The serious illness of Philip IV[11] in August 1627 had brought home to the *privado* his insecurity: the pattern of events anticipated Richelieu's similar crisis of 1630. Like Louis XIII then, with Richelieu, when Philip recovered, he put his authority squarely behind Olivarez and his unpopular domestic programme. A successful military action offered the prospect of a welcome diversion: abroad *reputación* was enhanced; at home the silencing of vociferous critics. As the gambler in Mazarini would appreciate, two statesmen were taking the highest risks. If anything, Richelieu's was the greater. If Cordoba had been a better general; if the Huguenots had held out for another month, even Richelieu might have been deterred. On such chances the future of Spain, France and the Empire were to depend.

Richelieu's mid-winter march appealed to the imagination of Italians, as would a similar Alpine venture by another Frenchman of genius in 1796. Richelieu had selected the one vulnerable point in the Habsburg front which he could probe without incurring the immediate risk of counter-attack in the eastern provinces and of the open warfare where the Spanish *tercios* might be expected to defeat the relatively inexperienced French; and he was doing it with the blessing of the Pope. The subsequent diversion of Spanish and Imperial troops to an operation which proved both futile and costly, not least in the death of Spinola in the fever-stricken encampments around unlucky Mantua; the encouragement thus afforded to the watchful Gustavus Adolphus, now released from his war against Poland, to commit himself to the German war; the shipwreck of the Admiralty scheme which had done so much to focus his hopes of Baltic dominion upon a precise objective, Pomerania; and alteration in the military balance large enough to stultify the emperor's Edict of Restitution even before Gustavus' crushing, decisive victory of Breitenfeld (September 1631): in such outcomes of the Mantuan affair there is enough to justify the opinion that it was the turning point in the Thirty Years War.

Out of Mantua too, though not suddenly or irrevocably, came Mazarini's change of allegiance. It was the result in part of his reading of the trends, in part of revulsion from Spanish intransigence and the implications of the *pax austriaca* which seemed to Mazarini, as to the Pope, to point towards universal monarchs. The move probably owed more, however, to Mazarini's admiration for Richelieu than to any strategic calculation. As he encountered some of the leading men of Europe he began to see his Rome for what it was: a world of absorbing interest and rare delights, resplendent, even honoured but, in relation to the great political issues of the day, marginal. It was not what was being planned there, in the tense conclaves of Cardinal Francesco Barberini, that Mazarini saw would count, but the power of a country, in population more than twice the size of Spain,[12] and of a minister who was starting to govern it effectively, whose decisions would determine the course of events.

His encounters with Richelieu show that there was, on Mazarini's side, a degree of fascination, tinged with hero-worship. Baroque culture is permeated by the cult of the hero, whether secular or spiritual, in nostalgia for the ancients or in some modern adaptation of classical themes. Pervading all is the concern for order that was the *leitmotif* of Richelieu's career. To the impressionable Italian he appealed as heroic in intellectual and moral stature. As the embodiment of the French state he represented something of the romance of power. 'I had attached myself by instinct for his genius', he was later to recall. The potency was no less great for being envisaged in diplomatic terms. Diplomacy sought order in a disordered continent where lands were ravaged, where prince and peasant were dispossessed and burghers bullied. Richelieu's achievements at home represented an unfinished but already notable imposition of order and rationality. Patron of art, literature and music, above all architecture on an increasingly grand scale, he could not fail to appeal.

So much by repute. On 29 January, 1630, Mazarini first met Cardinal Richelieu at Lyons where he was en route for Italy. Accompanied by Montmorency, he was planning the campaign which was designed to aid Nevers and relieve the pressure on Casale, again under siege. Mazarini's mission was to explain the wishes of his master and to propose a truce. The minister was immersed in the practical problems of a winter campaign which, as we know from his correspondence with the king, he believed to be crucial to the outcome of the war. He had won the debate between what he saw as stark alternatives: *réputation* and *repos*. 'The esteem of the world' he told the king, 'is gained only by great actions.' This great action was a hazardous one and his political base was far from secure. The leading spokesman for the *dévôts*, Michel de Marillac,[13] was apprehensive about the fiscal and social consequences of Richelieu's hawkish policies: reports from the provinces supported his fears about the breakdown of social order under the pressures of war. Nor could Richelieu trust his generals. Montmorency was soon to rebel. Louis de Marillac,[14] Michel's half-brother, was to be arrested on suspicion of treason the day after he had been appointed to lead the army of Italy (November 1630). His predecessor, Bassompierre,[15] who had served the crown well, was sent to the Bastille.

When Richelieu met the man who was to succeed him, the supreme crisis was imminent: it originated in the king's severe illness and culminated, in November 1630, in the Day of Dupes.[16] The death of Bérulle,[17] whose saintly character had adorned the cause of the *dévôts*, in October 1629, had removed one restraining influence on Richelieu but had hardly affected the central issue: the continuance of royal support for his embattled minister, Louis XIII was virtually estranged from his wife,

Anne:[18] there were no children. The king's health could not be relied on. Gaston of Orléans,[19] his younger brother and heir, was an incorrigible intriguer. When Richelieu and Louis were out on campaign he was governor of Paris. It did not stop him spending the last months of 1629 in Lorraine, whose duke Charles[20] kept open house for French rebels. He had only been tempted back to Paris by the offer of the governorship of Orléans.

At times Richelieu was exhilarated by the challenges and risks: there was always business to engage his mind, and deferential service to feed his vanity. But he was under great pressure. Mazarini must have had misgivings before his meeting at Lyons. Would he brush the unknown Roman aside or offer him perhaps a few impatient minutes? The Frenchman's first reactions were certainly guarded: 'le Mazarini has come here to spy rather than to treat . . . I believe he is wholly inclined towards our enemies . . . he is so Spanish and Savoyard that what he says ought not to be taken as gospel'. Richelieu still saw Mazarini as Colonna's man. It is therefore surprising that he received him and, with the Venetian envoy, kept him for two hours.

It was Mazarini's feat to persuade Richelieu that his proposals were worth serious study. Before the interview he had been given good advice by Cardinal Maurice of Savoy, who knew Richelieu well: 'he is really a great person, but in all matters he wants the decision to appear to depend on him alone'. Mazarini's pliant manner, his readiness to listen and adapt his style were put to a prolonged test. Possibly however, what most impressed Richelieu was that the Italian remained firm in his refusal to be put down by first rebuffs: he was to secure further interviews between then and May, at Casaletto, Pinerolo, Grenoble and Chambéry.

It was a trying summer for the statesmen; no less so for the generals and their men, besiegers and besieged: dysentery and typhus made no distinctions of rank. Spinola died before Casale, Duke Charles Emmanuel in his capital at Turin, to be succeeded by Victor Amadeus,[21] husband of Louis XII's sister Christina:[22] neither death was bad news to Richelieu. But he was upset by the fall and sack of Mantua. He knew he was being undermined at court where some were defeatist, some openly pro-Spanish, a few avowed enemies. 'Everyone there' he was told 'asked with extraordinary curiosity when Mazarini was to return.' So the latter found himself in the forefront. With his useful contacts was he the man to arrange a settlement? Richelieu was at first sceptical. On the 2nd August he gave Mazarini a further audience. He had earlier said that he had 'good impulses but so little power that I do not believe the negotiations can produce fruit'. With alarming reports about the illness of the king Richelieu may have been at the end of his tether. Indeed peace would be more attractive if it were not being urged so vehemently by his enemies at court. If there were to be a peace it would have to be on his own terms: that meant first fighting a successful campaign. Mazarini's position was therefore most delicate. It was possible that he could win the confidence of each patron: the Pope, Savoy, France, even Spain; no less possible to upset them all. Sooner or later he would have to make a choice of masters. It would depend on the course of events – and that would be influenced by the way he handled the negotiations.

Predictably the meeting was fraught; it proved to be fateful. First Mazarini, who had already experienced the bully in Richelieu, saw an outburst of wild rage when the Cardinal threw back his chair and stamped on his red skull cap. Mazarini – but note that the account is his – stood his ground, 'firm and determined'. Richelieu regained self-control, apologised and asked him to resume his efforts to find a settlement. Afterwards, for the first time he wrote to him. The tone was both laudatory and confidential, as if he had been testing him and had now decided that Mazarini was to be his man. He would also be a dangerous man to have working against him, for a *dévôt* Paris-Rome axis. Immediately, he could see that Mazarini could exercise a valuable influence on the wavering duke of Savoy. Meanwhile he planned a new strike. Schomberg[23] and La Force, trusted veterans, were to raise the siege of Casale. Their army, like the Spanish, wilted in the dust and heat. Richelieu then looked to Mazarini as the man who could save it from humiliation, perhaps defeat; meanwhile the Spanish, deprived of their revered commander, their ranks decimated by dysentery, despaired of victory. This squalid scene, with both camps in low morale, was to be the background to an event as dramatic as anything that could have been seen on the Roman stage. To understand its significance, however, the reader has first to travel once more across the Alps, to Regensburg in South Germany, and to the Reichstag there in session.

4

EARLY FAME

At an interview with Richelieu, at Pinerolo, in April 1630, Mazarini had met Father Joseph,[1] the Capuchin friar who was already Richelieu's trusted agent. He was still pursuing his ideal of a European crusade against the Turks while directing his immediate efforts against the Habsburgs. In personality and outlook the two men could hardly have been more different. Inevitably they were to be, to some extent, rivals. The ascetic friar was to remain something of an enigma to Mazarini. At this stage, however, he was to serve Mazarini and the cause of peace better than he did Richelieu and his Italian ambition. Mazarini had been trying to bring the military chiefs together. When political control was so feeble, it was usually best to go direct to the generals. But the authority of the Emperor still counted for something, and he was presiding at the Diet of Regensburg, summoned in June 1630 to secure from the reluctant princes the election of his son, as king of the Romans and so heir, in due course, to the Empire.[2]

Richelieu's official agent at Regensburg was Brûlart de Léon,[3] with powers 'to treat of a general peace in Italy' and to bind his government to any treaty he concluded. Whether or not it was Mazarini who persuaded him to do it, Richelieu saw the wisdom of sending Father Joseph to Regensburg since he was more likely to respond flexibly to events in North Italy. The Emperor would grant a peace favourable to France only in return for her abandoning her allies, Venice, Holland and Denmark. Since the German princes had already obtained their main objective namely the dismissal of Wallenstein, they gave Father Joseph little support; so he found himself in a weak bargaining position. Addressed by Maximilian as a fellow Catholic, he found it hard to resist the argument for a general peace. Maximilian had gained what he wanted: the Upper Palatinate and title of Elector. The Emperor too was in favour for he needed soldiers from Italy to meet a new challenge: Gustavus Adolphus had just landed in Pomerania.

Father Joseph was uneasy about the connection between the Lutheran threat to North Germany and the ambitions of France. He was also too wary a politician not to realise that, at any time, the king, then lying sick at Lyons, might die, leaving the throne to Gaston. He was not informed that Schomberg's army was marching south from Champagne, to reinforce the army of Italy. Richelieu still hoped for victory; Father Joseph, more realistically, anticipated disaster. Believing that they already had the crucial concession in the shape of the Emperor's willingness to let Nevers keep Mantua, the French emissaries affixed their seals to a treaty (October 1630) which seemed to favour their cause: the Spanish were to withdraw from Casale, the Imperialists from Mantua. Nevers was to be installed. In return the French would withdraw from Italy, except for Susa and Pinerolo, and they would in no way assist the Emperor's enemies.

Mazarini received news of the treaty on October 26. There ensued the scene before the walls of Casale which was to become the talk of Europe – at least of the courts and chambers where the interested and well-informed discussed matters of state. First Mazarini extracted from the Spanish a promise that they would give up the siege. Then he galloped towards the front ranks of the advancing army of Schomberg crying 'Peace, Peace'. In a letter of 1638 Mazarini was to give his own account of what must have been a tense encounter. 'I spoke in public for about a quarter of an hour. Everybody agreed with what I said and began to embrace, so that one could no longer distinguish Frenchmen from Spaniards, but all appeared to be blood brothers – to the amazement of the armies, who believed that they had to engage in quite a different combat from embracing and courtesies.' It was an appealing scene, a gleam of sanity and humanity at a dark time.

Richelieu was delighted at first news of the treaty and grateful to Mazarini. The artist in him may have appreciated the *coup de théâtre.* So did the publishers of the popular almanacs which featured the gallant cavalier brandishing his parchment. Their concerted publication caused speculation that the affair was stage-managed after prior agreement. If so it is unlikely that Richelieu had any hand in it, for when he read and understood the full text, he was furious. He had seen Mantua as the means to a larger end, checking, if not reversing the Habsburg advance. He was especially concerned about Lorraine. Duke Charles gave asylum to some of Richelieu's most dangerous enemies, notably the duc de Guise,[4] whose very name evoked disturbing memories from the Religious Wars. In September 1630, with the generals, Marillac and Bassompierre, and spurred on by reports that the king was desperately ill, Guise held Richelieu's fate. Louis recovered, but seemed too unwell to resist the arguments of Richelieu's enemies.

They accused him of acting in Mantua against the interests of the church and squandering resources which would be better employed against heretics in France. Even without the Pope's moral support it would have been difficult for Richelieu to change his policy. He was playing for high stakes and could not afford to betray his allies for the intangible benefits of an Italian peace. The recent Edict of Restitution, which could only be effected by force, did not encourage hope that the one-sided action required of him by the Regensburg treaty would ensure peace in Germany. So he refused to ratify. The formal reasons were that the terms were too vague; furthermore, his envoys had been authorised to treat only of Italy.

Such an audacious demonstration of higher diplomacy could not fail to impress the watchful Italian. While the Habsburg courts simmered with righteous indignation, Richelieu's unofficial agent Charnacé negotiated with the Swedes: the eventual treaty of Barwälde,[5] in January 1631, was to provide Gustavus with funds for his advance into Germany. Anticipating that the Spaniards were about to surprise the citadel of Casale, Richelieu ordered a French garrison to occupy it. Meanwhile he had consolidated his position at home. In early November, the king 'duped' the *dévôt*, Hispanophile faction by confirming Richelieu in office: 'I honour my mother', he said, 'but my obligations to the state are greater than to her'. Richelieu, for his part, proposed to show the king 'by ever increasing proofs that he was the most devoted subject and most zealous that ever king or master had in this world'. Mazarini persuaded the Pope to send him to Paris to test ministerial opinion and work towards an Italian peace. Possibly, he could have worked with Marillac. In the light of subsequent events, however, Richelieu's triumph looks like a further milestone in Mazarini's fortunate career.

Little is known about Mazarini's first visit to Paris, in January 1631. According to the nuncio Alessandro Bichi,[6] he was received 'with joy in this court where his fame has already taken hold and where the memory of his courage is fresh.' He stayed for three months, before departing for North Italy and the next diplomatic round. Nothing in his letters conveys his feelings on first entering the city. Like Rome, it was the scene of much new building, none of it more ambitious than he palace Jacques Le Mercier[7] was creating for Richelieu in the rue St Honoré. No doubt Mazarini was absorbed in the business of winning people to his cause. Chief among them was Abel Servien,[8] War Minister from 1630 and destined to be the chief French negotiator. He was one of the ablest of the *créatures*[9] on whose loyalty the *premier ministre* depended. Now he helped establish the Italian as the man to be trusted to guard French interests. Mazarini knew that Servien would pass his news on to Richelieu, so took care to please: he confided every concern, from the revenue of a newly assigned French abbey to schemes for universal peace. The French may have thought that they had Mazarini in their pocket. But there are indications of mutual trust.

Another important friendship was that of Chavigny,[10] the young Secretary of State with whom Mazarini lodged. The two rising men thought that each could be useful to the other: Mazarini knew that Chavigny was as close as any man to being the Cardinal's favourite; Chavigny did not yet fear a rival. The dual role which Mazarini was to play until he could work unequivocally for the French king might have worried a man of less equable temperament; but he worked discreetly and ensured that he was kept well-informed. From Mirabel, the Spanish ambassador, he learned of secret dealings between Marie and Madrid. Richelieu was quick to see his potential value. Asking the French ambassador in Rome to secure for Mazarini the post of nuncio, he wrote: 'I know of no subject from whom the Holy See could obtain more service than from him.' Aware that his enemies would present an unfavourable picture, Richelieu was clearly anxious that nothing should deter Mazarini from allegiance. So he asked Servien 'to assure Mazarini that everything he has been told about me is false and that I love and esteem him as much as he could possibly desire'.

'The Pope cannot be served by a worthier or cleverer minister'. The treaty of Cherasco, in June 1631, gave Italy the peace for which Urban had prayed: like Servien, he had nothing but praise for his legate. The French minister trusted him sufficiently to require that he should go over each clause with Feria, Spanish governor of the Milanese. This was the first of the diplomatic settlements on which Mazarini's diplomatic reputation would rest secure. It was important as much for the experience he gained, which he was to use in larger arenas, as for its actual terms. Events in Germany were reducing the little duchy to a sideshow. With Tilly besieging Magdeburg and Gustavus pondering his next move, they were content to let Nevers preside over his ruined palace and plague afflicted people. The Spanish were enraged, however, and threatened to stop negotiations when Richelieu, claiming a right to Pinerolo, secured it, despite an ancillary treaty, negotiated by Mazarini.[11] Richelieu blandly announced that the occupation was temporary. By the end of the year he was concerned with Germany, and his troops stayed in Pinerolo.

It was another diplomatic mission that brought Mazarini, in April 1632, to Paris, this time for only six weeks. He was presented to queen Anne by the king himself. His looks and manners appealed to the queen. 'You will like Mazarini', Richelieu supposedly said to her: 'he is like Buckingham'.[12] Among the characteristics that endeared him to women was his zest for life, expressed in a letter to Servien, who was in Turin, which reported how much the ladies there missed him: describing a visit to a 'villa' at Saint-Cloud he enthused: 'most beautiful ladies, magnificent collation, everything to perfection'. It is the more impressive because he never lost sight of the main purpose of his mission, nor shrank from work. He had come to persuade the French government to back the new duke of Savoy, Louis XIII's brother-in-law, Victor Amadeus. Richelieu was anxious to keep Savoy on his side but not prepared to pay a high price for it: for example, a quarrel with the now friendly Swiss. The recent campaign had shown that Savoy could be brought to heel by a show of force. So, when Mazarini presented him with the proposal that Savoy should be given Geneva in return for Pinerolo, Richelieu responded warily that, if Savoy should conquer Geneva, France should receive it; the duke would be offered the Vaux instead. On his way back to Rome, Mazarini visited Turin to persuade the gullible Victor Amadeus that the plan was dead; he listened politely while the duke expounded another project: Mazarini would, he hoped, ask the Pope to support him in a crusade to recover Cyprus.[13] Meanwhile, as ever doing some of his important business through the honeyed exchanges of the social round, Mazarin cultivated the duchess.

The episode further strengthened Mazarini's relationship with Richelieu, for whom, with other important ministers, he ensured a flow of Roman presents: toilet water, jasmine-scented gloves and, for the Cardinal, fine works of art. Looking constantly for ways of strengthening ties and supports, he played a balancing act between the court of France, openly allied to Protestant Sweden after 1631, and the interests of Rome: there the Spanish faction strove to thwart Richelieu's designs. It was no longer clear to Urban VIII that he should be the ally of France. Nor can Mazarin have been without misgivings about the soundness of Richelieu's policy: it was open to question after the death of Gustavus at Lüzen (November 1632); still more after the crushing defeat of the Swedes at Nördlingen in August 1634.[14] But there is no evidence that Mazarini wavered. To the Spaniards he seemed to be an open accomplice of France. It is of this period that Victor Cousin writes: 'one feels that he is in despair over having no one round him but timid and mediocre people: he finds energy, resolution and consistency only in France'. That is hardly a fair description of the Pope, whose dreams of peace and crusade shimmered, as in the heat haze of a Roman summer, far beyond the sordid realities of dynastic war. Nor does it fit the diligent Francesco Barberini, who sought the middle way, emphasising discretion and impartiality in his instructions. Mazarini did not want to lose his patronage. He wrote to inform him of every step, to justify his actions: the tone is warm, the excitement and sense of urgency barely controlled.

At the same time Mazarini continued to cultivate the more malleable Antonio Barberini. He enjoyed his company and appreciated his taste. Antonio could command the services of the best architects, painters and musicians, and had money to spare for lavish entertaining and large presents. Finding him a less exacting master and warmer friend than Francesco, Mazarini had already tried to propel him towards the centre of the stage. 'The time has come', he wrote in 1630, 'for the cardinal-legate to leave his peaceful residence in Bologna and to make his appearance among the princes, generals and plenipotentiaries who hold the fate of nations in their hands'. Antonio's thoughts dwelt however on easier planes: for a man of sensibility the embellishment of Rome was indeed no mean ambition. Mazarini's attention to his new patron failed to make a statesman of him. It did provide him with much delight, an education in the higher arts and, at critical moments, with the material support he needed for the advancement of his own career. All that, when the Barberini cardinals fell on hard times, he would not forget.

During the years spent in formal service to Cardinal Antonio, Mazarini became more of a connoisseur, also more of a churchman. It is hard to write about another's faith except by way of his own statements and intimations. Mazarini left little evidence of his thoughts. He was plainly not interested in theology for its own sake; perhaps a Jesuit training had left him sated. Again, unlike Richelieu, he left no corpus of devotional writing. The correspondence with his sister Anna Maria was mostly one-sided, as she plied him with advice about faith and works. He seemed to value her advice. Yet he was plainly no *dévôt*. His religion, it may be surmised, was that of so many Italians: unquestioning, natural as soil and seasons; comfortable, as if an extension of domestic life; undemanding. It came with the sun and the bounty that was God's evident pleasure to bestow on those who laboured in His vineyard – most abundantly on those who managed it. He was of the generation touched by he saintly life of Carlo Borromeo[15] and his imitators in a pastoral style that was notably humane and practical. He would be familiar with the work, early translated into Italian, of the favourite saint of Frenchmen, François de Sales.[16] A large part of the teaching of Sales, was that the life of piety should also be a happy life, since to live in accord with the will of God was to live with reason and God-given instincts. The ideal Christian should not eschew the world but work with it in the way that suited him best.

Mazarini's God was far removed from Him whom Father Joseph served by schooling his mind and punishing his body; far too from Him whom Jansenists served with rigorous scruples and suspicion of those who, like Mazarini, seemed to be taking their faith too lightly. Here were not only nuances of understanding or style, but fundamental differences which would matter in the French political context. Meanwhile the amiable face of Christian faith, displayed in generous actions and conciliatory manners, was what the young diplomat, counselling peace through compromise, seemed to display, with a faith less shallow, and moral foundations less unsound than critics were soon to allege.

As yet the canon of St John Lateran and Santa Maria Maggiore was not moved to seek ordination. Popes often used to provide income from such benefices for relatives and officials. News of the first came to him in Paris in 1632, with advice which suggests the relaxed way in which Rome regarded such transactions. 'It would be appropriate for you to take at least the first tonsure': so the nuncio Bichi cut a token patch in his hair, which left virtually unscathed his luxuriant cavalier locks, but

27

marked his clerical status. It was his first, and last sacerdotal step. He would sometimes speak of becoming a priest, but probably without serious intent. For his purposes, and for those of his masters, Pope or king, such a vocation was unnecessary. He wore contentedly the ecclesiastical garments, the badge of service to the church. He accepted promotion, becoming protonotary apostolic and domestic prelate of the Pope, so entitled to the violet cassock and title Monsignore. He had the means to sustain, not only the dignity proper to a valuable official, for his family as well as for himself, but also the necessary staff for his work. It was not poverty that made him unsure about his future in Papal service. In August 1634 he wrote with understandable satisfaction of two contracts which brought the names of Martinozzi and Mancini into the family: 'I have married off two of my sisters with a dowry of 40,000 *livres* each.'[17]

Providing for sisters, later nieces, was a responsibility which Mazarini always took seriously. The *casa* had to be maintained and strengthened. Honour and wealth were two sides of the same coin. The dowries came from the Pope, through Cardinal Antonio. Was it for such dealings that the faithful paid their tithes and rents? A Pope seemed able to accept as easily as his self-indulgent nephew and his ambitious new prelate the logic of a political institution that was also a business: that valuable benefices had to be used to maintain the bureaucracy of church and state and to secure the services of talented men. Still less would Monsignore Mazarini have any qualms about the ways in which he might be required to serve. He would be no less sound a Catholic, no less zealous a servant of the Holy See, for finding his *métier* in the arduous tasks of diplomacy. Duty and inclination pointed in the same direction in what must, at times, have seemed to be the best of all political worlds.

A fair proportion of Mazarini's time was spent in the *palazzo* Barberini, or in his younger patron's villa at Bagnaia, near Viterbo. Francesco was jealous of his brother's enhanced reputation and the larger political role which Mazarini envisaged. Urban saw, however, the advantages of a rivalry between the brothers which might make them more sensitive to their uncle's wishes. Maintaining Antonio in his accustomed style taxed the Papal exchequer. Mazarini did well therefore to persuade Antonio to act, along with Cardinal Maurice of Savoy, as co-protector of the French interest at the curia, for which Richelieu then contributed some of the costs. Mazarini thus retained an escape route which might have been barred to him if his service to France had been of a more direct nature. Antonio was bound, in his formal capacity, to represent French interests. If the result was unfavourable and Papal policy were to take a more pronounced Spanish turn, no blame could attach to Mazarini, since his patron was only performing his proper function: no more than to an advocate who loses a case in a court of law.

Playing the political game that suited him, Mazarini also entered *con brio* into the cultural life that was making Rome such a stimulating place, especially to those privileged to enter the *palazzi*, gardens and private theatres; but a free show too, for ordinary citizens, who could admire the exuberant facades, watch the artists at work, enter churches resplendent in fresh stucco and paint, saunter round the new squares and linger by the cooling spray of fountains. Surely they experienced some of the delight of the modern visitor at the monuments of the glorious city that was being created around them. There was little in the private life of the great that escaped the eyes of Romans. When Mazarini purchased the *palazzo* Bentivoglio,[18] in 1641, a crowd came every evening to admire it, to inspect the alterations, even to play football in the courtyard. Romans were proud of their city. It was the foundation of a self-respect, even of consciousness of a civilised superiority, which was to sustain the vice-legate in the remoteness of Avignon, the cardinal-minister in the trials of high office, and in exile. Where, he could ask of one who might disparage his country, were the greatest French painters perfecting their technique? Where was the greatest and most exciting sculptor in the world to be found? Where would men come to hear the finest music, to sample the new delights of the opera?[19]

Mazarini's own commitment to the arts was neither superficial nor mercenary. An aesthetic sense trained by keen observation and a delight in objects of beauty was to survive his later mania for collecting them. For a man who depended much on the company of friends, who expressed himself characteristically, when alone, in long effusive letters, Mazarini had also a degree of self-sufficiency, with a toughness and resilience which became more marked as he matured into the statesman. In part that can be ascribed to his early successes and the experience of meeting great men on equal terms; in part to the enrichment of sensibility which turned an accomplished *galantuomo* into a man of well-rounded personality and proven staying power: qualities he would need if he were to succeed in his next assignment.

5

NUNCIO EXTRAORDINARY

In August 1634, appropriately on the feast day of St Louis,[1] Mazarini left Rome for France. With a small entourage, he travelled in a sumptuous carriage drawn by six mules: paintings, including four Titians and a Pietro de Cortona, and chests full of scents and trinkets, were destined for Richelieu's gallery, the gifts of Cardinal Antonio. To him Mazarin owed his new appointment – to follow his friend Bichi as Papal representative at the French court. Urban had refused to award him Bichi's title of Nuncio, but satisfied Richelieu by allowing Mazarini to come as Nuncio Extraordinary.

Mazarini's leisured progress reveals much about his ability to learn from important people: convincing each of his special interest, while keeping an open mind and freedom of action. In Florence he met the exiled Charles of Lorraine, who had paid the forfeit for possessing lands of strategic importance on France's vulnerable eastern frontier and for involvement in French court politics. At Modena he lost his favourite violinist Michelangelo to the service of its duke and learned of the Habsburg triumph at Nördlingen. Mazarini took a typically optimistic view: he was 'certain of being listened to with more courtesy and attention after this event'. At Turin he spent agreeable days in the company of duchess Christina. At Avignon he was advised by Louis XIII's governor in Languedoc that the formation of an Italian League would aid universal peace talks.

When Mazarini eventually arrived in Paris at the end of November, his carriage was escorted to the Porte St Antoine, thence by the usual ceremonial route to the Place de la Grève,[2] past the Hotel de Ville, and along the right bank to the Louvre, by the hundred carriages of the official party of welcome, led by the Comte d'Alais. It was customary for new envoys to be accorded a grand formal entry. Where the church was involved, further dignitaries would grace the occasion. The lavish scale of this reception indicates the importance attached by the French to good relations with the Papacy. Richelieu could rely on the new nuncio to report in fulsome terms. Nördlingen had brought him nearer to the necessity of open war. Mazarini's mission was therefore as delicate as it was important and he needed all his buoyancy to overcome anxiety about unrealistic objectives: 'You can well believe', he wrote to Servien, 'that I have not wanted to occupy myself with negotiations which cannot succeed . . .' But to be in Paris, close to that man of genius in whom he saw personified the expansive destiny of France – that was enough to still doubts.

The Pope had given his nuncio three objectives which, separately, would be hard enough to achieve: to make Louis XIII accept the marriage which Gaston had secretly contracted with Marguerite of Lorraine;[3] to persuade France to restore Lorraine to her brother Charles; and to prevent Richelieu from engaging in open war against the Habsburgs. Richelieu could only, however, be guided by his assessment of military risk or advantage. Till now his strategy had been to work through allies, the Dutch, latterly the Swedes, while taking steps to strengthen his vulnerable frontiers, occupying first Lorraine, then Trier. He was aware of weaknesses in his armies extending to the top, where generals might put political interests before loyal duty. Spain had to be confronted however, and subsidies were expensive: armies based in the eastern provinces might be more cheaply deployed in enemy territory. Studying developments, and discussing policies with officials, Mazarini enjoyed a privileged apprenticeship in statecraft. He began to venture into the master's field. One day, in March 1635, he pressed the case for Lorraine's duke and, as he reported, made an eloquent plea for peace. 'His Eminence rose and retorted that I courted peace as if it were the lady of my dreams and, pressing my hand, concluded: "you have not yet abandoned France".'

Richelieu was becoming resigned to the near-certainty of a war which Olivarez seemed positively to welcome.[4] Lorraine was a vital piece on the strategic board. The alliance between Gaston and Marguerite was one which Richelieu was bound to oppose. The marriage was moreover invalid, according to his ecclesiastical lawyer, because it had not received royal consent, that being a custom of France 'affirmed by legitimate prescription and authorised by the church'. Here the Papal diplomat was encountering the obstacle of Gallicanism,[5] that corpus of law and tradition, drawn upon at need by the crown, not always prominent on the surface, but iceberg-like, massive beneath. It was an early lesson in the singularity of French institutions, a useful warning against relying on the ultramontane assumptions of the Vatican experts, indeed on their ability to achieve anything substantial against the sovereign's will.

What that will meant, affecting immediately the fate of millions, was displayed on 26 May 1635 when, with formal trumpeting of heralds, in the *grande place* in Brussels, Louis XIII declared war on Spain. Mazarini had then apparently failed in each of his objectives. Soon, barring extraordinary events, the death of Richelieu or a heavy French defeat, he would have to choose between service of the Holy Father and that of 'le roi trés chrétien'. Meanwhile, at Rome, Cardinal Antonio, labouring to persuade Urban not to declare for Spain, was emphatic about the value of his client. As he wrote to Richelieu: 'there is no one in whom I place more confidence than Mazarini . . . I have always found him the best servant that His Majesty or you could have'. Mazarini, in turn, was to report Richelieu's favourable response in the awkward French he was learning to use – and which gives the reader some idea of the pronunciation which brought smirks from the French listener: 'le Cardinal Antoine et for generos el il aeme bien le France'. He was partisan but realistic. In October 1635, for example, he wrote that Paris, like all France, was full of people sympathetic to Spain: they were 'dominated by the belief that change of government will improve their condition'.

Ever an enthusiastic shopper, Mazarini sent home presents and recommended purchases to his patrons, such as a Flemish tapestry, 'very rich in gold', which reflected his taste for the sumptuous. He turned his love of music to good effect to win Richelieu's respect as one of the *cognoscenti*. To provide proof of taste, by presenting him with the finest paintings, was also a way to share Richelieu's guarded hours of privacy in the Palais Cardinal. No matter that the Frenchman could still patronise and tease him in ways which must have left Mazarini wondering where he stood in Richelieu's highly cerebral scale of valued relationships. A man less resolved to rise might have resented the use of familiar names, *nunzincardo*, or *Colmardo*.[6] Mazarini could clearly not reciprocate in that bantering vein: he had to keep his place. It was worth reporting to his superiors that he had 'made His Eminence laugh'. Committed to no faction and uninhibited by office under the crown, it was a positive advantage that he was foreign – for Richelieu was more likely to confide in him. Mazarini, the tyro statesman, can be seen as some perfect secretary, attending to Richelieu's needs and moods. But behind the compliance was an independent mind. His views about diplomacy were sufficiently well informed to command respect, even if they did not always coincide with those of Father Joseph. So this year, although barren in terms of diplomatic achievement, was to prove seminal in Mazarini's career, founded as it was on the trust of the most powerful man in Europe.

Meanwhile in Rome Cardinal Antonio remained loyal. Mazarini encouraged his patron's ambition with proposals that were also intended for the eye of the Pope: a well-considered diversion from his failure to restrain Richelieu from his aggressive schemes. There was a prospect, Mazarini suggested, that Rome might acquire the duchy of Castro, which lay just north of the Papal states, under the rule of Parma: if, assisted by France, the duke of Parma were to gain Spanish Milan, he would show his appreciation by giving Castro to the Pope. There were flaws in this optimistic projection, as Mazarini must have known.[7] Cardinal Francesco took a less sanguine view of the French connection. He inclined more openly than before to the Spanish party in Rome who were putting their weight behind plans to convene the peace conference which Mazarini was plainly failing to promote. It looked to Francesco as if the nuncio was so dazzled by Richelieu that he was losing sight of the prime object of his mission. So he called for talks about arrangements for a congress and ordered Mazarini to leave Paris for Avignon.

The Papal city, imposing and beautiful, where fourteenth-century Popes had once spent their 'captivity', was the traditional seat of Papal legates; Mazarini was, however, pointedly designated vice-legate. He accepted the move, in March 1636, with extreme reluctance. In Avignon's painted chambers he could neither shine nor manipulate. Richelieu wrote to him, expressing concern about an illness, in a courtly style that suggests a gently mockery of Mazarini's own style; but he concluded in words which might convey to the woe-begone exile that he sympathised: 'I am much afraid that this good Italian lord has been so much affected by his situation that his state of mind is more sick than his body'.

At Avignon Mazarini succumbed to uncharacteristic depression. During this period he is seen to have had no inclination to pursue learning for its own sake, or even to equip himself more fully for the world in which Richelieu shone so brightly. When he might have been studying theology or venturing into the stirring world of the philosophers, he was complaining to Chavigny that his 'life in this country is the most melancholy in the world'. We hear nothing of Mersenne,[8] for example, who had recently founded his mathematical academy in Paris, nor of the Provençal Gassendi,[9] the priest whose speculations were becoming so influential. Mazarini left no devotional writing. His letters betray no speculative interest. If retreat meant an opportunity for reflection or more systematic cultivation of his faith, we do not hear of such things. The friendship of Bichi, now bishop at nearby Carpentras, could do little to sustain his spirits. He converted one of the ancient drawing rooms into a gambling den: 'but after playing for an hour I am more bored than ever'. He assured Richelieu that 'he would exchange his life for the gardener's, at Rueil'.[10] The frustrated nuncio, for whom the point and savour of life were to be found in human relationships, was becoming anxious about his standing with Richelieu and he suspected *surintendant* Bullion[11] of fostering prejudices. The *surintendant*'s main offence was, however, that he did not pay the money due to Mazarini.

Richelieu's indifference to the fate of the exile is easy to understand. Sixteen thirty-six saw the summer of Corbie,[12] when Spanish and Imperialist armies crossed the frontier in strength. The French attack of the previous year had ended in failure, as remnants of the army pulled out of Flanders in demoralised disorder. The campaign had exposed the

33

defects of an army still in some respects feudal, relying on the skill of individual generals, lacking professionalism. Imperialist and Spanish veterans of the German and Netherlandish wars believed that the French had no stomach for a fight. As in 1940, deep political divisions had an enervating effect. The hasty surrender by the governors of La Capelle and Le Câtelet, towns lying in the path of the advancing Spanish troops, suggested treason: La Force's unpaid army in Alsace was mutinous. In Italy Marshal Créqui's Franco-Savoyard drive on Milan had come to nothing and Victor Amadeus threatened to defect. In early August the Spanish captured Corbie, near Amiens, while the Imperialist Werth's vanguard of Croatian horse, ill-reputed for savagery, pushed on as far as Compiègne, two days' ride from Paris. With refugees thronging the streets of the capital and Richelieu talking of evacuation, the vice-legate in Avignon may have wondered if he had backed the wrong horse.

It was not merely a military crisis. *Parlement*, as ever a sensitive political indicator, objected strenuously to edicts creating new offices. The measure was designed to supplement inadequate taxes and it was ominous that it was deemed necessary after only a year of war. *Intendants* were starting to impose forced loans on towns.[13] At Rennes, in September, the riotous Breton mob supported the stand of the Estates against higher taxes. Heavy taxation was the main cause of the Croquant revolts[14] which disturbed some of the more remote and ungovernable provinces in the southwest. So it was fortunate for hard-pressed ministers that the military threat had lifted by Christmas. As in 1792, as in 1914, enemy commanders lost their nerve as their lines of communication were stretched. The French did indeed rally bravely: spirited attacks recovered Corbie and the rolling plains around the Somme. Louis XIII rode off to join his troops at Senlis. Richelieu's *Gazette*[15] puffed each French success but he had been shocked by the failures of the summer. He had been forcibly reminded of the proximity of Paris to the frontier. Nightmares from the days of civil war and a Spanish presence in northern France were revived. He faced the urgent need to reform the armies and strengthen his grip on the administration.

Meanwhile Mazarini had been eating his heart out at Avignon, observing the crisis in a war which his master had expected him to prevent, aware, even after the rolling back of the Habsburg armies, that Richelieu might be overthrown at any time and French policy come into the hands of men like Châteauneuf,[16] a lover of Mme de Chevreuse,[17] disgraced by Richelieu in 1633. Mazarini dispatched a load of gunpowder for the army's use. But it needed more than Richelieu's letter of thanks to dispel his sense of insecurity. He would rather lose his head, he wrote, than lose the support of the Barberinis, 'for then what solution would there be for me, persecuted by the Spanish, deserted by His Eminence, and without any assurance of being well received in France, where the situation can change in no time at all?' Francesco Barberini might indeed have left him to stew, but now he reaped the reward of his cultivation of Antonio – for it was he, in November 1636, who obtained leave for Mazarini to return to Rome.

The rigours of seventeenth-century travel and the man's agitation can be seen in Mazarini's behaviour when, after a month's journey, he arrived in Città Vecchia and rode post-haste to arrive early in the morning and fling himself at Antonio's feet. He was received with affection and reassurance. Perhaps Antonio was amused that anybody could care so much as to so exert himself at such an hour. Mazarini could not trust overmuch to this pillar of the church, whose own position was being undermined. But he never forgot Antonio's timely aid; when their positions were reversed, he in power, Antonio in disgrace, he was to provide for him generously out of the revenues of the church. There were many cases where Mazarini's kindness was clearly calculated; others where it was magnanimous; others where it was disinterested and warm-hearted. Marshal Toiras,[18] defender of Casale, had befriended him during those anxious days when he was making his career. Subsequently disgraced, Toiras might have seemed a risky subject for support. Mazarini interceded to gain permission for him to serve Savoy. When he died soon after, Mazarini's praise for him was ingenuous: the marshal loved Italy and in his esteem for men of virtue he made no distinction of nationality. Nor, Mazarini evidently hoped, would Richelieu.

Mazarini went to Rome armed with instructions from Richelieu which made him, in effect, Louis XIII's personal agent at the Papal court. Mazarini was empowered to assure Urban that France would exchange the now useless alliance with England for one with Bavaria. As a weapon of last resort he was provided with a memoir on the subject of 'a Holy War'. Seeing a more promising goal than was provided by the temporarily inert bulk of the Ottoman Empire,[19] Mazarini worked, nominally under Antonio's direction, for the revival of the peace congress at Cologne. There his steady friend, Zongo Ondedei,[20] became the recipient of detailed letters, full of practical advice, reflecting throughout his concern for peace. Mazarini also kept Ondedei informed of Richelieu's views and encouraged him to anticipate imitating his own progress 'from legate's desk to more exalted office'. For Ondedei there was frustration, as the congress never assembled; only after his patron's elevation to power in France was he to have a significant political career. Meanwhile Mazarini was assiduous in caring for his own interests in Paris where his agent, the amiable *abbé* Charles,[21] assured him that the people who mattered were his friends. He might not receive the abbey of Saint-Avold, for Condé had laid claim to it. But he should take heart from the news that Richelieu had instructed his official entertainer, Boisrobert, to keep his new play in production until his return to be nuncio. Mazarini could also count on the friendly concern of Father Joseph, Sublet de Noyers,[22] the new war minister and, above all, Chavigny, who became his principal political correspondent.

The letters of these years between two aspirants to high office, the one, in his own esteem, virtual director, under Richelieu, of foreign policy, the other hoping to put his talents at the service of France, are a prime source for the diplomatic history of the time. Their style was high-flown, as Mazarini strove to emulate the exaggerated expression favoured by *habitués* of the *salons*, not least by this rising star. Thus writes Chavigny: 'I hope for your return to France as for that of a beloved' and in answer, Mazarini: 'He that would tell me I should never return to France would pronounce my death sentence'. Chavigny's affectation beyond the conventional hyperbole of correspondence between patrons and clients,[23] need not suggest insincerity. The young Secretary of State, father of many children, looked to the Francophile Italian to further his career. The interest of the Spanish cardinals was strong enough temporarily to keep Mazarini at Rome. There he served France while still working, ostensibly, for the disillusioned and increasingly dissatisfied Pope, and for Antonio, whose credit waned with receding hopes of German peace.

These were frustrating but important years for Mazarini, furthering his political training as he endeavoured to reconcile the interests of his masters in Rome and Paris. He tried unavailingly to secure for Father Joseph the Cardinal's hat. It was sobering to encounter the prejudice in the curia against those who acted too openly in the interests of a foreign sovereign. The Pope was reluctant to promote a friar and critical of Father Joseph's intrigues within the Empire. In vain Mazarini stressed the Capuchin's efforts to reduce the power of the Huguenots. He despatched a stream of presents, worked to build up a pro-French party in the Sacred College and tried to mediate between the haughty French ambassador d'Estrées,[24] and the Barberinis, who were offended by the Frenchman's temper. He took soundings among agents of the warring powers for the possibility of a truce, as preliminary to a general peace; in particular he sought to create good relations between the Italian states and France.

Savoy, always unstable, critically important in the delicate Habsburg-Bourbon balance, provided Mazarini with a way out of his impasse. Richelieu ordered that the correspondence of the French ambassador at Turin should be made available to him. Mazarini had carefully cultivated his relationship with Christina and her tolerant husband Victor Amadeus. It was largely due to him that the duke had made an open alliance with France by the treaty of Rivoli in July 1635. It proved hard to ensure cooperation between the French and Savoyard commanders. At the battle of Monbaldone however, in September 1637, the duke defeated a Spanish force and comported himself bravely. A month later, after a banquet given by Marshal Créquy, the duke and his chief minister, Mazarini's ally

Verrue, died, both after violent convulsions. Sudden and mysterious, though to one man highly convenient, the deaths inevitably gave rise to dark rumour. Christina herself did not escape suspicion, if only by association with her lover Philippe d'Aglié.[25] Her son, Charles Emmanuel,[26] was only five years old and a long regency was in prospect. She now did nothing to enhance her authority by installing Philippe as governor of Turin: virtually ruler of Savoy, he professed neutrality but pleased none of the powers most closely concerned. The Emperor challenged Christina's regency on the grounds that Savoy was an Imperial fief. Once again Mantua was involved in a train of events which was to prove significant for the contest between France and the Habsburgs, now so finely balanced, and for Mazarini's career.

Charles of Mantua's daughter-in-law Maria, inclining towards Spain, signed a treaty, in March 1638, by which she agreed to deliver Montferrate, with Casale, to Spain. The French, still garrisoning Casale, saw to it that the Savoyard governor was imprisoned before he could execute his orders. Olivarez rose to the bait and invaded the principality. The subsequent devastation scared Christina, and she resorted to placing her army under French command. The lines were now more clearly drawn. Maurice of Savoy,[27] uncle of the child duke, was not to be tempted from his allegiance to the Emperor. Thomas, the other uncle, already an officer in the Spanish army, was sent to enforce the imperial decree removing Christina from the regency. In 1639, two French generals, La Valette,[28] then Harcourt,[29] failed to prevent the loss of her capital Turin. 'That wretched woman', as Richelieu called the duchess, refused to hand over her son to the custody of Louis XIII or let France become 'protector' of her country. With the fate of Lorraine in mind, her reluctance is understandable. The situation was made for Mazarini's diplomacy – and by then he was again working from Paris, unequivocally, for Richelieu.

Mazarini had always been more sympathetic than Richelieu to the ducal family and more sensitive in handling Savoyard affairs. When the question first arose of a separate peace to end the war of France and Savoy against Spanish Milan he advised against it. Apparently inconsistent with his earlier concern for peace in Italy, indeed for a general peace in Europe, his change of front is specially significant. He had been converted to the French ministerial view of Olivarez as the inveterate warmonger: it had been reinforced by his experience at Rome. The obduracy of the Spanish cardinals did not encourage negotiation. Behind them the ebullient Olivarez was still acting, against accumulating military evidence,[30] as if Spain could yet emerge with credit from this war. Mazarini became disillusioned therefore with the prospect of peace on any basis other than the complete defeat of Spain. He came to see the Italian peninsula as the 'sensitive point' of the Spanish ulcer, draining her power, as it had in the Mantuan war. He moved warily towards the thinking of Father Joseph. Also he was coming to cherish the idea, long dear to Urban VIII, of liberating the north of Italy from the Spanish presence: Rome would then be relieved of concern about her own northern frontier, Savoy tied to France, French influence paramount in Italy. All would depend, of course, on the ability of Franco-Savoyard armies to win a decisive victory. That proved elusive and when, in 1638, France and Savoy signed a truce with the Emperor, the Spanish held back. That was how matters stood when news came, in December 1638, that Father Joseph had died.

Father Joseph had been a legend in his lifetime. 'Is it not a strange thing, that a demon should be so near to an angel?' This anonymous tombstone graffito expresses the enigma that continues to fascinate. Several views are possible of the unkempt, red-bearded figure with the prominent blue eyes who plodded about his master's business, carrying under drab cloak and cowl the sealed instructions of the king of France, creating webs of alliance, leaving trails of misunderstanding, working with but sometimes behind the backs of the king's accredited envoys. All was directed towards a European crusade which he hoped the Habsburgs would lead when they had been forced to abandon their secular objectives in Germany, Italy and the Netherlands. Ten days before the declaration of war in May 1635, Father Joseph spoke of his king's wish for a 'universal peace'. He was perhaps less anti-Habsburg than anti-Spanish – intensely so, like so many of the generation which had known the presence of Spanish soldiers on French soil. To the austere Capuchin may be attributed the sincere confusion of a man of God trapped in a moral maze: corrupted in some measure by politics, he retained to the last a certain integrity, and a touching humility.

In Mazarini, who had sought, but perhaps not too hard, to further Richelieu's request for a Cardinal's hat for Father Joseph, the latter recognised an expert and also possibly a rival. Mazarini certainly suspected that Father Joseph was jealous of his favour with the Cardinal. Yet Richelieu remained devoted heart and soul to the Capuchin, whose outlook on affairs of state was in many ways so similar. Father Joseph's death was a severe blow. 'Next to God, the principal instrument of my fortune' Richelieu had once called him. The would-be crusader left his memorial in the *Turciad*, a verse epic which Pope Urban called the 'Christian *Aeneid*'. The mystic, in the demanding school of Mme Acarie,[31] and Benet of Canfield,[32] could relate to the Cardinal in words and ways with which Mazarini was unfamiliar. 'Breisach is ours' Richelieu is said to have whispered, anticipating a report which would bring joy to the dying man. Love of country had never displaced in Father Joseph the greater love. In one part of his life's work, guiding the Congregation of Our Lady of Calvary,[33] through letters and meditations, he had written several million words. Richelieu could understand it. During the years 1636 to 1639, fraught with anxieties, he found time to compose his *Treatise of Christian Perfection*.

Theirs was a world of mutual sympathies and shared perceptions, as much *dévôt* as *politique*, alongside which Mazarini could only be, in most important respects, an alien.

The death of Father Joseph left a void – which the Italian could not fill. He could, however, take over the diplomatic role. He was sufficiently well established in Rome to anticipate the Cardinal's hat which Richelieu now sought for him. The *premier ministre* himself was far from robust: the question of succession could not be neglected, if for no other reason than to ensure continuity in diplomacy at a critical juncture of the war. Because Richelieu had taken pains to guard against the possibility of any one becoming strong enough to challenge him, there was no obvious successor. All was therefore to play for. Mazarini had been dealt a good hand. He played it with consummate skill.

6

THE CALL OF FRANCE

'I was twenty-two years old ... I had absolutely never had any business with the French when a servant of the duke of Parma, who was considered a great astrologer, asked me why I laboured serving the Spanish, since all my fortune, honours and advantages would come to me from France': so wrote Mazarini to Chavigny in 1637. By then French service had begun to seem to Mazarini an attractive option, with something of inevitability about it. Years before Urban VIII had allowed himself to be persuaded to embark on the foolish war against Parma (1642),[1] which depleted Papal finances and compromised his role as peacemaker, it was becoming clear to his disconsolate servant that little was left of the authority that had enabled a Pope, as recently as 1598, in the Franco-Spanish treaty of Vervins, to exercise a decisive influence. The Pope could not compel rulers to heed his voice. The peace initiative at Cologne had foundered because none of the principals had thought it timely: each still looked for advantage.

Mazarini had tried to engage the princes, through their chief ministers, in serious talks. He hankered after a meeting at the summit, where the possibility of peace could be considered in a practical spirit. When there was so much fatalism about, Mazarini's persistence was admirable. He was always looking for a reliable contact; first the nuncio in Madrid, Campeggio, in May 1635; then the count of Salazar, prisoner of the French but released at Mazarini's request to use his influence at Madrid, in July 1636. Then Francisco de Mello, a young soldier and, Mazarini believed, 'Olivarez's confidential friend' was approached in November to act as a go-between for the making of a truce which Mazarini saw as the first step. All to no avail. As Mello assured him, Olivarez would have none of it. As for the old Emperor, the Electoral meeting at Regensburg in December 1636 saw the culmination of his life's work when the Electors approved the peace of Prague, elected his son Ferdinand king of the Romans and so guaranteed his succession to the Empire. When Ferdinand II died in February 1637, a Habsburg victory still seemed to be worth waiting for.

As France first withstood the Austro-Spanish onslaught, then fought

back, Olivarez became obsessive about Richelieu's hand in moves that
thwarted him. He might assure a French agent that 'there was no outstanding difficulty between the two crowns', only then to harangue his
junta to the effect that 'Richelieu wishes only to fool us and the answer
is to prosecute the war with greater fury than ever'. Even after the Catalan
revolt, when the veteran Oñate told him that there was no future in war,
he persisted in his European strategy. Mazarini could not have seen the
future with the retrospective clarity that is the historian's advantage.
Indeed there are still divisions of opinion as to the extent of Spanish
decline in these years.[2] He could however have discerned enough from
favourable reports of Bernard of Saxe-Weimar's operations in the Rhineland, or even from the increasing stridency of the Spanish party at Rome,
to justify his open commitment to France.

Making a judgement about military prospects and relative resources,
Mazarini was abandoning his neutral ground for the apparent security of
the chosen camp. Does that mean that he was no longer sincere in his
pacific professions – or that he had never been? The evidence of
his correspondence and actions during the next few years suggests that
he saw a better chance of achieving his goal from a position of strength:
first let the Habsburgs be defeated, then let there be peace. In terms of
country the move was not such a great one. When sense of national
identity, limited in France, non-existent in Italy, is discounted, the Alps
seem but another physical barrier. They had not deterred French kings,
from Charles VIII, from pursuing Italian claims, nor Italian notables from
seeking their fortunes. Great names, Gondi and Particelli (soon to be
surintendant), not to mention two Medici queens and the favourite of the
latter, Concini,[3] are a reminder of financial enterprise and political ties.

Intermittently there had been a special relationship between the French
crown and the Papacy. Mazarini was well placed to appreciate its value.
He had already been captivated by France, not so much by the idea of
the *patrie* as a Frenchman might cherish it, the beloved homeland, the
realm to which he rallied at times of crisis, as in 1636, when insurgent
peasants laid down their arms rather than be of aid to the enemies of
their king; more by French men and women as he found them: by their
manners, ideals, *esprit*. The qualities of heroism and magnanimity celebrated by Corneille[4] he found in the soldiers, Créquy, Schomberg and
Toiras, whom he encountered in his diplomatic missions. What diplomacy
could achieve he recognised in the professionalism of Servien and
d'Avaux,[5] talented exponents of his own *métier*. In ministers like Chavigny
and Sublet de Noyers, in the virtually hereditary legal establishment, he
saw skills of management applied to a widening range of responsibilities,
offering unprecedented rewards. Above all he saw in Richelieu one who
used his sovereign's authority so effectively that he himself had something
of the sovereign about him: manipulating a small army of clients, amass-

ing a fortune, presiding over a splendid court, creatively involved in the refining of a distinctive civility. There was much for the Italian to identify with and to emulate. He had seen the cardinal depressed. He knew him to be an invalid, fighting against distressing ailments and the butt of cruel jokes on this score; a prematurely ageing figure beneath the scarlet cassock. But he could see nothing pathetic about Richelieu. Richelieu's own propaganda in the sponsored *Gazette* and *Mercure*,[6] in the work of pensioned or specially commissioned political philosophers, poets and playwrights, embellished the picture of royal authority imposed with increasing force on a country turbulent and prone to revolt, but of vast potential when firmly governed.

Undoubtedly Mazarini was dazzled by his own ambition: what he wanted to see in the haven he chose, so profitable and so civilised, he did see. The material rewards were real; the *douceur de vie* beckoned. There was also the challenging aspect of French society, the penchant for fine gestures and bold actions in love and war, the absolutism in matters of faith and honour. He had yet to experience its irresponsible, spoiling spirit that was to infect the Fronde. Meanwhile, some of his comments on the French say more about him than about them: 'that nation is by nature adventurous and relies on its courage' and 'no other nation on earth succeeds more happily in bold and dangerous actions'. His focus was not only Catholic but Mediterranean; he knew little about England, except what he might have gleaned from Walter Montague.[7] That sentimental nobleman had long cherished a romantic attachment to queen Henrietta Maria.[8] He hoped to win the queen's favour and further the cause which he made his own: the conversion of England to Roman Catholicism.

Mazarini enjoyed Montague's friendship and apparently subscribed to his sanguine view of English politics. In September 1636, when Montague was staying with Mazarini at Avignon, the latter had gone so far as to predict that Charles I 'would be touched by the divine hand and driven . . . to return to the old devotion and obedience'. Mazarini would learn more about England, soon to be wracked by civil war. At this stage his knowledge was superficial. Nor was he yet well acquainted with the affairs of the United Provinces, though keenly aware of their strategic importance. There is a way in which, arising inevitably from the nature of their dealings, diplomats skim over the polished surface of societies. Their calculations may however be upset by disturbances arising from those conditions in society which they have been unprepared or unwilling to study. When the view is also, like Mazarini's, that of the outsider, who has not acquired through upbringing the instinctive grasp of particular institutions and mentalities, the risk of miscalculation is greater. When he is not merely advising but directing, it is potentially catastrophic. Meanwhile we can notice a disturbing superficiality in Mazarini's outlook, reflected in sometimes trite remarks about people and issues. Yet when he praised the 'openness of mind which is peculiar to the French nation', surely he was not simply being glib. Was there not an element of disillusion with his own people, the deviousness, myopia and petty conceits that can pervade privileged officialdom – all of which were to be found at the Papal court? Was he not expressing the venturesome side of his personality which warmed to aspects of Richelieu's France: its educated men and women sharp in debate, appreciative of wit, willing to innovate, responsive to excellence, cruel to mediocrity?

After Father Joseph's death the Chavigny connection proved its value. Richelieu had entrusted Chavigny with the delicate task of keeping Gaston under surveillance. Richelieu's *créatures* tended to be too much concerned to maintain a good relationship with the Cardinal, to risk adopting too independent a stance. But they could follow their patron's example by building up their own *clientèles*. In the first years of his secretaryship Chavigny had specialised in Italian affairs while Father Joseph handled relations with Germany and the north; dealings with English ambassadors, held to be relatively unimportant, were left to Bullion. Chavigny was now coming to look like a foreign minister. Mazarini can therefore be excused if he attached weight to his private opinions, significantly conveyed in Italian to evade the Cardinal's spies. He would have been displeased to hear (December 1636) that 'Christendom ought not to believe that peace encounters obstacles on our part . . . It is necessary to preserve our reputation and announce the departure of deputies [for Cologne] as soon as we know the final decision of the Swedes [about the renewal of the alliance with France]'. Chavigny's thoughts mattered less, however, than his continued interest in Mazarini and the latter's views. They can be seen as a trailer for eighteen years of statecraft devoted to his adopted country; otherwise there would be something comic about Mazarini's ardour. Richelieu's waspish, condescending references to the ardent Roman suggest some laughs in the *salon* at 'Monsieur Coupe-chou's' expense. Yet Richelieu knew his value. When he had put him up for promotion as French candidate to the sacred college, in January 1639, he wrote: 'Monsieur Colmardo is well aware how useful it is to have good friends and that I am not the least of them'. Mazarini was grateful: 'it would have been the end for Colmardo if he had not been upheld by Your Eminence's affection'. He made a further step towards his goal by applying for French naturalisation in order to enable him to move freely, bequeath property and possess ecclesiastical benefices in France: for example, he could be nominated abbot of St Médard at Soissons, whose revenues were already reserved to him. In the introduction to the letters of naturalisation sent to Rome, Louis XIII referred to the 'important services of *le sieur* Jules Mazarin to the public in diverse negotiations, treaties and affairs concerned mainly with peace and tranquillity among the most powerful princes of Christendom'.

Richelieu had been reluctant to go to war. He would have appreciated the strength of Mazarini's argument (December 1637) that 'peace would bring him the love of all the French people while His Majesty would enjoy the advantages of success brought about by the war'. But he now saw advantages in pursuing the war. The Cardinal-Infant, embattled in Flanders, could expect little help from Spain after the destruction of the annual treasure fleet, in October 1639, at the battle of the Downs.[9] In the same month a treaty was signed with Erlach, the successor in command of the forces of Bernard of Saxe-Weimar. Since his capture of Breisach in the previous December, Bernard had shown signs of independence. His death in July 1639 secured the vital Rhine fortress and his army for France. The revolt of the Nu-Pieds[10] of Normandy in the same year reinforced *surintendant* Bullion's warning that 'he had reached the bottom of the pot'. Yet France could better afford than Spain to hang on in this war of attrition. Was it a sign of desperation that Olivarez sent his emissary Jacques de Brecht to negotiate? A key proposal was that Holland should be made to return to Portugal that part of Brazil that she had conquered. Olivarez hoped to split the allies; but Richelieu was resolved not to jeopardise the Dutch alliance. Moreover grievances about Brazil would inflame Portuguese opinion against Spain. The Papal legate in Paris, Ranuccio Scotti, came to discuss the Pope's proposals for peace; he found Richelieu busy with plans for taxing the Church and marshalling Gallican arguments so convincingly that Urban believed that he contemplated schism.

In November 1639 Jules Mazarin, as we should now call him, as did the French, was formally invited to come to France. For frustratingly slow months he had experienced the venom of the Spanish party and the temper of d'Estrées, who was unhelpfully fierce in defence of the interests of France. In September he was saddened by the death of his brother-in-law Geronimo Martinozzi, which left his sister Margarita with the care of two young daughters, Laura and Anna-Maria. Mazarin would not neglect them but he was impatient to get away. Denied a passport through Spanish Italy, he took the risk of travelling by sea. A strongly-armed French ship and following winds gave 'that security which the Spanish had denied me'. From Cività Vecchia to Marseilles took but three days. At the end of the year he was in Lyons. On the 5th of January 1640 he was in Paris to kneel before king and cardinal. He was never to see Rome or his parents again.

Part II

FRENCH SERVICE

'I had attached myself to the Cardinal by instinct, even before
understanding from experience his great qualities.'
Jules Mazarin

7

CARDINAL MAZARIN

'To a gentleman (*galant homme*) any country is his homeland'. So Mazarin had written in 1637, in the equable spirit that supported him in many trials. He had begun to see himself as a Frenchman 'by gratitude and by temperament'. During his last Roman summer, he had been willing to serve in any capacity so long as it would afford escape. In June 1639 he had written to the king: 'I have no duty or greater desire in this world than to be able to appear in fact the servant of such immense devotion and respect as the goodness of Your Majesty gives me the glory of being'. Anxious to please, he worked on plans for Richelieu's projected theatre but soon became immersed in politics. To help effect a reconciliation between new master and old he secured the recall of d'Estrées. As if testing Mazarin's commitment, Richelieu first nominated him envoy to the proposed congress at Cologne, then held him back. At Easter he was required to attend the court at Amiens, established there to maintain contact with the army besieging Arras.[1] The Spanish defended it with a tenacity that suggests they were far from demoralised. If they had already sunk to a condition of irreversible decline, the history of the next two decades, and that of Mazarin, would have been very different. The city held out till August.

In the South too the French experienced failures. In August 1637 the Spaniards had besieged Leucate, on the frontier between Narbonne and Perpignan. Schomberg had eventually relieved the place, after a bold night attack on the Spanish lines. In the following year however his successors, Condé[2] and La Valette, had failed dismally to follow up their advantage. After a long siege, in September 1638, they assaulted Fuentarrabia; their undisciplined troops were first repelled, then fell back in panic. The episode is revealing. La Valette declined to confer with archbishop de Sourdis,[3] then, when his troops were replaced by the archbishop's, refused to join in the assault. Rightly fearing Richelieu's rage, he fled beyond his reach to England. This episode illuminates the attitude of noble commanders who regarded war as a private sport. It was one of the practical concerns that drove the 'absolutist' process.

Materials for war were hard earned; they were too precious to be squandered; on both counts the machinery of the crown had to be strong. Representing the state in the front line were the *intendants de l'armée*,[4] responsible directly to the war minister. The best, like Michel le Tellier, learned the hard way that successful government was about mobilising resources and bringing them to bear in the most effective way. There would be a revolution before the way was clear for a thorough application of absolutist principles. Richelieu could only hope that courage and enterprise would make up for the chronic indiscipline of French troops. Meanwhile he could find consolation in the success of his nephew Pontcourlay, operating off Genoa, under his personal instructions, with a fleet of galleys.

It may be deduced that Richelieu's ambitious designs were furthered more by Spanish failures than by the military competence of French troops. Yet the picture conveyed by the memoirs of Henri de Campion,[5] a young nobleman serving almost continuously in these campaigns, is of resource and heroism, of dashing attacks and heavy casualties, particularly among young nobles. He praises the expertise of the Spanish general, the younger Spinola, as well as that of his own commander Schomberg. Even when allowances are made for French logistical problems, the impression is again one of Spanish resilience in the face of Richelieu's aggression; all the more significant therefore were Spain's economic problems and in particular the crippling revolts of 1640. Alarming though the revolt of the Nu-Pieds was, it was confined to one part of one province: it was not exploited by noble dissidents; it did not become a serious separatist movement threatening the integrity of the realm; it did not offer the enemy a chance to open up a second front. Those were precisely the characteristics of the Catalan revolt which, followed by that of Portugal, was to be the prime pre-condition of the defeat of Spain, crucial therefore to the career of Mazarin. His diplomatic record can be properly assessed only in the light of this momentous alteration in the balance of power.

The revolt of the Catalans was the direct result of the war and of Olivarez's attempt to finance it. Trying to achieve both constitutional and military objectives, he was confronted by the multiple crises which were to lead to his downfall. After Condé had captured Salses, on the frontier of Roussillon, Spinola invested the town and, after a huge effort, succeeded in recapturing it (January 1640). The Catalans had long refused to contribute to the cost of empire; they were detested by the Castilians who bore the brunt, even after the Union of Arms.[6] In 1639 the province was chosen by Olivarez as the main front: he hoped Catalans would see the sense of paying for their own security. For many of them however, encouraged by Richelieu's agents, Castile, not France, was the enemy. The quartering of troops in Catalonia led to peasants taking up arms, then to a more general rising. In September 1640 the *diputacio* of Catalonia requested French aid: by the subsequent agreement French ships were allowed to use Catalan ports and 3,000 troops were sent in, to be paid for by the Catalans. Richelieu could afford to be ungenerous because the revolt had its own momentum. As Olivarez grimly said, Spain now had another Holland to deal with.

Richelieu had no love of rebels. There were French provinces, notably in the south, which might follow the precedent, if only to gain relief from tax burdens. When however the republic of Catalonia, so confidently proclaimed in January 1641, collapsed in anarchy, he had no alternative but to send in French officials to direct the war and levy taxes. The people soon wearied of such protectors. Long before the province was subdued, the revolt had ceased to be of service to the French and they had reduced their military presence. The revolt had become a sideshow, secondary in importance to that of Portugal. In December 1640 the palace of Lisbon was stormed by a crowd shouting for 'King Juan IV'. The subsequent war was to outlast Mazarin's life.

In a sense Portugal was on the fringe of Mazarin's Europe; but in some ways its concerns were central. The nobles who supported the duke of Braganza[7] in his bid to recover the throne lost by his forebears sixty years before had much in common with their restless counterparts in Catalonia, Sweden, England, indeed France.[8] There was national pride tinged with feudal spirit and there were material grievances. The Portuguese empire, so far-flung, so hard to defend from the resources of a country of barely a million and a half inhabitants, had always been a *tour de force*. Decline, in some measure, was inevitable. Involvement in the ambitious operations of Castilian imperialism had assisted the process. Portuguese antipathy towards Castile was no new phenomenon: the states were different in ways that England and Scotland were different, their frontier an area of dispute and violence. Xenophobia was now made more venomous by anti-Semitism.[9] The failure of the Pernambuco expedition to recover Brazil was the disaster which concentrated the minds of the Portuguese on the practical problems of staging a *coup d'état*. Their pride and sense of national identity ensured that it would be sustained with fanatical ardour. Long before the final defeat at Villa Viciosa in 1565, the prelude to their official independence three years later, the Portuguese, assisted in turn by the United Provinces, France and England, had conducted themselves as a sovereign nation. Meanwhile the Spanish were committed to another gruelling war. Indeed it could be said that that Rocroy was won on the fields of Iberia.

Catalonia, Portugal, finally Savoy: there was the remaining area of the southern fringe of the great European conflict which contributed to the decisive alteration of the diplomatic balance, through the intolerable cost to Spain of efforts to hold on, or to recover lost ground. It was in

Savoy that Mazarin's knowledge and cherished contacts were of the greatest use to his new master. So, in September 1640, Richelieu ordered him to go to Turin to bring about a settlement of Savoy's disordered affairs. It called for tact but also the nerve required of those who served the *premier ministre* – and the king. Mazarin was on trial. 'Colmardo must remember that powers greater than his [Richelieu's] take notice only of performance and scorn those who have more capacity for airy proposals and vain discourse than for useful actions'. So Mazarin was sent to inflict the punishment Richelieu had decided that count Philippe deserved for his mismanagement. Trying to ingratiate himself with the Piedmontese, he had refused to hand over the Alpine forts demanded by the French army which had been sent to relieve Savoy after the Spanish invasion the previous summer. The result had been the fall of Turin (July 1640) and narrow escape of the duchess herself, largely indeed through Philippe's presence of mind. A few days before Mazarin arrived, having shown his sense of urgency by reaching Savoy from Paris in the remarkable time of four days, Harcourt had re-captured Turin for the duchess. Mazarin at once arranged for Christina to return to her capital. On the last day of 1640 Philippe was arrested and sent to do penance in a French prison. He had to await Richelieu's death before the more sympathetic Mazarin could order his release: then he would return to find that Christina had taken another lover – though she did make him commander of her army, later finance minister. Meanwhile, in May 1641, Mazarin had returned to Paris, reasonably confident that Christina's regime would survive, though the treaty that guaranteed it, by which the towns held by France and Spain were returned to Savoy, was not confirmed until 1642.

During his nine months in Savoy Mazarin chafed sometimes at his absence from court at a time when Richelieu was ailing, and the king was in brittle health. Court speculation about the future had a sharper edge than ever. But it had been a gratifying role: a woman whose company he enjoyed, an element of conspiracy, a coup requiring daring and finesse – and all with the chance to strengthen the idea that he was indispensable. Impatient for results and anxious about the future, Richelieu had cause to appreciate his protégé's talents and manifest loyalty. The year 1641 saw another episode in the sequence of plots which makes up so much of the domestic history of France at this time. Its origin once again was the duchy of Lorraine. The treaty by which duke Charles received back his estate in return for accepting the status of vassal, the cession to France of Clermont and other strong towns, the provisional occupation of Charles's capital Nancy, and a promise that he would not make any treaty with France's enemies, appeared to give Richelieu all that he could reasonably expect. But the duke, anticipating his enemy's early demise, simultaneously provided his lawyer with a private disavowal of his concessions on the ground that they had been made under constraint. He would take the first opportunity to renege.

It came with the resurgence of noble plotting, stimulated by events in Savoy. The convergence of forces from Lorraine, Champagne, where Soissons[10] was governor, Sedan and the Spanish Netherlands was dangerous enough. It looked worse when Soissons and Guise, Thomas of Savoy's brother-in-law and co-leader of the rebels, had the better of a scrappy battle against Châtillon, at Marfée (6 July 1641). Then Soissons blew his brains out. It was reported that he had been careless, lifting his visor with his loaded pistol. His death was enough to dampen the ardour of the remaining rebels. Charles of Lorraine reverted to his previous role of imperialist general. Bouillon[11] made his peace with the crown and ceded his principality of Sedan. Within months he was conspiring again; Sedan was sequestrated, this time, in September 1642, by Mazarin in person on behalf of the king. In 1651, after a further ducal lapse, Mazarin would have to make a deal, costly to the crown but necessary in the dire circumstances of that year, by which the crown secured Sedan in exchange for other lands actually within France. The first episode in the saga provided Mazarin with a foretaste of conflicts to come and a lesson in the strategic interests of his adopted country.

Sedan was a vital piece on Richelieu's geo-political board. It commanded a bridge over the river Meuse and was a centre from which roads went to Paris and Dijon, and also into Germany, to Aachen, Strasbourg and Luxembourg. Nominally a sub-fief of France, it came under the lordship of the La Tour d'Auvergne family, entrenched for centuries in its own county in Quercy. They were Huguenots. They held land from the bishop of Liège, were princes therefore of the empire and in that title virtually independent sovereigns. The present head of the family, Bouillon, already a seasoned rebel, was soon to be a *frondeur*, as was his younger brother, Turenne,[12] whose precocious military talent Richelieu was so anxious to secure. The nature of feudalism in this, its last phase, was thwarting royal authority; the threat to security posed by magnates who owned the largest pieces of the mosaic of estates which composed France's eastern frontier, not so much a line as a zone, owing little to logic and everything to history – were together displayed in high profile by a family, too small in means to create an independent state, even in the fluid conditions of the German war, but too big to be mere subjects. They could exploit ambiguous status but then risked forfeiting the prizes to be obtained by service to the greatest lord of all, the king of France. So much greater their resentment when they saw his authority being usurped by a chief minister.

If anything were needed to demonstrate the rationale of absolutism, justifying arbitrary actions, the case of Sedan might be said to have provided it. Yet it is unlikely that Mazarin's thinking was so much changed that the security of frontiers or loyalty of subjects was uppermost in his mind, as it had to be in Richelieu's. In September 1641 he wrote to a Roman friend: 'I have good reason to think that at the end of the month I shall be on my way to Münster'. It was noted by Henri Arnauld[13] in October that Richelieu was 'working every day on the instructions for the peace embassy. Mazarin will be taking a suite of more than eighty people with him'. The Pope needed no further persuading. Mazarin had earned his cardinal's hat. He heard the joyous news on 30 December and hurried to the king to thank him and to savour his fame in the eyes of the *beau monde*. In January 1642 he received his brief. He can have been under no illusions as to the difficulty of even starting to make peace. Stubbornly attached to his high notions of royal rights, Louis XIII was unwilling to give up a single conquest: indeed he was looking forward to more, starting with Perpignan, capital of the now vulnerable Spanish province of Roussillon. Mazarin had to attend him as he set up court and head-quarters for that operation. But he had more pressing concerns.

The death of Urban VIII was thought to be imminent and Mazarin was expected, as leader of the French party among the Cardinals, to prepare the ground for the election of a suitable successor. After the death in July 1641 of his friend cardinal Bagni, devout humanist and widely esteemed even by the enemies of France, there was no obvious candidate. As it turned out Urban was to live for two more years, wracked by pain and grief. Meanwhile on 26 February, 1642, in the church of St Apollinaire in Valence, Louis took the square, scarlet biretta from the hands of the Pope's chamberlain and placed it on Mazarin's head. The Cardinal kneeling in humble obeisance before the Most Christian king: the symbolism was apt.

With his new prestige and much good will, the time was surely favourable for Mazarin to return to Rome. It would have been easy for him to cross Provence and take ship from Marseilles. The reader may be sceptical about his protestation in a letter to Bichi that he had only one wish, to serve the king in Rome. His standing had never been higher, in Rome or in France; he was negotiating the purchase of the Bentivoglio palace, the 'mad desire' he confessed to; he wished to see it, and his family; his ailing mother longed to see him. Yet his position was delicate. In France the supreme prize was his to bid for: the succession to Richelieu. He was not alone in wanting it; nor was the power of Richelieu secure even now. To absent himself from court, even briefly, might prove fatal to his chance of promotion; equally it might remove him from the danger of disgrace by association with a fallen minister. In the event Mazarin deferred his departure until the point when Richelieu, supported, after some anguish of mind, by Louis, had struck down his enemies and could ponder an orderly transfer of power. By then, having stayed by king and Cardinal, having done all that was required of him, Mazarin had strengthened his claim to high office.

Characteristically Richelieu's enemies had encompassed their own destruction. If Gaston of Orléans had been more determined or consistent he could have given a lead. No longer, since the birth of the dauphin in 1638, heir to the throne, he had great wealth and the disposal of patronage on a larger scale than any other subject. He was ready to be persuaded that it only required his backing to release his brother from the malign influence of the Cardinal; but he was no less ready to cooperate and reveal all when it became clear that Louis would back Richelieu against all comers. Irredeemably selfish, even cowardly, or so much a product of his upbringing and situation that he found it impossible to choose between two kinds of loyalty and policy, Gaston was in a most difficult situation. He was well placed to value the increase in royal power; at the same time no one was better able to understand the grievances of the magnates. The strained language of manifestos issued in his name, rehearsing the miseries of the poor, may have been no more than conventional rhetoric;[14] yet it is possible that Gaston acknowledged a higher claim to his sympathy, that of the French people, whose condition seemed to reinforce his own injured pride. Since neither Louis nor Richelieu usually shared their thinking with him or divulged their policies, he became the confidant of plotters. They, Vendôme, Soissons, Bouillon, Guise, bearers of the greatest names in France, lived in a world little touched by considerations of state interest, as it was understood by Richelieu. So they interpreted loyalty to the person of the king, which all professed, as requiring them to act against the minister who had usurped royal authority.

The conspiracy of 1642, in which Spanish aid was sought and the murder of the Cardinal considered, raises questions however, as much about the conspirators' judgement as about their morality. Henri d'Effiat, marquis de Cinq Mars,[15] Louis' spoiled favourite, was prepared to drive a coach and horses through royal policy to avenge himself on the minister who sought to reduce his influence over the king. He demanded a place on the council and would not be bought off by Richelieu's contemptuous offer of a governorship. Bouillon, fresh from negotiations over Sedan following his last revolt, saw a chance to recover his city and insisted on a treaty binding Spain to give troops and money to that end. Gaston let himself be persuaded that the king was now prepared to dismiss Richelieu. But Richelieu was gravely ill. Mazarin's letters to his niece, the duchess d'Aiguillon,[16] provide a commentary on his suffering and fortitude no less moving for being tinged with his own concern about the future. It is surprising that the conspirators were not prepared to let nature take its course. It is not surprising that Olivarez, facing political eclipse, hesitated before committing himself to the treaty which Fontrailles,[17] tracked there and back by Richelieu's spies, brought to Madrid for his signature. Another friend of Cinq Mars, François-Auguste de Thou, obtained from the queen blank, signed letters which could be drafted as orders to royal officials. It is possible however that queen Anne herself saw to it that Richelieu obtained a copy of the treaty. She was looking to the future: motherhood and the imminence of a greater political position gave her a new sense of responsibility. Fontrailles was discouraged by the public rift between Cinq Mars and the king: sensibly he left for England. Before other hawks could take wing, Richelieu acted with decisive speed to get royal warrants for the arrest of Cinq Mars, de Thou and Bouillon. Gaston cooperated as usual by divulging all he knew, then took refuge with his sister Christina before being coaxed back to court to sign the declaration which, with Bouillon's denunciation, was to be the death warrant of Cinq Mars.

Mazarin was responsible for Bouillon's contribution, coupled with the sequestration of Sedan, and Richelieu acknowledged his skill: 'M. le Cardinal Mazarin has negotiated so cleverly that M. de Bouillon has said enough to make our proof complete. His mediation is so necessary in these matters that I have asked him to return tomorrow in order to see that what is necessary is done to Monsieur and also to the sieur de Bouillon'. The picture of the amiable man of the world, who could reduce the awesome matter of treason to a little local difficulty among friends, is well conveyed by Mazarin's response: he was specially pleased at Bouillon's pardon since he [Mazarin] was 'the particular friend and servant of the vicomte de Turenne'. He also knew how vital it was to Richelieu that Turenne should remain committed to the regime. His victory at Kempfen in February had shown that he was at least the equal of the veteran Imperial generals.

There is nothing more remarkable in Richelieu's life than its last months when he toiled through the intense heat of the Rhône valley summer, for the state and for himself, body and soul, to accomplish the destruction of his enemies: not, be it noted, by summary justice, but through the patient sifting of evidence and due legal process. The suppurating ulcers that ravaged his body were painful reminders of mortality; he slept fitfully, but his mind was at full stretch. For liaison with the king and for the day-by-day conduct of diplomacy he relied chiefly on Chavigny; for the control of military operations on Sublet de Noyers; for the successful conclusion of the trial which led to the execution of Cinq Mars and Thou, in September, on chancellor Séguier; for confidential matters and special missions, increasingly on Mazarin.

A significant feature of the last decade, the corollary of Richelieu's pre-eminence in government, which gave him power to control and confidence to delegate, had been the development of a team of ministers, bound by ties of common interest, specialising and building up their own political empires. The prevalence of *clientèles*, in which men were bound to serve a patron by quasi-feudal ties, defined in formal terms expressive of fidelity and the expectation of reciprocal benefits, could have divisive effects when no one had overall control. In Richelieu's period it was plainly conducive to more efficient administration and consistent policy. In these months Mazarin, always a quick learner, had the opportunity to see, first, what could be achieved by the cooperative efforts of able ministers; but also, through the manoeuvres typical of politicians in any regime when change of leadership is imminent, the scope for disruption when there was no acknowledged principal to direct on the sovereign's behalf. The performance to date, with *intendants* active in most of the provinces, was impressive; the prospect, with the near-certainty of a long royal minority, was clouded.

Meanwhile circumstances and Richelieu's personal needs were drawing Mazarin closer to the inner circle where the crucial decisions would be made. On 23 May he witnessed Richelieu's long and detailed will. To be thus involved in the intimate detail of legacies, the expression of his thoughts about the future, redolent too of his philosophy of life and government, could only strengthen the bond between the two Cardinals. What they shared, so that it hardly needed to be spoken, as men of the Church with awesome secular responsibilities, was becoming more important than differences of character and style. Intimacy grows where one is ailing, the other tactful and considerate. Mazarin's being foreign, to some extent the outsider, capable of objectivity, his sympathetic manner and ability to find time for his patron, free as he was of the administrative load of the ministers, may have helped to ease suffering and provide reassurance. So it was in these months that Richelieu could envisage Mazarin as his successor, if not as First Minister, certainly as director of the great diplomatic effort that would be needed to bring peace to Europe and security to France.

8

ANNE, QUEEN MOTHER AND REGENT

The future was clouded; the present situation was abundantly clear. Richelieu was in control. That was the message of the sombre procession of barges, carrying musketeers and officials, with pikemen marching along the bank, guarding Richelieu's own barge, richly caparisoned in scarlet and gold, on the slow journey up the Rhône. From his bed, draped in purple taffeta, a wasted figure, his right arm already paralysed, he ordered the affairs of the realm. At Lyons in September, he supervised the final stages of the trial of Cinq Mars and Thou; here too he heard the news of the fall of Perpignan. From Nemours to Fontainebleau he had to submit to the painful jolting of a carriage; there he met Louis for one of the rare private talks in which these unlikely partners established the common ground which was always more important than their differences. In October, in the Palais-Cardinal,[1] he wrote a memorandum, setting out the conditions which the king should accept in future dealings with ministers: he must not let favourites interfere with political matters; he must check the truth of charges against ministers and punish those guilty of slander. To the end Richelieu had to play the political game according to the rules: the king ruled, the minister was his subject. Early in November, not having heard from Louis, he offered his resignation. Not till the 20th did Louis respond, but then exactly as Richelieu wished. He should stay in office and act with such freedom and authority as he required. A week later Cinq Mars's remaining associates were expelled from court.

When Mazarin returned, in mid-October 1642, from his mission to Sedan to receive Bouillon's castle for the king, he was given the task of drafting the instructions to d'Avaux 'for the treaty of peace'. It was work that Richelieu, in health, would have entrusted to no subordinate. Since 1636 Corbie had been a resonant name to Frenchmen: its abbey was also one of the richest in the land, worth 80,000 *livres* in peacetime.[2] So its gift now to Mazarin was no small mark of confidence. A minister would, of course, need a large income if he were to build up a *clientèle*. Mazarin was a late starter in this field; his need was correspondingly great. On November 18 Richelieu wrote to his niece, the duchesse d'Aiguillon, herself Mazarin's regular correspondent and keen ally: 'I was giving instructions to a minister of state when you were at the theatre'. If his reference to an official post which Mazarin did not yet hold was a slip, his subsequent words may explain it: 'I know only one man who can succeed me, though he is a foreigner'.

Exactly what Richelieu hoped the king would do cannot be established merely by such references. It matters more that Mazarin was given every mark of confidence. Richelieu would have known, because he knew the king, that whether Mazarin stayed in the ministry as one of a team, achieved primacy or fell to ruin, would depend on chance as much as on skill. What he could do was to help his trusted henchman to make good use of his opportunity. Writing to Prince Maurice of Savoy, nine days after the death of Richelieu, Mazarin was unequivocal about his debt: 'My great obligations to His Eminence are well known since, on his deathbed, he wished to demonstrate his affection for me by . . . representing to His Majesty that, due to the fidelity and zeal that I had for his service, I was not incapable of serving him. So just when I believed I had leave to return to Rome, I received the order to stay here and I was called to the council.'

In his last hours Richelieu was composing his own epitaphs. 'I have the consolation of leaving your kingdom in the highest degree of glory and reputation which it has ever had . . .' he said to the king; and, to the curé of St Eustache, that he prayed God to condemn him if he had ever had 'any intention other than the good of the state'. Historians will not quarrel with the first judgement and need not qualify the second. Few statesmen who have remained so long in power have held so faithfully to their principles, nor gone so far towards achieving their aims. Several of his last actions were to ensure that gains would be consolidated. He recommended for the highest commands Turenne and Condé's elder son, the twenty-two-year-old duc d'Enghien.[3] He advised that ministers be kept in office and singled out Mazarin for praise. He did not specifically request that Mazarin succeed him as *premier ministre*. Most likely he envisaged him as French plenipotentiary in charge of negotiations for peace: that he would have seen as the major task. There is no reason why he should have expected the king to die so soon. Louis had not committed himself to appointing any minister to the prime position; nor did he during the few months left to him. It was Chavigny and Sublet de Noyers who, on 4 December, took the news of the Cardinal's death to the king at the Louvre. Each of them had reason to hope that he might be the man. So surely did Mazarin when Louis actually asked him to carry on and devote the same care to affairs of state as his predecessor.

Meanwhile it looked as if the king intended to be in the saddle. Richelieu's *créatures* knew their work and they had experience of working together. In February however Louis fell ill and it became clear that tuberculosis was too far advanced to allow any hope. So he had to make immediate provision for what could only be a long period without an adult king. For regent there could only be two candidates, his brother, and Anne.

At different times Gaston had shown spirit on campaign and sense in council. His faults were part of the history of recent events. For him could be argued a manner distinctly more gracious than his brother's, a way with words that could charm seasoned lawyers in *Parlement* and, *au fond*, a loyalty to the family: that he was a Frenchman he might forget; not that he was a Bourbon. He was to show undoubted devotion to the young king. Mazarin had helped him extricate himself from the Cinq Mars affair which had found him so ambivalent: 'sa trop facile Altesse', as he appears in Richelieu's coded letters. To cultivate Gaston was one of several policies with which Mazarin insured against the uncertainties of his own future. Gaston must, of necessity, play a leading part, though not as regent. To that office, following tradition, Louis appointed Anne, but under precisely stipulated constraints. Gaston was to be lieutenant-general of the realm; Condé head of the royal household. Basic state policies were to be approved by majority vote in the council. There, Anne, Gaston and Condé were to share power with the ministers. Mazarin was to have a place but with no special duties and only such precedence as was due to his rank as Cardinal. Ecclesiastical benefices were however to be his responsibility and the regent was to take his advice in making appointments. The formal registration of the will in *Parlement*[4] added a last humiliation to Anne's last days of married life.

On 23 April councillors and courtiers assembled round the royal death-bed to watch the king receive the last unction. The next few days were bound to be tense; they brought surprise, even drama. Before Louis' death the dauphin had received his official baptism in the Louvre's Gothic chapel: he received his name, by the king's order, 'Louis le Dieudonné'. Significantly Mazarin was a godfather. When he went, with Pothier,[5] the Grand Almoner, to report to the king, the Dauphin returned to his nursery. It was reported that his father asked: 'What is your name now?' 'Louis XIV' he replied. 'Not yet', the king replied sharply. The story is probably apocryphal – but conveys, by way of projection, a courtier's feeling of suspense as the king hovered between life and death. He died on 14 May. Not quite five years old, Louis was too young to appreciate fully the splendour and peril of his situation. Anne of Austria did.

Neglected wife, proud mother, Regent of France, Anne was determined to protect his rights. She had found a role and she knew her mind. She was reputedly indolent, but since Richelieu's death she had worked hard to improve her position. She took pains to secure the support of the Vendôme family.[6] Illegitimate son of Henry IV he might be – but Vendôme was still a Bourbon: his son Beaufort was happy to pose as her champion. She won the allegiance of Condé: the prince agreed to the dissolution of the king's council. She found a sympathetic response among some *parlementaires* bruised under Richelieu, now scenting an opportunity for change. Omer Talon had already been alerted as to what she expected of *Parlement* when the king should die. She summoned a *lit de justice*.

It was the traditional name for a solemn session of *Parlement*, at which the king presided, attended by princes and peers. Held on his initiative, it represented the essential fact about this highest of legal corporations: its courts were royal courts, its members royal officers. In that no edict could become law without registration by *Parlement*, this court, with jurisdiction over a third of France, partook of sovereignty. Though in no political sense a representative body, it had a further constitutional role as guardian of the fundamental laws which defined certain rights of sovereign and subjects. Its prestige was enhanced by the long-established practice of purchase of office and the recent development of hereditary succession, through the *paulette*.[7] *Parlement*'s principal members, *noblesse de robe*,[8] had titles which might go back several generations. In all *Parlement* embodied an authority which even the strongest king was bound to respect. Although the crown had enjoyed, since 1439, the right to levy the *taille* without consent, it was not powerless in financial matters. It could speak for particular interests, corporations and officials. It could at times obstruct royal business.

The *lit de justice* had been used by Louis XIII to overcome resistance to financial edicts. In 1635 a session for the registration of edicts creating new offices, twenty-four of them in *Parlement*, had led to protests over the head of the *premier président*, the arrest and exile of the culprits, a subsequent strike by one of the courts and conciliatory action by the government, including cancellation of some offices. The incident reveals both the kind of issue that could generate a contest and the nature of monarchy, some way from absolute when it came to enforcing edicts which the magistracy believed to be arbitrary or injurious to legitimate interests. In February 1642 a *lit* had limited *Parlement* to judicial matters. The preliminary lecture dwelt upon the disorders of the Religious Wars, the restitution of royal authority under Henry IV, when France became 'the perfect model for accomplished monarchies', lapses during the regency of Marie de Médicis, and the elevation of the crown in the person of Louis XIII. It represented Richelieu's view, that it was only when royal power was fully recognised that 'France recovered her true strength'. Even then *Parlement* was allowed to keep its right of remonstrance about matters of finance 'if they find any difficulty in verifying them'. That clause would soon prove to be of crucial importance.

A regency provided the situation in which *Parlement*'s powers could be tested, in which militants could see to declare new principles and discover new precedents. While Louis XIII had been browbeating *Parlement*, the English parliament had been defying Charles I. The two institutions were wholly dissimilar in composition, function and tradition: it did not prevent young Parisian lawyers from looking enviously across the Channel. It was prudent of Anne, following the precedent of Marie in 1610, to seek a good relationship at the outset. She bid boldly for *Parlement's* support. On 18 May the judges were confronted by an imposing display of court solidarity: the little king on his throne in the *salle de justice*, was flanked by Condé, Orléans, Vendôme and other grandees. It was noted that bishop Pothier stood to the king's left: was he intended for high position? The Chancellor, Séguier, speaking for the crown, made a confident submission. Without demur *Parlement* voted to amend Louis' will. Anne was given powers to choose ministers and to decide policies on her own authority. There was irony in the spectacle of judges who had been so obstructive in the past now granting the Spanish queen mother the absolute authority she sought. Here can be seen the tactical plan which was to lead her to the Fronde.

That course was not inevitable. She was being invited to cooperate. Anne undertook to seek advice 'about the welfare of the state'. *Président* Barillon,[9] suggested that *Parlement* be empowered 'to discover some means of relieving the state and making remonstrances on the conduct observed in past affairs'. From that position it would be a short step to demanding the reversal of recent measures. The *intendants* had always been in the front line, government's trouble-shooters, over-riding local officials, particularly since their fiscal role had been extended. Their continued existence was an issue which could disrupt apparent harmony. The central one was finance. Since 1635 the cost of war had far exceeded the yield of taxes. So long as the war continued, there could be no end to the arbitrary exactions which had fouled relations between crown and *Parlement*.

From the outset therefore there were ambiguities about Anne's authority and doubts about her ability to use it. Even if peace had been imminent and financial moderation a prospect, she would still have needed *Parlement* more than would an adult king. Co-existence was feasible but would call for compromise and finesse. If she were to govern, Anne would have to make controversial decisions. Delegation of authority must be unpopular: in fact it was inevitable. Anne had been trained to domestic command, not to political management. To choose any one of the leading contenders for the position of *premier ministre* would be to offend the others. She did not delay. On the very evening of *Parlement's* session she announced that Mazarin would remain as minister and act as head of the council whenever Orléans or Condé were absent. To soothe ruffled feelings she said that she acted to ensure continuity in vital diplomatic dealings. But the message was plain: Mazarin was *premier ministre*.

It was not only offended *Importants*[10] who would view Anne's decision as a case of heart ruling head. She had however had months to ponder, and good cause, even without recalling her husband's good opinion of Mazarin, to trust his diplomatic capacity. There in any sovereign's choice of principal minister, an element of personal preference. In this relationship, characteristic of a phase of political development, half-way between personal and bureaucratic forms of government, the sovereign had to be comfortable with the man. It was not so much an official or contractual relationship, more a trust with such elements of partnership as are possible when one is sovereign, the other subject. The unique feature of the partnership that was to form between Anne and Mazarin, which sets it apart from those, for example, of Philip IV and Olivarez, James I and Buckingham, or Louis XIII and Richelieu, was the extent to which they relied on each other: the regent having an incomplete authority, the foreign cardinal beset by enemies and rivals. Both inherited strengths however: she from the French people's profound respect for monarchy, he from Richelieu's creative statecraft, with the instruments he had forged for his successor to use.

Mazarin's course of action was less straightforward than subsequent events might suggest. A year or so before it might have seemed as likely that he would become Pope, as *premier ministre*. In the dangerous world soon to be exposed by the *Cabale des Importants*, the gruesome precedent of Concini would remind him that Anne's patronage alone stood between him and disaster. Yet his inclination is clear enough. During the king's last illness he had been quietly turning to Anne. Through Pothier he had intimated his devotion and willingness to serve. Anne was grateful. 'I am persuaded', she wrote, 'that Cardinal Mazarin is my servant. It would be reassuring to have someone who could inform me of any intentions the king may have at his death so that they can be followed. For that I wish to avail myself of a person who is not in any way dependent on Monsieur or the prince de Condé'. She could have added, 'nor on one who has been Richelieu's zealous agent in the arrangements made to isolate me from the king and prevent my being queen in anything but name' – and in that way indicated, with reference particularly to Séguier and Chavigny, further reasons for Mazarin's rise to power.

Anne had responded shrewdly to the first challenge of her son's reign. First she had lulled suspicion by talk of dismissing Mazarin; then she distracted the council by seeming to favour the duc de Beaufort, Vendôme's vacuous son. She had flattered *Parlement* by according privileges which she knew they would demand. Once armed, she had acted promptly and decisively. These first actions were in character. She was not, like two previous queen mothers, a Médici, but a Habsburg, conscious of a long tradition of international rule at the highest level, in the grandest style. Now tasting power she revealed some of the autocratic traits to be expected when a proud woman has long been denied the chance of controlling any but her immediate circle, mostly female, mostly devout, and inclined to sympathise with her wrongs.

All royal marriages are to some extent matches of convenience. They cannot always be expected to produce loving partners. A sovereign would commonly feel justified in keeping a mistress. Successive wives of French kings had to accept such situations. Anne of Austria was married at the age of thirteen in 1615, to a boorish adolescent who did not conceal his preference for the company of soldiers and horses. She was now forty, having had her first child at the age of thirty-five. There had been several miscarriages much earlier in the marriage. The birth of the dauphin, followed by that of a brother two years later, did little to repair their relationship. Anne seems to have been repelled by the king's gauche manner and sullen moods, the repressed violence, intense attachments and emotional infidelities. He was a stammerer, hard put to hold his own with the quick-speaking people around him. Chronically unwell, too insecure to find fulfilment in state business, too conscientious to be able to relax without diversion, he seems to have needed and looked for a steady attachment. For some years he had found it – though it was not reciprocated – in Mlle d'Hautefort.[11] In 1635 he had fallen obsessively in love with one of Anne's ladies in waiting, Mlle de la Fayette,[12] 'la fille' of his carefully coded correspondence with Richelieu. It was to be to her, not to Anne, that he gave his crucifix on his deathbed. She had shrunk from his ardour however and sought the veil: he visited her in her convent to talk for hours through the grille. La Fayette's innocent love was noted by Mme de Motteville:[13] 'it ought to have brought happiness into his life but that prince was in no way destined to be happy'. 'He had nothing of the lover but jealousy', was Tallemant des Réaux's cruel comment.[14]

At the end of his life, Louis expressed remorse for the way he had treated the queen. Yet he had shown no more natural tenderness towards the mother of his children than towards the childless wife of twenty years. Offended pride may have led her into complicity in plots against Richelieu, whom she held responsible for the anti-Spanish direction of royal policy. She responded warmly to friendly women, notably Marie de Chevreuse, who was irreverent, sharp and shameless, teasingly different from her own more staid but profoundly religious nature. Between 1635 and 1637 she was under surveillance by Séguier's agents after the discovery of her clandestine correspondence with her brother Philip IV. After the reconciliation of the royal couple in 1637, with formal pledges, still more after the birth of the dauphin, followed in 1639 by that of a second boy, she was more contented. From Anne's experience certain desires of her middle age may be adduced: to exercise power, to have a reliable partner in that power, one who could stand as a father to the king. She would be queen but she would not abrogate the rights of a woman or the responsibilities of a mother.

Mazarin had won Anne's approval from the time of their first meetings in the *dévôt* circles of the two queens and Marillac. His role as Papal peacemaker had commended him; his considerate manners and fluent Castilian were further advantages. He was a great bestower of 'bagatelles', jewels, perfumes and the like. The story that, having made 5,000 *écus* at the gaming table he promptly conveyed them to the queen may be apocryphal; it is revealing that it should be told of him. With her well-rounded features and appearance of glowing health, Anne had never lacked admirers. As a young queen she had provided Rubens with the subject of a striking portrait; she was made, it would seem, for his generous brush. The mature woman still had power to attract. But it was perhaps the queen as much as the woman that Mazarin first admired. In the early days of the regency council he needed Anne's tendency to see matters in a simple light, and her brisk words to cut short debate. 'She was born to govern' he wrote. He saw too that 'her passion was for the king' and that this helped her to put the interests of France before the temptation to press for peace. He had the kind of tact that enabled her to believe that she was in control.

On several public occasions, Parisians could observe the partnership evolving. On 27 June a memorial service was held at Notre-Dame to mark the end of forty days of mourning for the late king. Mazarin was one of the two masters of ceremonies who offered Anne holy water at the cathedral door and led her to her pew. On 18 August he was prominent in her part at thanksgiving in the cathedral for the latest French victory, the capture of Thionville. On August 25, the feast day of St Louis, he shared in a significant rite: vespers in Louis XIII's recent foundation, the Jesuit church of St Louis. Mazarin meanwhile was working hard to convince her that he was a reliable adviser. Like the perfect servant he created the impression that he was indispensable. He saw that she could only act decisively if she understood the processes of government and knew about the men involved. Every evening, for two hours, in the queen's private cabinet, he briefed her on matters of foreign policy. The sessions provided an opportunity for him to range widely. They were tutorials in government.

His notebooks of this period reveal how thoroughly he prepared for his role.[15] The pages of minute script, in Italian, sometimes Spanish as well as French, show the dedicated professional, diplomatic and political questions never far from his mind, even when he was travelling (if that is the reason for scrawled entries in pencil). They do not show a shallow or a conceited man; rather one aware perhaps of the shadow of the great Cardinal; aware certainly of awesome responsibilities. Mazarin wrote voluminously, studied despatches far into the night. He was thorough, but he was also subtle. His professions of devotion may have gone beyond the conventional language of client to patron: having left home and family, his prime interest lay in service to the queen. Periodic suggestions that he might return to Rome if she were not content with him may have reflected his own misgivings. The scarcely veiled suspicions around him, the knowledge after mid-summer that a plot was forming to remove him, would have tested the strongest nerves. But taken together, the sedulous attention, the self-deprecating manner, the sheer efficiency of the man worked powerfully to convince the queen that he must stay. In these months the strands were woven and knotted that were to last through the gravest of emergencies. The evolving relationship of mutual trust and affection is not the least of Mazarin's achievements. He had not had the time or resources to build up a solid *clientèle*. He would now have that opportunity. Meanwhile he had already made some useful friends. His preferment meant from the start that they would be outnumbered by his enemies, casualties of the ministerial shuffle before and after Louis XIII's death.

Sublet de Noyers,[16] minister of war since 1636, devout, loyal, austere, was one of the stock of which good government is made, Sublet was versatile in the way of the great manager-ministers of Louis XIV's reign. His 18,000 surviving letters witness to a dogged struggle with the malad-ministration of an army that was still semi-feudal in structure and atti-tudes. Lacking trained staff either at headquarters or in the field he had to attend to the smallest details, as well as to the crippling problems arising out of false musters, mutinies and desertion. If he does not enjoy the reputation of his formidable successor Michel le Tellier, that is partly due to the chronic lack of funds which forced him to resort to short term expedients. By 1643 the armies were already operating more efficiently. It was a cruel irony that Sublet was dismissed only weeks before victory at Rocroy brought reward. His fall was due to a manoeuvre which, by itself, it enough to dispose of the idea that Mazarin was a reluctant candidate for the highest office. Mazarin and Chavigny[17] joined forces to destroy Sublet. They hinted that he had an understanding with Anne over the question of the regency. The confederates played on Louis' reluctance to accept that he was mortally ill and on his coolness towards the queen. On 10 April Sublet was discharged, to be replaced by Mazarin's man, the reliable Le Tellier.[18]

Chavigny was then left as strongest contender for his patron's mantle. As Richelieu's *créature* he had shown capacity and tireless energy. Mazarin seems to have been grateful for aid and confidences; but theirs was essentially a political friendship, not built to survive competition. They could cooperate when their common interest dictated it, but the Sublet affair left Chavigny wary of Mazarin's intentions. After the king's death one of them had to go: an inferior position was unacceptable to either man. Mazarin's advantage lay in the favour of the queen mother. Even so it was an achievement, having secured the dismissal of Sublet by the king because he appeared to declare for Anne too soon, to edge out Chavigny because Anne was persuaded that he was trying to curb her powers. With Mazarin presiding at council and conferring daily with the queen, Chavigny was soon considering where his future might lie. Mazarin had shown once more the gamester's ability to weigh risks, matched by a strong instinct for the right time to declare his hand. The study of one's opponent at cards, or across the diplomatic table does not necessarily, however, provide understanding of human behaviour at its deeper levels. Mazarin's very successes were preparing him for facile misreadings of complex situations. He had much to learn.

It was well that the immediate question of authority within the council was settled in the early weeks of the regency for it soon became clear that the spirit of faction had not died. The precedents of earlier regencies were ominous.[19] A council containing the names of Condé and Gaston, alongside ministers whose attitude towards Mazarin ranged from Séguier's guarded cooperation to Chavigny's open hostility, offered a poor prospect of stable government. After the vigorous exercise of royal power by Richelieu a reaction was again to be expected. These were 'times of shaking'. A civil war was already raging across the Channel, yet Charles I's government had been mild and cautious by comparison with that of Louis XIII. A crucial element in earlier French revolts was missing, for the Huguenots had been disarmed after the peace of Alais in 1629. Their leadership now tended to see security in a stable government. There was however a serious complication in the situation: foreign war.

War had traditionally an initial unifying, or at least diverting effect, since those mainly involved were those most likely, in peacetime, to be rebellious. There had been, for example, a close connection between the end of the Habsburg-Valois War in 1559 and the outbreak the year after of the first of the Religious Wars. In the seventeenth century the pattern was altered. Armies were much larger. After 1635 France had altogether around 80,000 under arms.[20] Richelieu was also building a large navy.[21] The economic and social effects were correspondingly severe. The combination of arbitrary, novel, even fraudulent ways of raising revenue, with the draconian measures needed to support them, offended powerful interests. Dissident magnates had already shown that they were not averse to engagements with Spain. Richelieu had eliminated some, most notoriously Montmorency (1632). By offering high military command he had neutralised others, though that was no guarantee of continuing loyalty. But there were a significant number who now welcomed the prospect of a long minority. It would be, they hoped, a time of recompense for alleged injuries, punishment of upstarts, and a reversion to happier times. Unhistorical in its claims, unprincipled in its plan, muddled in action,

65

the *Cabale des Importants* provided Mazarin with his first important challenge. It also takes us to the core of the continuing problem of government in France.

The *Importants* were so called because of the pretentious way in which they conducted their intrigues. They included enemies of Richelieu who had been counting the days till his death. Châteauneuf had been Keeper of the Seals from 1630 to 1633. Under a cloud for dalliance with Mme de Chevreuse and suspected pro-Spanish plots, he had been dismissed, briefly imprisoned, and later pointedly excluded by Louis XIII from his death-bed pardons. As with Bishop Pothier, who looked to be a cardinal, it is easy to see how ambition could tinge more altruistic concerns about the cost of war and the condition of the people. Where there was also an instinct for revenge it focused naturally on Mazarin, successor in place and, it was assumed, policy – moreover, a foreigner. The duc de Mercoeur[22] represented the interest of his father, Vendôme, whom Richelieu had deprived of the Admiralty, which he abolished, and his governorship of Brittany, before taking it for himself. Beaufort, his brother, had more personal reasons for hostility: thinking himself, in Mazarin's opinion, 'to be a Mars and an Adonis', he had first been fooled by Anne's apparent favour and he was now led on by Mme de Chevreuse. An inveterate plotter since her first dramatic appearance in the Chalais plot of 1626,[23] happy to let infatuated gallants risk their lives on her behalf, she had survived only by favour of the queen and privilege of her sex and – when that had not been excuse enough for the exasperated Richelieu – by long periods of exile. The admirer now was Alexandre de Campion;[24] the ally, the duchesse de Montbazon;[25] her grievance, exclusion from Anne's court, as she assumed, at Mazarin's request; the plan, to assassinate him and to replace him by Châteauneuf. There would then be a more urgent approach to negotiation for peace.

Another aim of the *Importants* was to support Charles I, represented in France by his wife, Henrietta Maria, Louis XIV's aunt: she believed that he could still win the day. In this respect however the conspiracy was flawed. Walter Montague, her chief agent in France, put his faith in Mazarin and urged his cause with Anne. Mazarin however availed himself of Montague's contacts to track the conspiracy. It was deadly enough. Beaufort's bravos were ready to ambush the Cardinal. By rich irony he owed his life to Gaston who gave him a lift in his carriage. The conspirators had to hold their fire.[26] The plot was revealed and its authors sought refuge. In September 1643 Beaufort was arrested and sent to the Bastille, remaining there for five years.

On 19 May, the day of Louis XIII's interment at St Denis, Condé's son the duc d'Enghien, barely twenty-two, had attacked the Spanish army of Flanders under Don Francisco de Mello and defeated him in a gruelling and ferocious battle: by the end 8,000 Spaniards were dead, 6,000 taken prisoner; 200 flags and 60 standards were captured. It was, said Mazarin, 'the most signal victory for many years'. It was the fruit of Sublet's planning, Richelieu's policies and one of his last appointments: the remarkable promotion of a very young man. First Rocroy, now the débâcle of the *Importants*: Mazarin could count himself fortunate – and he needed to be. The summer also saw a peasant rising in the Rouergue, incited by a few nobles: it did not spread, like those of the Croquants of 1636, and it was put down with a few executions and the dispatch of others to the galleys.[27] It served however to warn the government that there were limits to what the French would pay for an unpopular war.

To preside over council was one thing, to exert real authority another. Mazarin's apparent modesty and willingness to listen made an emollient change from Richelieu's sharper style. But there were uncomfortable moments in council, where he was at first unfamiliar with procedures, and at court, where he could not be unaware of scorn and insult. Vendôme's boast that he would 'pull his moustache off' was no doubt well received. From the outset Mazarin was convinced of the necessity of having a bodyguard. He also took early steps to build relationships with well disposed nobles at court. His method can be studied in the case of the duc de Liancourt, first gentleman of the king's chamber, named *duc et pair* in 1644. He was influential in securing for Liancourt the coveted *honneurs du Louvre* (the right of entering the palace courtyard in a carriage). Liancourt was to prove steadily faithful to Mazarin. Meanwhile debate raged in *Parlement*, in the *cour des aides*[28] and in pamphlets about the precise nature of Anne's authority, in particular whether she had the right, as Séguier maintained, to hold a *lit de justice* and thus force through measures which *Parlement* might oppose, or whether, as most lawyers argued, she was merely a caretaker for the king and therefore not allowed to make innovations. In practice, argument turned round new taxes and levies through edicts which *Parlement* would be disclined to register. It was inevitably linked to foreign policy and so to Mazarin's judgement in that sphere. It was generally held that the effect of Rocroy had been to encourage Mazarin to raise his demands and so postpone serious negotiation. The possibility that France might benefit from such tactics was obscured by the allegation that he was guided solely by self-interest since so long as war continued, he would be indispensable. Such jaundiced views may have done less than justice to past efforts for peace. But it is not surprising that he aroused mistrust, concerning his position in the first place, now about his use of power.

9

THE ADOPTED LAND: POVERTY AND DISORDER

Mazarin could not yet have known a great deal about his adopted country. He had not had the chance to acquire the native Frenchman's nuanced sense of what was possible. His acquaintance was with the summit where diplomats operated. The point may be reinforced by comparing his training for power with that of an *intendant*, like Le Tellier or Servien, who could learn, in the daily grind of provincial administration, about justice, taxation, social conditions and the workings of the official mind. Mazarin now had to concentrate on the day-to-day problems that came through at the end of the process; there was little time for considering how they were engendered. His concern was with measures, to soothe or suppress. He leaned on the experience of those, like Séguier,[1] who knew the system from the inside. He had to make decisions – and there follow his own judgement. But he might have avoided blunders if he had known more.

Richelieu's philosophy and statecraft had been tempered by his knowledge of the worlds of the law and the Church, above all the Poitevin world of his youth.[2] If, then, he had continued in power, would the Fronde have occurred? It is fruitless to speculate. The Fronde reflected disorders and tensions at all levels of society. They had manifested themselves already in resistance and riot, conspiracy and revolt. France was not ungovernable, but government rested on a basis of compromises. Whether it was the *élu*[3] trying to raise taxes from a village, or a minister trying to impose *élections* on a *pays d'états*,[4] an *intendant* dealing with a general or the chancellor dealing with a *parlement*,[5] the process of government appears to be one of continuous bargaining, punctuated periodically by the use of force. Long before the Fronde there was a kind of administrative civil war. It was not new in Richelieu's time – but he raised the stakes. The lower the social level, the more effective the bullying; the higher the level, the more likely the collusion. One reason for Richelieu's success, and a prime reason for the hostility he aroused, was his skill in using the traditional weapons of the grandee to create a fortune and a *clientèle*.[6] He exploited the system that he knew so well.

At this point it becomes clear, with every assertion raising further questions, that it is time to pause and take stock. Some brief account is needed of the society and institutions of the largest country in Europe: one in six Europeans, united only in allegiance to the young sovereign whose fortunes must, to some extent depend on the judgement of his *premier ministre.*

There is a question at the outset about the most important thing governments need to know: the size of the population. In 1707 Vauban's report would contain the most reliable estimate to date, based on thorough surveying of the country.[7] His nineteen million almost certainly represents a decline of around two million from an earlier peak; similarly the nineteen million of 1643, if that figure be chosen as a reasonable estimate, was to be reduced by the same amount in the next ten years before recovery and the acquisition of new subjects in annexed lands. The reason for such large swings lies in the occurrence, periodically, of great mortalities which contained the rising trend otherwise to be expected in a society that was ignorant of artificial means of birth control, yet had an average life expectancy of around twenty-five.[8] Its bounds were set by limits of production that reflected agricultural methods and modes of transport and marketing that were little advanced since the fourteenth century, and by the 'chronic morbidity' of this pre-scientific age.[9] A sequence of poor harvests, with famine and epidemics, such as occurred between 1648 and 1652, exposed the vulnerable condition of the mass of the French people.

Those are among the few generalisations that it is safe to make about the country. For there was a variety in its geography, history, law, language and other aspects of popular culture as great as that within the German empire, that loose confederation of many sovereignties still almost unimaginably far from being a single unitary state. 'The irregular and picturesque growth of centuries', to borrow Bagehot's description of the English constitution, can be seen in the mosaic of provinces which composed the realm; also in the pattern of growth around the original royal domain. It reveals how the feudal inheritance affected the nature of the state. The absorption of independent fiefs which had owed only nominal allegiance to the crown, and the acquisition by marriage or conquest of large territories, such as the duchy of Brittany,[10] did not mean assimilation or the abandoning of old loyalties. The imposition of royal officials tended to have a superficial effect. It was not simply a question of size and distance, though these were important factors, as anyone knows who has travelled across France. The English in particular should beware of equating the shire with the French province. If they look beyond the central and northern parts, the old Ile-de-France and its earlier additions, they should think rather of a Wales, an Ireland, a Scotland. If language be taken as the test, there simply was no one France. If the idea of the state be chosen, it seems that only a minority could truly be said to belong to it: those who could speak, write or understand the literary or Parisian French which was generally replacing Latin as the language of government and learning. They were the political nation. Outside it were the common people who spoke the local version of one or other of the dialects, northern and southern: each consisting almost entirely of such terms as were needed for the business of living.

Mediterranean France was quite different from the rest in ecology, language, laws and customs. Besides the more spectacular and isolated mountain fringes, sub-Alpine or Pyrenean, the high hills and plateaux, dense forests and remote valleys of the Massif Central created another world apart. In the eastern provinces laws and customs which strongly favoured the *seigneurs* showed Germanic influence and the consequences of the lax rule of the dukes of Burgundy. Even in Normandy, concessions to cities like Rouen[11] represented the original price paid for control. The slow growth of the kingdom had left its most striking legacy in the shape of the *pays d'états*, retaining their Estates and enjoying their distinctive system of taxation. Among other provinces tolls levied on road and river further emphasised the physical fragmentation: one realm, many *pays*. Where the sea did not mark it beyond doubt, there was nothing like a modern frontier to tell the traveller when he left or entered the realm. France's eastern border represented a feudal pattern of estates, not yet reduced to order by the rationalising action of the state. There was no line behind which all was French. The utter confusion of land and lordship explains the concern of both Cardinals for the acquisition of strong bases in lands of divided sovereignty.[12]

With a relatively high proportion of inhabitants to the area of land, about forty to the square kilometre, with extensive fertile areas and a climate which did not generally run to extremes, it might seem that the country could have provided sufficiently for its people. The reality was otherwise. The landscape was certainly a stable one and peasants held with fierce attachment to their communal sites. Most French men and women lived and died in the community in which they were born; there were fewer deserted villages than in England. There were forest clearances, draining of swamps, some enclosures; there was local wartime devastation; yet the overall picture was one of equilibrium. Markets were local within a limit of around a day's ride on horse or mule. Nearly all Frenchmen would be within reach of some kind of town, having a market for the surplus produce of largely self-sufficient communities. The isolation of so many particular, virtually separate economies was ensured by numerous obstacles to the flow of trade.

Work proceeded on making rivers navigable. Richelieu was interested in canal building and in 1642 the important Seine–Loire link was completed. Sully[13] had promoted an ambitious road and bridge building programme, but it was still not unusual to hear of merchants making a hundred-mile detour to avoid a bad road, or a district infested by bandits, like Périgord during the heyday of the notorious Pierre Grellety. It was still often cheaper to travel by sea than by land and no more dangerous. Richelieu had secured the reduction of most road and river tolls, but they remained an obstacle, expensive in time and money. A bale of cloth would be a month in transit between Rouen and Lyons, a man two weeks between Paris and Bordeaux. Mazarin's journey of January 1640, five days from Lyons to Paris, was exceptional: such could be achieved when an important man, sparing no expense, travelled with relays of horses. Favoured regions were those around navigable rivers or near a big city with a large appetite for grain, meat, fruit, vegetables and wine; or where there were manufactures, most commonly textiles, which could provide ancillary employment. Peasants were specially vulnerable in districts where there was no alternative employment; but even where there was, as among the peasant spinners and weavers of the Beauvaisis,[14] a slump in demand could bring disaster to households reduced thereby to dependence on their few strips of land, commonly a dozen acres or less. Anywhere peasants could fall into debt, through improvidence, accident, whether to man or beast, sickness, a baby and another mouth to feed; the path of the borrower led, through selling of land, to pauperisation, the condition of the insecure day labourer. So a more distinct peasant hierarchy was emerging, with a growing number among the *bas peuple*, as they were often described in official documents, landless, unable to pay taxes, whose ragged squalor in times of dearth aroused revulsion and fear.

The social countenance of poverty would have been clearer to contemporaries than the underlying economic trend: towards a recession whose worst consequences were to be experienced in the second half of the century. It was not only a French problem. The condition of Castile was more distressed in almost every respect.[15] By the 1640s many parts of Germany were ravaged by a war in which the movements of armies were dictated as much by the imperatives of commissariat as by considerations of strategy. France's frontier provinces were already experiencing the 'Misères de Guerre'.[16] Even without war's disruption of markets and trade routes, the decline in the amount of bullion coming in from the New World after 1600, by depressing the money supply, would have led to a flattening of demand.[17] This was apparent in France from around 1630, just when government was increasing taxes to pay for its enlarged armed forces.

Social crisis, as perceived at times of special disorder, was rarely engendered by a single or simple cause. A tax on wine brought riots in Dijon in 1630; rumour of new taxes was as potent as the pressure of the old ones in stirring up the *Croquants* of 1636–7; the salt tax was the main grievance of the Nu-pieds of Normandy in 1639. Anywhere the billeting of troops might spur desperate people to violence. Conditioning all, were the remorseless, inelastic conditions of the agrarian economy which determined the level of demand and would continue to do so, as Richelieu had realised, until capital was accumulated through trade and manufactures. It was his, therefore France's, misfortune that the effect of his policies, with higher taxation and extensive creation of offices for sale, was actually to divert capital from productive use. Without large investment by agencies of the state, improvement depended on the initiative of the more substantial peasants and landowners. The evidence of the tax returns from this time is that many of the former were in trouble.

The development of peasant capitalism was bound to be slow and uneven. Why, however, were the larger landowners unable to apply themselves, like some of their English counterparts, to the improvement of farming – and therefore to returns from the land? Explanations are many: the widespread system of *métayage*, share-cropping; the equally safe income that could be derived from feudal dues; the weight of those dues, with the tithe, in the many areas where they were exacted with full rigour,[18] the preponderance of very small holdings; prevailing *mentalités*: the conservatism of the peasant and the scorn of the nobleman for the occupations of the soil. Whatever the causes, the consequences are beyond doubt. The rural economy which encompassed the lives of 85 per cent of the people lacked the resources and techniques for increased production. Crop yields, as measured by the ratio of seed to harvest, averaged around one to five. That bleak statistic represents the poverty trap in which the peasant farmer was caught. No wonder he treated bread with almost religious respect.[19] Because of the pressure of population on resources, more land was being cultivated. It might be waste or scrub that would otherwise be used for grazing. In any case it meant less manure to go back on the land. With declining yields came further pressure on the marginal land. The trend was towards monoculture of cereals and accompanying malnutrition.

The plight of the people disturbed some of the *seigneurs*, officials and priests who saw it, in afflicted communities, and in the evidence of declining rents, dues and taxes. Their poverty was a commonplace of political rhetoric, used to reinforce objections to royal policies. The worst years of famine, and further suffering from the movement of armies in the civil war, were yet to come when Omer Talon,[20] *avocat général*, thus addressed the *lit de justice* of January 1648: 'For ten years the country has been ruined, the peasants reduced to sleeping on straw, their furniture sold to pay the taxes, so that to maintain luxury in Paris millions of innocent persons are forced to live on bread made of bran and oats'. Ministers might be moved more by the frequent reports of tax collectors – 'there are here only those who are useless for taxation' – and the recurring nightmare of peasant risings which could reduce entire provinces to fiscal sterility.

'The history of France in the seventeenth century', wrote Tapié, 'is truly that of the rural community'. Yet to think of government, starting with the perennial question, how was the crown to extend and uphold its authority, is to see the vital role of the towns. A town was likely to be of strategic importance, the key to securing communications or the surrounding countryside. Military operations during the Fronde were to revolve round their control. Even those towns that were not important provincial capitals like Rouen, Toulouse or Dijon, had their privileged groups, dominating the urban worlds of trade, property, finance and law. As officials or merchants, by the ways in which they made their capital work for them, and as landowners through the collection of rents and feudal dues, they loomed over the local countryside;[21] as *seigneurs* they tended to introduce a more efficient, therefore severe feudal regime; as lawyers they would support it against any appeals based on traditional, though often unwritten right.

That certain urban groups were prospering did not mean that their communities as a whole were healthy. Already urban autonomy, sustained through the weakness of the crown during the Religious Wars, was becoming a thing of the past. From the start of Henry IV's reign there had been an unremitting assault on the privileges of towns. Political control was the crown's objective, most clearly at times of revolt; sometimes religion was an issue, as in the exceptional case of La Rochelle; there were usually financial motives. Where the state's interests are concerned, the lines between justice, finance and politics are so blurred as to be indistinguishable – as no doubt they were to contemporaries. The fewer the elected magistrates, the more appealing would be the offices of the crown. Towns like Abbeville, Poitiers and Limoges all saw drastic reductions in the magistracy: one line of attack was on the method of election. Another was fiscal, through curbs on the towns' right to levy their own taxes, or the levying of new royal taxes. In the village, the wealthiest *laboureurs*, usurping the power of more representative assemblies, often used it to enhance their own standing with the authorities. In the town, the tendency towards oligarchy, with wealthy families consolidating their position, suited ministers and furthered absolutism. A dual process can be seen: coercion, with fines and threats, softened resistance; meanwhile office and honour beckoned the ambitious along the route of royal service.

There was another side to the crown's apparent political advantage. As government came to rely increasingly on urban élites, the danger grew that they would try to call the tune. If it sought to exploit its position by raising taxes and creating new offices, the local prestige of the courts, particularly *parlements*, could provide a focus for resistance to which not only peasants but disaffected nobles might rally. Leading the Languedoc revolt of 1631–2, following the establishment there of *élus*, Montmorency[22] and Orléans had their own political agenda but their rising was rendered more dangerous by the initial support of the province for its governor. Through kinship and other ties of interest, members of Estates or *parlements* could see what threatened to be more important than the possible rewards of royal service – or indulging in the rivalries of faction which, as in Aix,[23] often allowed government to divide and conquer. As Mazarin would find in 1648, there were limits to the loyalty of even the highest legal officers, determined by the extent to which they felt that their rights, and their role as guardians of the rights of others, were threatened.

Around seven per cent of Frenchmen lived in towns: some forty of them had populations of more than ten thousand. The history of one city, capital of a province which had been subject to the French crown for four hundred years, a metropolis of law and the church, reveals more about the experience of 'creeping absolutism' and the mentality of the French people before the Fronde than any statement about the country as a whole. The case of Angers, a city of 30,000 souls, is not unrepresentative. An eighteenth-century traveller was to say that 'there are few cities in the French dominions that afford the curious a larger field of enquiry'.[24] Apart from the interest to an Englishman of its Plantagenet past, that enquiry might have included examination of the policies that had contributed to its becoming a picturesque backwater. Traditionally Angers was a little republic, possessing its own administration, with assemblies representative of the parishes, and municipal officers who became hereditary nobles by virtue of their office. The corporation raised the town militia, of which the mayor was captain, and levied municipal taxes. The citizens as a whole were exempt from the *taille*, the *gabelle* and the quartering of troops. After 1600 clashes over rights and interests created an unhappy atmosphere. The more privileged, near-monopolists, were attacked for proposing new royal taxes and then taking a percentage of the proceeds. Leaders of the popular party were professional men outside the close circle of royal officers, also merchants, protected by their particular *corps*. Their support came largely from artisans, organised in twenty-seven guilds; they were the chief sufferers from the taxes on consumption. Angers had a number of religious houses besides its cathedral and sixteen parishes. The clergy had long-running disputes over jurisdiction with the magistrates, as did the university. The city lay in the path of opposing forces during the civil wars of 1614–20 and had to pay ransom money three times: the magistracy were blamed. As debts mounted and unrest grew, they appealed to the crown for support.

Richelieu relished the situation. After 1635, with a mayor who was in effect a royal agent, he disregarded Angers' financial immunities, levied new taxes, increased the old ones; then made the unfortunate city pay for its remaining privileges. As at Bourges, where, in 1633, the municipality was punished for failing to buy the new office of controller of the communal funds, by the seizure of its remaining funds, the indebtedness of the city led to the imposition of direct rule. Besides other burdens Angers was made to guard and feed prisoners of war. The prime motive of Richelieu's commissaries was to raise money as expeditiously as possible. So the imposts fell mainly on the richer citizens. The magistracy, royal officers in the main, still clung to allegiance to the crown – and would continue loyal during the Fronde. The rest struggled against increasingly draconian authority; there were riots and assaults on tax-officials; few paid their taxes: troops were billetted and ransacked the place. In places like Angers the Fronde had been well rehearsed. When it came the people would be on the side of the rebels.

The agents of wartime government, encroaching ever more brusquely on rights and properties, created severe dilemmas for local dignitaries. There were numerous urban revolts, usually concerned with indirect taxes, or with forced loans. Rumour was often important. It was thus that Agen was suddenly roused to violent and bloody revolt in June 1635, as its council reported: 'On Sunday 17th of the month at 9 a.m. the riot and popular sedition began on the rumour of the *gabelle*...'[25] Plenty of people assembled and began to muster together, shouting 'we must kill the *gabeleurs*' and 'long live the king without the *gabelle*'. In such a situation, when prominent citizens were butchered trying to restrain the mob, the authorities were quick to rally. The *parlement* of Toulouse condemned the activities of 'certain unknown persons, disguised as travellers and pilgrims' who were spreading false reports of certain *gabelles* and impositions, even on children to be born and the bodies of those who had just died. *Parlement* assured the people that 'His Majesty's paternal goodness wishes only for the relief of his subjects... He has no wish to establish new *gabelles* or other taxes but merely to obtain the help that is absolutely necessary to sustain the expense of several armies beyond the frontiers.' Combined with the threat to property inherent in any urban riot, that was probably enough to deter most citizens from taking the path of sedition. It was usually specialist groups, like coopers or tanners, who took the lead against new taxes. Their action could be useful however as the first move in a bargaining process: local leaders would seek to secure, along with pardons, the reduction or abolition of the offending tax. They could claim to have suppressed the riot with their own militia; or to have disassociated themselves from the popular demands. The crown agents would respond sceptically, noting how useful to the wealthier classes was this kind of 'controlled violence'; also that it was their main concern to secure the gates against peasant bands.

The urban revolts were generally less critical than inconvenient to the crown. They could however be serious in the wider context. They engendered a spirit of disaffection with royal authority which appeared, in the shape of its *intendants* and tax officers, intrusive, bullying and contemptuous of local sensitivities. It also set limits to what money could be raised from the towns, necessitating therefore still greater reliance on the *taille* and burdens on the peasants. Their risings offer the most spectacular evidence for the discontents of the people. They provide the other flanking panel of the triptych of disordered France, whose vibrant centre was to be the Fronde. Like such panels the Fronde can be taken apart and studied as a series of episodes, each having its own motivations, principles and passions. But, as in the artist's conception, there is an underlying organic unity. The Fronde was the product of certain circumstances and acts. They cannot be properly understood without reference to the society in which the protagonists were grounded. It had experienced in several forms, and at each social level, violent protest and open revolt.

In 1636–7, at one time or another, from the Loire to the Garonne, over a quarter of France was affected by the risings of the Croquants. Much of the rebel country was remote and inaccessible: forests and hills made it ideal terrain for resistance, as was again to be found in 1940–5, in a struggle against another kind of 'foreigner'. In 1636, to the small town official, *hobereau* or peasant, that man was the *intendant, traitant,*[26] or any of the proliferating horde of officials who practised 'fiscal terrorism'.[27] Behind all was the sinister figure they learned from dissident propaganda and rampant rumour to envisage as the oppressor and perverter of justice. Mazarin was to inherit Richelieu's image and odium. Meanwhile royal troops were concentrated on the frontiers, facing the invasion of Spanish and Imperialist troops. There could be no prompt response to the mustering of peasants from the Saintonge and Angoumois. When their motley force assembled, there were deserters as well as old soldiers to give a lead; many had arquebuses and pikes; they marched in formation, accompanied by fifes and fiddles. La Force[28] wrote to Séguier to warn that 'in the great disorder of this *canaille* there was a dangerous kind of order'. Overall there may have been as many as 30,000 under arms. There were some isolated acts of violence, sometimes no doubt the settling of old scores. There was insufficient overall control: but the movement did not degenerate at once into aimless forays. Towns were blockaded; emissaries were despatched to other provinces and there ensued serious risings in Poitou, Périgord and Quercy. There is little evidence for concerted moves by the Huguenots. But individuals' experience from earlier civil wars may have been useful. In Périgord the peasants secured a base, Bergerac, whose walls had recently been razed on Richelieu's orders. A commune enforced severe discipline. Here the rebels were formidable. But they were gradually isolated, as other provinces were subdued by measures both firm and conciliatory. On 1 June 1637, the royal commander, La Valette, defeated the rebels at La Sauvetat. The survivors dispersed, for safety – and the harvest. After the recovery of Bergerac the revolt was effectively over: a general amnesty showed good sense; the execution of ringleaders was deemed sufficient example. Who were they? What induced them to risk a traitor's death? What did the rebels want?

There were several nobles, most notably La Mothe la Forêt,[29] but there is no sign of an entente between the peasants and the privileged classes, however much individual *seigneurs* might sympathise with their people, or bewail their own tribulations: revenue lost when *censitaires* were too poor to pay their dues, or the dreaded *arrière-ban*; revived by Richelieu in 1635.[30] No single grandee made a move to support the insurgents. There was no mistaking the solidarity of the noble order in the face of popular risings. There was a general loathing of the new political order they saw taking shape under the all-powerful minister, upheld by a swelling band of *créatures*. There may also have been appreciation of the need for a contented rather than destitute peasantry. La Force expressed his dismay at their wretchedness: La Valette was reluctant to pursue them after defeat with the rigour commonly used against rebels.[31] Equally there is no sign among the rebels of antagonism to those whom they were accustomed to see as natural leaders in their communities. There was little looting of châteaux; nor did seigneurial dues seem to have been a grievance. The political tone too was loyal and conservative. There was no demand for new constitutional safeguards, regular States-Generals for example.[32] Nostalgic recollection of an imaginary golden age, so often potent in the idiom of political resistance, played its part: the king should live as of old, with his traditional rights and a levy of the *taille* such as had been sufficient for his father.

In some places regulations for the fair apportioning of the *taille* were drawn up in the presence of the *curé*. There were some radical *curés*. Should that be attributed to hostility towards wealthy or absentee bishops and abbots, sometimes expropriators of tithes, often remote from the lives of the rural priesthood? Was a 'Marillac factor' at work, as *dévôt* hostility at court towards Richelieu and his Protestant alliances filtered down to the parishes? Mobilised by Gondi, it was going to be an important force in *frondeur* Paris. The *curé* was well placed, if he so wished, to be the leader of his simple flock. Some turned out at the head of the village contingents. In Normandy the Nu-Pieds were directed by a council of four priests. There is further interest in the composition of the rebels there – not only was there complicity between leading officials and the insurgents, some gentry afforded them protection. The revolt was confined to one part of Normandy and did not spread beyond its borders. The sternness with which government repressed the revolt, the reprisals they thought necessary, suggest however that they conceived it to be particularly dangerous. To see why is to gain further insight into the condition of France before the Fronde.

Normandy had experienced serious outbreaks of plague. In some villages two-thirds of the inhabitants had perished. Fields lay unploughed and unsown. Trade declined. With a clumsy system of assessment, the tax officials were slow to take notice of local conditions. Prices rose. Regiments were billeted in the province: it also had to support levies, each parish having to equip three or four soldiers. Office-holders had salaries withheld; some offices were devalued by the creation of new ones; a higher charge was made for reversion. All these afflictions befell different provinces at different times. In Normandy they combined to bring the province to the point of explosion. Its Estates were an anachronism and had not been called since 1635. Its *parlement* had all the keener sense of being responsible for the well-being of the people. It was slow to register edicts and ready to espouse the cause of merchants and artisans when they protested against new taxes: the lawyers could enjoy popularity; the tanners and coopers could do their work for them. For government it was the critical conjuncture: all classes were aggrieved, only the occasion for revolt was missing. It was supplied by rumour: Lower Normandy was to become *pays de grande gabelle*, so it would pay the full rate of salt tax, paid by the rest of the province. An unfortunate official, who had nothing to do with salt, was lynched by a crowd on a July market day in Avranches. So, with the familiar mingling of the tragic, ironic, brave and petty, began the revolt which took its name from the salt-panners who walked barefoot about their work.

There are signs of intelligent direction behind the revolt. Inevitably however it was patchy, depending on local circumstances and tempers. In the *élection* of Avranches only twenty-seven parishes rose out of ninety-seven. It was however at Avranches that the semblance of an army gathered, under the standard of John the Baptist and the orders of 'Jacques Nu-Pieds', an anonymous name for collective leadership. The province had long been an awkward piece in the jigsaw of the realm. The League[33] had been strong here. The vicomte de Coûtances, subsequently indicted for spreading false rumours, was the son of an old Leaguer. When the leaders appealed for support they invoked loyalty to the *patrie*: not France but Normandy. There were the makings here of a lively autonomous movement: the Fronde would reveal the threat that such a movement could pose when it was led by an ambitious magnate who was also governor. Meanwhile targets, some of them murdered, were mainly officers of finance. Petty squires might drum out their men for the hunt for human prey: 'mort aux gabeleurs'. But as elsewhere the magnates stood back. There were no respected nobles, no prominent clergy; even among the peasants there were few substantial proprietors. It was a rising of the *ménu peuple* with a smattering of the resentful and dispossessed. But it might never have started without the compliance of *parlementaires*. It therefore provided the government with an ideal chance to administer a lesson in the realities of power. With only a small force, but moving fast, Gassion put down the revolt at the end of the year. Chancellor Séguier then arrived in person, with retinue and pomp to represent the offended majesty of France. The *parlement* of Rouen was suspended. There were numerous executions; some were broken on the wheel, some had their houses demolished, some fled.

Richelieu had struck at the weak point in resistance to absolutism. No popular rising could succeed without the cooperation of towns. There the local officials, much as they hated the plutocrats of office, with their Parisian backers, knew that their own offices were held of the king. The crown had strained the relationship of mutual interest to breaking point, but so long as it commanded enough military force, it could bring the officials to heel. Yet it will be clear that royal government faced, by 1643, a crisis of authority more serious than the inconsequential conspiracy of the *Importants* might indicate. The forlorn pleas of the Croquants, the murderous rage of the salt panners, would not decide its fate. Whatever happened in the provinces of France, it would be, as ever, at the centre, in Paris, that the crisis of authority would be resolved.

10

PUBLIC FINANCE, PRIVATE ENTERPRISE

Whatever the particular reasons for individuals or communities being brought to the point of rebellion, the common cause was financial. The state was nearly bankrupt. In 1639 Bullion had warned Richelieu that the '*traitants* were deserting us' and that there was danger of a general tax-strike: 'the masses will not pay either the old or the new taxes'. He instigated an inventory of the property of the church. Fearing Gallicanism and the erosion of its independence, the church put up a stout defence. At the Assembly of Mantes[1] in February 1641 government demanded 7 million *livres*: it got little more than half. There was to be little help from that quarter. In August 1641 Bouthillier, sole *surintendant* after Bullion's death the previous winter, noted the effects of the failures of two leading financiers: 'Our tax contractors can scarcely find credit'. At Amsterdam Lopez, Richelieu's agent, was having to offer ever higher rates of interest to attract the cautious Dutch investor.[2] The government was trapped between the exigencies of war finance, and a fiscal system which could only operate with relative efficiency under peacetime conditions.

It cost some four million *livres* a year to supply Bernard of Saxe-Weimar's army between 1635 and 1639: the king's own troops, based on French soil cost far more. Military expenditure overall was running in those and subsequent years at around thirty-five million. Armies were not only great consumers: their discipline depended on prompt and regular payments. The pressure was relentless. The system could now only work, as Bouthillier admitted, if government, alternately bullying and bribing, worked with 'the money-changers who are really notorious usurers . . . An investigation against them, would be justified according to good morals and the observance of law, but we are constrained to tolerate them; they do bad things at Rome in order to avoid worse ones'. His last words were apt for the financial administration of Richelieu: even more for the next twenty years. Yet the system, grounded for two centuries in the principle that the king had the right to tax without consent,[3] served, by contemporary standards, by a sophisticated apparatus and experienced personnel, had the potential, as Colbert was to show, for producing a revenue to support the pretensions of a great power. In a century when statesmen did not generally allow their policies to be influenced by prior calculation of money available, it appears therefore to provide a familiar case of political abuse: a financial system required by its masters to provide more than it was capable of doing.

The crown relied on three main types of revenue: direct taxes, indirect taxes and extraordinary revenues. The main direct tax was the *taille*, riddled with exceptions and anomalies, levied annually to raise a total fixed by the council of finance.[4] Supplements, *crues*, could be raised: there was also a military tax, the *taillon*; wartime brought the hated subsistence tax *du quartier d'hiver*. The principal indirect tax was the *gabelle*, salt tax, which, with its range of assessment and its small army of functionaries provides a cameo of the financial regime at its most ambitious and most grotesque.[5] Other indirect taxes included the *aides*, trading and consumption taxes, principally on wine, and the *traités*, customs dues levied at the frontiers but also between certain provinces. The collection of the *taille* was the responsibility of the *trésoriers*,[6] within a *généralité*, and of the *élu*, within an *élection*. Inevitably from the hazards of the assignment and the incentive to make money to justify the cost of the office, there was favouritism and peculation. At the bottom of the ladder was the unfortunate collector, elected by the village, who might end up in gaol if he could not find the sum required.

Indirect taxes were farmed out to *traitants*, who undertook to administer them and to pay an agreed sum for the privilege. The same men might also be involved in the contracts, *traités*, through which the government raised its 'extraordinary' revenues, selling *rentes* or offices. The former word, signifying the interest payable to the *rentier*, comes to signify the whole system by which the crown had progressively raised capital sums, at the cost of increasingly high rates of interest. It was estimated, in 1644, that 700 million had been raised in *affaires extraordinaires* since 1620, on which financiers had made 172 million. The *rentier* was in the front line when a minister sought to reduce or withhold interest payments. So was the office-holder, since the periodic renewal of the *paulette*[7] provided the hard-pressed *surintendant* with the chance to raise revenue by increasing the payment required: the temptation to do so would prove fatal in 1648.

War was responsible for what amounted, after 1635, to a continuing state of emergency, during which the main criterion for the assessment of old or imposition of new taxes was the capacity of province or town to pay without rebelling. In real terms, in the decade ending in 1640, taxes, indirect and direct together, had more than doubled. Bullion complained that he was given an impossible task. He had acted sensibly to devalue the currency in 1636, a move which made French trade more competitive, and significantly reduced the cost of foreign subsidies. But lacking the stamina or will to undertake more far-reaching reforms, busy securing his own vast fortune, he furthered the development of a world of private gain within the larger official system, as Bonney describes it, 'the worst of all worlds: an illogical and unpopular system that worked to the advantage of few at the expense of many without any real gain to the crown.' With more *rentes* being created than buyers found, and with the saturation of the office market it was inevitable that he, and his successors, would have to think of new taxes, increase existing ones, and persuade more individuals to lend more. The first would bring head-on collision with corporate interests: that meant riots and risings. The second would encounter the basic feature of the situation, sheer inability to pay. The third would involve entering the vicious circle of faulty finance: the more precarious the credit of government, the greater risk to the financier; the higher therefore the interest rate; thus the greater need, in the next round, to borrow more. Risky, but lucrative, investment in the state was coming to involve the highest in the land, usually hiding behind agents or within a consortium, acquiring an interest in the very regime of which, in other capacities, they might be destructive critics. Taking the institutions that ruled France, the councils, the court, the sovereign courts, central and local administrative elites, senior figures in army, church and diplomatic services, Dent concludes that about a third were involved in financial deals of some kind. That will be found to be part of the reality lurking behind the rhetoric of the Fronde. Meanwhile there could be no certainty about the outcome: much depended on the expertise of ministers; even more on the ending of the war. But it was not unlikely that these three routes, however followed, would lead, by way of bankruptcy, to the revolutionary conjuncture.

Ministers were aware of the faults of the system. The ever-present spectres of mutiny, desertion and defeat, frayed ministerial nerves and sharpened the tone of correspondence. In October 1641 Richelieu wrote to Bouthillier and Séguier: 'If Messieurs of the council continue to allow tax farmers and contractors the freedom to treat the king's subjects according to their unruly appetite, then it is certain that a disorder similar to that in Spain will happen in France'. The latest expedient, to which Richelieu was referring, was a sales tax, the *sol pour livre*.[8] It was farmed out at rates which reflected the hazards of collecting; eventually it proved impossible to administer, mainly because some provinces preserved constitutional rights which enabled them to claim exemption: others then refused to pay. The scheme was withdrawn in February 1643.

The inconvenience of a dual financial regime had again been demonstrated. It did not however inspire ministers to renew the effort to make France a unitary state by abolishing the privileges of the *pays d'états*. Besides the political risks already encountered, there was concern about the integrity of the system of *élections*. Some *trésoriers* were also *receveurs*: that made nonsense of verification of accounts. Indeed it could be argued that the system of *taille personelle* was so flawed that it should be replaced everywhere by the *taille réelle*.[9] However that system was associated with the independence of the more distant provinces. So the main thrust of reform was to bring *élections* under the control of the *intendants*.

Among expedients, prime place had long belonged to the sale of royal office. The practice had been so long established and exploited by government that talk of its abolition, as the young Richelieu had advocated, had become academic. He had urged that it was 'prejudicial to your authority and the purity of justice' but it had since been bringing in an average twenty million *livres* a year. Richelieu's policy and mature view expressed reality.[10] The price inflation of the sixteenth century had enriched many *bourgeois*; fortunes had since been consolidated; there was surplus capital available and this was a way of mopping it up. With prestige, tax exemption and the prospect of a safe income the *bourgeois* won a position which they would not willingly put at risk. Richelieu had done more than acquiesce. Wholesale creations had devalued office and provoked revolt. Ministers admitted a connection between the decline of standards among *élus* and *trésoriers* and the creation of unnecessary offices. Extensions of government were not generally as constructive as the creation of a royal postal service (1630) or as uncontroversial as the creation of a new *parlement* at recently acquired Metz: all were used as opportunities to create new offices. Nor were traditional institutions immune. There were twenty-four new *secrétaires du roi*.[11] In the Chambre des Comptes alone there were eighteen new masters, seven checkers and ten auditors. The law of diminishing returns had to be reckoned with. During Mazarin's ministry returns from office sales slumped disastrously. With diminishing returns from the *pays d'états* and provinces afflicted by war and billeting he would have to rely increasingly on the *taille* from the central *pays d'élection* (they always bore the brunt) and from loans. There was also a political cost, exposed by struggles with *Parlement*: the reckoning came in 1648.

In 1648 *Parlement* went so far as to exclude from membership of the courts *traitants*, their agents, their sons and sons-in-law. But the worlds of law and finance remained closely interwoven. Though Holland, enjoying a buoyant trade, was showing the way to greater efficiency, no seventeenth-century state could raise money without resort to private enterprise. While *traitants* were operating in a seller's market, abuse of the system would persist. An administrative revolution was half what was needed; the other half was a sustained attempt by government to live within its means: neither was possible under present circumstances. Ideal scenes could lie ahead, to hard pressed ministers unimaginably remote; now they trudged through the morass, trying to keep to the only routes they knew, dealing with obstructions as they appeared. At a time when prices were static or falling, when there was a growing monetary famine, interest rates were actually rising. Thus trapped by the inexorable laws of the market, the crown was forced to raise more money from taxes. The more hazardous the collecting, the more *traitants* required in commission. Now they moved from the indirect to the direct taxes.

To keep the cash flowing the government was reduced to farming receipts of the *taille* against advances by *traitants*. The figures are revealing. The levy of the *taille* and other direct taxes, including after 1637 the *subsistence*, trebled between 1620 and 1642 to around fifty-five million *livres*. Indirect taxation from all sources rose correspondingly to around thirty million. The figures are approximations: they represent moreover the nominal income, that which in theory was levied. The gap between that and disposable income, that which was in ministers' hands to spend after all charges, commissions and expenses had been paid, widened steadily from around 1630 until it was little more than a third of nominal income. The increases and new taxes were consumed largely in higher interest charges and collection costs. Meanwhile projections were rendered increasingly fallacious because of resistance, passive or otherwise, and the destitution of many communities: arrears could stretch back for several years or so. After a spectacular rise in 1635–6 royal expenditure, of which military costs accounted for about seventy per cent, was thereafter steady, running at about twenty-five million *livres* above disposable income. That large annual deficit represents the category of *affaires extraordinaires*,[12] about which little precise can be known: ad hoc borrowing, office sales, certain *traités* with financiers can often be identified. But the picture is blurred by the use of special accounts, the lack of audit, the kind of private deals in which Mazarin was at different times involved, in general a lamentable confusion between private and public accounts.

To ministers the conclusion was inescapable. The system could not be altered fundamentally but one area could be selected for reform: the *élections* and the *taille*. *Intendants* all knew of abuses: protection of favoured communities by their *seigneurs*, unfair assessment within villages. The decree of the *conseil des finances* in March 1640 was explicit: 'the richest and most important inhabitants have thrown the main burden of the *taille* and other taxes on the weakest and poorest inhabitants'.[13] So the state must intervene to ensure fair and efficient collection, through its own agents. In August 1642 Richelieu took the plunge with a measure as radical as anything he had essayed. The power to make the *assiette*, the basic assessment of *taille*, was transferred to the *intendant*. In many cases he was also authorised to replace the *receveurs* by agents of the *traitants*. Backed by special brigades varying in size from a few archers to a force of musketeers and light cavalry sufficient to strike terror, the *intendants* claimed successes. The yield of the *taille* actually rose slightly between 1643 and 1648. But they were in the front line, more exposed than ever to attack.

In the *Code Michaud* (1629) the role of *intendants* had been formally defined: evidently Marillac envisaged them primarily as investigators. Richelieu's view was enlarged, first by conspiracy and revolts, then by the exigencies of war, till he saw them as essential instruments of government. The *intendant* was, in fact, the sharp end of the evolving body of public law, relatively free to act because bound by few other considerations than *raison d'état*, as interpreted in the terms of his commission. During the 1630s they became a normal rather than occasional part of provincial government. The year 1635 could be seen as the critical date in this process, as in much else. It had become the rule by then that there should be one *intendant* in each *généralité*. Only seven *généralités* out of twenty-two had *intendants* continuously since 1630; only seven had gaps after 1635. Local officials in the hierarchies of law and finance who had bought or inherited their offices resented the intrusion of a young man from Paris, armed with sweeping powers – following in often arbitrary ways the instructions of his political master. Their loyalties would be in the main to their province, town, *parlement* or governor. The *intendant* was likely to be alien in sympathies, ideas, even style. Typically he would be seen as smart, articulate and knowledgeable, imbued with that impatient Parisian spirit that can still offend provincial people.

In a way typical of the period, the means of reform came from within the existing regime: the majority of *intendants* were recruited from the ranks of the *maîtres des requêtes*, wealthy office holders in their own right, usually from well established *robe* families. Few were self-made. Some came from families distinguished in public service: d'Aligre, Molé, Phélipeaux among them. Many could lay claim to noble status of varying degrees of authenticity. Not till 1644 however did Mazarin's shrewd measure, extending the privilege of nobility, already enjoyed by *secrétaires du roi*, to the *maîtres des requêtes*, make this a general state. The *clientèle* was already by then much in evidence. Séguier was connected to eight *intendants*, Bouthillier to six. With much of their capital tied up in their office, they responded to the needs of the expanding state because it offered a chance for distinction at a time when *parlements* were being barred from any kind of political role. They were also losing business to the councils, with the relentless growth of administrative law. As one *parlementaire* put it: 'there are more affairs in petty justice decided by commissions than by ordinary judges'. That *maîtres* were attracted to this risky, relatively ill-paid form of service says much about the growing appeal of royal service. With the king's commission they would not be venturing unarmed even into the wildest regions of France. To bring royal law to the lawless, and order, even probity to the cosy empires of local finance, were not ignoble ambitions. Nor was it easy work. Between the ministerial hammer and the anvil of local recalcitrance, *intendants* could fall into oblivion or disgrace. They could also, like Particelli d'Hémeri, Servien, Le Tellier or Séguier, lay the foundation for a subsequent ministerial career. The value to the state of having men in council experienced in the problems of provincial government, when enactments had so often to be particular, with reference to a single province or town, can hardly be exaggerated.

The control and supply of troops and, more specifically, watching their senior officers, remained a prime function. Inevitably this brought the *intendant* into areas of civilian life and into clashes with judicial and financial officials. Abel Servien, *intendant* in Guienne in 1628, was violently opposed by the *parlement* of Bordeaux whose *Premier Président* was then summoned to appear before the king. He stood – but briefly, since the king seized him by the collar and said 'On your knees, little man, before your master'. Under wartime conditions the *intendants* began to exhibit some of the characteristics of a permanent organisation. While a man of character might have ideas of his own, the *intendants* as a whole formed a homogeneous group. They held office by appointment, not by purchase. Short commissions, usually for three years, kept them on their toes. The long stint of François de Villemontée, in Poitou from 1631 to 1644, was a rare exception. Their main problem was finding reliable and honest local agents, with knowledge of the province. So the office of *subdélégué* became established. As the *intendant* became more effective, with more influence over local affairs, he gained allies: sometimes the governor or general, more often some lower official, who might help uncover corruption or negligence. The more successful he was however, the more opposition could be expected to develop. In particular this occurred when *intendants* were given a larger financial role.

The personal commission which defined the *intendant*'s role enabled the crown to confer additional powers according to the needs of a given situation: Huguenots at La Rochelle, supplies for the Val Telline, the *parlement* of Toulouse, the nuns of Loudun, each required a distinctive brief. The *intendant* was expected to be resourceful and ruthless. During the *Croquant* risings in the southwest armed force had to be used to collect taxes. *Intendants* were thus cast in a new role, responsible for the special companies of fusiliers raised for the purpose. It was a bad precedent. Mazarin's government would have little option but to leave the *intendants* to manage the collection of taxes as best they could. They had to work with the *traitants*, tax farmers, to the point on occasion of dismissing the *receveurs des tailles*, in order to be sure that the advances would be renewed. The humiliation of the old officials, the disreputable look of the new arrangements and the increasingly brutal methods of some of their number made the *intendants* as much loathed as the *traitants*, whose too visible fortunes had made them the traditional scapegoats for the faults of the system. The reformers of 1648 demanded the recall of the *intendants* for their abolition. It was a kind of tribute to their success, for when they were withdrawn government was effectively crippled.

Thus the stage was set for the manipulations of Particelli d'Hémery which were convincing enough to encourage Mazarin to live dangerously, that is to pursue foreign policies as ambitious as those of his predecessor, as if credit would be forthcoming for as long as he needed to settle accounts with the Habsburgs. Such a sanguine view made insufficient allowance for the fact that the new absolutism, together with resentment of Particelli's new taxes and methods, was bringing all groups and interests together in a common front. At the summit it was Particelli and Mazarin who were hated. But it was the *intendants* who drew fire from all sides. They represented an assault on rights of property and the subversion of established law. They embodied the principle, not new but endowed by Richelieu's government with new significance, of *raison d'état.* They were blamed for numerous tax revolts. They could only be a source of strength to the regent so long as she could maintain her authority.

The family of Particelli was now no more Italian than that of Gondi though the name did nothing to allay suspicion. Particelli gained the normal reward which this society of orders, always more mobile than it appears in legal definitions, allowed to the rich: a *seigneurie,* that of Hémery en Brie. Through his wife he was related to important *traitants;* other family connections linked him to the world of office, first through the Colbert family, then through his daughter's marriage, to that of Phélipeaux de la Vrillière. He was the kind of young man, energetic, resourceful in bargaining, prepared to stand his corner against generals and grandees, whom Richelieu liked to send on difficult missions. In 1629 he was made *intendant de l'armée* in Italy, in 1631 *intendant des finances* in Languedoc, and in 1633 ambassador in Turin. By then Mazarin knew him well. He became a regular correspondent. Meanwhile Particelli was consolidating his position, buying land, building a fine *château* at Tanlay in Burgundy. The death of Bouthillier in 1643 gave Mazarin the chance to promote a friend – and a man of proven ability. He bought for 800,000 *livres* the new office of *contrôleur-général* and set about using his business contacts to find money for the state. Particelli has not enjoyed a favourable press, either from contemporaries or historians. He can seem to epitomise the 'blood-suckers', to be the ugliest of the detested race of *traitants.* He was unrestrained in his own pursuit of wealth and pleasure; dismissive of tradition in search for new revenues: not a wholly admirable man. But he did not create the system within which he was required to work; nor the virtual bankruptcy of 1643, nor the policy which required him to find even more money. The expense of the war actually rose in the first two years. His task was to fund it.

11

PREMIER MINISTRE

Since the flow of money was all-important, the finance minister was bound to be prominent, increasingly so as events moved towards the confrontation of 1648. Mazarin was seemingly content to leave him a free hand to propose and carry out his policies. To an even greater extent than Richelieu's, his interest in fiscal measures was limited to simple considerations: the amount that could be raised, the trouble that would be caused. For the reckoning, he deferred blandly to the expert.

Fiscal policy cannot however be treated in isolation. Judgements were necessarily made in council, with the reports of *intendants* to hand. Conditions at the front and in the provinces influenced the outcome. The views of the chancellor and war minister would therefore carry weight. But Pierre Séguier and Michel le Tellier were both much occupied with their own departments of government. Having the regent's ear, Mazarin may have felt less need to assert his authority. Diplomatic training had made him a good listener; to claim competence outside the bounds of his own experience was not one of his faults. Undoubtedly Mazarin's way with his fellow ministers was less authoritarian than Richelieu's. Of course their whole-hearted response was tinged with self-interest. They shared values and interests to an extent that ensured a degree of harmony. It could also breed complacency. In the gilt and profusion of their *hôtels*, served devotedly by clients and servants, sheltered by bureaucratic routines and the conventions of a society that valued politeness, ministers could come to underestimate the threat of rebellion. In those reflections contemporaries would have seen reference in particular to Pierre Séguier,[1] *dévôt*, humanist, bibliophile, for thirty-seven years chancellor of France.

Séguier's career completed the evolutionary process, characteristic of France, by which the greatest lawyers became senior functionaries of the state: his grandfather had been *président à mortier*, his father, Jean Séguier, one of Henry IV's *fidèles*, had been rewarded by being made *lieutenant-civil* of Paris. Pierre was one of the new school of absolutists, who took their line more from Cardin le Bret than from Bodin.[2] Richelieu had

seen a man after his own heart, who strode confidently over those awkward fissures that kept opening up between traditional rules and rights
and the interests of the state. Séguier had been blooded in an early
commission (1621) as *intendant de l'armée* in the Limousin. We are
reminded that Richelieu was not the first to appoint *intendants*, though
he did extend their powers. There was greater continuity in the absolutist
process than has been realised. Nor was there a significant break when
Mazarin took over from Richelieu. Séguier exemplifies that continuity,
grounded as it was in well understood principles and pressing needs.

He had already held the seals for two years when Aligre[3] died in 1635
and he replaced him as chancellor. He was briefly to lose the seals during
the Fronde; thereafter to serve with full powers until his death in 1672.
The *premier ministre* might outweigh the chancellor in political debate.
But there was more than dignity in the latter's position; and the dignity
was incomparable. When a king died, the chancellor alone, as personify-
ing his authority, did not go into mourning. On some ceremonial
occasions he acted for the king; at a *lit de justice* he sat immediately below
the royal throne. Sometimes a picture conveys more than its ostensible
subject: Le Brun's superb portrait of Séguier, riding in the heavy splendour of his official robes, under canopies held aloft by running pages,
says more about the ethos of French government, the concern with form
and precedence, than any list of his functions can convey. They are
impressive enough – he normally presided over the two lesser councils.[4]
So long as he retained the function of sealing royal edicts he possessed
a powerful check on anything he deemed prejudicial to the interests of
the crown. Bellièvre had used it in 1602 to signify his opposition to the
establishment of the *droit annuel*. In 1656 Séguier was to refuse to sign
an edict ordering the sale of royal forests in the Ile-de-France. That was
sound law. Alienation of the royal domain was contrary to the ordinances.
That principle would also provide justification, by daring extension, for
annexations on the frontiers.

The chancellor also had legislative powers. Marillac had been renowned
for his concern for regulation. Séguier was less creative, more concerned
with the steady maintenance of order – not surprising in one bred to
Roman Law and imbued with the notion of the lawyer as a royal officer.
A tendency to authoritarianism was further stiffened by his early experience. He had found appropriate candidates for Richelieu's new courts
and commissions and supplied legal arguments for prosecutions in which
the interests of the state took precedence over the rights of the subject.
He had interrogated the queen about her Spanish liaison in 1637;[5] also,
at different times, Gaston and Cinq Mars. He had presided at the inquest
that followed the revolt of the Nu-pieds. Outside his own circle he was
mistrusted, even by some detested, as the embodiment of the new order:
absolutism parading in the dress of law.

Séguier's role would be different under the regency. He had to hand over presidency of the lesser councils. Gaston and Condé (father and son in turn), as princes of the blood, presided – but infrequently. One effect was to accelerate the process by which major decisions were taken by the inner group of ministers sitting in the *conseil d'en haut*. There his knowledge of the law and, through *intendants'* reports, of the country, his stamina and instinct for survival proved invaluable to Mazarin. Séguier, in turn, could be grateful to Mazarin for representing his virtues to Anne, who had cause to dislike him and would have preferred Châteauneuf. He was ready to accept second place to a second Cardinal, but quick to act if he saw any serious threat to his position; after the exile of Mazarin he gave his allegiance to the princes – in the interest of political stability, he could argue. He was of course no *frondeur*, but deferential to the authority of the king as he expected others to be to him. He was always prepared to be a harsh executor of justice, but took care to protect clients, even tax-shy tenants on his estates. Altogether Séguier typifies much of royal government, the dignified face and principled assertions, and the bargains and compromises.

Centuries of history had gone to making the office of chancellor. Less than twenty years had seen the exercise of power by a *premier ministre*, in ways, moreover, which had created precedents without establishing rules. With the title of Cardinal went the acknowledged right of precedence in council. It ensured too a degree of protection, since the French Church would interpret any attack on Mazarin as an attack on the Church. Richelieu's success prepared the position for Mazarin, but also ensured that he began with a ready-made opposition. Mazarin did not have to win power by displacing a sitting minister, as Richelieu had La Vieuville[6] in 1624. He also had the assurance of Anne's support, while Richelieu had always to contend with the possible counter-influence of a royal favourite.

Anne too had a mind of her own; her temper was imperious. But her relationship with Mazarin was bound to be different for, in a sense, Mazarin was her 'favourite'.[7] So long as his health held good, Mazarin's position was secure. Given his life of incessant work and gnawing anxieties, that could not be taken for granted. He had had his first attack of fever, probably typhoid, in 1635. In October 1644 a further attack brought him so low that some thought he could die. He did not have to reckon with a potential intermediary, unless it be the confessor.[8] Richelieu had not availed himself of the authority he used so freely in ecclesiastical matters, to direct the conscience of the king: he had therefore been vulnerable when his policy could be interpreted as being contrary to the interests of Rome. Mazarin also had much to fear from the *dévôts*; it was to be one of several factors working against him during the Fronde. But so long as the pious Spanish queen trusted and supported him, and the *dévôts* were represented by Gondi,[9] whom Anne distrusted, the *dévôt* factor would prove to be of limited significance. As in other cases, it will become plain that Mazarin was fortunate in his enemies.

The role of Mazarin, like that of Richelieu, will be seen to evolve continually in response to changing circumstances. From the start he could, and did, act over a wide field. It is no more an exaggeration to talk of Mazarin's government than it was to talk of Richelieu's in the previous reign. He was the prime mover and coordinator of policy. He issued instructions to ambassadors, generals and governors. He soon overcame initial hesitation when dealing with business in council though it exposed his limited knowledge of procedures. It is unlikely that it harmed his standing with fellow councillors that he was at first diffident, then more confident, but still invariably tactful, indeed solicitous, about the interests and feelings of others. It is to be noted that those who knew him best generally liked him most. It did not reduce his standing that he could exercise much patronage, from his own growing resources, but also by influence over the crown's. Le Tellier, Fouquet, Colbert and Lionne are but four of the most eminent examples of men, intensely ambitious for themselves, whose ability would be at his service. After the Fronde he could afford to build his *clientèle* more ambitiously: by his death there were 114 *créatures* in the finance ministry alone.[10]

Much of Mazarin's time was spent in reading and composing despatches. As with Richelieu, diplomacy was for long periods an overriding concern. It should be taken to describe his dealings not only with foreign powers but with magnates at home: men like Bouillon and Condé had at times to be treated as if they were independent powers rather than subjects. A volume could be composed on the relationship of Mazarin and Gaston alone.[11] Richelieu had secured discharge in 1626 from the duty of hearing private grievances in order that he could concentrate on affairs of state: ill health was his convenient pretext. It meant, not that he stopped dealing with such matters but that he could choose his ground and see whom he wanted to see. It was also a sign of his growing authority after 1630 that he was able to delegate, even in areas of policy where he was most concerned: foreign affairs and war. With the mobilisation of resources for war, along with the increased use of *intendants*, had come the development of specialist departments, with trusted men taking more decisions and finding new opportunities for creating their own *clientèles*. The outstanding examples of this tendency were the two men who aspired in 1643 to fill his shoes: Chavigny and Sublet de Noyers, specialists, respectively, in foreign affairs and war. It had perhaps been easier for Richelieu to let his *surintendants* regard financial affairs as their own. For example Colbert would be able to extend the range of the finance ministry to include commerce, colonies, the navy and royal buildings, because Louis XIV would become his own first minister, practising his *métier* with absolute faith in his right and ability. That, of course, was something that Mazarin could not know.

Five years separated the elevation of Mazarin from the outbreak of the Fronde. There is a tendency to assess the prelude to a revolution in terms of what later transpires, as before an opera, when the music of the overture first falls on inattentive ears. The themes, soon to become familiar, are there to be identified: the financial shufflings on the brink of bankruptcy; the posturing of those who for differing reasons were out of the game: ex-ministers, magnates whose hopes of a lax regency were disappointed by the appearance of 'business as before'.[12] When constitutional issues emerged from the medley of grievances, Mazarin did not stand back and leave such domestic matters entirely to the chancellor and finance minister. It was however inevitable that his prime concerns should be military and diplomatic. Negotiations were endlessly considered, belatedly begun: their progress and conclusion, together with the campaigns and battles of the last years of the German War will be related in a later chapter. It will be seen that Spanish armies did not collapse after Rocroy; that the Imperial and Bavarian commanders were still able to keep the field; that Mazarin's envoys did not therefore have an easy task at the conference tables; that his nerve was tested to the utmost by the need to keep French troops supplied and to resist the war-fatigue which only stiffened resistance to taxes and other financial devices. At the same time he exercised overall control over affairs. It was his judgement that the domestic front could be held for as long as was necessary to conclude war against the emperor on terms that would fulfil his mentor's vision of a secure eastern frontier; also that it was worth pursuing the war against Spain beyond 1648. Particelli may have provoked the Fronde by measures too clever by half. But the Fronde was about a whole system of government: it was the legacy of Richelieu but the commitment and responsibility of Mazarin. The basic instinct of the *frondeurs* was therefore to be correct. It was not only because he was an Italian favourite of a Spanish queen that they attacked him with such vehemence, but because he held, without misgiving, to the absolutist course.

12

ROYAL ABSOLUTISM: THEORIES AND TRADITIONS

Richelieu's tremendous image looms over the early Mazarin years. Mazarin's fellow ministers, like Colbert in a later generation, would refer to him as a final authority: 'what would the great Cardinal have done?' *Frondeurs* were to make it an objection and a taunt that Mazarin did not understand what was legitimate in the way that Richelieu had done. The past came to seem more attractive, of course, in the glow of present resentments. In the same way Henry IV was already acquiring his almost legendary status as the good king, presiding over a land of plenty. Richelieu's ministry was however fresh in men's minds. Some had been injured and looked for recompense. Respect for the man did not mean that all accepted the measures he had taken. The immediate question does not however have to do with particular measures but with the trend towards a centralised royal authority, enlarged inevitably at the expense of the rights of individuals and corporations. To what extent did educated Frenchmen accept the absolutist trend? Had Richelieu and his subsidised school of writers[1] won the political argument? Upon answers to those questions, among other factors, would depend the outcome of the Fronde.

Coming closer to the world in which Richelieu operated, away from that depicted by the neat formulations of the jurist or political theorist, historians have come to be wary of seeing absolutism as a system – even if they still see it as a useful way of describing a political process: a series of frequently arbitrary, sometimes hesitant, even contradictory, but always pragmatic attempts to promote royal authority.[2] To recognise the realities of government, that, for example, the privileged classes came to realise that their interests were best served by collaboration, and that ministers stood to profit immensely from the extension of royal powers, is not to invalidate the theories of those who sought to rationalise or to justify high royalism. To the footsore soldier the fifes and drums of the accompanying band may not be an adequate commentary on his experience of the march. The tunes may be lost on him, yet the beat gives a sense of disciplined direction: so it is with the political philosopher in relation to those who have to keep their feet on the ground. Those who served the king needed firm principles to hearten them for the struggle and could see them in the light of reason now shining so clearly above the messy landscape of politics. Not for nothing were Le Bret,[3] Balzac[4] and Priézac[5] contemporaries of Descartes,[6] the mathematician who, in the words of Fontenelle,[7] 'gives the tone to a whole century'. *L'esprit de géométrie* was the religion of some of the best minds of the time and pervaded every realm of thought and art.

Foremost among the philosophers of absolutism was Cardin Le Bret who combined practical experience in government with the ability to give cogent expression to the principles which underlay his various employments. He defined sovereignty in unequivocally absolute terms: 'it is no more indivisible than the point in geometry'. Of course absolutist principles represented more than intellectual fashion. Le Bret, Balzac and others who wrote in the same vein, worked in a climate of opinion that had been strongly affected by the centrifugal forces at work during the Religious Wars, and again during the regency of Marie de Médicis, when powerful subjects were holding the state to ransom; when religious language and structures, whether Huguenot, League or latterly *dévôt*, reinforced the spirit of faction: periods associated with massacres or assassinations; and with the intrusion of Spain. Men who might deplore the execution of Montmorency might then recall the murder of Henry IV; Huguenots who had found arguments for resistance to an 'ungodly ruler', had reason, since 1629, to appreciate the virtues of political loyalism. Required to choose between individual rights and collective security, Balzac opted for the latter. An arbitrary execution could be lawful, and represent divine inspiration, through the agency of the king, if it was required for political survival. Just as the observations of the empirical scientist would break free from the rules of deductive logic, so the rationale of absolutism was countered by reference to the possible, inherent in the art of politics. Yet there was more to it than mere calculation of advantage. Early seventeenth-century royalism was in most respects in accord with traditional views.

Monarchy was supported by the facts of history, and the sentiment they engendered; by myths, but also by law. When the realm had been small and beleaguered, the king had come to be seen as protector and justiciar. The disunities within the realm, reflecting the uneven process of conquest and assimilation, emphasised the fact that he alone represented unity. With awareness of mutual dependence, characteristic of feudalism and responsible for the demands made by great families on the generosity of the crown, went also a sense of intimacy, a family spirit that extended beyond the confines of the court. In his unashamedly flattering treatise, *De l'excellence des Roys et du Royaume de France* (1610), Bignon[8] had stressed the accessibility of the king: 'it is this which attracts and wins Frenchmen's hearts and makes them affectionate and devoted to their prince'. The physical presence of the king in Paris was of crucial importance. When living at the Louvre or, after 1643, the Palais-Royal, he was within short walking distance from *Parlement*, Notre-Dame and the Hôtel de Ville, not to mention those informal centres of Parisian opinion, the markets and the place de Grève. It is the fact that emerges most vividly from narratives of the Fronde. It was a nightmare for those concerned at the palace with the king's safety: indeed the chief dilemma for the court during the Fronde was to choose between the king's presence as a focus for loyalty, and the freedom of manoeuvre that he could enjoy in the provinces. The years when his young authority was in jeopardy were also however to be the years when the people's love for their king was to be most effusive and valuable.

The idea of Divine Right played a large part in the royalist thinking of Louis XIII's reign and was to be further embellished for the benefit of his successor.[9] The principles were long established. Literary arguments had reinforced holy writ when patriotic writers stressed the legitimacy of the Valois and hailed eventual victory as God's blessing on the *fleur de lys* and the dynasty. The king was sacerdotally endowed from the moment in the coronation at Rheims when he was anointed with oil from the holy phial of Clovis.[10] At the ceremony he wore his tunic 'like that of a sub-deacon at mass', his mantle 'raised on the left as one raises the chasuble of a priest'. *Le roi thaumaturge*, thus set apart, was constantly assured that he was like a bishop: 'the first in your kingdom after the Pope, the right arm of the church'. He was *très chrétien*, an appellation which became almost a formal title. Like the kings of England he touched for 'the king's evil'.[11] No assessment of Louis XIII, that troubled, scrupulous man, should omit the profound sense of religious calling which coloured his views about government. Nor can Louis XIV be understood without what would be for him, boy and man, an unshakeable premise: kingship was a trust for which its holder was responsible to God alone. When however the royal behaviour was also conditioned by views like that of du Boys:[12] that 'kings were masters in the obedience that a subject owes them, as owners of the goods and lives of men', when policy could be decided on grounds as subjective as the promptings of conscience, was there not a danger that Divine Right could assume the form of a blank cheque upon which the sovereign could write as he pleased? The question loses some force from consideration of other sources of royal authority.

In Louis XIII's reign a party had come into existence calling themselves *bons français*,[13] signifying that their views were inspired by nothing other than the good of France, as against the *dévôts*, who gave priority to the international interests of Catholicism. They held that the king should be obeyed as the supreme representation of the state. At the start of the seventeenth century, the catholicism of many courtiers, most *parlementaires* and a significant number of bishops, was robustly Gallican. Henry IV's conversion,[14] which appeared to confer authenticity on what many Catholics had regarded as a dubious claim to the crown, had however left some unconvinced. Henry's assassination (1610) had therefore been more than the isolated gesture of a fanatic: Ravaillac only took to their logical conclusion widely held views about heresy and the case for tyrannicide. The shocking act reflected suspicion of Henry's motives and intentions. Was he not about to go to war against Spain? Fuelled by the emnity of many Frenchmen towards that country, conversely by the zeal of others for the Habsburg princes' crusade against European heresy, the opposition of *bons français* and *dévôts* became a central ideological issue, painfully embarrassing to Richelieu as it would be to Mazarin.

In 1635 Matthieu de Morgues[15] was sentenced to death after trial *in absentia*, for plotting against the state and the Cardinal's life, by the *Chambre de l'Arsenal*: the special court, the extreme, and unsubstantiated, charge, the ultimate penalty, together illustrate the chasm that was opening up between the parties – both were in deadly earnest. In his *Catholicon françois*, Morgues condemned Richelieu's use of religious principles, as 'your preceptor Machiavelli showed the ancient Romans doing, shaping them, . . . applying them just as far as they aid the advancement of your designs', to justify a foreign policy that had brought 'enemies, wars and disorders such as France has never seen'. Morgues remained a persistent enemy of Richelieu and subsequently of Mazarin, the source of scandalous stories and a contributor to the black legend: two unscrupulous Cardinals betraying the trust of the king and the interests of his realm. Even more serious consequences were to flow from the dispute aroused by Jansen, in *Mars Gallicus*,[16] also in 1635. His sweeping attack on French policy provoked Richelieu into reprisals which set the pattern for royal policy towards Jansenism for the rest of the century. He commissioned Priézac to write his *Vindiciae Gallicae*,[17] a study of *raison d'état* as being consistent with Christianity, and an uncompromising defence of the king's right to act as he thought fit to preserve his realm. It was not for subjects, 'those who are born to obey, to insinuate themselves into affairs of state'. It is, of course the thinking of the Cardinal, elaborated in his *Mémoires* and *Testament Politique*.[18] Where did it leave *Parlement*? Excluded from affairs of state? Magistrates' rights were clear in their own minds, their constitutional place sanctioned by tradition. Reacting to policy, in particular concerning religion and foreign affairs, their stance was bound however to be ambiguous: that could only be to the advantage of the crown. Judges claimed, even when protesting at some manifestation of royal power, that they were defending the crown's authority against usurpations.

In what might have been a nursery of political opposition, magistrates continued to emphasise the dependence of the Church upon the protection of the king: so his secular authority was enhanced. The contrast with

England is indeed striking: for there the royal supremacy was a material fact and Puritan opponents of Charles I's moderately absolutist policies used religious arguments against royalist high churchmen. In the absence of a central representative body comparable to the English parliament, the predominance of Roman Law in the practice of the French courts was a prime reason for the diverging political courses of the two countries. Roman axioms lend themselves to absolute government.[19] The contrasting emphasis in Common law on the rights of subjects, the reliance on precedents, the historical circumstances which led to the 'third estate', the House of Commons, becoming powerful in its own right, and the presence there of a large number of lawyers, together created formidable obstacles to the growth of royal power. It does not follow however that there were no restraints on the king's power in France where, as generally in Europe, 'liberty' meant liberties, particular and exclusive, rights and franchises, so many monuments to centuries of bargaining between sovereign and subject. To be found throughout the realm, in forms as varied as the customs and laws of its provinces, fiefs and towns, they were protected by law which *parlements*, at the summit of corporate privilege, could usually be relied on to maintain.

As a royal court, composed of royal officers, *Parlement*[20] claimed to share in the absolute sovereignty of the crown. In its legal capacity, it also lent its unique authority to the defence of particular rights: the ambivalence was to be starkly exposed during the Fronde. Meanwhile, given the Gallican sympathies of leading judges, it is not hard to see why the Third Estate should have proposed to the States-General of 1614–15 the elevating into 'a fundamental law of the realm' of the thesis that 'the king is sovereign in France and holds his crown of God alone': it was aimed broadly against those ultramontane Catholics who held the authority of the Pope to be superior, even in temporal matters, to that of the king. It is paradoxical that the crown should have rejected so loyal a declaration. Evidently ministers wished to avoid the differences within the church from developing into schism. Even so the episode illuminates the way in which *parlementaire* Gallicanism fed the growth of ultra-royalism.

To one influential writer, C. Loyseau,[21] author of the influential *Traité de Ordres* (1613), questions about rights and usurpations would have been meaningless. The king, as God's vice-regent on earth, as embodying the state, was the sole law-giver, bound by no human ordinance. The sovereign's 'absolute power . . . perfect and entire in all particulars' enabled him to make laws, confer and remove offices and privileges, do justice, coin money and raise taxes; all without the consent of the Estates. 'The power of a prince', he concluded, 'extends over goods as well as over persons' and he can command both 'for the proper necessity of his people'. Was the role of *Parlement* then to be confined to debate over what constituted such 'necessity'? That would be, in effect, to license *raison d'état*, to reduce registration to an empty formality. Not surprisingly *Parlement* remained committed to the traditional interpretation of royal authority: the king was not free to dispose of the kingdom as he wished, for he was not owner but administrator of the *corps politique et mystique* which was so constructed, the king being head and the members of the three orders the limbs, so that if any part were injured, the whole would be injured. The organic metaphor might grow stale with use, but it came close to the realities of the situation. For there were limits to what the sovereign could do without arousing resistance which would then be offered in the name of 'the fundamental laws', would reflect those entrenched positions which restrained ministers' ability to act decisively, and would be most obdurate when it appeared that the king's cause was being damaged by those who professed to act in his name.

That these were not merely academic questions becomes clear in the periodic tussles between crown and *Parlement*, like that of 1632, which followed *Parlement*'s refusal to register the edict setting up the *Chambre de l'Arsenal*[22] and led to its humiliation. Salt was rubbed into the wounds when, after the outbreak of war in 1635, a *lit de justice* was held to register edicts creating new offices, twenty-four in *Parlement* itself. The edicts were registered, but certain members of the *Enquêtes* demanded that they be considered by a plenary session. When their leaders were arrested, in January 1636, and banished from the capital, their colleagues staged a judicial strike that lasted till March. Peace was restored when the king consented to restore the exiled magistrates and to reduce the number of new offices to seventeen. Providing the essential background to the constitutional Fronde, the affair well illustrates the positions of king and *Parlement*, the boundaries within which each could operate. These would shift according to the authority of the crown at a given time. In 1638, after a protest against the crown's failure to honour certain *rentes*, five magistrates were banished; a second strike ensued – but the crown stood firm; *Parlement* gave in, without exacting concessions. In February 1641 the august body was forced to register an edict defining its role: edicts of a political rather than specifically financial or judicial nature were in future to be registered without prior discussion. Only the prestige of a resolute king could ensure the compliance of *Parlement* in such unpalatable measures. The taste lingered. Goodwill had been sacrificed. A reaction could be expected.

Richelieu was generally most effective in striking against individuals. In developing the power of the *intendants* or creating new courts, he might by-pass but not usually replace existing officers and courts. When he mounted an assault upon an institution, it was likely to be the first move in a bargaining process from which some form of compromise could be expected to result. If any minister was pursuing the goal of fiscal uniformity by introducing *élections* into *pays d'états* it was his rival, Marillac, rather than Richelieu, whose record on that issue shows him to have been the supreme pragmatist, concerned primarily with the provision of money and increasingly aware of the shortcomings of the *élections* in that respect. In the event Burgundy, Provence, Languedoc and Brittany all kept their Estates, and with them the *taille réelle*, though only Brittany escaped punitive action.

Richelieu's own authority and scope for action was derived from exploitation of his *clientèle*, enlarged so massively that it could be identified with the royal administration. His single-minded pursuit of land and office was not novel; it was the scale, resulting in a fortune eventually larger than either Gaston's or Condé's, that shook the high nobles into opposing – or coming to terms with – the great minister. Montmorency died and with him some of the spirit of the old feudalism; Condé, more realistic, or simply more mercenary, arranged for his son's marriage, in 1641, to the Cardinal's niece:[23] the contrast is telling. The Fronde would show that the old values, loyalties and cries still appealed; but for every one noble prepared to go the whole way, whether to glory, death, or disgrace, there was another ready to collaborate. The lucrative marriage of Condé's younger son, Conti, to another *Mazarinette*[24] would reveal more of the future of society and government than the gentlemen of Poitou rallying to the duc de la Rochefoucauld.

If Richelieu had something of the ruthlessness in pursuit of clearly defined goals that characterises the intellectual in politics, he also had the common sense to stay within the bounds of what was practicable: witness his treatment of the Huguenots and his policy of limited objectives in the search for security of frontiers. His religious faith was neither extreme nor narrow but surely comprehended some of what was finest in this 'great age of souls'. So far from being coarsened by wealth and power, the author of the *Treatise of Christian Perfection*,[25] the devoted friend of Joseph du Tremblay, seems actually to have grown in spiritual insight and serenity (and the capacity to bear physical suffering) in the last years of his ministry. Of course such statements can only point to certain tendencies; they cannot delineate the complicated man who in one day could appear cynical, caustic, harsh, hysterical, magnanimous and tender. They highlight ways in which he differed from Mazarin; they do little to blur the clear impression, whether it comes from domestic or foreign policy, or the evolution of political ideas in the context of royalist tradition, of continuity. There would be setbacks and times of wavering. But in what Richelieu himself would have regarded as the main work of government, there would be no wavering.

Part III

THE FRONDE

'A deuce of a want of light and grouping to it.'
R. L. Stevenson

13

CLOUDY SKIES

Early episodes in the regency suggested essential continuity rather than abrupt change. Ministers had much to worry about but the mood at court, after the defeat of the *Importants*, appears to have veered between relief and mutual congratulation. There was little sign of a break or of reassessment, in principles or in administrative procedures. There was however a new situation. War was no longer the issue of security that it had been before Rocroy, when the enemy threatened the eastern provinces – and the estates of prominent Parisians. The strident propaganda that Richelieu had successfully sponsored now had negative effects. If his enemies had 'shed their blood like water',[1] if the royal armies were victorious by land and sea, why did peace seem as remote as ever? Were ministers pursuing the war because it was profitable to them and to their financial associates?

Such questions were not the concern only of the 'political classes'. Each year saw riots or risings in some part of France. A new tax on wine was enough to rouse the people of Tours in October 1643. In June 1644, at Montpellier, the familiar grievance was a demand for *subsistance* for billeted troops. Marseilles, Valence, Clermont-Ferrand, Angers, Toul, Grenoble and Toulouse were convulsed at one time or another during these years. Bakers' shops were a common target of clamorous mobs, with women usually to the fore. Mutilated or killed, tax officials were the usual victims.[2] To read accounts of the frenzied violence is to wonder what extremes of suffering people had endured to bring them to such a state. Where troops were not available, as at Tours, the *intendant*, Heere, had to arm a force of *bourgeois*: only when they saw that the city might be pillaged did they cooperate.[3] Government could rely on the instinct of men of property to defend themselves, on the particularism of the French town and the mutual antagonism often found between town and surrounding villages – but only until some overriding cause or influential local magnate should stir up a general insurrection. There were warnings enough in the *émeutes* of the pre-Fronde.

Rumour was always a potent agent. Stories were about that government would launch some kind of attack on the financiers. That was exactly what they could not do since they relied on the flow of loans: it was the trap that continued to inhibit ministers during the Fronde. The expectations of the sovereign courts had been raised by the advent of regency and Anne's promises of cooperation: again, resentments were correspondingly keen. It was thus that the general perception of Mazarin was so important. He was at his best when smoothing out personal differences and questions of etiquette, such as those which revolved round the perennial feud between the duchesses Montbazon and Longueville.[4] In the matters that meant most to the upper echelons of official Paris, he seemed to be weak, indifferent to the abuses of state finance or, worse, party to them.

In fact, Mazarin was working diligently for the successful prosecution of the war and for a satisfactory peace. Critics may have failed to appreciate the complexities of negotiation. But Mazarin had himself to blame for the mistrust that grew around his personality and ministry. A politician's chance remark may be given undue weight because it seems to fit with some trend or policy, or with the popular view of the man. So Mazarin would have cause to regret referring to *Parlement*'s concerns as mere 'bagatelles'. Europe's most famous tribunal, this court of peers and arbiter of rank, took itself very seriously. None were keener than the young councillors of the *Enquêtes* and the *Requêtes*, hungry for briefs and promotion, who were to be the shock troops in early conflicts with the crown. It was the apparent nonchalance with which Mazarin met their concerns, with a contempt for proper procedures which reflected his own hazy understanding of French law, together with a well-founded suspicion that Anne would encourage him to override opposition, that exasperated moderate men. Two of them, in key positions, Omer Talon,[5] *avocat-général*, the crown's representative, and Mathieu Molé,[6] *premier président*, and so the leader and voice of the whole body, could have been valuable allies. They would be forced into positions ranging from Talon's outspoken criticism to Molé's espousal, at least for a time, of the opposition's cause.

Inevitably the main arguments developed over finance and the measures of Particelli d'Hémery. He came to represent the hated class of *traitants* and the deviser of policies designed to enrich them and himself. He developed the practice of direct, unaudited payment from the revenue till it amounted to about a third of total expenditure, all unaudited; he worked closely with a select group of financiers and made a huge personal fortune. Yet he managed to borrow money needed to keep the armies in the field, at a relatively favourable rate of interest: around fifteen per cent. Mazarin did not initiate, though he generally approved his measures. He was careful to keep some distance between himself and his unpopular *contrôleur général* but he sustained him in office, indeed promoted him:

in 1647, he became *surintendant*. In general terms Hémery worked to Mazarin's brief.

Finance was a recurring cause of quarrels between the crown, *Parlement* and other privileged groups. They revolved round material grievances as much as constitutional rights and practices; they were as much about the property and status of office as about the condition of the people. They culminated in the Fronde. It was appropriate that Hémery should be one of its earliest victims; yet he should not be held solely, even mainly responsible. He inherited a chronic deficit, a mountain of debt, a year's revenue pledged in advance, an official establishment already seething with resentments. Nor was he responsible for the all-consuming war, impelling him to plan for the short term: one purpose of his hated new taxes was simply to show creditors that the crown still had the initiative and could raise money. Devising the tactics to overcome the resistance of *Parlement* he acted for the regent and Mazarin. Only when matters came to crisis point did Mazarin break with him. In the end it was the very ingenuity of Hémery's schemes that caused such political damage.

A council decree of March 1644 ordered that all occupants of buildings built in Paris since, and in contravention of, a sixteenth-century ordinance forbidding further construction within the precincts of Paris, should pay a fine fixed according to the space occupied by the building concerned. The cleverness of the *toisé* lay in the fact that it was indisputably legal. *Parlement* could hardly deny the validity of such a decree. But Hémery tried to be too clever. To avoid the obstruction and delays to be expected from *Parlement* it was ordained that disputes arising from the *toisé* should be heard, after appeal to the *Châtelet*,[7] by the royal council, not by *Parlement*. Encouraged by certain *parlementaires*, in July 1644, victims of the decree, generally the poorer citizens, came swarming out of their tenements in the districts of Saint-Antoine and Saint-Germain, and clamoured to *Parlement* for redress.[8] The regent met *Parlement*'s request by reducing from eight to one million *livres* the total to be raised. Even that did not stop a flow of petitions against the levy or mollify members of the *Enquêtes* and *Requêtes*, who believed that they should be dealing with them. *Parlement*'s procedures were too slow. Meanwhile Hémery was left to find the money in some other way.

In August 1644 Anne warned Talon that a *lit de justice* would be held in September to enforce the registration of an edict compelling the richest citizens of Paris to lend money to the government through investment in the *rentes*: a forced loan in all but name, Talon alleged that 'it was an extraordinary and unparalleled act for a king who was still a minor to hold a *lit de justice* and to have edicts verified by the exercise of his absolute power'. That Talon should make an assertion of such doubtful constitutional validity indicates the extent to which the crown was rousing alarm by its extreme measures and arbitrary methods. Anne drew back from the brink and a compromise was reached. The proposed *lit de justice* was abandoned on condition that *Parlement* nominate a commission to choose the citizens who were to make loans. Magistrates were exempted so that the weight landed on the financial community, *gens d'affaires*. A deputation of financiers went to the palace to demand fair treatment. Their spokesman warned Anne that 'they would take no further part in financial business'. If 'the gentlemen of *Parlement*' went on trying 'to spoil her affairs' it was time she imposed her authority. The example of England should make her careful! She was, and the idea was subsequently dropped in favour of persuasion; there Hémery was relatively successful: it was his forte.

Hémery might placate his friends. While he went on cutting or withholding official salaries, he could only expect hostility in the courts. In 1645 he farmed the collection of the *taille* and then deprived the *trésoriers* of the right to allot the farms. Nor did *rentiers* escape the general squeeze; the withholding of interest payments and reduction of rates alarmed many bourgeois. Magistrates sensed a gathering of support. They were in a position to become champions of the people. Ministerial retreats had shown that opposition could be effective. Anne still rejected requests from *Parlement* to restore to the *Enquêtes* and the *Requêtes* the right to hear *toisé* appeals. In March 1645 members of those courts defied her express ban when they called for a plenary session of *Parlement*.[9] Anne responded by exiling three of the main protestors and imprisoning the man regarded as their ringleader, president Barillon.[10] That he was a relative of Bouillon and a friend of Gondi did not endear him to the court. He had offended at the outset of the regency when he warned the sovereign not to delegate her power to a sole minister. His subsequent death in prison did nothing to improve relations between Mazarin and the *coadjuteur*; it also deprived the ministry of a chance to offer a concession in the form of his release and created a martyr for the cause of opposition to arbitrary power.

In September 1645 Anne held her long-threatened *lit de justice*. The *toisé* was dropped but only as part of a package consisting of several new taxes and the creation of new offices. The distance between court and *Parlement* remained as large as ever. The magistrates declared that their consciences did not permit them to register edicts which they had not examined. Séguier clarified an aspect of *raison d'état* when he replied that there were two sorts of conscience, one for private matters, the other for matters of state. The chancellor was receiving reports from the provinces that revealed the difficulties that confronted the *intendants*. For ministers, government was now fundamentally about force, with advances, entrenchments and retreats to meet the changing circumstances. The magistrates clung to an older conception of legal monarchy. Where they saw principle, Séguier saw pedantry. It is the measure of the change that was being wrought by war. It was not only reluctance to make financial sacrifices that inspired the intense longing for peace.

In September 1646 a new tax was decreed: a tariff on goods entering Paris, either by land or river. It was a clever amalgam of old and new, some duties being based on rights belonging to the crown, others deriving from laws which had already been registered; others were temporary excise duties, verifiable therefore by the *cour des aides*. The whole group was sent for registration to the *cour des aides*: its members were no happier about the tariff than were the *parlementaires*: they feared the precedent. The crown was little more successful in another cynical exercise in social manipulation. The offer of 'perfect nobility'[11] for membership of some provincial sovereign courts and for *trésoriers* did not impress those who already enjoyed the significant privileges, like tax-exemption, while it offended the lesser officials. Meaning to exploit differences of status ministers managed only to provoke a more alert and united opposition. Placards outlining *Parlement*'s case brought popular interest to a dangerous level.

The government could derive comfort from *Parlement*'s own dilemmas. An edict registered in September 1645 had required rent in return for an extension of the lease from proprietors of alienated lands formerly in the *domaine royale*.[12] *Parlement* now found itself compelled to decree imprisonment for non-payment, as notably, in the case of one Croisset, *procureur au Châtelet*. Like others he was given time to get away. Looking back on the strains and clinches of this prolonged wrestling match, it is still possible to see elements of theatre, as if neither party were in deadly earnest, each looking for ways out. Negotiation was still possible. In September 1647, *Parlement*, unbidden, registered the edict imposing the duties, but with the reservation that it was only to last for two years – and only that long if peace were not concluded earlier. So they safeguarded their right of registration and asserted the principle that additional taxation was merely a temporary wartime expedient.

It is hard to see Mazarin's next action as anything but a blunder. He could be obtuse when required to read the popular mood. On technical grounds it could be urged that *Parlement* had exceeded its authority. On other occasions, however, Mazarin showed that he could waive principle to secure a material objective. He could have listened more carefully to his opponents. Foremost among them was Gondi, well placed by his position as effective director of the clergy of the diocese, to gauge Paris opinion. For all his conceit and eccentricity, Gondi was realistic about city politics and sensitive to the popular mood. He looked forward to putting his knowledge and skills to the service of the regent – or to rebellion – as circumstances should dictate. Mazarin brought the latter eventuality a step nearer when he issued a conciliar decree annulling that registered by *Parlement*, but retaining the tax.

The people were now invited to choose between two conflicting pronouncements on the same tax; two interpretations, if they cared to ponder them, of sovereign authority. Mazarin was opening doors when he should have shut them. Danger had always lain in the too precise defining of powers which had long been regarded as opposed but complementary, in a situation in which peace could best be assured by recognition of common interests. Now, without benefit of the effective action that it could deliver, he was inviting the worst interpretation of arbitrary power. To compound error, he then allowed Hémery to go ahead with a plan to create twelve new offices of *maître des requêtes* and another batch in the *maréchaussée*,[13] and to use a further *lit de justice* to secure its registration, along with that of other taxes.

Just at the time when the future of the *maîtres* as *intendants* was open to question, when he had most to gain from retaining their support, Mazarin was antagonising them. He was forcing the lawyers most closely associated with government to look for support in *Parlement*. He appeared to be disregarding the warnings of Talon and Molé, who had repeatedly argued against the use of a *lit de justice* and the packaging of assorted edicts for this process. Meanwhile his *surintendant* was threatening to suspend the *paulette* unless *Parlement* approved his financial edicts.

Salaries, *rentes*, tariffs, now offices: the pressure appeared to be inexorable. Ministers were haunted by fear of mutinies in the armies, a rising in the provinces. Magistrates, hurrying home from hot debates in the Palais de Justice, to their houses in the Marais, the rue Saint-Honoré or the newly fashionable Faubourg Saint-Germain, saw another face of the country's crisis: famished people, many of them new arrivals from the stricken countryside; beggars more numerous than ever,[14] tradesmen out of work, women unable to feed their children; a volatile city close to eruption: in short a situation in which the magistrates must lead or be themselves the targets of the people's rage. The *lit de justice* of 15 January 1648, may or may not be held to be the beginning of the Fronde. It is the moment when the discontents of the several disparate groups, who had reason to believe that they could no longer trust the crown to defend their rights, come into a single focus, as their leaders sense the people's desperation, find a representative voice and identify with a common cause.

14

THE GATHERING STORM

On 15 January 1648, Louis XIV, aged nine, held a *lit de justice* at the *Parlement* of Paris. Flanked by his mother, his ministers, the princes of the blood and *ducs et pairs*, he declared his will: the judges must register the seven financial edicts. The majesty of France spoke in treble tones, but it was not the child's voice that weakened the emphatic words. Neither the argument about the rights of the regent, whether the *lit* was acceptable when the king was not of age, nor the fact that the crown was insolvent was, by itself, sufficient reason for *Parlement* to make a stand. Together however the constitutional and financial questions interwove to create a new political pattern: it was possible for sober, moderate men of property to envisage open opposition.

Mazarin might not be interested in the finer points of fiscal policy. The general issue of confidence was however inescapable. The *traitants* were withholding advances, waiting for a signal that it was safe to resume. Unpaid troops were faltering before what it was hoped would be the last campaigns; diplomatic advantages, so dearly bought, were lost in the last rounds: alongside such frustrations, in the world of high risks to which he was accustomed, the argument for a bold attack was irresistible. Anne too liked the idea of a comprehensive parcel which would both assert her authority and tap the resources of some affluent subjects. *Parlement* was required to accept the Paris tariff, the sale of new offices, the fee on feudal property acquired by non-nobles, including arrears back to 1634, and a clutch of other taxes. With the royal family and the greatest men in the realm it now heard a memorable response from the *avocat-général*.

Omer Talon was no radical. Philippe de Champaigne's portrait shows a man of some dignity: in his gown of scarlet and black, with his regular features, close cropped grey hair and severe look, the embodiment of civic responsibility, he was a worthy subject for that great artist.[1] Although he may have relished the opportunity to preach to Anne and the court about the condition of the land, he cannot have been comfortable. To plead effectively for the crown, he had to be assured of a reasonable case and sympathetic audience. Since he had neither, he had to use immoderate language to make a case for moderation. He denounced the use of the *lit de justice* to enforce the financial measures and warned Mazarin not to withhold the *paulette*. His conventional, rather old-fashioned rhetoric[2] rehearsed familiar themes: the duty of *Parlement* to assist the king to govern, excessive taxes, the wickedness of financiers. Crucially, he declared that edicts were not valid till they had been examined by the sovereign court. To hold that they were verified when the king had caused them to be read in his presence, he deemed 'a kind of illusion in morality and contradiction in politics'. His description of the miseries of the people was near enough to what many of his audience had seen themselves.[3]

Men, Talon declared, could not be fed 'by the palms and laurels' of a ruinous war. For Anne and Mazarin he certainly went too far when he urged her to ponder these horrors 'in the solitude of her oratory'. She had already had a trying time. For weeks, before Christmas, Louis had been seriously ill with smallpox: she had nursed him. The physical and emotional strain showed when Anne herself succumbed to a feverish complaint. Now she looked forward to a better year. She was in no mood to be trifled with. If the Cardinal had preferred a more gradual approach he had to reckon with Anne, angry at a seemingly gratuitous insult and now yearning for a civil Rocroy. The *maîtres des requêtes* heard her in scathing mood: 'truly you are fine people to dispute my authority'. She knew enough of French history and of her husband's way with stubborn magistrates to expect that they would defer to the royal will.

They did not openly defy the king, nor resist registration. Instead, deferring to the king's right to require it, they indulged in a parade of protest which aired their grievances to the world and made the decrees virtually unenforceable. While Parisians rallied to their supposed champions, *Parlement* itself closed ranks. Anne and her ministers had helped create essential pre-conditions for revolution: their opponents were under a united leadership, capable of action which they could take without the need or inclination to stray far from the path of constitutional rectitude and, behind them, was an effectively solid body of popular support. Here indeed was a reversal of roles: the crown so offending the most conservative in the land that they were ready to make common cause with impatient young lawyers, besides those in Paris and the provinces, from proud noble to reckless mobster, who had an interest in disorder. In this fraught and confusing situation the crown was vulnerable; but so was *Parlement*. Its direction called for fine judgement and a strong nerve. Those pre-eminently were the virtues of the *premier président* Matthieu Molé.[4]

Molé was born in the purple, a legal aristocracy that had no equivalent in any other country. With *Parlement*'s mechanisms for retaining office within a narrow circle, its integral place in the formal processes of royal government and personal links with the élites of finance and administration, went inevitably an interest in maintaining property and privilege.[5] (Typically Molé's wife was the daughter of another *président*; his son, Champlâtreux, was a rising *intendant*.) It was the very strength of that interest, however, that gave it an independent voice. How effective the voice would be at any time would depend on the character of its *premier président*. He had stood up to Richelieu, for example, over the imprisonment of Saint-Cyran.[6] His intimate links with Jansenism through friendship with the Arnauld family might have worried Richelieu. However he had respected Molé for his principled conservatism and found the Gallican tendency in *Parlement* useful on occasion. Doctrinal questions aside, it is not hard to see Molé as a friend to Port Royal and to the Jansenist set – legalistic in argument, puritanical in morality. But he seems also, in his probity and respect for conscience, to have drawn strength from his own reading of the tradition of *Parlement*.

As a staunch royalist Molé was determined to recall monarchy to a proper sense of responsibility for the public good. His eloquence witnessed to his perception of a world out of sorts and of a tragedy waiting to unfold. He saw that the young king would inevitably be the principal focus for the action, even if others had to speak his lines: 'It is a fatal moment when the majesty which is graven on his countenance, which alone separates him from common men, is not respected for the tender and true sentiments which it conveys to the hearts of the people but is seen as the means to gain what is wanted, just or unjust'. Molé did not question the authority of the crown but simply wished that the king be well advised. Others were less deferential or scrupulous.

In these defiant months Pierre Broussel[7] became the beloved tribune of the people, rallying point for magistrates who might otherwise have been less bold, and target for royal counter-attack. Molé may have hoped that the opportunity for magistrates to examine the now registered edicts would absorb their energies. He pointed out to Anne that Louis XIII's *réglement* of 1641 permitted remonstrances after a *lit de justice*: they must be preceded by scrutiny and discussion. However Omer Talon saw further. 'Freedom to debate', he said, 'will result in the option of modifying laws and adding conditions which will nullify their execution'. It also signalled to other aggrieved groups that they should add their weight to the protest.

First among them were the *maîtres des requêtes*. When the crown deprived them of their functions in the councils, councillors of state[8] then refused to work in their place: protest was spreading to the executive. January also brought news of peace between Spain and the United Provinces.[9] It was a setback for Mazarin since it made it harder for him to secure the best terms; however it put pressure on him to conclude negotiations with Austria, so might have been well received; yet it did not seem to impinge much on the magistrates. It was not the least of Mazarin's difficulties that he was working constantly in a diplomatic field which was rarefied and remote to most Parisians: they tended all the more to think that he was indifferent to their legitimate concerns. Few outside the small group of ministers and those who actually had something to do with policy had a conception of interests of state which might override those of individuals and factions.

Foreign news could however excite Parisians if it seemed to be relevant to their concerns. Masaniello's short-lived Neapolitan rising, in origin a bread riot, no longer had the appeal which had once caused Parisian rioters to shout '*Napoli*'.[10] It was more significant that Charles I of England had failed to recover power by his increasingly desperate manoeuvres and that Cromwell and his army were now controlling the political process. Soon they were to bring that 'man of blood' to his trial and execution.[11] Meanwhile the citizens, accustomed to think of Paris as the centre of the universe, became absorbed in the rare spectacle of a battle between crown and *Parlement*, whether welcoming or apprehensive of the prospect of anarchy, or simply aware that here were issues that concerned them all.

After warm debate and a remonstrance against the edict concerning tax on the alienated royal domains, *Parlement* banned the proposed advances. Anne then raised the fundamental issue of right. Unfortunately, instead of stating the royal case, she phrased her demand in the form of a question: did the judges mean to deny the principle of royal absolutism? Mazarin, whose letters show how much he was taken up with foreign affairs, may have been swept along by the vehement queen or may himself have failed to see the danger of such an invitation to constitutional debate. Gondi apparently did. 'A veil' surrounded the 'mystery of the state': tear it away and the respect naturally felt by subjects for the sovereign might fade away. Lefèvre d'Ormesson[12] was appalled. Was Anne trying 'to push *Parlement* into committing itself to extreme action'? Inevitably radical judges became more hostile to the regent with every session. Molé tried to serve the crown by suspending discussion. Anne helped her critics by insisting on a reply.

On March 3 the oracle of the *Palais de Justice* delivered the verdict in cleverly ambiguous terms. Modification of an edict was 'subject to the king's good pleasure'. It had however been made and in a manner so public that the crown had been forced on to the defensive. Anxious about the narrow majority that kept the radicals at bay, Talon added a reassuring gloss. Séguier responded helpfully. He had been engaged for several years in heated dialogue with leading *parlementaires* about the place of the royal councils and *intendants* in the judicial field. He understood, however, magistrates' concerns about the combined effect of the erosion of traditional business and the devaluation of offices through new creations. 'Provided that authority remained with the king he would be glad to receive counsel from *Parlement*'. His smooth words could not however deflect the judges from exploiting their advantage. They subjected the hated Paris tariff to conditions that rendered it ineffective. Anne hinted that she might be driven to use force.

Meanwhile Molé used every device, procedural and verbal, to keep the hounds of *Parlement* under his control. They scented blood, he feared reprisals. By elastic interpretations, he was able to blunt the thrust of successive decrees as they were conveyed to the court. By a skilful manoeuvre, which his enemies saw as vote-rigging, he secured a significant concession to the regent: on March 17, the amendment to the tariff edict was re-phrased so that it became a written remonstrance. With this document, the *parlementaires*, obeying Anne's summons, marched as a body to the Palais-Royal. Their reception was frosty until Anne was satisfied that they were indeed bowing to her authority and that the principle of absolutism was unimpaired: that formal decisions could only be made by the king. Both sides had bought a little time. Magistrates looked for some sign that ministers would go some way to meet their demands. They looked to the end of the war and the opportunity to exert their authority. Meanwhile *Parlement* had found that it could oppose the king, and get away with it.

On April 23 Séguier gave Anne's answer to *Parlement*'s remonstrances. More money had to be raised: the crown would not withdraw any of the edicts. Guessing what the reaction would be, Molé postponed reporting the royal message for ten days. Meanwhile Anne, who had already cancelled the country holiday she usually took at this time, took the initiative with a new move. On 30 April the *paulette* was renewed: for *Parlement* on nearly traditional terms, for the other sovereign courts on condition of a fee amounting to four years' salaries, for the *maîtres* not at all. To the tactics of 'divide and conquer' the aggrieved parties had their own answer. On 4 May the judges of the *Enquêtes* burst into the *grand chambre* and demanded a plenary session. The *paulette* was now to be the issue.

In all these exchanges the role of Mazarin can only be a matter of conjecture. He was not inactive. In May he had a long interview with Talon in which he explained his concerns about the effect of inflammatory speeches on opinion abroad. He had other means of persuasion: he was soon to offer Talon's brother an abbey. Molé was not to be touched by such means. Mazarin was not being sarcastic when he said that 'he loved the state'. At times however he was critical of Molé's efforts. He may have under-estimated the difficulties which Molé faced or suspected that the *premier président* was playing his own, that is *Parlement*'s game. He knew that Molé had long campaigned to recover for its jurisdiction those domains of law which had been poached by *intendants* and the royal councils; and that he argued that *Parlement*'s authority could only be maintained if the crown were to support its traditional functions. Was the *premier président* therefore less than whole-hearted in his resistance to the hot-heads who complained that Anne acted as if she were the late king – and Mazarin, as if he were another Richelieu?

In fact the differences between the two cardinals were never clearer or more crucial. Mazarin did not know enough about the traditions and principles of that aristocracy of office, entrenched on the Ile de la Cité. His own experience of the road to power made it hard for him to recognise altruism when he saw it. He inclined too easily therefore to the prejudices of the regent. In the final analysis, the widening gap between ministers and magistrates was as much about priorities as about principles. *Parlement's*, primarily legal, concerned with rights and status; the crown's, no less properly concerned with the prosecution and conclusion of foreign war. It is easy to see the drift of palace opinion, the disparaging terms in which matters were discussed: Molé a hypocrite, Talon a pompous ass, *parlementaires* generally seditious. Frustration poisoned judgement. Seasoned ministers, wanting results, become impatient with debate. If that is true of democratic regimes, how much more when the chamber is not representative but an adjunct of the executive process? Yet there were limits to what could be done. The crown could threaten action – but who would carry it out? The troops were fully committed on the frontiers to what was hoped would be the final campaigns.

The *paulette* issue showed Anne, Mazarin, and indeed Séguier at their worst. It was disingenuous to suppose that *Parlement* would detach itself from the members of the sovereign courts, besides the *maîtres* and the superior financial officials, all of whom had suffered from the non-payment of salaries. The political climate was quite different from the 1630s when Séguier had learned to appreciate the smack of firm government: then ministers could take initiatives which had visibly altered the balance between executive and legal establishment because they saw Richelieu working in partnership with an adult king. It is surprising, however, that more attention was not paid to the clannish nature of the legal and financial hierarchies, in which brothers, nephews, cousins and friends spanned the echelons.

Within the halls of justice there might obtain what Aguesseau[13] called 'the majestic silence of the tribunal; the respect, the reverential dread with which the litigant faces the judge; all these things seem to lift him above the level of ordinary men'. Outside however was the *bas peuple*, raucous, curious, awed, yet not to be left out of the reckoning. The magistrate, gowned and bewigged, attended by his page, walked out into corridors lined with stalls selling everything from clothes to chestnuts, and crowded with litigants, lawyers, clerks, officials, hangers-on, prostitutes and spectators of all sorts, the fashionable among them – but those evident mostly when there was some great political or religious issue.

From this busy, intimate place, as from an exchange or a canteen, flowed gossip and rumour to nourish the political awareness of ordinary Parisians. It was a world in which reputations rose and fell like commodities on an exchange; in which the principals, schooled in Roman history as well as law, were encouraged to make fine gestures, tempted to play theatrically to an audience that reached out to homes all over the city. It was a school for demagogues. Many Parisians were hungry and angry enough to accept at face value phrases that came as much from classical themes as from understanding of the current crisis or sympathy with its victims. They were also coming to think that nothing good could come from the Palais-Royal. Ministers were startled by the furious reaction to their proposal for the *paulette*. When representatives of the *Grand Conseil*, the *Chambre des Comptes* and the *Cour des Aides* met in the chamber of the latter, they did not wrangle over precedence. They resolved to ask *Parlement* to join them. The magistrates inclined warmly towards their fellow courts. There was talk of extending support to officials within *Parlement*'s jurisdiction. The *maîtres* were also assured of continuing protection. On 13 May *Parlement* issued an *arrêt d'union*.

The crown's tactics had rested on the assumption that *Parlement* would never ally itself to the other courts. The decision to convene a fifth body 'without legitimate authority' was, as Séguier recognised, 'dangerous and prejudicial to the good order of public government'. The council's *arrêt* declared that 'to permit any extraordinary assembly without the king's consent and will would be tantamount to creating a new power'. Behind the stern words there was nervousness. In what areas would this union seek redress and reform? More pertinently for some, whom would it attack? That there would be some agitation in the provinces was certain. It may be that provincial governors who sought to placate local *parlements*, like Longueville in Normandy, did good work: their influence is hard to gauge. Certainly opposition was hardening as news came to provincial capitals of stirring events in Paris.

In Toulouse *parlementaires* issued *arrêts* and *remonstrances*, calling, for example, for the suppression of any edicts not verified by *Parlement*, reduction of *taille* arrears, and jurisdiction over appeals concerning municipal elections. What did not happen was any country-wide union of courts. It had long been a theoretical possibility since first enunciated by Chancellor l'Hôpital[14] in 1560 – only then from the criterion of a more efficient authority: 'If the king could exercise his supreme judicial authority through a single *parlement* he would do so. The different *parlements* are only divisions of the royal *Parlement*.' However, provincial spirit was so strong that the magistrates of Dijon and Toulouse, for example, saw dangers at this juncture, in action which might expose them to future subordination to the *Parlement* of Paris. The general reaction was to remain watchfully neutral. The Breton *parlement* ignored orders from the council. Meanwhile there were some old scores to be settled: a royal tax official was hanged at Rennes. That, the cynic might think, summed up the provincial response to news that the government was in trouble.

15

THE CHAMBRE ST LOUIS

Following the crown's ban on meeting, selective arrests of members of the *Grand Conseil* and the *Cour des Aides* strengthened the resolve of the courts. Séguier, stung no doubt by the public scorn for 'the dithering chancellor', spoke to a *parlementaire* delegation about the danger that the Habsburg powers might seek a last-minute victory when they heard about 'the disaffection of the people'. Mazarin, writing to Longueville, professed himself puzzled as to what the sovereign courts wanted, but determined to stop their activities: 'we must push this matter to a conclusion'. He was concerned about the effect of lack of money, 'this famine we are now experiencing' as he described it to Turenne, on his diplomatic team at Osnabrück. On June 7 the council quashed the *arrêt d'union*. *Parlement* responded by calling for immediate sessions of the *Chambre St Louis*.[1] Anne bridled at a further affront. It was decided to summon the entire *Parlement* to the Palais-Royal, bringing the register which recorded their *arrêt*.

On 16 June the judges marched there in a body, in full ceremonial dress, while thousands of Parisians thronged the route along the river, shouting their support, then crowding around the palace. The royal stroke fell flat when it was found that the judges had left the register behind in *Parlement*. Instead of tearing out the offending pages, Anne could only request that they obeyed her council's *arrêt* forbidding the *Chambre St Louis*, and threaten those rebels who opposed her with punishment. 'In all her dealings with the *Parlement*, whose organisation and pedantic spirit she never understood, she always wanted to ride rough-shod over the court, and expected that company to carry out everything ordered in her council.' Anne's angry words on the subject might have been ringing in Madame de Motteville's ears when she wrote those lines. Molé was convinced that he was right: *Parlement* was indivisible. Either all its members were rebels, or all were loyal subjects of the king.

The episode raised the magistrates' profile among the people. They were fortified by the heady notion that they were serving the larger interest of the community. Debate expanded volubly to encompass

117

finance, economic matters more generally, law and government. There were divisions over tactics. Radicals were unmoved by the risk of sedition in Paris and the provinces, indifferent as to the effect on military operations. Omer Talon was barracked when he urged that it would be best for *Parlement* to secure legitimacy for the *Chambre St Louis* by pleading its case with Anne. The anarchic regency of Marie de Médicis was a disturbing memory for older men, among them Broussel, who expressed what might be termed a loyalist radical position: it was still for individual courts to consider what the *chambre* could only propose. With characteristic bravura, he appealed to colleagues to place the *fleur de lys* on their hearts and save the monarchy by convoking the *Chambre St Louis*.

Mazarin's instinct for the soft answer now weighed in council. Ministers should wait for cooler days, perhaps for peace. Meanwhile there were encouraging reports from the markets where the price of flour was falling: it was around fifteen per cent lower than in January.[2] Bread was expensive but well below the highest prices recorded four years before. On the other hand, there were still many Parisians who could scarcely afford a crust. Their threatening presence accounts in part for the revival of traditional protectionist arguments. In July the *Chambre* would hear proposals to take action against foreign textile imports which 'have reduced an infinity of the *menu peuple* to unemployment'. The reality behind the rhetoric was the trickle of peasant weavers coming to find work or charity in the city. There, demand for goods and services was slumping because of the exodus of wealthy families anticipating trouble: another argument for conciliatory gestures. After the war, or even during winter remission from combat, troops would be available for coercive measures. Meanwhile, thought Mazarin, a few concessions would do no harm: they could always be revoked. Still happy to be of service, Orléans was sent to ask for a recess of *Parlement* to allow for negotiation. On June 21 he offered restoration of the *paulette* and release of imprisoned *trésoriers*. Séguier spoke of curbing the powers of *intendants*.

On June 27 a royal declaration would actually anticipate many of the reforms eventually proposed by the *Chambre*. But *Parlement* was sceptical of the value of ministerial professions and sensed that it was now riding a flood tide of public opinion with its proposals of 'reforms of state'. Blancmesnil[3] declared that 'an act of God' had led magistrates to champion fellow citizens who were being tortured or killed for not paying their taxes: he became a marked man at court. On June 26 the die was cast as *Parlement* voted for an assembly of the four sovereign courts. Anne had little room left to manoeuvre. The *surintendant* must have his money; *traitants* were still withholding their advances, fearing cancellation of contracts or confiscation of profits. Each report from Paris strengthened the signal that now reached every corner of the land: with relief in the offing, why should subjects pay their taxes? Respect for government had been eroded to the point at which the crown must surrender to *Parlement* or risk mutiny in the armies.

Mazarin was fighting for his political life. His letters continue to reveal his pursuit of diplomatic and military objectives, with his usual care for detail. His *carnets* show that it was now only half the story. They suggest that he was listening, to an unsettling degree, to the voices of rumour and of his own heated imagination. His unpopularity was becoming a crucial factor, tarnishing the image of government. As Broussel was elevated to be the idol of the populace, so Mazarin became its bogey. In one of those outbreaks of xenophobia to which the Parisian, no less than the Londoner, was prone, his character was vilified, his intentions placed under the worst possible construction. For personal enrichment, it was charged, he was prolonging the war.

While his patronage of the new musical theatre was reinforcing the *macaroni* image, his wealth was highly visible as Italian sculptors and painters worked on the hôtel Chevry-Tubeuf, in the rue Neuve des Petits Champs, opposite the walls of the Palais-Royal. He had bought it, in 1643, from the financier Tubeuf; typically he saw to it that early extensions were carried out under Tubeuf's name. Walking along its great gallery, decorated by Romanelli and his successors with mythological scenes from Ovid, presiding delightedly over this 'Baroque offensive' (M. Laurain-Portemer) he had come a long way from his first lodging chez Chavigny, from the Hôtel de Cluny, the usual lodging place of the nuncio, and the Hôtel de Cleves, to which he moved when he became Cardinal. He still saw his Palais Mazarin, (which today appropriately houses the Bibliothèque Nationale which has grown around the core of his original library), in Motteville's words, as a retreat 'where he was sometimes able to relax in the midst of the wonderful objects he had accumulated' and as a place in which to lodge his nieces, the 'mazarinettes'. He continued, when in Paris, to operate mainly from his pied à terre on the second story, the Pavillon du Roi, in the Louvre.

His qualities became his vices. He was handsome, so he was corrupting the queen-regent. He was clever, so not to be trusted; he was polite, so necessarily hypocritical. One important psychological pre-condition of the Fronde was thus established. 'His name itself became an insult' writes Mousnier.[4] The Paris coachmen urged on their horses – 'or Mazarin will get you!' Mazarin's previous experience, largely of rational discussion in polite circles, was now of little help to him. Confronted by the *esprit de corps* of *Parlement* his negotiating skills were frustrated. Whom could he trust? Was he to be another Concini? No wonder that he was overwrought. Anne's loyalty had yet to be proved. Orléans, on whom he had worked so hard, would bend before any storm. Fellow ministers would not sacrifice themselves for him. Those whom he had displaced or debarred, notably Chavigny and Châteauneuf, had reason to attack him. Beaufort had

119

recently escaped from prison: was the *cabale des importants* re-forming? His spies were busy: evidence came to hand in the form of an anonymous letter to Broussel from 'a nobleman of high rank' hinting at support for *Parlement* if it could sustain its opposition. Such straws could show which way the wind was blowing. At this stage however his suspicions went too far. *Les Grands* were still, in the main, loyal. Some were even hostile, as they were to become again, to the pretensions of *Parlement*. Mazarin did not entirely lose his nerve. He was always prepared to probe an individual *parlementaire* and test his price. But he was perhaps too jumpy to make sound judgements. His state of mind can be gauged from his treatment of President de Mesmes. This conservative royalist, who had persistently argued the absolutist case in *Parlement*, was watched by Mazarin's spy simply because he was the brother of the comte d'Avaux[5] whom Mazarin had recently recalled from the delegation at Osnabrück.

A chasm was now opening between magistrates, patrimonial and corporatist in outlook, and absolutist ministers. Differences had been accentuated by recent debate: positions tentatively adopted, hypotheses advanced to test the opposition, can become entrenched lines. It was a process that Molé struggled to resist, to maintain flexibility. His position was not however a simple one. He had tried to defend the administration but had received little help from ministers – and that haughtily given. He had been insulted by radical lawyers for his pains, with suggestions that there had been bribes, in the form of pensions and offers of advancement. Molé had indeed been the agent for the *surintendant*'s distribution in June of 25,000 *livres* to certain senior judges. Was it butter too thinly spread, simply therefore accepted as of right, like any other *douceur* slipped during legal proceedings? Mazarin derived one definite benefit: every day he received, from some *parlementaire* who had taken the oath of confidentiality, a written report of the court's supposedly secret proceedings.

Molé may have decided that he had to try to satisfy the expectation of colleagues. The *Chambre*, he declared, was legitimate and it would meet: that was a statement, not a request. It was the royal ministers who had been acting illegally; *Parlement* was simply fulfilling its historic role as defender of the rights of subjects. There was an unmistakeable reference to Mazarin in his comment about the evil influence of foreigners on the regent. In the sense that the Fronde was the climactic expression of a long-evolving constitutional conflict, it had now begun. The acts of violence which were to come, the civil wars that were to ensue, only brought the issues to a sharper focus and advertised them to the wider world.

On 29 June Séguier gave the regent's approval of the *Chambre St Louis*: using Mazarin's emollient words, he expressed the hope that the courts would serve as loyally in the new chamber as they had in the past, and that their work there would be speedily finished. The next day the *parlementaires* and six representatives from the other courts sat down to work. Their draft, completed in five weeks rather than Séguier's suggested one, was as clever and comprehensive as might be expected from experienced lawyers. Though they rejected the claims of the *trésoriers* and *maîtres des requêtes* to be represented, they proposed reforms which answered to their grievances and those of lesser officials in Paris and other sovereign courts in the provinces. Ministers did little in the way of cooperation to match their honeyed words. When Mazarin wanted to draw the magistrates into negotiation he called them, not altogether convincingly, 'restorers of France' and 'fathers of the fatherland'. However, even to envisage genuine accord is to overlook Anne's anger, tinged with something like incredulity that such things could be happening.

The *Chambre St Louis* did not have *Parlement*'s right to register laws which therefore had to go, by due process, through *Parlement*. The reform proposals were moreover too far-ranging and general to be translated readily into specific enactments. There were too many occasions for delays in such technical proceedings. Nor could members of the *chambre* act as if nothing were happening outside. For every pedestrian fact there was a host of rumours. No one word – fury, fear, hope, despair – can sum up the popular mood: with the conversational small change of grumbling and jokes, all were there. Suspicion was too general, the stakes were too high, for peaceful settlement. *Parlement* found itself the clearing house for every kind of plea and submission. It was practical, day-to-day considerations rather than any constitutional theory about limitations on the royal power, that went to shaping proposals for reform and the making of this Parisian revolution. While the other sovereign courts waited for the completion of the work of the *Chambre St Louis*, and *maîtres* negotiated their own deal with government, *Parlement* rose to the occasion. Spurred by the noisy sounds of public approval, rather than wait for the whole parcel from the *chambre*, they took each of the twenty-seven articles of reform as it was drafted, discussed and acted on it. *Parlement*'s status ensured that its lead was followed by many provincial courts. Its decisions were automatically binding over the third of France over which it had jurisdiction. Experience gained in earlier battles was not wasted. Moderate voices prevailed when there was a question of procedure. It was agreed that *Parlement*'s *arrêts* should not be used to alter contracts between *surintendant* and *traitant*: the granting of a lease was accepted to be the prerogative of the crown. *Remonstrance* remained the only legitimate instrument which *Parlement* could use to secure reforms which went beyond present laws. So far in spirit from Westminster and its representative parliament was the venerable corporation of the Ile de la Cité!

Events across the Channel undoubtedly affected some of the principals in the Fronde. Any attempt however to view the efforts of *Parlement* in 1648 in the light of the protracted struggle in England should be discouraged by the case of the *taille*. If control of taxation were the key to power, *Parlement*'s reiteration of the traditional position, that it had no right to review this tax, meant that, even at this tempting moment, it would let it remain with the crown. There was no precedent for deciding otherwise. So *Parlement* proceeded, by *remonstrances*, with *arrêts* only where they were indisputably justified, in ways that display tactical ingenuity and so mature a sense of what was possible that Mazarin could do little about it.

Orléans was sometimes given the crown's negotiating brief. He was steered by the judges into the position of accepting the case against the *intendants*, that their commissions were illegal. Carefully briefed at the Palais-Royal he could speak of financial problems that made it imperative that the *intendants* continue their work. He appeared now to be a model of loyalty and could carry himself, and speak, with princely grace, but his own chequered record was against him. Was he to be taken seriously? One can imagine Richelieu aloft, savouring the irony, as his inveterate enemy defends the absolutist legacy. The late Cardinal, whose spirit seems sometimes to hover over these mortal struggles, might however have recognised a finer instinct as Gaston sought to serve his dynasty.

Once Anne had conceded reforms in Paris she had to send declarations about them to the provincial *parlements*. One such had an immediate impact: on 10 July, with the exception of those in certain frontier provinces, 'where they were to assist the governors in their functions', the *intendants* were recalled. The result confirmed Mazarin's worst fears as *traitants* realised that they had lost their protection and any chance that their contracts would be fully honoured. On 12 July the crown authorised a *chambre de justice* with powers to investigate 'the exactions, violences, and extortions carried out in the provinces of our kingdom'. It had been sought at the start of the regency, but some *parlementaires* now saw it as a dishonest move, to forestall prosecution. Likewise the dismissal of Hémery on 9 July was interpreted as a move by Mazarin to prevent the embarrassing disclosures which the *surintendant*, on trial, might have made.

However *Parlement* still had the upper hand, and it took up the cause of the *trésoriers*. At once those incarcerated in the Bastille since May were released; funds were provided for the payment of their salaries. The knowledge too that *Parlement* might take up their case prompted ministers to offer generous terms to the maîtres. They thanked the regent, but pointedly refused to pay their respects to Mazarin. After the restoration of the *paulette* to the sovereign courts, *Parlement* kept up the pressure on behalf of the other officials until they too had gained the concession. So July passed, with ministers retreating, till the point at which a stand had to be made. On 31 July Anne responded to a further batch of remonstrances by holding another *lit de justice*. Mazarin may have persuaded her that Marshal Schomberg's victory at Tortosa had made a favourable impression. Further, to allay disquiet, she promised an Assembly of Notables,[6] when external affairs should permit.

Mazarin wrote that day of the royal session and of the king's deportment: 'so full of grace and received with so much respect'. Did he think that all was settled with the magistrates' applause? He sounded optimistic. Of taxes, the main cause of the crisis, he wrote: 'we have consumed all the current year's and the two following years'. At the *lit* the young king probably saw admiring faces. He certainly saw *Parlement* register, but not before he had heard Molé warning him that his throne would be in danger if reforms were not begun in earnest and Talon informing him that kings 'were indebted for their fortune and the grandeur of their crown to the diverse qualities of the men who obey them'. One day, Louis may have thought, he would command and those men would really obey. Meanwhile the boy had to respond, with what self-possession he could assume, after Mazarin's schooling, to the heavy words of those dignitaries of the *robe*. Moreover, as if to show how little the royal wishes meant to them, the judges then resumed their debate. Anne sent Orléans to order them to desist. They agreed only to postpone for a short time their examination of the articles of reform. In mid-August they resumed work and served notice that certain *traitants*, 'members of a shameful profession', would be named for investigation. They issued a series of *arrêts* listing certain taxes which could not be collected until registration, 'subject to the king's good pleasure', a phrase which they hoped would insure them against punitive measures.

The *lit de justice* had failed. The ministry was being forced to choose between the financiers and the magistrates. There is a direct relationship between *Parlement*'s action against the *traitants* and the events of 26 August. To add to the pressure for a counter-attack there was disturbing news from the provinces. On 20 July *intendant* Lauzun had written to Séguier: 'rumours coming from Paris are so prejudicial to the king's service that I do not know if we will dare to demand from the people the *taille* for 1647 or 1648. A general discharge of taxes is expected, as if the silver mines of Peru had suddenly been found in the Treasury.'

It was around now that the opposition acquired its name. One day Bachaumont, son of the outspoken Président Le Coigneux,[7] announced that he intended to be a '*frondeur*': soon the word 'fronde', denoting the sling with which Parisian urchins catapulted mud or stones, was on everyone's lips.[8] The word was singularly appropriate to so much that would be trivial and frivolous; not however to the deeper issues behind the words. Would the people confine themselves to a war of words?

In the context of what Lloyd Moote describes as 'a country with a unique potential for widespread upheaval' and Mousnier as 'a permanent state of unrest', there was always the chance of a *jacquerie*. The Nu-pieds of Normandy had apparently taken their cue from official protests.[9] More recently, in 1643, the peasants of the Rouergue had undoubtedly been spurred on by local *gentilshommes*. Now peasant action came to their doorsteps to remind Parisians of the menacing reality behind the lawyers' rhetoric. Even in France's largest city, with its 400,000 inhabitants, the rural world lapped round that of the bourgeois and artisan: one moment there were crowded streets, the next, cultivated fields. The contrast was accentuated by the congested nature of the city. Nearly all Parisians looked on to streets or courtyards. A bare five per cent had a garden. The two worlds converged in the markets where country men and women daily brought their produce, set up their stalls and tuned in to the gossip. One day's debate in *Parlement* was the next day's story in the tavern. *Parlement* was guardian of the Parisians' material concerns, having powers of government concerning markets, prices and food supplies, the state of roads and bridges, hospitals, charities, crime, beggary and prostitution. Since it was apparently being opposed by the royal ministers, there was a rough logic as well as rough manners in the peasants' partisanship. On 20 July about six thousand peasants converged from the direction of Meudon. The next four days saw concerted and noisy demonstrations: the reduction of the *taille* was the insistent cry.

16

THE DECLARATION OF SAINT-GERMAIN

Condé, on a brief visit from the front, was one of the grandees who observed the crowd. He stayed only for brief consultations with ministers. Back in Flanders he failed to prevent the archduke Leopold from relieving the Flemish fortress town of Lens. Ordered by Madrid to seek a battle, on 20 August, Leopold experienced a crushing defeat. Since the treaty of Munster the Spanish had been relieved of the burden of fighting on two fronts. The French fought furiously to sustain, the Spanish to recover, their reputation. Condé's generalship was superb: no wonder the hawk-faced prince came to see himself as the pillar of monarchy, deserving of a special place in the realm. Besides the 4,000 left dead on the field he took 6,000 prisoners and all the Spanish artillery.

As the carts lumbered home with Condé's seventy-three captured standards, ministers considered the implications. Mazarin saw the way cleared for the final round of negotiations with the emperor, leaving Spain to be dealt with. It was from Spain that the most valuable territorial gains could be won. Artlessly revealing the mood of the court, the young Louis thought 'how sorry *les messieurs de Parlement* will be at the news'. With studied ambivalence Gondi preached a far from triumphalist sermon at Notre-Dame on 'the political will of St Louis'. After praising Louis IX for his rigour against heresy and commending his example to the king he criticised the government for their arbitrary attempts to tax the church. The *coadjuteur*, the most powerful clergyman in Paris, thought it more important to strengthen his party than to win the favour of the court. Mazarin thanked him. He was never likely to start a quarrel for want of a gracious word; Anne however thought Gondi insolent. She took little persuading that the time had come for a decisive stroke.

On the morning of 26 August Parisian notables went through streets lined with musketeers to Notre-Dame to attend the official thanksgiving for victory. The ancient cathedral, with banks of candles reinforcing the light that filtered through the smoke-dulled crimson and azure of its mediaeval glass, casting their glow on the array of captive flags, provided its own sermon on the pomp of kings and the fortunes of battle. A few who knew or suspected what was afoot may have been too tense to appreciate the solemn words and chants. As the queen mother left the west door, acting on the plan concerted in council, she gave the word to Comminges, commanding the *gardes de la reine*. The scarlet-gowned magistrates scattered in confusion as his men tried to effect their arrests. The troops were only able to secure *président* Blancmesnil: Broussel had prudently stayed at home, supposedly taking a purge. Comminges found him – 'the people's saviour' – at dinner with his family. By the time he had managed to hustle Broussel into his carriage, an angry crowd was thronging the street. Comminges's carriage was overturned and he was fortunate to find succour, and another carriage, to get him and his prisoner on the road to Saint-Germain.

It was market day, a factor that may have been overlooked in the planning of the coup.[1] A crowd soon formed to support the boatmen of the *quais*, porters and artisans, the *petit peuple* who had so quickly rallied round their hero. There were always plenty of women in such crowds. Even children were seen to be carrying *poignards*. Stones and clubs were the most common weapons but some had muskets. Clamour, rumour, panic and rage marked the ensuing hours. As in the smoke of battle, conflicting reports make it hard to establish precisely what happened. Matters looked different from the palace perspective of Mme de Motteville, the *parlementaire* of Molé or Talon, the conspiratorial of Gondi. The events that can be located precisely in time and place are relatively few, but they are important. Confusion does not, in any case, detract from the drama or significance of this uprising. It was a frightening time for the royal family and ministers; no less for *les bons bourgeois* who saw how vulnerable they were to the people in arms.

The *gardes françaises*[2] were concentrated outside the palace. Detachments were sent to guard the Pont Neuf and the Quai du Louvre. Meanwhile chains were being drawn across streets, particularly in the Ile de la Cité. Typically this was the work of shopkeepers, concerned to protect themselves against looting, but it also hampered the movement of troops. La Meilleraye made two sorties from the palace: missiles were thrown and there was an exchange of fire. Gondi claimed that La Meilleraye was thrown from his horse and that he tended him, keeping the mob at bay. The marshal was however active early the next day, mounting a rescue operation for the chancellor. Séguier had tried to reach *Parlement* with the regent's orders forbidding them to assemble, but had been obstructed by a mob of artisans and forced to take refuge with his daughter in the Hôtel de Luynes.[3] Eventually over a thousand barricades were counted: chains, paving stones, carts and barrels turned the city into one great statement of protest and defiance. Molé led a procession of *parlementaires*, in ceremonial robes, to request the release of the prisoners, accompanied to the Palais-Royal by a shouting crowd: when he first came out of the palace without the desired guarantee they became vicious. When Molé tried again he could refer to his own experience: the mob could have killed him, they could attack the court or ransack the city.

Mazarin had spent the night fully clothed, ready for flight. He was well aware that he was the prime target of the insurgents. Contingency plans had been made for an evacuation of the court under armed escort: for nights the horses were kept saddled. The queen would have liked to stand firm, trusting to the protection of her *gardes*. Had she not earlier told Gondi that she would rather strangle Broussel with her own hands than release him? She was brave as ever, but feared for her son. Molé secured concessions. *Lettres de cachet*[4] were issued, ordering the release of Broussel and Blancmesnil. The next day, 28 August, there were further disturbances. Broussel returned to a triumphant reception but there were rumours of a royal plan to remove the king and unleash a punitive military onslaught on the city. Clearly there were some who had an interest in keeping the pot boiling: the court suspected Gondi. It is likely now that he was standing, offended and frustrated, on the side-lines. He would subsequently claim the credit for the release of Broussel. In truth it lay with the mob who had successfully defied their sovereign. Here was food for thought, not only in the Palais-Royal but in the Palais de Justice.

It can be argued that the plan was merely bad in its execution, that a clean, efficient swoop would have had the intended shock effect: Charles I's bungled attempt to arrest the five members of parliament comes to mind.[5] But awkward questions remain. Why did ministers imagine that *Parlement* would take lying down the arrest of several of its members? Why was Broussel chosen? A man of the people who prided himself on his plain dress and manners, spokesman for the radicals, mainly much younger men, he was responsible, with Molé, for the relatively restrained conduct of *Parlement*. If ministers intended to provoke open defiance and so justify more drastic action then should they not have waited till more troops were available?

This was one of those times in the history of Paris, July 1789 being the most momentous, when a sequence of happenings, arising out of some economic malaise, with specific political grievances, contributes to a crisis of authority: arousing such passions, involving so many interests, fuelling so much personal ambition and raising so many issues, that it stands out from the ruck and acquires a symbolic character. The heroic and tragic aspects of the Fronde were to mingle, as in the comic episodes that relieve tension in a play, with elements of the sham, petty, even at times absurd. The reader will judge how well or badly Mazarin emerges. It is impossible to know whether he approved of the Notre-Dame coup or was persuaded by Anne against his better judgement. Only intermittently was he in control. On occasion he can be seen to have paid for Anne's affectionate support by compliance with her will. Over the August coup it may not have been difficult. Parisians blamed him of course. Their instinct may have been sound for it was not out of character, nor exceptional in his career, built as it was upon chances boldly taken. The Broussel affair was a personal rebuff. In his nervous exhaustion Mazarin had wept before the magistrates. But there was no doubting his physical courage, nor his resilience. He was ready with his usual argument: concessions made now could soon be revoked. Meanwhile there were greater things to be done.

Within two months of the August Days his emissaries had completed the peace of Westphalia. They were well served by his clear briefings. Some would then have allowed that he served his country well in foreign affairs. Few however would have been found to defend his domestic record, justify his position as *premier ministre* – or expect him to survive. He had reached the position, normally fatal in political life, when even close associates were unnerved by the volume of hostility and looked to save themselves. They would however serve the king, therefore the regent. On her favour Mazarin was absolutely dependent.

One significant feature of the August Days is that *Parlement*, as a body, neither instigated nor led the popular agitation. Another is that no important nobleman seems to have been involved, either causing or exploiting disorder. Condé, flushed with victory, scornful of *Parlement*, which he thought to be undermining the war effort, was loyal. He discussed the political situation with Mazarin, but thought it wise to keep his visits secret. Up to a point Orléans too was trusted by Anne: he was also keen to ingratiate himself with *Parlement*, and this added to his value as mediator. Such prominent figures apart, interest centres upon Paul de Gondi.[6] In all but name, he was the head of the church in Paris, with everything that meant in a city where the church had long provided, through different individuals or groups – *dévôt*, Gallican, Jansenist, for example – models for emulation in the country at large. If his role remains uncertain, that was not because of any reticence on his part. This egregious ecclesiastic lived by such ambiguous standards that it is hard to know what principles informed his policies. That he later covered his trails with memoirs that were both an artistic personal testament and, to say the least, an imaginative reconstruction of events, compounds the difficulty. For some well-documented moves and words there is sufficient evidence. Otherwise we can say only what is likely to have happened.

Evidently Gondi wanted to be the conspirator-general. He had shown since youth an interest in the mechanics of subversion that went well beyond the academic. By the beginning of the regency he was a seasoned plotter: he had supped with assassins. He had been lucky not to have experienced the Bastille. He had learned to be circumspect and acquired, if not in court circles, a cloak of respectability. Fascinated by the political game he responded now with energy, charm and a certain panache, to the challenges that faced him as self-constituted *chef de parti*. That might not in itself preclude his becoming *premier ministre* in Mazarin's place. It did, however, involve confrontation with Anne which, in any situation short of a revolution, must prove fatal to his chances. Naturally, therefore, Mazarin and Anne believed that he was planning such a revolution. He had already shown a particular skill in building up his interest in Paris: it might be seen as an irregular militia, in which noble adventurers, disgruntled officials and certain activist priests provided the officers, while the rank and file were drawn from the tradesmen, artisans and labourers who needed little encouragement or bribe to form a mob. He had contacts with leading radicals in *Parlement*: Longueuil,[7] Viole[8] and Blancmesnil. Though it is hard to distinguish between friends, acquaintances and the agents he cultivated in his regular forays about the streets, it is clear that he was more than a superior kind of gangster. In the sense applicable to the circumstances, he was a politician. His information system was extensive, serviced by such seasoned plotters as Montrésor[9] and Laigues.[10] He had *entrée* into some of the best houses. The Church provided him with a biddable following and invaluable lieutenants among the traditionally militant priesthood.

The diffuse nature of his following and his own defects of character fitted Gondi better for agitation than for authority. One day those features would be exploited by government, to neutralise and to win him over. At this stage he could only be an object of deep suspicion. Forgetting perhaps that the government had created the opportunity in the first place, Mazarin thought that he encouraged the riots, that his ostentatious interventions and his benisons to the crowd were his way of signalling his readiness to lead them. He had certainly come forward with surprising alacrity, as if well prepared for the capacity in which he offered the regent his services, to calm and control the people.

The ideal of a coalition of noble interests, with sword and gown making common cause, which he would, of course, direct, provides one thread through the maze of Gondi's manoeuvres. From the start individuals can be seen coming together in informal groups. For Chavigny and Châteauneuf there was one paramount reason for working with Gondi: they yearned to recover ministerial office and sought allies in *Parlement*, like Viole. Sometimes personal friendships drew men together; opposition to the regent's policies was another bond. Dislike of Mazarin was a common factor. Without the discipline of a genuine party, and with few agreed objectives, alliances were likely to be shifting and unreliable. *Les grands* needed military power to be effective; activists in *Parlement* had to persuade their more cautious colleagues. When such negative factors predominated, Anne and Mazarin might have been wise to avoid giving offence. Not surprisingly, after the turmoil of the August Days, they could not see matters in that light. Under the barrage of taunts and slurs it was hard to be patient, let alone conciliatory. On 13 September Anne, with Mazarin and her family, left Paris, first for a visit to Richelieu's niece at Rueil, then Saint-Germain. From the château, with no more reason than their known links with prominent *frondeurs*, Anne ordered the arrest of Chavigny and Châteauneuf.

Who would be next? It was in Mazarin's mind to besiege Paris, but he needed the assent of Condé. For sound military as well as political reasons the general was reluctant: the operation was deferred, as ministers watched Paris. There *Parlement* rejected the royal order to leave the city and turned the attack specifically on to Mazarin. He was accused of arbitrary justice and military repression. *Parlement* threatened to convoke a special session and summon to it the *ducs et pairs*; further, it invoked an *arrêt* of 1617 against alien ministers. Mazarin swivelled: he recalled Concini's fate. As if to test the magistrates' resolve, ministers agreed to release Chavigny and Châteauneuf and to resume negotiations. *Parlement* responded with alacrity and sent delegates to Saint-Germain to bargain over the remaining articles of reform. Inept counter-moves had helped them to retain the initiative. The regent's range of options was narrowing. The latest fiasco had brought the financial administration near to collapse.

The dismissal of Hémery had been a popular move, as had been his replacement by marshal de la Meilleraye.[11] It was of course a political appointment, designed to impress *Parlement* and to please Condé, rather than the *traitants*. Unfortunately it was they who could actually deliver the goods. They were already sore after the verbal drubbing they had received in *Parlement* and resentful at the failure of ministers to defend them. In 1647 they had advanced four-fifths of the expenses of the state. In 1648, however, they had virtually gone on strike. That had been the background to the decision in July to annul all existing contracts, and the subsequent reduction of interest rates from fifteen to six per cent. 'A bunch of roses thrown at *Parlement*' Mme de Motteville had called it. Mazarin had claimed that the move would save the Treasury fifty million *livres* a year. He exaggerated wildly. In effect the move served notice of bankruptcy and the problem remained: in the short term to find cash for the troops, in the long run to restore fiscal credibility in the country at large. In the buoyant moods which tended to follow times of special anxiety, Mazarin could sound positively complacent: 'His Majesty has gained incalculable advantage from the divisions and antagonisms of his foes'. He knew that many *parlementaires* were involved in the money-lending process, so he knew that they would be among the sufferers from a more severe financial regime. Behind the scenes some financiers, keen to make their money work for them, were quietly furnishing funds; Anne pledged her jewels, Mazarin produced several large diamonds, and ministers and financiers began to draw together.

The Saint-Germain conferences dragged on until the regent made sufficient concessions to satisfy the delegates of *Parlement*. On 24 October the royal declaration, embodying those reforms on which *Parlement* had been able to insist, was registered. On the same day Mazarin's envoys signed the treaties which brought to an end the Thirty Years War. Church bells rang to bring joy to Germany's ravaged communities. France was now at peace with the empire but the war with Spain continued: it was that which had impinged most on the eastern and southern provinces and would continue to do so. From a settlement which brought lands and influence to his king, Mazarin gained therefore virtually no domestic advantage. The *Comptes* and *Aides* courts registered the Declaration on 27 October after stiff amendments. Provincial chambers dragged their feet, confused but also resentful at the continuation of the war with Spain: was the 'peace dividend' to be postponed indefinitely? The case of Bordeaux, as it appears in the reports of the Mazarinist governor Epernon, suggests that the magistrates there were using ratification of the Declaration as a pretext for slicing local taxes – to which that document had not referred.

The Declaration of Saint-Germain was based on the proposals of the *Chambre St Louis*, framed in articles referred, through *Parlement*, to the royal council. There were three main components: first, twenty-seven articles, technical in character; second, royal declarations; third, *arrêts* by various corporations. From this mass of material a picture emerges of a programme of reform, embracing most of the grievances arising out of three decades of royal absolutism: intrusions upon corporate rights, creation of extra bodies, and fiscal extortion. There comes into view a valid alternative programme, that of legal absolutism.[12] If 'programme' is too definite a term for such a miscellany, it is still clear that the parcel as a whole transcended the sectional interests of those who compiled it.

There were significant omissions, the *paulette* for example: its re-establishment was taken for granted. The restoration of official salaries and abolition of recently created offices expressed immediate concerns. Satisfaction came in piecemeal fashion as ministers were forced to make one concession after another: for example sovereign court judges and *trésoriers* were promised three-quarters of their salaries, *élus* half. Many offices were abolished. The regent promised that no new offices would be created for five years; thereafter any new creations would be verified, without coercion, by a *lit de justice*. A prolonged struggle over the *intendants* had already ended with a declaration abolishing all but six frontier commissions: Picardy, Champagne, Burgundy, Lyonnais, Provence and Languedoc. Even there the *intendant* was to have no control over civilians: supply and surveillance over the troops were to be his function, as in the 1620s. *Parlement* insisted on the right to scrutinise commissions.

The issue of arbitrary imprisonment and punishment was revived by the swoop on Châteauneuf and Chavigny. Séguier's defence of the crown's right might have been written by Richelieu. 'When persons can disturb the tranquillity of the state through cabals . . . though their crimes cannot be proved, formalities are useless.' The chancellor combined great knowledge of the law with a notable readiness to lend the authority of his office to political justice. He was stoutly rebutted by Molé, who wanted a guarantee that the regent would not abuse her undoubted right. She conceded *Parlement*'s specific demands: no official to be deprived of office or liberty by *lettre de cachet*; a trial to be guaranteed within twenty-four hours.

Humane concerns, economic sense and, even here, an eye to the *seigneur*'s interest influenced the demand for the reduction of the *taille* by a quarter, and another, for the suppression of a number of indirect taxes. From the debris of Hémery's too ingenious efforts, the *toisé* and the tax on alienated domains were scrapped. The *Bureau de Ville's rentes* were to be supervised by the judges; the *Bureau*, in turn, was to supervise the Paris tariffs. Of course the *traitants* drew fire. Farming of the *taille* was to end; its management was to return to the *trésoriers* and *élus*. New contracts for other taxes were to be awarded on a competitive basis. The *Chambre des Comptes* would then be able to audit such transactions. Speculators who had dabbled in the *rentes* were to be fined. To investigate questionable dealings between the state and its creditors a *chambre de justice*[13] was to be set up.

An interesting article, calling for the abolition of trading privileges within the kingdom and prohibition of the importation of certain foreign products, indicates a wider view of the needs of the economy. In any case *Parlement*'s concentration on fiscal questions need not be interpreted as reflecting narrow class interests. The *traitants* needed scrutiny. The measures envisaged might be crudely discriminatory but they were not novel. Indeed they were arguably less tainted by political calculation than previous exercises in scapegoat justice mounted by government to focus blame on selected individuals, such as Semblançay[14] in 1527: he was hung. La Vieuville escaped the likelihood of a similar fate in 1624 by fleeing the country. The methods of *Parlement* in 1648, which were to provide the model for Colbert's highly productive onslaught on Fouquet[15] and other leading financiers in the early years of Louis XIV's personal reign, were designed to prevent subjects being sacrificed for the benefit of the state's creditors.

How could ministers respond to an onslaught which appeared to represent fiscal common sense and judicial probity, but was actually introducing a new principle: that no levy was legal unless registered by *Parlement*? The implications of complete acceptance were horrifying. Many impositions had been authorised by conciliar *arrêts*; all *aides* and *gabelles* registered at the *Cour des Aides* were at risk until a concession, suggested by Broussel, saved them for the time being. His committee drew up a revised list of tariffs. Anne may have wished him behind bars – but she had sanctioned the committee and had to accept its recommendations. She was able to save only five of the twenty-five per cent cut in the *taille*; she also had to authorise cancellation of most arrears. The rest of the programme was accepted, either through action or vaguer commitments. *Traitants'* powers were restricted. The *trésoriers*, strongly re-established, were given a role in the auctioning of new tax leases. The *comptants*,[16] that invaluable financial device, though in theory only for 'secret and important matters of state', were restricted to three million *livres*.

Out of a battle of attrition *Parlement* had gained a signal victory. Some certainly grumbled when the *chambre de justice* was abandoned in favour of a state controlled chamber: for the time being that meant that the *traitants* were safe. Generally however euphoria reigned in the *Palais de Justice*. Of course there were unresolved constitutional issues. Mazarin thought that 'the best part of the monarchy had been abolished'. The tenor and content of *Parlement*'s reform programme seemed to him to point ominously to the English experience. The parliamentary measures which led to the civil war and the destruction of monarchy belonged to a world apart from anything that French history had known or constitution could allow. That did not prevent French radicals gaining inspiration from what they thought they saw. Anne would not allow the subject of England to be mentioned. Humiliation and a kind of moral imprisonment were again her lot. In her husband's lifetime it had been the king's ministers who had been responsible; now it was *Parlement*. The experience strengthened the bond with her *premier ministre*, equally under pressure. They were two outsiders who would not give up. Her son's inheritance was always in Anne's mind: whatever mealy-mouthed protestations of loyalty they might make, those who opposed his authority were traitors. There could be no forgiveness of these acts of political rape; therefore no genuine acceptance of their outcome.

Such concerns are unlikely to have troubled magistrates savouring their political achievement. By devoting themselves to financial reform and by holding firm against royalist attempts to modify or evade their demands, they had achieved one of the few serious victories, on behalf of subjects, over the seventeenth-century French state – only a minority of subjects, it must be emphasised. They did not even consider curtailing or abolishing the privileges of office holders and nobles which contributed to the plight of the common people. That could not be expected of men steeped in the values and practices of the corporate state. They would have concurred with the argument of Montesquieu,[17] a century later: their corporate and individual rights were the first line of defence against arbitrary rule.

Finance was, of course, the central concern of government. Measures of the sort described were therefore bound to have a direct impact, not merely in its efficiency but on its principles and institutions. The work of the *intendant*, barring appeals to local courts, raising taxes, taking direct action, on the strength of his commission, had been linked directly to the *traitant* and his lease from the *surintendant*. They were 'valets of the partisans, not king's men' (Le Coigneux). The *lit de justice*, absolutism's ultimate deterrent, and the *lettre de cachet*, which could render a citizen defenceless, had lain at the end of a line which started with an edict or *arrêt* announcing a new tax, increased tax, or other money-raising device. The abuse of otherwise accepted procedures had been held to justify *Parlement*'s eventual stand. Does it therefore follow that the lawyers failed to appreciate the short-term needs of the state in their concern for the balance of powers within the traditional concept of sovereignty? The question is unanswerable since it relates to distinct, ultimately incompatible ideas about the rights of the crown. Most *parlementaires* were aware of the need to tread warily in a field which had few accepted boundaries. They could not forget that they held their offices from the crown. They avoided the charge of being revolutionaries by acting scrupulously, according to precedents or to formulas which stopped short of curtailing specific royal rights. Even during demagogic flights they preserved a certain dignity, as representative, not only of the fundamental law, but also of the well-being of the people. Professional expertise and high moral tone ensured that they were, for the time being, unassailable.

But for how long? Behind the reform programme there was a disparity of interests, concealed until this time by certain common objectives now largely achieved, and by a common enemy, Mazarin. By its very success the *chambre* had put a question mark against the further utility of a temporary coalition. Other individual groups would now try to exploit the Fronde for their own ends. A resolute regent and ministers could still work together, and they had every incentive to preserve the regime. On the other hand it would never be easy for *Parlement* to hold the *Cour des Aides* and the *Chambre des Comptes* to the cause. Those courts were upset when *Parlement* insisted that their registration of some taxes was invalid without *Parlement*'s verification. The *Grand Conseil* had been an awkward partner from the start, jealous of *Parlement*'s pre-eminence. The ambivalent position of the *Maîtres des Requêtes* presented a chronic problem. A number of them still looked to the royal administration for an executive career, now largely blocked by the abolition of the *intendances*. The fact that Molé's son, Champlâtreux,[18] was an *intendant* exemplifies the dilemma that faced a number of *parlementaires*: as *intendant* of Champagne, he was one of the lucky ones to escape recall. *Maîtres* stood also to suffer from *Parlement*'s objection to their recently extended legal functions. Mazarin tried to win them over. He would have liked to give them old-style commissions to fulfil some of the duties of the *intendants*.

Some would indeed go out to the provinces but without their titles and with a tactfully limited brief.

Some of the reforms therefore proved embarrassing to the reformers. Official salaries depended on the payment of taxes. The vigour of *Parlement's* challenge encouraged disrespect for the law. The hardened tax evader would be unlikely to distinguish between unverified and valid commissions, proper or irregular courts. The relationship between *trésoriers* and *élus* reverted to the normal when the latter raised local assessments to improve their profit margins: old habits died hard. Somewhere between *Parlement's* estimate that reversion to the old system would add forty million *livres* to revenue, and the ministers' estimate that it would actually cost nine and a half million – but nearer to the latter – lies reality. Reforms could not change attitudes overnight: the balance between public service and private gain could not be adjusted by laws or rhetoric. The administration's estimate was based on experience. It also reflected current observation. Orléans was advised that forty million *livres* would be lost by cancellation of arrears (that assumes that it would have been possible to collect them); another ten million by the twenty per cent reduction; five million by the reduced tariffs from Paris and other towns. This was not a dynamic economy in which the reduction of taxes would stimulate extensive activity. There was an immediate loss, exacerbated when the administration honoured its undertaking to pay official salaries in full.

With *traitants* having to accept lower payments and therefore reluctant to advance more; with the *intendants* withdrawn from most of the provinces and with the knowledge that new levies would be blocked by the courts, the regency was suffering in the worst of all worlds. Without benefit from previous developments or hope from a new financial regime, with a war to be financed – there was every incentive to fight back. The revolt of *Parlement* would not be the end of the story.

17

THE FIRST CIVIL WAR

The Fronde has been treated so far as a Parisian affair. The sullen, precarious equilibrium that followed the Declaration of Saint-Germain was vulnerable to a major upheaval in a province, a challenge by any set of magnates or a royal counter-attack. Each was to occur. Meanwhile tax-payers everywhere tucked away their *sous* and appreciated a short-lived tax holiday: this ill wind blew some good. Officers came home on winter leave. Their commanders had to cope with disgruntled troops, confusing loyalties, conflicting advice. Most dazzling star in the military firmament, Condé now looked for recognition and reward beyond anything he had yet received. Orléans craved popularity, resented Mazarin and talked unhelpfully about harmony between crown and *Parlement.* Anne could not be sure what he meant by it; she distrusted him anyway. While Longueville was still serving the crown in his own heavy fashion his wife enjoyed the chance to play political and amorous games. Her brother, Armand de Conti,[1] needed little persuading to find a role more prominent than he had yet enjoyed as the unregarded younger brother of the famous general. His name, wealth and position as governor of Champagne, on France's vulnerable eastern flank ensured him a prominence his personality and abilities did little to deserve. Marcillac would be better known as the duc de la Rochefoucauld the older,[2] perhaps wiser author of the *Maxims.* In hot youth he now embraced the cause and person of Mme de Longueville. Longueville's Normandy, Conti's Champagne, Marcillac's estates and connections in the southwest: here were formidable bases and resources for the rebel cause.

What made the aristocratic plotters more dangerous was that they had friends in *Parlement.* Particular grievances or ambitions may have drawn senior lawyers into a riskier game than they had so far played. *Présidents* Novion and Viole may have fancied the role of English parliamentarians, authors of a political revolution compared to which the Fronde, so far, had been a mere play. The men themselves may hardly have known what tempted them to sedition. Was it irksome to be directed so emphatically by Molé and Talon? The social instinct was surely not dormant: it was no small thing to entertain a Bourbon prince in one's house. The Parisian mood was conducive to bold words. Bread continued to be expensive, rumour abounded, the winter promised to be cheerless. *Mazarinades* reminded magistrate and mercer alike of the true enemy: to be opposed to the Italian who was so blatantly misdirecting regent and king was salve to tender conscience.

Mazarin was invariably well informed. At one point he dangled before Gondi the prospect of being governer of Paris, in place of the octogenarian Montbazon.[3] Gondi was not tempted so Mazarin turned instead to ensuring, as best he could, the allegiance of Orléans and Condé. He invited the abbé de la Rivière,[4] Orléans's politically-minded confessor, to attend the council. He encouraged Condé to think in terms of supreme power at court, vaguely defined but given substance in the form of fortresses on the eastern frontier. It was probably the only policy he could adopt, but it was short-term and flawed. Was there room for both Condé and Orléans? How would other magnates view the Condéan apotheosis? How would it improve Mazarin's tarnished image to be seen so willing to abase himself? Without a supply of fresh grievances it is unlikely that *Parlement* as a body, as distinct from a few malcontents, would have endorsed independent action by a covey or two of magnates: without such endorsement it would have been a rash nobleman even now who would venture on military action. Montmorency's failure and execution in 1632, as had been intended by Louis XIII, had served notice of the danger of open rebellion. In this situation what Anne and Mazarin did, whether conciliatory or provocative, would make all the difference between peace and war.

Certainly inaction had little to commend it. All reports were gloomy and ministers felt beleaguered; the ground was slipping under their feet. It was not in Anne's nature to accept defeat, nor in Mazarin's to stop thinking about new ruses. Uppermost in his mind was still war against Spain; a strong campaign in 1649 might make Spain sue for peace. Open repudiation of the reforms enacted or promised in the Declaration was not conceivable. Séguier advised Mazarin to proceed gently, without patent breach of law. So *traitants* were reminded of a worse alternative: to withhold money would be to ruin the state, and to expose themselves to revenge. Any advances La Meilleraye could obtain were sent at once to the armies. Interest and salary payments were delayed. Registration, and with it occasion for protest, was avoided by making no formal increase in taxation. The *Cour des Aides* was asked to approve the flexible use of the *taille*, the *Chambre des Comptes* to remove controls on the *comptants*. Mazarin hoped that the courts would fall out over their respective briefs and rights. Indeed the common front was soon a thing of the past. But they resisted separately: they registered – but with crippling amendments.

Meanwhile *Parlement* had no formal business so their plenary session of December was a provocative act in itself. They maintained that they had authority to enforce reforms, therefore the duty to investigate complaints about evasion. Molé, under pressure, defended the legality of the proceedings. Orléans and Condé appeared for the crown and were told that there had been breaches of the Declaration. Several firebrands attacked Mazarin for his reluctance to make peace with Spain. *Président* Novion went so far as to claim that *Parlement* was the proper forum for the authorisation of war, treaties and alliances; novel doctrine indeed. Mazarin was aware that he was a client of Condé and would not have been impressed by the latter's profession of disgust. However Condé was responsible for the royal household and may have been sincere when he rebutted charges of extravagance. He was further incensed by complaints about the indiscipline of his troops now stationed round Paris. He had little time for the magistrates, 'those devils in square bonnets'. He was probably sincere when he declared: 'my name is Louis de Bourbon and it is not my wish to unsettle the throne'. He mistrusted Gondi and, no doubt, enjoyed telling him that his fellow-conspirator Noirmoutier[5] was secretly corresponding with Mazarin. The special problem for Mazarin was posed by Condé's overweening pride: the king excepted, he would be second to none. Orléans was more amenable and actually managed to work out with Broussel a formula to avoid further disputes by the device of a committee to examine alleged breaches of the Declaration. More than this would be needed to keep the peace.

By the end of December 1648 *Parlement* was issuing *arrêts* on its own authority and pressing for inquiries into breaches of the Declaration. Acceptance by the *Comptes* and *Aides* courts of the crown's right to take advances on revenues represented a success for Mazarin's policy of 'divide and conquer': it brought violent objections and Molé announced that there would be a plenary session on January 8. Anne, meanwhile, was receiving distressing reports from England, where the deposed king was to be put on trial. Charles I, as Mazarin saw it, had invited his fate by his preliminary weakness: he had allowed his minister Strafford, to be put on trial, subsequently to be executed.[6] Anne was touched by the sad story of her sister-in-law, Henrietta Maria.

Charles I's downfall had begun with financial failure. Still conciliatory towards *Parlement*, La Meilleraye initiated a new round of bidding for tax contracts. The process did not however lead Mazarin to think there was any sound alternative to military action. He believed that *Parlement* could be isolated and that the Hôtel de Ville could work effectively for the crown once given a lead. If the government moved out of the capital and left *Parlement* to face the music, hungry people would come to see it as the author of distress: the king would be welcomed back. All therefore pointed to an attack or a siege. Anne declared that she preferred 'Paris lost to Paris disobedient'. There were, however, differences about tactics. La Meilleraye urged a drive through the capital, starting from the Bastille. Condé spurned the idea of street-fighting against civilians and amateur soldiers. A siege, he thought, would be more honourable and efficacious: it would either lead to the surrender of the city or to an open battle in the event of attempted relief. Le Tellier preferred an economic blockade. The eventual plan was an elaboration of that idea. A sovereign waging war against her own subjects had to avoid needless bloodshed. It was notoriously hard to keep soldiers from fraternising or from helping themselves to their property. To approach the business with too much delicacy would however be self-defeating. Since the army had to re-deploy on the frontier in the spring, victory had to be swift and decisive.

On the evening of 5 January the royal family celebrated Twelfth Night in traditional style. Dividing 'the Cake of the Three Kings', submitting cheerfully to being crowned 'queen of the bean', Anne was in high spirits, as if revelling in the adventure. Even Mme de Motteville was excluded from the well-kept secret, and left behind to experience the anger of the people: 'for two days and nights we heard the incessant cry, "aux armes".' After the palace doors had been closed for the night and all was quiet, Louis was awakened. With Villeroi[7] and Mademoiselle[8] completing the party, the royal carriage quietly made its way out of the city and on to the road to Saint-Germain, where Mazarin and La Meilleraye were to meet them. At the château there was nothing ready, neither beds nor fires, for preparations would have alerted Paris. Mazarin produced camp beds, however, for the queen, her two sons – and himself. Mademoiselle was less than enchanted, but observed that Anne 'could not have been happier if she had won a battle, taken Paris, and hanged everyone who crossed her'. Secrecy, surprise, consternation in Paris: all had gone well. The elated queen ordered Condé to secure key positions round the capital.

Anne proceeded to overplay her hand, sending a message to the capital which accused certain *parlementaires* of conspiring to seize the king. She may have believed it. Mazarin's agent, Lionne,[9] wrote that, if the royal family had not left Paris, the mob would have had them at their mercy. But it was injurious to accuse without being specific; insulting to send the despatch to the Hôtel de Ville rather than to *Parlement*; reckless to force the issue by ordering the sovereign courts to remove themselves to four cities, none nearer than sixty miles from Paris: Montargis, Orléans, Rheims and Mantes. Even if, as Moote suggests, Anne was driven by 'determination to prevent the pattern of the English civil war from spreading' it was folly to bring up the republican issue, for which Mazarin must share responsibility, for it reflects remarks in his *carnets*. He would have preferred a quieter style than Anne's but his intention was clear, Lionne's memorandum was explicit. 'We hold firm in wishing that the authority of the king be fully restored; that is, all that has occurred during the past eight months be deleted from its [*Parlement's*] register and all memory of it obliterated.' It was to be as though 1648 and the Declaration, issued at the very place where Anne and Mazarin now declared war on *Parlement*, had never happened. *Parlement* now became rebels in order to sustain their claim to be loyal.

Seventeenth-century war was an ugly business. Wherever, as in the border lands of eastern France, sieges, ambushes, raids set the scene; wherever villages lay within the range of the foraging patrols, the normal hazards of life were compounded by the random violence of the soldier. Calloused by life beyond the civilised fringe, he lived by rules of his own. He might behave no better towards his fellow countrymen than towards the foreigner. Many of the troops in the pay of the French king were not, of course, Frenchmen. It made little difference. The most beneficent achievement of the military revolution, the bringing of armies under efficient civilian control, with the provision of adequate billets and magazines, was yet to be accomplished. To unlease an army in a domestic conflict was to incur a grave responsibility. Meanwhile, the harsh tone of Anne's letters spoiled any chance of the settlement which might have been effected by compromise on principles, and pardons for individuals. Molé's reaction was ominous. He would show repeatedly that his main purpose was to sustain the authority of the crown. Yet he wrote about Condé's move towards Paris: 'those who have given this advice cannot be sufficiently punished; this blow will shake the crown; it won't recover for a long time'. How could those who had so clear an interest in peace and order lose sight of it, unless they were peering at an uncertain future through eyes bloodshot with pride and anger? How else could men of the law, more used to the war of words, be drawn into an engagement in which they would have to accept the aid of great nobles who did know something of war and were all too ready to fight? Once committed, how could they extricate themselves?

Meanwhile there was some clever legal fencing on both sides. *Parlement* avoided receiving the orders for their exile by sending them unopened to the royal attorneys and ordering them to go to Saint-Germain to request chapter and verse for the general charge of treason. After keeping them waiting for hours, Anne refused to see the attorneys. Séguier pointed out that *Parlement* would have no legal authority till it was established in Montargis. *Parlement* stayed solid under this assault. According to Ormesson, barely a dozen were truly radical; yet the most royalist of judges were now arguing for a united front. There was no wavering even in the *Grande Chambre*, which had earlier shown its distaste for opposition to the throne. Underlining the administration's blunder, Molé now told Mazarin's agent that those who had slandered *Parlement* should be punished. 'Unprecedented oppression' was how he described the situation to secretary of state Brienne.[10] Only the *Grand Conseil* supported Anne, but ineffectually, since their efforts to leave Paris for Mantes were blocked by order of *Parlement:* suspending their work in a futile gesture of loyalty, the councillors could but wait for a royal victory.

Not since the first years of Henry IV's reign, when the still Huguenot king was fighting to gain his capital, had such powers been invoked by the city authorities. Then a radical network and executive, the League, and the *Seize,* had imposed their will.[11] The precedent embarrassed the *frondeurs,* who were determined to do all legally, through a union of bodies representing the crown. Committees dealt with defence, finance, propaganda and communications. Most financiers had left, but La Rallière, Hémery's favoured *traitant,* was secured and imprisoned. *Parlement's* prestige proved sufficient to back loans and raise taxes: ministers noted wryly that *Président* Novion could now contribute 200,000 *livres.* Royal funds were confiscated, Gondi called in the silver of city churches. He also raised his own regiment, his Corinthians.[12] 'Selling his cross for a sling' ran a popular song. The city establishments, mercantile and militia, were dragooned into cooperation. The voice of the mob was tuned by Gondi's agents. Molé worked tirelessly to coordinate and invigorate the war effort.

The Conti faction was joined by important recruits. To the fore were Bouillon, gouty veteran of rebellions and younger brother, Turenne. The latter supported his brother and his claim to Sedan but was sincere in his avowed reason – disapproval of the siege of Paris. Though Mazarin ensured, by a swift payment, that the troops of Turenne's Rhineland army obeyed his German second-in-command, Erlach,[13] the defection of such an accomplished general was a serious matter – and a personal blow to Mazarin who had helped promote Turenne's career and was now told that 'he could no longer count on his friendship'. Marshal la Mothe-Houdancourt[14] was another who turned rebel. The Guise family, and a long tradition of aristocratic revolt, was represented by Elbeuf.[15] Offering their swords and retainers, such great men could be relied on to be brave. But to accept second place, to act together, let alone as an alternative government – was not to be expected. From the outset of the noble Fronde, intelligent collective action was wanting: individual leadership was therefore at a premium. Gondi manipulated *Parlement,* whipping up the mob to a show of rage at the delay in selecting a commander, distributing money and even, for sentimental effect, parading the duchesses of Longueville and Bouillon before the magistrates. He secured his goal, the appointment of Conti. Broussel's son was installed as Governor of Paris.

That Conti was manifestly inadequate for a role which would involve him in operations against his distinguished brother, was a secondary consideration to the *coadjuteur.* Gondi was primarily interested in political

141

control. Beaufort was amenable, expecting that he would be the true leader in the people's eyes. Elbeuf, who had boasted that he would manage the Fronde 'better than Mayenne did the League', nursed a grudge from the start. He was given command of the token attack on the Bastille: the royal commander surrendered at once, so there was little honour in the affair.

Reports of divisions within the *frondeur* leadership might encourage Mazarin in the face of ominous signs of contagion spreading to the provinces. Circular letters from *Parlement* to its provincial counterparts kept local magistrates informed of the causes and course of its quarrel. When Longueville followed his wife's prompting and turned *frondeur*, the Norman magistrates followed their governor's lead. When the Mazarinist comte d'Alais,[16] governor of Provence, with crass ill-timing, revived a scheme to create new judicial offices, no letter of support from *Parlement* was needed to bolster resistance by the *parlement* of Aix. By March, Provence was engaged in its own little *fronde*, with the governor, together with some nobles, confronting the people of Aix who, in the main, supported their *parlement*.

The steep rise in the price of flour in the Paris markets indicates how severely the siege affected the people.[17] Stalwarts of the *robe* kept their nerve, however, in face of royal inducements, threatening or alluring; kept some kind of hold over their aristocratic allies; kept the loyalty of the people of Paris. The judges remained sensitive to the conventions that had governed relations between sovereign and subject for centuries. They drew a firm line between loyalty to Louis XIV, repeatedly assured, and obedience to his ministers. They were tested by a stream of orders in the name of the king. They evaded the issue of authority by finding pretexts for not opening letters whose contents would be known, as copies were sent to other bodies.

The execution of Charles I on 30 January 1649 enabled the judges to display royalist credentials when they issued a letter of sympathy to Queen Henrietta Maria (who had remained at the Louvre when the court had gone to Saint-Germain) and denounced the regicides as 'wicked men who have violated every ... law and dipped murderous hands in the blood of that most just king'. Attempts to provide the widowed queen with a pension were less happy; either the money was not forthcoming because wanted for the defence of Paris, or she refused to accept it. She may have suspected hypocrisy. 'Warn the queen,' she told Motteville, 'that Charles died because he would not accept the truth.' Nothing deterred *Parlement* from attacking Mazarin. A solemn declaration of January 1649 charged him with usurping and abusing royal authority. He was formally tried for crimes against the state, found guilty, denounced as 'disturber of the public peace and enemy of the king and state' and sentenced to be expelled from the royal councils and kingdom.

'This foreign rogue, juggler, comedian, famous robber, low Italian fellow only fit to be hung': that was Mazarin, in the view of the usually dispassionate Guy Patin.[18] It was loathing for the minister, largely irrational, but grounded in the assumed extent of his influence over Anne, that held together the coalition of *Parlement* and magnates. To keep the nobles in harness to their cause, *Parlement* required of them an oath to defend *Parlement* and take orders from them; warily the magistrates had the document committed to the *premier président*, not being entered in the court's register, it did not bind *Parlement* to the nobles' cause. Of course the latter had to make the military decisions. They had their clients among the magistrates. *Ducs et pairs* also enjoyed the right to sit in plenary sessions. They were to that extent involved, not as brothers in a common cause but rather as allies of convenience.

The aims of the great nobles do not admit of simple definition. Clues abound however in the record of previous risings, when they rehearsed injuries to property and slights to status; when governorships, places in council and pensions all figure largely among their demands. At least one now, the duc de Brissac,[19] was open in assuming self-interest: he would join any party that offered material gain. Honour made conflicting demands. La Boulaye[20] resisted Mazarin's eloquent appeal to loyalty and followed his patron Longueville. Unlike *parlementaires*, nobles did not shrink from the prospect of anarchy. Lawyers who had maintained the rights of the crown against foreign authority, notably that of the Pope, might respect local rights, not least those of fellow *parlements*. They were royal officers however and their justice was royal justice. Therefore their ideological position remained centralist.

The opposite was the case with the magnates, whose standing was derived from the surviving strength of family fiefdoms and their corresponding local influence. Their rights and claims pre-dated those of the absolute state. There was therefore more than a difference of style or policy. There was a profound difference in *mentalité*. The time would come when the two kinds of nobleman, sword and gown, would so interrelate that they would be consolidated into a single upper caste, or plutocracy.[21] At this stage, they were different kinds of Frenchman, with different notions of allegiance. That aspect of the 'society of orders', in which social distinctions were more strictly defined than they were across the channel, is only one of several that point to fundamental differences between the Fronde and the Great Rebellion. It helps however to explain the tactics of the magnates which, from the start, alienated them from the majority of the magistrates and provided the royalists with their strongest argument.

Conti had to find a way of breaking through the ring of steel with which his brother was enveloping the city. It seemed to him a poor thing to be required to protect convoys of food; it was also very difficult. His troops were of indifferent quality. The rank and file of the cavalry was largely recruited from city coachmen: their commander, la Boulaye, was soon called 'Monsieur Carriage-way'. The *co-adjuteur*'s regiment was mauled on 28 January. One squadron, under Renaud de Sévigné,[22] was overwhelmed by Condé's superior forces, the rest fled. 'First Corinthians', said Gondi's detractors. The Fronde was open season for the wits.

In February Conti invited the archduke Leopold[23] to enter France from the Low Countries. A letter, clearly devised by his aides but signed by Leopold, was sent to *Parlement:* Mazarin was alleged to be offering peace with Spain in return for Leopold's aid in crushing the *frondeurs;* the archduke sought nothing but peace. Therefore *Parlement,* 'natural tutors' of kings, sole legitimate authority, should act as mediator: a well-baited trap indeed, treason under another name. The habit of mind acquired over centuries served the judges well. Negotiations with a foreign power were the prerogative of the monarch: Molé sent the letter to Saint-Germain. In the same spirit, still clinging to the legal high ground, refusing to issue orders beyond their authority, they thanked the *trésoriers* and *présidial* judges of Poitou for their offer of help – and refused it.

Parlement may have been short-sighted in failing to lay a base for common action with provincial *parlements*. A critic might see more concern for traditional pre-eminence than the will to bring the administration to terms – but the balance between constitutional rectitude and effective resistance was desperately hard to hold. So it was within the beleaguered city where the city government had to be accorded its rights as well as its duties. The *prévôt des marchands*, Le Féron,[24] a member of *Parlement,* had been appointed by Anne in 1648: he led the *échevins* in cautious royalism, obstructing defensive measures when he could. Merchants were losing business through the siege; the *échevins* represented them – but in practice that meant only some of the richer citizens. The six major guilds[25] were in any case faithful to *Parlement.* Special bourgeois companies of militia were formed to aid the defence of the city.

The fact that a number of the regent's *arrêts* were aimed specifically at the interests of the wealthier citizens, for example the tax on their country estates, suggests that ministers assumed that most of them were on the side of *Parlement,* or at least that it was unnecessary to bother over much about their interests. *Parlement* could have allowed the mob to attack the Hôtel de Ville, it if had been held to be incorrigibly Mazarinist. Instead Molé, the true statesman of the *fronde parlementaire,* kept the initiative for *Parlement* and helped to reassure anxious citizens. *Parlement,* he proclaimed, 'should not so satisfy the people's appetite'. So the Hôtel de Ville was incorporated, under duress, into the defence system of the city, and two dangers were circumvented: the slide into mob rule which would provide a pretext for royalist attack, and the collapse of the city's defence if the Hôtel de Ville was allowed to sabotage it.

Condé's strategy was to seize the small towns, whose markets might supply the city, and maintain patrols between them. Dire threats were issued to peasants who might take food into the city. Royal decrees sought to undermine the authority of *Parlement* by entitling lesser criminal courts to take over its appellate jurisdiction. Orders went to town councils and tax officials to send tax proceeds direct to Saint-Germain. There was, all the same, a trickle of supplies and money into the capital, from sympathetic areas or officials prepared to run the risk of reprisals. The peasant economy was fragile enough without such disruption. Reports like those of *mère* Angelique Arnauld[26] convey that it was not only the people of Paris who suffered in this grim winter.

Attempts to concert *frondeur* strategy were foiled by the recklessly competitive conduct of commanders. Beaufort was rash and vain but he did earn the glory he craved. He successfully covered the passage of a vital food convoy from Étampes. After rumours that he had been captured his return was greeted by an ecstatic crowd and a *feu de joie*, with lighted candles in every window. A further success, when he captured Villejuif and brought in another convoy was however outweighed by the one major battle of the first war. On February 8 Condé trapped the Charenton garrison and his mainly German mercenaries slaughtered them and threw their bodies into the Seine. Elbeuf was censored for failing to relieve the place. La Rochefoucauld fought bravely at Brie-le-Robert. Paris didn't starve – but Condé held the field; merchants were unable to trade and artisans had no work.

Mazarin had maintained contact throughout with a number of moderate *parlementaires*. Anne let it be known that her main concern was the authority of her son; that assured 'she would prefer mildness to violence'. If sincere, she was in a more conciliatory mood than in January. Molé held secret meetings with ministers. He insisted that there be free entry of supplies during the negotiations, knowing that it would improve his chance of winning Parisian support for negotiation. Formal conferences took place at Rueil, near Saint-Germain. On 12 March, after only a week, a preliminary settlement was signed. News of the archduke's invasion of northern France brought some urgency to proceedings. Modifications were followed by registration by *Parlement* in April, then promptly by the other Parisian courts and by the *parlements* of Aix and Rouen.

Serious deficiencies in Mazarin's political armoury had by now been exposed. In these negotiations, however, he used tried and familiar weapons with accustomed skill. He was well matched by Molé, who could argue that he had served monarchy better by staying and restraining *Parlement* than he would have by joining the court. He could argue from strength as representative of *Parlement*, which had not been defeated. He had the self-assurance to ignore last-minute orders from Paris not to treat. Noble *frondeurs* had persuaded *Parlement* that Mazarin was treating the conference as a blind. Molé could be flexible because his basic position was that of traditional royalism: *Parlement* should be guardian of the law, not controller of the king: its assumption of powers had been provisional, implying no permanent right. Mazarin was always prepared to sacrifice forms and appearances to achieve his ends. Among people inhibited by considerations of rank and etiquette this could confer a valuable flexibility of action. In these negotiations however neither principal had a free hand. Anne had much to thank Molé for but tended to resent his lofty stance of impartiality.

Molé and his fellow delegates refused to negotiate directly with Mazarin; so the two delegations met in separate rooms and conferred through messengers. Mazarin had always to reckon with Anne's temper and desire to assert herself. Molé's delegation included radical *parlementaires*, besides representatives of other courts and of the Hôtel de Ville. The nobles stayed outwardly aloof from such mundane proceedings. The Crown's main goal was revocation of *Parlement's arrêt* of July 1648 which forbade taxation without its approval, together with the amendments added by the *Comptes* and the *Aides* to the royal declaration of October, guaranteeing the salaries of judges in those courts and protecting tax officials against the revival of the *intendants*. Meanwhile La Meilleraye requested authorisation to float a loan of twelve million *livres* as an advance on the *taille*, at ten per cent interest, to be paid through *comptants*. Mazarin also stipulated a restriction on the number of times assemblies could be convoked, and then only under conditions, notably the approval of the *Grande Chambre*, and exclusion of radical elements from *Enquêtes* and *Requêtes*.

In the end the opposition had to concede very little; revocation of the decree of banishment; a short-term advance on the *taille*, whose collection was, however, to be administered by *trésoriers*, not *traitants;* and the repayment of interest under the *Comptes*, not by way of the secret *comptants*. The Regent's general amnesty was to include those radicals she would like to have punished. *Parlement* could continue in Paris. The reforms of 1648 would be protected. If there were to be any breach, *Parlement* would then convoke a plenary session: from 1650 such sessions could be held, whatever the circumstances. Relief was gained also for Aix and Rouen, with the abolition of new judicial offices. So Molé's strategy was vindicated. *Parlement's* honour saved, its conception of its place in the royal constitution confirmed, Mazarin remained in office. He had won another round in the battle for his political life. But there was no security; nor was there any question about the price the crown was paying. If the Regent had chosen to make him negotiable, better terms could have been won. As it was, *Parlement* had won on most important points. The Regent withdrew all the punitive measures ordered during the blockade.

The victory of *Parlement* would not have been seen in that light by noble allies whose interests it did nothing to promote; they were too particular to be translated into a single measure or even a statement of rights. Noble *frondeurs* had, however, expected solid benefits to accrue from their military service to the cause: now they were left in the air and the possibility of an independent noble fronde had to be considered. It might enlist popular support, even be directed against *Parlement*. There was talk in the circle of Beaufort, relishing his popularity in *Les Halles*, of mobilising the Paris poor against the magistrates' leaders who, it was bruited, had betrayed them. Gondi's line was more cautious: he had played for an alliance with Spain, then no less secretively worked for peace; he now counselled that Rueil should be endorsed – but unofficially wrecked. Divisions among the leaders typically hampered the adoption of a common policy. Mazarin was so well informed that he could usually keep a step ahead. For example, he now ensured that Longueville was detained in Normandy. Turenne went by himself to await events in Spanish Flanders where he found archduke Leopold un-cooperative. The latter had begun to cool towards the *frondeurs:* in early March he had moved towards the frontier with deliberate slowness. Even that had been enough to bring Mazarin to sign the preliminary treaty.

The nobles ineptly underlined the differences between them and *Parlement* by rousing a mob to demonstrate outside the *Palais de Justice.* Shouts of 'Pas de Paix!' and 'Pas de Mazarin!', even, and possibly unscripted 'République!', assailed the judges and swung the debate – for the treaty. *Parlement* was never so visibly united as when its own security and dignity were threatened. Its leaders could also use the affair to impress Mazarin with a sense of their worth as potential allies. Leopold was so exasperated by the 'continual changes and slight effect of promises' that he announced that 'he wished to waste no more time' and retreated to Flanders. The nobles realised that they must look after themselves. Those whom Mazarin most needed to win over asked a high price: for Conti, entry to the council: for Longueville, 800,000 *livres* and the right to transmit his offices to his heirs. There would be a time for retribution. Meanwhile, with military strength so delicately balanced, Normandy was worth that small fortune to the crown. Most of the nobles were less fortunate. When *Parlement* contented itself with registering the relatively few declarations relating to them, they sent their own delegation to bargain with Mazarin; he refused to concede anything further. Molé then dismissed with contempt Conti's plea to suspend the treaty till the nobles were satisfied.

The treaty of Rueil was registered on 1 April 1649. The fools on this day seemed to be the nobles: to all but a few of the committed *frondeurs,* or their particular clients, they appeared incurably factious. To the nobles however, it seemed that the magistrates were interested only in their own offices and fees. The *Fronde parlementaire* was over. That of the princes was soon to start.

18

DIVIDE AND RULE

Reports from Paris had not come to Aix, Bordeaux, Rouen or Angers as news from another world. They represented, according to the recipient's position, a threat or an incitement. They described events which struck a chord and related to issues of local application. What happened in Paris would, in the long run, prove decisive for France. What happened in the provinces affected the action in Paris: the response of ministers, *Parlement* and *frondeurs*.

Never far from Mazarin's mind, for example, would be the situation in Provence. He knew the province well and kept in touch through his friend Bichi, bishop of Carpentras. It was a vital piece on his strategic board. Marseilles was the port of embarkation for troops for Italy and winter quarters for those returning. It was the most independent and unruly of provinces. Between 1596 and 1715 there were 364 'insurrections' in Provence,[1] small affrays mostly, but they acclimatised the people to armed defiance of authority – and the authority was local. In Provence Louis XIV was *comte*, not *roi*. No royal official could touch its money, no troops march through it, without leave from the *procureur du pays*. Taxation of the peasantry had risen steeply but towns limited the amount of their annual subsidy to 200,000 *livres*. To that paltry sum Arles and Marseilles gave nothing, rather than infringe on 'liberties' which, in the latter city, could be defended by a ferocious mob. No *lettre de cachet* could prejudice the privileges of the province. Dealings with Provence belong more to the realm of diplomacy than of administration and were suited therefore to Mazarin's skills.

The governor, the comte d'Alais, was authoritarian and tactless. He was also Condé's cousin, which inhibited Mazarin in his dealings with him. The policies which caused him to fall foul of the *parlement* of Aix were, however, the crown's: to create new offices in *parlement*, to impose a semester,[2] and to insist, in Aix, on choosing the consuls,[3] with the result that they were seen to be puppets of government. Not surprisingly no one was prepared to buy a new office since the first who did was promptly murdered. The *intendant*, de Sève,[4] one of those allowed to remain, could

149

not prevent the development of a miniature *fronde*. In January 1649, the consuls were expelled, the *parlement* recruited peasants to defend their cause, and Alais, with 2,000 troops, besieged the town. Both *parlement* and governor claimed to be acting for the crown. Evidently, the crown was becoming a virtually neutral agent alongside the two warring powers, each owing their authority to the crown, each seeking to exploit it. In March 1649 Mazarin sent Bichi to arbitrate. He conceded the cancellation of the semester, but could not secure peace. In July Alais, encouraged by support from other municipalities, set about the siege of Aix. This time Mazarin commissioned d'Etampes[5] to mediate but he faced the same fundamental difficulty. Mazarin could order the governor to withdraw – but the crown had no means of executing its orders. Here were lessons for the young king to ponder. One day the Provençal authorities would pay for these disorders. Meanwhile, as usual, the people paid, when Alais gave up the siege and allowed his troops to pillage the province. The affair tightened his bonds with Condé when his daughter, under Condé's instructions, married the duc de Joyeuse.

Guienne had certain features in common with Provence: remoteness, seven days' ride from Paris; a great seaport, Bordeaux, with an active and independent-minded *parlement;* and a governor, Epernon,[6] who reacted aggressively to all problems. The province was to be the most effective in resistance to the crown and the last to yield. It had suffered gravely from the increase in the *taille*. It was on the fringe of *Croquant* country,[7] so no stranger to peasant revolts. Epernon had warned Mazarin in April 1648 that trouble was brewing from office creations and demands for *subsistances* for billeted soldiers and, ominously, that the *noblesse* was becoming involved. In May placards appeared in Bordeaux inciting sedition. It was claimed that the governor, in league with merchants, was exporting grain to Spain. So prices rose in Guienne.

Developments mirrored events in the capital. In July 1648 Epernon complained to Séguier that it was impossible to prevent the *parlement* of Bordeaux assembling and passing edicts. In August he wrote to justify its attitude towards the taxes on wine. By the winter however he was preparing for war, strengthening the Château Trompette, Bordeaux's Bastille, and marshalling troops. In March 1649 he declared his hand. *Parlement* proclaimed union with the city government and, with *bourgeois* support, raised a force of artisans and local peasants. There ensued a guerilla war against Epernon's force till Argenson,[8] Mazarin's arbiter, patched up a settlement. Unable to control its supporters or maintain the peace, the *parlement* issued an *arrêt* which says much about Epernon's pretensions: he was no longer to style himself '*très puissant prince*' or to coin money with his effigy and arms. But when the Bordelais army failed to capture Epernon's stronghold, Libourne, the moderate party in *parlement*, made terms amounting to virtual capitulation. Mazarin then committed a capital

150

blunder. Having given Epernon full powers in July 1649, he suspended the *parlement:* punished, it seemed, for moderation, *parlement* now called the people to arms.

There ensued a scrappy civil war. Only the reluctance of the peasantry to become involved kept it within bounds. A familiar cry was: 'We will fight for you – but not till after the harvest!' Reinforcements sent by Mazarin, but unpaid, ravaged the lands they were supposed to defend, but Epernon was about to bring the siege of Bordeaux to a successful conclusion when Mazarin again changed his policy. At Christmas the king signed a declaration giving Bordeaux most of its demands. It represented a tactical shift in Mazarin's position: at this point his prime concern was to regain the favour of Condé. That policy was to prove short-lived, as was the peace in Guienne. Mazarin's policies had provided the Condéans with a ready-made party and powerful southern bastion.

The governor's ability to exercise effective patronage could be a vital factor in determining whether a province remained loyal. In Burgundy Condé worked initially with the *parlement* in Dijon to encourage loyalty and secured, in return, remission of a tax, as well as letters of nobility for leading councillors. It was in his interest to cultivate a following and to have secure base there. In Brittany the *parlement* of Rennes made no move. Since Anne was nominal governor and La Meilleraye, acting for her, usually absent, there was no provocation. Proud of its traditions, the Breton establishment was wisely content to stay aloof from civil conflict. In Languedoc too, where Orléans was another absentee governor, caution prevailed. Bitter experience from Huguenot revolts and the rising of Montmorency, countered any desire to pursue local causes. The with-drawal of the *intendant* was popular, as was Mazarin's gesture of goodwill, the withdrawal of the edict of Béziers.[9] That the *parlement* of Toulouse devoted much effort to curtailing the powers of its old enemy, the *Chambre de l'Edit*[10] illustrates the primacy of parochial concerns, the obstacles that hindered the creation of any kind of common front against government; indeed, the absence generally, of any idea that it was needed.

In two provinces there were serious moves towards the *frondeurs* and *Parlement.* Partly it was a matter of traditions of protest; mainly the actions of the local magnate. In Anjou,[11] where the duc de la Trémoille declared for the Fronde, Angers opened its gates to him. Following the peace of Rueil in April 1649 he made peace with the crown. The legitimate gover-nor, Maillé-Brézé then installed a traditional-style municipal government. It would not be the end of the story.

Anjou was important to the crown, Normandy vital. It was the richest province, accordingly the most highly taxed.[12] The severe treatment of the province after the Nu-Pieds' rising left much bitterness. The *parlement* of Rouen suspended in 1639, had been re-established on a semester basis, with new officers dividing the duties. The *parlement* quarrelled with the governor, Longueville, over his creation of new offices to establish his *clientèle*. He used his influence to keep the province quiet until it suited him to make trouble. When, in January 1649, he joined Conti and the *frondeurs* he tried to rouse the province. Support was patchy but Longueville's friends in Rouen closed the city's gates to Mazarin's newly nominated governor, Harcourt. Longueville got in by boat and a postern gate beside the Seine and was acclaimed by the crowd. The *parlement* submitted, and the Norman *fronde* began. It ceased with the peace of Rueil. Small concessions were all that was needed to secure the loyalty of *parlement* and of the city: cancellation of the semester and a promise to raise no more levies without verification by the sovereign courts. Normandy would remain calm, unmoved by its former governor's going to prison in 1650, his emergence in 1651. There was little enthusiasm for revolution in this province which apparently had most cause for complaint: its *fronde* was reluctant in inception, half-hearted in progress and easily killed.

Mazarin was proved wrong in his fears that the Fronde would follow an English, even republican course. It had remained an essentially moderate movement for two principal reasons. Crown and *Parlement* shared, *au fond*, a view of monarchy as indispensable. *Parlement* and nobles were never effectively a single force. Their brief period of attempted cooperation had exposed incompatible values. One privileged elite must master the other. If the nobles were to go their own way, only serious blunders on the part of the crown would induce *Parlement* to give a corporate lead or even selective support. The Peace of Rueil certainly ended on phase of conflict between crown and *Parlement*. It did not, however, bring ease to the regent or security to Mazarin; nor evidently did it bring peace to the country. Indeed 'peace' proved to be an inappropriate name for a treaty made under duress, not regarded therefore by Anne and Mazarin as definitive or binding for any longer than suited their tactical purposes. Most of the nobles engaged intended to fight on: new men were constantly joining this or that faction, glorying in the name of *frondeur:* vague as it was in meaning, the name still had a distinct cachet. Some politically minded noblewomen were charmed by the idea of engagement in high politics. Nor could *Parlement* help being involved in the complex patterns of intrigue.

The country thus drifted into a further self-destructive period. The years 1649–53 rank with the darkest days of the Religious wars of the later sixteenth century as a time of factious violence. Causes and motives are variable and idiosyncratic, identifiable mainly in terms of the loyalties engendered within family *clientèle* or feudal nexus, along with individual ambition and amatory adventure. Though coloured by the contemporary cult of the hero, who finds self-fulfilment in the pursuit of glory, in essentials the aristocratic Fronde is an extension of the reactionary struggle of a handful of great families and their adherents, sustained by the vision of an alternative regime which should allow them the import-ance due to blood, tradition and great estates. Within their uneven ranks there were several groups, each recruited from the original *frondeur* factions. Gondi's party took from its leader the conviction that it was the true Fronde. Since, after April, it eschewed force it was early deserted by most of the military men. Its declared purpose in sustaining resistance was to reinforce the reforms accepted at Rueil and to purge Anne's government. Evergreen, altruistic but relishing his unexpected fame, Pierre Broussel continued to sound like the honest voice of Parisians. The favourable impression gains by contrast with that created by the *frondeurs'* self-constituted champion.

'He has a talent for mixing gunpowder with his oils' muttered Molé as Gondi entered *Parlement* for the registration of the treaty of Rueil after performing the ceremony of the Holy Oils in Notre-Dame. When Gondi delivered a moving sermon on Christian charity in St Germain d'Auxer-rois, beside the Louvre, he was suffering painfully from venereal disease, the result of his recent liaison with the duchesse de Brissac. Currently his mistress was the pretty daughter of Mme de Chevreuse.[13] Hypocrite and charlatan he allowed himself to seem; unscrupulous and devious, he undoubtedly was. For the zealous *curés* who kept alive the political tra-dition of the Parisian clergy he could be the dévôt: for fashionable congregations he could preach an elegant sermon: for political confeder-ates he could play 'Machiavelli'; for flattering hostesses, the Roman hero, or even the *honnête homme*, embodying *generosité* and *virtu*.[14] It is easier for the reader to admire the imaginative energy with which he acted his parts than it was for Anne, who resented his self-importance and bare-faced plotting, or for Mazarin, who stood to lose most from his jealous rivalry.

In the end Gondi was to become a figure of scorn, not only at court, or in the camp of Condé, but among other *frondeurs*. On occasion he seems to have been lost in his own maze. In March 1649, he had edged towards an understanding with the Spanish in Flanders, only to find that Bouillon and Elbeuf were ahead of him. When they tried to make an open treaty with Spain he retreated, fearing that he would lose credibility in *Parlement*. His grand conceptions were to boil down in the end to a fervent desire to be a Cardinal. In satisfying that ambition Mazarin would be able to neutralise him until such time as he could be removed. Then he was left only with the satisfaction of composing his *Memoirs*. It was there, ironically, in a story of personal failure, glossed over in highly subjective reminiscence, that he achieved a kind of greatness as he joined the select band, with St Simon, Proust and Mme de Sévigné of French writers who have revealed themselves in the depiction of others. That was for the future. Meanwhile he had to be taken seriously.

Another name to conjure with in the steamy gossip of the courts and hôtels of *frondeur* Paris was that of Châteauneuf, already a veteran of intrigue as he was of more constructive political activity. Disappointment had only sharpened his ambition to achieve power, as Chancellor, if not *premier ministre*. He had hoped much from Anne, in whose circle he had formerly moved by favour of Mme de Chevreuse; he was only one of several admirers, whom that vain woman kept on a string for her conspiratorial games. Marazin whom she detested, not least because he stood so well with Anne, blocked his way. Châteauneuf's imprisonment, in 1648, had enhanced his status among *frondeurs*. He did not believe that his hour of destiny had passed. The duc de Beaufort, with his mane of fair hair and easy manners, and now some military successes to boast of, the darling of the Paris crowd, may have thought that his had arrived. He too had suffered from participation in a plot, having been a principal in the *cabale des importants*, and spent five years in prison for it. Loathing Mazarin but resentful too of Condé, Beaufort now carried the standard for his father, Vendôme. Beaufort sought to recover for the family the governorship of Brittany, and the Admiralty: Richelieu had taken them, Anne had kept them. For all his bonhomie there was nothing gentle about this sprig of the Bourbon tree: he had not shrunk from planning the murder of Mazarin and he would fight a duel on the slightest pretext.

Birth had given the prince of Condé an even better start – but it was his rapid mind and startling self-confidence, triumphantly vindicated in battle, that made him the most talked of young man in Europe. There was nothing fortuitous about his victories. He was brave on the battlefield, but he kept his head. Notoriously slovenly, with manners that combined aristocratic insolence with peasant roughness, callously indifferent to his wife,[15] he underwent swings of mood that suggest a manic streak. Wilfully careless about his reputation, he was yet as quick to take offence as he was ready to give it. Condé was a profoundly complicated person whose behaviour cannot be explained merely in terms of precocious fame. Self-centred and greedy for recognition as he appeared during the later stages of the Fronde, he was also to show that he could be loyal and understanding, as toward the king and Anne during the early years of the regency. He let prejudice so cloud his judgement that it is hard to see what he wanted or intended. Yet he seemed to have ideas beyond the usual concerns of the nobleman, with an analytical tendency which grew on him till his gouty old age, when he was patron of writers and philosophers at his château of Chantilly. His advice, as against a military onslaught on Paris in 1648, could be wisely moderate. Later he was apparently torn between duty to the young king and personal ambition, vaguely but passionately expressed in claims to untrammelled authority. He may have been a subject; he was also a Bourbon and – let Vendôme and Beaufort remember – of the legitimate branch.

Despite his ultimately futile course in the Fronde it is not hard to see why men called him 'le grand Condé'. In another setting, where there was a higher ideal to be pursued, he might have cut a finer figure. Indeed he was later to serve his king with distinction – and win more battles. To command on the field, where none could question him, was one thing; to work with others for a political goal quite another. Meanwhile, epitomising the Fronde in one self-dramatising, self-destructive personality, he was deeply frustrated, without a focus for his gifts. For negotiation he had neither patience nor inclination. Rather he appeared to gain satisfaction from pushing his demands to an outrageous limit. Perhaps the estates, titles, offices which he demanded – and received until Mazarin thought that the time had come to challenge him – were a substitute for the reality of power, such as Mazarin seemed to enjoy. Contemptuous towards the brother who had dared to oppose him, having little time either for his cousin Orléans, he became increasingly resentful of Mazarin, the more vulnerable therefore to the prompting of the one woman who had some sway over him – his sister, the duchess of Longueville. She, more than the diminutive princess of Condé, who was to fight so spiritedly for her husband's cause, was best equipped, by instinct and upbringing, to understand him.

In 1649, when defeat was still unimaginable, the Condé faction's strength lay not in Paris but, in the tradition of *les grands*, in the country: in the east, Burgundy and Champagne, where he and his brother Conti (who defected from the original *frondeurs* after Rueil) were the respective governors; after 1651, when Condé had exchanged governorships, in Guienne. Though many Parisians never forgave him for the siege of 1649, he maintained a base in the capital. The judge Deslandes-Payen and *présidents* Viole and Nesmond were his prime agents. The latter supervised his estates while he was in prison, in 1650. In that year Condéan propaganda was effective and sympathy strong. Molé, briefly at the outset, and Broussel, unworldly, perhaps dazzled, were two unlikely men who came under the Condéan spell. The former's son was *intendant*, before the Fronde, with Condé's army: the veteran *frondeur* was to become *prévôt des marchands* in Condé's Paris in 1652. Such unlikely liaisons only show what might have been if Condé had been capable of working with men of lower rank.

Lieutenant-general of the realm, Gaston of Orléans seemed to be a wiser, perhaps sadder man after 1643. Mazarin was the object of his envy and what was left of his ambition. It was to lead him to sympathise with both *frondeurs* and Condéans; checking such wayward tendencies was his sentimental devotion to Louis and a readiness to serve Anne in the difficulties of regency. Overall he was effective neither as champion of the crown, nor as a credible alternative to Mazarin. Latterly he became much involved in the business of *Parlement;* sometimes his opinion swayed debate: he rarely commanded complete confidence. For all his undoubted distinction of bearing, with a saving humour, he emerges as a figure of some pathos. The impression is heightened by comparison with the vigour and forthrightness of his redoutable daughter, la Grande Mademoiselle.

Clearly Mazarin did not have to reckon with a coherent body of enemies, nor an undisputed leader. They could however unite on one issue: his continuance as *premier ministre.* He could not rely solely on Anne's favour; nor, when so much was at stake, even ultimately the safety of the king, would he wish to place her, as it were a human shield, between him and those who clamoured for his disgrace. He therefore sought every opportunity to enlarge his own party. It remained substantially intact even during his periods of exile. At times indeed, so fragmented was the political nation that the Mazarinists seem merely to be a faction, like any other of the period. The essential difference was that some of Mazarin's *créatures* were the key men in royal government.

Mazarin at least knew precisely what he wanted: to remain in a position to serve the king, indeed to be indispensable to him; to ensure that the crown retained sufficient authority to govern; ultimately, to complete his *politique* by ensuring the defeat of Spain. Within the compass of these aims he sifted and assessed the information which trickled in from well-placed agents and decided on the action to suit the occasion. Sometimes it would be drastic, sometimes self-effacing, always unpredictable. He was not above making mistakes, but he was learning all the time. How else could he now play his hand? There was no question of his making a broad coalition out of such disparate, mutually hostile groups. His central concern, beyond mere survival, was to make domestic alliances serve the needs of his foreign policy. But how could that be when, as Turenne had shown, he could not rely on a military commander, once provided with the resources to wage war, to use his army against Spain? It was natural therefore for him to fall back on the diplomat's last weapon: to divide and rule. His tactics served to heighten the tensions, exacerbate enmities, and encourage resort to force.

19

THE WAR OF THE PRINCESSES

Mazarin was always capable of learning from experience. He realised after Rueil that it was expedient to work with the courts and the financial officers. With each development in the noble Fronde it would become clearer that there was more to bind than to divide them. Becoming inured to the threats that had once unnerved him, Mazarin had been able to ignore the last essentially *frondeur* gesture of *Parlement* when, in January 1649, he was tried and sentenced to be expelled from the king-dom. Following his lead and their own desire to keep the administrative wheels turning, ministers turned to a policy of appeasement, with selective targeting of likely troublemakers. *Rentiers* were to be paid interest due, *officiers* their salaries. Late in 1649 *Parlement* would be offered the chance of staging trials of prominent *frondeurs*. It became policy to keep *Parlement* informed of seditious conduct by nobles: also of negotiations undertaken with provincial *parlements*. So *Parlement* was offered what, for many of its members, was the main point behind their protests: a sense of being partner with the monarchy.

In the spirit of rapprochment, the *lit de justice* was set aside, for the time being, as a coercive instrument; no *lettres de jussion*[1] were employed. Mazarin was too keenly aware of the advantages that money could bring: he could always find it for deserving *parlementaires*. One early assignment of the young Colbert,[2] Mazarin's personal agent, was to investigate the affiliations of individual judges to noble factions.[3] Despite the tactical shifts which were designed to baffle, there can be no mistaking the main thrust of Mazarin's policy. It was imperative to cut *Parlement* off from *Les Grands*; at least to make it as hard as possible for Condé and others to build parties within *Parlement*. So they were increasingly isolated: it was a pre-condition of their eventual failure.

Parlementaires are unlikely to have seen a real change of heart behind Mazarin's courteous approaches. Their position remained delicate. From each committed individual within its ranks, *frondeur*, Condéan or Mazarin-ist, came fervent appeals. Upholding the rule of law became increasingly hard in a country where the crown and its opponents conducted themselves by the simpler rules of war. The instinct to support royal government was strengthened by every revelation of irresponsible noble conduct. It was countered by the realisation that Anne was bent on escaping from the constraints so recently imposed. *Parlement* could strengthen its political position in the short term if it responded positively to the factious spirit of the few; or it could look beyond the *mêlée* towards a secure future as respected guardian of law and tradition. Early in the Fronde of the nobles, when it was impossible to predict the outcome, the dilemma was acute. Only when their costly follies seemed to most magistrates to outweigh the faults of Mazarin, would the scales of justice settle on the royalist side.

Even the short winter war had created havoc in the affected areas. It was always easier to raise troops than to discipline or disband them. Semi-independent companies looked after themselves by pillaging the countryside. There were 15,000 refugees in Paris, contributing to existing scarcity. The unconcealed ambitions of certain nobles kept quarrels simmering and soldiers hopeful of employment. Restless *hobereaux*,[4] with more pride than money, constantly renewed the pool of recruits for their grand patrons. The capital witnessed serious affrays. Business was slack. An idle crowd might soon turn from spectators of a noble brawl to participants in a riot. One reason for the plight of the craftsmen and shopkeepers was the prolonged absence of the court. Whether through concern for the king's safety or desire to keep a free hand, Mazarin still advised against an early return to Paris. The delay exacerbated the disorder he professed to fear, as nobles and their followers swaggered, expressing their contempt for the 'peace', denouncing Mazarin and working on the citizen's fears. Acknowledged chief among these tavern soldiers was Beaufort. It is typical of the Fronde that one trivial, if bloody combat, when Beaufort and his friends had drawn swords on their mocking rivals, should be described in detail by memoirists.[5] Meanwhile Mazarin had more serious engagements in mind than the 'affair of the tablecloth'.

Mazarin put his faith in a successful offensive against the Spanish. It is an indication of the damage already caused by the Fronde that Mazarin could give the command of the attenuated force, brought together for the spring campaign, to the comte de Harcourt. Turenne was out of the reckoning; Condé was held to be too great a risk. Harcourt was a loyal Mazarinist, but an uninspired commander. The Spanish took heart and avoided engagement while Harcourt exhausted his men in futile pursuit. He failed to capture either Cambrai or Courtrai. This was hardly defeat; nor was anything disastrous recorded from Catalonia or northern Italy. But failure to secure any victory which could be puffed up in the *Gazette* was enough to fuel denunciations of the war. While the court was at Arras, Mazarin attended the Flanders campaign himself for some weeks.

Typically he was accused of besieging Cambrai in order that he could establish a governorship there: a possible bolt-hole. Failure there certainly upset him: 'however carefully we work at things, we do not seem able to bring them to a successful conclusion'. The cost of the war could be counted. Why was it being fought? Mazarin knew well enough. One day he would have the complete answer for his critics.

Meanwhile 'warmonger' remained part of the indictment, giving heart to all who refused to pay their taxes. In Paris *Mazarinades*[6] poured from the printers, mostly from Gondi's stable, more boldly offensive than ever, with private enterprise bringing ingenious variations to themes serious or scurrilous. Condé did not escape attention, but Mazarin was the chief target. 'Nothing', wrote Guy Patin, 'pleases so much as those libels against this wretched tyrant, cheat, fraud, clown, buffoon, Italian thief, here held in detestation by all'. Anne was of course his accomplice, '*la Mazarine*'. Even there the more scabrous pamphleteers did not stop, but took the relationship to the queen's bed. It is unlikely that such libels were actually read by the king. His valet La Porte[7] was however sufficiently jealous of Mazarin to have hinted to Louis what he thought about the queen's indiscretions. If so, it plainly did nothing to lessen the king's respect for Mazarin.

Mazarin might laugh at such *canards* but the deliberate tarnishing of the image of royalty could only exacerbate the problems of ministers. Bad that monarchy should be disliked, it was worse that it should be despised. The *arrêts* of *surintendant* La Meilleraye were largely ignored. As Mazarin's chief anchorman and correspondent in Paris Le Tellier was gaining experience by the day; he made sensible efforts to allay Parisian fears. Orléans wanted to be comfortable and was genuinely concerned to create goodwill. Molé urged ministers to attend to the reforms and to expedite the return of the court – but to no avail. So it was left to *Parlement* to maintain order. The conservative majority trod warily between the regent, who demanded more severe sentences, and *frondeurs*, who thought that *Parlement* should turn a blind eye to pamphleteers and other malefactors. Its own members might be involved in brawls, but considered it best not to investigate an attack on two royal servants, when blows were delivered with such shouts as 'That's for the king, that's for Mazarin and that's for *la Mazarine*'. But obscenity among the lower orders could not be overlooked – then *Parlement* was prepared to prosecute. Only intervention by the mob in the Place de la Grève saved the author of *Le Custode* from the hangman. An obscure scribbler was unlikely to cause serious embarrassment; a political case involving a leading nobleman was quite different. Anne wanted to prosecute Beaufort for assaulting her friends in the affair of the tablecloth. In law her case might be sound: her political judgement was less so. The *frondeurs* relished the prospect for publicity and the chance of contriving the humiliation of the regent.

As *duc et pair* Beaufort would expect a plenary session: Molé, Talon and Séguier, were all opposed. No one could be sure how the case might affect the standing of *Parlement,* nor what an enraged mob might do. Anne was persuaded to drop the charge.

In its responsibility for the provinces that came under its jurisdiction, *Parlement* was faced by the same difficulty: that of keeping to a middle way. They could not further curb the tax officials without jeopardising the security of the state – and their own salaries. To appear indifferent would be to nullify their own reform programme. Their decrees were therefore aimed impartially at preventing the abuse of powers by tax officers and evasion by tax-payers. They rebuffed the *frondeur* La Trémou-ille,[8] who asked leave to arm noblemen in Poitou; tough *arrêts* were aimed at stopping royalist plundering. A good harvest brought cheer to peasants; the consequent fall in wheat prices, relief to the city poor. With evidence of *Parlement*'s sound restorative work, and with some lifting of the poison-ous cloud of malice that seemed to hang over Paris; with the perceived advantage of being close to *Parlement* at a time when its loyalty might be tested by the demand of the *parlements* of Aix and Bordeaux for a plenary session. Anne and Mazarin decided that they should return to the capital.

On 18 August 1649, the royal cavalcade entered the city. No doubt anticipating a revival of business, loyal *bourgeois* welcomed this chance of expressing their detachment from unsavoury *frondeurs.* Behind one account one can detect a royalist hack, anonymous, earning his fee: 'Everyone has come from all around to see this glorious spectacle . . . the air is full of acclamation and joy and all hearts have uttered these loving words . . . : "Long live the king, long live Louis!" ' Interestingly, along with an echo of the contemporary physics, the theme of 'the Sun King' appears already in this account: 'this radiant sun, this day without night, this centre to which all lines of the circumference aim . . . this driving force which gives movement to all others.'[9] The decision to go to the Palais-Royal rather than to the Louvre, which the soldiers would have preferred as a traditional fortress-palace, may have inspired confidence. Within days Mazarin was walking with his bodyguard about the streets, renewing old contacts, looking in at churches, advertising his self-confi-dence. He was treated with guarded respect. It was to the young Louis however, that men looked with affection and hope. On 4 September the municipality celebrated his twelfth birthday with a ball, a feast and a display of fireworks. Rarely had the sovereign been more important. After eight bewildering months, he now represented the tried and familiar, tradition and unity, past and future, source and sanction of law and order.

One reason why Mazarin wanted the court to return to Paris, was that the provinces were in turmoil. Not for the first time, Frenchmen were fighting Frenchmen with a relish that might owe little to religious or political conviction. Across a wide band of southern lands peasants and artisans, often now with nobles, sometimes *curés* at their head, were looking for heads to break. At a higher level of these rites of violence,[10] Mazarinist governors or lesser officers wrangled and fought with *parlements* and other officers. The *parlement* of Aix, challenged their governor, linked with the *parlement* of Bordeaux, and called on Molé for a plenary session of *Parlement*. On 2 September Anne called twenty-five judges to the Palais Royal to inform them that d'Alais had been cautioned and that a settlement would soon be reached in Guienne: *Parlement* expressed solidarity with provincial *parlements* but desisted from calling a plenary session. These responses came too late to prevent the contagion spreading to Languedoc and its *parlement*. The administration's nightmare was that a revival of such political activity would fan the South into a rebellious blaze. It was compounded by awareness that military action of the kind taken by Richelieu was unlikely to succeed. Indeed it was too hazardous even to move troops across much of the country: whether deserting or looting, their own discipline was as much a problem as any foe they might encounter. It was safer to send a regiment from Flanders to Guienne by sea. There was nothing more likely to provoke a local rising than the presence of an army demanding food and billets.

Failing the military option, Mazarin had to rely on his political skills. Condé presented the crucial problem. He had either to be aggrandised in order to be useful, or neutralised, so as not to be dangerous. With the autumn leaves fell Mazarin's hopes of resolving the problem. In September Condé attacked the government for its mismanagement of the war. At once he became the champion of the *frondeurs*. To limit the damage, Mazarin had to minister humiliatingly to his pride. He was accorded what amounted to an overriding power in government, having the right of veto over most major government appointments: armed forces, governorships, the royal household. Dispatches were to pass through the *conseil d'état*, where he was influential, rather than through Mazarin's personal office. Finally, astonishingly, in November, Mazarin had to yield to Condé control over financial policy. It was confirmed, by one of those ironies in which the Fronde is so rich, by the restoration of Particelli d'Hémery whose policies had done so much to cause the Fronde – and who had been its first casualty. He was in poor health: only out of rancour was he now a Condéan.

The use that Condé made of his power was to be the main factor in determining the course of events up to his dramatic arrest in January 1650. Also significant was the issue of the southern *parlements*, with the pressures their demands brought on *Parlement* and the opportunity for *frondeurs* to revive their campaign against Mazarin. Condé can be seen as agonising, like some Corneillian hero, between his *amour-propre* and his obligation to the young king. Of course, *frondeurs* who had hailed his assault on Mazarin now hated him for his apparent deal with the regent. The grievances of the judges of Aix and Bordeaux, the level of interest rates, were not for him worth close attention. Where, however, his interests were involved, he was quick to act, without regard for consistency or effect. So Condé supported the *parlement* of Bordeaux, whose governor Epernon was being courted by Mazarin as a possible husband for one of his nieces, and where he intended building up his power. He opposed that of Aix, because another governor, Alais, was his relative. When it sent a deputation to the council he declared that the judges were 'republicans' – and threatened them with his cane. As for those of Bordeaux, when the hapless Villeroy queried their actions, he told him with heavy sarcasm 'to lead an army against them'.

While Condé made enemies, Mazarin tried to make friends. Pamphlets put the case for the government. A typical assertion was that since the declaration of Saint-Germain had been forced on the regent, she did not need to adhere to its terms. Arguments of absolutist tenor were inappropriate at a time when royalist *parlementaires* were under increasing pressure to adopt a more aggressive stance on behalf of their sister *parlements* and of aggrieved *rentiers*. On 25 October a deputation from that court which sat when *Parlement* was in recess, the *Chambre des Vacations*, went to the palace to state their case. *Président* de Novion told Anne that all France's troubles stemmed from breaches of faith. Séguier argued that the *parlement* of Bordeaux was in that position itself when it demanded the dismissal of its governor; the Provençal judges were likewise, when protesting against the removal of suits from their jurisdiction. By focusing on the question of the provincial *parlements*, which he knew to be embarrassing to *Parlement*, Séguier secured nothing more than a legal victory, of little political importance. To retain the cooperation of *Parlement*, he had to attend – and did, with placatory measures – to the concerns of Aix and Bordeaux. Financial questions were harder to resolve. Again Hémery was at the centre of a storm.

A recurring theme of Mazarin's letters of 1649 is the urgent need for money: 'We need great sums ... do everything you can' was a typical plea. The limited funds had to be divided between the armies, official salaries and the payment of interest, as promised in the Declaration of Saint-Germain. Political advantage, or 'justice', it might be called, against the military argument, 'necessity of state' as ministers might see it: as ever a hard decision. Some *parlementaires* had been paid interest secretly and could afford therefore to counsel patience. Some had divided loyalties, like Gondi's hitherto forthright associate, *président* le Coigneux who had just made a lucrative match for his daughter with Hémery's son. *Frondeurs* staged demonstrations in September in front of the Hôtel de Ville. *Parlement* responded by proceeding against the *traitants* to get cash with which to pay interest on the *rentes*. Gondi's hand can now be seen clearly in the concerted *frondeur* attack: behind the unfortunate Hémery was the real target, Condé. Guy Joly[11] led a syndicate of his fellow *rentiers*, a body without legal status, formed ostensibly to supervise payments – in reality, for political action. Joly was Gondi's secretary and the syndicate included several of the most radical *parlementaires*, among them *président* Charton.[12] Molé persuaded the *Grande Chambre* to declare the syndicate illegal. The *Chambre des Enquêtes* affirmed that only a full *Parlement* could so pronounce. He therefore invited a special assembly, representative of Paris authority, *prévôt des marchands*, *rentiers* and delegates from every court of *Parlement*, to meet at his house.

There ensued one of those episodes which, like an electrical storm after days of brooding heat, occur periodically during the Fronde and contribute to its character of theatricality, encompassing the deadly and the grotesque.[13] Armed with knives and pistols, a crowd of *rentiers* and sympathisers, some five-hundred strong, turned up at Molé's house. The *premier président* spoke firmly: he would espouse their cause, but would not countenance their syndicate. Joly shouted that Molé and his fellow conservatives were Mazarinists. Blows were exchanged. The *prévôt* was lucky to get out of the building alive. The result of this brawl was a widening of the breach between *Parlement*'s moderates and *frondeurs*: the latter were determined to secure the reforms. They chose a strange way of opening the fight.

On 11 December news spread round the city that Guy Joly had survived an attempt to assassinate him. Charton – 'brusque, turbulent... a great *frondeur*' Mazarin called him – rushed to *Parlement* and declared that he had been the intended target. La Boulaye ran about the streets urging the people to set up barricades. Was it the August Days all over again? Broussel demanded that the gates of the city be closed to prevent another royal evacuation. That evening Condé's empty carriage was shot at. Suspicion rested on La Boulaye. Was this impulsive young nobleman, realising that he was on the list for prosecution, trying to win reprieve? Was he indeed a double-agent, acting for Mazarin? It is virtually certain – *pace* Gondi and la Rochefoucauld – that Mazarin did not instigate the affair. Naturally however, he sought to exploit the rivalry, now intensified, between Condé and the Fronde. He probably suggested to Condé that he send his empty carriage through the streets to see what would happen: that bore the stamp of his imaginative approach to awkward problems. If he had been a Greek he would not have let ten years elapse before deploying tricks to capture Troy. Beyond doubt, the *frondeurs* had staged the initial event to win sympathy for the *rentier* case; they now felt the backlash of opinion. *Bons bourgeois* could thank heaven that there had been no rioting. Talon persuaded Le Tellier to let Orléans guard the streets with the city militia. *Parlement* voted for an investigation. It discovered that Joly's wound was self-administered.[14]

The weapon of ridicule, so potent against Mazarin, could now be turned against the *frondeurs. Parlement* had never seemed stronger. On 22 December Molé and Orléans announced terms between the government and *parlement* of Bordeaux which promised an end to the southern Fronde. In Paris a syndicate of eighteen *rentiers* would deal with questions concerning the *rentes*. With a nod in the populist direction, it represented a victory for the legal approach. The *rentes* issue was defused, the radical element contained. The judges as a whole had declared firmly for monarchy and for peace. Did Mazarin fully appreciate it? Was it through a misreading of an admittedly confusing situation that he chose this moment to counter-attack? Believing that *Parlement* would now stand with the regent whatever happened, had he now concluded that Condé was the real enemy? This turn of events might have provided one kind of opportunity – to re-build a royalist party on the strength of sympathetic dealings with *Parlement,* waiting for extremism to burn itself out – but it seemed to him quite another: to deal decisively with his most dangerous rival.

Mazarin's feelings towards Condé are hard to gauge. He realised that he would be of more use to France as the king's ally than as his enemy. Condé seems however to have welcomed any chance to thwart and insult the Cardinal: one occasion was provided by Mazarin's plan to hold a great supper to celebrate the marriage between his niece Laura Mancini and the duc de Mercoeur; another when Mazarin gave the Admiralty to Vendôme. Mazarin was prepared to eat humble pie. The marriage was put off, the Admiralty appointment was frozen, the queen taking temporary charge of it; Longueville, at Condé's request, was given the governorship of Pont de l'Arche.[15] Mazarin bided his time, seeing how far Condé would go towards self-destruction. 'Adieu Mars', Condé flung at him after one meeting in the queen's chamber. Having had much practice Mazarin could endure an insult more patiently than the queen. She was deeply offended after the youthful comte de Jarzé, Beaufort's antagonist in 'the affair of the tablecloth', carried his loyalty to Anne too far and declared his love; but less by that – he was merely rusticated – than by Condé's uncalled-for defence of the young courtier. To ministers Condé was simply a liability: decades of statecraft could be wrecked by his erratic management. It made sense, following the setback to the *frondeurs*, to devise ways in which they and Condé would destroy each other.

Mazarin's moves had never been so tortuous. He worked through a small company of informers and spies; hardly a body or meeting was without one. While he encouraged Condé to take legal action against certain *frondeurs*, he made overtures to those whom he saw as useful allies. Gaston was helpful: he could wield influence in *Parlement* denied him in the regent's council. Mme de Chevreuse returned, with a new card to play, her pretty and marriageable daughter.[16] Her clique of great ladies, Rohan-born or sympathetic to that family's interests, united in detestation of the Condés, was almost a political party in itself. Its tone is revealed by Madame de Montbazon's threat to mutilate La Rochefoucauld and offer the pieces to Mme de Longueville on a silver tray. The air was thick with foreboding. Many *parlementaires*, forgetting convention, went to their courts carrying daggers or pistols.

Mazarin's game was bold and subtle; but flawed, for it depended on the cooperation of *Parlement*. That divided body was too much concerned about its own security to be a willing accomplice. It was therefore essential that Mazarin should move with caution. He could hardly have been more precipitate. On 13 December a full session of *Parlement* was attended by Condé, Orléans, Bouillon and Vendôme; they were bent on the destruction of Gondi through investigation of the assassination plot. Mazarin hoped that Gondi would be sufficiently scared to offer the crown a new tactical alliance. So he put the crown's resources behind the prosecution and recruited men who would commit perjury for cash or security. On 22 December, the *procureur-général*, under ministerial orders, asked *Parlement* to try Gondi, Beaufort and Broussel. For evidence there was little but hearsay. Only scraps of conversation could link Broussel with the Joly affair. *Avocats-généraux* Talon and Bignon therefore refused to sign the deposition. *Président* de Mesmes evoked disturbing memories when he called the affair a new conspiracy of Amboise.[17] Sympathy for the *frondeurs* grew when Gondi exposed witnesses for the prosecution as low fellows in Mazarin's pay who were inventing their stories. A principal witness, 'the sieur Pichon' had been, in effigy, broken on the wheel at Le Mans where he enjoyed a reputation as thief and arsonist. English history affords similar examples – the trial of the Seven Bishops notably[18] – of the boomerang effect of a political trial that miscarries, and the folly of employing rogues as witnesses: there is sport for the crowd in the public process and a hero to be made out of the victim. 'Vive Monsieur Beaufort' was again the cry in the markets.

Disconcerted, Mazarin turned to Mme de Chevreuse. Through her mediation, a form of reconciliation took place in a hidden oratory by the church of Saint-Honoré: there Gondi, in disguise, met the queen and Mazarin. A new deal was hammered out. In effect the crown was entering into alliance with those elements in the Fronde whom Mazarin believed that it could manage. The houses of Rohan and Vendôme were to be the principal beneficiaries, in governorships, military promotion and pensions. Gondi would have the nomination to the sacred college, at present reserved for the *abbé* La Rivière. Condé however assumed that the *abbé*, as a *protégé* of Orléans, would know what was going on and therefore discounted rumours of a plot against himself. Mazarin and Anne were justifiably nervous about the intended coup and put it off for several days. By good fortune as much as good planning, they achieved a complete surprise.

On 18 January 1650, the two princes, Condé and Conti, with the duc de Longueville, were seized at the Palais Royal and dispatched to the fortified château of Vincennnes.[19] 'Further patience', Mazarin wrote to Bichi, 'would have put the realm in danger of destruction'. No less characteristic of Mazarin's *politique* than the boldness of the *coup* was the insurance policy that he took out against its failure. Two days before, he had assured Condé of his 'constant attachment and . . . obedience'. The queen's orders made it look as if she had pushed him into it against his better judgement. So Anne wrote to him: 'I am resolved at last not to follow your advice in this matter nor the advice of anyone else who would persuade me to gloss over any longer the encroachments that the princes are making on the authority of the king . . .' Indeed if Mazarin went on opposing her she would not only 'be displeased but forced to doubt his loyalty'. It was a vintage performance and Orléans was sprightly in his appreciation: 'Here's a good catch, they have taken a lion, a monkey and a fox'. Molé expressed outraged traditionalism: 'Ah Madame, what have you done? They are children of the royal house.' The charges were of treason; but vague and insubstantial. Conti had been, with Longueville, a principal in the *fronde parlementaire*. But Condé, feathering his own nest, had not unduly fouled the king's. He had played the political game with conventional moves. Condé's friends had always had a military hero, a prince of the blood, a family clique and an extensive *clientèle*; now they had a martyr, a cause, a treacherous set of enemies – and a villain to execrate. So they rode off to their châteaux to raise support for a rebellion of a more extensive and deadly kind than had so far been seen.

Richelieu had not shrunk from acts of executive justice, but his preferred method might have been directed towards a single individual, followed by trial, perhaps execution: he would not have tried to justify it in law before *Parlement*. Imprisoned without trial or term, the princes advertised Mazarin's weakness. He had bid high for *frondeur* support; but he could only hold out the prospect of a Cardinal's hat for Gondi. Meanwhile the *coadjuteur*'s capacity for mischief was unrestrained. There was a price too to pay for promises that could be honoured. In March Séguier resigned the chancellorship, having been left with little power when Châteauneuf was made Keeper of the Seals. Energetic, brusque, at seventy ambitious as ever, Mme de Chevreuse's favourite now hoped to become *prémier ministre*: there was no comfort for Mazarin in that quarter. Another political debt was paid to *président* de Maisons[20] fulfilling a promise made earlier to secure his support: when Hémery died in May, de Maisons became *surintendant*. The Fronde was to see other such deals and realignments; it was extraordinary nonetheless to see Beaufort and Gondi leading soldiers through Paris and earning applause and celebratory bonfires for the overthrow of the tyrant Condé.

It must have been a relief to Mazarin to leave the unquiet city when, in February, he went, with the king, to Normandy. Mme de Longueville had gone to raise the province for the princes. Its *parlement* was luke-warm.[21] The royal progress ended with a triumphal entry into Rouen while the duchess, after being nearly drowned, and after fifteen days of hazardous travelling about Normandy, made her escape from Dieppe.[22] The royal success in Normandy at least ensured a secure retreat and base if matters became desperate. At best, for crown and Cardinal, it was bound to be a hazardous year. No single force was strong enough to defeat the royal army, but the wide spread of revolt, with interspersed patches of passive resistance, posed a formidable logistical problem. The charm, energy and personal following of la Rochefoucauld secured a sizeable force in Poitou. Bouillon recruited in the family lands in the southwest. Marshal Brézé, Condé's father-in-law, raised the standard in Saumur. There was resistance in Burgundy when Vendôme claimed the governorship from Condé; that eastern province, potentially dangerous as a base for foreign troops, was the next target for the royal army.

More dangerous was the force collected by Turenne who, on 30 April, at his headquarters at Stenay, with Mme de Longueville by his side, made an agreement by which Spanish money and troops were to be provided to assist Turenne's force to liberate the princes and secure peace. A treaty which envisaged at least the temporary Spanish occupation of conquered towns would, if Turenne had succeeded, have weakened France's bargain-ing power in any peace-making process. This alliance shows how *frondeurs* could believe themselves morally justified in making an engagement with a foreign power: Mazarin's aversion to peace was allegedly 'so great that it has obliged him to go to the extreme and violent lengths of seizing the Princes because he feared that they would hamper or thwart his unjust design of keeping Christendom in a state of blood and fire, solely for his own selfish interests.'

Meanwhile Condé's closest relations excelled themselves. In April his mother went to *Parlement* to make a personal appeal for support before the embarrassed judges. It was only by a narrow majority that she was allowed to speak, against the regent's express wishes. Condé's wife sur-prised those who had patronised or pitied her when she went to Bor-deaux, with her little son, to lead the city in revolt. A great crowd greeted her with shouts of 'Vive les Princes, Point de Mazarin'. She declared that she had returned to their midst to protect her son 'from the violence of Cardinal Mazarin'. She begged their aid 'to protect the only prince of the blood who is out of this foreigner's power'. Typical of those who responded to the call was the chevalier Thodas who arrived at Libourne with a thousand men. Chivalric instincts could still move men to serve.

In May Turenne joined the archduke Leopold and besieged the Châte-let, then Guise. Both towns surrendered but there was no significant advance. Royalist tactics, threatening their communications and supplies, were successful. After returning from Normandy and a brief spell in Paris, the court had spent June in Compiègne to be close to the Flanders front. The immediate danger there being over, in July they moved to Poitou, thence to Guienne and the siege of Bordeaux; it did not capitulate till 29 September. Even so brief an account of the royal itinerary gives some idea of the vigorous lead that Anne and Mazarin were giving to the cause of the young king. For him it was an invaluable training. For Anne, it can only have been a prolonged ordeal; she became ill in October, again, alarmingly, in December.

Mazarin was sufficiently anxious about Anne to insist on having daily medical bulletins. By the end of the year she was recovering. He had been suffering from gout but it had not deterred him from joining the royalist troops engaged in the siege of Rethel, on the Aisne, some ten miles northwest of Rheims, in that country of rolling plains which offers such an inviting route to the Ile-de-France and to the capital. The battle, on 15 December, in which maréchal du Plessis-Praslin defeated Turenne as he tried to relieve the town, leading to its capitulation, was momentous. It had some impact even in Paris. Vallier[23] noted in his journal: 'the principal credit for the battle and recapture of Rethel is rightfully due to the care and resolution of Cardinal Mazarin, without whose presence and orders two such great enterprises, so necessary to the peace and security of Champagne, could not have been undertaken.' Mazarin had cause to be proud of his personal contribution to a remarkable royalist effort. Events of the year had sealed the bonds between minister, queen and her impressionable son. He may even have dared to think that the Fronde, that unnatural monster, was over.

While the court was out on campaign, Orléans had been left to look after government and *Parlement*. Anne had been advised to explain her action against the princes to the courts. It might have been better to have left it in the area reserved for a sovereign's private judgement and let supposition stand for evidence; as it was, *Parlement* was invited to consider the law, and was uneasy about it. Had there not been a violation of the reform article of 1648? Meanwhile the *frondeur* trials collapsed. Beaufort, Gondi and Broussel went free. The trial of lesser dependants was left to the criminal court, *Chambre de la Tournelle*. The renewal of war again brought the financial question to the fore. Mazarin's latest ruse was to persuade the *Cour des Aides* to take responsibility for the collection of taxes: its commissaries were *intendants* under another name. The government was probing all the time to find a way of infiltrating the defence line guarded by the reform articles.

The record of administration in the provinces complemented that of the war: no clear pattern, but numerous local initiatives; local *officiers* matched by new men from Paris, generally supported by small detachments, as much for protection as for tax-levying. Some of the '*intendants*' were driven away. In the *pays d'états parlements* refused to recognise the authority of Mazarin's agents. Vendôme, now Mazarinist in sympathy with his son, brought in a *maître* from Paris to administer Burgundy; then the *parlement* resisted all attempts to raise taxes and supplies. Provence was another area where magistrates looked for any chance to extend their liberties. Unrest was not confined to distant provinces. *Trésoriers* gave trouble in Bourges, Châlons and Limoges. How could the *taille* be collected in the Limousin, where echoes of the Croquants were roused by the gatherings of *hobereaux* and peasants? They took their cue from western Languedoc and Guienne where was brewing the most alarming concoction. It is there that royal authority looked most tyrannical, was most grimly resisted and was in danger of being destroyed completely.

As much to find food and shelter, as for coherent military reasons, royalist troops, accompanied sometimes by *intendants*, spread terror and earned hatred for Mazarin's officials. Particularly notorious was Etienne Foullé.[24] He was besieged in Tulle by thousands of peasants and forced to free a local *seigneur* who had been ringleader in concerted resistance to the *taille*. The *trésoriers* of this region refused to support Foullé who was called to the *parlement* of Toulouse to answer for his actions. Epernon's *ordonnances* were quashed by the high court. As if despairing of decisive action from the top, he had taken the law into his own hands. All was not plain sailing either for the *parlement*. In June, for example, it registered the royal declaration outlawing the Condéan generals. Bouillon, Turenne and la Rochefoucauld. But in July it raised 2,000 troops to attack Epernon's *intendant* Morant,[25] protested against the detention of Condé and violations of the reform programme. In Bordeaux *parlement* refused to register the declaration of outlawry and the city filled with Condéans. Incited by the princess the crowd urged their magistrates into open support.

It will be apparent therefore that the military victories of the crown, even the recovery of Bordeaux and the defeat of Turenne, tell only half the story. Sustained by an alliance that rested on the good faith of Gondi, the public spirit of Orléans, and the consistency of Mme de Chevreuse, Mazarin may have felt that he was well out of Paris, away from *frondeur* scowls and whispers, savouring again the military life. In the year he made only three brief visits to the capital to see that his agents were in good heart, his potential enemies kept in check. No concessions that he could make were sufficient to satisfy the leaders who found that real power still eluded them. Vendôme, now admiral and governor of Burgundy, and his son Mercoeur, viceroy of Catalonia, were enthusiastic for the royal cause; Beaufort, the other son, was still frustrated, craving more action. Holding in his hands the title-deeds of revolution, but unsure what to do with them, Gondi was offended by Anne's reluctance to ask the Pope to make him a Cardinal. Orléans, always vulnerable to conspirators' flattery, was closely watched on Mazarin's behalf by Le Tellier: the war minister worked to sustain Orléans's sense of importance by sharing military information and plans.

Mazarin's position rested essentially on the *frondeurs'* vehement opposition to the Condéans: he was simply for them the lesser of evils. They continued to agitate, mainly to secure more concessions. Châteauneuf and de Maisons did their best to keep *Parlement* content and Paris quiet, though by trying to implement the reform programme rather than standing firm as Mazarin would have preferred. In this approach they were surely being realistic, indeed constructive. Every month brought closer the happy day when Louis could be declared of age.[26] How large a place it had in court thinking can be seen from the agreement of 3 July, drawn up by Le Tellier, to which Orléans was persuaded to put his name. 'The queen and Monsieur are agreed that when the king attains his majority they should secure his agreement that the said Princes should be detained for at least the first four years of his majority.' Meanwhile the more harmonious the political climate, the more likely it was that the regime would survive.

The Condéans could not win *Parlement* to their side: the Spanish connection stuck in the gullet of these lawyers, with their keen sense of *patrie*, as the foundation of political morality. Mazarin needed more than that, however, to build a solid party in *Parlement*. Some of its members might accept the substantial *douceurs* that came their way, but most still realised that he had no sympathy for their original cause. They realised that he was still pressing persistently at weak points or sympathetic individuals. They could not rely on cooperation from the Hôtel de Ville. They had secured the appointment of Antoine Lefèbvre,[27] as *prévôt des marchands*, only to find out that he was as much Mazarin's man as his predecessor.

20

THE FIRST EXILE

The crown was apparently emerging victorious from 'the War of the Princesses' but there remained unresolved issues, notably the future of the princes, which dulled the prospect of a lasting peace. Mazarin's tactics had changed at every turn; but he remained set upon certain goals. Indeed he could not imagine working for the crown in any other way. Nor could Molé do much for him, torn as he was between legal scruple, sympathy for Condé and concern for the king. Nor was Orléans the ally he would have liked. Mazarin still looked for military victories over the Condéan-Spanish party: Orléans and Le Tellier favoured diplomacy and Orléans could be forceful. In the critical summer debates in *Parlement*, deaf to the clamour of a bribed mob, he argued strongly against the early release of the princess. *Parlement* had rejected pleas for support from Bordeaux – instead Orléans was mandated to try to persuade the regent to work out a compromise with the Guienne rebels, that being what Talon called 'public business' which only she could handle. A delegation of *Parlement* was to accompany the duke, to consider their grievances. So *Parlement* maintained its rights while deferring to royal authority.

Atrocities on both sides had made peace harder to achieve. Hurt by a demand by the Bordeaux rebels for his banishment, Mazarin would not at first consider amnesty for the Condéans; nor did he like the intervention of *Parlement* following Turenne's invasion of Picardy (August, 1650). Turenne planned to march towards Paris and secure the freedom of the princes. The *frondeurs* failed to persuade Orléans to move them to the Bastille:[1] since Broussel's son was governor, it would effectively have placed the princes at their mercy. Instead, *Parlement* and Orléans negotiated a peace plan. Orléans meanwhile worked with the capital's authorities to organise a second defence of Paris. To provide funds the sovereign courts advanced their *paulette* fees for three years. The prisoners, following Orléans's proposal, were moved to a safer château, Marcousis, on his own domain.

After Turenne had withdrawn his troops, Mazarin had entered more seriously into negotiations and worked with characteristic care for detail.

Orléans managed to persuade the judges to assist. The outcome was the treaty of 1 October. Mazarin believed that *Parlement* had given too much away. Noble followers of Condé were banished from Bordeaux and made to renounce their treaty with Spain; but otherwise they escaped scot-free. Mazarin thought it a bad precedent; he also deplored the chance missed to endow the crown through confiscations of property. They had however ignored demands for his banishment and for the release of the princes. Now a peace existed, at least on paper, for virtually all of France. There was a chance of negotiating with Spain with a relatively free hand. It was even possible that the king's supposedly grateful subjects would start paying their taxes again. The initiative rested once more with the regent and Mazarin, but with it a delicate problem. Was it politic to release the princes? If so, when?

At all cost the *frondeurs* should be prevented from casting their lot with the Condéans. *Parlement* could not be relied on indefinitely to endorse such an arbitrary act as the arrest of the princes; yet some of its members accepted the absolutist doctrine of royal justice, even arguing that Turenne should have been one of the prisoners as well. Such issues were raised by the prolonged trial of the *intendant* Foullé, whose robust defence centred on the fact that he used force only to subdue rebellious subjects. Those, like Broussel, who believed him to have acted with unnecessary cruelty, could turn against the ministry which had authorised it. That he did not appreciate the vital part *Parlement* had played in containing conflict and restoring peace, took their compliance for granted, and failed to see that the issue of illegal detention might lead to another noble Fronde, was to become the charge against Mazarin: it deserves consideration.

Between October 1650 and February 1651 Mazarin lost friends and made further enemies. He had spent effort and money in building up a party in *Parlement*. Such tactics might do more to confuse, than to build a reliable system of support. Now he was untypically inactive. Had he, as Moote suggests, lost his nerve? 'The politics of duplicity had given way to the politics of indecision'. It is likely that he was simply exhausted. The sheer physical effort of campaigning under the conditions of this confusing civil war had taken a toll. It is possible too that he was sometimes out of his depth. Resourceful though he was, he could still have been baffled by the complexity of the issues. His information tended to be of the sort that induces irrational fears rather than provides reliable evidence. Paranoia is too strong a term to use in relation to a man so evidently sane. But some misapprehensions and suspicions, bordered on the obsessive. They were focused on one man seen correctly to be an enemy, but perhaps incorrectly, as a dedicated and deadly one. In fact Gondi was an incorrigible intriguer; he was also vain and capable of almost any arrangement that would lead to personal promotion. He was not the kind of opponent most to be feared, the implacable, single-minded fanatic.

The effect of the *Mazarinades* has to be reckoned with. There was no precedent for such a battery of hostile propaganda to be directed at one man, about whom there was simply nothing bad or absurd that could not be said. Insecure from the very nature of his position, Mazarin needed reassurance but received abuse. English events played their part too. European opinion was used to state trials, as of an Oldenbarneveldt[2] or a Montmorency; even to an assassination, a Henry IV, a Concini. A state trial and execution of an anointed king, the formation of a republic – these were different – shockingly so. Mazarin had reason to feel vulnerable. His temporary accommodation with the *frondeurs* had not allayed his hostility towards them. Was malignant conspiracy not their nature? Was republicanism not their principle? Le Tellier had reported to him that Gondi had claimed to have heard the cry 'République' during the winter siege of Paris – and that it would have been easy for the *frondeurs* to have proclaimed a republic by removing a few monarchists. It is more than likely that the scare was also a hint, to Le Tellier's master, that he, Gondi, could be won over to the crown – at a price. Le Tellier and Colbert, having no love for Gondi, and with something of the bureaucrat's literal-mindedness, assured Mazarin that he was indeed a republican. Undoubtedly, as his writing and reported conversation witness, it preyed on the Cardinal's mind.

Condé also loomed large. Only the argument that he was extremely dangerous could have justified his imprisonment; only the idea that he was no longer so could justify his release. Before this simple logic, consideration of the tactical advantage to be gained by an act of clemency could hardly stand. Mazarin's subjective view was coloured by his awareness of responsibility for the initial act. As for Turenne the *frondeur,* as opposed to Turenne the great captain, it must be stressed that he had not acted under Condé's direction: he had been his own man. Ever the reluctant rebel, he never forgot the greatness of his family nor, sustained by his devout wife, the claims of his Protestant faith. Like Cromwell, he could be expected, in his laconic, deliberate way, 'to make some conscience of what he did'. Like many soldiers caught up in politics, he also tended to be pragmatic. Now he was having second thoughts – and they were turning towards his duty to the young king, as well as to the material gains to be expected from such a *volte-face.* Meanwhile, to Mazarin, Turenne was still an unknown quality.

Encumbered with this mental furniture, Mazarin was reduced to playing a waiting game. That meant a loss of initiative just when others were all too keen to seize it. He tried to make each group feel that he was on their side. Each therefore believed that he could not be a worthwhile ally, that a way must be found of combining against him. In opposition to him they could sink their differences. Mazarin blocked the way to power: together they could shift him. He meanwhile stood back from any Condéan or *frondeur* proposal of alliance. He did not follow up a suggestion that Condé be allowed to go into voluntary exile. He would not press on Anne Gondi's fervent wish for him to become a Cardinal. He advised Anne to delay her return to Paris till November because he was concerned about her health. He might have thought of her previous enthusiastic reception and its tonic effect. Her delay fed hostile rumour. Tradesmen suffered from the absence of the court. By November the city was seething with discontent. How far, too, Mazarin was from encouraging a conciliatory mood is shown by his having the princes moved a second time, from Marcousis to Le Havre. Now under Mazarin's control, it was the fortress which Condé had tried to secure. So poisoned had the atmosphere become by December, that when the minister did act with determination against the traditional enemies of the state and helped secure the victory of Rethel, the military success was acclaimed only by committed Mazarinists. Most were indifferent. Meanwhile his motives were strongly impugned.

It was widely assumed that he was bent on keeping the war going to secure his power. Condéans expected him to follow Rethel by another coup, so they began to treat with the *frondeurs* for a defensive pact. The situation was tailor-made for the conspiratorial genius of Mme de Chevreuse. Resourceful as ever in the pursuit of family interest, she planned a double marriage to further the alliance of the two grandest representatives, after the king himself, of the royal house of Bourbon. Her daughter was to marry Conti; Condé's son and heir was to marry one of Gaston's younger daughters. In the delicate process of soundings and bargainings, Mme de Chevreuse could now count on the formidable Princesse Palatine. Bishop Bossuet would one day recall 'the ceaseless fertility of her political expedients' and 'her ability to penetrate the secrets and win the confidence of all parties'.[3] Behind this Parisian stage, where several would-be directors were vying to shape the story according to their own interpretation of the text, with variants of plot and roles, but a single ending in mind, all the Princesse's tact and charm would be required if the play were to come into production.

Mazarin now faced the possibilities that he had always dreaded: Condéans and *frondeurs* in concerted opposition, acting with *Parlement*, committed to freedom for the princes; a ministry headed by Châteauneuf; a Cardinal's hat for Gondi. The argument for a new ministry was reinforced by the evident breakdown of the old. It would be argued by Séguier and Le Tellier that the blame lay with the removal of the *intendants*. Séguier, already a veteran of office, now displaced by Châteauneuf, would keep his options open. Le Tellier, indebted to Mazarin, implicated in most important government business, some of it decidedly irregular, would remain attached: holding high office, latterly as Chancellor, for forty-two years, he would never have cause to regret it. Mazarin's *clientèle* remained substantially intact. They could see that he was still persona grata with the queen. But for those outside the loyal circle, Mazarin had become a convenient label for whatever in government was specially resented: the insolent dominance of Parisian officialdom, the corruption of private deals between ministers and financiers – or simply attempts to raise tax at levels which would have been regarded as light three years before. The Cardinal might have countered the hostile wave more effectively if he had been better served in the provinces, and not involved in local quarrels which led back directly to the question of his patronage and judgement.

In some provinces there was virtually a vacuum in government – in Languedoc, where Orléans was titular governor, but ineffectual because he had to be in Paris; Guienne, where Epernon had caused so much opposition; Provence, where Alais lingered, though officially dismissed; Champagne and Burgundy, where Mazarin's agent's exercised temporary powers till the fate of the imprisoned governors should be decided: efforts to raise taxes, billet or supply troops had therefore a look of irregularity, if not illegality, that compounded officials' problems. When those provinces demanded a moderate governor, they meant a man sympathetic to the concerns of *Parlement* and tax-payers. The *parlement* of Toulouse led the sovereign courts in Languedoc in resistance to royal officials by all possible means: *arrêts* against the unpopular *intendant* Morant, reversal of decisions of the royal council, appeals to Anne and, most seriously, to the *Parlement* of Paris. The old cry of 'union' was raised again. Well might Mazarin have felt that he was under siege. His sudden decision to go to the army in December may have answered a desperate need to break out.

How wide the movement for reform had again become is illustrated by the hardening attitude of a body which had not yet, at least in its corporate capacity, become involved. A group of nobles had revived the time-worn call for a States-General. The Church, which would provide the First Estate in that body, had long kept a wary distance from *Parlement* which was generally Gallican in outlook and liable periodically, to bristle with anti-clericalism. Now the Church Assembly, convoked in October 1650 to approve the *don gratuit,* heard the language of reform. These assemblies, in effect national religious councils, received the *cahiers,* lists of grievances from each province, and could make formal remonstrances to the crown. In 1645 Gondi had been summoned to court to receive Mazarin's demand that he retract a speech to the Assembly that had so offended her. This early encounter had been influential, both in confirming the court's view of a troublesome prelate, and in promoting the *dévôts'* picture of Mazarin as alien, secular and cynical. It was usual at these assemblies for some individual group of clergy to raise issues which

175

called for action; so they could establish the most favourable position from which to bargain over the amount of their 'gift'. It was inevitable that political questions should now impinge. Interest was generated by numerous personal relationships: most noble families had an ecclesiastical member. The greater the family, the higher he was likely to be in the church hierarchy, even if his benefice was a source of income rather than a place of work. So it was that the issue of Conti's imprisonment was raised, since he was *abbé-général* of the order of Cluny:[4] thus a member of the First Estate. Anne and Mazarin were still at Mantes, when delegates came to request Conti's release. They were sent on their way with a brusque refusal. In November the Assembly renewed its claim on Conti's behalf – and refused the *don gratuit*.

With royal government widely foiled and abused and many looking to *Parlement* for leadership, it was inevitable that the temperature on the Ile de la Cité would rise again to the point at which judges would consider further controls over the government. First judges examined and denounced cases of unregistered taxes, assaults by soldiers on communities and individuals and secret deals between ministers and *traitants*. When appeals on behalf of the princes flowed in, Mazarin was forced to weigh the balance of risk. To release them would encourage further excesses on the part of nobles whom he regarded as beyond redemption. To stand firm might be to bring about that union of *Parlement* with *frondeurs* and Condéans that could be the basis of another Fronde, more dangerous, because of the mood in the country, than anything yet seen.

Mazarin's main strategy, up to this point, had been to manipulate *Parlement* through key appointments and individual overtures. He seems to have thought that *parlement*'s interest lay so demonstrably with the upholding of the king's authority that, with good management, they would resist the appeals of the rebellious nobles. For such management he relied on chosen men, like the precocious and personable young Nicolas Fouquet, who replaced the retiring *procureur-général*, Blaise Méliand. Fouquet's elevation was resented and his ignorance in procedural matters exposed. At a critical time, while Fouquet consulted and stumbled, the anti-Mazarinist judges proceeded with their plan of campaign.

Meanwhile Mazarin failed to win Molé to his side. That conscientious man still believed that *Parlement*'s duty was to maintain law and order. If he wished to serve Condé, it was as a way of exercising a restraining influence. Mazarin had suggested expedients such as the summoning of a grand assembly in Paris. The council had opposed it. He had therefore fallen back on delaying tactics – the excuse provided by Anne's illness, which he hoped would arouse sympathy. By Christmas she was convalescing. *Parlement* merely postponed the debate by four days. It was then hectic and rowdy as arguments were launched from prepared positions,

Condéan, *frondeur*, Mazarinist; few minds were changed. Some compromise was inevitable, and eventually *Parlement*'s remonstrance was limited to the matter of the princes' release.

Parlement's correct language hardly hid the fact that it was now putting its authority behind the central demand of the opposition. They required Mazarin to accept what he could, with some credit, have done in October. By Christmas *Parlement*'s successful defiance had put fresh heart into the rebels' cause. On 20 December Gondi went to *Parlement* to call for the liberation of the princes and was followed home by a procession of carriages as members of all factions queued to subscribe to the cause. At first Anne and Mazarin angrily refused to give anything further away but eventually Anne promised to free the prisoners, on condition their friends disarmed: as for *Parlement*, it was their duty to hold subjects to their obedience, not to encourage revolt. The menace of Spanish troops on the frontier was invoked to lend point to a lecture on duty which served only to convince *Parlement* that it must stand up for the princes.

Orléans had been uncomfortable for some time in his delicate role as spokesman for the crown. Old friends and habits ensured that he was constantly unsettled. He had come to regret acceding to the arrest of the princes. He resented Mazarin's position, standing, it seemed, between him and the queen. His wife said that he laboured more in making a decision than she in giving birth to her children. In this case Mme de Chevreuse's match-making, the devices of Gondi, the mediation of the Princesse Palatine, were influential. On 30 January 1651 Gaston, with the Princesse, de la Mothe-Houdancourt, Viole and Nemours[5] as co-signatories, resolved 'to withdraw from the counsels of Cardinal Mazarin, as the true cause of all the disorders of the state and divisions within the royal house', and pledged himself to secure the freedom of the princes.

A separate agreement reinforced the treaty: Gondi received an assurance that Conti would renounce his ecclesiastical ambitions and would espouse Mlle de Chevreuse. On 1 February Gaston informed Anne that he would not come back to court until the Cardinal was dismissed. Mazarin apparently enraged him by declaring that he, Orléans, was as much at risk as the minister from men who would stop at nothing till they had deposed the king. Mazarin was provoked into pardonable exaggeration: but Orléans probably needed to lose his temper to give him courage. It was reported that he had shouted 'madman' as he stormed out of the room; that Anne had been in tears. Gaston's breach with the minister with whom he had worked for nearly eight years, along with Mazarin's unguarded charge that *Parlement* was anti-monarchist, was enough to make that body throw caution to the winds. On 3 February they remonstrated again for the release of the princes and for the banishment of Mazarin. The law had now pronounced what the majority of the political nation appeared to want.

Anne and Mazarin agreed on a strategy. It is at such critical junctures that they seem most obviously to have behaved like partners. Mazarin left the city on 6 February, to lodge at Saint-Germain. Anne and her family, it was planned, would make their secret departure if Orléans and *Parlement* remained uncooperative. Mazarin did not intend to lose control. He thought that he could play on the hopes and fears of the different groups while relying on Molé to secure order in Paris. He saw that they had fundamentally different objectives and would eventually fall apart. Meanwhile neither Orléans nor Condé was prepared to forgive him. Nor could Anne escape. Supported by the vote of *Parlement*, Orléans had ordered the city authorities, civil and military, to take their orders from him. He was possibly alerted by Mme de Chevreuse; in any case rumours abounded and it was only common prudence to set the civic militia to guard the Palais-Royal. Anne believed that Gaston planned to seize the king: his pretext would be to prevent Louis from leaving for the country. On the night of the 9–10 February, she told him that he must calm the people who, by midnight, were milling round in the courtyard. Then she took a calculated risk. She invited a group to come in, to see for themselves.

The doors of the king's chamber were opened, people crowded round the bed. As they watched the boy sleeping, or pretending to, their hostility turned, in embarrassed fashion, to admiration. They shuffled out to reassure the rest outside. Gradually, the crowd began to disperse. Anne's coolness, her instinct to trust to Parisian sentiment, had served her well. It did not however relieve her political difficulties. Gaston was still truculent. With civic guards placed at the gates of Paris, she had no option but to accept her virtual imprisonment: she was, in Talon's delicate phrase, 'in libera custodia'. To win Parisian hearts, she must now accede graciously to the requests which she had hitherto rebuffed. So she received *Parlement*'s thanks for removing Mazarin from power – with what feelings can be imagined – and issued a declaration excluding from the royal councils all foreigners, including those who had been naturalised, and those owing allegiance to foreign princes. The latter phrase included the Pope. Anti-clerical and xenophobic in tone, it was aimed specifically at Mazarin. Believing that Anne intended to take refuge in a general promise of compliance. *Parlement* added an *arrêt*, to the effect that if Mazarin did not leave the country within two weeks, his life could not be guaranteed.

So cornered, on 10 February, Anne gave orders to the sieur de Bar to effect the princes' release: privately he was told to place himself under the orders of Mazarin. Meanwhile Mazarin was travelling to le Havre to negotiate their release on his own authority. Did he hope that he could win reprieve in this way? Condé was not to be swayed by his genial approach – by some accounts obsequious. He rode off towards Paris, with Conti and Longueville, in what became a triumphal procession. They entered Paris on 16 February; on 28 April *Parlement* registered a royal declaration of their innocence. In the presence of Gaston and Condé, they ordered Mazarin's arrest. If he were captured he was to be detained in the Conciergerie prison and subjected to judicial inquiry: the same applied to friends, associates and servants. The Norman *parlement* rebuffed him. Slowly and reluctantly he made his way across northern France, from one secure place to another, with an escort of a hundred cavaliers to ensure that no zealous official sought to carry out *Parlement*'s order. At Péronne he had the reassuring company of marshal d'Hocquincourt,[6] one of those soldiers who had little time for the follies of Paris, wanted to pursue their trade and respected Mazarin for his contribution to the war effort.

His mood swung with news, or lack of news, from Paris. He wrote every day, at length at first, as if still in control. To Le Tellier, for example, from Normandy, he had urged strong action to secure the city, then offered detailed plans for the escape of the royal family. Le Tellier, Servien and his nephew Lionne, the queen's *secrétaire des commandements*, were offered varying analyses of the situation, as if he was arguing in council, with exhortations to be loyal and diligent, interspersed with complaints about the way he had been treated. From these daily epistles, bearing the marks of haste and worry in their loose phrasing, certain main concerns stand out. Gondi was the arch-enemy, 'with no other plan but to rouse sedition'; Molé had a majority in *Parlement*, with substantial support outside it among *bons bourgeois* and *honnestes gens*; everything should be done to wield a party among them; even among the princes there were potential allies. La Rochefoucauld, for example, was worth working on, having the ear of the princes; Lionne was urged in tones near desperation; 'if you can, by whatever means possible, win over Viole and *président* Perrault,[7] it would be a great coup'. Certain reliable men were named: a number of soldiers likely to see their future in service to the crown, Schomberg, Grancey, Candâle, Fabert[8] among them; clergy, like Gondrin, archbishop of Sens and de la Feuillade, archbishop of Embrun.[9] His letters have a constructive side as, besides tactical points, he was defining a strategy, based on the coherence and loyalty of his chosen agents and the knowledge that the king would soon be of age.

Inevitably however Mazarin saw politics more than ever in terms of animosities towards him. Typically he discerned a new female influence, a Mlle de Beaumont 'who does the worst she can against me' on behalf of Châteauneuf. Self-justification, even self-pity also featured. To Anne he felt obliged to recount the records of his service to the state since 1643, to stress his attachment to the nation that he 'had always honoured and cherished with so great a tenderness', to assure her that he would not do anything to prejudice the state or displease her. But people 'would be astounded that a cardinal who has the honour of being godfather to

179

the king should be treated in this way and that twenty-two years of faithful service should not have been sufficient to acquire an assured retreat in some part of the realm whose bounds have been so notably increased by his efforts'.

In her personal dealings it is likely that Anne accepted Mazarin's guidance: for example, 'she should make much of marshal de Gramont but not trust Mme d'Aiguillon'. For a man who had won power by assiduous attention to the inclinations of individuals, the need to work by proxy was surely frustrating. It was hard to influence, let alone control, the political process from three or four days' ride away; there were hazards and delays involved in the use of agents, like Millet or Bartet,[10] men of indifferent repute, necessarily working under cover. Mazarin was being over-anxious when he inferred that Le Tellier was working against him, but there were considerations beside client loyalty for any minister with his career to make, and his own *clientèle* to support; no favours could be sought from Châteauneuf, Chavigny, or even Séguier. Whatever her personal feelings towards Mazarin, Anne would do nothing that might put at risk her main object, the preservation until his majority of her beloved son.

At Sedan, which he had known under happier circumstances as Richelieu's emissary, now governed by the dependable Fabert,[11] Mazarin was joined by his nieces and nephew, from the refuge which Anne had provided in her favoured monastery, Val de Grace; with them came the faithful Ondedei. He also received articles required to keep him in his usual style, silver, plate and linen; he already had some jewels and gold, squirrelled away before he left Paris. He was particularly sensitive to the charge that he had despoiled the crown jewels. He referred ironically to 'all the millions of *les Halles*', where indeed rumours abounded that he had banked abroad vast sums, nine million according to one account. Any such arrangements, then as now, are likely to be private. It appears that they were on a relatively small scale and that he was justified in claiming, at this stage, that his fortune had been 'sacrificed freely to assist the king in the most pressing necessities of his affairs'. The time of the great treasure hunt lay ahead. If he had disappeared from the history books at this point, he would not have left a name for greed or avarice. Those unpleasant traits were encouraged by the humiliating circumstances of exile.

When Mazarin crossed the frontier, Habsburg hospitality gave no cause for complaint. Archduke Leopold provided a grand escort for a man whom he would rather see in exile than in office, who might even serve Spain. Like a victorious general he was accorded a triple salute by the fortress cannon of Juliers before the Elector's chamberlain escorted him to palatial lodgings at Brühl. His exile would last from early April to December. It would be frustrating; it was not uncomfortable. The Rhineland Electorate of Cologne was, moreover, well placed to be the centre for the operations to which he now had to devote himself: the defeat of the Fronde and his rehabilitation.

In Paris the promised enquiry was set up, and it continued for the rest of the year. The charges were familiar: Mazarin had mismanaged the finances, wasted revenues, sent money out of the country; had misled the regent and the king about political and diplomatic matters; had prevented the making of peace with Spain. The popular view was less restrained. This year saw the production of the *Mazarinades*, already a thriving folk industry, rise to new peaks of ingenuity and slander. With over five thousand titles in all, they were anonymous, though it is possible in some cases to identify authors and patrons; the latter included Gaston, Condé and Gondi, though it is unlikely that the first two took much personal interest in their production. They ranged from the subtle to the crude, from the naive to the personal, from *pièces d'occasion* to considered statements of political principle. Clearly some of them enjoyed an audience larger than the circulation of printed copies as stories were passed on, no doubt embroidered. Nothing to do with Mazarin escaped notice. No interest, including Mazarin's, went unrepresented.

A composite picture of the Cardinal, as portrayed by the hostile majority of the *Mazarinades*, might run as follows. Born to an obscure Sicilian family, his father being variously described as oyster-seller, button-seller, pirate, inn-keeper or bankrupt, he had wormed his way into Richelieu's confidence, then persuaded the queen mother that he was indispensable. These feats he had achieved by the tricks of the mountebank; by playing on her vanity with scents and knick-knacks, by capturing her affections by his love-potions. So he contrived to rule France from the royal bed. He was a usurer, scrounger, hypocrite, charlatan, lecher. A recurring word is *mollesse*: it suggests effeminacy. Much was made of 'unnatural vice'. In descriptions of his *créatures* as 'perfumed minions' there was a harking back to another period, the late 1580s and early 1590s, when civil war, the absence of one king, Henry III, evidently degenerate, then another, Henry IV – a Huguenot – saw folk fantasies inflaming the sense that all was out of order, as Paris sought to govern itself. Now it was an alien minister whose alleged sins were a metaphor for anarchy at large. 'He disrupted all of nature in order to destroy the state.' As with Henry IV's becoming Catholic and recovering his capital, the state would not be whole until Louis XIV were to rule – and dismiss his minister. A corrupt regime was further conveyed by the allegation that he sent back French money to his family and brought them in to share in the cornucopia of his illicit dealings. The queen might be 'a whore', but the king was safe from all aspersions. In this popular fantasy which owed less to ascertainable facts than the tales of winter firesides, the gossip of tavern and vestry and the enterprise of back-street printers,

Louis was the object of loyal sympathy, soon to be released from the grip of his wicked godfather. In January 1649, for example, Mazarin had 'kidnapped the king'. It was allowed that the queen, though Spanish and sensuous, was capable of redemption – if only she could be made to renounce Mazarin. But as for him – exile was not enough. He merited the death of an enemy of France.

The *Mazarinades* were part of Parisian entertainment: it was a relief to some to be able to hiss at the villain. One predictable element was xenophobia. National stereotypes flourished long before the sentiment came to serve nationalist politics. There was shameless demagogy. Popular religion played its part in the hands of Gondi's well-schooled priests, notably that archetypal zealot, Rousse,[11] *curé* of Saint-Roch. There was crude political calculation; also advocacy of a particular interest or tactic. What was largely missing was political argument. If the term '*Mazarinade*' be stretched to include a long treatise, *Collection of True and Important Maxims for the Instruction of the King*, a case could be made for Claude Joly[12] as a serious political commentator. Canon of Notre-Dame, sympathetic at different times to Gondi, Condé and, more consistently, *Parlement*, Joly harked back to the Renaissance monarchy in the spirit of such neglected writers as Balzac, revived the constitutional ideas of Claude Seyssel,[13] and urged the sovereign to eschew Italian, Machiavellian politics, to seek good ministers, and not to overtax the people. In this somewhat anodyne homily, the one novelty is that the ministers should be elected; the king would choose from three candidates put forward as honourable and experienced men by the sovereign courts.

An imaginary address by *Eight Peasants from Eight Provinces* represented not the rural mass, but what might be called 'the country programme' or typical concerns of the *noblesse de campagne*. The calling of an Estates-General, the opening of royal offices to nobles, reduction in the number of lawyers and administrators, abolition of pensions to great nobles, a special levy upon the wealthy for the improvement of the Louvre, contributed to an interesting list of demands. The maintenance of the Edict of Nantes was balanced by a call for the banishment of Jews and restraint of the Jesuits. Foreign soldiers were not to be employed, nor of course foreign ministers. The sheer range of proposals, amounting to a comprehensive programme, sets it apart from the mass of pamphlets. Picking up various provincial prejudices en route and with them a distinctly chauvinist tone, it still finds its focus in mistrust of Mazarin. History was pressed into service, as in the *Chronology of Queens brought to Misfortune by the Insolence of their Favourites*. Sometimes the impression is of a column in a popular newspaper, making a sensation out of a topical issue. *The Queen's Convulsions the Night before Mazarin's Departure* has her waking from a nightmare in which Paris has become a desert, her subjects like wild beasts. Appalled she cries: 'I am losing my son's state, my reputation, and my subjects' hearts, and all for the sake of a wretched foreigner ...' A number took the form of lay sermons, with titles which convey the flavour: *Truth Speaking to the Queen* or, more ponderously, *The Laughter and Tears of France at the Conduct of the Queen and the Council of State.* It will, of course, have been clear to Anne that her popular reputation suffered by her association with Mazarin. It may be however that she had the wit to see that the farcical elements in the orchestrated campaign of vilification could only discredit its conductors.

Mazarin may have won Anne's heart: more important he had won her head. The insolent advice of his avowed enemies only strengthened her conviction. Even Mme de Chevreuse was losing her power to enchant: there was little left of the friendship of younger, more frivolous days. Hardest to resist must have been those closest to her. For La Porte,[14] typical of the old servant who could tolerate no rival for his mistress' affections and regarded it as his privilege to speak his mind, nothing was too bad to believe about Mazarin. He was the source of many libellous stories. In the end he tried Anne's patience too far – and she dismissed him. From her ladies-in-waiting, Mme de Senécy and Mme de Hautefort,[15] she had been receiving the message almost from the start of the regency: the necessity for prudence was reinforced by the concern of *dévôts* for the spiritual health of one whom they regarded as their own. Inevitably such a message was political, reflecting at best the desire for peace, but also the interests of Spain. Most difficult of all, perhaps for that reason most exasperating to Anne, must have been the admonitions of Mme de Motteville, so sensible and staunch. When she ventured to say, in February 1651, that she thought the queen to be well rid of Mazarin, Anne, as she recalled, explained that it was hard to find a minister who did not, to some extent, serve the interest of a faction. She believed that she was 'duty bound to defend a minister who is taken from me by force'. In her own way that is exactly what she would do. Meanwhile she had no option but to wait for his enemies to overreach themselves.

Parlement had won a Pyrrhic victory. It had made the regent reverse policies and surrender key points in her proudly held position: it had done this by legal process, without violence and without yielding too much to noble allies. But *Parlement* made a costly error when it adopted Broussel's anti-clerical declaration.[16] It aroused old prejudices and created a new and divisive issue. Aimed at Mazarin, it antagonised not only Gondi, but also Châteauneuf: it was not so inconceivable that the septuagenarian *garde des sceaux* should become a Cardinal: Mazarin once considered promoting it as a tactical move. So the declaration disrupted the unity of the alliance and contributed to the anarchy into which the country was drifting. Instead of congratulating *Parlement* on securing the release of Conti, the General Assembly denounced it for attacking the Church. Lesser nobles, then gathering in Paris for an informal assembly of their own, supported the clergy: they in turn voted, on 15 March, to unite with the nobles in calling for an Estates-General. *Parlement* detested the idea of an assembly in which the Third Estate would be subordinate.

The political stalemate could only be to Anne's advantage. She was determined to seize it, so she set about creating an inner council of Mazarin's henchmen, Le Tellier, Lionne and Servien. They worked in his interests, building bridges with individual *parlementaires*, or sowing where possible the seeds of division. Anne also showed tactical skills which reflected Mazarin's tutoring. On 24 March she announced that an Estates-General would be called after the king's assumption of full regal powers on 8 September. That event would create the power which could at once be used to defer its meeting. So, with *Parlement* opposing, and with smooth words from Orléans, the nobles dissolved their gathering. Anne would also find encouragement in expressions of loyalty from the clergy. After their Assembly had voted a small *don gratuit*, their spokesman was unctuous in his address to the king: 'Sire, your minority, very wisely conducted till now by the admirable care of the queen, although it has not succeeded in avoiding the occurrence of agitations within the state, has seen our body remain steadfast in the fidelity which we have sworn to it.' That might seem more like a marker for a future regime than an expression of satisfaction with the present, for *Parlement* secured its clause about French and foreign Cardinals. The Declaration of 19 April, to which Châteauneuf at first refused to put his seal, was so drafted that it looked like an undertaking unwillingly ceded by the queen, one that could, therefore, be overruled in September.

The most certain prospect of better days to come for the crown lay in the quarrels of *Les Grands*. Gondi responded to the ban on ecclesiastical ministers by assuring Anne that she did not have to give in to *Parlement*: if he were Cardinal he would soon get the better of *Parlement*. With Orléans standing bemused in the wings and Condé disputing every point with the *frondeurs*, Anne was emboldened to resume the initiative. She rarely showed to better advantage than during these months, her pride tempered by humbling experiences, her resolve stiffened by the absence of her devoted minister, her hopes buoyed by the prowess and promise of her elder son. In April she made a sweeping change in her ministry: Molé was given the seals, Chavigny made a minister and given a place on the council. The appointments upset the *frondeurs* whose frantic negotiations with Condé achieved only the removal of Molé, which left chancellor Séguier with full powers. Apart from what the discomfited Gondi called 'the legitimate *fronde*', Orléans lost the most. He was not consulted about the initial appointments; he was left looking ridiculous as Condé moved into the central position. He enjoyed far-ranging powers, such, on the face of it, as no subject had before. He could claim credit for not doing what some followers urged, assuming the regency and sending

Anne to Val-de-Grace. Having exchanged the governorship of Burgundy for that of Guienne, through his own estates, his offices and those of his associates, he controlled a quarter of France.

21

MAZARIN RETURNS

Mazarin thought that Condé had been given too much. Insatiable, Condé still found grievances to nurse, notably that Conti had not been given the governorship of Provence to complete the southern bloc. He may have feared assassination: some *frondeurs* even believed that Anne might be sympathetic to such an event. He certainly never felt at ease in the capital. In July 1651 he left, to seek the reassurance of his strongholds and the adulation of his partisans. *Parlement* was left with the disagreeable after-effects of its heady political ventures. To endorse Condé's actions now would be to create a new civil war: to support Anne would be to incur the risk of her recalling Mazarin; to do nothing would be to abdicate from hard-won authority. At the heart of the predicament was the fact that *Parlement* was neither an executive nor a representative assembly. Only Anne could appoint ministers: they were beholden only to her. By summer she appeared to be moving back on to her high ground, sufficiently confident to be able to accept temporary setbacks. Her inner council, all Mazarin's men, Le Tellier, Servien and Lionne, needed no prompting from Cologne to expose and exploit the grievances and divisions of the coalition that pretended to power.

Condé bombarded *Parlement* with appeals for support, even, on occasion returning to make his statement in person. His line was always the same: Mazarinists and *frondeurs* were the true enemies of the state. He avoided seeing Anne. She did not take his insults lying down, but engaged with spirit in the propaganda war. She turned the argument about arbitrary penalties to her advantage when urged to dismiss her Mazarinist ministers whom she had the undoubted right to appoint. Some judges may have taken more kindly to that argument since they were being won over by *douceurs* from Mazarin's agents. Molé was not to be bought, as Mazarin seems to have hoped. Taking views of past and future of a length to match his famous beard, Molé also had his own goals to pursue. No longer impressed by Condé, contemptuous of the *frondeurs*, he looked to have a leading role under a king whom he could use to fulfil his own conception of legal absolutism. Molé was not a *dévôt*, belong-

186

ing rather to the politique and Gallican tradition, opposed to foreign interference in church or state. But there was common ground with the *dévôts* in the cherishing of an idea of France which is still alive today in the idealisation, even among people far removed from it, of the peasant culture; also in his conviction that the crown was bound by the same moral laws as those governing the conduct of its subjects. A Mazarinist *politique* based on *raison d'état* could not therefore now be acceptable to him merely because Mazarin's opponents were themselves so reckless about the interests of the state.

It was difficult for *Parlement* to deal with Mazarinists when there seemed to be a steady seepage from the ranks of the righteous. Marriage was the new weapon in the Cardinal's armoury. The duc de Mercoeur was threatened with legal action if he married Mazarin's niece, Laura Mancini: it did not deter him.[1] The judges could try to assure the exclusion of Mazarin by securing a written promise from Anne: she eventually gave it – in September, when the forthcoming royal majority made it a meaningless gesture. 'Banned for perpetuity', Mazarin would 'be guilty of *lèse-majesté*' if he dared to return. But what if the king himself recalled him? The stern words meant little to Anne, as is shown by her private letters to Mazarin, conveyed through Millet. Accustomed as he was, however, to the half-truths of diplomacy, he could still not be sure that distance was not lending disenchantment. There are notes of anguish in his pleas to the queen. He wondered in early September, why she wanted him to go to Rome, where it was anticipated that there would be a Papal election. What use would he be there when he had no official position? He begged her not to send him 'into the hands of my enemies, to ask for charity in my birthplace, banished from France with shame'. He saw his enemies at work; she may merely have thought Rome a more becoming place of refuge. She gave up the idea and it was he who revived it, a sign of desperation, when he heard of *Parlement*'s registration of the letter of banishment: 'The king and queen, by an authentic act, have declared me a public thief, incompetent and an enemy to the peace of Christendom . . .' He said that he felt so ashamed that he wanted to die, and demanded a trial. How much of all this was play-acting on the part of both principals? We are left with his uncertainties: his hopes resting on her affection, and the king's, his fears for his standing when he no longer had ministerial allies. For in July Molé had got Anne's undertaking that she would dismiss her Mazarinist ministers.

Their loss, especially that of Le Tellier, would be a blow to government. That the responsible Molé could think that it was justifiable shows the extent to which domestic political issues were governing men's thinking. Back in Paris, Condé was obsessed by the tantalus of domestic power and the pretensions of the *frondeurs*. Matters came to a head when Parisians were invited to read the Condéan pamphlet: 'Articles agreed upon by M.

the Cardinal Mazarin and M. Châteauneuf . . . the Coadjutor of Paris and
Mme the Duchess de Chevreuse.' The title was the message. Anne charged
Condé with treason. On 21 August he swaggered into the Palais de Justice;
Gondi appeared at the same time: their followers shouted insults and
drew swords. Gondi was trapped near the door and could have been
killed but for prompt action by Champlâtreux.[2] It was hardly the way to
win support from sober magistrates. The most that could be achieved by
Molé was to extract from the reluctant regent a declaration exonerating
Condé. Since it was registered at the *lit de justice* in September, held to
mark Louis XIV's assumption of full royal authority, it was anyway worth
little. To Anne the fact that her thirteen-year-old son was true king was
worth everything. Cares remained, but some of the burden was lifted
from her shoulders.

The queen's successful defence of royal rights at the centre was not
conveyed in any way to the country at large. If this were peace, what
would civil war be like? Soldiers made no nice distinction between friend
and foe: if they were kept under arms but not paid, they might desert or
fend for themselves. The *arrêts* of *Parlement* were worth little when officers
connived at pillage and protected their men against the law. Inevitably
Parlement found itself leaning towards the executive's view. The excesses
of soldiers would continue till money were found to pay or disband them.
When *surintendant* des Maisons explained the basis of a new contract with
the *traitants, Parlement* stopped investigating its legality. Even a self-evident
case of breach of law, the levying of *gabelle* from the nobles of Poitou,
took weeks to resolve before a declaration confirming traditional exemption could be registered. If the *élus* could not collect the taxes unaided,
then *commissaires* had to go out, acting like the former *intendants*, but
under the aegis of *Parlement* and respectful towards local courts. Where
there was a royalist army and an *intendant* attached, there would be a
flurry of complaints and appeals. *Parlement* could then issue *arrêts* but
there remained the difficulty of restraining the *commissaire*'s activities to
the military sphere.[3] If, as *lieutenant-général*, Orléans took any view at all,
it was a military view: commanders must have control over discipline. If
they operated inside the frontiers, that must include supply, and so
requisitioning: taxation by another name – or plunder, it often seemed.

Nor could *Parlement* rely on local courts to be cooperative. There
were as many variables in the relationship between the crown, governor,
Parlement or other courts, as there were provinces. The *parlements* were
losing their enthusiasm for the Fronde as the hope of a union faded. All
over the country, specially where armies made their presence felt, there
was a mood of disillusionment with all distant or nominally legal authority.[4] The old parochial France of private deals and ties was reasserting
itself; the man to be trusted was the local *seigneur*, who could afford
protection, or the petty official who might turn a blind eye. 'A plague

on both your houses' was a natural reaction to the aimless violence which filled the worm's eye view. Condé cared little about what the worm felt. Anne might have pious regrets and charitable instincts, but little in her training had made her sensitive to the people's sufferings. She could not fail however to be gratified to see how they looked to the one *seigneur* they could all recognise: the king.

Louis XIV entered the *Parlement* of Paris on 7 September 1651, two days after this thirteenth birthday, under his mother's watchful eye, to deliver to the assembled courts his carefully rehearsed assertion of full royal powers.[5] The constitutional significance was beyond doubt. From being regent, with limited authority, she became the representative of the absolute powers vested in the king of France. The occasion was splendid even by the high standard that Parisians had come to expect. Bells rang from every church, cannons boomed from the fortresses, public fountains spouted wine. The young English gentleman, virtuoso, diarist and royalist, John Evelyn,[6] standing with the philosopher Thomas Hobbes[7] (soon to offer the world his own unsentimental notion of absolutism), watched a cavalcade which impressed them all the more by contrast with the recent 'execrable wickedness' of Evelyn's own sovereign's trial and execution. He saw

> The king himself, like a young Apollo, in a suit so covered with rich embroidery, that one could perceive nothing of the stuff under it; he went almost the whole way with his hat in hand, saluting the ladies and acclamators, who had filled the windows with their beauty, and the air with *Vive le Roi*. He seemed a prince of a grave yet sweet countenance.

Parisians too were impressed. The impact on the country is harder to judge, being measurable more by mood than by any immediate alteration in the terms of power. Condé was declared innocent *in absentia* but continued in defiance. It was what Mazarin wanted. Anne's conditions for peace, as suggested by Mazarin, were that he should hand his army over to the crown, stay in the country and await the outcome of a States-General. Even if Condé pride had let him accept, his associates, too far gone in rebellion and too insignificant, in the main, to get out on good terms, would have held him to his course. His sister, the duchesse de Longueville hankered after civil war, with its promise of liberation from marital control. Louis XIV identified that beautiful woman as one of the most mischievous of *frondeurs* and would never forgive her. Meanwhile the queen rejected the idea of an accommodation to meet Condé's requirements. It was even harder now for *Parlement* to support Condé than it had been before. The question of arbitrary imprisonment had gone; he was now simply a rebel, leading others on a course which could only cause further distress. On the other hand, to be overtly supportive

189

towards Anne would be to surrender much of what had so far been gained. They had no reason to suppose that there had been any significant shift in Anne's view of the situation. Her tactical moves were however conciliatory.

On 8 September a new administration was formed. Molé was given the seals, La Vieuville the *surintendance*. Châteauneuf was to be chief minister, Chavigny was rejected. His probity and moderation commended Molé; he balanced the *frondeur* Châteauneuf. La Vieuville was Mazarin's choice to replace des Maisons: wealthy, influential, a steady man from a traditional background of high office, he might find acceptable ways of raising money. The Cardinal's main agent in government however remained Le Tellier: in December he would be reinstated as Secretary of State, but meanwhile he worked assiduously as ever to keep the royal armies in the field. Without Chavigny, Condé had apparently no friend in the administration and Molé was becoming disenchanted. Nor was there much comfort for Mazarin. Even le Tellier thought that restoration was premature. Châteauneuf would not lightly surrender what he had worked for. Orléans, no longer required as *lieutenant-général*, hung around, decided only in opposition to Mazarin.

It would have required a subtlety beyond Anne's capacity, to have worked with the ministerial coalition so as to use their talents and make them an effective force for peace. In particular, Molé's position as minister but still *premier président*, could represent either an awkward ambivalence or a valuable opportunity to win the sympathy of *Parlement*. Anne's thinking was in any case dominated by the question of Mazarin. Could he return – and when? Meanwhile, how could his advice be implemented? Anne's expectation, underlying all her actions, was that Mazarin would resume his ministerial position. There were some encouraging signs. He advised La Vieuville's giving priority to the payment of salaries and interest to *officiers* and *rentiers* to cultivate an amenable and sound public opinion. He kept in touch with governors of provinces. Without an effective body of *intendants* and in the fragmented condition of the country, the governor was all-important. The duc de Mercoeur, now attached by marriage, was intended for Provence. La Meilleraye was secure in Brittany. Even Longueville was a Mazarinist prospect as he now had little to do with his errant wife. Still more important than the governors were the generals. Mazarin remained determined to win over Turenne and used his contacts among other generals to build up the royal forces. With the end of the German war, there was a buyer's market in mercenaries. He planned restoration, when the king should give the signal, with a military campaign to deal a double blow, to Condéans who might try to bar his troops and *frondeurs* who would contest Paris.

Condé's military prestige, his still considerable personal following and his ability, when minded, to impress and please, were no substitute for the numbers of trained men and regular supplies needed for a full-scale campaign. He held Bordeaux, where the Mazarinists had abandoned the *parlement* to his faction and, less certainly, Guienne. The chance of a concerted campaign with the Spanish and Turenne in the northwest disappeared when Tavannes[8] failed to bring over more than a fraction of his force. Then, in October, Turenne returned, tardily but, as it proved unswervingly, to his duty under the king. It was a natural movement by a consummate strategist, quick to recognise that the tide had already turned. He had already written, on Mazarin's first exile, that he hoped that he 'only left to return'. In his mature judgement, Mazarin's designs were 'just and regular' whereas Richelieu's had been 'greater and less concerted'. Neighbouring Languedoc was anarchic, with the *parlement* of Toulouse following the lead of the absent Orléans and one of Condé's generals, Marsin,[9] raising troops in the province, while the *parlement's* officers went about destroying bridges: an effective means, in that country of fast rivers and deep valleys, of checking the progress of an army.

Condé's captains used forced levies of money and men to sustain their army. Government forces, with so many foreigners in their ranks, were no less brutal, but Anne began to have the better of the propaganda war as *Parlement* came to see the activities of Condéan officials as infringing on their own rights. The Mazarinist *intendant*, Denis Marin,[10] was therefore given a free hand in actions which two years before would have elicited a storm of outrage. Increasingly sure of her standing in the heartlands, Anne was emboldened to leave Paris, on 27 September and to make her base at Poitiers. The situation was indeed unusual: the authority of the state represented by Anne and the war cabinet at the front, with a group to provide anchorage in Paris, *surintendant* de Maisons, Châteauneuf and Guénégaud,[11] secretary of state: it was the latter's task to keep Orléans and Gondi under control.

Gondi's critical failure in these months had been to build up a *frondeur* party of judges, nobles and *bons bourgeois* to hold neutral ground in sufficient strength. He looked to Anne for the cardinal's hat and she had presented his name to the Pope; but he had still to project himself as leader of the opposition to Mazarin. In *Parlement* his attacks on Condé were interpreted by the latter's adherents as indicating secret support for the court. There were justifiable misgivings about his character. Only in his own imagination was he in any way the leading player. Meanwhile Condé's refusal to seek peace with Anne was pushing *Parlement* into a quasi-Mazarinst position. In October 1651 it forbade the levying of taxes and conscription of soldiers without explicit royal authority. On 4 December, after much hesitation, *Parlement* registered the vital document, by a majority of three to one, declaring Condé an enemy of the state. To balance this, they ordered frontier officials to be on their guard against

Mazarin's return and begged Anne to repudiate him. They sent *commissaires* to Picardy and Champagne, but no troops.

Mazarin knew by then that this return would be welcome to Anne and Louis, whatever ministers said. In October the king had written to invite him to rejoin the council. He had considered, before rejecting, the proposal that the *parlement* of Metz should legalise his re-entry. Anne had been against it because it would publicise his recall. If *Parlement* were to accept a *fait accompli*, the less said about law or right the better. Mazarin's re-entry must not look like an invasion, but it had to be accompanied by a sufficient force to deter his enemies or those provincial officials who still heeded the *arrêts* of *Parlement*. Preparations completed, having heard of *Parlement*'s vote, on Christmas eve, Mazarin slipped across the border and began his journey across France to join his queen. There was an attempted ambush; perhaps more were planned. Soon he was at the head of some six thousand green-scarved soldiers,[12] many of them Germans. He was not seriously impeded as he made his journey through Champagne, Berry and Touraine, seeing for himself the consequences, patchy but in places devastating, of the sporadic civil wars. When he got to safe loyalist territory he sped on to Poitiers, with his personal bodyguard of three hundred light horsemen.

Whether for his counsel or companionship, Anne had eagerly awaited his arrival and did not pretend otherwise. She had learned much – but perhaps not enough. If the rebellion was really on the point of expiring, the intrusion of Mazarin's controversial personality could only embarrass the would-be peacemakers. Paris was as volatile as ever. The December demonstrations against the Cardinal had been enough to persuade *Parlement* to condemn Mazarin for *lèse-majesté* and to put a price on his head.[13] It was not only Châteauneuf who urged Anne to change her mind: Molé was exasperated at the prospect of new confrontations. His position was delicate, as he was reminded when a *frondeur* deputation arrived at his house: he warned them off or 'they would be hanged'. Le Tellier also thought it untimely. He could afford to take a long view. It was not as if Mazarin brought a new strategic initiative. It had already been decided to attack Condé in the southwest: the time had come for a trial of strength. It made sense to concentrate the administration in one place. So Anne ordered Châteauneuf and La Vieuville to join her at Poitiers. Administrative logic or political risk: the balance was a fine one. In any case, Châteauneuf was dispensable: he had represented a phase and a need, part of the price paid for the cooperation of Mme de Chevreuse. He had already found that his position as head of the *conseil des dépêches* did not make him *premier ministre*. His military plans were outvoted in council. After Mazarin's arrival at Poitiers, he left for Paris, to brood over the mirage of power, so long beckoning and pursued. It was an anticlimactic end, possibly undeserved, for he had been a competent minister.

When Mazarin approached Poitiers, Louis went out of the city to meet him: a signal mark of respect, usually accorded only to a fellow sovereign. There can be no doubt about the feelings of the fatherless boy towards his godfather: constant protector when in a position to be so, devoted servant, tutor in public business and tactful friend. That Anne was fond of Mazarin did not impair Louis' affection and gratitude. It says much for the Cardinal's sensitivity, in a situation which can breed resentment, that he seems to have aroused no such feelings in the young king. That they had been to war together was much; that Mazarin had suffered in the royal service, was more; that he was devoted to Anne, yet without taking advantage of her reciprocal feelings, may have been most. Now there was the appearance of a family reunion. But there was little in it to suggest that Mazarin and the queen were lovers. The historian can only guess at the nature of their relationship. Yet a matter so important to contemporaries, so salaciously enjoyed by the *canaille* – and those who sought to influence and amuse them – cannot be ignored.[14]

Conscientiously, in some ways superstitiously pious, scrupulous about confession and regular in sacramental life, intensely proud of her lineage, perhaps schooled by her early frustrations to accept a greater degree of restraint than most of those around her, seemingly placid in nature though capable of sudden bursts of passionate anger, with her strongest feelings focused on her son. Anne was either chastely fond or so exceptionally discreet in sexual encounters that she fooled all around her. The record of his life shows Mazarin too to have been more sensitive in temperament than his preferred pose of ironic detachment might suggest, but also controlled and objective in the conduct of his life: he enjoyed the company of women in the way of a man who is coolly unafraid that his judgement will be overturned by untoward passion. In the absence of firm evidence for an affair or a marriage, it may be well to leave the last word with a renowned expert in such matters and one well placed to know – Mme de Chevreuse. She was not convinced that there was any sexual relationship between Anne and her minister.

In her political management, as we have seen, Anne had not been invariably so cool or prudent. But at least one important lesson she had learned. Whatever she might think of its conduct she was now resolved to secure the loyalty of *Parlement*. The council continued to issue *arrêts* for the needs of the judges and *rentiers* and to hold *traitants* to their contracts for supplying cash for payment of their salaries. Apart from a *frondeur* or Condéan rump the anti-Mazarin noises were just that – and no more. For one man, however, there could be no continuing in the royal camp. For Orléans the recall of Mazarin was the last straw. Under-valued, as he thought, now offended and suddenly decisive, he signed a treaty with Condé and joined him in revolt. At last the dividing lines, connections and interests were becoming clearer: to all intents and purposes there were two parties, not three. Both men were to fight against the crown until Mazarin was banished. Orléans's troops marched South to join the rebels while he remained in Paris as Condé's lieutenant. Beaufort and Broussel supported him. Between them they commanded enough support to ensure that the queen would not recover her capital without a fight.

22

THE DEFEAT OF CONDÉ

On 18 January 1652, a *parlementaire* delegation was informed by Anne that the king personally had asked Mazarin to rejoin the council. On 23 January a royal decree quashed *Parlement*'s anti-Mazarinist declaration. Anne could intimate the king's will but that was a different matter from an adult king, unmistakably his own master, speaking his own mind. *Parlement* issued a statement asserting that Mazarin had usurped the authority of the king: therefore orders issued in his name were acts of tyranny against king and subjects alike. It gave the semblance of a moral authority to the rebel cause but did not improve its prospect of victory. *Parlement* was not, as in 1649, being attacked. Few, even among the Condéan magistrates, relished the prospect of war coming again to the gates of Paris. Meanwhile all *Parlement* would do for Condé was to suspend the royal declaration against him. Their main concern was to preserve the neutrality of their zone of jurisdiction. How little they could sway the course of events was shown when Nemours led his troops on a destructive *chevauchée* across the centre of the country. They wanted Condé defeated and Mazarin expelled. They feared putting resolutions to the vote since that would only expose those irreconcilable aims. The more legality was flouted in general, the more they clung, to particular legal forms. For instance, they condemned the duc de Rohan for seizing a Mazarinist head of a *présidial* court.[1] They scrutinised such accounts as could be obtained. Yet the political instinct was still strong and the hotheads had to be appeased. So in March the *Chambre St Louis* was reconvoked.

As old issues surfaced, talks broke down in squabbling between *Parlement* and the *Chambre des Comptes*. The one policy that could have given a base for effective political action was neglected. Instead of attempting to work with the provincial courts, the Paris judges merely kept them informed. Local *parlements* had their own difficulties. At Rouen the duchesse de Longueville was working for Condé; her estranged husband, rather less vigorously, for Mazarin. Aix was no less divided. There was a straw in the wind from the Dauphiné in the form of a letter to the king asking him to restore peace by 'any measures thought necessary'. The magistrates of Brittany were absorbed in their conflict with La Meilleraye. Only Toulouse, Bordeaux and Dijon conformed to the Paris line: Mazarin must go. Generally, other considerations were secondary to fear and distress about the spread of war. The crown afforded the only hope. Typical of the general confusion was the way in which Nevers, for example, welcomed the news that the royal family was coming to the town – but petitioned the king to leave Mazarin behind. Ominously reflecting the recent German experience of civil war, some towns offered cash to both sides to leave them alone.

Sixteen fifty-two saw the last and deadliest military phase of the Fronde. In January the Condéans had been defeated at Tonnay-Charente. In February and March they lost, one by one, the towns which they had earlier gained. On 29 February Rohan, governor of Anjou, who had declared for Condé and secured Angers, surrendered the key to the city to Mazarin's troops. Its bishop[2] pleaded successfully that it be saved from pillage. But the crown imposed fiscal penalties. Already familiar with the province, *intendant* de Heere[3] lost no time in installing royal officers of justice and finance. Till Condé took control, the rebels' effort was paralysed by the failure of Beaufort and Nemours to agree about strategy: Beaufort wanted to block the road to Paris, Nemours to cross the Loire at Blois and attack the royal army in the rear. Only victory would persuade cautious city governments to join them. Agen opened its gates to Harcourt when he assured the citizens that the crown would respect its property and privileges.

Bordeaux was a law unto itself, remaining obstinately embroiled in its own internecine feuds. As is usually the case in civil war, the larger conflict subsumed local feuds which proved to have a separate life: here it was the battle for control between radical and conservative elements which acquired the name of the *Ormée*[4] from the elm-lined square in the centre of the city. Though governor, with numerous clients in the province, Condé had indeed little more influence in Bordeaux than Mazarin. An erratic politician he may have been, verging at times on the absurd: but Condé remained the soldier, deservedly respected for his military judgement. He saw that the issue would be decided in Paris. As in the 1590s, he who controlled the capital controlled France.[5] At the end of March he rode north to lead his confederates to the decisive point.[6]

Two great commanders contended for the mastery. On 1 April Condé defeated Hocquincourt at Bléneau. Voltaire would write of this skirmish, with its four hundred casualties: 'There can hardly have been a smaller combat accompanied by more imminent danger and with greater interests at stake'. Important too was the action of the next day when Turenne drubbed Beaufort and Nemours at Jargeau. By-passing Orléans, where la Grande Mademoiselle[7] held excitable sway on behalf of her father Gaston, barring the city gates to both sides, he managed, moving warily along Condé's flank, to protect the court and block the road to Paris.[8] Juggling military and political objectives and urged on by Chavigny,[9] Condé then rode for the capital, leaving his army to sustain the campaign. Both armies laid waste the countryside as if it were foreign soil. Blazing villages taught Louis more than could any lessons of Mazarin about the needs of his realm.[10] On 11 April Condé entered Paris. A sufficient number lined the streets to give him a noisy welcome. But the soaring price of bread may be a better indicator of Parisian sentiment and of the problems that lay ahead. The peasants in the surrounding countryside were shy of the roads and markets. The city authorities guarded their stocks, anticipating siege: individuals hoarded; traders profiteered; the poor were suffering. Condé did not long honour them with his presence, but embarked on the campaign of the Ile-de-France which saw both Condéans and royalists terrorising whole districts, pillaging, burning and spreading disease. Into this nightmare world, with old scores to settle, plunged Charles of Lorraine,[11] nominally on Condé's behalf. His motley, unpaid troops ran amok. The cost of buying him off was a further factor in determining the royal policy: Mazarin and Turenne realised that they must bring Condé to battle.

Mazarin had therefore some advantages when he worked to increase support for the crown. The young *procureur-général* Nicolas Fouquet now proved his worth. Charming, generous with the crown's money as with his own, he used his influential position to build up a royalist *clientèle*. It was La Vieuville however who played the leading role in these vital months. He gave priority from his slender resources to the payment of salaries and interest. Recognising the tension between ministers and magistrates over the continuing use of *commissaires*, he had their commissions registered as *maîtres des requêtes en chevauchée*. He attacked abuses by *maîtres* such as Balthasar at Limoges.[12] So he persuaded *Parlement* that he was their ally, that financial officials were to blame. As a tactic for splitting the *frondeur* front by turning *Parlement* against the lower corporations, it served well at this juncture. It was once more a time for choosing sides, for some simply because they could see no other way out. When monarchy had become partisan, where was the true authority?

The history of Paris in the next few months can only be recorded as a formless sequence of demonstrations, pleas, threats and brawls. Loyalties depended on particular interests or connections. The *bons bourgeois*, like those belonging to the wealthy guild of silversmiths, were still mainly against Mazarin. The fevered atmosphere of the city can be gauged from a clash between two marches. The cry of the one was 'Union of *Parlement* and People and Down with Mazarin' while the others were all for 'Peace at any Price'. *Parlement* collectively behaved with restraint. It stiffened the

resolve of the city fathers not to allow the troops of either side to enter
the city.

On 2 July war came nonetheless to the streets of Paris. The events of
that day epitomised the spirit that has made the Fronde synonymous with
so much that was heroic and self-destructive. Turenne had managed to
trap Condé between the heights of Charonne and the Porte St Antoine,
barred to the latter's troops by order of the municipality. Louis, Anne
and the court were installed at St Denis, in whose abbey so many of the
king's ancestors were buried. While the queen knelt in fervent prayer
before the high altar of a nearby Carmelite convent, Mazarin and the
young king went up to Charonne and climbed a windmill to survey
the battle. In furious fighting, under a broiling sun, Condé's men were
pressed back along the Faubourg St Antoine towards the gates where
Turenne expected them to die or yield. Frantic messages were sent to
Gaston at the Palais Royal, but he would not give the order to open the
gates that would save the prince. While he whistled through his teeth,
his habit when beset by doubt, his daughter played the man's part she
so much enjoyed. Wresting from her father the necessary order, she went
in person to see that it was carried out, then mounted the battlements
of the Bastille and, it was said, persuaded the commander of the fortress
to turn his guns on Turenne's milling troops below. Thus covered,
Condé's men reached the safety of the city whose narrow streets made
further pursuit impracticable for the royal troops. There is a poignant
image of the Fronde in the young Rochefoucauld, in his loves and
loyalties the epitome of noble life as so many aspired to it, riding away,
slumped over his horse, blood streaming from his terribly wounded face.
He would live. To Mazarin's bitter distress Paul Mancini, his nephew, died
of his wounds. The uncle's letters reveal again a humane man, who
understood the recklessness that was part of the nobleman's creed – but
deplored the cost. Now the Fronde had indeed come home to him.[13]

Thwarted by what he saw as *Parlement*'s legalism and fearing a settlement
between *Parlement* and the crown, Condé now adopted the crudely demagogic course that seemed to his impatient spirit the only one that was
feasible. On 4 July he appeared before an assembly of judges and other
Parisian notables at the Hôtel de Ville to demand support for his rule of
the city. His strongest argument was the great crowd of soldiers and
citizens outside: many had been tippling, all were excited and noisy. They
heard that the city authorities had opted for neutrality. The Hôtel de
Ville was set on fire and a number of deputies killed or severely beaten
as they tried to escape. In the short term, Condé, who expressed no
regret for the behaviour of his followers, seemed to be the beneficiary as
moderate *parlementaires* lay low or left for the country. Even so it was only
by a small majority that the rump of magistrates gave Condé effective
control. He retained the semblance of legality by investing Orléans with

emergency powers as *lieutenant-général* of the kingdom. Orléans was prepared to do everything that Condé required of him, as were Beaufort, now appointed governor of Paris, Broussel, in charge of its administration as *prévôt des marchands*, even, at first, Séguier. The pretext for these actions, constituting a clear case of *lèse-majesté*, was the usual one: that Mazarin had the young king in his power, the royal will was therefore in abeyance and Orléans, as his closest adult male relative, was therefore the proper person to execute it. The young king experienced once more that sense of outrage that was so strongly to colour his absolutist views. His respect for Mazarin was stronger than ever. With Parisians yearning for peace, with their leaders looking for a way out, the situation was tailor-made for the minister's diplomatic skills.

Certain judges, notably Le Prévôt,[14] were now actively working for Mazarin, with money to dispense for sweeteners or for royalist demonstrations. More direct pressures came with the king's order that the sovereign courts be transferred to Pontoise, with the withholding of payments of interest and salaries from those who stayed in Paris and threats to levy special taxes on their country estates. Pontoise, forty miles northwest of Paris, was then a fortress city of some importance, guarding the traditionally insecure border with the Vexin. If there was now a trickle back to the royalist cause, beside the twenty-five who actually went to Pontoise, it was not to be attributed to any sudden surge of enthusiasm for the king; rather a choice of the lesser of two evils, inspired by little more than *sauve qui peut*. Anne was therefore forced to do what she had most wanted to avoid: to offer the second dismissal of Mazarin. It was to be the pre-condition of peace. She had already, in June, made a conditional offer: he would withdraw if the rebels laid down their arms. *Parlement* had then insisted on unconditional dismissal. Now the Pontoise clique – for its members were little more than that, though headed by Molé and staffed by senior judges such as Novion – drafted an emollient remonstrance. Anne acted on it, though her order, commending the minister for his services, surely reflected her understanding that the banishment was but temporary.

On 19 August Mazarin set out, if not jauntily, at least in more contented mood than on the previous occasion, for the German frontier. In effect his journey was the end of the Fronde, for it was now only a matter of time and terms before crown and *Parlement* made their peace. Mazarin directed by correspondence, Condé tried to negotiate on his own behalf but was rebuffed. 'See how the civil wars have reduced the position of the princes of the blood, and how unhappy they are to be forced to act with deference towards men who are so far beneath their rank.' The words of his lieutenant Marigny[15] might have been his own. Times were indeed changed when rebellion could not be made to pay.

Among those who had been affronted by the massacre of 4 July was

Gondi, now Cardinal de Retz, as he was titled after having at last, on 19 February, been made Cardinal – though he had yet to receive the insignia of his office. During the summer he had worked to secure peace, keeping his distance from the Condéans, but handicapped by Anne's reluctance to deal with him. In the second week of September he set out for Compiègne and the ceremony of investment, at the head of a retinue of Parisian notables, over a hundred-strong. Since the king was required to carry out the formal investment he could not refuse him audience. Retz adopted a high moral tone, speaking to the king of the desolate state of his land and recalling how Henry IV had been advised by his forebear, Cardinal de Gondi, when pursuing the policies that led to peace and recovery. As Le Tellier reported to Mazarin, he was received with disdain. With ministers and a growing body of officials, besides other agents, working for Mazarin, Retz[16] had become almost irrelevant. The people of Paris could speak for themselves.

On 24 September a crowd of some four thousand surrounded the Palais-Royal, with slips of white paper in their hats to distinguish them from the remaining Condéans, with their straw badges. They resolved to keep on meeting until the lawful government of the city was restored. The city council took note, its Condéan members were made to resign and the rest sent a delegation to the king to ask him to return. He stipulated that remaining Condéan troops and supporters leave the city. Their prince rode off to join the Spanish army in Flanders. Did he reflect on those other, more heroic, days on the battlefields of Rocroy and Lens? What he could not have known, in his angry pride, was that he would again have the chance to serve and to win battles for his king.

All conditions fulfilled, Louis graciously consented to return to his twice-rebellious capital. No pains were spared to ensure that his people understood that he had come to stay. The spectacle of 21 October was magnificent as Louis rode into the city, preceded by Turenne with his troops and accompanied by his cousin, Charles Stuart, the English king in exile as well as a company of peers and marshals of France. Anne followed with her twelve-year-old younger son and with leading courtiers and ministers of the court. As Le Tellier described the scene in a letter to Servien, the king 'was received with all the acclamations and signs of joy and affection that can be imagined. Nearly all the people of the town came out as far as St Cloud to welcome him'. One who did not was Gaston, in an agony of indecision, threatening to raise the barricades, but doing nothing. He had reason to be apprehensive. Royal letters banished Beaufort, Rohan, La Rochefoucauld; other decrees deprived Condé, Conti, Mme de Longueville and others of their honours and dignities. Gaston signed a declaration of submission and relieved the city and king of the embarrassment of his presence by taking flight for Limours. Mademoiselle followed him. Having been so blatantly partisan she could no longer even think of the once seriously mooted match with the king. Her fate, little palliated by the fact that she was still the richest heiress in France, was to endure exile with her father in the country. Under the circumstances Louis had been magnanimous.

No doubt Retz hoped that his belated efforts for peace and his Cardinal's hat would save him. He could neither maintain the image of unequivocal and straightforward loyalty that he sought to present to the court, nor give up the wheeling and dealing that had been so typical of his public life. Trying to secure posts for his friends like Brissac and Guy Joly, he let it appear that he was secretly in league with Condé. In an atmosphere thick with rumours of *coups* and assassinations, Anne issued a secret order for his arrest, to a copy of which Louis added his own postscript: 'I have commanded Pradelle to execute the present order against the person of Cardinal de Retz, and even to arrest him dead or alive if he offers resistance.' That the arrest did not occur till December 19, and then only after Retz had gone to see the king at the Louvre, gives some idea of the perceived strength of Retz's following in the city; the posting of armed guards along the route of his carriage to imprisonment at Vincennes, shows that they were leaving nothing to chance. Anne had, of course, to consider how Rome would react. When Henry III had had the Cardinal de Guise arrested and murdered, the Pope had excommunicated the king. Actions were now less drastic, the times less bloody. But Pope Innocent X could hardly ignore such treatment of a prelate who had so recently been recommended for promotion by the government that now condemned him. As the other French cardinal, Mazarin was clearly vulnerable to papal displeasure after this 'great scandal' and violation of 'the sacred immunities of all within the church'. Excommunication of Mazarin was considered at Rome but cautious voices warned against providing ammunition for Gallican or Jansenist critics of the papacy. For fifteen months, without help from Rome, Retz was left to fret and plot at Vincennes. Indeed, once Mazarin's spies had won his confidence, he was of use to the government, a freely flowing tap of information about the state of parties past and present.

23

UNFINISHED BUSINESS

Mazarin did not hurry back to Paris. It suited him to wait until Retz and Châteauneuf were out of harm's way. He busied himself with the raising of supplies for Turenne, who was engaged in Champagne, clearing the board of the remaining Condéan fortresses. The delay did not please Anne. The queen might appreciate the wisdom of restraint; with every day that passed, sentiment improved as Mazarin was seen to be working for the crown, not rushing back to enjoy his share in its victory; the woman looked perhaps for evidence of his being eager to see her again. By the end of January she was writing of what she 'suffered on this subject'; that she had been disappointed so often that she would only believe that he was coming when he fixed a date. It was on 3 February that he eventually arrived. As at Poitiers, Louis went out to meet him, three leagues outside the city walls. He entered the city in the king's carriage and was given quarters in the Louvre. The minister's return had come to represent to Louis the vindication of royal right.[1] The theme of triumph had a human face in the young king's obvious gratitude: the godparent had proved his right to the place of father by his self-effacing devotion. Following the royal lead came deputies from *Parlement* which recognised the debt which France owed to his 'great and illustrious efforts' and came to assure him of their 'joy at his happy return'. The celebratory supper, followed by fireworks, completed what must have been among Mazarin's happiest days.

No less satisfying or significant was the great feast of 29 March at the Hôtel de Ville, at which the city fathers honoured the statesman whom so recently few had dared do other than condemn. Ministers had successfully maintained links with the city government, working on their common interest in efficient policing in the city. It is still surprising, unless one subscribes to Shakespeare's view of the mob as naturally and basely fickle – and the Roman crowd that acclaimed Coriolanus might well serve as model for the Parisians of 1653 – to read accounts of Mazarin's ecstatic reception. Jean Vallier described how the crowd shouted ceaselessly for the first minister and redoubled their applause every time he appeared at the windows of the *Hôtel de Ville*: 'what flattery and what abasement were indulged in by the most notable frondeurs to efface the memory of past affairs and to propitiate this divinity whom they have but lately so abused . . . as if they were regaling the king on his return from conquering a great province.' That was the point, of course. 'This proscribed man, this disturber of the public peace and obstacle to the general peace, on whose head a price of 50,000 crowns has been put' was believed to have brought peace within reach. If Parisians had known that there would be six more years of war they might have been less inclined to cheer.

Mazarin desired peace, but realised that it would be harder than ever to achieve. It was that item in the balance sheet of the Fronde of which ministers would be most aware. As was brought home by the loss of Catalonia and Dunkirk,[2] the Spanish war effort had revived in proportion to the diversion of royal resources to the task of defeating the rebels. Pursuit of the war would continue to be Mazarin's main preoccupation. It was a war of attrition which only a decisive victory could bring to to a speedy end. First the country had to be subdued. Civil Wars rarely have the tidy ends allocated to them by historians.[3]

Why, when Paris had welcomed back their king, did resistance continue in Guienne? Why in particular did Bordeaux prove such a tough nut to crack? Answers lie in the geography and tradition of the province and in the peculiar situation within the city itself. The patronage of the princes, and particularly the implication of Condé, links the *Ormée* to the Fronde – but the episode has its own distinct vitality. Deriving its name from the elm-fringed square in which meetings were held, the *Ormée* was a genuine radical movement, recruiting support from artisans and tradesmen, under a leadership mainly of minor lawyers and officials, with a few clergy and nobles. The prime concern was to protect the privileges of the city, not so much against the crown as against *parlement*, with its well-established judicial oligarchy. It was also anti-Mazarin, associated as he was in Bordeaux with intrusive officials and taxes. There were undoubtedly some extremist influences emanating from England. The Cromwellian soldier and agitator Edward Sexby[4] was sent on special mission to Bordeaux and stayed there for two years (1651–3) with the express intention of making trouble for the French government. He had the radical pamphlet, *The Agreement of the People*, translated into French for this purpose.

In the summer of 1652 an *Ormeiste* government was set up, with a political council of five hundred. The Hôtel de Ville was taken over, *parlement* was chased out and the red flag raised on the bell towers. With the official establishment here actively on the side of the government, Mazarin knew that he must act decisively. The danger was that Bordeaux would achieve independence, with its returns from commerce, particularly the profitable wine trade, to finance its garrison. It was compounded by the interest of both England and Spain in the revolt. Condé secured a Spanish force to garrison Bourg. As in 1627–9 there was a danger that the revolt would spread to other areas of the south. As Richelieu had done over La Rochelle, Mazarin decided to bring to bear the maximum concentration of force. Holding the north-eastern front with modest forces, Turenne was worth his weight in gold to the king, while the presence of Louis, with Mazarin, in camp with the army of the South, had a significant moral effect. Soldiers of mixed provenance and shaky discipline, engaged in a civil war on their own soil, needed to know that rightful authority was not only behind them, but with them in person.

If the *Ormée* was disturbing to the crown, it was more so to Condé. Struggling to hold together his attenuated forces and uncertain allies, he had the worst of both worlds. The *Ormée* rebuffed him but their reputation for extremism damaged his cause, frightening away potential supporters.[5] While a fleet under Vendôme blockaded the Gironde, the king's soldiers, under the duc de Candâle,[6] recovered, one after another, the towns of Périgord. The damage to the wine trade, with losses to merchants, coopers, tavern keepers and *vignerons*, led to splits within the *Ormée*, as citizens began to question its aims. Mazarinist white flags replaced the red. Bordeaux opened its gates to the royal army on August 3. Condé had already left for Flanders, with his wife and son. Marsin went to join the Spanish in Catalonia. The duchesse de Longueville returned to her husband and a life of Jansenist piety: no half-measures for her. (Louis was not convinced and her patronage brought fresh suspicion on the sect.) Conti's belated surrender made possible his long-planned marriage with Mazarin's niece, Anne-Marie Martinozzi. He was contemptuously refused the office of constable and the governorship of Brouage which he also demanded. Instead he was given command of the remaining French in Catalonia, a lost cause to which he could do little harm. A large dowry added to his fortune; to his wife he gave syphilis. There was little room for sentiment or humanity in the aristocratic marriage market.

Clearly the crown had to pay dearly for the allegiance of those of its rebellious subjects whom it needed to win. The case of the comte du Daugnon is instructive. The southwest coast was vital to the crown. Daugnon, *lieutenant-général* with authority over vital ports, was able to make a hard bargain. In November 1652 he exchanged his office for 530,000 *livres* and a dukedom, with a complete amnesty for him and his *fidèles*. Perhaps it was inevitable, under the circumstances, that bribery should be as important as force. It had been so too for Henry IV in the last stages of the religious wars. In a diffused way it was to be part of the political establishment of Louis XIV's personal reign: the discreetly rationed cornucopia of Versailles. But it had unfortunate consequences. It made inroads into already inadequate funds, reduced provision for the army, slowed the progress towards peace and pushed into the distance the re-ordering of the finances without which the regime could never achieve stability. It also disgusted loyalists, like the comte d'Harcourt, one of the king's most successful commanders. His case illuminates a chronic concern of government, most acute at times of restoration when the means of gratification are insufficient to meet the demand;[7] also the continuing and delicate interaction of domestic and diplomatic business.

Expecting large rewards for his services, but disappointed, Harcourt took himself off to Breisach and there negotiated with the emperor for an independent principality. The episode reveals both what Mazarin was up against – and the value of his patient methods. After a year of negotiation, during which Mazarin bought the services of the Philipsburg garrison and paid off the mercenaries of Breisach, Harcourt came to terms. He received back all his offices and governorships of Upper and Lower Alsace since the king wished 'to show goodwill in restoring affairs to M. de Harcourt in the condition that they were before'. The iron fist had still to be concealed in a glove of softest velvet.

For lesser mortals and communities guilty of rebellion the treatment could be less sensitive. The Bordelais were granted an amnesty but certain named individuals were excepted from it: those who could be caught were executed; a new city government was nominated by the crown. To reinforce royal authority the *château* Trompette was rebuilt. The *parlement* remained in rustication till the end of 1654. Prosperity eluded the city for several years more as both English and Spanish harassed ships and poached trade. At every level rebellion was seen not to pay. And yet, by contemporary standards, German, Swedish, indeed English, the treatment of Bordeaux was far from draconian. Magnanimity, calculation of fiscal advantage, plain common sense – however the policy of the crown be judged, it reflects creditably on Mazarin. His policy of selective punishment was unlikely to be misinterpreted. There was to be no weakening towards Retz, nor yet towards Condé, whose actions proclaimed him traitor long before *Parlement* received the official verdict of the court of peers. In September he evoked the glory of ten years before when he retook the town of Rocroy: humiliation for the French government and a reminder that Spain, thus reinforced, was still a power to be reckoned with. In June 1654 he was declared guilty of *lèse-majesté* deprived of the name of Bourbon and title of 'prince of the blood' and sentenced to death *in absentia*.

June also saw the event to which all else had been leading. In the heart of France's most afflicted province, where many villages in the rolling plains were still deserted, enveloped by the sublime Gothic of Rheims Cathedral, and at the climax of a ceremony of some five hours, the sixteen-year-old Louis was crowned king. Tradition had been studied but all could not be as formerly. As if to emphasise the persisting abuses in a church that was both alight with movements of the Holy Spirit and encumbered by the weight of aristocratic tradition, it was objected that the archbishop was not a priest: the bishop of Soissons officiated in his place. Noticeable too, reflecting the Fronde, was the absence of lay peers of old creation; other nobles who had not been *frondeurs* took part in the ceremony. There could be no better way of binding them to the royal interest. As if to emphasise what the exiles (Gaston most notably) were missing, the highest among nobility and officers were present in force, a collective demonstration of the unity which was to be found nowhere but in the king's person: on that day he was the realm, its soul, its pride and consciousness of law, right and proper custom.

Charlemagne's crown, the jewelled sword of state, the sceptre and hand of justice, the brooch for the king's mantle, his spurs, all accoutrements for royal investiture, were brought from the abbey of Saint-Germain. From the abbey of St Rémy, for the anointment of the *dieu-donné*, came the sacred phial of Clovis.[8] Mazarin was seated by the side of the high altar, on the cardinals' bench where Retz would have yearned to be, only less conspicuous than the queen and king's brother on the raised dais. With something of a choreographer's instinct for form and movement, Mazarin had ensured that the clerics and court dignitaries responsible for the ritual had missed no chance to impress participants with the sense and symbolism of the day. With no less keen an instinct for political advantage, he saw to it that the *Gazette* carried a full description and that accounts would reach every part of France: from the exhilarating entry to the sound of drums, trumpets and oboes, and procession into the cathedral which spelt out with every shuffling footstep the grades and values of this hierarchical society, through the solemn rites of investiture and anointment, to the cloud of white doves released from the west door to signify to the people the end of the ceremony, all gave symbolic force to the claims of Europe's most hallowed crown.

Anne declared that coronation week should be celebrated as an octave, in which there should be fitting religious observances; during that time Louis, *roi thaumaturge*, went to the shrine of St Rémy and there touched two thousand sufferers from the king's evil, reciting over each bowed head the timeless formula: 'the king touches you, may God cure you'. After that he may have welcomed a different part. Before the coronation could take place, Champagne had had to be cleared of soldiers – Condéan or other bands fending for themselves. Now the king went with Mazarin to Stenay: the last surviving Condéan fortress on the Meuse, its capture denied the Spanish army entry to Bar and Champagne. The idea of a soldier king would spread quickly in the military fraternity, and so to court. That was important, for events in the provinces showed that the symbolism of Rheims had yet to be translated generally into the disciplined subjection it implied.

Imbued with tones of romance and farce – as if Retz were committed to living out, in his personal odyssey, some picaresque novel – his latest effort was not one which Mazarin could take lightly. Given the known militancy of Paris clergy, one danger of his arrest had been that his cause would be more widely adopted. Retz was not a disinterested champion of the Church, but the issue of ecclesiastical authority was important to the bishops in France, even more to the Pope and to the large pro-Spanish interest at Rome. News in August 1654 that he had escaped from Nantes gaol,[9] to which he had been transferred from Vincennes only a few months before, was enough to provoke Mazarin to a rare display of pique. 'What has upset me in this affair', he told the loyal but uncharacteristically lax governor La Meilleraye, 'has been to see that, by the cunning of these people . . . you have come to trust them more than you trust me, who could never have any other interest but that of the state'.

Retz went to Spain, after his assurance of devotion to the king had been spurned. By then Mazarin was able to treat the affair with heavy sarcasm: 'It is a mark of the charity of this great luminary of the church that, after having shed his beams on France, he should extend his rays over Spain whence, surely, he ought to go to Rome.' He did – and there mounted a campaign among the French clergy for his reinstatement to the archbishopric which was being administered by Mazarin's nominees. Innocent X pensioned him and refused to accept his disqualification. Alexander VII,[10] who succeeded Innocent in 1655, gave him the pallium that signified that he was indeed bishop. In July de Sève, *prévôt des marchands*, was being required to find evidence in the registers of the Hôtel de Ville for Retz's criminal actions during the Fronde. He explained to Le Tellier that it was in the records of *Parlement* that such evidence should be sought: proof should in any case be easily obtainable since he had paraded openly in the streets, in his distinctive beige cloak at the head of his regiment. Mazarin took Retz sufficiently seriously to want to discredit him. It was partly a question of unpleasant memories and natural suspicions. The Jansenist controversy had yet to provoke him into acting against Port Royal, but its links with *Parlement* and certain notorious *frondeurs*, together with its Hispanophil ancestry in the person of Jansen, bishop of Ypres, were sufficient grounds for vigilance. Retz had already been instrumental in the defeat of the French candidate for the Papacy and the elevation of the anti-French Alexander VII. Planning alliance with Cromwell's England, equivalent in its shock effect on *dévôt* opinion to that of Richelieu with Gustavus Adolphus, Mazarin could not ignore the contacts and cash with which Retz was maintaining his party: the assortment of Parisian *curés*, covert *frondeurs*, noisy gallants and sympathetic ladies undoubtedly looked more menacing in reports on ministerial desks than it has seemed to historians, though one has taken it sufficiently seriously to label it 'the ecclesiastical *fronde*'. The half-crazed street rhetoric of Simon Morin[11] could be left for the time being to the discretion of the city authorities. The fiery radicalism of Jean Rousse, *curé* of Saint

Roch, was another matter; author of a pamphlet (1649) in which he asserted that 'a king must rule justly or face deposition', representing what was clearly, for some Frenchmen, the unfinished business of the Fronde, he had to be closely watched. 'He has always been seditious' wrote Mazarin, in 1656, observing the connections with Jansenism for which he was expelled from the Sorbonne. Ministers have to deal with the information available to them – and spies, to justify their existence, usually make much of what they are investigating. It is also a rare politician who does not allow his policy to be influenced by the events he has lived through. The Fronde cast a long shadow.

Ecclesiastical politics created ripples, compelled attention. More important however, for present peace and the future balance of power within the constitution, were the proceedings of *Parlement*. Held in the afterglow of the king's triumphant entry of the day before, the *lit de Justice* of 22 October 1652 did not prove the crushing defeat of *Parlement* that might have been expected from the stark words: 'Henceforth members are prohibited from taking any cognisance of the general affairs of the state and the direction of finances.' With the return of the men of Pontoise *Parlement* was whole again, ready to resume its functions, to capitalise on its recent moderation. Superficially it was the former balance that was restored, allowing *Parlement* scope for the amendment of royal edicts; but much water had flowed down the Seine since that February day in 1641 when Louis XIII had used a *lit de justice* to define its powers. The letter of law, as edicts pronounce it and historians record it, can say little about the thinking of the parties concerned: its reading will alter with circumstances. Constitutional history has to take note of the dynamic forces within a given situation: that of the first years after the Fronde was highly volatile.[12]

Parlement registered the document defining its powers: like that of 1641 it would be worth as much or as little as the political situation would allow. If *Parlement* were likely to stop short of an open challenge, equally the crown would be wary of provoking it. The Fronde produced more, not less of a partnership. After confrontation, consensus. So there was to be no dangerous quarrel till the early eighteenth century – and then over the Gallican issue. After two centuries when Gallicanism, as a set of principles and convention, had generally served the ends of monarchy, it would then be Louis who would step beyond accepted bounds and *Parlement* which would stand firmly within them in refusing to register the bull *Unigenitus*.[13]

So much for the future and the paradoxes that lurked within the principles of Catholic kingship by Divine Right. About certain immediate measures there would be no difficulty. No judge was to enter into the service or join the party of a nobleman. An extra lock was put on a door which no judge, after the experience of Condé's clients, was likely to open again. The exile of certain leading radicals, notably Broussel and Viole, took its tone from the dire threats issued by Anne at critical moments during the Fronde. However, exile was not execution, nor even imprisonment – and yet there had been a bloody civil war and an unauthorised rebel administration. From across the Channel the purge might look strikingly moderate. Le Tellier, for one, wanted stronger action. Again we see Mazarin's hand. He was always likely to counsel restraint. But this limited, selective form of punishment, like similar actions in the provinces, reflects as much the fragility of the crown's position as its strength. The balance within *Parlement* remained roughly the same, for the tilt away from the radicals, following their leaders' exile, was balanced by the death of two leading conservatives, Omer Talon and Henri de Mesmes, both in 1652. Before he died, 'after serving for twenty-two years in office without the loss of a single day', Talon committed to paper the *Nunc Dimittis* of a faithful servant of the crown. He believed that he had been out of favour at court because he had 'never flattered the first minister' but had also offended the party of the princes because he had 'spoken too strongly in favour of royal authority'. His words convey a more telling criticism of Mazarin's policies than the wilder denunciation of open opponents. 'Faction, parties and undertakings must be avoided so that the king's authority may be defended . . . It is the duty of a good man to oppose strongly the insolence of ministers, who abuse the name and power of the king in order to do wrong. However this must never come to a schism. Nor should it break the union which ought to exist between the king and his office-holders . . .' Self-righteous as such words might seem to ministers they do provide a text for Louis XIV's personal reign. If actions be held to speak louder than words, it must be significant too that Molé gave up the office of *premier président* but worked on for the administration as *garde des sceaux*.

Notably missing from the *lit de justice* was any repudiation of the specific reforms of four years ago. *Parlement* was still able to defend those reforms, as it had done during the Fronde. The crown would try to claw back its power, especially through the restoration of the *intendants*. They were to be opposed, as were new taxes and conciliar justice wherever, in lesser or provincial courts, this was possible. Mazarin's administration was as absolutist in spirit as Richelieu's: the letters of Séguier, Le Tellier and Colbert leave no doubt about that. But caution now prevailed. Mazarin was not anxious to travel again and kept a restraining hand on the young Turks. Séguier too would show new sensitivity to the interests of the sovereign courts: the trend towards conciliar justice was halted. Nicholas Fouquet, who was *procureur-général* and surintendant showed himself to be in the same pragmatic mould, content to work within the system that rewarded him so handsomely. Obstacles were to be got round, not tackled by frontal assault. The tone was thus set for the reign. For all Colbert's assaults on the financial establishment in the early sixties and the steady growth in the powers of the *intendants*, the institutional legacy of the Fronde was the preservation of the entrenched corporate society, with its overlapping jurisdictions and franchises.

Dealings between the crown and *Parlement* had the semblance of a tug-of-war. Each side needed to hold its ground and strained periodically to win some of its opponents. A *lit de justice* in December 1652 re-imposed some of Hémery's ill-fated expedients, tariffs and fees on alienated domains. The king's brother attended the *Chambre des Comptes* to overrule restrictions on the use of *comptants*. There were some noisy demonstrations. Members of the sovereign courts called for the return of exiled colleagues. Behind the crowd were *rentiers*, angry at the suspension of interest payments. They figure prominently in the letter of Le Tillier, an *intendant des finances*, to Mazarin, on 21 January 1653, which recalls the mood of the Fronde. 'The *rentiers* hoped for better things from the return of the king to Paris . . . We are in the fourth week when no payment has been made at the Hôtel de Ville. The revenue farms on which the payments are assigned are abandoned and without farmers. This produces such ill-effect . . . Paris is on the eve of some great sedition.' Learning too that the Swiss were 'dissatisfied but waiting patiently for Your Eminence's return, hoping that you would protect their interest', Mazarin knew that he should return to Paris – yet did not hurry.

Government responded by wooing the merchant guilds, promising reduction of proposed taxes and the preservation of their monopolies. Popular resistance continued: so taxes on wood, meat and other necessities were reduced or abolished. The *rentiers* were satisfied by concessions, but not till *Parlement* had authorised a meeting of their representatives. Prompted by Séguier Mazarin forbade such intervention. The new *premier président*, Pomponne de Bellièvre[14] warded off pressure for a plenary session. So both sides drew back from the brink. The sovereign courts continued however to block or delay government business. In July 1654, 'behaving in an insufferable way' and 'following each other's lead' wrote the angry Colbert, they set out on a course of obstruction. *Parlement* exploited to the full the judicial review procedure. In March 1655 the king held a *lit de justice* to force registration of fourteen fiscal edicts. Again, to secure simultaneous effect and prevent collusion, his brother attended the *Comptes* and *Aides*. When *Parlement* went on discussing the edicts regardless, some were reminded of the atmosphere of January 1648. But the king was no longer a child. He resented the challenge to his authority and decided that the time had come to assert himself. On 13 April 1655, he did so in no uncertain terms.

If Louis was coached by Mazarin, to judge from the cardinal's nervous reaction, he exceeded his brief. It is more likely that he listened to the queen, or perhaps to Séguier: the chancellor would normally have conveyed the king's wishes. When Louis rode straight over to the Palais de Justice, still in the morning's hunting clothes, he gave the impression of speaking for himself, impetuously, perhaps angrily:

> Everyone knows how much your assemblies have troubled my state and how many dangerous effects they have had. I have learned that you presume to carry on with them on the pretext of discussing the edicts which were recently read and published in my presence. I have come here expressly to forbid you to carry on, and you, M. *premier président,* to allow or to agree to it, whatever the *enquêtes* judges may request.

The impression of spontaneity is heightened in the eye-witness account which describes him pointing, first to the row of *messieurs des enquêtes,* then to the *premier président* himself. Bellièvre was hard put to assuage the *parlementaires.* Mazarin tried to help by explaining that the king was but speaking paternally and would welcome remonstrances, though only after a tactful delay. When ministers objected that it would appear like a repudiation of the king, Mazarin then informed the assembled *présidents* that they must postpone further consideration of the edicts: they remained in force. Mazarin could not forget 1648 and the debilitating experiences of the Fronde. He was now inclined to hand out carrots. It was the king, not the Cardinal, who had the confidence to use the stick.

Louis might have impressed the judges; he had not persuaded them that they were in the wrong. The next battle, in 1656, revolved round the issue which, along with the employment of *intendants,* most concerned them: conciliar justice. They issued an *arrêt* recapitulating the sixteenth-century restrictions on conciliar interference with the judiciary. They resolved to question *maîtres* who, they alleged, had acted irregularly. It was even proposed that the chancellor should be summoned for questioning.[15] Master-tacticians, the judges had timed their action to coincide with negotiations over the renewal of the *paulette.* The smooth outcome, a royal declaration confirming the restrictions, conveys little idea of the heat and clamour aroused. Royal absolutism was at stake: that is, the extent to which the crown could implement its theoretical rights. It would soon go further and the restrictions would be evaded, but only where *parlementaires* might be expected to accept a valid political interest.

Meanwhile even Colbert, working now to build the Cardinal's fortune and his own, realised that further moves must be cautious and subtle. Until he had the powers of *contrôleur-général* and the support of a king who ruled as his own *premier ministre,* he had to fall in with his patron's view.[16] One reason why *Parlement* was so obstreperous is that radicals had been allowed to come back from exile, some even making contact with Condé. So close-knit was the institution that it had responded to strikes against individuals by closing ranks. Then the policy of direct assault was

211

found to be counter-productive: so it was better to work on individuals than on institutions: persuasion was more effective than coercion – and none the worse for a polite word, a *douceur* or a promise that did not have to be fulfilled; where there was need, a suspect – indeed an entire family, like the Potiers – might be kept under surveillance. That was all a long way from the high royalist precepts of pulpit philosophers. But ministers were prepared to compromise with *Parlement* because their main object was to secure taxes. The *trésoriers* presented an easier target – though they had their own syndicates, they had less of a support system than members of the sovereign courts. In 1653 they ventured a pre-emptive strike in the form of an *ordonnance* which, in effect, warned officials against working with *intendants*. Séguier then suspended the syndics and ordered all officials to obey the king's orders. The *trésoriers* were deprived of their right of remonstrance except in the form of 'very humble prayers and supplications'. They objected naturally and held meetings, as did the *élus*. It was not until 1661 that a conciliar *arrêt* banned all such gatherings. With an overriding interest in preserving their offices, the *trésoriers* were in no position to resist the progressive reduction in their powers. On the other hand their offices were to prove secure, like those of the judicial establishment. It would be as impracticable for Louis XIV to abolish, even significantly reduce, venal office as it was to overcome the passive but effective resistance of *Parlement* to the fundamental reforms in the law that were needed if the state were to realise its theoretical powers. Monarchy emerged from the Fronde stronger and in a position to acquire further strength – particularly in the military and diplomatic spheres. But the security and prestige of the crown rested on a consensus, subscribed to by the elites of sword and *robe* largely on their terms and for their own benefit, which was effectively to inhibit the freedom of action needed for fundamental reforms. Strengths and limitations: they were Mazarin's two-sided legacy to his king.

Most Frenchmen did not belong to any kind of *élite*. Most nobles certainly did not belong to any noble *élite*. Of those heads of families, around 100,000, who could claim nobility, relatively few were rich enough to live fashionably, let alone at court; fewer still to play a leading role, to raise troops or sustain the costs of royal service. While the most thorough of recent studies of nobles in one province shows a noteworthy degree of stability within the order, Normandy may not be typical;[17] anecdotal evidence suggests that a fair number were slipping below the level at which they could make even a pretence of 'living nobly'. Evidence from the *ban* shows that a surprisingly large number could neither serve themselves nor pay much in lieu. That they were often willing to accept the patronage of some magnate is evident from the composition of the private armies of the Fronde. The nobility are only of marginal importance in the popular risings before the Fronde. It created a new situation, open season for unaccustomed political sport, offering gatherings of nobles the chance to list grievances and propose remedies.

A number of *gentilshommes* were in Paris in the summer of 1649, airing their complaints. If he did not actually prompt them, Mazarin did not discourage their meetings. He was content to hear the discordant voices which suggested that if there had to be a States-General it would be divided and ineffectual. To many of these country gentry, overmighty princes, pretentious lawyers or ambitious clerics were as obnoxious as any minister. In 1651 there was a large number in Paris, about 460, of whom the majority were mere *écuyers* from North of the Loire. The offer of a States-General which brought them to the capital was, we have seen, if not a deliberate blind, an open cheque, without date or valid signature.[18] First Louis's coming of age, then his return to Paris relieved him of the necessity to sign it. It was to remain an idea, in its abeyance symbolic of the constitutional basis of absolute monarchy, that there was no obligation for the king to summon subjects to consult and be consulted. Meanwhile however the prospect of a States-General encouraged a number of groups to meet to prepare *cahiers*:[19] from documents such as that drawn up by the nobility of Champagne, listing their complaints and *remonstrances*, it is possible to see what nobles expected from the crown and what drove some of them to rebel.

Nobles called for a reduction in the number of venal offices. They were concerned about the burden of the *taille* – not least because it made it harder to secure their feudal dues. The *ban* stood high among other grievances, as did the *aides* and *gabelles*. They condemned financiers, typically described by the Champagne nobles as 'gorging themselves on the blood of the people as a vampire does on that of children'. Though some resented the periodic *recherches de noblesse* that might discover an unsound title, and so liability to the *taille*, others wished for a stricter definition of nobility. In several *pays d'états* they regretted the withering of the Estates. Loyalty to the crown was not in doubt, nor their sentimental concern for the well-being of the peasantry. In general they looked to a king who would sustain them – but require little in return.

As it became clear that the crown was not going to honour its pledges, hopes so widely roused gave way to frustration. In the grim early months of 1652, riding about a blighted countryside, nobles met in informal groups, calling for an early meeting of the Estates and repeating their grievances. The number involved was considerable, the tone respectful, but the crown took a poor view, was if these gatherings were a further extension of the Fronde. A meeting at La Roche-Guyon, under the auspices of the duc de Liancourt, received a *lettre de cachet* ordering its members 'to cease from making unions, addresses and useless assemblies', to come instead to his aid to defeat his enemies. Some rode to court to offer their service, but were coolly received, and sent home to await the royal summons: in vain. The episode sheds light on the suspicious climate engendered by civil war, with the instinct of a governing clique to close ranks, to be wary of any unofficial activity, especially of private gatherings; to assume an enemy if friendship could not be proven. Clarendon would tell the same tale of the embattled Charles I.

As if to justify government's suspicions, some of the nobles, encouraged by Condé, turned to secret assemblies, 'conspiracies of the forest'. They were to be part of the pattern of the 'post-Fronde': the harder it was for government to discover what was going on, the more it feared contagion, the greater its vigilance, the more secretive therefore the meetings – the harder to judge the extent of the movement. It centred on western provinces, notably Anjou and Normandy. In 1657 a widespread movement was reported. There was an impressive organisation. Each province was divided into cantons. In each canton two deputies were charged to call assemblies, collect grievances and formulate demands. At one gathering at Trun, near Argentan, in March 1658, 700 horses were counted: allowing for menials and followers that would argue a substantial number of nobles. Colbert was much concerned. A recurring term in his letters is 'malintentionés'. Though sometimes assisted by special brigades, *intendants* found it difficult to track the conspiracies. A special council was set up to supervise the operation, consisting of Séguier, Villeroy, Servien, Fouquet and Colbert, acting for Mazarin himself. In June the king forbade any further assemblies. But they continued, mostly in the depths of forests where hunting rights ensured privacy, or in remote *châteaux* and inns: sometimes more boldly at fairs, usually at night. At one meeting in the Vendémois deputies came from as far as Burgundy.

Grands seigneurs were involved. Condé of course; also Harcourt and Saint-Aignan.[20] The crown could have made greater use of governors – but Mazarin was reluctant to give them more power: again the experience of the Fronde inhibited action. Colbert wrote to Mazarin in August 1658 that 'a league of lesser nobles might gain all the provinces of the realm . . .' He was informed that certain *parlementaires* promised support. Several Protestants were involved, most prominently the sieur de Bonnesson. In 1659 he was active inciting a peasant revolt which threatened to spread fast. The ageing Gaston used his authority to good effect and the *Sabotiers* as the peasants were called were persuaded to disperse. That there was no real fight helped ministers play down an episode so much at variance with official pictures of a land of peace. Mazarin's unusually stern response tells another story. Bonnesson was executed, other nobles condemned *in absentia*, their goods confiscated, their *châteaux* razed. Rebellion was to be seen not to pay. The evidence of the years after the Fronde shows that it was a hard lesson, not readily learnt. With ministers acting as a team Mazarin was however able to give most of his time to the conduct of war and the peace process on which ultimately domestic order would depend. There too the way forward was far from smooth.

24

THE FRONDE CONSIDERED

The return of the king to his capital, the flight of Condé, the departure of the Spanish from the Gironde estuary, the arrest of Gondi; each of these events can be chosen to represent the end of the Fronde. However its end was not as tidy as is indicated by such landmarks in the restoration of royal authority. The Fronde had a further life of some years as a continuing spirit of resistance, patchy but at times erupting in revolt; also as a general climate in which the crown had to work hard to consolidate its victory. There had to be elements of compromise. The restored monarchy was not that of the Declaration of Saint-Germain; nor however was it that envisaged by Richelieu and bequeathed by Louis XIII. The story of the Fronde will have made plain several of the reasons why that should be so; also why, when set against the aspirations of resisters and rebels, it can still properly be described as having failed.

Foremost among the elements that went to the making of the Fronde, and most dangerous to the crown, was the determination of *Les Grands* to maintain, or, where lost, to restore their traditional place: in court, council and, more realistically, in the province, where they had a territorial stake and, commonly, the authority and influence associated with the still potent office of governor. Their vision was that of a society bonded by ties of fidelity, where they were seen, by local officials as well as by the *gentilshommes* with whom, naturally, they had most affinity, as proper leaders, as guardians of the customs, laws and institutions of the province. Associated with this reactionary stance, reflecting too some bruising experiences in Richelieu's time, were the aspirations of that larger number of the nobility who might look to the local magnate for patronage, but had pride of lineage and a distinct set of values to which they saw to be doubly threatened; directly by state fiscality, in the shape, for example, of the *arrière-ban*; more insidiously, by the wealth and pretensions of despised *robins*, whom they saw benefiting from the explosion of office holding and the relentless rise in the scope and overall weight of taxation.

Acting as catalyst for rebellion had been the concerted action of *Parle-*

ment and other sovereign courts to protect the interests of office holders and *rentiers*, and to reverse the recent trend towards the growth of conciliar justice, together with the burgeoning powers of *intendants*: both seen as intrusions on traditional rights.[1] The protests of *Parlement* were essentially conservative, framed in reaction to the radical initiatives of royal absolutists, and in response to particular interests. A minority, however, had made novel political claims, notably, through the function of registration, to exercise control over taxes. Hard to quantify but plain to see, responsible for much of the violence of the times, helping therefore to bring about the revolutionary conjuncture, were the distresses of peasants and the *petit peuple* of the towns. Helping to shape opinion, representing again the essential continuity of opposition to royal policies, were the religious factors, as they appeared in the unease of those *dévôts*, some Jansenists, or inheritors of old League loyalties, or members of the *Compagnie du Saint Sacrement*, tending to unite in opposition to a foreign policy which, since 1630, had been turned against Catholic Spain.

Pretext and opportunity for revolt had come with the death of Louis XIII and the prospect of a long minority, and with the ministry of Mazarin, hated as foreigner, queen's favourite and director of a foreign policy and a war which was held to be the prime source of the country's ills. Ensuring that the various combustible elements in the political and economic crisis flamed into revolt were the personal ambitions of men as various as Gondi, Beaufort, Broussel, and of the most spirited of an extraordinary generation of *grandes dames*, politically minded and liberated from the conventions which might have confined their energies to sexual affairs and the cultural politics of the *salon* by the emergencies of the time and the ambitions of husbands and lovers.

The very characteristics that made *Les Grands* so troublesome – their feudal mentality, their family histories reaching back to a state of virtual independence or boasting the tincture of the blood royal, with the idea that was bred in the bone that they were fellow princes with the king, in some measure therefore sharing in, rather than subordinate to his sovereignty – also made them vulnerable to determined royal action, whether it took the form of coercion or appeal to loyalty and self-interest. An important part of Richelieu's achievement had been to persuade the educated Frenchman that his kind of government was justified by both reason and experience. It did not need the Fronde to make a man like Pascal,[2] himself no stranger to controversy, write that 'the worst of all evils is civil war'.

Parlement's position too had been ambivalent. As royal officers, unrepresentative, with a personal investment which inhibited independent action among all but the most reckless or altruistic, its members had a natural bias towards compromise. There was a profound contradiction, inhibiting decisive action, between their responsibilities, as lawyers, for the rules

217

and traditions that underlay the good order of the realm, and the aspirations of at least some of their members to provide political leadership. For the obstacles to such leadership, which must appeal to a wider constituency, there is no need to look further than the metropolitan mentality of *Parlement* whose members were jealous of its rights in relation to other sovereign courts and chary of proceeding, beyond vague gestures, towards any form of union with other *parlements*. Each of those bodies, having its own *ressort*, local patronage, and influence, might add to the sum of the crown's problems but not necessarily concern other parts of France outside its jurisdiction.

All goes some way to explaining the alternation, which can be charted in the career of Molé, between political initiatives; for example the *arrêt d'union*, and the lawyer's business of trials, judgements, codification and interpretation – or, as it would be seen from the perspective of the Palais Royal, between irresponsible and proper actions. Moreover *Parlement* was far from being a cohesive body representing a common interest. There were party men, some, for example, open Condéans; some, particularly among the younger, more junior judges were tempted towards a populist course by what they heard from across the Channel; some belonged to families so enmeshed in the worlds of finance and administration that they were bound in the end to support the crown; some in any case were simply careerists, open, as Mazarin found, to persuasion. In the small Parisian world of the *haute bourgeoisie* one *parlementaire* himself, or through his relatives, could have an interest in the *paulette*, *rentes*, another sovereign court, a *ferme*, a country estate, even an *intendance*. Such were the ambiguities which Mazarin had learned to exploit.[3]

In this world of discrepancies the lack of a single unifying ideology was particularly important. There was no equivalent to English puritanism, giving a sense of God-given purpose, uniting men and women, stiffening the will to fight for right. There was religious feeling but no central issue of faith to compel men to choose sides comparable to that of the high Anglicanism which Charles I made his controversial cause. The self-defeating intrigues of *coadjuteur* Gondi helped ensure that the militant tradition of the Parisian *curés*, monks and friars, which was responsible for much of the propaganda against Mazarin, never developed into a coherent force. The *dévôts* were well-placed in influential houses; yet they could never develop from the medley of pious interests and pressure groups that periodically found common aims, opposing the Cardinals' foreign policy for example, into a party capable of concerted action.

The Jesuits stood four-square for royal authority and were generally sympathetic to their former pupil, while the Carmelites basked in the devout patronage of the queen. Her sympathy towards the *dévôts* sometimes worried Mazarin, but it was also one of his greatest assets, staying the hand of pro-Spanish zealots, some of them members of the *Compagnie du Saint Sacrament,* who might otherwise have combined to destroy him. Drawing its vitality from the hallowed status of *le roi très chrétien* and the rights that went with it, Gallicanism, with its many advocates among the bishops as well as in *Parlement,* acted as a further counter-balance to the *dévôts.* Vincent de Paul,[4] was critical of the secular and opportunistic tendencies of Mazarin's ministry, but his main concerns were social rather than political. Inspired by him, a significant group among the *dévôts,* recruiting notably from upper-class ladies, concentrated on the charitable services which were so desperately needed in beleaguered Paris, whose population was swollen by homeless refugees.

Another potentially subversive faction within the Church was that of the Jansenists,[5] whose quarrel with the Jesuits constituted one of several sub-plots within the main drama of the Fronde. Their controversial theology and sectarian tendency, cutting across Gallican and ultramontane positions, served to divide rather than to unify. While therefore Mazarin was disapproved of by some churchmen as a cynical and unworthy leader, the combination of divisions within the Church, and the support of his friends both at Rome and in France, rendered ineffectual what could have been one of the most powerful forces ranged against him.

So it was that the main threat on the religious front to Mazarin and royal government could be expected to come not from within Catholic ranks but from what had been the mainspring of rebellious activity since the start of the Religious Wars nearly a hundred years before: Huguenotism. In May 1643 rumours, false as it turned out, that a mob was on the way to burn down the temple of Charenton,[6] were enough to cause the congregation to panic while noblemen waited with drawn swords: St Bartholomew's Day[7] was not forgotten. In 1653 a conflict over the rebuilding of a temple at Vals in the hills above the Rhône valley led to the setting up of an armed camp of some 6,000 men; Cromwell's Ironsides would have recognised the mood there as the Huguenots sang their militant psalms. A Huguenot nobleman, Bonnesson, was a ring-leader in the assemblies of noblemen and the rising of the *Sabotiers*[8] that troubled Mazarin in the post-Fronde years. There can be no doubt about the potential for violence, nor about the way in which trouble could have spread. In the first years of the minority, Balthasar, *intendant* in Languedoc, thought that a conspiracy was hatching there; his proposal, to exclude Huguenots from office, being in breach of the edict,[9] might well have precipitated it! If any incident during the Fronde had triggered a major Huguenot rising, more specifically, if the west and southwest where, from Anjou to Bordeaux, the provincial Fronde was most active, had also been the scene of concerted Huguenot action, the course, and possibly the outcome of the Fronde would have been different.

The head of the Rohan family – principals in the revolt which led to the siege of La Rochelle, the subsequent defeat of the Huguenots of the south and the Grace of Alés – had been treated with politic generosity; yet he eventually threw in his lot with Condé and the Fronde. In 1660 Turenne was startled to find that Rohan was still a folk hero, inspiring talk of rebellion in the south. Turenne was of course himself a leading *frondeur* at the outset, as was his elder brother, head of the house of la Tour d'Auvergne, the duc de Bouillon. The provinces in which Condé and his allies found most support were also those where the Huguenot population was relatively dense: about a third of the whole number of about a million and a quarter lived in Poitou, Saintonge, Angoumois and Guienne. A number of them were nobles, a potential cadre in case of recourse to arms. There was another sizeable group in Normandy, a province which gave the Fronde some early support. Most Huguenots lived however in the southern provinces, those which, notably Languedoc and the Dauphiné, were most remote from Paris and hardest to control. This was where, with the influence of mountainous Dauphiné's Swiss neighbours in mind, the government was haunted by the fear of separatist movements, 'cantonisation' as James I's ambassador, George Carew, had called it. There the atrocious experiences of civil war lived on in the mentality of the families and communities who feuded over rights defined by successive edicts which were argued over by the lawyers, and defended or denounced by the religious authorities.

At the Catholic summit, when bishops pronounced or debated in assembly, the rhetoric embraced the images of persecution and war. That could be discounted as the exhibitionism common at such gatherings, when speakers are unconstrained by such mundane considerations as how such a policy could be implemented, or how it would affect the finances of the state. When, however, successive speakers at the Church Assembly of 1651 demanded action against heresy, they were not just making political points about Mazarin's apparently cynical adoption of a policy of *laissez-faire*, but voicing the fervour of Catholic revival, with which went a keen sense of the spiritual unity of the realm as a positive value and goal to be achieved. Under such pressures Huguenots might well feel beleaguered. Some were attracted towards Catholicism's gentler face, that of Vincent de Paul; some succumbed to worldly arguments for conversion. Yet to this period, forty years on, many would look back, as to a golden age. There were features of the Huguenot situation in mid-century which explain why there was no general rising; why, in 1652, the crown could officially thank the Huguenots for their loyalty.

His mind turning to the greater game abroad, Richelieu, after the fall of La Rochelle, had resisted the pressure from the *dévôts* to deny the Huguenots freedom of worship. Still locked in war against Spain, his pupil Mazarin was to show that he had learned the lesson well. To aid him there were already pronounced trends within the Huguenot body which made for peaceful co-existence. A high proportion of its membership was *bourgeois*. It reflects the importance of literacy in a cult that drew inspiration from the reading of the Bible. It meant that there formed groups of *bien-pensants* who did not find that the claims of their faith conflicted with those of the state or with profitable forms of service and employment. The patronage of Sully had been responsible for a high concentration of Huguenots in the financial administration. The appointment of Hervart[10] to be *contrôleur-général*, in 1657, would ensure that it continued to be so. With Mazarin's encouragement he had already used his international banking connections to provide cash in the preceding years; he was indeed one of the saviours of the monarchy.

Huguenot strength was not limited to the world of business. A startlingly high number of Huguenots were prominent in the Parisian world of the arts, architecture and literature. Some operated at the heart of the cultural establishment. Chancellor Séguier was one of several prominent patrons whose new hôtel was built by Jean du Cerceau, *architecte des bâtiments du roi*. At the Tuileries and Saint-Germain, Anne and Louis walked in gardens landscaped by Jacques Boyceau, *intendant des jardins du roi*. Vincent de Paul was one of many painted by the prolific and talented Sébastien Bourdon. When in 1648 the *Académie Royale de Peinture*[11] was founded, nearly a third of its members were Huguenot, as was its secretary, Louis Testelin,[12] who painted the murals for the Palais-Cardinal. For forty years after its foundation in 1634, the secretary of the Académie Française was another Huguenot, Valentin Conrart. Such men were well-placed to influence opinion, likely too to be moderate, undogmatic and drawn to policies of *détente*.

The change in the nature of Huguenot leadership from the noble, and militant, with ministers advocating and soldiers manning the hard line that corresponded to their theological views, to that of the *bourgeois* establishment, wealthy and moderate, reduced the chance of a general rising. The new social orientation was mirrored by trends in teaching and writing that encouraged hopes of peaceful co-existence, even possibly some kind of reunion. The debate in France reflected the wider malaise of Calvinism, torn, as in Holland, between Arminian doctrine,[13] stressing duty to the ruler, and Calvin's uncompromising view of sovereignty as belonging to God alone. Unlike their co-religionaries of Holland and Scotland, where results appeared to justify faith in election, the Huguenots had the sobering experience of wars which left them defenceless, a small minority in a Catholic state of growing prestige and power. There was no encouragement for them in Germany where the unhappy experience of the Elector Palatine taught the dangers of rash revolt. As for England – though some Huguenots rejoiced at the dismantling of the Anglican church, almost all, like the Scottish Presbyterians, deplored the republican and millenarian spirit that brought Charles I to execution.

221

Among the most influential was Moise Amyraut,[14] director of the leading Huguenot academy at Saumur, a scholarly humanist who was willing
to be unorthodox if that was where textual study should lead him. Influenced by the teaching of Grotius on natural law, he believed in man's
capacity to rise above differences of creeds, a seminal notion but one
that sat well with the ideas, for example, of François de Sales, whose
Introduction to la Vie Dévote was to be found in most literate households
(and many a Huguenot one; there were forty editions by 1656). When
Amyraut urged his fellow Huguenots to cultivate 'the affability which
makes us easily accessible one to another' he was speaking the good-
tempered language of de Sales, still compatible, the saint showed, with
the most profound piety. When Amyraut wrote his timely *Apologie pour
ceux de la religion* in 1647, arguing that the Huguenots had never intended
to set up a separate state, and when he condemned the regicides of
England in *Discours sur la Souveraineté des Rois* (1650), he served the
interests of Mazarin and the absolutists. One of them, Guez de Balzac,
paid the erudite theologian Turenne's protégé – but acquaintance too of
Mazarin – a telling compliment when he said that Amyraut showed the
qualities of the court rather than the consistory.

The consistory fought back, in the person chiefly of Pierre du Moulin,
pastor of Nîmes, leader of orthodox opponents of Amyraut's 'deviation-
ism'. The terms of the controversy, and its uncertain outcome, matter
less than its effects. The Huguenots were weakened by their divisions. By
their general retreat towards an Erastian[15] position they discouraged the
idea of revolt and contributed therefore to the triumph of absolute
monarchy. They secured their position in the short-term, but in ways that
left them vulnerable if, and when, monarchy should have a change of
heart.

How quickly that might happen is illustrated by the text of two royal
declarations. In May 1652, at a critical juncture of the war when there
was anxiety about the south, Mazarin's 'little flock' was praised for its
loyalty, the edict of Nantes was reaffirmed and all judgements made by
parlements since 1629 conflicting with its letter and spirit were annulled:
it was the Huguenots' reward for 'the devotion and loyalty, notably in
the present circumstances, with which "We are highly satisfied".' In 1656,
however, a much cooler document projected the appointment at a future
date of two commissioners for each province, one Catholic and one
Protestant, to enquire into breaches of the edict. By then the most acute
danger had passed. In 1653, in the Vivarais, an armed band of some
7,000 Huguenots had tried to establish the right to hold services at Vals.
A local nobleman, the comte de Rieux, came up to prevent it, with a force
nearly as large. The Huguenot bluff was called. If they had succeeded they
would have asserted their right elsewhere: a formula for religious war. A
commission was sent out in 1654 to investigate alleged breaches of 'edicts

of pacification' in Languedoc, Haute Guyenne and Foix. It was the start of a hardening of attitudes on the part of government.

In 1659, at Turenne's behest, Mazarin gave permission for a national synod to meet at Loudun. But Huguenots were told that it was to be the last. Prevented from meeting at the summit, Huguenots would thence find it harder to concert a national policy. When, in 1661, the Declaration of 1656 was put into effect and the first temples were destroyed, Huguenots as a body were in no position to mount effective resistance. In this, as in other transactions, Mazarin was responding empirically to current needs and pressures. He had been concerned, first to ensure that there was no widening of revolt, second to alleviate English concerns about their fellow Protestants because he needed an alliance with Cromwell.[16] That secured by 1656, he listened more carefully to his agents in the field. They warned him about the excited state of southern Huguenots, particularly in Languedoc. Mazarin emerges from this part of the story as not so much tolerant as realistic and wisely moderate, though perhaps more by necessity than conviction.

It can be argued that the Huguenot issue was marginal to the outcome of the Fronde. The passivity of the 'separated brethren', as Vincent de Paul called them, is only one among several factors – but one to which Mazarin, short of friends, naturally attached high importance. In the end he was to owe nearly as much to his enemies as to his friends. In part, evidently, that was due to the nature of institutions; in part to personal failings. We have seen a fissiparous and self-destructive tendency in Mazarin's opponents, contrasting markedly with the tenacious and often skilful performance of those who served the crown. So long as they retained ministerial office, military command or a place in the royal household, even the opportunity to serve in some unofficial capacity, the latter enjoyed crucial advantages. Despite the enormous difficulties in raising taxes and the enforced abandonment of the *intendants*, the crown held on to its long-established right to tax without consent. In September 1653 Séguier made that plain when he laid down the law to *trésoriers*: only sovereign courts could even remonstrate.[17] Nor did the mechanism for raising loans fall apart; it was in the interest of finance ministers and *traitants* to work together and of *Parlement* to ensure that salaries and interest continued to be paid. The more uncertain the world around them, the more solid appeared the credit of monarchy. Though *frondeurs* were twice driven to set up an emergency government of Paris, there was no viable alternative body to assume the powers of government over the country. Neither *Parlement* nor the States General could fulfil that role.

Older men could remember the last meeting of that occasional body (1614–15) and its protracted, ultimately futile debates.[18] It was representative and capable of speaking for the interests of each order of the realm. But it lacked a tradition of continuity, with the practice in responsible debate that it might have brought. Above all it had no levers to pull, not just to ensure that ministers took notice of its submissions, but to compel summons in the first place. The crown had promised it, preliminary local meetings had taken place, but all had come to nothing. Time gained and support bought was shown to be the crown's only concern. The green shoots of representative government withered beneath the spreading tree of monarchy. *Parlement*'s was a more robust growth – but not independent. Molé's brave and skilful balancing act had ended with his leading senior *parlementaires* to Pontoise in order to maintain the legal front until the king should come into his own. Along the road to Pontoise there had been some bold initiatives. But neither the union of sovereign courts, which enjoyed a brief life and seems, with its programme of reforms, to have been the Fronde's most striking achievement, nor the wider union with the other *parlements* which never came into being, could have overcome the essential problem; the range and potential conflict of interests which allowed ministers to divide and rule.

They were exposed by successive developments which can be seen as landmarks along the royal road to success. The *maîtres des requêtes*, whose temporary siding with others of the *robe* had underlined the mistakes of government, soon drifted back to their former position, wedded to the crown as the prime source of its *intendants*. The *grand conseil* was never happy to be aligned with *Parlement* and by 1649 had suspended its sittings to show its loyalty; in 1652 it followed the royal entourage. The *chambre des comptes* and *cour des aides* stayed in Paris during the first siege, against royal orders, but they made only token contributions to its defence. Throughout, fear of the mob weighed more with them than enthusiasm for the cause of *Parlement*. The provincial *parlements* responded to initiatives from Paris only when it seemed to be in their particular interest. Even the *parlement* of Rouen, appealing for aid in its clash with monarchy, delayed registering the decree of outlawry against Mazarin. Only Toulouse and Bordeaux did so in the end. It is not surprising that Bonney concludes: 'The provincial sovereign courts' concern for local power was a fundamental reason for the absence of a united opposition to the policies of Richelieu and Mazarin'.

Paris was proud to claim leadership – but dismissed the possibility of including provincial representatives in the *Chambre St Louis*. Paternalist – some would say patronising – in style, it never came near to a national view of representation. It is not surprising that royalists took heart when, for example, Aix asked the king if he wished to retain or to banish his minister. That was not the language of revolution. There was least cooperation at the lowest levels of the judiciary, between the *présidiaux*, *sénéchaussées* and *bailliages*. There was little in the way of practical aid for the officials of the lesser courts. So there was always the temptation to such courts to hoe their own fields. The crown encouraged them, asking them at one stage to make sovereign judgements in all suits while banning the normal right of appeal to Paris. Given the splits within *Parlement* itself, which ministers were so well-placed to exploit, it may be concluded that the structures and mentalities for that solidarity of opposition, without which the *robe* could not achieve a significant change in the constitutional balance, simply did not exist.

The very features of French society that made it so hard to govern and tempted ministers to resort to arbitrary methods also made it hard to mount a concerted resistance. There was no lack of *esprit de corps*, but it was to be found within each *corps*. The notion of 'class interest' is out of place. Misused in 1648, the *paulette* was still a valuable tactical weapon in the hands of the crown. Despite some devaluation of office currency after two decades of over-issue, underlying demand remained strong. The conditions of civil war, unfriendly to other forms of investment, only increased the hunger for the security that royal office could provide. The insignificance of most offices in law and finance meant that their holders would naturally look to the authority of the crown as the best protector of their interests. Between the *élites* of gown and sword there remained fundamental differences. The academic, literate world of the *robe*, respectful towards scholarship, proud of their libraries, sensitive to the claims of religion and familiar with the idea, at least as it was expressed in classical texts, of civic responsibility, was increasingly unsympathetic towards the feudal values of the military aristocracy. Considering a marriage alliance or other business arrangement, they might respect the name and like the idea of 'living nobly' – while despising the man.

Successive phases of the Fronde, which had begun with gestures of unity, brought the culture clash into sharper focus as the party of the princes showed its scorn for the nice formulas of the law, and judges were outraged by reckless resort to arms and insatiable demands for governorships and pensions. Although the Hôtel de Ville was hardly typical of the leading merchants, since the *prévôts des marchands* were openly Mazarinist when it was safe to be so, it did represent the *bourgeois* concern for stable trading conditions. Merchants supported *Parlement* in initial opposition to royal taxes, but, as had been shown during the August Days, soon came to fear the mob more than they did the officers and policies of the crown. Indeed it is not absurd to claim that the common people of Paris, who relished the spectacle of great men at odds, intruded into the royal palace, jostled the *parlementaire* dignitaries who, they supposed, betrayed them, took the pay of partisans of both sides – and, at the *dénouement*, showed so vociferously their love for their king – were his final, conclusive argument.

The fact that *frondeur* hostility, especially after the peace of Rueil, was directed so largely at Mazarin, at the man who allegedly abused the system, rather than at the system itself, is revealing; no less so is their

225

failure to secure his permanent removal. Mazarin had reason to feel insecure when his position depended solely on the support of the queen. But she was not forced to go through more than a show of giving him up. What happened in Paris always affected the rest of the country. But again its provincial fragmentation enabled the regime to survive. Anne took the court to the country, gave what support she could to her loyal generals, and waited for her opponents to destroy themselves. She could afford to play a waiting game because her son was soon to come of age. How different, she might reflect, was the destiny of young Louis, secure in his subjects' loyalty, and that of his adult cousin, 'King Charles II', a penniless exile, now even denied the support he might expect from his mother's country because Mazarin needed the alliance of Cromwell against Spain. Hereditary right, the principle which served Mazarin so well, could not be allowed to stand in the way of France's territorial interests.

Personal factors have been seen to count; the follies and blunders of some of the principals, the sense and strength of others. From one angle, that for example of Gondi, Châteauneuf or Condé, the Fronde can be seen as a frustrating sequence of opportunities for personal aggrandisement; from another, that of Talon or Séguier, crown law officers of different stance but sharing a common interest in good order, it appears as an unseasonable storm; from another, that of Molé and most of *Parlement*, as a necessary, if at times embarrassing attempt to halt absolutist trends, not in the end an entirely unsuccessful one; from another, that of Le Tellier or Lionne, pragmatists both and not averse to necessary wheeling and dealing, as a disagreeable interruption to the proper business of government. Each of these men, representing here many others, had a chance to influence events. No one, unless it be Anne herself, had more chances than Mazarin. He was for long periods the *premier ministre* in fact as well as title; even abroad he could influence and manipulate. The failures of the Fronde, seen in personal terms, are the successes of Anne, once persuaded to swallow pride, control her temper, make deceitful concessions and wait for Louis to come of age. They are also the sensible actions of those ministers, Mazarin foremost, who served the crown and their careers by ensuring that money was raised and armies kept in the field. Indeed it may be that the most important aspect of Mazarin's personal survival course was the logistical: supplies for the troops. For in the end all came down to success or failure in battle and siege. Though they employed their own *intendants* for recruitment, pay and discipline, the *frondeurs* were never able to levy enough troops. The crown was. Turenne's return to the royal camp, the consistent loyalty of other generals, would have been less significant if they had not been provided with men, nearly as many foreigners as Frenchmen, and the cash to pay them.

Yet they pillaged, no less than their opponents, damaging the crown's cause, because funds were always inadequate and priority throughout was given to the *corps d'élite*, the royal household troops, Mazarin's own guards and to the Swiss. When times are adverse and allegiances uncertain, loyalty, long-term contracts and professional competence are at a premium. The 12,000 Swiss in royal pay, household guards or companies serving with other royal regiments, were, in this respect, uniquely important. Their service had long been as valuable to the Swiss cantons whence they were recruited, with their surplus population, as to the French monarchy. Now they showed their mettle, manning the front-line against insurrectionary Paris. Louis XIV did not hesitate to acknowledge his debt to these Frenchmen by adoption, who stood firm against armed mobs, defended the Palais Royal and protected the flight to Saint-Germain.

If a kind of order was restored and monarchy preserved by the efforts of its soldiers, it is unlikely that they were appreciated by the mass of the ordinary people of France. Soldiers were always enemies to the people on whom they were billeted, whose houses they pillaged, whose crops and livestock they seized. The years 1648–53 were years of exceptional misery. 1652, the climactic year of the Fronde, was about the grimmest of the century. Wide-ranging armies had little option but to live off the land. It would appear therefore to follow that they were the prime reason for social distress. But the case is not so simple. The impact of war was regional, not general: among French provinces, Picardy, Champagne, Burgundy and the Ile-de-France were worst hit; patches of country between Anjou and Bordeaux and around Rouen suffered cruelly at times. The eastern provinces were specially afflicted because of the continuing war against Spain. They had been suffering, like neighbouring Artois, Flanders, and Lorraine, since the 1630s. Indeed the Fronde made relatively little difference to Burgundy, long inured to the bitter 'war of the two Burgundies', the other being that part of the original duchy that had remained Spanish – the Franche-Comté.[19] The nobles on both sides raided and plundered in ways that recall conditions on the Anglo-Scottish border in the Middle Ages. They would stop at nothing. An attack by Comtois on the church of the frontier village Mailly l'Eglise, during midnight mass in 1642, yielded them forty prisoners. With reports from the years before the Fronde of wolves roaming and killing, of peasants found dead in the fields with grass in their mouths, the campaigns of the Fronde could do little to extend their experience of the miseries of war.

Evidence for famine and epidemics in burial registers recording a steep rise in deaths in these years, with a peak in 1652, is to be found in provinces virtually untouched by civil or foreign war;[20] indeed the 'grain crisis' of 1652 affected communities from Exeter to Cracow, from Stockholm to Naples.[21] Evidently other factors were at work; they include a sequence of wet seasons spoiling crops, bread scarce and expensive, prolonged malnutrition weakening resistance to disease. Related, as both cause and effect, was the general economic recession, with the slowing down in the growth of the money supply. Against that background, a near-doubling of taxation in real terms since 1635 had been sapping the vitality of the peasant economy. Revolts would continue to erupt. It was a song of the Fronde that the insurgents of the Vivarais would chant: 'Peasants to arms, down with all vultures and taxmen. You must howl with the wolves . . .' – but this was in 1670.[22]

One trend, already beginning to affect the social balance in the countryside, and set to continue, was the increase in peasant debts. When a peasant lost his horse and cart, the precious assets which were most in demand by foraging soldiers, he lost the working capital which might have enabled him to remain solvent. If he borrowed beyond capacity to repay and the richer *laboureur* or local *bourgeois* foreclosed, one more unfortunate became a *journalier*, a dependent and landless labourer, or a beggar. Consolidation of estates around big cities was not caused but accelerated by war. It was most evident in those areas most severely affected, around Paris, Rheims and Dijon.[23] Specific points made by Lescot, *échevin de Paris*, charged with a mission to find food for the capital in March 1649 were the scarcity of grain, and the depredations of soldiers while peasants hid. 'The countryside will soon become a desert' warned Molé. There is no need to see hypocrisy in descriptions which gave emotional force to *parlementaire* protests, any more than in the charitable efforts of great ladies to relieve the suffering.[24] It is ironic though that what they deplored was part of the process – the enlargement of estates, which would increase the fortunes of their class. Meanwhile however, as Chéruel pointed out, there was a political consequence: *parlementaires* returned to the crown because of the threat to their lands.

War falls then into place in a larger scheme; important but not uniquely so; affecting the European economy, and so France; devastating at particular times, in particular areas – never more so than during the Fronde. Statistics confirm what contemporaries attested to, Jansenist ladies inditing leaflets pleading for money for relief, *curés* heart-sick from visiting the sick and burying the dead, officials explaining why it was impossible to raise more taxes. Where campaigning was most intense, as in the country south of Paris round Etampes, which suffered terribly during its siege in the spring of 1652, there can be no doubt of its impact. Vincent de Paul and his *filles de charité* found utter ruin there, amid the stench of dead bodies. It did not even need fighting, as Monsieur Vincent makes clear: 'We have undertaken at Palaiseau, where the royal army has been encamped for 20 days, as great an operation as at Etampes; there is extreme sickness and poverty'. The incursion of hungry, undisciplined men, with their horses and mules, into a rural community precariously balanced at the point of self-sufficiency, could only be devastating. They stripped it bare. Often, for the hell of it, they raped the women and burned the houses and barns. Their encampments bred disease, typhus, dysentery and the plague.

Peasants found ways of surviving. Refugees at Rheims, with their cattle, would slip out of the gates at curfew time, returning at dawn with fodder for their animals. Nor were they always passive. Writing to Le Tellier, in October 1652, Mazarin was delighted to hear of a Spanish defeat in a skirmish at Grandpie when 'peasants hiding in the woods fell on the Spaniards and inflicted great carnage'. With peace, and a new sowing, could come speedy restoration. Crude dwellings could soon be rebuilt. Some villages would never, however, be re-occupied; some towns never recover former vitality; some peasants never regain their former status as independent landed proprietors; some nobles would fall into indigence, and become objects of charity. There is enough, both in the records of suffering and in the wider social consequences to justify the description of the Fronde as a time of special distress. Black patches in the chiaroscuro of the larger portrait, lose only a little of their effect against the sombre colours of the whole.

Part IV

WAR AND PEACE

'Le Cardinal trompait; mais il ne mentait pas.'
Talleyrand

25

TOWARDS WESTPHALIA

The very day, 24 October 1648, that the declaration of Saint-Germain was registered by *Parlement*, also saw the signing of the two treaties, at Munster and Osnabrück that together were to be known as the peace of Westphalia. Bewailing the ingratitude of his adopted country, Mazarin would hardly have appreciated the ironies of that October day. Yet Frenchmen, all, that is, but the handful who were in a position to appreciate the finer points of diplomacy, were likely to be concerned more with the costs of the continuing war with Spain than they were with gains of land, fortresses and rights which, unless they lived in one of France's eastern provinces, were as unimaginably remote from their lives as if they had been colonies overseas. For the dynasts and the diplomats who served them Europe was a vast estate map: war was an acceptable means of acquiring property, only more expensive and hazardous than marriage.

What even ministers and diplomats had to strain to see, beyond the diplomatic maze, would yet prove to be something which future generations would take for granted. The longest, most extensive, bloodiest and most damaging of wars, involving in some way every important state except Russia, had left France – though burdened with taxes and now disrupted by revolts – as strong in relation to the hitherto dominant Habsburg powers as in 1559, when the peace of Câteau-Cambrésis had ended an earlier phase of dynastic wars, it had been weak and vulnerable. Then, with the successive deaths of Henry II and Francis II, a long minority had set the scene for ineffectual government and civil wars. Now, with another minority and prospects again clouded, it was more likely that Frenchmen would fear the worst, than share in Mazarin's vision of glory and power. What sustained him?

One part of the answer lies in success in battle. The impact on the domestic scene of two particular actions, Condé's victories at Rocroy and Lens, has been seen. As the sun went down on the carnage of that May day in 1643, when the flower of the Spanish infantry was destroyed, the elated victors might well envisage the sunset of Spanish power. Since the Catalan and Portuguese revolts, the Spanish were committed as well

233

to war on two fronts in their own peninsula. Under the circumstances, it is the tenacity of the Spanish government that astonishes, with its capacity to find the means for further campaigns, rather than the remorseless process of decline.[1] Moreover Thirty Years War battles were rarely decisive[2] and after 1643, French success was not unbroken. Since the fall of Breisach in 1638, the country had enjoyed a greater degree of security: the fortress protected Lorraine from the raids of its freebooting, exiled duke Charles and his Bavarian ally; it also provided a base for offensive operations in Germany. But here the French encountered resolute commanders, notably the Bavarians, Mercy and Werth, who were now effectively managing the Imperialist war effort in the interest of duke Maximilian as much as of the emperor. At this late stage in the game, Maximilian still hoped to secure his Electorate along with the Upper Palatine. For these ends he was prepared to change alliance, as Mazarin realised and exploited.

What seems in the end to have counted, as much as particular victories, was the ability of the French to sustain several fronts and continue to put relatively disciplined troops into the field, under competent commanders. For this was a war of attrition designed to use up the enemy's resources, weaken his resolve and so give more weight to the diplomats at Munster and Osnabrück. Theirs was another kind of war, more civilised but little less intense. Their weapons were papers and procedures, lobbies and bluffs; their skills those of the lawyer and the politician. The delays and postponements before and during the actual negotiations were due partly to the tactical moves of the principals, looking for some advantage from military or political events. Mainly however they reflected the sheer complexity of the issues to be resolved. Because Richelieu had recognised this, and saw that they must be handled by one who had already mastered the *métier* of diplomacy, he understood the interests of states – and, no less important, the mentality of statesmen – he had envisaged Mazarin as his successor. It will become apparent that his confidence was justified.

Studying his foreign policy, Pagés concludes that 'Mazarin played the part of first minister to an even greater extent than Richelieu'. He was certainly his own foreign minister. Managing the council, building up a clientèle which included potentially useful foreigners cultivating individual good will, he corresponded with ambassadors and generals without consulting Loménie de Brienne or Le Tellier, respectively secretary of state for foreign affairs and war. If the account of domestic business has left an impression of insouciance, with a preference for the private deal and the dramatic stroke, that is dispelled by the record of Mazarin's expert, tireless engagement with military and diplomatic business. His contemporary, Priolo,[3] wrote that 'he rested rarely and slept little and dealt personally with all matters of importance'. That is not to say that his judgement was always faultless. It can be argued that he knew, or cared, too little about Holland, too much about Italy. He had a tendency to get carried away by the ingenuity of some scheme. When he erred, it was usually in the way of daring, of optimism; the spirit of 'a bridge too far'. Realism quickly asserted itself. He might be voluble in complaint and self-justification, but he was equally resourceful, ready to plan afresh and to fight back. He was usually a good judge of soldiers, of their needs and capabilities. Early acquaintance with generals of the calibre of Spinola had helped to form his judgement. His choice of Turenne, brought from Italy to take over the demoralised remnants of Guébriant's[4] Rhineland army, was crucially important: he was an astute general, as befitted a former student in the prime Protestant school of war, the camp of Frederick Henry of Orange.[5]

Imperialists exaggerated when they claimed that the defeat, in October 1643, of Guébriant, with a mixed force of French and Bernardines, made up for the Spanish disaster at Rocroy. In any case, the German balance was partially restored when Turenne, collaborating with Condé in a three-day battle near Freiburg in July 1644, eventually overcame the Bavarian, Mercy. Casualties were high – the remaining Bernardines were disgruntled at being used as cannon fodder for France while Mercy, Ferdinand's most capable general, lived on to fight another day. In May 1645 Turenne was surprised in camp by Mercy and suffered heavy loss, but he had his revenge in August when, with Condé, he won the second battle of Nördlingen. No one team of diplomats representing Austria, Spain, Sweden, Holland and France, beginning to assemble for the first talks about peace, was yet able to use overwhelming military strength as the clinching argument. For Mazarin, the Swedish and Dutch alliances were of the highest importance; the inclination of either to a separate peace would be the greatest misfortune. The majority of Queen Christina[6] (1644), and her pacifist inclination, made it all the more important that her generals, still subsidised by France, exploit Austrian weakness. That, the fiery Torstensson,[7] Wrangel's successor in command, was happy to do. With brutal logic he adapted his style to the state of Germany: for pay his troops were promised victory and loot. But first he had to deal with the Danes who had provoked war by raising Baltic Sound dues. This he achieved in no uncertain manner, but it needed Mazarin's diplomacy to bring the combatants to terms at Brömsero in August 1645; in November, by the treaty of Copenhagen, he secured the opening of the Sound to French trade.

Sweden had already renewed its alliance with France at the Hague in March 1644, accepting that each might negotiate individually with the Habsburgs but not make a separate peace. The Dutch stood on the same footing, but their alliance with France, long the mainstay of French security and a significant factor in their own success, entered an uncertain phase as they anticipated the day of formal independence. It was important therefore that nothing should suggest that Mazarin had a secret agenda concerned more with French ambitions in Flanders than with the security of the United Provinces. There was a growing rift there between the military and dynastic wing, represented by Frederick Henry, *stadholder* of six out of the seven provinces, and the republican wing, which represented the commercial strength of Holland and the financial dominance of Amsterdam, with its interest in peace – or such a war as might further its economic interests.

Mazarin was inclined to deal with the power he understood, in the person of Frederick Henry as sovereign. He accorded him the sovereign title *altesse*, underestimating perhaps the strength of Dutch pride in their unique constitution, with its balance between provincial autonomy and federal executive. He could do little to allay the fear of Dutch Protestants that France was their enemy, since Dutch Catholics – still around fifty per cent of the population, but generally submerged beneath the dominant Calvinist groups in towns and Estates – appealed to Anne for protection and found a sympathetic ear in *dévôt* circles. As Richelieu had known when he had had to persuade *dévôts* that his alliance with a Protestant state was not damaging to the Catholic cause, while assuring that state that it had nothing to fear from the opposition in his own camp, one false move could undo a policy. Ironically this was made by the diplomat, d'Avaux, who should have understood the sensitivities of the Dutch after his service as negotiator at the Hague and in north Germany. On his way through the Hague to Münster, in March 1644, he informed the Estates that the king would be gratified if they would tolerate Catholics.

Mazarin deplored his envoy's *faux pas*, but only as a tactical blunder that might jeopardise a larger strategic design: that Philip IV should exchange Catalonia for the Spanish Netherlands. It was Mazarin's favourite scheme. 'The satisfaction with which he outlined his plan leads one to think that he was intoxicated by its beauty'[8] – and there was an elegant rationality about it. Spain could only with difficulty hold on to the Netherlands, and France was experiencing problems in Catalonia. There were, however, certain dangers as d'Avaux and Servien pointed out. France had promised the Estates-General of the United Provinces that the two powers would engage in the joint conquest of the Spanish lands. Spain could divulge the plan to the Dutch, thus facilitating its own negotiations. The betrayal of the Catalans would damage the French name and trading interests in the Mediterranean world. Mazarin countered these arguments by a new move. His envoy, d'Estrades,[9] made secret overtures to Frederick Henry about the transfer of Antwerp, with the Scheldt trade, to the Dutch; all in vain, since the Spanish behaved as predicted. The Dutch were unlikely to take kindly to the Antwerp proposal, for the last thing that the prospering burghers of the north wanted was a revival of commerce in the south. They were now determined to make their own peace, without regard for their cavalier and devious ally.

Thus treated, Mazarin's policy can seem merely fanciful, even reckless. Yet it deserves to be studied in the larger context of French tradition and strategic concerns. His letter of January 1646 to Servien reveals how his mind was working. 'The acquisition of the Spanish Netherlands would give the city of Paris an impregnable rampart and it could then truly be called the heart of France . . . so much blood and money would be well spent if . . . provinces were annexed to the crown of France which, in the past, have provided the means to individual rulers, not only to resist France, but to trouble her to the extent which we all know.' Was Mazarin carried away by his sense of the renaissance of French arms, or by the rhetoric of official publications, to envisage the monarchy being extended to the limits of ancient Gaul? He does not mention those frontiers, 'natural' or otherwise; rather he emphasises. 'the side from which we have most to fear' which suggests that his view was essentially defensive. One day Sebastien Vauban[10] was to be given the commission and funds to create a fortress ring round France's 'meadow square'. The opportunity would come with the series of acquisitions, starting with Westphalia. The evidence, in the targets chosen for negotiation and the gains secured, points definitely to a realistic military policy, like Richelieu's, giving priority to existing strongpoints and defensible sites.

One area where Mazarin allowed his imagination to luxuriate was Italy. A challenge was provided by the keen disappointment of the Papal election of 1644. Innocent X[11] had been opposed by the French interest and was expected to favour Spain. To compel him to reconsider and to crush the Spanish power in Italy, an amphibious operation was planned; a fleet under Brézé[12] and a landing party under Prince Thomas of Savoy was to seize Orbitello and the Spanish *presidios* on the Tuscan coast. The immediate object was to cut Spanish communications between Milan and Naples. As with the Netherlands there was a hidden agenda. Prince Thomas, whose conversion to the French cause was a fruit of Mazarin's carefully cultivated relationship with Savoy, was to incite the Neapolitans to revolt against Spain. If successful, he was to let the French have Gaetano and other Sicilian ports. He might even succeed his nephew (Louis XIV's cousin), the infant duke of Savoy,[13] in return for the cession of Nice and Savoy, 'everything which lies on this side of the mountains close to France'.

The years 1645 and 1646 were in many ways sobering ones for Mazarin – and Italy brought little comfort. Prince Thomas's expedition was a fiasco. He did not, as Mazarin urged, take Porto Ercole, Orbitello's link with the interior. After Brézé was killed in a naval fight, Thomas raised the siege (July 1646). He did little to incite the Neapolitans to revolt; when they did, the following year, it was to be a largely home-grown affair. After a deceptively easy start, Mazarin now experienced the frustration that Richelieu had known, the slips between plan and execution.

He showed however the energy and spirit which were repeatedly to redeem mistakes. Fresh troops were mustered and sent to Italy under marshals de la Meilleraye and du Plessis-Praslin. They set siege to Porto Longone on the island of Elba, and Piombino on the Tuscan coast. Both capitulated in October 1647. Restless Neapolitans noted the further dent to Spanish reputation.[14] The French were well placed to prey on Spain's lines of communication. Mazarin would have preferred not to become involved in Masaniello's revolt: neither his republicanism nor the murderous activities of his followers commended him. When, however, Masaniello persuaded the duc de Guise to be their captain-general, Mazarin sent a small fleet to his aid (December 1647). Since Guise was by then a prisoner, all he could do was secure his honourable release. Mazarin was anxious to disengage from an affair which at best could only be a small diversion, at worst a serious embarrassment. Italy had ceased to have priority as negotiations at Münster and Osnabrück reached the critical phase.

26

THE LONG HAUL

Peace had been talked about since Mazarin first came to France. As early as 1641 Swedish and French envoys had met at Hamburg to discuss preliminaries. The French maintained that the Emperor Ferdinand III[1] was insincere in his professions; the same could be said about them. A typical pretext for delay was the French demand for a title for duchess Christina of Savoy. When the Danes, as intermediaries, produced a solution, both the emperor and Richelieu were annoyed: neither side could however repudiate it. The Austrians then proceeded to ratify the preliminaries in a document so vague that the French could not accept it. It would seem that Ferdinand had more to gain from negotiation than his opponents: since his defeat at the second battle of Breitenfeld in November 1642, Maximilian had been able to call the tune – and he could not be relied on to be loyal. Even more serious, with effects the opposite to those of the close entente earlier in the war, was the drifting apart of the two Habsburg partners.

Spain's assertive pride seemed to grow with defeat. In psychological terms, the brave face, the stiff manners can be accounted for, when behind them was the growing realisation that the grand design had failed: there would not be a Habsburg Germany, or a wholly Habsburg Netherlands. The alliance of Austria and Spain was now damaging to both partners. So Spain looked to her own salvation. Without the Dutch to contend with, Spanish troops could surely give a better account of themselves in what was emerging as the main struggle, that with France. The new mood is reflected in the apparently inept decision to appoint Don John, Philip IV's twelve-year-old son, to be governor in the Netherlands. Vienna's choice was the archduke Leopold. The Spanish deferred sending Don John; meanwhile Don Francisco de Melo pursued the aggressive course that led to disaster. It was only after Rocroy, in June 1643, that Ferdinand gave Imperial sanction for negotiations to begin.

It was not until December 1644 that the Congress of Münster opened, with fanfares, processions and every kind of competitive gambit, ranging from the formally polite to the maliciously subversive: all time-wasting.

When the French delegation arrived at Münster[2] it was to find the Spanish alongside the Imperial delegate. It held up negotiations by contesting Philip IV's title as king of Navarre and Portugal, putting forward the claims respectively of Louis XIV and John of Braganza.[3] The Emperor meanwhile caught at any straw that might suggest a change in the wind: one was the death of the duke of Brunswick and the quick peace made by his successor: another, the relief that came with the war between Sweden and Denmark. Ferdinand was a man of faith, but tinged with a salutory pessimism, an ability, unlike his cousin Philip IV, to recognise facts and trends. The weakness of Spain required that Piccolomini[4] was deployed in the Netherlands. After the end of the war with Denmark, Sweden resumed the aggressive course. While Torstensson's licensed bullies taught the new law of Germany, that it was safer to be in camp than in nearby city or countryside, his queen urged her envoy, Oxenstierna[5] the arrogant son of the Chancellor who had contributed so much to Swedish greatness, to press Swedish claims without delaying the peace. Finally the French army was proving its capacity to sustain war on several fronts.

Germany was in the grip of famine but the diplomats of Münster and Osnabrück kept high state as the months passed. Most business was done outside the main conference chamber where it took six months to arrange a seating plan and order of entry. The Spanish ambassador, Peñaranda,[6] could never enter because suitable formalities could not be arranged. That did not deter him from discussing with the Dutch the outlines of a separate peace. The French quarrelled at different times with the envoys of Sweden, Brandenburg, Spain; the delegates of the Hanseatic League, the Venetian mediator, Contarini – and among themselves. The comte d'Avaux was strong on theories of diplomacy and he had much knowledge, particularly of northern Europe; a devout Catholic, he was opposed to anything that would weaken the faith, even if that were to France's secular benefit. 'The great count', as the poet Voiture called him, was seen by Mazarin as providing an emollient presence alongside his colleague, Abel Servien;[7] Richelieu-trained brusquely authoritarian, Servien was close in his philosophy and objectives to Mazarin, his friend and correspondent of many years. Did Mazarin consciously lean on characters opposite to his own, like Colbert's or even Turenne's, as if he needed the reinforcement of a direct and ruthless man to complement his own suave and ingratiating style.' He certainly looked for a balance in those who served him and saw advantages in this dual arrangement since he controlled the strategic moves; but his opponents exploited the prickly relationship of the two emissaries.

In April 1648 d'Avaux was recalled, according to d'Ormesson, because he had been saying that the French, Spanish, Germans and Swedes all wanted peace, but that the Italians did not. The reference to Mazarin was clear enough. But neither his personal feelings, nor Servien's ambition to have sole charge need have been the reason. Mazarin probably thought that it would be most efficient to work through one man in the last delicate stages of negotiation. The head of the delegation, the duc de Longueville,[8] was a figure-head, sent to give rank and weight to proceedings – and possibly to keep him out of trouble in France. He could play his part in the game however: when he arrived he had a garden planted to show that he was prepared to stay indefinitely. He could only negotiate officially with someone of equal status, so nothing went beyond preliminaries till the arrival, in November 1645, of Trautmansdorff,[9] a tactful grandee, the emperor's closest adviser. Reflecting that the mood induced by defeats in the desperate battles of Jankau and second Nördlingen (February, July 1645), was realistic, but not despairing, Trautmansdorff deserves credit for an eventual settlement that went as far as was practicable to satisfy the claims of the interested parties.

How difficult that was bound to be is illustrated by the decision of delegates, after a year, to hold a debate to determine the *subjecta belligerantia*. They grouped them under four headings: the complaints of the Imperial Estates, the conditions of amnesty towards rebels, satisfaction of foreign allies, and compensation of the dispossessed. Even a small selection of the issues thus treated illustrates their complexity: first, internal causes ranging back to the Cleves-Jülich succession crisis, besides the vexed question of Calvinism, and more broadly, the distribution of lands between Catholics and Protestants: second, that of the original rebel, the Elector Palatine: third, Sweden's demand for Pomerania as against, fourth, Brandenburg's claim, as of right, to that land. Holding all in mind, constantly checking, advising and sometimes negotiating on his own, Mazarin was in his element in this rugged diplomatic terrain. With each report of victory he urged Servien and d'Avaux to ask for more. Relentlessly they wore Trautmansdorff down. By May 1646 he was offering Alsace in full sovereignty, with Benfield, Zabern and Philipsburg. Then Breisach was put on the table. In October the northern deadlock was broken when Brandenburg accepted the principle of partitioning Pomerania. Sweden was to get the less-impoverished western half with the port of Stralsund, but young Elector Frederick William[10] could be satisfied with compensating gains. Halberstadt, Minden and the reversion to Magdeburg. It was to French diplomacy, and Mazarin's desire to secure a second ally to counter the intrusive power of Sweden, that he owed this advancement, greater than that of Saxony whose Elector John George had to be content with Lusatia. After Wrangel and Turenne had pillaged his hitherto peaceful lands, in March 1647, Maximilian signed, with France, the treaty of Ulm: under duress certainly, but seeing in Mazarin's guarantee that he would have the Upper Palatinate and the electoral title, something more solid than the much-abused goodwill of the emperor.

Sheer soldierly professionalism and a Spanish reluctance to admit defeat could still surface to mount a disconcerting challenge. They had been able to reveal to the Dutch that Mazarin was talking of taking over the Spanish Netherlands and of a marriage between Louis and the Spanish Infanta: a diplomatic gift. When archduke Leopold came to Brabant in early 1647, Mazarin ordered Turenne to concentrate his forces on the Netherlands. But a double mutiny endangered his strategy: Werth deserted his duke to serve the Emperor, and the Bernardines marched off to serve the Swedes. In a desperate move Maximilian then rejoined the emperor. More significant was the formation of a 'German party', at the instigation of Melander, Ferdinand's new commander-in-chief, with the object of opposing a foreigners' peace. Issues were at least narrowed down when, at Münster on 30 January, 1648, Spain and the United Provinces signed a definitive treaty. Since this relieved Spain of part of her military and financial burden it could only be a setback for Mazarin. That it was partly his fault made it no more palatable.

The Eighty Years War had bought the Dutch independence at the cost of the southern provinces, which remained under Spanish dominion. Mazarin believed that they were highly vulnerable and that it was therefore worth pursuing the war with Spain. A technical excuse sufficed: after Peñaranda's departure, it was asserted, there was no Spaniard of sufficient rank to treat with. We have seen that Mazarin consistently underestimated the strength of domestic feeling about the war, taxes and his own position. At first, however, it looked as if his gamble was justified. In May Turenne co-operated with Wrangel to defeat the remaining Imperialist army at Zusmarshausen. In August the unfortunate archduke Leopold spoiled the effect of a promising opening to his campaign, the capture of Lens, by moving headlong towards battle with Condé, with the consequences already described, on the battlefield and later, fatefully, in the streets of Paris. Beset by the Fronde, Mazarin gave his emissary the order to settle. Maximilian reverted to the treaty of Ulm and the French alliance he had so rashly forsaken. As Swedish guns pounded the walls of Prague Trautmansdorff too was ready to allow all the separate deals to be incorporated in one comprehensive treaty. So October brought peace with terms broadly similar to those which had been mooted as much as two years before. Bells rang and beacons blazed: the fires of war had been extinguished – but the fires of peace lit up an uncertain future.

At this stage, with the Spanish conflict still to be resolved, it is easier to accept Maurice Schuman's view of Mazarin as a good European[11] than one which sees him as succumbing to more crudely dynastic interests. Instructions to ambassadors continue to contain arguments of a juridical nature and to show concern for traditional rights, often embodied in characters and clauses of previous treaties. 'Negotiate unceasingly, openly or secretly, anywhere'. Richelieu's words might have been Mazarin's. With his prime strategic concern in securing bases he should be seen as staying true to Richelieu's principles rather than as anticipating the more aggressive policies associated with Louis XIV. Louis' values were more conservative, his policies more realistic, his methods more scrupulous than has usually been allowed.[12] The essential difference between master and pupil was that Mazarin was of the generation which had experienced the year of Corbie, which still feared the military might that could mount such an invasion. Security was the overriding objective; it would not be achieved until Spain were forced to concede substantial parts of the Netherlands. Those aims had been accomplished when Louis embarked on personal rule. War to him would be an attractive option promising good returns with relatively small risks. With several mis-judgements along the way, it was to prove in the end a grand illusion. Both the Cardinals could have told him that, just as there could be hidden benefits in diplomatic solutions that appeared to be moderate, so there were hidden costs to be reckoned with in every campaign plan: to sacrifice diplomatic standing in the long term could be too high a price to pay for any immediate advantages that military might could win. The essence of Mazarin's thinking was that it looked to a future when France would wield a political influence based as much on the attractions of French culture as on force of arms.[13] It is a bold claim to make, but it can be substantiated in the resolution of the main German questions and its effect on the Empire.

Richelieu and Mazarin regularly declared, as had Gustavus Adolphus, that they intervened in the German war to safeguard German liberties. The unbounded aggression of the Swedes soon exposed the hollowness of their claim. It is a mark of the skill with which the French managed affairs that their propaganda could actually be believed. German princes did not gain the complete sovereignty which would have been incompatible with the constitution of the empire. But two articles of the treaty of Münster re-defined *Landeshoheit*, a form of territorial sovereignty, which was thereafter guaranteed as an Imperial law: princes could make treaties with one another and with a foreign state, so long as 'these treaties be not directed against the emperor nor against the public peace of the empire'.

The Imperial Diet continued to exist. It could only be convened by the emperor and its resolutions only became law if promulgated by the emperor. But two clauses of the Osnabrück treaty rendered it virtually powerless, as a political instrument either of the emperor or the princes. It was mandated to establish a 'permanent settlement', in other words to define and to regulate the very nature of the settlement: that meant that it had to be in permanent session. Another clause dealt with the religious question in a way that ensured the prince's autonomy in that respect, according to the formula, *cuius regio, eius religio*, but also the impotence of the Diet, since 'the Catholic states and the states of the Confession of Augsburg are to be permitted to form two separate bodies, and in this case any dispute can only be settled by a friendly compromise, without taking the majority vote into account' – and that, besides religion, 'in all other matters in which the Diet cannot be thought to be a united body'. So the stage was set for the wrangles which would make the Diet so powerless that foreign diplomats would tend to ignore it and to treat with individual states. The winners within Germany were the larger states. Outside, too, it was the largest and wealthiest that most clearly gained.

From several particular arrangements France stood to benefit. The acquisitions of Brandenburg and the ability of the Elector Frederick William made possible the construction of a stronger north German state. Sweden, with West Pomerania, Bremen and Verden, was now a German power, but its stance would be defensive. The new balance of power in the north could serve France well. In the south a stronger Maximilian, with the Upper Palatinate and Electoral rank, owed in the end more to France than to the emperor, could be expected, like his successors, to be an ally and useful makeweight against Austria. Geography, strategy and material interests combined with the impressive performance of French armies to persuade the rulers of the truncated Palatinate, the restored Trier, always-friendly Cologne and Mainz, that France would be their natural patron. Rather than leave things there, Mazarin would give thought to creating his League of the Rhine, a solid bridgehead of French influence, capitalising on the wish of the Rhineland princes to be independent of the emperor and of the fact that individually, without outside support, they would not count for much. It was, however, in the settlement of the vexed question of Alsace that patient diplomacy achieved the ideal outcome, short of complete annexation.

27

GERMAN APPROACHES

From the end of 1634, following Richelieu's negotiations, through his agent Feuquières,[1] with the separate interests involved, France had been mistress for military purposes, of much of Alsace. After the flank had been secured with the capture of Breisach, in 1638, it was the base for offensive operations. To the cities who placed themselves under protection, to France's allies and to anxious neutrals, Richelieu's double pledge – that France would respect particular liberties and did not intend permanent annexation – was an important consideration. But the passage of years, with the marked swing in the balance of military strength, made it unthinkable that France should throw away her advantage. Possession was here nine-tenths of the law. In December 1647 Mazarin wrote to Turenne: 'I trust that you consider Alsace a country which belongs to the king no less than does Champagne'. Bidding high, he claimed for the king the whole of Alsace, with Philippsburg, Breisach, Breisgau and the four forest towns above Basle; then proceeded to bargain, discarding Breisgau and the towns, but standing firm, successfully, for Philippsburg and Breisach.

What exactly Mazarin got is less simple than a list of lands and towns would suggest. Alsace was not a province, but rather a land; a congerie of estates and towns notable, even by German standards, for its diversity. Near the Vosges the peasants spoke French; most however spoke German or an Alsatian dialect version of German. A third were Protestant, Lutheran or Calvinist, so Catholics were in the majority. Within Alsace there were seven distinct political entities. One, in the Upper Alsace, was the *landgraviate* of Archduke Charles Ferdinand, nephew of the emperor. Some land was directly ruled by Austria. Haguenau, with some forty villages, was a separate bailiwick. There were 'free cities', owing allegiance to the emperor; there were also independent republics, of which Strasbourg was the most important, whose allegiance to the emperor was nominal. There were ecclesiastical principalities and dioceses. Finally, outside princes had estates: the duke of Württemberg for example had Montbéliard.[2]

In its gaps and ambiguities, the disposal of Alsace at Münster reflects the variety of lordships and privileges that provided a field-day to the jurist and diplomat of Servien's tough stamp. No less than ten clauses of the treaty dealt with the matter. The emperor surrendered to the king of France everything he held in Alsace as Habsburg and the rights he enjoyed as emperor. What did that mean? If the key term *landgraviate* referred, as the emperor claimed, only to certain rights, then he had no right to cede land; if however it pertained to lands, then they became French anyway. A separate list of the lands to which Louis was entitled, including the ten free cities, was provided, but with a rider, that the king could not claim 'territorial sovereignty but must be content with whatever rights had belonged to the House of Austria; then with another, that 'it should not be understood that the right of *supremum dominium* ceded above is in any way diminished'.

Evidently both Trautmansdorff and Servien, anxious to settle but unable to agree a precise formula, were content to leave matters thus vague. As Servien wrote: 'I believe that we shall have to be content that everyone should keep their claims and interpret the treaty as they see fit'. He could afford to be complacent. Two blank cheques were left, made out, as it were, to the emperor and the king of France: the future of Alsace would depend on their relative strength. As Isaac Volmar [3] said: 'the stronger will win'. 'Stronger' for a time meant the Habsburgs whose forays into Alsace between 1649 and 1657 show that they treated the terms of 1648 in an aggressive way. Fulfilment of Volmar's prophecy would come in 1681, when French troops marched into Strasbourg: the last of the annexations, which they had been pursuing on the pretext of *réunion*[4] of lands once held as fiefs, it completed the process by which the French gained sovereignty over Alsace. It would not be the end of the story: further chapters were to be written in 1871 and 1919. With Lorraine it was to be a bone of contention between France and the new Germany. Meanwhile, dealing with the old Germany of over three hundred sovereign powers, working in a world which could hardly imagine the force of nationalism, Mazarin was content to see Alsace maintain some ties with the emperor. That might be used to gain admission to the Diet without spoiling the law-abiding impression of restraint and respect for local law that would appeal to the German princes.

Mazarin's Alsatian manoeuvres have, therefore, to be seen in the larger context of his view of French interests in Germany: a degree of security for France's eastern provinces compatible with the maintenance of good relations with neighbouring princes. During the Fronde, France benefited – and he, personally, during his two periods of exile – from the goodwill earned in the Rhineland. After the Fronde he was able further to capitalise on France's reputation and the value of French patronage. Mazarin was encouraged, briefly, to think that some might go so far as to abandon their traditional preference for a Habsburg as emperor. Like subsequent historians he may have underestimated what Ferdinand III had achieved during a reign of apparent misfortunes and retreats.

The shattered statue of St Wenceslas, found in the church of Jankau on the eve of the Imperialist defeat in the fields outside the village, stood for so many hopes and people destroyed during a war for which Ferdinand's father had been so largely responsible. But Westphalia was not a terminal disaster for the Habsburgs. The momentum achieved by Ferdinand II's policies, with the consolidation of rule in Bohemia and the all-pervading presence of the Counter-Reformation, Austrian style, imparting through church, court and chancery the principles of centralisation, was irreversible. The dynasty had lost its political pre-eminence in the empire: that was what Germans could attribute to Richelieu and Mazarin. In return the Habsburgs had gained authority within the family lands. They represented order in central Germany; there was no obvious alternative. Was there an alternative for the *Reich*?

When Mazarin heard of Ferdinand's death, in April 1657, he sent a strong French embassy to promote the claims of Louis XIV. Fifteen months elapsed, time for Mazarin to take advantage of the doubts of some, and the mercenary instincts of other Electors. Mazarin had great faith in the efficacy of gold and lamented that he could not find more: 'I would like to be able to use a million gold [crowns] ... for being distributed liberally and carefully ... one could do such great things as it would be hard to hope for in several centuries.' More than gold would however be needed to alter tradition: that apart, the Electors would vote for a Habsburg as much because he would leave them alone as because of the force he represented. They could not know, but might anticipate, that all that force would soon be needed to repel the Turks: when they invaded, in 1664, even more threateningly in 1683, the Germans may have decided that they were right. In no area, not even in his invasion of the United Provinces in 1672, would Louis XIV depart so harmfully from the policy of his mentor, by neglecting to cultivate German opinion.[5] For a bloc of friendly, Francophile German princes was the cornerstone of Mazarin's policy, his guarantee that France could continue to enjoy influence – and with it security – without the need to go to war. He might fail to raise his king to be the second Charlemagne. As he wryly observed, to make a non-German emperor 'would be much like aspiring to defeat a great fleet with two or three brigantines'. But his envoys did not come away empty-handed from Frankfurt, scene of the second convocation of the Imperial diet.

The Electors voted unanimously for the young Leopold.[6] They did not vote for a stronger emperor. It was not hard for the French to persuade the princes to impose 'capitulations', weakening his authority still further. Mazarin encouraged von Schönborn[7] archbishop-elector of Mainz and Imperial chancellor, to create a confederation of princes to safeguard the liberties of Germany. The League of the Rhine, as it came to be known, completed in August 1658, was the positive answer to those dire questions not addressed in the terms of the peace of Westphalia: about the security and freedom of a confederation of states, mostly so small, when the emperor himself had breached the constitution and foreign princes had seized German lands. By ensuring the membership of France, along with that of Sweden, in a league of German states, Mazarin served both Germany and France.

Altruist, visionary, realist and mercenary: the contrasts are all there in this design, as in its maker. Included at the outset were two Electors, the archbishops of Mainz and Cologne and several Imperial princes, duke Philip-William of Neuburg, three Brunswick dukes and the landgrave of Hesse-Cassel. Concluded for three years, but early renewed in 1660 when Württemberg and Münster joined, it came eventually to include Trier, Hesse-Darmstadt and Zweibrücken. When, in 1665, Brandenburg acceded, it reached from the Elector's Berlin, to Neuburg's Dusseldorf. It was however centred in the Rhineland – with a permanent directory at Frankfurt-am-Main, a treasury well supplied with French money, and hired troops to ensure its purpose: the maintenance of the German liberties which kings of France had claimed to guard since Francis I had first bid for power in Reformation-divided Germany. Now Mazarin, in Hauser's words, had extended 'the true frontier of France, that of political influence, beyond the territorial frontier, to the Rhine'.[8] It was one of the most significant achievements in French diplomatic history. Mazarin's skill may, however, have been less in creating the alliance than in exploiting it to French advantage. Implicit within the principle of protection bequeathed to Louis XIV was that of domination which would, in the end, be fatal to Louis' name and cause in Germany and cast a long shadow over the future of Europe. But Mazarin had taught a lesson, imperfectly learned and followed by his royal pupil, in what could be achieved by sensitive diplomacy which took account of prevailing sentiment: when territorial goals took second place to the maintenance of friendly relations.

Future patterns can be seen emerging from Westphalia: the decline in the political influence of the Papacy which could only, ineffectually, denounce its proceedings as 'null and void'; the potential of Brandenburg to set against the heavy German presence of Sweden; the weight of Holland in the world's markets; indications of the future collapse of Poland; the accelerating decline of Spain; the beginnings of re-orientation in Austrian policy as emperors faced the renewed Ottoman challenge and focused more narrowly on the hereditary lands; correspondingly, the predominance of France. Two powers – one mature, with a long tradition of involvement in continental affairs, the other on the fringe, emerging but slowly; both destined to exercise enormous influence in the eighteenth century and beyond – were out of the reckoning at Westphalia. Through support of the Ukrainian rising against the crown of Poland, Russia was gradually to be drawn towards the mainstream. England's isolation, by contrast, was due to exceptional circumstances. Since the failure of Buckingham's attempts to aid La Rochelle, England had been virtually a spectator of the Thirty Years War. Since 1642 and the outbreak of civil war, there had been no question of a coherent English foreign policy.

28

THE ENGLISH ALLIANCE

The failures of Charles II to recover his father's throne, signalised by defeats at Dunbar and Worcester (1650 and 1651) meant that his political stock had declined to the point at which Mazarin, pressed always by Queen Henrietta Maria, found him more embarrassing than valuable as a diplomatic counter. Legitimacy, apart, the prime fact of the political scene, judged by the visible authority of government and the size and professionalism of a victorious army, was the power of its general Cromwell. He was effectively, though harnessed to Parliament, ruler of England after 1649, Lord Protector, even, as some thought, would-be king after 1653. As Mazarin started to assess the problems involved in defeating Spain, an English alliance became increasingly desirable. Logic and sentiment were also directing Cromwell in that direction. He was lord of all the lands that the Stuarts had ever ruled, with a stronger army and fleet than they had possessed, more absolute, after his brisk dismissal of the 'Long Parliament', than Charles had managed to be; ironically, he could raise more money in taxes than had the king, with or without Parliament. Going to war in 1652 with the Dutch, he had responded to mercantile interests in Parliament and the big cities. Two years later, the first Dutch war brought material advantages. The English were 'perfectly lords and masters of the narrow seas'. Enlarged by prizes, the navy was at least equal to the Dutch, superior to all others. Advantageous treaties with the Scandinavian powers enhanced prospects in the Baltic and German trade.

The furtherance of trade was always important to Cromwell. The cost of maintaining a large army was never far from his mind. Now there were even higher priorities. Expediency and ideology were served by measures to prevent the restoration of the Stuarts and to promote the Protestant religion. Mazarin was undisguisedly cool towards royalist advances and grudging even over the modest pensions and grants meted out to the royalist court to fulfil the claims of hospitality and honour. The Spanish listened more readily and eventually, in 1656, made a treaty with Charles by which they offered to finance a small royalist force. In so doing they invited retaliation. Spain offered tempting targets to English seamen. A war against Spain would still command English popular support. So all came together to provide Mazarin with the ally he needed.

Spain clung to the hope, expressed by the minister Oñate during the Fronde, that France was 'so subject to faction and unrest' that 'future events would considerably improve our prospects'. Mazarin endeavoured to put new life into the war effort. In 1653 he had been able, for the first time since 1648, to use the bulk of the royal troops against the enemy. Conti, the returned prodigal, had a successful campaign in Catalonia. Mazarin knew how to express his gratitude: 'Those good successes do no less for your own glory than for the good of the king's affairs and reputation of his armies'. For three years the French had the upper hand on the northern front, targeting and acquiring fortresses in campaigns of siege and manoeuvre suited to Turenne's calculating, meticulous style of generalship, but galling to Condé, who yearned for the clash of arms on open battlefield. Among the sappers who were busy in Turenne's camp, a willing student of his doctrine of the impregnable frontier, perfecting his knowledge of the science of fortification, was the young Vauban. For the next half century, he was to leave his mark, handsomely and indelibly on the landscape of the frontier.

One little walled town after another – in 1653, Monzon and Sainte Ménéhould, in 1654, Stenay, Quesnoy, Clermont-en-Argonne, in 1655 Landrécies – rewarded the patient investor: they were useful assets in the diplomatic bank, but insufficient to compel the Spanish to come to terms. On one occasion, in August 1654, attacking in the light of a harvest moon, Turenne had routed Condé's motley force of Lorrainers, Italians fighting under Spanish banners, and mercenaries. The action, with the subsequent relief of Arras and capture of strongholds, was noted by Turenne's fellow Protestant, Cromwell, to whom France became more appealing as an ally with every military success. But thereafter, the decisive blow eluded Turenne and 1656 showed him, perhaps weary, losing his way, while Condé scored a success, of more symbolic than tactical significance, when he recaptured eponymous Condé. That Condé could still win adherents had already been shown when marshal d'Hocquincourt threatened to hand fortresses under his command over to the enemy. Professional jealousy, love of the imprisoned Condéan duchesse de Chatillon, or plain greed, may have brought him to the point of treason. Mazarin had little choice but to accede to his demands: 600,000 *livres* and the liberty of the duchess.

Mazarin was always prepared to adapt policy to circumstances. Indeed he had little choice if he were to make peace in his lifetime. When he heard that Condé had gone on to maul the army of de la Ferté–Senneterre,[1] hitherto a successful general, and to relieve Valenciennes which the French had been besieging (July 1656), he wrote to *abbé* Fouquet that 'this misfortune of Valenciennes' was not sufficient reason for winning the

251

favour of Condé 'and those of his party would be greatly mistaken if they thought otherwise.' Fouquet was often the recipient of his private thoughts: Mazarin was coming to the conclusion that France could not defeat Spain without an ally. England was already at war with Spain. Though his greatest coup was still to come, the destruction of the treasure fleet at Tenerife in April 1657, Admiral Blake had already struck blows which would affect the Spanish ability to supply their troops. However Spanish statesmen were notoriously reluctant to relate military planning to economic resources and, with Lionne reporting that he could make no headway at Madrid, Mazarin decided that it was time to harness English power to the campaign in Flanders.

He had no illusions about the political risk. Heretic, usurper and instigator of regicide, oppressor of subject Irish[2] and of dissident English, Cromwell was anathema to loyal French subjects and to good Catholics everywhere. He made no secret of his Protestant mission, indeed gloried in it. His alliance would therefore be a propaganda gift to Condé. It would come as justification to Retz and his friends at Rome and in Paris. It would mortify the queen of England and test even the loyalty of the queen mother of France. Mazarin could quote precedent, recently in the shape of Richelieu's alliance with Sweden. But would Richelieu have dared – or wanted – to make such a compact with the heretic? Mazarin himself had been explicit in his detestation of the proceedings of the English rebels; at times during the *Fronde* his expressions of disquiet had verged on the paranoiac. But he believed, with Turenne, his ministers and, most important, his king, that the military argument must prevail.

Whatever chivalrous feeling he may have had for his cousin Charles, Louis was easily persuaded. It is interesting to compare his attitude now with that of the mature sovereign who, in 1702, would jeopardise peace by acknowledging the right of another exiled Stuart – James III.[3] Insecure, eager for renown, carefully tutored by Mazarin, the young king was naturally less scrupulous. Peace beckoned; the frontier must be strong; Cromwell would not be served, but used – for the security of the realm. Already, cautious steps had been taken. Cromwell had first tested the ground in a project delivered to the French ambassador in July 1654. A treaty was signed at Westminster in November 1655, but was limited to ending acts of piracy between the French and the English. Months of arduous negotiations preceded the signing of the treaty in Paris in March 1657. Articles in French and Latin envisaged joint action leading to the conquest of fortresses in Flanders: Graveslines was earmarked to France, Dunkirk and Mardyke to England. Like Gustavus, Cromwell only engaged himself to guarantee free exercise of the Catholic faith in those places.

Events brought swift justification. The combined French and English forces defeated Condé, who had 14,000 troops, including Charles II's little force, among the sand dunes around the town; then Dunkirk surrendered and was handed over to the English to be, in secretary Thurloe's words, 'a bridle to the Dutch and a door to the Continent'. The English earned Turenne's admiration as their red-coated pikemen stormed the sand-hill that was pivotal to Don Juan's position.[4] Dunkirk was a seal set, before the most critical witnesses, upon the reputation of an army whose discipline and regular footing had founded a tradition and a weapon which was to survive all vicissitudes and to be of lasting significance. Charles saw in the loss of half his force the wreckage of his hope of restoration. In reality, it was improved by his release from engagement to Spain: better that he should be a free agent. Dunkirk, meanwhile, was English upon false premises: Charles would shed no tears when it was returned to the French, in 1662, for money which he needed more than a continental base. By then he had been king for two years, a prospect which he can hardly have envisaged on the bitter sands of Dunkirk.

That human affairs were unpredictable would be no news to the statesman who was endeavouring to give them order and direction. Within weeks of the battle of the Dunes, the French camp was plunged into gloom by the serious illness of the king: reports suggest that it was pneumonia. At the height of his fever, Colbert, ever vigilant for signs of disaffection, was taking military precautions in the capital. Mazarin knew that those who might grieve at a royal death might also see it as a time of opportunity.[5] Fortunately Louis' constitution was robust. Nursed devotedly by Anne, he made a swift recovery; Turenne drove on, exploiting his much superior strength to win place after place: Graveslines; in August 1658, Furnes and Dixmunde before the autumn rains brought mud and standstill. News came in September of Cromwell's death. His son Richard[6] was diffident, ruling without legitimate right: the succession question now came to the fore, but of more immediate significance for Mazarin was the second Spanish reversal of the year, one that meant more to the now deeply pessimistic Philip IV. The Portuguese victory at Elvas meant not that he was yet prepared to let go of Portugal – the cause now dearest to him but that he would let his minister, don Haro, move seriously towards peace. With opposition silenced by news of victory, the chance of peace on French terms so much improved, there was enough to inspire Mazarin to take personal charge of negotiations, whatever the cost to his failing health. The stage was set for the most testing, and in many respects the finest, transactions of his career.

29

PEACE WITH SPAIN

The first encounter of Mazarin and Don Haro took place on 13 August 1659. The peace of the Pyrenees, eventually embodied in a weighty document of 124 articles, with a number of matters reserved for further consideration, was concluded on 7 November. Preliminaries had already cleared much of the ground by August. Both sides wanted to make peace. Mazarin knew that Turenne was right when he argued that there were pickings for the asking in Spain's increasingly vulnerable Netherlands; but he preferred to use that knowledge to press his case rather than license another campaign. Indeed there was a cessation of hostilities from the start of negotiations, unlike 1648 when armies fought to the bitter end to win concessions at the table. Mazarin would surely have nodded appreciatively to the axiom of Sun-Tzu, mentor of Chinese war-lords: 'Those who love warfare will inevitably perish. Those who forget warfare will certainly be endangered.' He had his share too of that saving grace of *ancien régime* diplomacy: there was no wish to turn the knife in the wounds: the spirit of revenge, which tends to inform the diplomacy of the age of democracy, was missing. Since the privileged suffered least, the unrepresented people most, from war's savagery, that is not surprising: diplomacy was the occupation and art of a cultivated *élite*, having an idea of the state, with its interests and demands, which would have meant little to the masses unacquainted with the chambers of power. As for the views of people in territories considered for transfer between states – such matters were to be decided at the only appropriate level, that is between sovereigns, their ministers and envoys; only then were corporate rights and local laws taken into account – but then scrupulously. Certain intangible, but influential notions were taken seriously. Points of honour were understood. Appreciating that Spain's main concern was now maintaining her hold over Portugal, whose legitimate sovereign was Philip IV, for which crown he was prepared to let Artois go, with parts of Catalonia, Mazarin undertook not to aid the rebels in Portugal. Spain also recognised an obligation to Condé, on whose honourable reinstatement it insisted, delaying other matters in the process.

254

Crucial for peace which could be advantageous to France without being humiliating to Spain was the desire of both sides to bring about the marriage of Louis XIV and the Infanta Maria Teresa. Since Louis XIII had also been given his Spanish bride, the balance of power had so shifted that the French motivation was no longer defensive. Since Philip IV had only a daughter, Maria Teresa,[1] from his first marriage, while the first child of the second marriage had already died, and a second, Philip, was sickly, there were already uncertainties about the succession; nor would they be resolved when his son Charles[2] was born in November 1661, for he was so feeble that he was not expected to live long. Faced by the consequences of persistent inbreeding, with the poignant contrast between the magnificence of their rank and the wretchedness of their condition, Mazarin could see potential benefits from the marriage, with more to gain by hereditary right than could ever be won by the sword.

By the end of 1658, Louis was ready to play his part. That had not been the case a year earlier. Woven into the diplomatic story, threatening to spoil all calculation, was an unexpected flaw. Mazarin had staged an elaborate bluff, through the unwitting agency of a princess of Savoy, to bring pressure on Spain. What he could not have foreseen was the human factor of love: natural, touching, to Mazarin acutely embarrassing, ultimately painful as it could only be when one party to this most public romance was the prime player in the diplomatic stakes, the king himself; the other, Mazarin's own niece, Marie Mancini.[3]

Marie was the fourth 'Mazarinette' and had not been esteemed the prettiest. For two years, her sister Olympe had enjoyed Louis' favours, though not exclusively. Neither Louis' religion nor the influence of his watchful mother were enough to curb desire or bring decorum to the courtly rites of spring. A young noblewoman up from the country, not discouraged by her elders, might regard it as a privilege to share the king's bed – and a servant girl was unlikely to refuse him. However, Marie found in this strenuous young man a deeper need and finer sensibility. He was perhaps lonely and anxious in the face of the awesome responsibilities which Mazarin taught him to take seriously. With her abundant, curly, dark chestnut hair and olive skin, her look, posture and manner entirely Italian and so different from the French women around him, she was vivacious, appealing without being classically beautiful, apparently modest, genuinely clever, well read, proficient in languages and, like Louis, music-loving. She was naturally ambitious, but seems to have loved the king for his own sake; she would not be his mistress, but allowed herself to think of marriage: he was encouraged rather than deterred by her virtuous restraint to the point at which Anne became seriously concerned and Mazarin decided that he must intervene. Another man, the cynical adventurer of *frondeur* propaganda for example, might have been tempted by the prospect of such glory for the *casa*: indeed some observers believed that he was encouraging the affair. Up till then, his nieces had been used for important alliances. But Mazarin intended to use his power to confirm his fame and exalt the crown by a conclusive peace. In that scheme a family match, however spectacular, had no part.

Mazarin was left therefore with a very complicated game to play. He had to bring the Spanish, dilatory as ever, to see that the French marriage was in their best interests. He had to ensure that the king was free and willing to play his part. He may have relished the challenge. The intellectual problems involved in the later stages of negotiation may even have provided relief, or at least sustained him, in excruciating pain and growing weakness. His tactical skills showed to advantage in the elaborate exercise of December 1658. In November the court had left Paris and proceeded down the eastern provinces, first to Dijon, then to Lyons. There they welcomed Marguerite of Savoy with her sister and suitable entourage. Marguerite was the daughter of Christina, herself the daughter of Henry IV, so a cousin: whether rank or strategy were considered, evidently a suitable match. Lodged at the sumptuous house of the financier Mascarani, the king played his part: he was taken with Marguerite, and was charmingly polite – as often when his feelings were elsewhere. She was sensible, demure, 'softly spoken and cultured . . . with sweetness enough for all the world'. Reports flew back to Madrid, as was intended, that marriage was being planned. Philip IV was roused to send his envoy with instructions to offer the hand of Maria Teresa. Mazarin accepted with alacrity. Anne was delighted. As Spaniard, queen and mother, she could desire no more. Since Louis' illness, which she had treated as a sign that God was displeased, though on that occasion merciful, she had been impatient for peace and resolved that Louis should play his part in the reconciliation of Bourbon and Habsburg. The king seemed willing – but he continued to see and correspond with Marie: he was still infatuated. The Savoyard princesses were sent home, laden with gifts. They had played their part.

On 21 June, the Mancini idyll was formally terminated when Louis said farewell, sadly, publicly and, Mazarin hoped, finally, to the tearful Marie. It was a scene worthy of Racine: duty overcoming passion, stern resolve, unavailing tears. Its effect was spoiled, however, when Mazarin learned that they continued to correspond. In a letter from Poitiers, on 6 July, he begged the king to overcome his desires:

> La confidante [Anne] has written to me about the state you have been in and I am near to despair, for it is absolutely vital that you should find your own remedy unless you are to be unhappy and the death of your good servants. . . . And if you do not find the resolve to change your conduct, your malady will worsen more and

more. I urge you for your glory, your honour, for the well-being of the realm.

Four days later he returned to the theme: 'You always manage everything better than others when you have a mind to apply yourself and decide that all your passions should yield to that you should have, to be a king, so wise and capable of governing your realm that you are great and already very glorious.'

His syntax and style can be faulted but there is no mistaking the minister's intention: he used every device to appeal to the king's sense of duty and destiny. The tone, so direct, familiar and bald could only not have offended if the king had a profound, if not filial, respect for the minister with whom he had shared so much. Mazarin had built up, in camp, in council and in patient hours of private tuition, a relationship of trust suffused with the older man's instinctive feeling for the trials and temptations of kingship. Worldly-wise and of proven toughness, Mazarin had still never lost the gift of imaginative sympathy. He might recall Louis' words at the worst point of his illness at Mardyke: 'You are a man of resolution and best friend I have. That is why I beg you to tell me when I should be in extremities.'

August saw Mazarin locked into the final intense process of bargaining and defining. Believing that Louis had made the expected sacrifice, unaware that Louis had just seen Marie Mancini, he wrote to congratulate the king (13 August) on the assurances he had given him and went on to describe the opening ceremonies, and his personal escort of thirty carriages and two hundred gentlemen, on the little pancake of the Isle of Pheasants, chosen because it was midstream on the river Bidassoa which marked the Spanish frontier: therefore acceptable to both parties, a typical seventeenth-century triumph of protocol over convenience. Two weeks later, having found that matters were not as he had supposed, he wrote again: 'There is no matter so important as this, or one that demands with more urgency that it be finished.' Louis bowed to the inevitable. For Mazarin's niece there was little consolation, unless it were in the penning of her *Mémoires*. For her uncle the wry reflection of his comment to Luis de Haro: 'How I envy Spain, where women do not become involved in politics.'

The road to peace was cleared but the going was still hard. Seeing Mazarin's infirmity, that he was suffering constant pain, the Spanish counted on wearing him down, contesting article after article. In all, in seventy-nine folio pages, there were to be 124 articles. De Haro, was conscientiously aware of his obligation to his king and astute in bargaining, but he was up against a grand master, with patient courage to match his expertise. Typically, the talks came nearest to breakdown over the issue of Condé upon which Philip IV was adamant: honour required that

Spain fulfil her obligation to her ally; on the French side, propriety compelled respect for the principle that treason be punished; a liberated Condé might upset the equilibrium so dearly bought. Should Condé not pay the penalty? How better than by confiscation of his lands? It was thus that monarchies had grown in the past. But Mazarin had his eye on the frontiers and reckoned that concessions on the Condé question would make the Spanish readier to accept their losses. Pardoned, Condé was restored to his titles, lands and many functions, but not the governorship of Guienne. The territorial settlements, though, given the military situation, not unduly generous to France, proved Mazarin right.

Roussillon and the main part of Cerdagne, the Catalan lands on the French side of the Pyrenees, were transferred to France. Many clauses were devoted to the definition of lands and rights while details were left to subsequent negotiations and edicts. Most important was that of St Jean de Luz, of May 1660, by which the king granted the establishment of a sovereign council in Roussillon, like a miniature *parlement*: for some time its debates would be in Catalan. That helped to guarantee other concessions to ancient custom. Patriotic feeling was not to be underestimated: when the crown introduced the *gabelle*, the province promptly revolted. A governor would soon be writing: 'the people of Roussillon call themselves Catalans . . . they would feel degraded and insulted if they were called French'. Reference was indeed made in the treaty to 'the mountains of the Pyrenees which had in ancient times divided the Gauls from Spain and will in future also mark the divisions of the two kingdoms'. In the end it was legal arguments, invoking laws of property, not fanciful, nostalgic 'laws' of nature or imperatives of geography, which determined the frontier's course. Within that frontier the French crown had added another bundle of particularities to its patchwork realm.

The question of the eastern frontier was relatively straightforward. From journeys to and from exile, from the enforced vacations on the German side of the Rhine, recently from campaigns, with all the opportunities they provided to talk to experts, Mazarin had acquired a solid understanding of the tactical requirements of what was to be Europe's most formidable defensive system. The frontier would not be linear or continuous, but based on fortresses. A well-constructed, fortified town could hold up the enemy's advance and threaten its communications. The siege of Lille, in 1708, which cost Marlborough six precious months and thousands of lives, would provide justification for the theory. In 1659 Mazarin could not have anticipated the conflict of giants that was to come. His prime object, however, remained defensive. In February 1660, for example, he was studying the engineer's report on the state of fortifications at Philippsburg.

Realism was the key note, along with treaty obligations. Mazarin had had to honour his commitment to the English to hand over Dunkirk and

Mardyke. There had been remonstrances over the alleged betrayal of French interests. Servien had been required to draft an official response in which he recalled the constant interests of French diplomacy since Henry IV, and cited the precedent of Louis XIII's agreeing with the United Provinces for the division of Flanders, by virtue of which most of the larger towns were to remain Dutch. So France's gains were substantial, but not provocatively excessive. All of Artois but for Aire and St Omer, with its capital Arras, and ten further towns, from Graveslines on the sea, across those flat lands that were to become so familiar to British soldiers of the twentieth century, to Le Quesnoy and Landrécies; in Hainault, Thionville; Montmédy in Luxembourg. If ripe plums were left on the tree it was because there was already forming in Mazarin's mind the possibility that there would soon be other means to pick them. It did not prevent him securing Jülich from Philip IV, for France's ally, the duke of Neuburg; nor the humiliating cession, by Charles of Lorraine, of his duchy of Bar, with Clermont-en-Argonne, Stenay and Moyenvic. Nancy's citadel was to be demolished and French troops accorded the right of passage through his lands.

As his contribution to the marriage settlement, Louis renounced all claim to the Spanish throne, on condition that the Infanta's dowry were paid: it was fixed at 500,000 gold *écus* to be paid in three instalments. The sum would be beyond the resources of Spain's treasury; non-payment would become the pretext for 'The War of the Queen's Rights', launched in 1667;[4] so Mazarin has been credited with remarkable foresight in stipulating that sum. In fact, if there was anything like a trap, it seems to have been devised by Lionne.[5] European opinion tended to be cynical about French motives and actions. However, it should be noted that the dowry was not generous. Anne had brought with her much more when all precious goods were taken into account, with 'silver enough for twelve royal weddings' so the Spanish had reported. It would have been evident that Spain's financial position was parlous, but seventeenth-century governments tended not to make exact calculations on the scanty data available; rather to assume that kings could always somehow lay their hands on money.

That Spain was in decline is not open to serious doubt. Its full extent was to be revealed in 1667 when the French armies enjoyed something like a promenade through Flanders, with only a token resistance to satisfy honour before the white flag fluttered from yet another citadel of famous name. It is unnecessary, therefore, to credit Mazarin with anything beyond prudent calculation. Nature would play its part in the unhappy person of Charles II, variously called by Spaniards 'the Sufferer' or 'the Bewitched'. He would be twice married, but remain childless. The succession to his still vast empire would therefore be the prime diplomatic question of his reign, and the cause of bitter and prolonged war after his death. Much of this was present in germ in the peace of the Pyrenees, signed on 7 November 1659, which established beyond doubt the supremacy of France in Europe.[6]

In a characteristic letter of 1645 Mazarin had said that he wanted peace 'passionately' but one that was 'glorious and sure for the crown'. He had achieved such a peace in double measure. It was Mazarin's personal *nunc dimittis*, forged out of so much labour and suffering, his own not least.[7] Its significance should not be allowed to obscure his other diplomatic labours. He had already done much – and there was still more to be done before he could go to his final rest. Engaged for thirty years, in one way or another, to Sweden, France was directly involved in the continuing war of the north.

30

ARBITER OF PEACE

One effect of the Thirty Years War had been to draw the northern powers towards the mainstream of European politics. Reflecting the increasing demand for timber, tar, pitch, hemp and grain, the Baltic, with its river mouths and ports, was no longer just the scene of local rivalries, but the focus of interest of the major states. The intention of the Habsburg's Admiralty Plan, leading to the unsuccessful siege of Stralsund (1628) had been to secure a naval base from which to operate against the Dutch. Enjoying the lion's share of trade through the Sound, the busiest shipping lane in Europe, the Dutch had an interest in maintaining a peaceful balance within the region. One issue in the Thirty Years War, not resolved in Sweden's favour until 1629, had been the disputed Swedish succession, between Polish and Swedish branches of the house of Vasa. After the truce of that year, negotiated by Richelieu's envoy to prepare the way for Gustavus Adolphus' subsidised intervention in the German war, Sweden was a major player in the conflicts finally settled by Westphalia: it left Sweden a German power.

The accession, following the abdication of Queen Christina, of her soldier cousin Charles X (1654), was the signal for another bout of aggression, starting with an invasion of Poland which first prospered, then went disastrously wrong as the Swedes pulled out of the country, harried by a patriotic resistance movement. Charles was more successful when he hammered the Danes to submission and gained Scania and Halland by the treaty of Roskilde in February 1658. When, however, Charles renewed the war and attacked Copenhagen, Holland, England and Brandenburg rallied to Denmark's aid. Mazarin was already fully alert to the dangers in a volatile situation. As Richelieu had found before him, it was one thing to employ these Swedish hounds to hunt the common foe: quite another to control them once they had tasted blood. Fortunately for Mazarin Charles X, for all his Vasa courage, had little of the political judgement which Gustavus Adolphus had shown, which Charles XI[1] would show and which Sweden would need if it were to maintain its extended empire.

For Charles X it can at least be argued that he inherited a position which only calculated aggression could support and that he was right to see that Poland was vulnerable to attack. Following the revolt of the Ukraine in 1648,[2] that huge country had been at war with Russia: her disproportionately small army was always extended by the need to defend a long southern frontier against the Turks. Charles could hardly have foreseen that a more formidable enemy in the future would be Brandenburg. What could be seen was that peace and stability in the Baltic lands called out for outside arbitration. Once free of the Spanish business, his reputation further enhanced by the creation of the League of the Rhine, having the moral authority of a peacemaker and the power and resources at his disposal to lend weight to his judgements, Mazarin was clearly the man for the hour. He was helped by the sudden death, in January 1660, of the Swedish king. At the treaties of Oliva and Copenhagen in May and June 1660, his envoys were able to negotiate terms which went some way to satisfying all parties. Denmark's losses were confined to Scania, Livonia was transferred from Poland to Sweden. Poland renounced sovereignty over East Prussia.[3] The Great Elector would lose no time in using his new status to raise taxes, further to build his army and the state that was to become the mighty Prussia, heart and soul of the German nation that was destined to be France's greatest Continental rival. Even a rough guess at such a future would have required more a soothsayer than a statesman. Meanwhile the states confirmed the treaties of Westphalia and accepted the principle of armed intervention by France in the event of any breach of its terms. Finally the way was prepared for Russia's cession of Karelia and Ingria, settled, after Mazarin's death, in June 1661: like so much else, that was to be unfinished business. The end of the century would see Sweden fighting against all its neighbours to hold on to the outlying parts of its empire. For the immediate future it was secure in the patronage and subsidies of France. While ensuring that Sweden's own weight was balanced by that of Denmark and Brandenburg, Mazarin had extended the range of France's diplomatic umbrella. He seemed to have pulled off the most difficult of diplomatic tricks, providing for his country's security without arousing undue suspicion of his motives.

Opportunity came to Mazarin to add further pieces to his diplomatic ring with the restoration of Charles II to his rightful throne. The death of Cromwell in September 1658, the fumbling rule of his son Richard, the disarray of soldiers and politicians, the surge of public opinion, responsive to the logic of the situation and the initiative of General Monk, combined to bring about that event – but over a period of time which was sufficient for Mazarin to rid himself of the embarrassing encumbrance of his alliance with Cromwell. In any case, Charles was disposed to look, if not with gratitude, at least with admiring respect to his French cousin, so securely and splendidly installed. The marriage arranged for him with the Portuguese princess Catherine of Braganza[4] offered Mazarin a way to injure Spain without breach of his recently accepted obligation not to assist the Portuguese. It was however a natural step from that already taken when the young German soldier, Schomberg,[5] already in French service, was given command in Portugal. Economic arguments based on the rivalry of England and Holland, personally appreciated by Charles because of the chronic shortage of revenue which would lead to his decision to sell Dunkirk in 1662, also played their part in the arrangement. Mazarin smiled on the match, but should not be held responsible for it. It was to be of great significance. It helped enlarge the perspective and turn the direction of English foreign policy to the wider, beckoning horizons of a maritime empire: to distant Bombay and nearer Tangier – little though either of those parts of Catherine's dowry was valued at the time. That would not be to the advantage of France. In the short term, however, the marriage, formalised in 1662, strengthened the entente between England and France, pointing, with only short deviations, to what was to be Charles's steady preference and usual policy.

Mazarin rarely missed a trick when it was possible to use marriage to further diplomatic ends: hence the parallel marriage of Monsieur,[6] the king's younger brother, to Henrietta, 'Minette' as her brother Charles liked to call her. Monsieur may merit some sympathy as the younger brother and some respect as a man who showed judgement and courage when given the opportunity. Frustrated, idle perforce, since he was jealously denied a useful role in government or army, he came to behave increasingly in the effeminate and self-centred way that was to create the image of a degenerate fop and seem therefore to justify Louis' scarcely veiled contempt. So he was a poor husband for the sweet-natured and lively 'Minette.' Such considerations counted for nothing in the making of such matches. What Mazarin saw was that Minette, Roman Catholic, would make an excellent unofficial ambassador for France: her key part in the making of the Treaty of Dover (1670) would show that he was right.

To write of Mazarin's 'Eastern policy' would be to make too much of his responses to occasional events that served to remind Western statesmen that there was still an Ottoman threat. Venetians, Poles and Austrians would need no reminder since they manned Europe's vulnerable eastern frontiers and knew the daily reality of raids, skirmishes, piracy and banditry. For the French statesmen it would be only natural for Turkish affairs to have a low priority. The French tradition was one of compromise and expediency. Francis I had found Turkish aggression useful in diverting Habsburg resources. He had allowed cooperation to go as far as making a French port available to the Turkish fleet. Ambassadors had been exchanged and the diplomatic presence at the Porte had since been maintained to guard France's trading interests and secure the position of merchant communities in the several Islamic cities in which they were established. The achievement by successive sultans of a single authority over subjects of many different races, by 1600 some 30 million, for many of whom warfare brought honour and loot, had enabled them to create a war machine more formidable than any since that of imperial Rome.

There was always the possibility, the hope of the West, that this empire would disintegrate, victim, like others, of its own success. Of the sultans who succeeded Suleiman the Magnificent, only one, Murad IV (1613–40), did justice to his tremendous position. Since his reign coincided with much of the Thirty Years War, it was fortunate for the Habsburgs that he was mainly preoccupied with restoring order, conquering Iraq and making a lasting peace with Persia. His effete successor, Ibrahim (1640–8) was more alarming to Shi-ite zealots than the Turks' European enemies, while his successor, Mehmet IV (1648–87), virtually abdicated rule to his grand vizier. It might seem, then, that Turkey was experiencing its own version of the 'general crisis' of the mid-century when militants marched on Constantinople to demand a change of government. Eleven grand viziers, chief ministers, held office in eight years before the appointment of the grimly efficient Albanian, Mehmed Köprülü. He came to power in 1656: it was the year of the destruction of the Ottoman fleet by the Venetians. Hailed as proof of the empire's decadence, it proved to be the spur to reform. With a purge of some 50,000 officials and soldiers Köprülü created a leaner regime, competent to raise revenues and avid for war.

Surrounded by pirate-infested seas, Italians were alert to the inconvenience of Ottoman power which lent special force to the tradition of crusade. Crete was now seen to be only one piece on the wider strategic board: an attack on Transylvania in 1657 signalled more aggressive Ottoman intentions. That might seem to be the responsibility of the new emperor, as Crete was of the Venetians: but Mazarin was always concerned about the reputation of the king, '*le roi très catholique*' as official documents described him, in a way which Louis would later have done well to emulate. He was also particularly sensitive to opinion at Rome and was not prepared to stand back and do nothing. In 1654 he had allowed volunteers to go to Crete: in 1658 he sent 200,000 *livres* to Venice, with 3,000 troops to serve under a Venetian commander. In 1660, after the defeat of the Venetian fleet, he sent 600,000 *livres* to the Pope. It was politic rather than generous: his nieces could expect the same sum as a dowry. He refused to break with the Turks even after they had imprisoned his ambassador.

We can only guess what Mazarin's reaction would have been to the greater crisis of 1663–4, culminating in Montecucoli's victory at St Gothard over the Turkish horde, when Louis had again allowed volunteers to serve: or the climactic siege of Vienna in 1683, when Louis miscalculated so disastrously, withholding aid to the hard-pressed emperor. On his record, however, we can assume that he would have done enough to safeguard his standing as a good Catholic and friend to the Vatican, while allowing no chance to slip of furthering France's strategic interests. Though he might have been careful not to say it, he would surely have not disagreed with the comment of Louis' minister, Pomponne, who responded to Leibnitz's suggestion, that the French should join the emperor in chasing the Turks out of Europe, with the suave observation that 'Holy Wars have been out of fashion since the time of St Louis'.

Part V

MONEY MATTERS

'If the financier fails in his enterprise the courtiers say of him: "he is a bourgeois, a man of no consequence, a low fellow." If he succeeds, they ask for his daughter.'
La Bruyère

31

FOUQUET

Interwoven throughout Mazarin's diplomatic career are two contrasting lines: the visionary and the realistic. With the ability to identify and to seek the grand objectives, a larger, more secure French kingdom in a peaceful Europe, went the politician's devices, the engagements, bribes and threats that were the currency of public affairs. Between the elevated and the downright sordid was the mass of ordinary dealings in which his skills and those of his agents were stretched to exploit advantage or probe weakness. Success depended most on the military weapon, but somewhat too on the gentler arts of persuasion: both required regular funding. Urgent calls for money ring insistently through Mazarin's letters. Typical was one of July 1649, to Le Tellier:

> I await as a matter of life and death ... to know if and when we shall have the money necessary to start the siege of Cambrai ... I am sure you will not forget to speak to the businessmen concerned to see if we cannot persuade them to come to our rescue. ... I beg you to see that everything possible is done to ensure that on Monday or Tuesday we can have 100,000 crowns.

A *surintendant*'s worth would be judged not on any financial refinements he might propose, but on the simple criterion: his success or failure in maintaining the flow of cash.[1]

'Certain acts of mine may have been wrong. I do not excuse myself for them. I did things which had to be done and it was by doing them that I kept up royal business, which I could not otherwise have done.' In these frank words, writing during the trial which followed his arrest in May 1661, to Le Tellier, who was himself in no position to adopt a lofty moral stance, Nicolas Fouquet[2] summarised his line of defence before a *chambre de justice*[3] which would find sharp practice wherever it looked. He also wished, however, to stress that it was not only he but, posthumously, his superior who was on trial: 'and then, with Cardinal Mazarin one could not be certain of the rules in money matters. He never used to give precise orders. He blamed and nevertheless permitted. He disapproved of everything; and after one had convinced him of the impossibility of succeeding otherwise, he approved of everything.'

That *chambre de justice* was set up to represent the brave new world of Colbert's propaganda, in which the king would be his own *premier ministre* and would expect order and honesty in financial affairs which he, Colbert, would deliver. With royal support, six years of peace and a temporary improvement in the money supply, Colbert would enjoy initial success: while reducing the *taille* he managed to double the revenue available to the crown within six years.[4] He would be Louis XIV's *contrôleur-général* for twenty-two years; during that time he would enjoy an unprecedentedly wide range of powers over the economy. He arrived, a commissary of proven diligence and competence; he then revealed political skills of a high order; he was to show that he was something more, a statesman of authority and vision. His policies were designed to stimulate a more active and productive economy. Meanwhile they could not be implemented, nor could he attain the summit, while Fouquet was in power: he was therefore resolved to destroy Fouquet and did not hesitate, where necessary, to doctor the evidence. All that was to come – after Mazarin's death.

Since Colbert had worked for Mazarin as his *intendant*, and built his master's fortune by means as questionable as those employed by the *surintendant*, he would have personal reasons for ensuring a clean break with the past.[5] Fouquet should not now be judged, as he was by the *chambre de justice*, simply on the evidence that it was given to weigh, but with reference to the circumstances in which he took office, the financial world in which he had to operate and the methods he was forced to use. That there was a case for him, even within the narrow terms imposed on the *chambre*, can be gathered from the facts that the trial lasted nearly three years, did not bring sentence of death but only life imprisonment: that he was detained under conditions that ensured that he could neither state his case nor rally his friends; and that several of them, notably Olivier d'Ormesson,[6] had the courage to speak up for him.

Repeatedly Mazarin showed his flair for management in his choice of men to serve him, or indirectly to serve his ends. For financial management however, after the disgrace of Particelli, he was constrained by circumstances to accept someone who could command respect: the front was all-important. *Surintendants* La Meilleraye, de Maisons and La Vieuville had been too much concerned with immediate needs to look critically at the system or constructively to the future. With the restoration of royal authority there was need of a big man, as clever as Particelli, as well connected as de Maisons or la Vieuville, but personable enough to persuade men to lend and invest, and tough enough to withstand the strains of this demanding office. In essence his role would be to restore confidence. Reputation, character and ability pointed to Nicolas Fouquet. In many ways he proved to be the outstanding personality of the post-Fronde years.

After proving, as *intendant*, to be resourceful and loyal, Fouquet had gained Mazarin's backing when in 1650, at the unusually young age of thirty-three, he bought the office of *procureur-général* in *Parlement*. His role was to nurture the royalist party among the judges. He acted as intermediary between the government and Turenne in the negotiations leading to the general's return to the king. With his brother, the *abbé* Basile,[7] another valued Mazarinist, he worked to persuade Parisians that their interests too lay with the king. With Molé he led the move to Pontoise that was to prove crucial in securing the restoration in a seemingly legal manner. No wonder that Mazarin wrote in September 1652: 'I have the utmost confidence in him, without any reservation . . . I believe him to be entirely of my friends'. When, in February 1653, Mazarin appointed him *surintendant*, he encountered professional jealousy which he could afford to ignore. Handsome, pleasantly open in manner, appealing much to women, genuinely interested in the artists and writers whom he now had ample means to support, he could count on a large personal following, with friendships that went beyond the ties of the *clientèle*, substantial as that already was, and rivalling Mazarin's own.[8] Indeed, in many ways, interests, methods, pretensions and style, Fouquet's career complemented that of his *patron*.

To appease critics, perhaps for his own peace of mind, Mazarin appointed Servien to be joint *surintendant*. The veteran minister embarrassed Fouquet by attention to formalities which, to the impatient younger man, amounted to interference and caused delay. Mazarin eased the tension by dividing the duties. He wanted Fouquet to be his instrument and he intended to enlarge his own stake in the profitable business of the *épargne*.[9] How wasteful this could be is shown by figures for the alienation of certain royal taxes in 1658 which indicate that only eleven per cent of the amount raised actually reached the treasury. It was not an area that Mazarin wished to be scrutinised. In December 1654, Servien's role was limited to control of royal expenditure while Fouquet was left with the harder part, raising the funds. That remained the arrangement till Servien's death, in 1659, and left Fouquet nominally, as he had long been in practice, in sole control.

In 1653 the financial state of the monarchy was dire. Le Tillier,[10] *intendant des finances*, wrote to Mazarin in January 1653, noting specific dangers to the 'safety of the state'. *Munitionnaires* would not provide bread for the royal armies; *rentiers* had been waiting for four weeks for the payment of interest at the Hôtel de Ville; the revenue *fermes* on which payments were assigned were abandoned and without *fermiers*, Le Tillier's conclusion was ominous: 'With the ill-will and speeches of trouble-makers and malcontents who are still too numerous, Paris is on the eve of some great sedition'.

The withdrawal of *intendants*, on top of reports from Paris of *Parlement*'s open opposition to fiscal measures, had encouraged tax evasion. *Frondeur* hostility towards *traitants* and *fermiers*, with so many losses and grievances and such uncertainty about the future, engendered a surly, apprehensive mood. There had been widespread disruption of commerce. Occurring against the background of a long-term reduction in the bullion supply, the Fronde created a credit drought which called not only for firm measures by the crown, but also sensitive handling of the only men who could bring immediate relief, the financiers.

They had to be persuaded that they could invest their money with reasonable expectation of profit and guarantee of security. *Parlement* had to play its part: most members stood to benefit from the resumption of normal financial operations. The occasional clout, as administered by Louis XIV in the *lit de justice* of March 1655, was more effective because it was followed by a politic distribution of favours. At the head of the queue, receiving 300,000 *livres*, was the *premier président* himself, Pomponne de Bellièvre.[11] The equivalent benefit for the financier had to be high interest. Borrowing could keep the war machine in action, but at a frightening cost, as the proceeds went mainly to service the debts at rates that encouraged the financier to lend again. Loans commonly took the form of advances on revenue. Everything possible was farmed out. So weak was the bargaining position of the crown that returns to the crown averaged around thirty per cent of the amount extracted. It was not a formula for a contented country or a strong government. In the autumn of 1654 the government was already consuming almost all of its disposable income two years in advance: Mazarin was then proposing to earmark 1657 as well.

'Our principal care is to find cash promptly': Servien's words establish the criterion according to which Fouquet's financial strategy may look sensible, even responsible. It consisted essentially of two inter-locking operations. He used his own property as security for loans intended for the crown; he borrowed money on the security of the state. The scope there for personal enrichment needs little stress. It could be urged that he had to maintain a lavish front to reassure creditors that their money was safe. Vaux-le-Vicomte[12] was built for the *surintendant* between 1657 and 1661, at hectic speed and prodigious cost, exceeding the grandest of royal *châteaux* in its facilities for hospitality and entertainment. Conveying the impression of a rival court it sent a conflicting message. The last word in design at every point, it set a standard which only the richest could hope to emulate. In sum it was a monstrous challenge to the general view: that government was straitened and the people impoverished.

Vaux-le-Vicomte was also a public statement about the power of credit. Of course Fouquet knew, for example, from the high price of offices, that there were great accumulations of capital in private hands: much of it, like his own, was financing the purchase of estates and building of *châteaux*.[13] Only a fraction could be secured by taxation. The time would come for other methods: fines, confiscations and brutal cuts in rates of interest. Even now, Fouquet used the threat of action by a *chambre de justice* to extract sums, in effect protection money, from individual lenders. Meanwhile plutocratic fortunes had to be tapped through the well tried system of treaties and loans. It was the golden age of the *partisan*[14] but investment went far beyond the circle of the professional money men. There were the confidential clerks who did much of the business, like Jacques de l'Orme, who worked, first secretly, for Fouquet, while nominally Servien's chief clerk. De l'Orme was able to persuade financiers to lend under personal guarantee of repayment. There were also obscure agents behind whose names, as ostensible lenders, often concealed the great: the prince de Conti or Mme Palatine, for example, with large sums to offer and safe profits to make out of the exigencies of the state.[15]

As in the raising of money, so in its spending, much of which by-passed the main route through the *épargne* by use of *ordonnances de comptant*,[9] the involvement of important persons worked with the spread of investment through syndicates and sub-contracting to enhance Fouquet's importance as the man at the centre of the complex web. Auditing was defective or non-existent, as *contrôleurs* virtually abandoned their responsibility in that respect. The personal nature of the whole edifice and the hubristic element in his overweening self-confidence were revealed when, in June 1658, he fell critically ill. Unable to carry out the gruelling process of bargaining over money for the army, Fouquet was then reduced to selling his wife's estate of Belle Assize to raise funds. He survived this crisis. There is no foundation for Colbert's story that Mazarin, on his death-bed, decided to tell the king of Fouquet's misdoings. Two years before, Mazarin had snubbed Colbert when he presented him with a memorandum detailing the faults and abuses in the *surintendant*'s work. Whether through laziness, self-interest, or perhaps fellow feeling, Mazarin was loyal. He would appreciate Fouquet's argument that in current conditions any drastic attempt to reform would have been suicidal. In retrospect however the Fouquet regime can be seen to have been precarious, incompatible with the assertion of royal authority.

There was a carelessness, which no minister could afford (and a contrast, for example, with the behaviour of Le Tellier) in Fouquet's relationship with the king. Secure in his Parisian côterie, he came close to patronising the king. Seeing Louis still in political tutelage, he acted as if that would continue indefinitely. During the Fronde he had been loyal; now he was an agent of reconciliation; yet Louis saw him as belonging to that Parisian establishment whose view of monarchy seemed so demeaning. The king hardly needed Colbert at his elbow to associate disorder in the finances with the political disorders he had recently experienced. Even Fouquet's patronage offended. He 'forgot that Maecaenas would not have become a legend without Augustus' (Bluche).

Yet Fouquet loved life and office too much to be simply fatalistic. After 1658 he was at least contemplating the possibility that he might be dismissed. Anxiety can be sensed in his orders to step up the great building operation and in the continued purchase of land, over two million *livres* worth in all. He certainly considered plans to mobilise his friends in the country, governors of certain fortresses and the admiral commanding in the Bay of Biscay. Some nobles actually signed professions of loyalty to Fouquet. With Mazarin's consent, he bought the marquisate of Belle-Ile, off the Biscay coast, with the intention of creating a fortified stronghold. Unfortunately he committed these projects to paper: they would form the basis of the subsequent charge of treason.

The *chambre de justice* would find that around three to four million *livres* out of twenty-three had been spent in ways that could not be called royal service. Undeniably however he had given good service. His system, if such a medley of improvisations can be called a 'system', served its main purpose. It enabled him to secure sufficient funds for Mazarin to pursue victorious war. But it contained the seeds of its destruction, along with his own. Spreading upwards and downwards, compromising the very officials whose role it was to control the system, leading to Fouquet's delegating whole areas of business to minor agents, with more and more hands in the till, it was not merely corrupt but inefficient. Fouquet was too intelligent not to understand that. To his credit, he had begun the process of concentrating the *fermes* that was taken further by Colbert. He had resisted the temptation to juggle with the value of the *livre*. In grim circumstances he could claim that he had saved the state and contributed to its latter triumphs. In the view of his principal biographer he was a conscientious royal servant, the victim, as much as the manager of the crown's financial machine. That it could at least be made to yield more was what Colbert proved, not by his mean-spirited and vindictive vendetta against the man, but by his own more efficient management of what was, in most respects, essentially the same machine.

32

THE GREATEST PRIVATE FORTUNE

Serving a master who would be lauded in proportion to the gifts and favours he distributed, in an aristocratic society which prized the ideal of *générosité*[1] the seventeenth-century statesman did not usually expect to live frugally or to die poor. If he did, it might be because of some principle strong enough to counter the human instinct to acquire goods and endow a family. Religious zeal, republican virtue, perhaps domestic preference, might direct a Cromwell or a de Witt.[2] Such men were exceptional. The cases of Buckingham, Liechtenstein,[3] Lerma[4] or Oxenstierna, were more typical. The only prominent French ministers of this period who failed to leave a fortune were those, notably Concini and Fouquet, whose careers were prematurely ended by death or disgrace. Their fate underlines one reason for the amassing of spectacular fortunes by those in the best position to do so: political office was precarious – and so was life. Neither Richelieu nor Mazarin was an old man when he died. Calculations about careers were undoubtedly tinged by the awareness that death could come suddenly at any time. Anyone who reached sixty would know that most of his contemporaries had not. No view of the febrile quality of so much of life, with the tendency to extremes, in the spiritual as much as in the secular spheres, can omit that consideration.

Another is the all-pervasive influence of aristocratic values: the rank, title, rights, dress, household, position in a hierarchy and display that could be mounted: all were avidly pursued. Those who lost them, or saw them depreciated, while *nouveaux* flourished, were likely to be embittered. Those who enjoyed them in fair measure still strove to enhance them: at the highest level, as is illustrated by successive generations of the Condé family, there was little sign of any moderating sense of responsibility: they wanted all they could get. Those born *roturier*, whose education or native wit gave them the chance to rise, yearned for nobility: it was the most powerful single motive force in society. The occasional saga of successful elevation, like that of Gourville,[5] a very Figaro of his time, stands for a thousand aspirations: *laboureur* to become *seigneur*, valet to become major-domo. To expect a traditionally hierarchic society to be a necessarily static society is the greatest mistake.

Noble values were inseparable from noble requirements: land, fine buildings, clients, arms. The past hundred years had seen the wasting of numerous estates. The experience of poverty had lent a sharp edge to Richelieu's political ambition. A continuing factor, some would say the main thrust in his career, had been the desire to be 'considerable': measurable in estates as well as offices.

Corruption, greed and avarice feature much in the *Mazarinades*, with reference often to his family and his ambition to enrich it. In some respects, for all the crude prejudice, the foreign focus was sound. For Mazarin, the plutocrat, was also Mazarin the Roman, lover of books, pictures and sculptures, producer of dramatic and musical entertainments, patron and collector. The architectural and artistic splendours of Roman Baroque were financed by vast private fortunes and accompanied by such bravura in display and entertainment that the visitor who found himself, like the young Mazarin, moving in the right circles, might fancy that the city of St Peter was given over to a continuous festival of the arts. Political and social choice were to make Mazarin a Frenchman, but he remained a Roman in taste and in his view of business: no governing *élite* was richer than that of Rome – and the papal state was held to be the worst governed in Europe.

Long before Mazarin secured, with ministerial office, the funds to gratify his appetite for works of art, he had shown the instincts of the treasure hunter. It was recognised that he liked to receive as well as to give presents. He could be shamelessly manipulative in securing a coveted work of art: Cardinal Antonio was a rich source in the early days. So eclectic was Mazarin's stock that he can appear more as dealer than connoisseur, too keenly aware of the price and utility of works of art to develop a discriminating taste, content to receive what was best according to current estimates. His sources of information and natural bias meant that paintings and sculptures were generally Italian.[6] The choice of subjects was no less conventional. His large collection of Van Dyke[7] reflects that painter's typical choice of portraits, notable men and women, and the fortunate opportunity afforded by the sale of Charles I's pictures. There was a didactic side. In 1640 a mission to Rome under Chantelou[8] initiated a flow of Italian artists and craftsmen to France: it was the natural corollary of the young French painters' tendency to go to Rome to study the best models. There was however little apparent interest in the use of patronage to encourage the young painter at home. Le Brun,[9] Séguier's protégé, would have to wait for Colbert's ministry to receive royal commissions.

It may be fruitless to distinguish in Mazarin between the avid collector, the power broker and the lover of art. Yet it would be wrong to envisage him as having no more feeling about paintings, sculptures or tapestries than he had about precious metals or stones: or indeed to deny him an eye for beauty. Even where some political end can be recognised, there is sufficient evidence of a vision of the intrinsic value of art, as of music, literature and scholarship. The great library of 40,000 volumes, Naudé's[10] remarkable creation, was designed to be an instrument of learning as well as a demonstration of the Cardinal's munificence. From the start it was a haven for scholars. Like his works of art, it was to be a legacy to France of permanent value.

Besides the sheer attractiveness of great possessions to the minister, there was a further factor, perhaps the most important. Wealth was the means to obtain power, to hold on to it and, distinguishing the statesman from the adventurer, the opportunity to make good use of it. Mazarin might have expressed himself less loftily than Richelieu – and did the latter indeed say, on his death bed: 'I have no enemies save those of the state'? But he never ceased to claim that his prime concern was to be a good servant of the crown. That he thought first of 'le bien et la gloire de l'état' is a constant refrain in letters. To increase his sovereign's power he had to have the means: agents, security, the power to impress, and ready money for expenses. Between the state's need and the minister's, only he could decide. Therein, with the involvement of officials theoretically responsible for auditing in the primary business of money-raising, his direct access to money from the *épargne*, the virtual collapse therefore of any proper audit and control, lies the substance of charges of corruption.

Mazarin's financial philosophy, if his amiably amoral approach can be so called, was to be exemplified by his attitude towards state finance. The role of the appropriate minister was to secure sufficient revenue without provoking revolt. Mazarin cared apparently no more about its source, the manner of its collection or the damage its collecting might inflict on producer and taxpayer than might a Barberini or a Colonna. He was nurtured in a society in which political activity was largely an extension of family business, in which the interests of relations often took priority over higher interests and loyalties or, as in the case of successive Popes, co-existed with them in ways that discredited the institution and weakened its claim to universal sovereignty. Guilio, the Papal diplomat, was the clever son who made good, the family's chief provider and patron long before his father's death. His marriageable nieces played a part in his political game. But long before he was faced by the need to raise money for the kind of dowry required by a French nobleman when he decided 'to manure his lands' by marriage to a social inferior, he was conversant with the expense of maintaining the family in its proper state. His early correspondence shows him driven by personal ambition, but also by a sense of obligation to the *casa*.

In modern government all services are provided for the minister: place of work and entertainment, technical assistance, specialist advisers, facilities for research, swift and reliable transport, security: everything conducive to peace of mind, and the space, mental as much as physical, held requisite for balanced judgement and well-informed plans. All these a seventeenth-century minister had to provide, together with the means to create a *clientèle* to buttress power and implement policies. He could not have risen to eminence, unless, like Luynes, by the fast track laid out by the sovereign's special favour, without much preliminary grafting and spending. In Mazarin's case, starting late and without much of a *clientèle*, finding himself soon in a near-bankrupt regime, even uncertain for a time about his ultimate loyalties, committed to a war which would have gone disastrously wrong if he had not found the means to pay the troops, and surrounded by such enmities that it was essential to retain the loyalty of a *corps d'élite* – his Swiss guards[11] and musketeers – the needs were specially acute.

Mazarin started from a modest base, lacked the influence at first to enlarge it significantly through use of church patronage, and could not lean on his *surintendant*, Particelli, as later he could on Fouquet. He claimed frequently that he impoverished himself during the Fronde to save the state. Between 1643 and 1648, he had certainly found useful sources of revenue. He was remitting more than one million *livres* a year to his banker.[12] During the Fronde, these sources mostly dried up and he was pressed hard by creditors. Some of his goods were distrained by *Parlement* while that body subjected certain dealings, over leases for example, to judicial review. To secure allies he even surrendered benefices or granted pensions on their security. He returned to Paris in 1653 a relatively poor man. He had learned that it was essential to have wealth, not only in the form of lands and offices, but ready cash. There was also a festering sense of grievance which in another man might have fed a desire for revenge; in him it whetted the desire to be very rich. He had to make up for lost time. The speed with which his wealth was amassed is as impressive as its amount: easily surpassing that acquired over a much longer period by Richelieu (about twenty-four million *livres*) it was the largest of any minister's of the *ancien régime*. As in other respects, Mazarin had learned much from Richelieu, as relentlessly single-minded in the acquisition of wealth as in his political career, making no clear distinction between public and private business. His private household was virtually a department of state. Richelieu's official income came from varied sources, notably church benefices, salaries or other perquisites as governor or other titulary. His unofficial income was far more important. He became a great territorial magnate, with estates worth at least five million *livres*. Altogether he displayed the way in which power led to wealth. Mazarin would have seen that there was nothing accidental or inevitable about the process. In several respects, however, Mazarin's approach was different from that of his mentor. He was relatively uninterested in land as providing a power base and potential refuge. Nor did he share Richelieu's passion for building. He was particularly concerned to have large amounts of wealth in realisable, portable form.

Of Mazarin's fortune which, before allowing for the several millions allotted to the endowment of his remaining nieces, has been estimated at death at thirty-nine million *livres*, about a third was in the form of *argent liquide*, coin, bullion and precious stones, stored in Paris or at carefully chosen places about the country. There were several precisely enumerated hoards: 766,000 *livres* worth at the Louvre, for example; 663,000 with a financier, Picon; 1,500,000 at Vincennes, the royal fortress which Mazarin treated virtually as his own. Several particular chests were stored in fortresses, like Sedan, along the eastern frontier, where they could be easily obtained in case of emergency. About 2,500,000 *livres*, worth of precious stones represented shrewd buying in a market depressed by the spectacular misfortunes of great personages: notably Henrietta Maria and the Duke of Mantua.

Certain favoured recipients would benefit from Mazarin's shrewd buying with a memento of the Cardinal's affection and gratitude. One can imagine Mazarin's satisfaction in this part of a detailed testament, the ultimate act of service, the bequeathing of rare, in some cases already famous jewels to Anne, the king, the young queen or, a figure from the Roman past, Count Colonna. There were also nearly 500 paintings, a great library, half a million *livres* worth of tapestries, and silverware of similar value. Ebony cabinets were found stuffed with necklaces, crosses and chains, the precious trinkets that he had always been happy to give to appreciative women. Overall there is something uninhibited here that dismays the stoic who condemns excess or the puritan who submits his worldly accounts to divine audit. Stoical and puritan influences were not limited then to Protestant communities. Mazarin's ministry saw the establishment of Port Royal, standing for individual initiative in the search for God, with the sense of moral responsibility that permeated the legal establishment and had informed the early protests of the Fronde. To many Parisians at that time, Mazarin had represented a disturbing phenomenon, an intrusive and amoral presence, Mediterranean, sensual, pagan – to indicate something of the range of prejudices that those terms convey. The contents of Mazarin's treasure chests reveal that there was ground for concern, though what he had acquired by 1648 was only a foretaste of the final hoard.

Mazarin held no domain land till after his return in 1653. In 1654 he was granted the duchy of Mayenne; in 1657 he acquired the Nivernais and Donziois: all from the duke of Mantua. They represented under-utilised assets. It was the business of Jean-Baptiste Colbert[13] to ensure that they were fully exploited. When Colbert decided to make his career in Paris and, with Le Tellier's encouragement, began to serve Mazarin as a personal *intendant*, he was accepting a position that might appear menial. He realised that the way to power led to the capital and the household of the *premier ministre* : to be great he would 'be 'umble' though, unlike Uriah Heep, whom in his more obsequious moments and bullying ways he sometimes resembled, Colbert wished to elevate, not ruin his master; it was by making his master's fortune that he would make his own. Up till the Fronde, Mazarin's estate had been an untidy bundle, comprising as many liabilities as assets, a bran tub irregularly filled, into which he would dip, at need, when creditors pressed. With more contacts than cash, Mazarin had lived hand-to-mouth. Nor did he bring to the handling of his affairs Richelieu's or Sully's kind of sophisticated, consistent care. Careless in generosity as in greed, like the gambler who cares little about the balance sheet so long as there is coin to put on the table, he remained sunnily indifferent to the disciplines of financial management.

Mazarin gave Colbert general powers of attorney in May 1651, but was at first fussily interested and reluctant to let Colbert take over; the young man was brash, too emphatic in his views perhaps. He had to deal with Mazarin's creditors and regain control of leases and other contracts after two years of interference by the judicial processes initiated by Broussel. By December 1652 he was sufficiently exasperated at the lack of a clear plan, to challenge his master: either the Cardinal could let matters drift, without getting a grip, in this case, of his church benefices, and convey the impression that he was disinterested; or he could work (that is, let Colbert work in his name) 'to lay the foundations of a great establishment, worthy of a person of his condition, to bequeath to his successors and make his house considerable in this realm'. In a significant instruction of October 1653 Mazarin drew the lines between the two areas of their mutually beneficial enterprise: 'It is good that you should know, once for all, in requiring me to apply myself to my own affairs, that I am fifty years old; I have never been more pressed than now and it has never been in my power to make any effort to put my affairs into a good state. It is necessary that you should contribute where I am deficient . . . [attending to] particular interests which, for a long time, by nature and habit, I have been liable to forget for public affairs'. Perhaps he protested overmuch, knowing his own motives as he claimed to know Colbert's: 'He is my man and in my interest he would drown everyone he loves, without excepting Le Tellier. He professes honour and he is bound to me, and expects to do well for himself while furthering my concerns'. What mattered was that Colbert had a free hand.

If Mazarin was fortunate, Colbert was equally so. He had a unique opportunity to prove himself capable of higher office and to gain a first-hand knowledge, not only of finances, officials and agents at every level, but of the condition of the realm. His exceptional capacity to deal with detail, down to minutely itemised travel expenses, yet keep track of larger objectives, was given almost boundless scope; he could exploit the flaws in the system while gathering the evidence he needed for its reform, and recruiting the agents he would need to effect it. Anything lost to the crown, in his stewardship of the largest private fortune in Europe, would be recovered many times over when he took over the *contrôle*.

Along with the duchies that brought Mazarin the status of *duc et pair*, other lands accrued through grant or purchase, notably, and appropriately, lands in Alsace: these alone were valued at 2 million *livres*. Almost as valuable were the revenues that flowed from the alienation of certain royal domains, like La Fère and the forest of Saint-Gobain; also rights to certain *tailles, aides* and *gabelles*. His hold over the financial mechanism during Fouquet's ministry and his unrestricted access to the funds of the *épargne* meant that he could divert money almost at will to his private use. From 1655 to 1658 special payments from the *épargne* averaged 23 million a year: not all went to the prosecution of the war or other government business. No less hard to track were the sums of money lent by Mazarin to the crown and treasury. Other loans went to foreign sovereigns and French notables; it was thus, for example, that Mme de Chevreuse was enabled to live in her accustomed style. By 1661 around 10 million *livres* were earning interest in such ways. With salaries for offices that ranged from *surintendant* of the queen's household to governorships of Vincennes, La Rochelle and other lesser places, along with the capital value of his vast *palazzo* in Rome and the *palais Mazarin* in Paris, it is not hard to see how a total of thirty-nine million *livres* could be arrived at.

One important source of income was that which flowed from the Cardinal's collection of ecclesiastical benefices. The figure, 572,000 *livres*, which had risen by a fifth from 1656 to 1661, is seen to be an overstatement, when charges are deducted: that still left 342,000 *livres* of free income. In 1661, twenty-four abbeys and a priory were held by Mazarin. The first clutch had been acquired during the forties (when Mazarin's agent was the *abbé* Charles),[14] after the successive deaths of four principal pluralists, La Valette, the comte de Soissons, the duc de Guise and Richelieu himself, with sixteen, six, eleven and eighteen benefices respectively, had provided a rare opportunity to build up a holding. By 1648 he held thirteen abbeys. He had also begun negotiations for a bishopric, Metz. The story of this vital territory, confirmed to French possession at Westphalia, illustrates the interweaving of state and ecclesiastical business. Henry IV's illegitimate son, Henri de Bourbon-Verneuil,[15] had long been titular bishop. He was eventually persuaded to resign the see, with two abbeys, in return for one of Mazarin's. In October 1652 Mazarin wrote to Schomberg thanking him for assistance with his 'election' as bishop. Like Metz, most of Mazarin's abbeys were in north-eastern France; few escaped altogether the destruction of war. Several were resigned by Mazarin in favour of some potential ally. Others were seized at the request of an individual creditor. By 1653 he was in a mood to recoup with interest. In 1654 he acquired no less than ten abbeys, several, like Saint-Denis, among the most renowned in the land. His arrangement with Conti illustrates his way of combining political and personal business in one operation. Conti had married one of Mazarin's nieces, to his great profit; he had therefore to surrender his benefices; Mazarin was specially well placed to benefit from the transaction. Among the monasteries gained was that of Cluny, with which went generalship of the order, and which had been held by Richelieu. Its granting to Conti by Anne in 1643 had been a bitter blow to Cardinal de la Rochefoucauld's reforming hopes.[16]

It was Colbert's task to manage this empire in church property, with his own confidential agents, family members, like his brother Charles and Nicolas, but others too, groomed for larger responsibilities. Notable among them was Louis Berryer,[17] a factotum on whom Colbert increasingly relied for the demanding but lucrative work of administration. Some abbeys, like Corbie, yielded little because they had been pillaged by the Spanish; others, notably Chaise-Dieu, had suffered from the depredations of the local nobility. Colbert was often compelled to remit or reduce rents. After several *fermiers* had failed to meet their obligations he had to take a gentler line. Eventually he resorted to a *ferme générale* for all but two of the abbeys and a *recette-générale* for the accountancy. Revenue was the prime concern. But the innovating minister of the future can be glimpsed in his devising, with a Poitevin monastery, a scheme to drain local marshes. Furthering his acquaintance with the land, and its diverse patterns of ownership and tenure, Colbert was preparing for a time when he would enjoy larger powers. His stewardship was therefore of greater significance than the large increase in those revenues. It is unlikely that he would have been concerned about their diversion from the needs of the abbey for which the original endowment had been intended. By the practice known as commendation, freely used by sovereigns as a source of patronage, monastic lands had long served to supplement the incomes of the powerful and influential. To question the practice would have been to take issue with the Pope himself. Nor is there any suggestion that Mazarin had qualms, or scruples, any more than Richelieu before him. The latter had however taken seriously his responsibilities to the monasteries and devoted thought to wider church issues. Mazarin took much from the church; it is reasonable to ask what he gave back.

Part VI

CONSCIENCE AND POLICY

'God has given you so perspicacious a spirit that you have been able to distinguish between the temporal and the celestial.'
Anna Maria Mazarini

33

THE GREAT AGE OF SOULS

Mazarin's France was the France of Catholic reform. His years of power coincide with some of the most active and fruitful in that Europe-wide process for which 'Counter-Reformation', while defining one part, the unrelenting struggle against Protestantism, must be a wholly inadequate term. Brémond's phrase, 'The great age of souls',[1] better conveys the heroic aspects of a flowering of French spirituality which was so diverse in insights, gifts, and works that it cannot properly be called a movement. Yet, from Madame Acarie, Cardinal de la Rochefoucauld[2] and François de Sales, among early leaders, to Bossuet and Fénelon[3] at the end of the century, it so profoundly influenced successive generations that it cannot be treated simply as a single episode, or even phase, in the history of the church. Twenty-seven French men and women of the seventeenth century were to be canonised or beatified. It was an age of such extraordinary, path-finding personalities that the reader risks losing track of central themes in following the careers of certain individuals; yet he must, in order to appreciate a mental and spiritual ethos that is wholly intelligible in Christian terms, but remote from minds conditioned to see as irrational or 'neurotic' any behaviour which is seemingly at odds with the 'normal' impulses of nature. Faithful to the teaching of the Gospels about the denial of self and giving to others, seventeenth-century spirituality was grounded in the idea that chastity left one free to love many rather than one: *agape* promoted in place of *eros*.

No case illustrates the difficulty of interpretation more vividly than that of the duc de Ventadour,[4] founder of the Compagnie du Saint-Sacrement, who insisted on living chastely, as a 'brother' to his beautiful wife: she, no less influenced by the mysticism of Saint Theresa,[5] entered a Carmelite convent, while he set about drawing influential associates into a crusade for moral reform and charitable endeavour. It was self-sacrificing, generous and unworldly, inspired by the vision of a Christian society. The Company's lawyer members were charged to protect the poor in suits against the powerful. It distributed money, furniture and tools to the poor of the Paris suburbs. It also worked for the founding of the *hôpital-*

général which was eventually established in 1656.[6] Reflecting its ancestry in the Holy League[7] and its links with the Penitent companies of Paris, it was also secretive, political, censorious, apparently patronising and certainly intolerant. Ventadour secured the exclusion of Huguenots from Canada. Campaigns against prostitution, fairs on feast days, and theatre, laid the Company open to the charge of hypocrisy that was so memorably, if unfairly, delivered in Molière's *Tartuffe*.[8] The caustic voice of Guy Patin may have spoken for many *honnêtes hommes*,[9] even if they saw themselves as moderates in religion rather than sceptics: 'Paris is full of pharisees, knaves, swindlers, even in matters of religion. I never saw more religion and monkery, never less charity'. Mazarin had few doubts. He disliked the Company, suspected its motives and warned the king against it.

At the other end of the social scale, and equally significant, for spiritual fervour was no more the preserve of the upper classes than in Bunyan's England, was Henri Buch, a shoemaker, like the author of *Pilgrim's Progress*, and the originator of the pious congregations of men bound by craft and faith that were another feature of the period. Members of the *frondeur* crowds who hustled magistrates or demonstrated in the streets were not all untutored or thoughtless roughs. 'Henri le Bon' was himself no activist. Yet from apprenticeship in religion to mastery of political ideas was not an improbable progression. The spirit engendered by comradeship in faith helped prepare the ground for priests like Jean Rousse,[10] the unruly *curé* of Saint-Roch who was such a sharp thorn in Mazarin's side.

More dangerous for government than the piety of simple folk, were the extremes of spiritual ardour among those who had other reasons to oppose the regime. Between 1638 and 1643, Saint-Cyran[11] languished in prison. After Richelieu's death he was released, but only to die. Jansenism, the movement which he helped create, evolved in ways which would have confirmed Richelieu's forebodings: mystical excesses, covert political intrigues, all coloured by a pro-Spanish bias, were what Richelieu saw in this impetuous southerner, whose 'entrails were on fire'. Mazarin was no less aware of Jansenism's political implications.

Religious orders proliferated, old, reformed and new. Processions of hooded penitents took faith to the streets. Jean-Jacques Olier's seminary of Saint-Sulpice[12] witnessed to his own intense spirituality and inspired other priests. The missions of Jean Eudes[13] revived faith in the countryside. New styles of worship and objects of adoration appeared: the Sacred Heart, the Immaculate Conception. Louis XIII struck a chord when he placed the kingdom under the special protection of the Virgin Mary. Devotional manuals poured off the presses, none more popular than St François de Sales' *Introduction à la Vie dévôte*. Can such profusion of endeavours and graces be brought within any intelligible scheme?

It was a Christian age: the last before the exploring of new territories, physical and intellectual, eroded the conception of Europe as being synonymous with Christendom, and the faith as being unassailable. Effort went less into proving a case against scepticism than into attacking heresies within Christendom and converting pagans beyond it. Enthusiasts sought to persuade the nominally Christian to live as if Christ were present in their lives. Humanist scholarship, science and philosophy at least appeared to be reinforcing faith. There was a rapidly growing literate public and relatively cheap printing served its needs. The experience of wars might show the futility of fighting over different interpretations of the faith; but the message for many was the opposite to indifferentism: it was contrition, the need for a deeper spirituality, new ways of finding God. 'Shaking times' only fed the hunger for certainty and reassurance. Tridentine decrees[14] had provided that on the theological plane. Rival French traditions, embodying different views of Papal and royal authority over the Church, ultramontane and Gallican, and the party spirit they engendered, were, at this stage, a source more of enthusiasm for the faith than of the damaging conflicts that were later to weaken the authority of the church.

The most striking feature of the French revival was the role of prominent lay men and women, from the royal family and great noble families of sword and gown, to ministers in key positions like Séguier, intellectuals like Descartes and Pascal.[15] The importance of Paris can hardly be overstated: the commanding citadels of power and influence were there: court, *Parlement*, the Sorbonne, certain *salons*, cells and networks of devotion, bases for practical and pastoral initiatives. Here was the potential for controversies of the specially intense kind that occur wherever there is a concentration of intellectuals capable of abstract reasoning and lawyers trained to argue.

Catholicism was the soul of monarchy. Henry IV's conversion and his successors' piety exemplified the fact. Catholic rituals, most notably that of Coronation, enhanced the authority of the king. Secular and ecclesiastical conceptions of authority, patriarchal and absolutist, appeared to ride together, to reciprocal advantage. But a central objective of royal absolutism was political control. Over the question of the Huguenots this had given rise to little conflict between Church and crown, at least until Richelieu seemed to *dévôts* to be putting secular before spiritual considerations. But when the Church was also a vast propertied interest, providing scope for the building of fortunes and *clientèles* like Mazarin's, there was an inherent scope for conflict. It was exacerbated by the growth, since the Counter-Reformation, in the moral authority of the Pope and the recent increase in royal authority that was the prime achievement of Richelieu. It was sharpened by the exigencies of international relations, when two or more Catholic powers had incompatible territorial ambitions. It would be brought to the point of crisis when government pursued a foreign policy which was plainly dictated by secular rather than religious considerations.

Not the least extraordinary feature of Richelieu's ministry had been that he had executed and carried through essentially secular policies in defiance of opposition from reactionary magnates and disconcerted *dévôts*, often acting together. That had induced a chronic disorder, punctuated by periodic crises. He had survived, but left a dangerous legacy. The *dévôts* were unreconciled. Mazarin might seem at first to be so secular in spirit, so coolly detached from *dévôt* passions and programmes, that a case could be made for our setting them on one side. It cannot be sustained. For Mazarin, essentially a diplomat, the struggle to find the right balance between the secular aims of the state and the spiritual concerns of so many of his critics, may not have been as costly as it was to Richelieu. He was to an extent the outsider in the intense world of the *dévôts*.[16] He was all the more fortunate in retaining the support of Anne (for example, Vincent de Paul tried to secure his removal) whose life was such a textbook of *dévôt* principles, grounded in prayer and in the sacraments; also in that his arch-opponent, Gondi, was so manifestly a man of double standards that he served to discredit the cause of the militant clergy. Temperamentally inclined to take a cool view, both of the mysticism that underlay the rapid growth in religious orders and fraternities, and the idea of moral crusade, he was however forced to take note of *dévôt* opinion: his survival was due, at least in part, to his being sensitive to the prevailing spiritual climate and adroit in the handling of the inevitable conflicts. To appreciate that climate we have only to look around the capital as he would have known it.

Hard by the Place-Royale were the Jesuits,[17] in their new church of St Louis. The dedication marked Louis XIII's respect for the reputedly saintly character of his ancestor, Louis IX.[18] Richelieu had celebrated the first mass in the completed building in 1641; Louis XIII's heart was interred there. It symbolised the attachment of the monarch to the Church and the special niche in the hierarchy of power occupied by the Society of Jesus since its return to France in 1603; it provided the royal confessor, a crucial office when religion affected so many political decisions – and when religious policies could have political repercussions. The architecture of the church, modelled on Il Gesu in Rome, reflected the ultramontane stance of the Jesuits. Truly international in organisation and outlook, they served the Pope without question and without compromise. Few men knew their methods and style better than their one-time prize Roman pupil. Like Richelieu's before him, however, Mazarin's relationship with the royal confessor was bound to be ambivalent: his was a rival influence, and a secret one, hard to monitor. Père Paulin, Louis' confessor till 1654, was not informed, for example, about the decision to arrest Retz. The king would not have regarded such a matter as outside the confessor's province; Mazarin insisted on secrecy as a necessary pre-condition of success. Père Annat, Paulin's successor, was strongly anti-Jansenist, reinforcing in Louis the suspicions that were to harden during his reign into unrelenting opposition. Measures taken against the sect would be preceded, of course, by scrupulous theological enquiry to ascertain the truth: the interests of heaven would appear, conveniently, their enemies alleged, to coincide with the interests of the Society. With a number in *Parlement,* not only among Jansenists, firmly adhering to Galli-can tradition, theological questions were imbued for the Jesuits with the spirit of party.

The Jesuit church of St-Louis was Baroque, but in the relatively restrained French manner. It serves to remind us that they were not some alien body, but closely identified with and, some would say, at the very heart of the French Catholic experience. Half the ten provinces into which the Society was divided were in France. Jesuits had a leading place as spiritual directors of the great and educators of those aspiring to be great. Their Parisian college of Clermont, in the rue Saint-Jacques, was justly renowned. Corneille, Descartes, Molière and Bossuet were among those who would testify to the excellence of their schools. They were principally responsible for the formation of the devout upper-class laity, straddling the distinct worlds of gown and sword, that evolved with the Counter-Reformation in France. It is no accident that the first quarrel of Jesuit and Jansenist should arise over the treatment and reception of the Mass, for it was above all the Mass that provided focus and inspiration for the devout. From the great dome of St-Louis, above its single, aisleless nave, streamed the shafts of light to the high altar, at the intersection of nave and transept, where man met God in sacramental bread and wine. Jesuits did not believe that it should be hard for men to do so.

The Jesuits dominated education; they did not monopolise it. At the church of St-Jacques-du-Haut-Pas, by the Luxembourg gardens, with build-ings of the former abbey of Saint-Magloire, was the Oratory: with their daughter houses all over France, the Oratorians had so fulfilled the Christo-centric ideal of Pierre Bérulle that they can be judged to be second only to their Jesuit rivals in influence over the French mind. With his friend and spiritual mentor, Mme Acarie, whose mystical fervour, practical gifts and genius for friendship had done so much to persuade others to re-order their lives on religious principles, Bérulle must be accorded a high place among those whose work has left a lasting impression on society. His central idea was the reform of morals through a society of priests. 'Adherence to Christ' was the theme of his training, the staple of life. He had been instrumental in bringing the Spanish Carmelite order of nuns to their house in the rue Saint-Jacques, and been himself profoundly influenced by the fervent mysticism of the Span-ish school. Before he died, in 1629, he was disturbed at the prospect of war between France and Spain. Had he known that it would still be going on in the 'fifties, he would have been further dismayed. Mazarin faced by then a new generation of *dévôts*: many of them, like the young Bossuet, were proud to call themselves disciples of Bérulle, 'teacher of so many teachers, master of so many saints'.

Just beyond the Porte St-Denis, in the former abbey of Saint-Lazare, or by the Porte Saint-Victor, at the Collège des Bon Enfants, might be seen the slight, wizened, shabbily dressed figure of the most loved and respected man in the city. The name of Vincent de Paul – 'Monsieur Vincent' as he has always been known – has a special resonance for Frenchmen.[19] Son of a Gascon peasant, groomed by influential patrons for high office in the Church, he used his worldly advantages, notably the warm support of Philippe-Emmanuel de Gondi[20] and his brother the archbishop of Paris, to pursue his unworldly vocation, to serve the poor, the ignorant and the sick. As a *curé* in the Landes, he had encountered wretched lives and spiritual neglect. In the Gondi circle, rich, fashionable and devout, he had the ideal base to extend his knowledge of French society, deepen his spiritual life and plan works of relief and reform. At different times he was chaplain to the galleys and tutor to the Gondi children. He took one decisive step when he became superior of François de Sales' House of the Visitation in the Faubourg Saint-Antoine; another when the dying de Sales entrusted him with the spiritual direction of Jeanne de Chantal.[21] He embarked on one of his most ambitious projects with the creation of the Collège des Bons Enfants which, with the subsequent foundation of Saint-Lazare, was to provide systematic training for the priesthood. By 1660 there were thirty-three houses. From the outset, the Lazarists, as they were called, went out in teams to bring Christian teaching to the provinces.

'For your monastery, use the houses of the sick; for your chapel the parish church; for your cloister, the streets of towns or the wards of hospitals.' Monsieur Vincent's instructions to the Filles de Charité, founded to help 'our lords the poor', speak of the nature of the man and his unique achievement. Working in informal groups, wearing a greyish dress and the white *cornette* typical of peasant dress of the time, they founded hospitals for incurables, looked after the babies so often found placed in the doorways of churches, sent missionaries and nurses to the troops. Aristocratic ladies, like the duchesse de Nemours, sometimes Anne of Austria herself, worked among the *filles*, set up soup kitchens during the Fronde, nursed the wounded and buried the dead. They saw in him the inspiring example of a man who could move naturally in any circle. It was in the *conseil de conscience*[22] that he most often encountered Mazarin; with some reason Mazarin feared his influence over the queen and wished that he would keep out of politics. Vincent de Paul could be criticised for naivety and for accepting too readily the *frondeur* arguments of his aristocratic friends. Seeing the unhappy consequences of war and working constantly on his own front line of suffering and deprivation, it is not surprising that he urged Anne to dismiss her worldly minister, nor that the minister came to see him as a meddling priest.

34

THE CHALLENGE OF PORT ROYAL

On the outskirts of Paris, at the end of the rue Saint-Jacques, stood the new, spacious convent of Port Royal. Jacqueline Arnauld, Mère Angélique, had brought her Cistercian nuns there from the original abbey outside Paris,[1] and established an influential model of pious observance, infused by that intense, prayerful spirit that is so strongly conveyed by the nuns' portraits by Philippe de Champaigne.[2] The bold red cross on the nuns' white scapular speaks of a commitment that was overt, eccentric perhaps in the tendency towards self-mortification, but ostensibly orthodox. That could not be said of the abbé de Saint-Cyran who brought to his role as spiritual adviser to these nuns his concern with recovering the purity of the early church – and the taint of heresy. He had been in prison for two years when there appeared, in 1640, the massive tome that contained the thinking of his collaborator in plans of reform, Cornelius Jansen, the author of pamphlets denouncing Richelieu's foreign policy. From the start, Jansenism was to be more than an episode in the history of enthusiasm, more than a puritan sect within the Church: it was profoundly, inescapably political. Its importance for Mazarin, as later for Louis XIV, cannot be measured by the numbers involved, relatively few; or by the significance of disputes over doctrine. Jansenism induced nervous ministerial reactions because it touched sensitive areas of policy.

If evidence were needed of the extraordinary contemporary interest in theology it would be to hand in the interest roused by Jansen's *Augustinus*, based on St Augustine's refutation of Pelagian doctrines, but presenting what Jansen claimed to be a hitherto unrecognised synthesis of the demands of grace and free will, those terms defining the nature and extent of God's power and man's freedom which had loomed so large in the debates of post-Reformation Europe. To Jansen's critics his doctrines were simply Calvinist, a view eventually confirmed by Papal condemnation of the heretical 'Five Propositions' alleged to be contained in the *Augustinus*; to his admirers a just presentation of that severe view of Christian life that Saint-Cyran had already presented in his *Apologie pour le chapelet secret*: 'We have within us a perpetual source of sin flowing towards everlasting death, unless God places us within the fountain of life that flows into life eternal.' Saint-Cyran had written his book in defence of a slight devotional work by Agnes Arnauld, Jaqueline's younger sister – and sister nun. It had given a higher profile than was deserved to the theology of Port Royal, to the Arnauld family and to Agnes's book, originally criticised by the Jesuits as a move in their long-standing rivalry with the Oratorians.[3] Such links offer the essential clues to the story of Jansenism, marked, as it was, by a theology and devotional style that were repugnant to the Jesuits, and the political bias of significant groups in the Sorbonne and *Parlement.*

Jacqueline's father, Marc-Antoine, had led the opposition in *Parlement* to the re-admission of the Jesuits in Henry IV's reign. Along with his widow, six Arnauld daughters had entered Port Royal by 1640; one, a widow, Mme de Maître, brought with her four daughters. Three Lemaître sons, with Robert Arnauld d'Andilly,[4] now the eldest member of the family, were members of the associated community of Port Royal des Champs which had settled in the buildings vacated by the nuns. Antoine,[5] the youngest brother, was a rising star at the Sorbonne and did not reside, but was what might be termed a corresponding member, active in support. To that extent could early Jansenism seem like a family affair, with ramifications in those magisterial and aristocratic spheres where Mazarin could identify his most influential critics.

'There is no rule, no vow, no constitution, no community, no society, no cell . . . and we have no assemblies.' In these terms, stretching a point or two perhaps, Robert Arnauld d'Andilly defended the male community of solitaries at Port Royal des Champs against the charge of political activism. He had been commissioned by the family to represent the interests of Port Royal with Mazarin, in practice generally through the latter's *maître de chambre,* Claude Auvry. They were right to assume that Mazarin would take an unfriendly line.   It was important, therefore, for Arnauld d'Andilly to stress that the community was not a political cabal under the cloak of religion. It was however a hard case to make when Port Royal des Champs, the refuge of some thirty educated men, living voluntarily and informally in the austere and regular style of monks, writing, studying, teaching, praying, with its associated house of nuns in Paris, was also, in a way, *chic,* offering a style to admire, if not to emulate. It represented the antithesis of the materialism that many claimed to see in Mazarin's regime. If only symbolically, it became a living critique of the policies that led to the Fronde.

Jansenism, as elusive to us as, in some ways, it was to Mazarin, had already come to mean different things to different people. In certain respects a movement, when forced to be by attacks, and a theology refined in controversy, it was also a clique; it became a convenient pretext and ally for tangential causes, like that of Gallican lawyers who were quick to react to Papal bulls that over-stepped what they held to be proper bounds; of the Richerist[6] lower clergy, in conflict with their ecclesiastical superiors; or of Gondi, that most un-Jansenist of souls, in pursuit of his personal ambitions. Above all, like puritanism in England, it was an attitude. To put it more categorically, there was a theological, a political, a moral, a fashionable Jansenism. Never as distinct as such a list might imply, the interests and issues were fused in the heat of a sensational controversy, through the polemical spirit of Antoine Arnauld and the many-sided genius of Blaise Pascal.

'The great Arnauld', acclaimed scholar at the Sorbonne, was the youngest and cleverest of the family. He was profoundly moved by the theology and personality of Saint-Cyran and stirred by his dying challenge: 'the time has come to speak out; it would be a crime to remain silent'. While Mazarin was taking his first steps in government and confronting the *Importants,* Arnauld was writing the book with which he intended to answer the call. *De la Fréquente Communion* was published in August 1643. It purported to rescue the true doctrine of the sacraments from Jesuit 'casuistry', that is the judgement of particular problems with the aid of recorded cases which were recognised as having authority, and from its abuse in 'probabilism', taking that which can be 'proved' from such cases and using it as a guide to advice in the confessional. What could be seen by the busy priest as a helpful practice was suspect to the Jansenist as encouraging 'laxism' and confessions that failed to ensure that the 'penitent' received the sacraments in a properly contrite state of mind. Arnauld did not attack the practice of regular communion but the smooth counsel of confessors who recommended communion as a spiritual medicine without care for preparation. Much of the argument was sound. even traditional. A Jesuit Cardinal in Rome appeared unperturbed by the book. Indeed no one could argue with the need for reverence before the sacraments, but Arnauld's style was combative, some of his conclusions extreme. The Jesuits were wounded; they were not alone in seeing Jansen's views behind the assertion that only those should receive the sacraments who felt the definite call of divine grace. Monsieur Vincent wondered 'if there could be any man who held such a high opinion of his own virtue as to believe himself worthy to receive Holy Communion'. Rome issued a mild censure against which Arnauld wisely decided not to appeal. But the storm would not subside. The issues were too important, the corporate interests too powerful.

Between the parties some theologians were trying to establish the truth. Nicolas Cornet, syndic of the Faculty of Theology at the Sorbonne, extracted from careful reading of the work five 'propositions' which, he thought, summarised Jansen's thinking, and submitted them to the judgement of the faculty. The Arnaulds blundered. By obtaining an injunction from *Parlement* (July 1649) forbidding examination of the case they seemed to question the competence of the Sorbonne and invite their critics to lay the case before Rome. Urged by Monsieur Vincent among others, the majority of bishops signed a petition requesting the Pope to give judgement. Innocent X appointed a commission. It took care and time.

Meanwhile the Jansenist party grew. It had a significant following among the bishops: eleven had opposed the petition, one joined Port Royal. Responding to the adventurous, radical aspect of Jansenism as some of them had responded to the Fronde, fashionable women lent their support. The very names of four duchesses would be enough to cause frowns at court: Rohan, Luynes, Liancourt and Longueville. With them Jansenism entered the phase that has been called 'the ecclesiastical Fronde'.[7] The political Fronde was over when, in May 1653 Pope Innocent signed the bull *Cum Occasione*, condemning 'the Five Propositions'. Four expressed the view that 'efficacious grace' was indispensable to salvation, but that God did not give every man 'sufficient grace'. The fifth affirmed that Christ did not die for all men. If this Formulary represented a correct interpretation of Jansen's teaching, the *fact* of the matter, then Arnauld had little choice: he had to accept the *right* of the Pope to pronounce. A Jesuit almanac portrayed it thus: the Pope, under the heavenly dove, cast down the mitred Jansen who sped, on bats' wings, towards a corner where Calvin was making himself pleasant to a bespectacled Jansenist nun. Arnauld found a lawyer's way out, making the distinction between *fait* and *droit* which was to be the crux of the ensuing fight.

Mère Angélique, agonised by the way in which politics had overtaken her spiritual mission, counselled silent submission; so did Pierre Nicole,[8] the Cartesian, author of a book on logic for the Jansenist *petits écoles*. He represents the practical side of Jansenism and the rational spirit in which they were to make approaches to the Huguenots, prepare a fresh translation of the Bible and revise Catholic liturgies and manuals of instruction. By now however the main part of the ecclesiastical establishment was engaged. So, in the person of Mazarin, was the state. Mazarin's instinct had been to contain rather than to provoke opposition. Now matters had gone so far he preferred to work for a decision. He had to take diplomatic factors into account. His own interests and those of France made it desirable that the new Pope, Alexander VII, elected in 1655, should be supported, that no chance should be offered to his enemies in Rome to whisper that he was less than a good Catholic. He instructed the bishops to accept the bull *Cum Occasione*. Séguier kept him daily *au courant* with events in the Faculty of Theology. He had to tread delicately between the Papalists, now in full cry, led by Pierre de Marca,[9] archbishop of Toulouse, and *Parlement*. Only a handful of magistrates were committed Jansenists, but their chastening experiences during the Fronde made them all the more determined to stand up for their rights.[10]

When the Jesuits had earlier demanded of Anne that she should order Arnauld to go to Rome to defend himself, *Parlement* and the Sorbonne had protested and the order had been revoked. Now it seemed that the theologians of Paris could handle the affair. In January, 1656, a special and packed assembly of the Sorbonne, presided over by Séguier, formally condemned Arnauld. He had written a letter attacking a priest of Saint-Sulpice, Père Picoté, for refusing absolution to the Jansenist duc de Liancourt:[11] the Sorbonne declared it to be 'an insult to the Pope', while the distinction between *fait* and *droit* was dismissed as invalid. Some sixty Jansenists and sympathisers had walked out rather than be associated with the faculty's decision. More effective help was at hand. Before the Sorbonne moved to declare Arnauld's punishment, on 23 January 1656, there appeared, anonymously, the first of the *Lettres Provinciales*.[12]

The style was incisive, satirical; the argument forceful and clear. The writer purported to be a gentleman who wrote to a friend in the country explaining what was going on in the Sorbonne. Ostensibly reporting what he heard, he demonstrates the absurdity of the affair by trapping the experts into confused and contradictory statements. By contrast, the author's message was as plain as a pike-staff. No wonder Voltaire, a connoisseur of irony, a polemicist above all, expert in making a case into a cause, would hail the *Lettres* as a portent of Enlightenment.[13] They certainly illustrated the potential of the French language for conveying the significance of arguments that had formerly been left to experts. But Blaise Pascal cannot be thus transposed: in thought and sensibility he is firmly of the seventeenth century. His *Lettres* nonetheless were a sensation. His indignant point of departure was a sense of injustice and a kind of fraud, a misuse of scholarship for essentially political ends: he accused the Jesuits of acting out of malice and the Dominicans, allies on this occasion, as traitors to their theological principles. What else when they could be shown to agree with Arnauld in all but the use of terms? Like the modern reader, contemporaries who read the letters so avidly may not have been concerned about 'proximate power' or 'sufficient grace'. It did not matter, for Pascal's point was that these terms were so stretched as to be meaningless. Condemning such verbal juggling, Pascal's gentleman, 'Louis de Montalte', whose true identity long baffled his readers, offered true religion. Mazarin laughed at these early sallies, but approved when the Sorbonne went on to degrade and expel Arnauld from its ranks.

The next letters, the fourth to the tenth, appearing from different printers to evade detection, became sharper in tone. A Jesuit, seemingly well-intentioned, is gradually revealed, through his own words, as credulous, absurd, and enemy of true faith. By concentrating on the idea of casuistry, the writer struck at points where the Jesuits were most vulnerable: their sophistication and apparent lack of scruple in the pursuit of souls. He incurred the charge that he was damaging not the Jesuits alone, but Christian faith. Was he simply carried away by the excitement of the chase? Was he pursuing, with increasing anger, a personal crusade, projecting his own agonised questionings about faith? These questions can be considered, if not answered, because of what we know of the apparently disingenuous author.

Pascal had been in pain, racked by mental conflict, notably between the Montaignist humanism that he found attractive but inadequate, and the faith that appealed to the heart 'whose reasons the mind knows not of'. Only months before Arnauld's condemnation, he had had the mystical experience which had left him, in his own words, with a sense of 'certitude, joy, peace, forgetfulness of the world and of everything except God', words that were to be found, at his death, sewn into his doublet. Within this intellectual, spiritual and family context the inspired journalism takes on a new significance. Arnauld's writing and his defence had clarified for him the great question, one that has remained the point of departure for subsequent assessments, sympathetic or censorious, of the Jansenist cause: to what extent, should the Christian accommodate himself to the world? It brought a thinker of genius, who was also a literary artist, to ponder the related questions about life and faith that were to find expression in the *Pensées*.[14]

The Jesuits were not strongly represented in Paris: feeble and pedantic apologists did them more harm than good. Their ideal was not an ignoble one: to serve God, as his soldiers, with all the weapons he gave them. To the order which sent missionaries to Malabar, Paraguay, Japan, Canada, the clique of Port Royal supported in the main by private incomes, may have looked escapist, self-righteous and scrupulous because it did not have to encounter the world. The world was the province of the Jesuits. They haunted its most civilised courts, but they were not afraid of its wildest places. While the Jansenist controversy occupied France, Saint Ignatius's Jesuit followers were engaged in dialogue with the Chinese emperor,[15] devising a Christian-Confucian compromise that was eventually repudiated by Rome. They were establishing model settlements in Paraguay which protected the Indians against the rapacity of colonists,[16] Arnauld, living secretively in friends' houses; later, nuns holding out against ecclesiastical authority, represented one kind of martyr; others were the Jesuit fathers tortured and murdered by Indians in the forests of Canada.

Undoubtedly the Jesuits loved God: did they also love truth? Pascal's answer was that 'to refuse to love truth is also to refuse to love God'. It is the crux: an absolute standard of morality against the insidious idea of the relative – that the end justifies the means. Inevitable, confrontation may have been; so it was that the two attitudes should have become caricatured in the passions of the fight. In its absolutist spirit, tinged with a certain recklessness, it was characteristic of the age. Pascal may have been infected more than he knew, as was Port Royal, by the spirit of the Fronde. There was a deficiency of charity, if not self-knowledge, when he accused the Jesuits of spiritual power politics. Standing, a single writer, for a small body of solitaries and nuns against Church, court and a majority in the Sorbonne and *Parlement*, he dramatised, launched innuendoes, but did not falsify the facts. He came to realise that he was going too far and abandoned the *Lettres* after number eighteen. Rome had placed them on the Index in September 1657. Three years later Louis XIV would order that they be burnt by the public executioner. It was the final accolade.

Though Louis XIV would sometimes seem to be more irritated than really alarmed by the Jansenist defiance and the surrounding uproar, it becomes plain how the young king was being confirmed in those prejudices which would lead to the obsessive campaign against the sect which marred the last two decades of his reign, damaging not only religion, but also his authority.[17] In these years, however, Louis could count on the loyal sentiment of his capital and was sufficiently confident to give an interview to Arnauld and to attempt a *rapprochement* between him and a delegation of Jesuits. At this stage, Jansenism would not have been near the top of Louis' agenda if Mazarin had not ensured that it stay there. The Cardinal had alternated throughout between close interest and a show of detachment. Typically he worked through agents: he seemed at times to be responding to Arnauld d'Andilly; usually, however, he worked, through his own man, Auvry, to keep the movement within bounds. He had no quarrel with the nuns of Port Royal. But their refusal to accept the Formulary in any form forced him to act. He could not stand aside from what had become an issue of authority: that of the Church challenged by the nuns' stand for 'liberty of conscience'. Nor could he ignore the appeal of Jansenism to the *frondeur curés* and *parlementaires*.

Mazarin would not live to see even the temporary resolution of the issue. He did, however, show a way. In 1660, savouring peace, free from most anxieties, but not from pain, he summoned an assembly of bishops and theologians to sign a document approving the bull and to examine the *Lettres Provinciales*. Predictably they condemned the work. He raised again the question of the Formulary and secured its re-drafting in the form that was to ensure that it remained for a century to trouble scrupulous consciences: though bishops might accept it – and earn the scorn of the indomitable Jacqueline Pascal for doing so – not all students of the *Augustinus* could accept that the censored author 'had not understood the true principles of Saint Augustine'. Mazarin again closed the schools. He advised the king to distrust 'that refractory clique' and 'no longer to endure the Jansenist sect or even its name'.

Louis would act in this spirit. It becomes clear in the brutally insensitive words of the passage in his *Memoires*:[18] 'I applied myself to the destruction of Jansenism and the dissipation of the communities which fomented this novelty, which, though perhaps well-intentioned, were ignorant of or chose to ignore the dangerous consequences which might ensue from it.' The Jesuits around him encouraged this hostility. Mazarin could be more objective but was no less exasperated. Yet his concern was less with heresy than with the supposed political threat. The politicisation of a severe, but in no respect Protestant, theology, and of an intense, but in no way disloyal, devotional movement, was the true tragedy of Jansenism.

Mazarin may not have minded the discomfiture of a handful of Jesuits. He did not soften in his attitude towards Jansenism. There was need, however, for circumspection. The *Lettres* had won admirers beyond the Jansenist circle. Bossuet saluted them: 'the only modern work worthy of the ancients'. Jesuit attempts to counter the work, like that of the king's confessor, Père Annat, were lame and unconvincing. A timely miracle, in March 1656, could be taken to signify that God was on the Jansenists' side. Pascal's niece, Marguerite Périer, aged ten, suffering from a distressing ulcer of the eye, prayed before Port Royal's most precious relic, a thorn from the Crown of Thorns, to be healed. She was. Of course the community was convinced; so also were doctors, among them Guy Patin, not a man likely to be swayed by superstition. It occurred on that Friday in Lent when the Church sings at the Introit: 'Show me a token for good, that they who hate me may see and be confounded'. Whether or not Mazarin believed the story, he knew enough about Paris and the communal sentiment that could suddenly well up to stay his hand. In July 1656, the *petites écoles*, closed since February, were allowed to re-open; the solitaries, dispersed since Arnauld's condemnation, could return to Port Royal. It was not that Mazarin had changed his mind. He saw the political implications and preferred to let the Church act in its own way. De Marca had already drawn up a Formulary in which he condemned Jansenism and called on his priests to do the same. In August 1656, the Church assembly followed suit. The handful of Jansenist bishops, led by the archbishop of Sens, withdrew their previous opposition but secured some modification of the Formulary. It was sent to Rome and swiftly approved. Pope Alexander VII, was familiar with the arguments. His bull, *Ad sacram sedem* in October 1656, declared the Five Propositions to be contained in Jansen's book. The assembly of the Clergy made it compulsory for all bishops to sign the document, stating: 'with heart and mouth I condemn the five propositions of Cornelius Jansenius contained in his book *Augustinus*'.

For Jansenists to resist the Papal condemnation of the book which they believed to be true in its reading of Saint Augustine would be to move from unorthodoxy to heresy. Yet Pascal and his sister Jacqueline believed they had no choice. To accept would be to betray Jansen, the master. To sign, 'with mental reservation', would be dishonest in the Jesuit way that

Pascal had denounced. While Jansenists wrestled with their consciences, Paris was astir, as the debates in the Sorbonne, *Parlement*, the churches, *hôtels* and *salons* spilled out into the markets and streets. There was talk, fomented by Arnauld and his friends, of the Pope's reviving the Inquisition and limiting *Parlement's* jurisdiction in ecclesiastical affairs. Colbert wrote to warn Mazarin that registration of *Ad sacram sedem* would be difficult 'because the Jansenists have inflamed spirits in *Parlement*'. He was right. *Parlement* refused to register, Séguier, a veteran of such affairs, briefed Mazarin daily, a sign of ministerial concern. He thought that 'the opposition that is forming there in *Parlement* is only the work of a faction that takes advantage of its plenary sessions'. De Marca believed that 'the officials who compose *Parlement* have not lost the zeal of their predecessors... who registered the bull against Luther'. A *lit de justice* was required to secure registration. That was not the end of the matter. Mazarin was sure that Jansenism remained dangerous.

If he needed anything more to persuade him, it was the intervention of Retz. It is ludicrous to think of that master of deceits aligning himself with the scrupulous puritans of Port Royal. It was also inconsistent of him, latterly the ardent Papalist, to look to Gallicans to rescue him from exile. Naively, they thought he was their friend because he was Mazarin's enemy. They could not know that he also wrote to Anne, offering his help 'to exterminate Jansenism'. But his intervention serves to show how Parisian ecclesiastical politics had infected the religious spirit and confused the issues. When de Retz had escaped from prison, *curés* supporting Port Royal had infuriated ministers by causing the *Te Deum* to be sung. The Vicars general, whose role, in Mazarin's view, was to maintain the discipline of the diocese till the Pope would accept a new appointment, issued an ambiguous document re-awakening the distinction between *fait* and *droit*.

There was to be a period when disaster would seem to have been averted. The moderate archbishop of Paris, Hardouin de Péréfixe,[19] eventually took an initiative to break the deadlock by producing a new formulary for the nuns to sign; then, when they refused, took responsibility for closing Port Royal, provoking a further struggle, but preparing the way for the 'Peace of the Church' in 1668.[20] By then the factious spirit of the Fronde had evaporated and with it the fears that had unsettled the ailing Mazarin. For all his severe words, it may be that 'Peace' that most accurately represents Mazarin's thinking and policy towards the Jansenists – not the persecution of later years when Louis would rouse just the very temper of opposition in *Parlement* that Mazarin had been most anxious to subdue.

35

THE LAST YEAR

The marriage of Louis and Maria Teresa was first celebrated by proxy on 2 June 1660, in Fuentarabia. By custom a Spanish princess could not leave Spanish soil unmarried and a French king's wedding had to take place in France. The Spanish cortège, fifteen miles long, then moved ponderously towards the frontier, the Isle of Pheasants and further ceremonies. On both sides there was a desire to exhibit status while proving commitment. The sheer weight of significance attached by family and councillors might still have been less daunting to the little Infanta, to all appearances a docile doll, than the curiosity and comment of the French. She was only a few days younger than her cousin-husband, yet a child in experience. To one beady-eyed observer she emerged with credit from her prolonged ordeal – though Mme de Motteville's description has a sting in the tail: 'If her body were a little bigger and her teeth more beautiful she would deserve a place among the most beautiful women of Europe ... but her costume was horrible, neither cut nor style pleasing to the eye.' She also observed that the blue and gold of the French banners were more pleasing than Spain's predominating red and black.

In the second marriage ceremony at St Jean de Luz, on 6 June, that made the Infanta queen of France, she won admiration with a dress of red velvet embroidered with the *fleur de lys*, clearly a French choice: she, with her dowry and the promise of rich inheritance, was, in a sense, a possession of her king-spouse and of his realm; the sombre black of the Spanish courtiers no less reflected the sense of loss, even decline, that no politeness or presents could entirely dispel. They would go home to impoverished lands and the costs of an increasingly hopeless war against Portugal. There would be signs of distress too for the French to observe on their leisured northwards journey through now quiet and loyal lands – the evidence for 'the ruined state of commerce' that Colbert described in a subsequent memorandum to the king – but not so much as to affect the triumphalist mood.

On the eve of the wedding, d'Ormesson records, Anne had visited Mazarin and had been distressed when, throwing off his coverlet 'like

Lazarus rising from the dead', he showed her his legs, discoloured and ulcerated up to the thigh: 'See, Madame, these limbs have forfeited their peace in giving it to France'. Dramatic words – but Mazarin was scarcely exaggerating. Months of negotiation under the psychological pressure of knowing that the Spanish would take full advantage of any weakening on his part, had taken their toll. The month's journey home from St Jean de Luz was a sustained agony. Lying on a litter to minimise the jolting of the carriage, he could hardly stand for the pain. 'One could say that the rest of his life was a long death': his constant companion, at hand at all hours to write at the sick man's dictation, d'Ormesson wrote with hindsight, after Mazarin's death. Meanwhile he worked on relentlessly.

On 26 August 1660, the king, with his new bride, made his formal entry into his capital. Between the monks and friars of Paris's religious houses who led the procession and the royal falconers who brought up the rear, it took several hours to pass any point on the traditional route. Mazarin was too frail to take part in the procession. He was represented in the procession by seventy-two mules in twenty-four files, covered with rich harness, his carriage, with blinds drawn to indicate that he was not there, followed by the gentlemen and guards of his household, nearly as many as followed the king. He watched the procession from Mme de Beauvais' fine new hotel in the rue François-Miron,[1] with Anne, Turenne and Antonio Barberini: the group represented stages in his personal odyssey, the support he had received, the success he had won.

The nuptial route through the city was adorned with four triumphal arches, hugely elaborate constructions of wood and painted canvas, plaster and mock stone, embellished with every possible device, artistic, scholarly, literary, and with loyal messages in Latin supplemented by pamphlet commentaries for the man in the street. Reading there what he might crane his neck to see, yet still not understand, if not versed in Latin or classical lore, he was offered the official view: '*Et Mars quoque cessit Amori*', for example, Mazarin's answer, it could be said, to the *Mazarinades*. It was to be endorsed, in terms that the minister could not have improved upon, by Mme de la Fayette:[2] 'No minister has governed with such an absolute authority as Mazarin and none has used his power more effectively to establish his greatness.'

Mazarin was never more sincere than when he thanked God for having let him 'live long enough to see the conclusion of peace'. He could enjoy a general sense of fulfilment, of missions accomplished. He was uniquely well placed in the royal circle that was now enlarged in so propitious a fashion. He was as secure as the grateful king with whom his name was now associated, as architect of victory and fruitful peace. The arch that adorned the Porte Saint-Antoine, with Louis' bust, sculpted after Poussin's sketch, was dedicated to 'The peace gained by the victorious arms of Louis XIV, the wise counsels of Anne, the august marriage of Maria

Teresa, the diligent aid of Julius, Cardinal Mazarin.' It has fallen to few statesmen, at the end of their lives, to see such a consummation of hopes and plans: not even to Richelieu, who died in travail and uncertainties, but whose work his successor had brought to fruition. Would he not also have savoured some of the day's ironies: the presence of Condé among the princes who rode with their sovereign, two dukes of the house of Lorraine escorting the Spanish queen, the litanies and banners of priests who had worked so devotedly for the absent Retz, the acclamation of the same Parisians who had lapped up the calumnies of the *Mazarinades*?

Now the Fronde was expiated. Emotional loyalty, civic pride, politic generosity contributed to a display of which it was claimed at the time: 'It could only be Paris, and Paris flourishing as it is today, that is capable of producing enough workmen and the indefatigable supervision of the civil officers perfectly to second the intelligence and zeal of Sieur Noblet.' Architect to the king and overseer of the city buildings, he deserved the accolade. While all Colbert's efforts failed to ensure that Le Vau's new theatre in the Tuileries was ready for the projected performance of Cavalli's opera *Xerxes*, Noblet's designers and craftsmen had had every-thing ready in time for the procession, barely three months after its inception. Such affairs are of their nature ephemeral. The next day the workmen were busy dismantling the triumphal arches: each a masterpiece of Baroque symbolism and ingenious carpentry, with the statues, such as those that lined the bridge to the Ile-de-la-Cité: all are known only through contemporary drawings. the queues of civic dignitaries which proceeded all morning to the king's temporary throne outside the city gates, to pay their respects in speeches that vied in expressions of devo-tion; the cavalcade of courtiers, officials and soldiers that escorted Louis round the city marked political realities more solid and lasting than the fabrications of Melun and Lebrun.

The messages spoken or inscribed can be taken as a kind of festival hymn, with poetic images and musical flourishes expressing praise and supplication. But with the enthusiasm there is a theology: so it is worth identifying, in formal, classical phrase and Baroque image, the coded meaning and underlying mood. The *corps* and guilds, doctors of the Sorbonne, members of the sovereign and other courts knew they had to put on a show and that it should be the grandest imaginable. But they expected their words to be heeded. They acknowledged the gains of war, but, more insistently, the blessings of peace. They saluted the demure young queen and saw her as a pledge of a new age of harmony between France and Spain. The spokesman for the guilds acknowledged 'the true power of your arms', but declared that their love could not be won by force: 'in true obedience those who were most opposed to the grandeur of Your Majesty now come to offer the greatest and best love they have.' Here was no grovelling but a pride to match the tradition and present circumstances of a great city, anticipating a new prosperity. Implicit were the hope that the king had learned from recent lessons and the warning that he would only have the loyalty of free subjects if he deserved it.

There was enough in the courtesies of the day to convince the king that he had a mandate for traditional government: for legal absolutism; not enough to convince him that Paris was no longer the city of the Fronde, a place in which he could be at ease. The views that were to find fulfilment in the palace of Versailles[3] were already too strong for loyal words to alter them. Nor would ministers like Le Tellier and Fouquet, soon to be replaced by Colbert, hardened by their experience of civil war and the makeshifts of post-war years, be likely to moderate their policies or methods to suit all the concerns of the city fathers. No one cut a more splendid figure than the veteran chancellor, Séguier, as portrayed by Le Brun, in the golden robes of his office and black velvet hat with gold tassel, on his white horse, flanked by pages and equerries in satin and velvet, two holding violet parasols to protect him against the sun. He had narrowly escaped lynching on the day of the barricades. He had worked against *Parlement*, for the jurisdiction of the councils. He had taken a hard line over the Jansenists. He stood now for the full assertion of royal powers. Paris might mount a memorable display of old corporate France and fine words might convey the idea of consensus, but there was left wide scope for the interpretation of royal powers, with great appeal, to ministers and *intendants* bent on reforms, in absolutist principles and methods. For all his smiles and tactful words, Mazarin was of that school. In his methodical, skilful tuition of the young king, the implicit assumption was that the king must be free to rule without constraint.

The education of royal heirs has had its disasters. Even allowing for circumstances and for the character and ability of the pupil concerned, it seems that some pedagogic efforts have been inherently flawed, unlikely to succeed. Louis XIV's own elder son, the Dauphin, under Bossuet's intense and demanding programme, would prove an unrewarding pupil. In the case of a boy who is already king, as was Louis XIII, as would be Louis XV, there is the extra problem of fitting in the lessons with the training, in service, as it were, for the role. Among the temptations that might beset the royal tutor, would be that of trying to teach too much, hoping for the reflected glory of a royal paragon. Another, undoubtedly, would be that of trying to mould the pupil: to gratify vanity, secure a future protector or, more idealistically, to fulfil some ideal of rule. Among experiments in the latter kind of educational scheme, that of Fénelon, tutor to Louis XIV's grandson, the duke of Burgundy, was to be noteworthy. Nothing so original would be expected from Mazarin, or Hardouin de Péréfixe and his fellow tutors; in its way, however, the Cardinal's programme was no less ambitious than that of Fénelon, even if the latter, a noble and *dévôt* in the political tradition of Bérulle and Marillac, would not have approved of the Cardinal's values and priorities.[4]

When Louis XIII had appointed Mazarin to be Louis XIV's godfather, he evidently intended the position to be of more than religious significance. Mazarin was to protect and guide the fatherless boy. How well he did so, how he earned Louis' respect and gratitude, how he entered the family in a quasi-paternal way, will already have become clear. His position was bound to attract criticism. One contemporary view can be discounted, though it has been the source of much derogatory comment. La Porte,[5] who took it upon himself to teach the king lessons in history and deportment, avenged hurt pride in slanted memoirs: Mazarin appears in them as monarchy's evil genius. Péréfixe was nominally in charge of Louis' education from the start. Neither he, nor other tutors appointed for particular subjects, had made notable headway before the outbreak of the Fronde. Thereafter there were too many interruptions for regular study.

So it can be maintained that Louis XIV was poorly educated: by comparison, for example, with the typical product of the Collège de Clermont, that is the case. But he was not bound for a career in law or the Church. It could have been a serious handicap to him in the study of diplomacy that he was deficient in Latin, even more, that he was weak in Italian and Spanish. It was an important sign of his determination to be well equipped for the business of government that he set himself to master Latin and modern languages at the age when he might have been expected to think more of the pleasurable opportunities of kingship than of its intellectual demands.

Mazarin had only been dead for a day when, on 10 March 1661, Louis XIV informed the court that he intended to rule personally, without a first minister. He may have thought that he was following Mazarin's deathbed advice. In any case he was evidently resolved to take charge because he believed that there had been mismanagement. What mattered was that he believed that he was equipped for the role of manager. That he was prepared to wait till Mazarin died – and Mazarin was not thought to be on the verge of death till early in 1661 – before taking on this responsibility, is a tribute both to his patience and restraint and to his minister's towering authority. Few can have believed that Louis would continue as he had begun, regular in council, assiduous in the perusal of documents, decisive when firm action was called for, as over Fouquet, but also willing, even anxious, to listen to advice. His professionalism, reinforced by the knowledge that enabled him to direct and control, secured him respectful loyalty and continuity in the personnel and policies of government and brought fresh impetus to the processes of reform. One feature of his idea of kingship as a sacred trust was that he could not bear to be seen as incompetent in any respect. His perfectionism no doubt reflected traits of character as well as the testing circumstances of his youth. His skills were not however acquired simply by hard work, allied to a good memory and a shrewd understanding. They were the product of deliberate, intelligent training.

On one occasion Péréfixe told Mazarin that the king was not applying his mind to his studies and said that he would have to reprimand him, 'lest there come the day when he behave in the same way in matters of state'. Mazarin's answer illustrates his whole approach: 'Rely on my judgement and do not be too much concerned. He can know too much; as it is, when he is present at the council, he asks me a hundred questions about the subject in hand.'

Louis was at ease with Mazarin, who was happy to see him so active, whether hunting, fencing or dancing, but also encouraged him to give time to music,[6] as well as to his studies. Louis admired and trusted the minister, fellow-campaigner and guardian in difficult days. He had secured the monarchy during the Fronde, and was laying the foundations for its future greatness. Mazarin taught that there could be arguments of state that transcended all personal interest and feeling: so the king gave up Marie Mancini. The impressionable young man would have discovered the delights of kingship for himself. That they were associated inseparably from its duties was a harder lesson to learn. That they involved continuous application hardest of all. It appears that Mazarin had the light touch, the wit, the charm and the invaluable gift of making work interesting and rewarding. Whether during daily sessions in council or the regular private surveys and briefings that he used to instruct the king in all matters of government and to pass on the fruits of a lifetime's practice of diplomacy, he was consciously training the earnest young man, building up his confidence, influencing his ideas and taste. The reflective passages in the *Mémoires*, more mature than might be expected of a king under thirty, seem to be Louis' condensation of Mazarin's wisdom. It was years after the Cardinal's death too that Mme de Lafayette noted that 'the king sought to govern his politics by the ideas that he [Mazarin] had inspired'. In a sense Louis XIV, most commanding, most professional and among the most accomplished of kings, was Mazarin's masterpiece.

36

A CHRISTIAN DEATH

During the small hours of 6 February 1661, fire broke out in the gallery off the king's pavilion in the Louvre where workmen had been decorating walls and hanging pictures. The flames spread rapidly through the draughty rooms and threatened to engulf the palace. While servants and soldiers toiled with chains of buckets, Anne sent for the sacrament. By the time the priests arrived the wind was shifting and the fire was being brought under control: the enterprise of an Augustinian lay brother who was lifted by a makeshift crane to the burning roof timbers so that he could lever them out with a crowbar probably did most to avert catastrophe. Anne and Louis went to Saint-Germain, leaving the building to be cleaned and repaired. The incident may have served to strengthen them in the belief that they enjoyed divine protection, but for Mazarin it was a turning point in his struggle against grave ailments. He was carried out from his chambers next to the gallery, through dense smoke, shocked and gasping for breath. Twelve doctors examined him before one of their number, Guénard, delivered their opinion: he could hope for two months of life. The ordeal would be seen only to have hastened his demise.

If his correspondence were his only memorial it would give an idea of the relentless pressure of business. The physical and psychological trials of the Fronde, the vicissitudes of his life, had sapped the vigour of a naturally robust constitution. The pursuit of his business and artistic concerns would have been enough for many men; nor had he conserved his energies by limiting himself to a moderate social life. He had always found time for music, opera and the ballet, for suppers and cards. Undoubtedly it was constant travel, on often terrible roads, in all weathers, on diplomatic or military business, that had taken the greatest toll. Suffering from kidney stones, gout and breathing difficulties, with a chronic toxaemia and consequently swollen limbs, Mazarin had only been sustained through the long months of negotiation with Spain by his resolve to complete the work to which he had given his life. Anne had on one occasion been reduced to tears by his condition;[1] on his journey back to

Paris he had spent most of the time lying on the floor of his coach. He was mentally alert, however, worked incessantly on government papers and remained unshakeably in control. Ministers at home, diplomats abroad, artists and craftsmen working for him, agents carrying out his commissions and, above all, the king, in regular briefings, were left in no doubt about it: he was effective almost to the end. The fleeting notion that he might become Pope may have faded. But Rome was never far from his thoughts. In 1660 he launched the idea of a monumental staircase 'in memory of the peace' to join the Trinità dei Monti and the Piazza d'Espagna. He would have loved the result: the Spanish Steps. When he entertained the royal family to a Twelfth Night festivity in his palace on the rue de Richelieu, among the sculptures, pictures, tapestries and *objets d'art*, some hurriedly taken out of crate and store for the occasion, there was still hope that he might make some kind of recovery: almost to the end he showed the zest for life that had informed all his getting and spending.[2] After the fire however the end could not be long delayed.

When he was judged strong enough to move he was taken to Vincennes where Anne and the king joined him and stayed for all but the odd day's visit to Paris for some religious ceremony – or performance of the ballet that Mazarin would no less have approved. Anne tended him constantly and lived in the room next to his, until, as Motteville sympathetically recorded,[3] his agonised cries forced her to go elsewhere for sleep. Nor was Louis perfunctory in attendance as Mazarin sought to convey some of the lessons of his life in pithy maxims and practical advice. The young king, surely less confident of his own ability than he would allow to be seen, was to record them so faithfully that future generations could hear his master's voice.[4]

Anne's relationship with Mazarin had suffered at times from the differences of temperament that became more important when they were no longer bound by partnership in government. He found her piety excessively superstitious. She gave the impression of resenting the time he spent with Louis. She wanted – yet may have found it hard – to take second place to the young king who was so clearly capable of living and ruling without her advice. But the main impression left of Mazarin's relationship with Anne is one of touching tenderness and affection. In his testament he referred to her incredible steadfastness and fidelity. He bequeathed to her the finest of all his jewels, the Rose of England diamond. Another gift, a matching pair of inlaid cabinets, the work of Italian craftsmen whom the French could not yet match, was to be given pride of place in her apartments. Whatever the more intimate memories that remain locked in her heart, the exquisite workmanship of the two cabinets well symbolises an exceptionally successful partnership in government.

Public men then made public ends. Famous last words may owe as much to the sympathies of priest, relation or friend, who catches the last whisper and interprets it to an expectant world, as to the intelligence of the dying man. Sometimes it seems that last words have been well rehearsed to be the summary of a life's work or a philosophy. The reader may approach a death-bed report with caution, yet sense that the words ring true. Special interest attaches to Mazarin's last hours because the record is consistent with that of his last months. He was lucid to the end, courageous, stoical, and realistic. He could feel joy at an event which evoked memories of his Roman youth: the betrothal of his niece Marie to Count Colonna – and when he thought of his father's relationship to Colonna's father – some pride. He regretted leaving the treasures which he had had so little time to enjoy but did not dwell upon deprivations or pains. He had looked the world in the face and ventured forth; now he looked to the next world and made his preparations in the same resolute spirit. He found his faithful Theatine father, Angelo Bissaro[5] too emollient in bedside counsel and in his readings from Spanish mystics, so summoned Claude Joly from his Paris church to take him through a rigorous course of preparation for death in a truly contrite spirit. 'I am a great criminal', he said, 'and have no hope but in the mercy of God.' He asked to be treated as an ordinary penitent, knowing 'that there is but one gospel for the great and humble alike'. On 7 March he received the last unction in the presence of a crowd of bishops, courtiers, officials and domestics. That evening he spoke to the king, who came out weeping. On the 8th he followed the words of the mass: at Joly's prompting, he begged the forgiveness of any whom he might have injured. At midnight he was heard to say: 'My hope is in Jesus Christ'. At 2 a.m. he expired.

Mazarin had first expressed a wish that all his wealth should go to the king. Louis took time to ponder. On the one hand a clear benefit to the crown: policy and justice argued for it. On the other hand there was the prompting of gratitude. He rejected the money, and Mazarin proceeded to devise other ways of bequeathing his fortune. Louis believed that his minister had saved the throne during the Fronde and left it unassailable: that France, owing to his endeavours, was dominant in Europe. Mazarin's training had been so thorough that he was now resolved to be his own *premier ministre* and he had, to assist him, ministers of proven competence, all Mazarin's men.[6] For such exertions, such successes and such an outcome, no reward could be too great.

Louis XIV ordered full court mourning: the first and the last time that was done for anyone outside the royal family. Funeral orations, a studied art form, are generally of little more value as a sounding of informed contemporary opinion than the epigrams and *chansons*[7] which met a popular demand for some neat last words on the subject. Among the orators, the Carmelite père Léon, preaching at Rome, struck appropriate notes of paradox and puzzle in depicting 'the lights and shades' in his subject's career and 'the mysterious enigma' of the whole. 'He was French and Italian, soldier and doctor of law, layman and cardinal, foreigner and royal servant, exile and plenipotentiary, subject and friend of the king; a most notable victim, a phoenix; a Phoebus after the clouds have rolled away; the arbiter of great peoples and nations.' Père Léon's long acquaintance with Mazarin lends a certain authenticity to his words. From familiar imagery to political reality, his rhetoric had led skilfully to a conclusion that Mazarin would surely have valued. It fits with the project on which the dying minister set his heart, his Collège des Quatre-Nations.

His will provided for the building and lavish endowment of the college, to encourage learning and commemorate the four 'nations' which had been added to the realm of France by the treaties of 1648 and 1659. Here, under the direction of senior doctors of the Sorbonne, were to be educated sixty sons of gentlemen resident in the annexed lands: Alsace, Pignerol, Artois-Flanders-Hainault, Roussillon-Cerdagne. Here was to be installed his library. A chapel was to be built – and there his bones were to rest. Twelve days after Mazarin's death, the commission charged with executing his will met to decide upon the architect and the site. The architect was to be Louis Le Vau, who had been Mazarin's architect at Vincennes. Colbert proposed the site on the left bank, opposite the Louvre, involving the clearance of much old building and difficult drainage works. Whether its choice represented Colbert's idea of what was proper or Mazarin's stated wish, there can be no doubt about the significance of the outcome. In its sober grandeur, François d'Orbay's completion of Le Vau's design, complements the Louvre and stands still, after all vicissitudes[8] as a fitting monument to a great servant of France.

GLOSSARY

Aides. A variety of indirect taxes, mostly on drink, levied by the state.

Arrêts de conseil. Royal orders which did not require registration to give them immediate force of law.

Avocat-général. One of *gens du roi*, royal representatives in *Parlement*.

Ban et arrière-ban. Traditional summons to muster nobles for military service: becoming method of taxing nobles by making them provide for substitutes.

Bourgeoisie. Non-noble members of the upper échelons of rural or, more commonly, urban society sufficiently well off not to work with their hands and possessed of privileges, as distinct from the mere *habitant* – but the distinction is blurred at the lower urban levels: for example, it was common for working men to refer to the employer as *bourgeois.*

Bureau des finances. Sixteenth-century creations in the *généralités.* Administered by *trésoriers-généraux.*

Censitaires. Statutory provider of *cens*, labour or other dues on the *censives* or tenures.

Chambre des Comptes. Sovereign court, having important rights and duties, such as the registration of royal marriages and peace treaties.

Chambre de Justice. Special financial court set up to confiscate financiers' gains and to teach political lessons.

Champart. A feudal tax in kind, payable by the peasant to the *seigneur*, constituting around one twelfth of produce.

Clientèle. In political usage, a close-knit group of dependants, bound to the patron by mutual interest in advancement.

Coadjuteur. Ecclesiastical title, denoting an assistant to a bishop.

Commissaire départi. Royal official given a specific brief by letter of commission: so a term used for *intendants.*

Comptant. Cash payment made by the crown.

Conseil d'état. The original royal council out of which have evolved, with the growth of government, several bodies with specialised functions and, by Louis XIV's reign, the effective *conseil d'en haut.* For other councils see p. 344 note 4.

Contrôleur-général. Financial officer with supervisory powers. Not until the appointment of Colbert (1661), the supreme financial office, with powers ranging over the whole economy.

Corvée. Statutory labour laid down by custom.

Cour des aides. Sovereign court of appeal in matters of taxation.

Créature. In political usage, a person in dependent but often well established relationship to the *patron.*

Dauphin. Title of the heir-presumptive to the throne.

311

Dérogeance. Loss of status by nobles participating in certain occupations: notably manufactures and many trades.

Dévôt. Member of zealous Catholic party opposed to toleration for Huguenots, tending towards a pro-Spanish foreign policy.

Duc et pair. Nobleman of the highest rank, also enjoying the privileges of a peer (as possessor of a fief erected into a *duché–pairie* – as distinct from mere *duc*): enjoying therefore the right to attend *Parlement.*

Élection. Fiscal area presided over by an *élu*, responsible for apportioning the *taille* on the basis of personal income.

Échevin. Municipal officer (one of four in Paris) under the *prévôt des marchands* (q.v.).

Écu. A gold crown whose value depended on its declared value in terms of money of account – the *livre tournois*: typically three *livres.*

Enquêtes. One of the three main chambers of the *Parlement.*

Faubourg. A suburb – as in Faubourg Saint-Antoine.

Fermier. Leaseholder responsible, for a consideration, for collecting dues, seigneurial or royal.

Fleur-de-lys. The lilies of France: triple (in honour of the Trinity) stylised device on a blue shield; the royal arms.

Gabelles. Salt taxes levied on a basis which varied according to regions, exemptions and privileges.

Généralité. One of the major administrative areas (twenty-three in 1643) into which the country was divided. Becoming the seat of *intendances.*

Gloire. Reputation for noble deeds with contemporaries.

Grand Conseil. A branch of the *conseil d'état* (created in 1497), dealing with judicial business in which *Parlement* might be considered an interested party, therefore not proper to judge.

Grands. Collective, informal name for highest nobles.

Hobereau. Poor country gentleman: in court, *salon* parlance, signifying uncouth.

Intendant. Royal commissary, empowered to oversee financial, military and concomitant administrative affairs in the provinces. The *intendant de l'armée* had a more specialised role but matters of discipline and supply had implications for the civilians in his field of operations.

Laboureur. A prosperous peasant farmer.

Lettres de Jussion. First step in royal enforcement of legislation when *Parlement* delayed registration.

Lettre de cachet. A letter emanating from the sovereign, signed by a *secrétaire d'état*, containing an order relative to an individual (commonly for imprisonment), or a particular case.

Lit de Justice. Ceremony in which the king, attending personally, could enforce registration of edicts in *Parlement* or other sovereign courts.

Livre. Money of account, comprising twenty *sous*: each *sol* contained twelve deniers.

Maître des requêtes. A royal judge attached to the *conseil du roi.*

Menu peuple. The common people: often used in a derogatory sense.

Noblesse d'épée. Nobility of the sword: the military, not necessarily 'ancient' nobility, privileged supposedly by virtue of feudal service.

Noblesse de robe. Nobility deriving from office in the higher ranks of the judiciary and administration.

Octrois. Urban sales taxes.

Office. A permanent government post (as distinct from a temporary commission): generally for sale, sometimes conferring nobility.

Officier. Holder of an *office.*

Parlement. Sovereign, final court of appeal with wide powers of police (the latter word conveys both justice and administration). The *Parlement* of Paris, with three main chambers, had jurisdiction over more than one third of the realm, with responsibility for registering royal edicts, and administrative functions. Besides Paris there were nine provincial *parlements* in 1643: Toulouse, Bordeaux, Grenoble, Dijon, Rouen, Aix, Rennes, Pau and, most recently (1633), Metz.

Paulette or *droit annuel.* A form of premium enabling an *officier* to transmit his office in return for one-sixtieth of its estimated value.

Politique. Term used, notably to the Religious Wars, denoting one who might put French political concerns before those of religious allegiance.

Premier Président. Presides over *Grand Chambre* or *Parlement* (q.v.). Only post in *Parlement* (not an *office* but a *charge* and revocable) nominated by the king.

Président à mortier. One of eight judges of highest eminence in the *Grand Chambre* of *Parlement.*

Prévôt des marchands. Principal official of the municipality of Paris: like mayor.

Procureur-général. One of the *gens du roi*, royal representatives in *Parlement.*

Rentes. A government bond usually issued on the security of municipal revenues. A *rentier* was one who lived mainly off such an investment.

Requêtes, Chambre des. Court of appeal in *Parlement.*

Secrétaire d'État. From original secretarial role, holders of this venal office have become heads of ministerial departments, each with responsibility for designated provinces. (Only those who were summoned to sit regularly in the *conseil d'en haut* (q.v.) were designated *ministres*).

Seigneurie. The basic economic unit in rural France. The obligations of the tenant to the seigneur involved a widely varying range of dues and services. A *seigneur* enjoyed rights of jurisdiction within his lands.

Sol pour livre. A five per cent sales tax introduced in 1640.

Subsistances. A tax paid by townspeople to exempt them from billetting troops.

Surintendant des finances. Head of the financial administration.

Taille. The main direct tax: levied either on income, the *taille personnelle*, applicable to the *pays d'élection*, or on property, *taille réelle*, in the *pays d'états*.

Taxe des aisés. A wealth tax.

Toisé. A tax (1643, after resistance, abortive) on houses in the suburbs of Paris.

Traitants. Financiers who had made a contract, or *traité*, with the crown: usually to levy taxes or sell offices.

Trésoriers de France. Financial officials who headed the *bureaux des finances* (q.v.) in each *généralité*.

NOTES

1 THE YOUNG ROMAN

1 The Knights of St John of Jerusalem, or Knights Hospitallers, founded in 1114, had held their ground in Malta after the siege of 1565 and were established there as a sovereign state. They were esteemed as a traditional part of the defence system of Christendom against Ottoman attack.

2 Filipo Colonna, 1578–1639, was head of a Roman family, long distinguished for military prowess and latterly prominent in the service of Spain.

3 For the Jesuits see note 8 on Saint Ignatius.

4 Pietro Mazarini's complaints and demands became more insistent as his son began to make his way in the world. For example, in September 1629, he wrote: 'I have been waiting impatiently for you to send me some help... I can do nothing more... I desist [but he didn't] from describing to you the urgent demands of the *casa* so as not to increase your distress which I am content to carry alone.' He wasn't so content and the psychological effect of this family burden should be considered in the light of Giulio's later attitudes towards money and possessions. He did however enjoy a second marriage, in 1645, to Portia Orsini, and a fruitful autumn of his days, acting as an agent in Rome for his now famous son, keeping house grandly in the *palazzo* Mazarini on the Quirinale (though he had to give part of it to the French ambassador). To the end (November 1654) he made claims on his son's purse and attention.

5 Michele Mazarini (1607–48) showed some resemblance to his father in his discontented moods and uncertain temper. Educated by the Dominicans, and entering the order, he rose along with his brother's career. He was indeed elected General of the Dominicans, only to have the election quashed by the Pope because of irregularities in the process. His further promotion, to be Archbishop of Aix (1645), then Cardinal (1647) owed more to his brother's need for a well-placed ally than to his innate abilities.

6 Anna Maria Mazarini (1604–69) became prioress of the convent of Santo di Campo Marzo in Rome in 1657. Her brother's fame brought her celebrity and the Colonnas, Barberinis, even, latterly, the exiled queen Christina of Sweden, thought it worth their while to visit her – if, perhaps, more for political information than for spiritual advice. She was also at the centre of a little group, tending to mysticism, who constituted a spiritual resource whose value can be gauged by Mazarin's evident appreciation of her interest, prayers and letters.

7 Graphologists might deduce traits of character from Mazarini's rapid, flowing,

ill-formed and sometimes illegible handwriting. I will only suggest a mind fertile with expedients, moving faster than his quill, and a greater impatience to express himself and be on to the next necessary business. See also p. 335, n.15 for his *carnets*.

8 Ignatius Loyola (1491–1556) was a Spanish soldier who experienced conversion while convalescing from wounds; he composed the *Spiritual Exercises* and formed a group vowed to poverty and chastity which became the nucleus of the Society of Jesus. He was canonised in 1622 by Pope Gregory XV. By Mazarin's time there were over 15,000 Jesuits, working world-wide, primarily in education and missionary work. Their discipline, centralised authority and willingness to engage with the concerns of the world, made them formidable protagonists of the ideals of reformed Catholicism.

Drama was cultivated by the Jesuits as a means of disseminating doctrine. Originally pious, it came to have wider scope, with material from mythology and ancient history. Jesuit plays became increasingly elaborate and stagecraft kept pace with the newest developments in European theatre. Music was also important in forming the character and tastes of their bright pupil.

9 *Galantuomo*: the word loses by translation since neither 'honest man' or 'brave man' conveys its nuances: with soundness, sensibility; manliness as well as charm; particularly, honour. The young Mazarin may have gone out of his way to impress but it was in his nature to be friendly. Dethan writes, as always illuminatingly, of 'his passionate quest for friendship. It was through contact with others that Mazarin wanted to learn life'.

10 It is tempting to see Mazarin's career as 'Baroque' in its vaulting ambition and imaginative use of all possible resources. At least one can stress the impact of the spectacular creative effort that was visible all around on a young man of sensibility, moving in the circles of the great patrons. First manifestations of the Baroque (Italian, *barocco*, originally meaning any contorted idea) occur in Italy in the later decades of the sixteenth century. Its designs generally evoke emotion by appeal to the senses. Qualities associated with the style are grandeur, vitality, movement, tension and sensuous richness. It rode on a tide of technical virtuosity and inventiveness. Exponents aimed at the fullest possible interplay between architecture, painting and sculpture. The missionary impulse of the post-Tridentine church (see note 12) led patrons to call for designs that would lead the eye to the dramatic significance of the altar and the Mass, while providing a theatre for sermons to make the greatest possible impact.

11 Carlo Maderna (1556–1629) helped determine the style of early Baroque architecture. By adding the nave he transformed Michelangelo's Greek cross design into a longitudinal one, thus reverting to the scheme of early Christian cathedrals. Mazarini would also be familiar with his work in the *palazzo* Barberini. Gicacomo da Vignola (1507–73) died before his *Il Gesù* was completed (by della Porta, architect of the façade) but the basic plan was his. With its use of vast interior space, an effective instrument for the dramatisation of the Mass, it was widely copied. Giacomo della Porta (*c.* 1537–1602) was also responsible for the final design of the dome of St Peter's which became the prototype of the Baroque dome to be seen all over Europe.

12 The Council of Trent met, between 1545 and 1563 to define dogma and to propose measures for reform. It led, through clearer definitions of articles of faith, to a hardening of lines of difference between Catholic and Protestant. Pointing to greater centralisation within the church, it buttressed Papal authority, but, even more, the power of the bishops. Its conclusions combined

traditionalism with modern recognition of the needs of the church as an instrument of education and propaganda. Man's will was allowed to have a part in justification by faith through the grace of God: so the church put the seal of its authority on an interpretation which was bound to be rejected by Calvinists and which would become controversial within the church with the rise of Jansenism (see also pp. 292ff and p. 318, n. 14). The efficacy of the traditional sacraments was affirmed as was the 'true veneration' of saints. The Latin Vulgate bible was designated as the authentic text of the scriptures. With Italians in the majority among bishops and heads of religious houses it is not surprising that the reforms had most immediate impact in the Mediterranean world, nor that Gallican France was slow to receive or implement them. In general, however, the reform movement was bound to gain momentum because it was in tune with the secular tendency towards uniformity and coincided with the drive towards centralised political order. It can also be seen to represent the yearning for the absolute and extreme, whether expressed in the deliberate plainness of Puritanism or in the exuberance and colour of the Baroque.

13 Giordano Bruno (1548–1600), philosopher, astronomer, mathematician, occultist, was responsible for two theories which anticipated modern science: that the universe was infinite and that there was a multiplicity of worlds.

Galilei Galileo (1564–1642), mathematician, astronomer and physicist of a renown that needs no amplification, found himself in conflict with the church over the support of Copernican theory – that planets revolve round the sun – after writing his *Dialogues on the Two Chief Systems of the World* which, Jesuits claimed, could have worse consequences on the established system of teaching 'than Luther and Calvin put together'.

14 Francesco Borromini (1599–1667) was one of the chief formulators of the Baroque style. Irascible, original and daring sometimes to the point of perversity, he became latterly acutely melancholic. Yet he managed to cooperate with Bernini in one of the most fruitful of partnerships, the creation of the great *baldacchino* in St Peter's.

Giovanni Lorenzo Bernini (1598–1680) was a man of more sanguine temperament and deep religious feeling. Architect, sculptor and painter, prodigiously active to the end of his long life, he typifies the vital spirit of Mazarini's Rome. He served seven Popes in all, but it was the patronage of Pope Urban VIII that was responsible for his attaining a position of unrivalled dominance. He is most famous for his *baldacchino* in St Peter's (equivalent in height to a four-storey house), the grand colonnade enclosing the piazza before St Peter's, and his moving *Ecstasy of St Theresa*, a sculptural ensemble that seems to draw the worshipper into a deeply felt religious drama. He went to Paris in 1667, at the king's request, but offended Parisians by his derogatory remarks about French buildings and paintings. Mazarin would have been disappointed to know that Bernini's design for the Louvre was rejected – but would have approved the portrait bust of Louis XIV which set a standard for the future depiction of royalty.

15 Michelangelo Merisi da Caravaggio (1573–1610) led a life that was sensational even by the standards of Rome's Bohemia, the Campo Marzo. Violent, unstable, a boaster and brawler, he wounded one man in defence of his mistress and killed another in a dispute over a game of tennis. His painting was as ordered and masterly as his life was disorderly and impulsive. He introduced a revolutionary technique of tenebrism, with the dramatic, selective

illumination of forms out of deep shadow that was to be a hallmark of Baroque painting.

2 THE POLITICS OF ROME

1 Need we doubt Mazarini's sincerity when he wrote to Cardinal Francesco in 1636: 'I have no other ambition in this world, after that of God's grace, than the little glory that I may acquire in sacrificing myself for the public welfare and for the excellent house of Barberini'? On the election of Pope Innocent X in 1644 and an investigation into their misuse of church funds, the Barberinis left for Paris and the protection of Mazarin. He saw to it that they had benefices and then helped to effect a reconciliation with Innocent in 1653. Francesco and Antonio saw out their days (they died respectively in 1679 and 1671) in the magnificent palace Bernini had designed for them. Though adapted to French conditions, Mazarin's career reflects the model offered by this family, so blatant in its pursuit of wealth and power, yet not without fine ideas about its use.

2 The meaning of *dévôt* applicable both to an attitude and a party, is not adequately conveyed by 'devout'. To be *dévôt* was to embrace Catholic piety so intensely that it coloured language and behaviour; to oppose toleration of Huguenots and alliance with Protestant powers; to be generally pro-Spanish and 'ultramontane', recognising the Pope's superior authority, as against the Gallican tradition which favoured the secular rights of the French crown, (see also p. 322, n. 13; p. 327, no. 5.)

3 The Dominicans, or Black Friars, one of the four great mendicant orders, was founded by St Dominic in 1215. Bologna, where Michele Mazarini attended a Dominican school, was a leading Dominican centre. Dominicans adopted the theological system of St Thomas Aquinas in 1278; they never thereafter lost the reputation of unswerving orthodoxy.

4 Jansenists were so called after Cornelius Jansen (1548–1638), bishop of Ypres, theologian, whose master-work, the *Augustinus* (four volumes), seeking to prove that the teaching of Saint Augustine on grace, free-will and predestination was opposed to the teaching of the Jesuit schools, would have caused less controversy if the Jesuits had not been so powerful in France and Jansen had not also attacked Richelieu's policy with regard to Spain in his pamphlet *Mars Gallicus*. For Jansenism and the conflicts it engendered, see pp. 292ff.

5 Baldassare Castiglione (1478–1529), whose portrait by Raphael can be seen in the Louvre, learned the arts and manners of chivalry at the courts of Mantua and Urbino. The influential *Il Cortegiano* (1528), translated into many languages, deals with the perfect courtier, the noble lady and the relationships between courtier and the prince. The courtier was to be brave, a lover of the arts and something of a scholar; he was also to have an understanding of politics and diplomacy.

6 The dates favoured by Dethan. That Goubert tentatively suggests 1619–21 illustrates the difficulty that faces the biographer dealing with the years before his subject became famous, for which there is inadequate evidence. In any case Mazarini was back in Rome by May 1622 for the Ignatius play.

7 In 1609 Spain and the United Provinces put a temporary end to the war which had begun with rebellion against Spanish rule in 1566 and had developed into stalemate, by making a Twelve Year Truce. Its durability was already in doubt before the Bohemian revolt in 1618. The decision of the Elector Palatine to accept the crown of Bohemia exposed his lands to Spanish invasion: they

offered a strong position on the flank of the Dutch – and a more secure supply route.

8 The Spanish had taken advantage, in 1620, of a rising by the Catholics of the valley against their Protestant overlords, the Grey Leagues, or Grisons, to establish forts along the valley. In 1622 France, Savoy and Venice agreed to drive out the Spanish; Spain then handed over the forts to Papal troops. Louis XIII accepted this arrangement; for Richelieu it was not satisfactory. In November a Franco-Swiss army expelled the Papal garrisons. Urban shared Richelieu's misgivings about Spanish power in North Italy but wanted to ensure the protection of the Catholics of the valley. Meanwhile *dévôts* brought pressure on Richelieu to draw back from confrontation with Spain and a Huguenot rising forced the Cardinal to concentrate on problems nearer home. The resulting treaty of Monzón (March 1626), by which Spain accepted the sovereignty of the Grisons while France withdrew her troops, damaged Richelieu's standing with his allies, Venice, Savoy and the Dutch, but made possible his better understanding with the Pope. The episode contains the elements of problems which, at home and abroad, would one day be Mazarin's to solve.

9 Most important were Gian-Francesco, who prepared Mazarin for his diplomatic career, and Cardinal Guilio, another regular adviser, and later the favoured French candidate for the papacy after Urban's death (see p. 11).

10 It was painted c. 1622, and can be seen in the palazzo Colonna in Rome.

11 Ambrogio Spinola (1569–1630), Genoese, most renowned of Spain's generals, victor at Breda (1627) and subject of Velasquez's celebrated depiction of the event, and also of one of Van Dyck's most sympathetic portraits, was regarded as a model not only in military science but also in courtesy and humanity. Mazarini had the highest opinion of him, seeing him as model of Italian manners.

12 Charles, marshal de Créquy (1578–1638), was one of several French commanders whom Mazarini found impressive at a time when he was playing with the idea of transferring to the service of France. See p. 41.

13 Thirty years elapsed between the revolt of Bohemia and the treaty of Westphalia in 1648. The latter did not end the war between France and Spain. Several separate conflicts were subsumed into the German civil war which was at the heart of the conflict, notably the Polish-Swedish and the Dutch-Spanish. The description 'Thirty Years War' is inadequate to describe a complex sequence of wars for which even the initial religious divisions do not provide a sufficient cause.

3 MANTUA: CRISIS AND OPPORTUNITY

1 Ferdinand II, Holy Roman Emperor (1619–37), had succeeded in putting down the Protestants of Styria by force before being elected king of Bohemia, in 1617, and his coercive policies were among the causes of the revolt in Prague that led to widening conflict. Jesuit-educated at the University of Ingolstadt, clear-sighted in his pursuit of Catholic policies that would also advance the strength of the House of Habsburg, he followed up the defeat of the rebels by the re-establishment of Catholicism throughout Bohemia. His subsequent Edict of Restitution (1629), affecting ecclesiastical states 'secularised' since 1555, could be carried out only through the agency of Wallenstein, most powerful and feared of mercenary soldiers; with its divisive effects on Germany and consequent entry of Sweden into the war, it therefore supports

the view that he was the sovereign principally responsible for the spread and long duration of the war.

2 Maximilian, duke of Bavaria, after 1623 Elector, (1597–1651), another Jesuit pupil, was determined to use his power to promote the Catholic cause with that of his house of Wittelsbach. Founder of the Catholic League (1609) and subsequently Ferdinand II's most valuable ally, he had the resources of a well managed state to support a substantial army. His main secular objectives were securing the Electorate forfeited by Frederick of the Palatine, and that part of his lands, the Upper Palatinate, that marched with his own Bavarian lands. In both he was successful but at great cost to his subjects. See also p. 244.

3 Louis XIII, king of France (1610–43), was a conscientious ruler who brought to his role a keen sense of what his subjects owed him as their absolute sovereign, and of what he owed to God as *le roi très chrètien*. His complicated personality can be studied in Lloyd Moote's sympathetic biography. It may be claimed that his chief claim to a a high place among monarchs lies in his choice and support of Richelieu as minister. However theirs was a genuine partnership. Louis was no cypher. See particularly p. 91.

4 Gustav Adolf Vasa King of Sweden (1611–32), generally known by the Latinised name, was a highly accomplished ruler who seized the imagination of Protestant Europe by his invasion of Germany in 1630 and his decisive victory of Breitenfeld, in September 1631. After his death on the foggy field of Lutzen (November 1632) the Swedes retained a military presence in Germany and Richelieu, like Mazarin afterwards, anchored his foreign policy to this invaluable northern ally. Richelieu had assisted him to extricate himself from war with Poland in making the truce of Altmark in 1629, as the prelude to his alliance, sealed, with subsidy, at Barwälde, in January 1631). See especially p. 244.

5 In this year Mansfeld and Christian of Denmark were defeated, respectively, at the battles of Dessau Bridge and Lutter.

6 The edict of Nantes (1598), which brought to an end the Religious Wars of the previous four decades, had secured what was in effect, though in precisely stipulated places, freedom of worship for Huguenots, with the right of entry to royal offices and any profession or occupation. Special tribunals, *chambres de l'édit*, comprising Catholic and Huguenot judges, were set up to try lawsuits involving Huguenots. They were allowed to keep for eight years (the period was later extended) certain fortresses and a subsidy was allotted for their upkeep. The 'perpetual and irrevocable edict' represented an extraordinary admission on the part of the French crown that it was necessary, for peace, to grant privileges which made the Huguenots a separate estate in the realm; yet its position, resting on claims of religion that were rejected by the mass of the people, could only be precarious. The mentalities of civil war outlasted its formal end. Toleration was no more an ideal in sophisticated government circles than in passionately divided Languedoc. The fundamental assumption of both sides was that the edict was provisional; that of most Catholics was that Catholicism was the fundamental law of the state. When the crown's annexation of Béarn provoked a Huguenot rising (1620) Louis XIII failed humiliatingly and with severe losses, to quell it. The peace of Montpellier (1622) did however secure the destruction of all the Huguenot fortresses except Montpellier and La Rochelle. When the Huguenots rebelled again, under Rohan and Soubise, Richelieu staked all on the capture of a fortified seaport (Wallenstein's failure at Stralsund gave dire warning). The successful operation has been deemed a landmark in the absolutist process. The Edict

of Alés (or Alais) of June 1629, was not a treaty but a royal 'grace', an act of remission. The Huguenots lost their remaining political and military rights. They could worship as before but they were now plainly vulnerable, likely to be on the defensive, in action and mentality. That Richelieu could accept this situation and resist the pressures from the *dévôts* in the matter so close to his heart had a legacy in the cautious loyalty of the Huguenots during the Fronde – and an important lesson to Mazarin. See pp. 222–3.

7 Charles Emmanuel I (1580–1630), duke of Savoy, was one of Europe's more notable rulers. Though nominally, his mountainous land stretching from Nice to the St Bernard, was an Imperial vicariate, Savoy was a strong and independent state. It included an important fortress, Pinerolo, and it controlled two vital routes from Italy to the north: that by the coast and the Mont Cenis. Charles Emmanuel had inherited claims to Montferrat and Geneva, among others: he was a possible contender for the Holy Roman empire; more plausibly for the kingdom of Cyprus. Between the ambitions of France and Spain he tended towards the former, if only because of his greater fear and dislike of Spain, the resident foreigner. He was furious by what he saw as Richelieu's desertion in the treaty of Monzón. The death of the duke of Mantua gave him a personal stake in the Franco-Spanish battle for control, through his own Montferrat claim and that of his grand-daughter.

8 Gaspar de Guzmán, count–duke of Olivarez (1587–1645) was *privado*, in effect chief minister, of Philip IV from 1622 to 1643, therefore Richelieu's near-contemporary. Besides his major biography, *The Count-Duke of Olivarez: the Statesman in an Age of Decline* (1986), J. H. Elliott's comparative study, *Richelieu and Olivarez* (1984), reveals Olivarez' intelligence, resourcefulness and almost manic energy in pursuit of enticing prizes, not least the triumph of Catholicism in Germany, and latterly, in defence of crumbling positions abroad and a deteriorating economy at home. His last years, before he disintegrated into madness, have a heroic quality about them: his secretary Carnero wrote of him: 'Even with the water over his head he keeps on swimming'. See particularly pp. 48–9.

9 With his duchy in France, Charles Gonzague, duc de Nevers (*d.* 1637) was enough of a Frenchman for Richelieu to promote his claims to the Mantuan inheritance. With his interest in the crusade and his friendship with Father Joseph, he was also *persona grata* to the *dévôts* and the Pope. It was on the pretext that Nevers had not sought Imperial permission that Ferdinand II unleashed the Mantuan war. Nevers' claim eventually succeeded but it brought nothing but misery to the duke and his subjects. His Nevers duchy and many of his pictures would come eventually to Mazarin.

10 The edict, issued in March 1629, owed more to Ferdinand II's confessor, Lamormaini, than to Wallenstein, who foresaw the military problems that it would entail. It represented the Catholic view that the secularisation of church lands since 1555 (Peace of Augsburg) was illegal. Only those Protestants adhering to the Confession of Augsburg had been included in the provisions of the peace: Calvinists were therefore excluded. The Emperor could be pleased with the enforcement of Catholicism in five bishoprics and thirty free cities. But the measure was divisive. Saxony and Brandenburg feared that they would lose lands; even Catholic electors were doubtful about the legality of the edict and were concerned about the increase in the Emperor's authority; all distrusted Wallenstein and, in August 1630 they secured his replacement as Imperial commander, by the Bavarian Tilly, commander of the army of the Catholic League. This split in the Catholic front prepared the ground for

the successful Swedish invasion that followed – and for France to take advantage of it.

11 Philip IV (1621–65) presided over both the *época de triumfo* and the protracted and painful decline that followed the revolts of Catalonia and Portugal (see pp. 48–9). He has been widely seen as self-indulgent and ineffectual, though stubborn, with unfortunate consequences, where his royal rights were concerned. A recent biography, by R. A. Stradling, *Philip IV and the Government of Spain* (1988) has shown him in a better light, in particular being conscientious in council after the death of Olivarez, and showing some talent for management.

12 The population of France had risen by 1600 to around 18 million but was to fluctuate around that total during the century, with large swings due to periodic famine and mortalities (see pp. 69–70). That of Spain was starting to decline in 1600, after a disastrous plague in the nineties, below a peak of around eight million. By mid-century it was down to seven million, by 1700, six and a half. Meanwhile the resources of the Spanish Netherlands and of Milan and Naples should not be under-estimated. That was the logic behind Olivarez' Union of Arms designed, by securing proportionate quotas of troops from each of the king's territories, to reduce the burden on Castile.

13 *Dévôt*, authoritarian, dedicated to good order in the state, Marillac had first been Louis XIII's *surintendent* before becoming Keeper of the Seals in 1626. He and Richelieu agreed upon certain absolutist principles. The *Code Michau*, Marillac's compilation of rules for legal, administrative and commercial practice, contained much that stemmed directly from Richelieu's proposals to the Assembly of Notables in 1626. Marillac represents the course that French history might have taken, if Richelieu, for example, had been removed in 1630 (See note 16, below). War in Italy would have been averted, Spain appeased, the Huguenots coerced and taxes reduced. He would have wished to ride roughshod over vested interests, to curb *parlements* and to impose *élus* on *pays d'états*. Since he was arrested, after the failure of the Day of Dupes, lost the Seals, and subsequently died, his remains the alternative programme that was never put to the test.

14 Louis de Marillac was appointed to command the army in Italy to please Marie, just before the Day of Dupes which was to lead to his downfall. His alleged wish to see Richelieu dead and his connections with the group centring, after Marie's flight to Brussels, on Gaston of Orléans and Montmorency made Richelieu determined to destroy him – and Louis merciless. Although the specially picked court could not find much to discredit him, he was executed in the place de Grève, in May 1631.

15 François de Bassompierre, formerly ambassador to Spain, was a friend of the king. Mazarin too admired him for his warm personality and dashing manner. Although he was a capable soldier and had apparently done no more than correspond with Marillac, he was despatched to the Bastille. He was not to emerge till after Richelieu's death. The episode conveys the nervous atmosphere around government in the early 'Thirties.

16 The Day of Dupes, 11 November 1630, was so called because enemies of Richelieu and friends of Marie de Médicis were gathered at court expecting to hear news of the minister's downfall. Instead he was confirmed in power and the *dévôts* and their allies of convenience scattered, some to face trial, some, notably Gaston of Orléans, to raise the flags of revolt. Louis's renunciation of Marie and his commitment to Richelieu enabled the minister to

pursue his hazardous, costly, but ultimately rewarding foreign policy. It was a decisive day.

17 Pierre Bérulle (1575–1629), writer, preacher, teacher, gave Spanish mysticism a restrained Gallic look. The mystical ideal, 'adherence to Christ', was pursued with Cartesian method. Bérulle's contacts included Jansen but he was spared the pain of the Jansenist conflict. François de Sales and Vincent de Paul were among his disciples. When, in 1611, he founded the French Oratory, his object was to establish a new model for the priesthood. The Jesuits opposed it because of the looseness of its structure, and teaching methods at variance with their own. As father figure of the *dévôts* Bérulle was drawn into politics. He did not live to see Richelieu's alliance with Sweden but the rift between the two cardinals foreshadowed the tragic dilemma implicit in the statesman's attempt to be both sound Catholic and *bon français*.

18 Anne of Austria (1601–66) was the elder daughter of Philip III of Spain and Margaret, sister of the Emperor Ferdinand II. She married Louis XIII in November 1615: they were both barely fourteen, she having been born just four days before Louis. She brought with her implications about France's relations with the Habsburgs which ensured that Richelieu's anti-Habsburg policies would make her position uncomfortable even if she had received support from her husband. She has now received the biography she deserved. Ruth Kleinman's *Anne of Austria* (1985) depicts a woman sensible and dignified in a lonely marriage, resolute and single-minded as Regent and staunch in her support of Mazarin.

19 Gaston, duc d'Orléans (1608–60), younger brother of Louis XIII, was so named, unsuitably as it turned out, after the ancestral hero Gaston de Foix. He married twice: Marie de Montpensier, who died in 1627, and Marguerite de Lorraine. His position gave him a prominence in two reigns which his character could barely sustain.

20 Charles IV, duke of Lorraine (1604–75), ruled over a duchy nominally independent but vulnerable, with its strategically sensitive location, to more powerful neighbours, notably France. It exhibits too the variety of jurisdictions and types of sovereignty that could co-exist in a small state. The *Barrois* was a French fief and Louis XIII refused to recognise Charles as duke of Bar. The duchy proper, though in theory independent, contained many Imperial fiefs. In December 1631 a French army ousted Imperial troops from Moyenvic and in January 1632 Charles signed the treaty of Vic with France, by which he promised free passage to French troops. It was not to be the end of the story of Charles' increasingly embittered relations with the French crown. See p. 97.

21 Victor Amadeus (1587–1637) was duke from 1630–7. For Savoy and its ruling house, see chapter 3, note 7. As will become clear (pp. 36–7) his marriage to Louis XIII's sister did not create the stable alliance that Richelieu hoped for.

22 Christina (Chrétienne, 1606–63) was the youngest daughter of Henri IV and Marie de Médicis: she married the much older Victor Amadeus in 1619. His 'extraordinary affection' for Mazarini (the latter's words) may have reflected Christina's. Her lively court provided an agreeable half-way house between France and Italy for Mazarini.

23 Charles Schomberg was German-born but rose to high command in French service. Jacques de Caumont, duc de la Force, was more typical of the French commanders of the period: though a Huguenot, he was a friend of the king, remained loyal during the rising of 1625–8 and played a useful part in holding down his fellow southerners. For his command of the motley force

assembled before Paris to resist the Spanish-Imperialist invasion of 1636, see pp. 33-4.

4 EARLY FAME

1 François Joseph Le Clerc du Tremblay (1577–1638), nobleman, Richelieu's 'Grey Eminence', needs a biographer less drawn to psychological explanation than was Aldous Huxley, better versed too in the institutions and attitudes of seventeenth-century France and the Poitou which was home both to him and to Richelieu. His special value to Richelieu was that he could go anywhere, sound out anyone, act for the Cardinal, but unofficially – so that he could more easily be repudiated if necessary. His notion of a Catholic but French-dominated Europe can be studied in his correspondence with Richelieu.

2 Since 1356, when the 'Golden Bull' defined the constitution of the Holy Roman Empire, the college of seven Electors had held the keys to such power as the empire could exert. Without their consent, no *Reichstag* (diet) could be summoned nor tax imposed. Nor could the Emperor fight a war or make foreign alliances without their approval. That the emperor could not go far in the direction of *hausmacht* (putting dynastic before broader German interest), was shown in the Electors' insistence, in 1630, on the dismissal of Wallenstein. Though there proved to be no acceptable alternative, Ferdinand II was shown that he could not take the election of his son for granted. The Electors meanwhile could use the prospect of an election to exact concessions.

3 Charles Brûlart de Léon, career diplomat and member of the family which also produced an *intendant*, a chancellor (Brûlart de Sillery, 1607–24) and a Secretary of State for Foreign Affairs (Brûlart de Puisieulx, 1617–24).

4 Charles de Lorraine, duc de Guise, whose family had fought Henry III for supremacy during the Religious Wars and created an effective political instrument in the form of the Holy League, was governor of Provence. Already offended by Richelieu's taking over the office of Admiral, now having lost his governorship, he was thereafter an inveterate conspirator.

5 By the terms of this treaty, Gustavus agreed to maintain in Germany an army of 30,000 men and 6,000 horses in return for a subsidy of a million *livres* a year for five years. He promised to respect Catholic worship where it was practised, and the neutrality of the League, in return for its neutrality. Richelieu's risky strategy was exposed after the sack of Magdeburg by Tilly's troops in May 1631, the subsequent alliance of Saxony with the Swedes and their shattering victory at Breitenfeld, in September, 1631. Gustavus enjoyed Christmas on the Rhine; his guarantees proved to be worthless – and Richelieu faced another domestic crisis.

6 Alessandro Bichi (1596–1657) was among the most influential of Mazarini's friends. His 'spiritual sponsorship' (Dethan) and friendship were a vital factor in Mazarini's rise, in his promotion to be Cardinal and even in his decision to commit himself to French service – to judge from the eloquent force of a letter of 1642 in which he urged Mazarini, as a child of Rome, to consecrate himself to the government of France.

7 Trained in Rome, Le Mercier was Richelieu's favourite architect. The Palais Cardinal was massive, with two courtyards and extensive gardens in the middle of Paris. Le Mercier also designed the new church of the Sorbonne, a *château* at Richelieu and a new town beside it, whose severe rectangular design can still be admired. Just as the exuberance of the Baroque expresses the spirit of Rome at this time, the formality and regularity of Le Mercier's architecture

(Bernini thought it dull) evokes the principles of Cartesian philosophy and the spirit of absolutist government.

8 The career of Abel Servien, marquis de Sablé (1593–1659), reveals much of the way the state developed during the ministries of Richelieu and Mazarin. He served as an *intendant* in Guyenne in 1628 and with the army of Italy in 1630. At the end of that year he became war minister. He was dismissed in 1636 because of quarrels with his fellow ministers: the appointment of Sublet also reflected Richelieu's anxiety about the condition of the army. Thereafter Servien's main employments were diplomatic. He had corresponded with Mazarin since 1631. He held no secretaryship of state under Mazarin – yet was an important minister: joint *surintendant* after 1653. His nephew Lionne was to have an even more brilliant career.

9 The term implies nothing derogatory. As a term of politeness it appears often in the conventionally effusive endings of letters. Richelieu referred to himself as *créature* of Louis XIII and his ministers as his *créatures*. The relationship obligation and affection on both sides.

10 Léon le Bouthillier, comte de Chavigny (1608–52) was the son of Claude le Bouthillier (1584–1652), the most prominent member of the Poitevin family which was closely associated with Richelieu's rise to power and shared in his success. Claude became secretary of state in 1628, *surintendant*, with Bullion, in 1632. With family interests and money behind him, and Richelieu's interest and affection, Léon took readily to high office. At the age of twenty-four he took, by *survivance* (see p. 334, n. 7) the office his father vacated when he became *surintendant*. Enjoying increasing responsibility for foreign business, he would play a significant part in Mazarin's career.

11 Richelieu may have thought that a previous agreement with Savoy, ceding Pinerolo, justified his use of a trick to take the place. After the commissioners, Imperial, Savoyard, Spanish and French had inspected Pinerolo, the palace was seized again by a company of French soldiers who had hidden in the cellars.

12 George Villiers, Duke of Buckingham (1592–1628), minister-favourite of James I, escorting Henrietta Maria from Paris to the Channel, visited Anne, made brash advances to her and subsequently declared his passion in an embarrassingly public way. Though Anne had enjoyed a mild flirtation she could not be blamed for Buckingham's ill-mannered impetuosity. Far from being 'like Buckingham', Mazarin's courteous and sympathetic manner would have seemed agreeably different.

13 Victor Amadeus' father, Charles Emmanuel, had been asked by oppressed Christians to take Cyprus: revival of the idea was therefore not improper.

14 On this south German battlefield, on 6 September 1634, the combined armies of the archduke Ferdinand (future Emperor Ferdinand III) and the Cardinal-Infant (Ferdinand, the king of Spain's brother), crushingly defeated the Swedish army under Horn and Bernard of Saxe-Weimar.

15 Cardinal Carlo Borromeo (1538–84, canonised 1610), archbishop of Milan, reformer, ascetic, provided a model and inspiration for other reformers, as notably Cardinal de la Rochefoucauld, (see p. 332, n. 5). His life confronted the prevailing humanism with the demand that the church stand for a separate clerical culture, and his tussles with the governor of Milan, whom he excommunicated, have Hildebrandine echoes.

16 François de Sales (1567–1622, canonised in 1665) grew up near Annecy in Savoy; after a Jesuit education in Paris he worked as a preacher and missionary among the Calvinist Chablais. He was an admired bishop of Geneva but it

was as a writer that he was most influential. The popularity of his *Introduction à la Vie Dévote* was not confined to Roman Catholics.

17 Geronimo Martinozzi married Margarita in July 1634 in the Barberini palazzo; there, a few weeks later, Lorenzo Mancini married Girolama. Martinozzi was a young widower whose father had become major-domo to Cardinal Antonio. Mancini, a cousin of the Mazarinis, came of a somewhat grander family with a much frequented *palazzo* in the Corso. They can hardly have dreamed of the future in store for their daughters, the 'Mazarinettes'.

18 Mazarini's grand *palazzo* was on the Quirinale and Mazarini was familiar with it from boyhood when it was built by Scipio Borghese, nephew of pope Paul V. Mazarini justified the purchase in typically ebullient style: 'serving a great king and enjoying the protection of His Eminence the cardinal-duke. I feel no obligation to undertake ordinary things. Add to this reason the craving I have always felt to possess, before I die, a beautiful *palazzo* like that of the Bentivoglio.'

19 To Venice certainly, to hear the work of Monteverdi, *maestro di capello* at St Mark's until his death in 1643. Music was important in the Barberini circle. Mazarini was one of many who were entranced by the famous singer, Leonora Baroni whom he would one day draw to Paris and the favourable attention of Anne of Austria. He appreciated music and dance for their own sake; they were to play an important part in the upbringing of Louis XIV. Mazarini also realised the value of lavish spectacle for the entertainment and flattering of sovereigns and courtiers. The success of the first musical comedy performed at the French courts, *La Finta Pazza*, in 1645, was largely derived from the ingenuity of Giacomo Torelli's scenery and stage machinery. Some critics alleged that the music served to distract from its operations and drown its noise, others complained of the cost, or of foreign fashions. Many were impressed by the magnificence of subsequent performances, notably (1647) the memorable *Orfeo* of Luigi Rossi. The young king was delighted. Ammunition was provided however for sneering attacks, typically in the *Mazarinades*, on Mazarini's 'troop of castrati' and his 'effeminate' foreign ways.

5 NUNCIO EXTRAORDINARY

1 Louis IX (1215–70, canonised 1297), warrior, crusader, famed for justice and piety, was venerated as the perfect example of the Christian king, proof of Divine Right to rule. Louis XIII was proud of his royal ancestor and was attracted to the chaste and devout qualities which he found in St Louis, by contrast with his father's example of frank sensuality. He turned Louis IX's feast day into an annual religious celebration and, at dangerous times, chose 'St Louis' as the guards' password for entry into his palace. The name would be again much heard during Louis XIV's *dévôt* years.

2 The place de Grève, in front of the Hôtel de Ville, then lay lower than the present square and was frequently flooded by the Seine. Its more sinister reputation derived from the many public executions that took place there; owners of surrounding houses let out rooms for spectators of the beheadings (for nobles), hangings (for commoners) and burnings (for heretics and sorcerers).

3 In marrying Marguerite, Gaston broke the terms of the treaty of Vic and offered Louis XIII, who had not given his brother leave, a pretext for invading Lorraine. Richelieu started a process in *Parlement* for annulling the marriage. On behalf of the Pope, Mazarin upheld the validity of the marriage, which

earned him short-lived gratitude from Gaston; he was unable to persuade Louis XIII to let Marguerite come to France until after Richelieu's death.

4 Neither France nor Spain saw the outbreak of war in 1635 as signifying more than the earlier Mantuan war. It can be argued that, although France declared war first, Olivarez was the more belligerent of the two statesmen. The two sides drifted towards war, each testing the other's nerve. The French occupation of Pinerolo was seen by Philip IV to be a sufficient *casus belli*, but action was postponed. The arrest by Spanish soldiers of the Elector of Trier in March 1635 touched Louis XIII on the raw, since the Elector had been placed under his protection. Indeed, if responsibility for the war does lie at all with the French, it is with the king rather than Richelieu. In a secret memorandum to Richelieu of August 1634 he had argued the case for open war to secure a beneficial general peace. After Nördlingen Richelieu came to regard it as inevitable, but he did not share his king's enthusiasm.

5 The rights of the Gallican church (the Catholic church in France) had first been formally defined by the Pragmatic Sanction of Bourges in 1438. Since then 'Gallican liberties' had become an issue whenever a Pope or king had reason or opportunity to advance his cause. For example the Concordat of Bologna (1516) gave Francis I effective right of appointment to the 600 most important ecclesiastical offices in France. His *droit de vérification* enabled him to censor Papal bulls (through *Parlement*). Some members were ultramontane and *dévôt*, but it was in *Parlement* that the strongest arguments for the king's rights were to be heard. Louis XIV would find *parlementaire* and episcopal support was helpful when he took issue with the Pope over the *régale* (the king's right to the revenue of vacant sees) but that Gallican principles were an embarrassment when he needed the authority of a Papal bull to strengthen his hand against Jansenism. See pp. 299–300.

6 *Nunzincardo*, 'dear little nuncio'. *Colmardo*, the supposedly Italian equivalent to *coupechou*, the humble friar assigned to domestic duties.

7 Another loyal friend was Gian-Francesco, Cardinal de Bagni (1566–1641). He was sufficiently intimate to make private jokes: on occasion Mazarini was *gli occhione*, 'big eyes'. He despaired of his friend making a career in Papal service. At the same time he thought that Richelieu was wrong to be attacking Flanders and Germany. The Milanese should be the target if he wanted to bring pressure on the Spaniards.

8 *Père* Marin Mersenne, Minim friar (1588–1648) was a mathematician. His role as correspondent and agent, furthering dialogue between mathematicians and physicists like Descartes, Gassendi and Pascal, was specially important in this first phase of the 'scientific revolution' before the rise of the learned societies.

9 Opponent of Descartes, Pierre Gassendi (1592–1655), wrote mainly in Latin and was little known outside the savants of Europe, with whom he enjoyed a high reputation. He represented what Descartes never countenanced: the continuation of the humanist position within the new mathematical philosophy.

10 Rueil is a few miles northwest of Paris (now in the suburbs): only the church, with its fine facade by Le Mercier, reminds the visitor of the seventeenth century, when Richelieu settled on the place for his country retreat.

11 When Claude de Bullion (1659–1640) became joint *surintendant* with Bout-hillier in 1632 he was already a veteran of government. Under pressure, he was responsible for the development of a system, ultimately disastrous, which relied too heavily on *rentes* and therefore weakened the bargaining position of the crown in relation to the financiers. His chateau of Wideville was famous

for its elegance and splendour. Gambling need carry no moral connotation. In his *Suite du commerce du monde*, Chevalier de Méré, a recognised authority on contemporary mores, citing Mazarin, Anne and Louis XIV among other devotees, wrote that 'gambling has a good effect when a man indulges in it skilfully and with good grace; it is the means by which a man can obtain admission to any company where gambling is practised, and princes would often be extremely bored if they were unable to indulge in it.'

12 Corbie is in Picardy, sixty miles northeast of Paris.

13 For the *intendants* and their increasing use in the state's fiscal strategy, see pp. 85–6.

14 The word *croquant* means 'clodhopper' and it conveys the nature of these popular risings which aroused such massive support – but mainly among the peasantry. For details, see pp. 76–7.

15 The *Gazette* was founded in 1633 under the editorship of Théophraste Renaudot. It was given the monopoly of publishing news. Renaudot prided himself on his objectivity as a reporter of events but he tended to reproduce the official view. He also published articles commissioned by Richelieu or penned by the Cardinal himself. This controlled newspaper played its part, along with sponsored literature, drama and history, in shaping the views of literate Frenchmen, probably ten times as many as those thousand or so who actually bought the weekly *Gazette* for four *sous*. Mazarin would know from the start that he could count on Renaudot. He was slow however to make use of the editor whom Patin, representing no doubt the opinion of his circle, described as 'that spy of Mazarin, alchemist, charlatan, usurer like a Jew, perfidious like a Turk'.

16 Charles de l'Aubespine, marquis de Châteauneuf (1580–1657), was Keeper of the Seals from 1630 until his arrest in 1633); after repeated disappointments (for he thought that Anne would look favourably on him) he was to have a further political career during the Fronde. See p. 166.

17 Marie de Rohan, duchesse de Chevreuse (1600–79), was much loved, not least by those, like Châteauneuf, whose careers she promoted in order to achieve her own somewhat inconsistent ends. She was a pretty, clever, adventurous, malicious woman, nicknamed 'the devil' by Richelieu: her political importance rose in periods of instability and the Fronde would provide a fine opportunity for her manipulative talents.

18 Jean de Toiras' career was assisted by the warm favour of Louis XIII. He successfully defended the Ile-de-Ré against Buckingham in 1627. Mazarin saw in him some of the qualities that had appealed to Louis.

19 Inert only on the Danubian front – which mattered to the Emperor and released him for a forward policy in Germany. Wars with Poland (1620–1), with Persia (1623–39) and with Venice (1645–69) absorbed Ottoman energies. See pp. 263–5 for Mazarin's policy towards the Turks.

20 Zongo Ondedei (1593–1674), the recipient of some of Mazarin's most revealing letters, was a close ally, particularly useful when, as in 1636–7, he served on a Papal delegation exploring the possibilities of peace, of concern to Mazarin – though he was debarred from taking part. In 1649 he came to France and served in a confidential and invaluable liaison capacity during his patron's enforced exiles.

21 Nicolas Charles also received revenues recently granted to Mazarini from the abbey of Saint-Médard and acted as intermediary for the presents sent by him to Anne, such as perfumed gloves, oils, and orange-blossom toilet water. His role sheds light on the precious manners of the time, also on the methods

necessary to maintain a connection. With Mazarin perforce absent for three years, it was to prove of the greatest importance. Richelieu's friend, Bautru wrote: 'when I meet Charles, I feel a great happiness, as if I were seeing our good friend, M. Mazarini himself'.

22 François Sublet de Noyers (1588–1645) was war minister from 1636 to his fall (see p. 64) in 1643. He served Richelieu devotedly, grappled with the multifarious abuses in army administration and initiated some badly needed reforms. As *surintendant des bâtiments*, his enlightened patronage of architecture and learning (he set up the *imprimerie royale* in 1640), besides his exceptional industry (to which 18,000 letters and dispatches bear witness) and his *dirigeiste* tendency, justify the description of him (by Michaud) as a 'Colbert in a minor key'. Sarrat less flatteringly called him 'le petit bigot'. His reputation as a *créature* of the Jesuits would be useful to Mazarini in the manoeuvring for power in 1643.

23 Chavigny was an *habitué* of the *salon* of Madame de Rambouillet and cultivated the style of the *précieuses*, at once fastidious in its shunning of anything deemed vulgar and extravagant in the expression of feeling.

24 François-Annibal d'Estrées, marquis de Coeuvres (1573–1670), was Richelieu's choice for command in his first and successful Val Telline operation (1624). He was a less suitable choice for the Roman embassy where his hasty temper seriously compromised Richelieu's standing with the Pope and distracted Mazarini from his efforts on Richelieu's behalf.

25 Philippe, count d'Aglié (1604–67), was probably not Christina's first lover. Servien reported the liaison between Philippe and Christina to Mazarini in 1632; he was more relaxed about it than was Richelieu who saw in P. Monod's advice to Philippe, and Cardinal Maurice's interest, a plan to sever the links between Savoy and France. Mazarini was mortified when he received requests from Christina to use his interest to promote relatives of d'Aglié and he realised that damage was being done to French interests. He saw it as a challenge: 'one must flatter cunning people if one cannot get rid of them'.

26 Charles Emmanuel came of age in 1648 and ruled from then till 1675. Close ties with France were ensured by his marriage to Françoise de Valois, Gaston's daughter by his second marriage.

27 Maurice, prince of Savoy (1593–1657) was, like the Cardinal-Infant, an unordained Cardinal. He served for a time, with Bentivoglio, as protector of French interests at Rome, but was displaced by Antonio Barberini and thereafter, like his brother Thomas (1596–1656), served the Habsburgs: he saw them as the more likely to further his ambition to become regent of Savoy.

28 Louis de Nogaret, Cardinal de la Valette (1593–1639) was the soldier-ecclesiastic whom Richelieu entrusted with command of the army in Italy after the death of Créquy. His brother, Bernard de Nogaret de la Valette, after his father's death in 1642, duc d'Epernon (1591–1661), played a leading part in suppressing the *Croquants* in 1637 on behalf of his father, governor or Guienne, but was subsequently disgraced for his alleged incompetence at the siege of Fuenterrabia. He was rehabilitated in 1643. For his intransigence as governor of Guienne during the Fronde, see pp. 150–51.

29 Henri de Lorraine, comte d'Harcourt (1601–66), son of the duc d'Elbeuf, was the only prominent member of the house of Lorraine to be left by Richelieu with a responsible position. He was governor of Touraine. For his significant role during the Fronde, see p. 96.

30 The loss, in 1637, of Breda, the town whose capture in 1625 had marked the

nadir of Dutch fortunes, might seem to have signalled the end of the period when Spain could hope for a favourable military solution.

31 Barbe Avrilot, Mme Acarie (1566–1618), 'la belle Acarie', was the wife of a former Leaguer who maintained her husband's interest in Spain, and was responsible for the introduction into France of the Carmelite order (1604). She was most influential, as a hostess and patron, in the bringing together of devout individuals, notably François de Sales and Bérulle, whose influence was all the stronger for their having this source of contacts. From her religious *salon* Mme Acarie helped give the *dévôts* the characteristics of a party.

32 William Fitch came to Douai as a young man, with a religious vocation, took the name, from his Essex village, of Canfeld, and spent most of his life in Paris, as a Capuchin. 'Master of the masters' in Brémond's phrase, he became teacher, by example and writings, of a generation of mystics and enthusiasts.

33 Antoinette d'Orléans, co-adjutrix of Fontrevault abbey, the greatest but not hitherto the most exemplary in France, undertook the reform of the abbey to the point when her community (those nuns who accepted her reforms) was raised to the status of a new order, the Congregation of Our Lady of Calvary.

6 THE CALL OF FRANCE

1 This episode reveals aspects of papal government which conditioned Mazarin's political style. The Pope was not alone among the more important Italian rulers in seeking to absorb smaller neighbouring principalities. But the occasion was un-timely and the methods ill-judged. The Barberinis took advantage of the Duke of Parma's weak financial position and unwise borrowings to seize his city of Castro. When, however, Urban excommunicated the duke and declared his fiefs forfeited, Tuscany, Modena and Venice rallied to Parma's support. The ensuing war brought devastation to the states of the church. The peace eventually made at Venice, in March 1644, reinstated the duke. The 'War of the Barberini' – as it was significantly called – brought humiliation on the Papacy without corresponding gain to the confederate states. France, with Savoy, and Spain, retained the influence that counted.

2 It has been argued (notably by Henry Kamen) that the notion of decline is misleading because Spain had never risen to the status of a great power on a sound economic basis. It had however achieved a hundred years' political and military ascendancy. Moreover contemporary Spaniards were concerned about 'the *declinación* to which all republics are prone' (Cellorigo, writing in 1600) and saw economic reforms and peace as essential for recovery. Olivarez failed to achieve the first and presided over a period when Spain's military effort was wholly disproportionate to its resources Agrarian distress, the decay of manufactures, a steady decline in population, a falling away both in colonial trade and in bullion receipts from the New World, are some symptoms of 'decline' which were evident before the Catalan and Portuguese revolts advertised them to the world. The Fronde would postpone the hour of reckoning. Spanish soldiers did not over-night lose their skills and discipline. It is important not to exaggerate the extent of 'decline': it is hard to deny that it occurred. For more on this subject, which is so relevant to Mazarin's career, see pp. 259–60

3 Concino Concini, maréchal d'Ancre (?-1617), was the Florentine favourite of Marie de Médicis: his wife, Leonora Galigai, was Marie's confidant. Their attempts to monopolise patronage and, latterly, Concini's efforts to build up

a territorial bloc in the northeast of France outraged their circle of clients and toadies: in particular he antagonised Condé. Concini was assassinated in April 1617; the sixteen-year-old king had connived at the plot and rejoiced at the event. The Concini connection nearly proved fatal to the prospects of Richelieu who had become a minister in the previous year. When Mazarin became *premier ministre*, the Concini precedent hung like a sword of Damocles over his head.

4 Pierre Corneille (1606–84) was matched in France only by Racine as tragic dramatist. Though too popular in *frondeur* circles to be entirely pleasing to Mazarini, he was unwavering in loyalty to crown and country. His elevation of the heroic virtues appealed however to rebels for whom Cornellian *devoir* and *vertu*, as belonging to the realm of private conduct, was entirely compatible with faction.

5 Claude de Mesmes, comte d'Avaux (1595–1650), was employed in diplomatic missions from an early age, like that of 1638, to secure Sweden's continued involvement in the war: he was then described by the German jurist Pufendorf as being 'a man who, when you thought you had caught him, was found to have slipped through your hands'. He did not always enjoy Mazarini's confidence. See also p. 236.

6 For the *Gazette* see also p. 328, no. 15. The *Mercure françois*, founded in 1605, was the official record of the activities and achievements of the crown. Its usefulness was limited by the fact that it only appeared once a year: hence the foundation of the *Gazette*.

7 Walter Montague (1603–77), second son of the earl of Manchester, was a courtier, who first came to France in the embassy sent to fetch the Prince of Wales's fiancée, Henrietta Maria; he spent much of his subsequent life in France on diplomatic business, official or unofficial, acting generally for the English queen. He found in Mazarini a sympathetic listener and agreeable friend. In 1643 he appears to have had an important influence on Anne's decision to keep the Cardinal on her council as the 'complete opposite of Richelieu and the minister most likely to work for peace'.

8 Queen Henrietta Maria (1609–69) was the youngest daughter of Henry IV and Marie de Médicis. She was married to the future Charles I in 1624, and enjoyed, after an uncertain start, a relationship of mutual love and loyalty, rare among royal marriages. By her open adherence to Rome, she aroused the animosity of puritans. She worked resourcefully for Charles after the outbreak of civil war, but her uncompromising attitude towards Parliament had played a significant part in the final breach and his downfall.

9 A Spanish fleet with troops for Flanders appeared in the Channel and was attacked by the Dutch. When the Spanish took refuge in the Downs, Charles tried to use their predicament to secure money from them. The Dutch attacked and won a decisive victory. The effect on Spain's military and economic position was serious.

10 The Nu-pieds were the 'bare-foot' salt panners of Normandy who gave their name to the rising in that province of 1639 (and to its 'general', nicknamed Jean Nu-Pieds). For the details and significance of this revolt see pp. 77–9.

7 CARDINAL MAZARIN

1 Arras, capital of Spanish Artois, about twenty miles northwest of Amiens, would be acquired by treaty (the Pyrenees) at the end of the war with Spain, in 1659. Since Francis I surrendered suzerainty over Artois in 1529 the prov-

ince had been central in French strategic thinking: subsequent events were to show how important it was to secure key forts in the open country north of Paris and create a defensible frontier.

2 Henri II de Bourbon, prince de Condé (1588–1646), was a product of civil wars and the uneasy status of a royal relation. As a young man he showed himself to be as keenly adept at furthering the interests of his cadet Bourbon branch as apparently oblivious to higher claims, those of crown and *patrie*, upon his loyalty. He was a conspirator who could not keep trust with his confederates and a general who would never pay his troops. He tried to ally with the Huguenots, then fought against them, flaunting his piety; he took vast bribes from Marie de Médicis, then denounced her for mis-spending the crown's income; he raged against Henry IV (with reason) for trying to seduce his wife, but was unfaithful himself. The Huguenots, Spain, the States-General, any cause that promised to be serviceable he would make his own. After 1631 he was, however, the king's ally. He consolidated his vast fortune. He arranged, with Richelieu, the marriage of his son, to Richelieu's niece, Mlle de Brézé: such abasement, as it would formerly have seemed to him, is a telling commentary on the changing political balance. He served as general in several campaigns.

3 Henri de Sourdis, archbishop of Bordeaux, was a churchman in the family tradition (his brother was a cardinal) of Gallicanism and royal service. He was a friend of Richelieu and useful to him in several capacities, as ecclesiastical invigilator of his turbulent diocese, at times as admiral or, as at Fuentarrabia, as a soldier; even in more personal ways, as when he directed work on the cardinal's new château of Richelieu.

4 About 120 *intendants* were appointed between 1560 and 1630. During the next decade their use became general. 'War, above all the fiscal demands of war, was to prove the decisive factor in the establishment of the *intendants*' (Bonney). *Intendants de l'armée* (as opposed to those *intendants* who were made responsible for troops in winter quarters in their province) were given specific commissions: typically they were to watch and report on the conduct of the general to whom they were assigned, to provide for the needs of the army in regular ways that would prevent looting and violence, and to act as judicial authority. Their institution did something to mitigate 'la terreur des troupes': their absence from armies operating during the Fronde strengthens the point. For *intendants* generally, see pp. 85–6.

5 Henri de Campion (1613–63) was a Norman nobleman of ancient lineage, one of a number of French men and women in this period who diverted themselves in later years recounting their experiences, in his case as soldier and, reluctantly, drawn in by his brother Alexandre and the duc de Beaufort, conspirator. For his role in the *Importants*, see p. 66.

6 The Union of Arms was a plan devised by Olivarez in 1625 (see pages 321, note 8 and 322, note 12) to secure a military contribution, proportionate to its supposed resources, from each province of the Spanish empire. Intended to provide a common reserve of 140,000 men, it was wrecked on the rocks of privileged separatism.

7 The accession of Philip II to the Portuguese throne in 1580 had never been accepted by the native Braganza family, whose claim to the throne was now re-asserted by John IV, as he became, in December 1640: he ruled until 1656.

8 To which list could be added the Ukraine, where, in 1648, Chmielnicki led a successful revolt against Polish overlords, and Holland, where the young *stadholder* William II died, in 1650, in the throes of a conflict with the authorities

in Holland over foreign policy. Since his inclination was monarchist, this crisis, following the execution of Charles I, can be seen as a reflection of the Great Rebellion in England. Similar connections can be made between other countries which experienced crises and disorders and there were certain prevalent factors, notably the effect of war. However even the ecomomic evidence falls short of what is required to substantiate the once-fashionable theory of a 'General Crisis'. Every country's experience was unique, reflecting local conditions, and is best treated as such. For articles on 'The General Crisis' see bibliography, p. 389. For the influence of English events on the Fronde see p. 138.

9 The general position of European Jewry in the seventeenth century was that communities were strongest in countries where government was weak, notably Poland, or federal and limited, like the United Provinces. Some Jews in Portugal, as in Spain, chose to convert rather than emigrate. *Conversos* found that their financial services were valued and elicited a reluctant tolerance. It was the activity of the Sephardi Jews of Holland in financing Dutch activities in Brazil that most inflamed popular prejudice.

10 Louis de Bourbon, comte de Soissons (1604–41), Louis XIII's cousin, had a record going back to the Chalais conspiracy which ensured that Richelieu kept a wary eye on his activities: as governor of the Dauphiné he was 'assisted' by Marshal Créquy. Had his reckless career not been abruptly ended, he would presumably have been a *frondeur.*

11 Henri de la Tour d'Auvergne, duc de Bouillon (1605–52) was head of one of the greatest Protestant families in Europe. The family estates in the southwest of France (see note 12) were a source of revenue and extensive patronage and the fortress city and principality of Sedan, outside the realm, with his contacts with fellow-Protestants at home and abroad, made him a particularly elusive opponent.

12 Henri de la Tour d'Auvergne, vicomte de Turenne (1611–75) took his title from the *vicomté* of Turenne in Quercy which retained its autonomy and separate representative institutions until 1738. As a young soldier in Italy he had been favourably impressed by Mazarini. Admiration was mutual. Turenne believed that he owed his promotion, in 1643, to the fact that the new minister did not count his Huguenotism against him.

13 The *abbé* Henri Arnauld was sixth son of Antoine Arnauld: he became bishop of Angers and inclined, like the rest of the family, though less militantly to Jansenism.

14 The reader may judge from this example (1632): 'Less than a third of your subjects in the countryside eat regular bread: another third . . . languishes in such lamentable need that some die of hunger while others subsist like animals on acorns, grass and similar stuffs. I have seen these miseries with my own eyes since leaving Paris. . . . May God grant that the outcry from these wretches' hearts . . . will bring heaven's rage upon the head of the Cardinal, sole cause of their misery'.

15 Henri Coiffier de Ruzé, marquis de Cinq Mars, was appointed *Grand Ecuyer de France* at the age of nineteen and proceeded to live up to his familiar name 'Monsieur le Grand' with conceited impropriety – and the consequences described.

16 Marie-Madeleine de Vignerod, dame de Combalet, duchesse d'Aiguillon, Richelieu's niece, benefited from her uncle's affection, in status and wealth: she was a large beneficiary of Richelieu's will, including his château of Rueil. Widowed at eighteen, she was deeply pious. She stayed with Richelieu through-

out his last illness and was consoled by his words: 'Remember that I have loved you more than all the others'. Mazarin's respect for her was based on more than his knowledge of the influence she had over Richelieu: 'She has enough spirit to govern two kingdoms', he wrote.

17 Louis d'Astarac, marquis de Fontrailles, who would later be a *frondeur*, provides a good example of the persistent noble opponent of the cardinals who could be said to be motivated by political concerns, notably opposition to the war against Spain. As Mazarin would by now have learned, intrigue and rebellion were not simply 'de pures questions de personnes'.

8 ANNE, QUEEN MOTHER AND REGENT

1 The palais-Cardinal stood near the Louvre. The original *hôtel* d'Angennes in the rue St Honoré had been enlarged by two wings containing a theatre and, eventually (commissioned just before Richelieu's death) a library. To create a garden, he bought a neighbouring *hôtel* and demolished it, along with a stretch of the city wall. He bequeathed it to the crown. As the palais-Royal it would figure largely in the life of the royal family during the next twenty years.

2 The abbey was finally received by Mazarin, from the duc de Guise, after delays, in 1646. It yielded an estimated 25,000 *livres* a year. Ecclesiastical benefices were vitally important to Mazarin for their bargaining use and as a more or less dependable source of income: by 1648 he would have more than 200,000 *livres* a year income from thirteen benefices. For knowledge of this vital aspect of the Church as property, and its importance for Mazarin, we are indebted to the work of J. A. Bergin: see Bibliography, also pp. 281–2.

3 The elder son of the Prince de Condé, whose title he took in 1646 (see p. 99 and p. 345, n. 23), the duc d'Enghien (1621–86) would be better known as 'le grand Condé': deservedly for his generalship, less so for his political judgement or personal attributes.

4 The *Parlement* of Paris, a leading actor in the ensuing pages, will be referred to simply as *Parlement* to distinguish it from the provincial *parlements*.

5 Augustin Pothier (*d.* 1650) was a protégé of Cardinal de la Rochefoucauld and shared his reforming zeal. That he had succeeded his brother (in 1616) in the diocese of Beauvais is just one indication of the need of such reform. Appointment as *grand aumonier* and close association with politically-minded *dévôts* in Anne's circle gave him a perhaps unrealistic notion of his prospects: he was Mazarin's rival for the cardinalate and was thought of as a possible *premier ministre*.

6 César, duc de Vendôme (1594–1665) was bastard brother to the king (his mother was Gabrielle d'Estrées). Much favoured by his father, he was correspondingly disliked by the young Louis. He grew up with ambitions that could only be satisfied at the expense of his brother's realm. Henry IV's reign would come to be regarded as a time of promise – and he was admired, not least by Louis XIV, for his political skills. A family man of an irregular and callously promiscuous kind however, his legacy was unfortunate.

François, duc de Beaufort (1616–69), Vendôme's son, carried on the family tradition, suffered imprisonment for his part in the *Importants*, but eventually escaped (in 1648); then he offered his services to the Fronde.

7 The *paulette* or *droit annuel*, so called after it was established, in 1604, by Charles Paulet, was an annual premium, calculated at around a sixtieth of the value of an office, which enabled its holder to transmit it to his heirs. It was renewable every nine years, last in 1639. Renewal was usually treated by

government as a way, much resented, of extracting more money for the privilege; renewal time (early 1648) was therefore both a time of opportunity – and of danger – to government. For office-holding in general, see p. 83 and for the *paulette* and the Fronde, pp. 108 and 110.

8　The *noblesse de robe* enjoyed titles of nobility derived from the higher appointments in finance and judiciary. It was only the highest offices, like the Chancellorship, that conferred hereditary nobility; the remainder had titles for life – likely, however, to stay, with the office, in the family. Though the *noblesse d'épée* maintained social pre-eminence, their order was more open (in many cases less ancient in origin) than its representatives liked to claim; meanwhile, with numerous creations (over a thousand between 1550 and 1650 in Normandy alone), together with the virtual monopoly of the *robe* in council (for which they were better trained), the balance of power was tilting towards the *robe*. In Paris, and other great cities, the great families of the *robe* were the true aristocracy.

9　Jean-Jacques Barillon (1601–45), *président* of *Parlement*, died while in prison at Pinerolo. His treatment shows the government at its worst in the handling of office holders; his death provided a martyr for the cause of the more militant.

10　It was allegedly Gaston or Condé who coined the slighting phrase, *Importants*, registering their scorn for the Vendôme faction.

11　Marie de Hautefort was but fourteen, in 1630, when she caught Louis XIII's eye and was drawn into a tempestuous relationship. The king appears to have been less capable of uncomplicated love than of jealousy and self-abasement. For readers of *Mazarin*, the importance of the relationship may be in its humiliating effect on Anne, compelled to receive Marie as lady-in-waiting.

12　To Louise de la Fayette, the king's devotion brought no sustained happiness – but this pure-minded young woman was able to reciprocate in some measure. She brought out the better side of Louis' complicated character: to let his chaste companion go to a monastery was undoubtedly a painful sacrifice to Christian duty – as it may have been for her.

13　A felicitous introduction to the ready pen and shrewd observation of Françoise de Bertaut, Mme de Motteville (1621–89). Her early marriage to a ninety-year-old official left her a young widow. That reveals something about seventeenth-century notions of marriage (see also p. 204) but Anne, first drawn to the girl through her ability (from her half-Spanish father) to speak Spanish, thereafter gained the life-long attachment of her *dame d'honneur* and friend. Motteville's *Mémoires* provide invaluable views of the period: they represent a court view, Anne's view, a woman's view: she could be subjective – indeed the *Mémoires* would be less entertaining if she were not so. But there is a robust note of common-sense throughout her clear account, undertaken in honour of the queen whom she served so loyally; also, as she wrote, 'pour me divertir' and 'pour ma propre satisfaction'.

14　Gédeon Tallemant des Réaux wrote his *Historiettes* in the latter years of Mazarin's ministry, mainly between 1657 and 1661; they are the source of some of the best stories of the period – but not to be relied on except where they receive independent corroboration. Since he appears to have been interested mainly in private lives, loves and quarrels, it could be said that he was the historian the age deserved. As here about Louis XIII he could coin an illuminating phrase: so Gondi 'had gallantry on the brain'.

15　A complete definitive edition of the notebooks, the *carnets*, is awaited. There are difficulties of deciphering and interpretation. In essentials they are known from the work of Cousin and Chéruel (see Bibliography). They cover a period of eight years (1642–50). Accounts of expenses jostle with resumés of reports, and conversations, sketches of projects and concerns about intrigues. Their focus is the court and the queen, suggesting that the busy minister was preparing in brief memoranda, for the next meeting. Besides their value as evidence for the informal ways in which France was governed, Mazarin's preoccupations have a psychological interest. They recall Rochefoucauld's comment on his 'petty views, even in the midst of grand projects'. The example of Asquith comes to mind, playing bridge and flirting in the midst of another great war. Nor did Churchill neglect his black swans at Chartwell in 1940. So it may be unfair to see anything ignoble in these private jottings; they fill out the picture of a statesman resilient under stress, perhaps still capable of enjoying himself, but often, naturally, anxious.

16 For his career see p. 329, n. 22.

17 For his earlier career and friendship with Mazarin see p. 325, n. 10. He had been entrusted by Richelieu with responsibility for watching Gaston and reporting on every suspicious move.

18 Michel Le Tellier, marquis de Barbésieux (1603–85) was to enjoy high office, as secretary of state for war till 1677 and chancellor for forty-two years, till his death; the first decade was one of crisis and disorder, the last appeared to have been a time of fulfilment, power and glory. From 1640 to 1643 he was *intendant* with the army in Lombardy. His career was to benefit from his loyalty to Mazarin and was reinforced by his assiduous attention to the building of his own *clientèle*, but his high reputation is founded on his political and administrative skills.

19 Both those of Catherine de Médicis (1560–63) and Marie de Médicis (1610–15) had been the occasion of factious activities leading to civil wars, highlighting, through the activities of certain magnates and Huguenot rebels, persisting weaknesses of monarchy which were less evident when there was a strong adult king. The influence of both women, and 'regency conditions', lasted beyond the age (thirteen) when the king came formally of age and 'minority' ended.

20 Inadequate statistics, persistent fraud in the compiling of musters and a high rate of desertions make it hard to establish a precise figure. Many soldiers were tied down to garrison duties. Effectives, available for campaign, rarely exceeded 60,000. The nominal figure, according to L. André, would rise to a peak, in 1653, of 120,000; in that exceptional year there were six separate forces in the field: none of them would actually be able to count on as many as 15,000 effectives.

21 By reforming naval administration, improving recruitment, and port facilities and instituting a warship-building programme Richelieu extended the authority of the state in an area hitherto dominated by certain magnates (for example he abolished the feudal office of Admiral and took over responsibility for naval affairs) while creating a navy of some fifty ships capable of challenging the Spanish and earning the respect even of the Dutch and English. While financial necessity made it difficult for Mazarin to maintain effort at this level, his lack of interest in, and consequent neglect of the navy, points to important differences between his priorities and those of Richelieu – or indeed of Colbert, who furthered Richelieu's work.

22 Louis de Bourbon, duc de Mercoeur, later Cardinal de Vendôme (1618–69), younger son of the duc de Vendôme, would provide one of the several sub-plots of the Fronde when he incurred the wrath of Condé and censure of *Parlement* by declaring his wish to marry Laura Mancini – for reasons as much

to do with his inclination as with Mazarin's tactics of 'divide and conquer'. Vendôme *père* secretly backed the match and used it to regain the office of Admiral.

23 In 1626 the first serious plot against Richelieu brought together various aggrieved parties, including Gaston of Orléans.

24 Alexandre de Campion (1610–70), tireless in intrigue against the Cardinals, was the elder brother of Henri, author of the *Mémoires* (see p. 384) which are one of the main sources for the story of the *Importants*.

25 Marie d'Avaujour de Bretagne, duchesse de Montbazon (1612–57), a celebrated beauty, was second wife of Hercule de Rohan, due de Montbazon and was therefore step-mother, though younger, of Mme de Chevreuse. Mme de Motteville was sufficiently aroused from her usual calm appraisal to write, à propos the intriguing *grandes dames* of the Fronde, that women were ordinarily the cause of the greatest disorders in states. Certainly affairs like that arising out of Montbazon's jealous quarrel with the duchesse de Longueville could have a ludicrously disproportionate effect. Condé was furious at the slight to his sister, Beaufort saw in her exile from court a signal to rebel, and Anne and Mazarin spent days trying to resolve the quarrel and limit its damage. Retz wrote of the duchess that 'he had never seen anyone who preserved in vice so little respect for virtue'.

26 Mazarin certainly believed it. In his notebook he described his escape: 'M. Bellegarde has said that he knew that if I had not been in his Highness's carriage M. de Beaufort's assassination plot would have been executed'. Apparently 'forty armed men were waiting for him'.

27 The galleys, providing the main Mediterranean fleet, were also the country's prime penal establishment. His experience as chaplain-general to the galleys (1619–22) was a powerfully formative influence on the young Vincent de Paul.

28 The *cour des aides* was one of the sovereign courts of Paris outside *Parlement*, the others being the *cour des comptes* and the *grand conseil*. Though it had a lower status and its offices were generally less valuable than those in *Parlement*, it was all the more sensitive about its rights. Essentially it dealt with appeals arising out of taxation. The *Aides* and the *Comptes* were therefore in the frontline of resistance to arbitrary financial measures, whether the employment of *intendants* in a fiscal capacity or the introduction of new taxes or manipulation of the *paulette*.

9 THE ADOPTED LAND: POVERTY AND DISORDER

1 Pierre Séguier (1588–1672), *Garde des Sceaux*, 1633–5, Chancellor, 1635–72, the son of one of Henry IV's *fidéles*, was born to high judicial office and enjoyed a distinguished, though (in the Fronde) not unchequered career. His activity in selecting members for special judicial courts and commissions, and acquiescence in the transference of business from *Parlement* courts to the council, made him unpopular with his fellow lawyers.

2 The statesman in Paris whose imagination and interests are still focused sharply on the beloved *pays* of his early life: it is a recurring story in French political life. Note here the power base among family and friends, the *clientèle* that grows around it and – in Richelieu's case – the pride of the nobleman who wishes to be 'considerable' among his neighbours: satisfied by the elevation in status that followed the creation of a *duché–pairie* out of the *seigneurie* of Richelieu. Following extensive purchases, most of his land-holdings were in

Poitou: much of his resources was devoted to the building of his new château and the uniquely ambitious new town of Richelieu.

3 The *élu* was the official staffing the *élection*, the basic unit of fiscal administration for the *taille* which, in *pays d'élections*, approximately two-thirds of the realm and generally those provinces which had belonged longest to the realm, was paid on the basis of income.

4 *Pays d'états* were provinces with Estates, paying the *taille* on the basis of land by a sum periodically agreed between the crown and the commissioners of the Estates. The assessment included some land that was owned by nobles but was *roturière* therefore not covered by the principle of noble exemption. The *taille réelle* was fairer than the *taille personelle* (see above, *élus*), less susceptible to bullying or selective protection by powerful interests – but it yielded considerably less. So ministers periodically tried to impose *élections*. That the main *pays d'états*, Burgundy, Languedoc and Brittany, survived till the Revolution indicates a fundamental weakness in government; in the seventeenth century, more significantly, the 'short-termism' expressed typically in compromise solutions (a province kept its privileges in return for a larger payment) was typical of a regime under financial pressure.

5 One of the nine provincial *parlements*, varying in importance with the size of the province, each with jealously guarded jurisdiction, rights and powers and its own *élite* of *noblesse de robe*.

6 For the nature of *clientèles*: see also pp. 43 and 311. The work of J. Bergin (see bibliography) has altered and filled out our view of Richelieu, in particular the means by which he acquired wealth and power. The skills required of a man bent on extending his connections in the ecclesiastical and secular worlds, were those of the businessman which the *premier ministre* had to be. Mazarin did not have Richelieu's opportunities; his ascent is all the more remarkable.

7 It is possible to check contemporary estimates of population by other data, such as tax returns and registers of baptism and burials; also by reference to later figures derived from census returns and by extrapolation from other evidence. The European population was young, because of natural fertility and low because of high mortality.

8 A woman who managed to reach the end of her fertile period, say forty-five, had normally witnessed the death of both her parents, the majority of her brothers and sisters, more than half her children. She would often be a widow. Death was familiar: without means of subduing pain, terminal illnesses could also be ghastly. Accounts of Anne of Austria's last days, for example, or indeed Mazarin's, illustrate that rank gave no immunity. Such observations should affect judgements about seventeenth-century morality, sexuality and attitudes towards life. For more about these subjects see, for example, the work of Mandrou and, for the lot of women in particular, Wendy Gibson (see bibliography).

9 A reasonable description (Mandrou's) in view of the disorders of the medical *ancien régime*. Medical practice was a mixture of pedantic scholarship derived from revered tradition, primitive, though not always contemptible psychology, traditional and often worthless prescriptions. The common people continued to rely, perhaps sensibly, on time-honoured potions and remedies, herbs and spells. Overcrowding within old town walls created ideal conditions for disease, streets were latrines, water was polluted, wells unsafe; for the peasant, when families slept on straw that was rarely changed and ate with their fingers or unwashed knives and spoons, light and air were less important than warmth.

Lice and fleas abounded. Rickety legs, hunched backs and awkward limps, pockmarked faces, defective eyesight, congenital idiocy, witnessed respectively to malnutrition, crude methods of midwifery, the common ravages of smallpox, inherited damage from syphilis or the effect of in-breeding. Typhus, spread by lice, typhoid and dysentery, by infected water, were common killers among the poor – notably in army encampments. The plague still reminded people, in periodic visitations, that it was the deadliest killer of all.

10 The history of provinces cannot be explained by geography, common language, or even race: the examples respectively of Burgundy, Flanders and Brittany show this. Nor did acquisition mean assimilation. In the case of Brittany the process began with the marriage, first of Charles VIII, then Louis XII, to Anne of Brittany; the union only dates formally from 1532. The Breton Estates remained vigorous, the *noblesse*, who dominated the Estates, were as vociferous in defence of their rights as they were numerous, generally poor, and risible to the non-Breton world. The language of the ordinary Bretons was unintelligible to the Parisian official (he would find difficulty with the *patois* in other provinces too).

11 Much of this book is necessarily concerned with Paris. Angers has been chosen to represent a city of middle size. Rouen, also affected by the Fronde, exhibits features of the provincial capital which has a *parlement*, a substantial body of officials, and a cherished tradition of autonomy. Like Dijon or Bordeaux it was *sui generis*. It had close trading links with Paris along the line of the Seine. That river led, by way of le Havre, to the shipping lanes of an expanding world. With a quayside *bourse* and a growing stake in international finance, Rouen was sufficiently proud to resist attempts to milk its wealth through the creation of new courts and venal posts; yet with its own recent experience of the Nu-Pieds, it would be aware of the risk of being associated with revolt. The history of Rouen helps us understand both why the Fronde was dangerous to the crown, and why it failed.

12 For the example of Alsace and its treatment in the peace of Westphalia, see pp. 245–6.

13 Maximilien de Béthune, marquis de Rosny, duc de Sully (1650–41), Huguenot, friend and fellow warrior of Henry IV, became his chief and most effective minister. Holding the offices of *surintendant, surintendant des bâtiments, surintendant des fortifications* and *grand voyeur* (having responsibility for roads, bridges and canals), he came to enjoy, until his master's death and his own downfall, a degree of power over the economy which was unequalled until the ministry of Colbert.

14 The exhaustive study of Goubert (see bibliography) treats of this *pays* in northern France, a country of rolling open plains given almost entirely to wheat, exhibiting the tendency towards dominance by the few substantial peasants – *laboureurs* – and the pauperisation of the growing number of small proprietors or landless.

15 Citing 'the weight of taxation' and 'the oppression of the tax collectors' as the main cause, a member of the Castilian *cortes* wrote in 1621: 'Numerous places have become depopulated and disappeared from the map, in some provinces as many as fifty or sixty.'

16 *Les Misères de Guerre* of Jacques Callot (*c.* 1594–1635) are among the best known of his prodigious output of engravings.

17 A sign of this deflation is the general fall in interest rates, noted in French provinces as well as in Holland and England, where sophisticated financial systems would be more responsive to external influences. Meuvret (see

bibliography) argues that the general deflation was particularly difficult for the French economy because French exports, still mainly grain, wine, salt and linen, with various fabrics of medium quality like muslins and serges, did not enjoy high profit margins. Their export was based largely on the differences between French and Spanish prices. With the slowing down of the flow of precious metals, this difference shrank to insignificance. The Spanish did not gain; the Dutch did. France was to suffer for another fifty years a monetary famine.

18 The feudal regime has to be considered in the context of a wide variety of agricultural rents. A common form was that of *métayage*, favoured by the urban landowner: in return for his loan of seed and stock he received a proportion of the share-cropper's produce. But agrarian feudalism, though so far removed from the mediaeval military imperatives, still had power to inculcate a sense of mutual dependence: it influenced noble attitudes that were displayed, sometimes in extreme ways, during the Fronde. It also acted as a brake on agricultural improvement, encouraging conservative methods and inhibiting investment. Around 20 per cent of income was the average toll of feudal, church and royal taxes on the peasant holding.

A *seigneurie* was a property and area of jurisdiction of an individual or a corporate body: typically it was identical in extent with the village. A *seigneur* could be layman or churchman, noble or commoner. The *seigneurie* had two parts. The domain usually comprised the dwelling, not necessarily an imposing *château*, the home farm and a park, a chapel and a mill. The other, larger half was composed of the *censives*, tenures. The peasants who worked these lands, often without oversight but normally in accordance with communal arrangements, paid dues which varied in bewildering fashion even within the two-thirds of France, central and northern, in which some kind of feudal regime obtained. The advantage of the *seigneur* was all the stronger when justice was represented by the seigneurial court. There were also problems involved in control and exploitation. Feudal dues could supply a *seigneur*, particularly in Burgundy or Brittany, with a sufficient livelihood, and could be a sound business proposition for a landowner prepared to be thorough and ruthless. But they were often barely worth the effort to collect or the ill-will they engendered.

In much of southern and some of central France there persisted 'allodial' tenures, free of feudal obligation. There the familiar cry 'No lord without title' had the force of law. In eastern France, where German influences were strong, there survived forms of serfdom, affecting as many as a million peasants, clearly profitable to the landowner.

Tithe, its principles and terms first defined in the capitularies of Charlemagne, was a widely varying amount, anything between three and ten per cent, resented mainly when the *curé* was absent or when it went to a big tithe-owner, bishop, abbot or even noble layman – and not to his *vicaire*.

19 'The most necessary of all the footstuffs that God in his goodness created for man's sustenance' stated Chomel's dictionary (1718). It was a common practice, before cutting a new loaf, to make a cross on it with the point of a knife. Since bread was the main component of diet for all but the wealthiest, the storage and distribution of flour were at the heart of economic activity in village and town. The corn market was always close to the town hall; prices of bread were fixed in relation to grain prices in the market; millers, often suspected of cheating, and bakers, were always prominent in the public mind. So historians look for causes of riots and risings in the market price of flour

and measure the public temper by the incidence of attacks on bakers' shops. For the price of bread and the Fronde, see p. 118.

20 Omer Talon (1595–1652) figures in the ensuing pages – both as a leading protagonist and as the author of one of the *mémoires* on which the narrative is based.

21 Around Dijon for example, most of the land within twenty miles of the city was owned by prominent citizens: wine merchants and *parlementaires* being to the fore in the process of acquisition. Roupnel (see bibliography) says that land in thirty-two villages in the Dijonnais was owned almost exclusively by urban families.

22 Henri, duc de Montmorency (1535–1632), *maréchal de France*, '*premier baron chrétien*' in customary usage, was regarded as the most important nobleman in France, apart from those of the blood royal. His family had provided governors of Languedoc since 1525: his trial and execution were a striking demonstration of political will, and of the resolve of the king.

23 In 1648–9 governor Alais' demands for supplies for his troops led to a civil war within the province in which supporters of the governor were equally matched by those of the *parlement*. See pp. 149–50.

24 John Breval, in 1738.

25 The *gabelle*, or salt tax, was levied at different rates in five areas, a sixth being exempt. *Pays de grandes gabelles* were mainly in the northern and central provinces. There the salt was taken to royal warehouses, where it was taxed before it could be sold – every household was required to buy salt. For all its anomalies, the cost of its collection and the large smuggling industry that it fostered, the tax produced a steady revenue, around three million *livres* a year. The Nu-Pieds revolt in Normandy started with rumours of an extension of the *gabelle* to this hitherto exempt province. There was also a serious revolt, anticipating several of the issues of the Fronde, in Poitiers in 1642.

26 A *traitant* was a financier, one who made a treaty, or contract with the crown to raise certain taxes or sell certain offices. Because of the insistence of *traitants*, for their own security, on the crown's registering such agreements in the courts, and the courts' reluctance to do so, *les affaires extraordinaires* (methods of raising money beyond the customary direct or indirect taxes) became the focus of political controversy.

27 The phrase is Y. M. Bercé's whose *History of Peasant Revolts* (see bibliography) is essential reading for understanding the social background to government in this period. Emphasis has tended to be on the violence of rebels like the *croquants*: it has to be balanced by the necessarily forceful measures of government. The levying of taxation was a quasi-military operation.

28 Jacques de Caumont, duc de la Force (1588–1621) was head of a leading Huguenot family and governor of Béarn until he joined Rohan's unsuccessful rising in protest against the forced restoration of Catholicism in Béarn. His subsequent career illustrates both the danger such a man posed to the crown and the way it could be dealt with. In 1622 he traded loyalty for a marshal's baton: after another flirtation with revolt, in 1627–8, he offered his sword to the crown, and was rewarded by a peerage. He was happier, as a Huguenot, fighting Spaniards than fellow-Frenchmen – though prepared to fight 'this *canaille*', rebelling against their natural masters. Richelieu's foreign policy, in some respects so divisive, made choice simpler for men like la Force. But he might have behaved differently if Richelieu's attack on la Rochelle had failed. Like others, even Turenne, he should be judged in the context of the Thirty

Years War: mercenary, professional, responsive to appeals to serve the state only when it was strong.

29 Antoine de Puy, sieur de la Mothe la Forêt, was one of the few nobles who played a prominent part in any popular rising of this century – whereas so many were prepared to fight behind a Montmorency or la Rochefoucauld. He seems to have been able and honourable. Somehow discipline was imposed, a sense of common purpose instilled.

30 *Ban et arrière-ban* was the traditional proclamation to muster the nobility to the military service which was the duty for which, theoretically, they had the privilege of exemption from the *taille*. Such proclamations were now used as a way of taxing nobles by requiring them to provide for substitutes.

31 As by Cromwell in Ireland, the 'massacres' of the garrisons at Drogheda and Wexford (September and October, 1649) followed, in the first case, his deliberate decision, following the military convention of the day concerning garrisons who continued to resist after a breach had been made, and in the second, troops running wild after a furious and hotly contested assault.

32 There had never been regular meetings of the States-General. This body representing the three Estates of the realm. Clergy, nobility and commons, did not take its eventual form till the fifteenth century. Before 1614–15, its last meeting before the Revolution, it had met in 1484, 1560, 1576 and 1588. It was therefore associated, in the minds of seventeenth-century Frenchmen, with times of disorder and with the spirit of faction. It failed to secure a right to meet regularly, let alone exert any control over taxation or other aspects of policy.

33 In 1576, local organisations of Catholic noblemen coalesced into a Holy League. Thereafter dissolved, it was re-formed in 1584 under Henri duc de Guise and became an effective force, like that of Calvinism, because of the combination of religious zeal, rancour, inspired by fear, towards rivals, social discontents and political ambitions. After the assassination of Henry III in 1589 and accession of Henry IV it was the mainstay of opposition to the 'heretic' king. In Paris it was bourgeois in leadership, with a radical fringe, opposed not only to nobles but also to *Parlement*. After Henry's recovery of Paris and conversion to Roman Catholicism the League disintegrated but left traces in individual careers and in dévôt attitudes.

10 PUBLIC FINANCE, PRIVATE ENTERPRISE

1 François Paumier, in a remonstrance to the king in 1650, affirmed that the clergy of France owned half the land in the realm; subsequent estimates varied between a third and a fifth. It was undoubtedly wealthy – yet many *curés* lived on a pittance. For the Church it was argued that its property was held in mortmain, therefore inalienable: endowments had been given for the purposes of the Church. The Church was, moreover, an Estate, the first in the realm, as was acknowledged in royal pronouncements and in the proceedings of provincial Estates and the Estates-General. The regularly opposed position, that of ministers, was that, given chronic 'necessities' and the special conditions of war, the Church should contribute generously to meet the needs of the crown. The accepted compromise took the form of a periodic grant, known euphemistically as *don gratuit*, and decided at the meetings of the Assembly of the Clergy, held at regular intervals, on average every five years. The Assembly's proceedings were usually complicated by the Gallican issue (see p. 327, n. 5). The session of 1641 was unusually acrimonious, reflecting

the crown's desperate need for money: it lasted for a year before a compromise sum was accepted.

2 Leading the western world in banking, broking and insurance, reflecting the dominance of the United Provinces in international trade, Amsterdam provided the money market for states whether friendly or hostile.

3 The right was established in 1439 by Charles VII.

4 The chancellor presided over the *conseil d'état et des finances*. Like Richelieu before him, Mazarin did not attend the council though he would be informed of its decisions and they would be made in the context of strategies discussed in the *conseil d'en haut*.

5 For details see p. 341

6 Since 1577 *trésoriers* manned the *bureaux des finances*, with responsibility mainly, as assessors and accountants, for *receveurs des tailles*, the royal domain and funding of public works (The *élections*, by contrast, functioned mainly as law courts, judging disputes which could be referred to the *cour des aides*). With the increasing use of *intendants* in a fiscal role, that of the *trésoriers* declined. After a brief recovery during the Fronde (see p. 133) they lapsed into genteel obsolescence. The process is one of several by which the advance in government, the absolutist trend, can be measured. The magisterial work of J. P. Charmeil, *Les Trésoriers de France à l'Epoque de la Fronde* (1964) provides an approach to the whole world of finance and government.

7 For the *paulette*, see pp. 334–5, n. 7. The average receipts from the *droit annuel* during Mazarin's ministry were two million *livres*. Even that has to be set against the loss of taxes owing to exemption. Government had only three realistic options. One, the improvident, was to go on creating offices for the sake of the capital sums: the market was saturated, values had levelled and there was little room or demand for more. Two, politically risky, but adopted nonetheless, was to withhold salaries or pay only a fraction. Three, a dangerous resort, was to suspend renewal of the *paulette* as preliminary to raising the terms. Another alternative could not be contemplated until government was stronger: the abolition of certain offices, Colbert estimated, in 1661, that there were 45,780 offices, representing a capital of 419,630,842 *livres*, costing 8,346,847 *livres* a year in salaries. He managed to abolish some – but by the mid-seventies he was creating more.

8 The *sol pour livre* (a twentieth) was introduced following the withdrawal of the *Aisés* which, being in effect forced contributions from the 'well-to-do', were provokingly re-distributive in effect and aroused merchants and officials to make common cause. (Typically, they were eventually validated by *Parlement*, in 1644, on condition that they were levied only on merchants and financiers). The excise was more successful but no less hated. For example butchers, who were to the forefront in riots at Troyes and elsewhere, resented paying the tax on livestock entering the town. Some *intendants*, already burdened with supervision of the *taille*, reported that it was impossible to enforce the tax. Its withdrawal of the tax after Richelieu's death indicated the weakness of government in the face of determined urban resistance. Envisaging a total royal income of 58 million, Richelieu proposed, in the event of peace, that the *taille* should be abolished, to be replaced by an extended *gabelle* and the new sales tax of 5 per cent. Even under near-intolerable pressure Richelieu could think clearly, boldly – if perhaps unrealistically – and about the future.

9 For the system, the implications and the obstacles to change, see p. 338, n. 4

10 He called it 'a disorder which is part of the order of the state'.

11 This was becoming a sinecure. It conferred noble status; the privilege became

less valuable when, in the early years of Mazarin's ministry it was extended to most of the offices within the Parisian sovereign courts.

12 The 'extraordinary' taxes were raised by way of *traités*, the contractors undertaking to raise an agreed sum in return for a fixed rate of interest. For their role in the financial ministry of Fouquet and the growing use of special accounts, see p. 272–3

13 There was corruption at every level, from local officials to ministers like Séguier: his parish of Sully, to the disgust of the local *intendant*, Fortia, had its taxes halved in the years 1659–61.

11 PREMIER MINISTRE

1 See p. 337, n. 1.

2 If one man had to be chosen, with one book and, in it, one assertion, as prophet, foundation and text of absolutism, then it would be Jean Bodin (1530–96), his *République*, and its central idea, that there has to be a single authority in the state in which are united the legislative, executive and judicial powers: 'the principal mark of sovereign majesty and absolute power is essentially the right to impose laws on subjects, generally without their consent'. His conception of sovereign authority was however qualified, both by subject rights, those of individuals and of corporate bodies, and the realities of political life.

3 Etienne d'Aligre (1560–1635) was appointed *garde des sceaux* in January 1624 following the dismissal of Brûlart de Sillery: after the latter's death in October 1624 he became chancellor. He lost the Seals and had to retire to his estate in disgrace after a weak repudiation of royal policy towards Gaston was interpreted by the king as indicating favour to that wayward prince. He continued to call himself chancellor while Marillac, his successor as *garde des sceaux*, performed the main duties of the office. His son was also to become chancellor. Much is known about this family of servants of the Bourbon state from D. J. Sturdy's *The d'Aligres de la Rivière* (1986).

4 These were the *conseil des dépêches*, the *conseil privé* and the *conseil d'état et des finances*. The latter became narrower in its functions during this period, coming, after the Fronde, to deal only with finance, its offshoot, the *conseil privé*, hearing judicial appeals, and the *conseil des dépêches* taking over domestic affairs, with the four secretaries of state, each responsible for a group of provinces, hearing reports from the provinces. It was a slowly evolving process, with only a temporary break during the Fronde: continuity was provided by the overlapping of personnel in the councils. The supreme council, the forum for all important decisions, necessarily co-existing until 1651 with the regency council, with its small group of ministers working with Mazarin and the sovereign, was the *conseil en haut*: less formal than its title would suggest, it did not have official records and would meet *ad hoc*, as well as on a regular basis wherever the court happened to be. When the king was on campaign or other expeditions, as in the late fifties, a room was designated as a *salle de conseil d'état du roi* and laws were then verified in a ceremony known as the Audience of the Seal. Two secretaries of state were entrusted with the *cachet* (small seal) for the king's commands.

5 Richelieu had a full file of intercepted correspondence between Anne, Philip IV, the Cardinal-Infant, Mirabel, Mme de Fargis and Mme de Chevreuse. In August 1637 he ordered a search of her private chamber at Val-de-Grâce. Séguier was also responsible for the questioning of the mother superior and

nuns. Anne was compelled however to admit the authenticity of the Cardinal's documents: the affair was too humiliating for her to forgive or forget – even if she had not had the disgraced La Porte at hand to fuel her resentment. See also p. 255, n. 7

6. Charles, marquis and duc de la Vieuville (?–1653) was a *surintendant des finances*, 1623–4, but ousted by Richelieu whom he had been compelled to allow into the council as the price for the support of Marie de Médicis. For his recall to be *surintendant* during the Fronde, see p. 190

7 The word denotes a close companion, of either sex, whose position of influence, not necessarily translated into political power (as was Buckingham's, but not Louis XIII's friend St Simon's), was derived from friendship. Richelieu gained a certain objectivity, and freedom of action, from his distance from the always respectful king – but not peace of mind. For Lloyd Moote's valuable essay on the subject see bibliography.

8 Not merely the confessor but the *dévôt* group around him who might use him as their means of touching the royal conscience. Anne needed all her determination to stand by her commitment to Mazarin against the objections of Vincent de Paul, or Carmelite Mother Maria.

9 Jean-François Paul de Gondi (1613–79), Cardinal de Retz, was the son of Vincent de Paul's patron, general of the galleys and latterly devout Oratorian, Philippe-Emmanuel de Gondi, nephew of (and co-adjuteur to) Jean-Francois, archbishop of Paris. As will appear, he played an important part in Mazarin's career. Ultimately however his *Mémoires* would secure him a greater place in literature than his intrigues would achieve in political history.

10 Since, as Dent makes clear (see bibliography), his total recognisable clientage of 141 includes nobles, churchmen and others who also had 'financial uses', it is hard to be precise. Le Tellier proved an apt pupil of Mazarin in this respect. Approximately a third of all the important administrative commissions issued by the Le Telliers, father and son, between 1643 and 1691, went to their relatives. It is worth bearing in mind Kettering's judgement (see bibliography) concerning such patronage. With its informal staff of brokers in Paris and the provinces, it was 'a benign mechanism holding together an essentially unstable polity'.

11 It had several distinct phases. First, before Mazarin came to power, when Gaston treated him with a sometimes patronising geniality. Second, when, as chief minister, Mazarin was perceived by the touchy prince to be a rival or threat – but to be tolerated out of loyalty to the young king. Third, after Gaston had thrown in his lot with the princes, vehement opposition. Fourth, after the defeat of the Fronde, ungracious acquiescence.

12 De la Rochefoucauld, for example, was to look back regretfully to heady days, with expectations of a more liberal regime, appropriate to aristocratic expectations. Retz did not exaggerate more than usual when he wrote of the start of the Regency: 'all exiles were recalled, all prisoners set at liberty; all those who had lost their offices had them restored; every favour was available; no request refused.'

12 ROYAL ABSOLUTISM: THEORIES AND TRADITIONS

1 The *Académie française* and the *Gazette* (see p. 328, n. 15) were given leading roles in Richelieu's campaign to train the French mind in absolutist principles. In the *Académie*, for example, some of his *créatures* were employed to revise his speeches, some to write pamphlets. Mazarin at first neglected this aspect

of policy and suffered for it. The keen engagement of the printers of Paris in the *Mazarinades* was not however only due to benign neglect on his part. It also represents a reaction to Richelieu's use of the press. He had angered the influential Corporation of Printers and Booksellers by granting Renaudot his monopoly (see p. 331, n. 6). By 1644 Renaudot was running four presses. If the frustrated printers could not benefit from official patronage they would be all the keener to exploit the hunger for unofficial news and views. For the *Mazarinades*, see p. 181–2

2 For the work of Parker, Bergin, Beik, Kettering, *et al.*, see bibliography.

3 The career of Cardin le Bret (1558–1665), author of *De la souveraineté du Roy* (1632) and 'the greatest political theorist of his generation' (Bonney), shows us the evolution of absolutism in one long life-time. He was *avocat-général* in the *cour des aides* of Paris, then in the *Parlement*. He conducted the prosecution of Leonora Concini. In 1624–5 he served as *intendant* at Châlons to investigate the conduct of the duc le Lorraine and there invoked the principle of the inalienability of the royal domain. He was later commissioner to the Estates of Brittany and there enunciated a fundamental principle: privileges were held 'purely out of the great liberality of our kings'. In 1632 he became *premier président* in the new *parlement* of Metz. He believed that the sovereign courts must yield before the supremacy of the council. Subsequent employment in the trials of Marillac and the duc de la Valette would only have confirmed that view. It was to be a central issue in the Fronde.

4 J. L. Guez de Balzac (1597–1654) author of *Le Prince* (1631), wrote memorably about the restoration of France after the civil wars: 'No longer are the French the enemies of their country, idle in the service of their prince and scorned by other nations. Behind their faces I see other men; in the same realm another state.' That represents the aspirations of *bons français* and the sense of achievement of those who found fulfilment in royal service.

5 Daniel de Priézac's *Vindiciae Gallicae adversus Alexandrum Patricium Armacanum theologum* (1638) is described by Church as 'one of the most valuable studies of reason of state to be published with Richelieu's sanction during the later years of his tenure of power' (see Bibliography).

6 René Descartes (1596–1650), author of *Discours de la Méthode* (1637) was the most influential French thinker of his day. The method expounded was one of doubt: all was uncertain until established by reasoning from self-evident propositions, on principles analogous to those of geometry. It was serviceable in all areas of study. There was a mechanistic model for all things. It was significant, not only for scholarship but for Richelieu's France, that he wrote in French rather than in the customary Latin.

7 Bernard de Fontenelle (1657–1757) was a nephew of Corneille, but far removed from the heroic mood which, to him, was simply bombast. His philosophy was based on two things: 'first that we have inquiring minds, second that we have very short sight'.

8 Jérôme Bignon, humanist, was one of a group of talented bourgeois who bridged the gap between intellectual society and government, sought advancement in royal service and brought to it the intelligent devotion that did much to make absolutist principles respectable. As junior *avocat-général* he was present in *Parlement* in January 1648 when his senior, Talon, made his celebrated protest (see pp. 109–10). He was concerned about the precedents created by *Parlement's* resistance because he expected a rough royal response, then a public commotion.

9 Jacques-Bénigne Bossuet (1627–1704), theologian, historian, political philo-

sopher, tutor to the Dauphin and eloquent preacher, served God in a spirit of reasoned devotion, his king with a fervour of hyperbole that at times sounds strained. He became the greatest luminary of Versailles – yet preserved his integrity.

10 Clovis, Frankish chieftain (481–511), was baptised in 496 by St Rémy at Rheims, before making his capital in the defensible island in the Seine that was the original Paris. 'Magnus et pugnator egregius' (Gregory), he stood for conquest, piety and, according to later interpretation, the integrity of the Frankish state. Hincmar of Rheims first revealed the existence of the holy ampulla, that renewable source of spiritual energy, which was to be such a potent symbol of divine favour towards the kings of France. For Louis XIV's coronation, see pp. 205–06.

11 Marc Bloch's classic, *Les Rois thaumaturges* (1924), illustrates the way in which a gifted historian can illuminate periods, institutions, *moeurs* and *mentalités* through the study of what might seem to be a limited theme.

12 From Henri du Boys, *De l'origine et l'autorité des Roys* (1604).

13 The leading representative and voice of the *bons français*, those who followed in the *politique* tradition of putting country before creed, was François Fancan, canon of St Germain l'Auxerrois. His allegory, *France Mourante* (1623), written on behalf of Richelieu, made a powerful case for the re-alignment of foreign policy – against Spain.

14 The Huguenot Henry of Navarre, who had inherited the throne in 1589, fought to secure it against rivals of the house of Guise, and Spain, under the severe handicap of appearing to be a *chef de parti* until his conversion, in 1593. The suggestion that his motivation was more political than religious provided arguments for *dévôts* who mistrusted his foreign policy.

15 After the Day of Dupes, de Morgues, hitherto a partisan of Richelieu, turned bitterly against him. From Marie's exiled court at Brussels he indulged in forms of verbal assassination which set the tone for the later *Mazarinades*. The following is typical: 'Do not permit a puny man, sick in body and mind, to tyrannise over the minds and bodies of so many healthy persons, nor an apostate friar, his chief adviser, to treat you as galley slaves. Cast away these two evil instruments.'

16 See Jansen, p. 318, n. 4 and Jansenism, pp. 292–4.

17 'A war is just', wrote Priézac, when the intention that causes it to be undertaken is just'.

18 The *Mémoires* represent Richelieu's thinking, even if not invariably penned at his dictation: his secretaries would have been careful not to misrepresent him. They comprise a chronological miscellany, with supporting documents and letters. Under God and his lieutenant the king, the minister is seen guiding the realm through all dangers. All who oppose him are enemies of the state. The *Testament* conveys Richelieu's deeper thoughts about country and ministry.

19 The political implications of a corpus of law which had evolved originally to suit the purposes of autocratic emperors are conveyed in the much-quoted maxim: *quod principi placet legis vigorem habet*.

20 For its composition and functions, see also pp. 59–60.

21 Charles Loyseau (1564–1627), more jurist than political philosopher, conveys a static view of the categories of French society. He throws valuable light however on the principles and psychology of office-holding.

22 This arbitrary court was used for the trial of political prisoners. Its creation

in 1631 was a test case for *Parlement*, which resisted registration for several months.
23 Claire-Clémence Brézé: for details of this significant union see p. 99.
24 As the Cardinal's nieces were called.
25 His mystical faith, and penchant for order, are revealed by this work in which he advocated the practice of the presence of God. Whether his settling of accounts with God or heartfelt statement of what he felt he had neglected in his busy life – it is a wonderful accomplishment when it is considered what else occupied him in these years, 1636–9.

13 CLOUDY SKIES

1 The words are inscribed on a fountain at Richelieu's château at Rueil.
2 As in the Auvergne where, in 1636, *intendant* Mesgrigny reported to Séguier that there was 'a great league, from a number of parishes, of armed men'. Several tax officials were murdered there.
3 *Intendants* like de Heere could now rely on effective sanctions. In July 1643, 'tax rebellion' was declared *lèse-majesté*, treason. *Intendants* were to prosecute not only those participating in a revolt but those officials aiding and abetting. They could employ all necessary force. In 1643 de Heere was reporting rumour-mongering, disobedience and connivance from 'persons of quality'. In 1645 he reported quiet: 'everything is in a good state in this *généralité*. It seems that the tougher policy worked.
4 For one such affair, see p. 165.
5 The eloquent Talon (see p. 109, n. 10 and p. 346, n. 8) was expected, as senior of the two *avocats-généraux*, to fulfil several roles: authoritative source of legal judgements, reader of royal messages, interpreter of *Parlement* to the crown, and of the crown to *Parlement*. He had objected to Louis XIII's use of the *lit de justice* as a weapon to enforce royal commands. In his view it should be an opportunity for the king to hear his judges' opinions.
6 Matthieu Molé, sieur de Champlâtreux (1584–1656), was already a veteran of *Parlement*, where he had first sat in 1606. 'No procedural thicket was unknown to him' (Ranum). He would need all his experience and wisdom in the forthcoming conflicts between the crown and *Parlement*. Before he accepted and bought the office of *premier président* (the most expensive as it was the most prestigious of judicial offices) he had refused Louis XIII's offer of the joint *surintendance*. He was then *procureur-général*. It was an early indication of where his loyalties lay.
7 The *châtelet* was the tribunal of the *prévôte* and *vicomté* of Paris, immediately subordinate to *Parlement*. The *prévôt* (not to be confused with *prévôt des marchands*) had rank after the *premier président* and his court had jurisdiction for certain cases over the whole of France.
8 The *toisé* commotion saw the first appearance of the flags which, with other emblems, scarves, badges and so on were to characterise popular action during the Fronde. To Molé's disapproval the mob brandished a flag, 'formé d'un baton auquel ils avoient attaché un mouchoir'.
9 The three senior chambers had to decide whether a plenary session should be held. It would be attended by four *maîtres des requêtes* beside honorary councillors and *ducs et pairs*. During a plenary session, debate was initiated by the *gens du roi*: they were followed by senior judges. So a balance was achieved between experience and the kind of protest which could be expected from younger judges when there was a controversial issue.

10 For the man see p. 350, n. 12.
11 'Perfect' was hereditary nobility. The offer offended lesser officials who at the same time were losing immunities – like that from payment of the *gabelle* – by royal decree.
12 The 'rent' was in effect a fine, equivalent to a year's rent.
13 The quasi-military body charged with the maintenance of law and order: a police with a very top-heavy bureaucratic structure.
14 Forty thousand beggars was an informed contemporary estimate.

14 THE GATHERING STORM

1 Philippe de Champaigne (1602–74) was appointed painter to Marie de Médicis in 1628: the connection surprises since the queen mother is usually associated with the florid representations of Rubens in a style far removed from Champaigne's austere version of the Baroque. His portraits of Cardinal Richelieu, whose favourite painter he was (not however Mazarin's) use Van Dyck's and Rubens's heroic pose but in robes modelled on the lines of classical sculpture. Champaigne was attracted by Jansenism: Port Royal supplied some of his subjects; its ideals permeate his later work.
2 No less effective for all that. Anne was moved to tears by his comparison of France to the kingdoms of the Medes and Persians and his harrowing accounts of the condition of the people.
3 At least they would be aware of falling dues and rents from their country estates.
4 For a biographical note see p. 348, n. 6.
5 See also p. 217, n. 18 and p. 379, n. 11.
6 For the circumstances see p. 286.
7 With Pierre Broussel's age and his popular reputation, has gone the idea that the councillor was somewhat simple. The evidence of debates and his subsequent conduct during the Fronde show him to have been a sound lawyer and tactician. More than most he represented the valid causes obscured by the frivolity and self-interest of other *frondeurs*.
8 During the regency, royal appointments to the council, which enabled a man, in theory, to attend the lesser councils, were a way of gaining public support: there were thirty-one in 1624, sixty-three in 1640, one hundred and twenty-two in 1644. Séguier lamented 'the great confusion and disorder' when 'every day produces a new councillor of state'. It did not even have the desired effect of gaining reliable adherents. Semester arrangements only produced discontent.
9 For the circumstances and effects of the treaty of Münster see p. 242.
10 Commonly named after the fisherman who led his followers in an orgy of violence, the revolt was given coherence by the lawyer Genonino, whose demands for parity with the nobles in municipal government were to have echoes elsewhere, and notably in Bordeaux, in the rising of the *Ormée* (see pp. 203ff).
11 On 30 January, after a trial by special court, whose jurisdiction he refused to accept, Charles was executed outside the Banqueting Hall of the Palace of Whitehall. In his scaffold speech he said he 'did not believe the happiness of people lay in sharing government'. When the executioner struck, an onlooker wrote, 'there was such a grone by the thousands there present as I never heard before and desire I may never hear again'. The 'grone' and the unprecedented circulation of *Eikon Basilike* (fifty editions in a year, many of

them translations) represent the reaction at home and abroad. Nowhere, as Knachel shows, in his important book, *England and the Fronde* (see bibliography) was the shock felt more strongly than in France.

12 Olivier Lefèvre d'Ormesson (1616–86), son of André d'Ormesson, here referred to, like him a long-serving councillor and, periodically, *intendant*, wrote a journal which provides a commentary on the events of the Fronde from a relatively objective viewpoint. He would suffer later from his refusal to subordinate his integrity as a lawyer to the demands of political justice. Appointed *rapporteur* in the trial of Fouquet, which entailed the duty of summing up before judgement, he was led by dislike of arbitrary procedures to declare that the evidence was insufficient for a capital sentence. Colbert did not forgive him and Ormesson's career was blighted.

13 Henri-François d'Aguesseau, contemporary of Montesquieu, first *procureur-général*, later chancellor, was a distinguished lawyer, consciously representative of an older tradition.

14 Michel de l'Hôpital (1507–73) was chancellor at a time when, as was the case with him, a chancellor could also be chief minister.

15 THE CHAMBRE ST LOUIS

1 The *Chambre St Louis* in the *Palais de Justice* became in name, as in proceedings, the focal point of constitutional conflict. Ministers feared that *la cause commune de la robe* could become institutionalised in a new and perhaps lasting way as the basis for a regular opposition. Anne expressed her alarm in a typically dramatic way: 'They are trying to make a republic in a monarchy'.

2 The highest prices were in 1644. They collapsed in 1645. There was a slow rise up to January 1648. After that month prices fell markedly. In August an average of all cereals shows a rise of sixteen per cent in relation to the corresponding period (just before the new harvest, so usually the worst) of 1645; but in relation to August 1644 a fall of twenty per cent.

3 To judge from the precedents of the turbulent 1590s, which he liked to quote, Nicolas Potier de Blancmesnil, *président* in the *Enquêtes*, may have had a keen taste for radical politics. He embarrassed some colleagues by inviting all who had financial dealings with government to abstain from voting. Ministers may have thought therefore that he would be a safe target.

4 A sad little episode in July bears it out. An elderly judge, Boullanger, discoursed at length to a restive chamber before reaching the climax of his peroration with lines from Cicero about Italy's not being despoiled. Someone muttered that France was being despoiled for Italy. Amid noisy merriment the judge raised his voice – collapsed and expired. The session was suspended for the day.

5 After Molé, Henry de Mesmes was, perhaps, the most respected and prestigious of the *présidents*. He had been a representative for the Third Estate at the States-General of 1614. It seems likely that he was unnecessarily pushed towards resistance by ministerial intransigence. He gave support to the Fronde during the siege of Paris. Indeed he set a precedent by sending his silver to be melted down for money for the defending troops.

6 An Assembly of Notables was more acceptable to government than a States-General because it was small (fifty-five met in 1626), selected by ministers on the criteria of rank and office. There were no *cahiers*, so no link to potentially troublesome groups or chance of a party's forming. Voting was by head and in this exercise the representatives of the sovereign courts were likely to

outweigh court nobles and ecclesiastics. The intention generally was to secure support for specific proposals. The crown started with, and could be expected to retain, the initiative.

7 Jacques Le Coigneux represents the double standards and ambiguous position of some of the most refractory judges. Gaston's client, he was able to find the half-million *livres* required to purchase his presidency, on the resignation of his father, from the immense dowry, 600,000 *livres* that he received for his marriage to Angélique Le Camus, daughter of the celebrated financier.

8 Typically it was a leather thong, with a pouch for pebbles in it. The word and the mischievous connotations were a gift to writers of songs and doggerel verse. It quickly acquired the sense of a rough game, frivolous, yet dangerous; reckless, yet justified, the *frondeur* might think, by the irresponsibility of government.

9 For the significance of popular revolts in relation to social and economic conditions, therefore to the 'Pre-Fronde', see p. 75.

16 THE DECLARATION OF SAINT-GERMAIN

1 *Les Halles*, whose recent removal has saddened many, were a series of pavilions where merchants rented stalls to sell, principally, grain, leather and cloth. Through all their contacts with shops, businesses and other markets throughout the city, the markets performed as a central exchange of information about everything that might affect supply, prices and security.

2 The *gardes françaises* were an elite force in that part of the army (about 15,000) that was genuinely royal. Even here the crown's control was qualified by the right of the *colonel-général* to commend for commissions in certain infantry regiments.

3 Séguier did not lack courage. Several of his party were killed. The episode is graphically retailed by Jean Vallier, among others.

4 The *lettre de cachet* was a sealed order, emanating from the sovereign, signed by a secretary of state, containing an order relative to an individual or a particular case. Typically, but not invariably, the letter would be ordering exile or imprisonment or – as here – release.

5 'The only possible excuse for a *coup d'état* is success, and Charles failed dismally' (Godfrey Davis). Stung apparently by his French queen's challenge 'to pull these rogues out by the ears, or never see my face more', Charles went down to Westminster in person, with a company of swordsmen, only to find that 'all the birds are flown'.

6 Possibly the best guide to Gondi's conduct at this time is to be found in the memoirs of Guy Joly, his secretary, then a magistrate of the *châtelet*, who believed that his benedictions to the mob were designed to rouse, not to appease them.

7 The reference here is to the judge, Longueil. It could equally have been to his better known brother, René de Longueil de Maisons (?-1667), a wealthy *président* and one of several who opened their houses to *frondeurs* and concerted tactics with nobles. Maisons would show that he was capable of movement in both directions. In May 1650 he accepted the office of *surintendant*. Since he was acknowledged to have little experience beyond his personal finance, the appointment was clearly a political one. In July 1652 he committed himself again to the rebel cause by serving on Gaston's council after Condé's entry into Paris.

8 Pierre Viole was something of a firebrand, at least in speech. Gondi thought

351

him a fool – but he condemned Broussel in the same terms – 'des cervelles de ce carat'. He was at least consistent. He was another of the *frondeurs* who joined Gaston's council in July 1652.

9 The comte de Montrésor was a leading agitator, with his own following among fellow nobles of Périgord and ambitions to have a main part in any assembly. He represents one of the main dangers of the Fronde – that the resistance of *Parlement* would open the way to more general and noble-led risings.

10 Geoffroy, marquis de Laigues was another adventurer in the Gondi circle. During the siege of Paris, he established himself in Brussels as a link with the Spanish. He was involved in the 'attack' on Guy Joly (see p. 163). By 1650, now attached to Mme de Chevreuse, he was attempting a secret deal with the court. By 1652 he was an habitué of Port Royal and friend of Arnauld d'Andilly (for links between Jansenism and the Fronde see pp. 292–5). In 1661 he was being used by Colbert in machinations designed to discredit Fouquet.

11 Armand-Charles de la Porte, maréchal-duc de la Meilleraye (1602–64), Richelieu's cousin, was promoted by him and enmeshed in his *clientèle*. He had been a strong lieutenant-general in Brittany. It was now reckoned that he would have the prestige and nerve to deal with the more complicated situation in Paris. As senior officer during the days of the barricades, he was energetic in his handling of the troops.

12 'Absolutism' implies that the sovereign was subject to no institutional restraint – which is how Bodin, like others after him, envisaged him: exercising a legislative function above the civil law, the subject having no intrinsic right to resist. In practice however the power of the ruler was always limited by respect for the fundamental laws of his kingdom, obedience to natural and divine law and the obligation to protect certain rights, principally the right of private property in land. The exigencies of government, especially in wartime, made it hard for sovereigns to tread the righteous path between the 'licentious anarchy' which Bodin feared and the 'despotism' which *frondeur* critics alleged. The term 'legal absolutism' still fits both the ideal of all but the most extreme *parlementaires* and the 'absolutism' of Louis XIV. For more on absolutism see pp. 94ff.

13 The *chambre de justice* was the extraordinary financial tribunal resorted to periodically by monarchy, as in 1624–5, for political as well as financial reasons. The political motive might vary according to circumstances: in 1648, to blacken the regime by association with the generally detested financiers; in 1661, ministers would seek to disassociate themselves from financial malpractices which, in less favourable times, they had been forced to allow. In both cases the incentive was to raise money in fines from those who had enriched themselves at the expense of the state and, through summary punishments, to create a climate of fear in which the borrower, the state, might have the upper hand. Bosher (see bibliography) sees the relationship of the financiers to their clients as being akin to that of prostitutes: for them uncertain but sometimes handsome profits at the cost of moral censure and social rejection: for the client, the yearning to be free, even to take revenge, arising out of dependency, with associated feelings of shame and guilt. Contemporary language supports the idea. There lingered prejudice about usury long after Catholic teaching about it had ceased to be influential. The need for scapegoats appears to be a universal one. The 'dirty souls' (la Bruyère) provided them for seventeenth-century Frenchmen.

14 Jacques de Beaune-Semblançay, *surintendant* was tried, condemned and despite frantic appeals to Francis I for clemency, hanged, in 1527. Charles, marquis

de La Vieuville (1580–1653) likewise encountered royal justice at its most terrible, the penalty, in his case, for political failure. Ousted from council by Richelieu he would survive to serve again. Lublinskaya (see bibliography) writes interestingly about the significance of his career.

15 Nicolas Fouquet, vicomte de Melun and marquis de Belle-Isle (1615–80) *procureur-général* in *Parlement*, *intendant* at different times in Grenoble, Normandy and Burgundy, was *surintendant* from 1653 to 1661; besides Mazarin he was the most important political personality of those years. See particularly pp. 270ff.

16 *Comptants* were cash payments made by the crown.

17 Charles Louis de Secondat, baron de Montesquieu (1689–1755), author principally of *De l'Esprit des Lois*, was a *philosophe* who brought his experience of the role of *parlements* and a singularly keen and open mind to political and constitutional questions. His concern for the sanctity of human law and established custom in government and his idea of a natural harmony of interest between monarchy and nobility – 'The nobility enters in some way into the essence of monarchy' – would have appealed to many *frondeurs*.

18 Jean-Edouard, sieur de Champlâtreux (1615–82), was *intendant* at Châlons, 1648–9, under the dispensation that allowed *intendants* in frontier provinces. Neither he nor his descendants achieved his father's fame. A family fortune, in the eighteenth century, of seven million *livres*, was perhaps not conducive to political initiative.

17 THE FIRST CIVIL WAR

1 Armand de Bourbon, prince de Conti (1629–66), younger brother of 'le grand Condé, suffered from a shoulder deformity and an inferiority complex that was only enhanced by his brother's triumphs. For Gondi, Conti was 'a zero, only significant because he happened to be a prince of the blood'.

2 François, prince of Marillac, duc de la Rochefoucauld (1613–80), was head of one of the oldest families and a great landowner in the west. Of his father, it is related that when Louis XIII admired the large company he brought with him to the siege of La Rochelle, he replied: 'Yes, sire, and all my relations'.

3 Hercule de Rohan, duc de Montbazon, was father of Marie de Chevreuse and husband (by his second marriage) of the duchess whose beauty, immorality and petulant temper (see p. 165) made her the focus of some notorious incidents at court.

4 The *abbé*'s talents did not earn him a high place in the church: he was unfortunate to have received one of Gondi's most crushing dismissals: 'le seul et unique abbé . . . était le poltron le plus signalé de son siècle'.

5 Louis de Trémouille, duc de Noirmoutier, had been responsible for the administration of the army in Flanders but had resigned after a quarrel with Condé. This may have led him to offer his sword to the Fronde and he was one of its generals during the siege of Paris. He figures in one of Gondi's most memorable scenes when the memoirist recalls his coming in, with his fellow officers, to the duchess of Longueville's apartments from a foray in the suburbs: 'This mingling of blue scarves, of ladies, cuirasses, violins playing inside the room and trumpets playing in the square outside, made a spectacle to be found more in romances than elsewhere.' Even if he did not model his conduct entirely on d'Urfé's popular romance *Astrée* (in which fairy-tale adventures were mingled with abstract discussion of the psychology of love), as Gondi suggested, he does seem to have personified the aristocratic mood of the time, in his pursuit of personal fulfilment.

6 Thomas Wentworth, 1st Earl of Strafford (1593–1641), most formidable of Stuart ministers, was tried by the ruthless procedure of attainder in the House of Lords, found guilty and, in May 1641, beheaded. Like Richelieu, he had shown courage and a degree of consistency in the pursuit of some good, even noble ends, while carving for himself the fortune in lands and goods that the seventeenth-century statesman held to be the essential basis of power. Unlike Richelieu, he had chosen the wrong side in the constitutional conflict; unlike the Frenchman, he could not rely on the support of his king.

7 Nicolas de Neufville, duc de Villeroi (1598–1685), *maréchal de France*, was governor of the Lyonnais, and was to be appointed titular head of the new *conseil royal des finances* set up by Louis XIV after the downfall of Fouquet in 1661. One of nature's courtiers, and Mazarin's client, he earned this mark of trust by his responsible conduct during the minority, when he was governor of the young king.

8 This was the court title of Anne Marie Louise d'Orléans, duchesse de Montpensier, 'La Grande Mademoiselle' (1627–93), Gaston's daughter by his first marriage to Mme de Bourbon-Montpensier. Her high birth, the great wealth which made her such a desirable match, and her extrovert character ensured her a leading place in the social and political life of the period.

9 Hugues de Lionne (1611–71), Servien's nephew and Mazarin's client, was to crown a distinguished career in administration and diplomacy as secretary of state, and, in effect, foreign minister, from 1663 until his death.

10 The Loménie family, particularly Antoine, comte de Brienne, furnished secretaries of state under Henry IV, Louis XIII and Louis XIV. Henri-August de Loménie received the *droit de survivance* to his father's position in 1615; both men worked together as secretaries until Antoine's death in 1638; the son continued in office, with his son Henri-Louis until their resignation, following exclusion from the *conseil en haut* in 1663. None of them held a senior position nor exercised much obvious influence on policy though such continuity in confidential contacts may have meant more than the records convey.

11 The power of the League during the later stages of the Religious Wars was exercised in cities by groups, the best known of which was the *Seize*, named after the sixteen *quartiers* from which its members were elected. The *Seize* plotted against king Henry III in 1588 and expelled him from his capital. Essentially they represented the vacuum of authority caused by Henry III's weak direction and the initial absence of Henry IV. Once he had defeated the Guise, embraced Catholicism and recovered Paris, the *Seize* lost cohesion and vanished from sight – in a way that pre-figures the history of radical groups during and after the Fronde.

12 The regiment of Corinth was so-called after the special title bestowed by the Pope on its patron.

13 Jean-Louis, baron d'Erlach (1595–1650), had inherited Bernard of Saxe-Weimar's mercenary army, employed by Richelieu, after Bernard's death in 1639. He was now governor of Breisach, the vital Rhine stronghold whose capture had been Bernard's last military feat. Since he was a strong believer in the independence of the soldier from civilian – that is *intendants'* – control, his move came as a relief to Mazarin.

14 Philippe de la Mothe-Houdancourt, *maréchal de France*, was a capable general of the kind favoured by Richelieu and Mazarin as a counter-weight to the even more independent and unreliable grandees who led, almost as of right (though in the case of Turenne and Condé justifiably). Mazarin took pains,

as his correspondence shows, to work closely with La Mothe-Houdancourt and his defection was a serious setback.

15 Charles de Lorraine, duc d'Elbeuf (1598–1657), was the senior representative of the Lorraine interest. He had lost his governorship of the vital frontier province of Picardy in 1633.

16 Louis-Emmanuel de Valois, comte d'Alais, later duc d'Angoulême (1596–1653) was governor of Provence. Appointed to succeed Vitry, who had replaced Guise, he held his governorship from 1637–53.

17 When food prices were fixed by decree, a black market developed. The main purpose of military action was the covering of food convoys. In this the Fronde was quite successful. Grain prices did not rise to the height of 1593–4 and an earlier royal siege of Paris. The rage of the mob could in any case be turned against Mazarin and the besiegers.

18 Guy Patin (1602–72) had come from his native Picardy to win fame in Paris. He became dean of the university faculty of medicine, a platform which he used to obstruct change. He made a more positive contribution in meetings of the intellectual community 'where our conversation is always gay. If we speak of religion or of the state it is only in terms of history, without proposing a reformation or sedition.' From his own distinctively libertarian standpoint, his letters, often caustic in comment, provide a valuable picture of life and opinion in *frondeur* Paris. Detached from the côteries of court or *Parlement* he represents what he liked to call *le public*. Interestingly he believed that Gondi would have been a better *premier ministre* than Mazarin.

19 Louis de Cossé, duc de Brissac, was a co-signatory with Beaufort, Bouillon and other leading nobles, of the document forswearing the making of peace till the objectives of the Fronde should be achieved. He was prominent among those in the Orléans circle who set a tone of open debauchery. He was later involved in the successful plan to extricate Gondi from prison at Nantes (in a box: see p. 207). In July 1658 he was exiled for plotting against Mazarin during the king's serious illness of that month.

20 Maximilien Eschellart, marquis de la Boulaye, was among the first to offer his sword to the Fronde and he commanded the cavalry during the siege of Paris. He played a leading part in the 'assassination' plot of December 1649.

21 The relationship between the nobilities remains a controversial subject (see, for example Labatut and Coveney, bibliography, p. 386) and it is easier to describe a trend than to define positions. Divisions, jealousies and debts were all pushing the sword nobility towards liaisons with new rich financiers or the well-established *robe* families. Social barriers remained, along with the nuanced understandings and prejudices that are potent – but hard to weigh. The registers of *parlements* contain many disputes between *robins* and traditional nobles. Since wealth is rarely the most important factor in 'class' encounters it is likely that the barriers were strongest in provincial society. The civil wars in Provence and Guienne were partly between the *robe* and the sword nobles. The crown was not faced, during the Fronde, by anything resembling a homogeneous upper class. If it had been so, the prospect for Mazarin would have been bleak indeed.

22 René-Bernard-Renaud, chevalier de Sévigné, between bouts of *frondeur* activity, usually on behalf of Gondi, was periodically a Port-Royal recluse. His nephew Henri, marquis de Sévigné, pursued Ninon de l'Enclos, fought a duel in 1651, over another celebrated courtesan, 'the divine Lolo', was killed, and left a young widow and a daughter. His disordered life was to have a happy post-script: his widow, Marie du Rabutin-Chantal, marquise de Sévigné, wrote to

her then adult and married daughter some of the most revealing, touching and entertaining letters ever penned.

23 Archduke Leopold-William (1610–62), young brother of the Emperor Ferdinand III, fulfilled the ecclesiastical-cum-military role appropriate to a Habsburg prince. As governor of the Netherlands (1646–55) he had little time for the duties of a bishop in his several German dioceses. He did however manage to build up the magnificent collection of Flemish paintings many of which are now to be seen in Vienna.

24 Jérome Le Féron, *président* in *Parlement* and *prévôt des marchands* (the nearest equivalent to mayor in Paris) was representative (he was related to *président* Novion) more of the interests of *Parlement* than of the Parisian *bourgeoisie*. In Moote's words 'he was a notorious trimmer'.

25 The six major guilds, representing the dominant interests of merchants, were those of drapers, grocers, mercers, furriers, hatters and silversmiths. Offering their members, in a hereditary position of privilege, special honours and facilities, with their own hall, chapel and patron saint to reinforce the sense of corporate exclusiveness, the guilds helped preserve the divisions that made it possible for monarchy to manipulate and control. Tactical reasons may have dictated short-term alignments. In general however the guild member looked to the preservation of his status within a framework of order. There were around five hundred craft guilds keeping their distance from those groups clustered at the lowest level of this strictly hierarchical society: the numerous *compagnies*, for the relatively unskilled, the porters, water carriers, grooms and valets, who existed on the corporate fringe – but were likely to be found at the centre of any disturbance.

26 *Mère* Angélique Arnauld (1591–1661) was the reforming abbess of Port Royal. For the Arnauld family and for her place in the history of Jansenism see pp. 293–5.

27 When Mazarin left Paris he left behind certain agents, like Cohon, bishop of Dol. It was part of their job to lobby people on Mazarin's behalf, like Mme de Liancourt and Mme de Montausier (the latter one of the most celebrated of the *précieuses*). *Salon* and fashionable opinion was perceived to be important.

18 DIVIDE AND RULE

1 According to the calculation of R. Pillorget, *Les Mouvements insurrectionels en Provence, 1596–1715* (1975).

2 A system popular with government, anticipating capital returns from the sale of office, by which more judges would work for shorter terms.

3 As in Marseilles, and reflecting Roman tradition, the consuls were the governing body of the city.

4 Alexandre de Sève (1605–73), *intendant* in Provence (1647–9), was particularly experienced, having already been in the Boulonnais, Grenoble and Riom.

5 Jean d'Etampes (1594–1671) had been for some years a commissioner in Brittany, so was used to dealing with refractory bodies – notably the Estates.

6 For d'Epernon's earlier and stormy career see p. 329, n. 28.

7 For the *Croquant* revolts see pp. 76–7.

8 Again Mazarin was employing an officer of proven loyalty and competence. René Voyer, sieur d'Argenson (1596–1651) had already held five *intendant*'s posts when, in 1649, he was made commissioner in Guienne. By nature a conciliator, a *dévôt* who was later ordained, he represents an aspect of absolutist government, idealistic in its conception of good order, that can be overlooked

amid the opportunism and brutality that disfigured this period of 'fiscal terrorism'.

9 The edict of Béziers (October 1632) followed the revolt of Languedoc and abolished the *élections* in the province in return for a more regular source of income. The fact that the amount, 1.3 million *livres*, was found insignificant when set against the soaring costs of wartime government – and was yet regarded as unduly onerous – illustrates the crown's problem. Mazarin responded to pressure to revoke the edict because he could not afford to lose control in this vital province. In this saga of continuous conflict, successive compromises reflect his overriding concern for security. Indeed the contribution of the *pays d'états* to the treasury fell during the ministry of Mazarin to a third of the level under Richelieu.

10 The special tribunals, comprising Catholics and Huguenots, set up by the edict of Nantes to try lawsuits involving Huguenots.

11 For the turbulent recent history of the province see pp. 74–5. As in other provinces the Fronde in Anjou was more an episode in a continuing process than a novelty or aberration.

12 Inequalities in the incidence of taxation, not only as between *pays d'états* and *pays d'élection* (see note 9 above), but within the later regime are revealed by the figures of Normandy (the *généralités* of Alençon, Caen and Rouen) which provided twenty per cent of direct taxes from the *pays d'élections* during Richelieu's ministry and little less during Mazarin's. (See the tables showing tax proportions in R. Bonney, 'Louis XIII, Richelieu and the Finances' in *Richelieu and His Age*, ed. J. Bergin and L. Brockliss (1992)).

13 For whose subsequent role and unhappy fate, see p. 358, n. 10.

14 For definition of these terms, see p. 374, n. 1.

15 For whom, see particularly pp. 196–7,198.

19 THE WAR OF THE PRINCESSES

1 *Lettres de jussion* were a first step in the exercise of the king's power, before the summoning of a *lit de justice*. Both, in Colbert's view, were a sign of the weakness rather than the strength of monarchy – because a court might embark upon an open-ended debate on how it should respond.

2 Jean-Baptiste Colbert, marquis de Seignelay (1619–83), who came from a provincial family (he was born in Rheims) with useful positions and contacts in the legal and financial worlds, was one of a generation of aspiring royal servants who accepted the tenets of the new absolutism and sought promotion and wealth along the road to more efficient government. He entered the service of Le Tellier in 1645, acted, during the Fronde, as intermediary between that minister and Mazarin, and transferred to Mazarin's service in 1651. As Louis XIV's minister he pursued financial, commercial and social policies sufficiently distinctive and effective to add the word 'Colbertism' to the language of economic history.

3 Some judges, like Le Coigneux (Gaston's man), Deslandes-Payon (Gondi's) or Nesmond (Condé's) were long-term clients and partisans.

4 Expressive, but virtually untranslatable, *hobereau* serves to convey the kind of lesser country *gentilhomme* who inspired patronising jokes in polite society – like the rustic squires of English Restoration dramas. They were an unstable element until the expansion of the royal armies after 1661 provided them with the chance of an honourable career in royal service.

5 As typically by Vallier. Insulted by Mazarinist taunts about his generalship from

a neighbouring table, Beaufort snatched the cloth off, spilled food and plates over his tormentors, then, with his followers, drove them out at sword-point.

6 The name by which the mass of pamphlets in prose and verse inspired by the Fronde were called: appropriate since a high proportion of them were to do with the personality and policies of the Cardinal. See also pp. 181–2.

7 Pierre La Porte, cloak-bearer and confidant of Anne, was brave and loyal during the crisis occasioned, in 1637, by her correspondence with the Spanish court. For his role as go-between he suffered temporarily by imprisonment. Mazarin himself wrote that 'he would have cut his veins for her'. He took a proprietory interest in the young king and correspondingly detested Mazarin.

8 Henri-Charles duc de la Trémouille (1621–72) hoped to secure the governor-ship of Anjou. He also claimed Roussillon and Cerdagne, conquered but not yet officially acquired provinces, on the strength of fifteenth-century marriage contracts: claims could live as long as memories in the feudal world.

9 The sun theme was already well established when Louis XIV adopted it, not from a whim but, Bluche argues, from his keen sense of history. In 1623 Bérulle had argued, for the benefit of Huguenots, that the king represented the image of God, the light of His rays being imprinted on the royal counten-ance. The sun moreover illuminates, as reason does. 'The king is a sun which you should look up to. He is the Lord's Anointed . . . the true image of God.' His subjects should therefore render him homage and obedience.

10 Natalie Zemon Davies's telling phrase specifically applied to the religious riots of the sixteenth century: it seems legitimate to see the same instinct to abandon the normal restraints and promptings of the individual conscience at work in the *émeutes* that defied external interference, in the form of new taxes or offices, with the cherished rights of a community or corporation.

11 Guy Joly, a magistrate at the *châtelet*, did not abandon Gondi's service until 1665 – and then under circumstances which may account for the sour tone of his *Mémoires*. In Salmon's words, the work is 'tendentious and pejorative'. It may be seen however as a useful corrective, from the viewpoint of an insider, to Gondi's complacent account of his *frondeur* activities.

12 Louis Charton was recognised as being among the most extreme of *frondeurs*. He was a defendant in the December trials.

13 'Deadly' is hardly an exaggeration when applied to noble *moeurs* during these years. Nine hundred noblemen were killed in duels during Anne's regency: a hundred a year.

14 Apparently he stuffed his doublet with straw and fired a pistol at it, then cut himself through a hole in the doublet. Charton's surgeon pronounced the wound to be genuine and Charton, as colonel of militia in his quarter, sounded the call to arms. The anonymous author of the *Journal de la Fronde* wrote: 'All Paris believes that it is an incident that the *frondeurs* have contrived expressly to rouse the people; not having succeeded they are being mocked, everyone saying that *fronderie* is down and out'.

15 An important Norman fortress: its governorship would enhance Longueville's already extensive control in the province.

16 Charlotte-Marie de Lorraine, mademoiselle de Chevreuse, was destined, inevi-tably, to be a pawn in her mother's political games. Gondi preyed on her – though she was 'so stupid as to be ridiculous' and yet, at one stage, he planned marriage for her to Conti. Her habit of burning her discarded clothes (to the chagrin of her maids) and capricious behaviour to her lovers might furnish interesting material for the psychiatrist. The malady from which she died, in November 1652, was so sudden that some suspected poisoning. She can be

seen as glamorously amoral or as the pathetic victim of a callous, in some respects singularly unpleasant, society.

17 The Conspiracy of Amboise, in 1560, was a plot organised by a Huguenot nobleman, the seigneur de la Renaudie, aimed at securing the court for the Huguenot party and eliminating the power of the Guise.

18 In 1688 archbishop Sancroft and six fellow bishops were put on trial on the charge of seditious libel for refusing to allow James II's Declaration of Indulgence to be read in their churches. Their acquittal was enthusiastically received; James's throne was imperilled.

19 Beaufort, Chavigny already, Gondi later, were among the distinguished men to be confined in this formidable fortress-prison, conveniently close to Paris.

20 René de Longueil, marquis de Maisons (?–1677) had been a cautious, perhaps reluctant *frondeur*; now he was an ineffectual minister, witness to the temporary preponderance of political over financial necessities. Gondi's description of a man 'blackened by countless thefts and betrayals' merely reflects the *coadjuteur*'s concern about the disintegration of his *fronde*.

21 In 1648 there had been support for Longueville. However there were uncomfortable memories of repression after the Nu-pieds rising. Meanwhile Mazarin had taken care of the Norman judges' interests. Unsentimental Norman magistrates found reasons for resisting the appeal of the beautiful duchess. Their attitude marks a significant turning-point in the course of the Fronde. There was psychological as well as strategic value in the crown's victory.

22 Ordered to present herself at the Palais Royal, the spirited lady had refused, fled to the coast, tried to get away from Pourville in a gale and been rescued from rough waters by some fishermen, made her way to Dieppe, secured an English boat and sailed to Rotterdam, thence eventually to the Spanish governor's court at Brussels.

23 If one could choose only one contemporary account of the Fronde (though it would be hard to dispense with Motteville), it would be that of Jean Vallier whose journal provides eye-witness accounts of some of the main episodes, with illuminating detail about others. He reproduces much that could be gleaned from pamphlets and the *Gazette* but also gives the impression of having his ear close to the ground.

24 Etienne Foullé was one of the *intendants* who represented the cutting edge of government policy in the provinces. He had been entrusted by Richelieu in 1637 with the punishment and re-ordering of Quercy and Périgord after the revolt of the *Croquants*. His extraordinary powers represent a landmark in the development of the *intendant*. He could levy forced loans, preside over the *bureau des finances*, prosecute leaders of the revolt on his own authority, even demolish houses. There was no appeal against his tribunal's sentence in criminal cases. The local governor was ordered to send him troops. For his personal safety he was authorised to carry arms. After his contentious experience as commissioner at Limoges and the charges laid before the Bordelais judges, he elected to present his case to *Parlement* where he carried out a stout defence over some months.

25 Thomas Morant, was re-introduced, in January 1650, as *intendant* by another name, by being sent to Bordeaux *en chevauchée*. For such circuit tours there were respectable precedents, with commissions legitimised by reforming ordinances. He was to go out again after the Fronde. In 1658 he became involved in a dispute with governor Longueville over the billeting of troops in Normandy. It was a sensitive issue with implications for local power and patronage

and settled by Mazarin with a typical compromise, which left the governor with the formal right, the *intendant* with sufficient room to manoeuvre.

26 His father had also declared his majority, at the traditional age of thirteen. The formal acquisition of full powers did not effect an immediate change in the reality of government. Louis XIII, at his coming of age in October 1613, had actually declared that he wished Marie de Médicis to continue as regent. Pursuing a traditional course (previous queen mothers, Catherine and Marie, had tried it before their sons, Charles IX and Louis XIII respectively, achieved their majorities), the king was paraded about the country and introduced to his subjects in a series of carefully rehearsed ceremonies. There was more to it than royalist propaganda – though that was important. Impressively resilient in adversity, Mazarin sought to relieve the crown of the weight of his own unpopularity. At the same time with his fellow ministers he did useful work, hearing petitions, strengthening ties through exercise of patronage, resolving disputes and arranging alliances. Military and political objectives went together. For example Mazarin took the king to see the siege of Bellegarde in Burgundy. When Tavannes' troops inside the fortress took up the besiegers' cheers for the king it could be read as an omen of the likely outcome of the Fronde – collapsing before the personal authority of the crown.

27 Antoine LeFèbvre, seigneur de la Barre, was Gondi's friend and nominee. It did not prevent his acting for the court and he was subsequently rewarded with the post of *intendant* in Paris (1653).

20 THE FIRST EXILE

1 No Parisian could be unaware of the Bastille's presence or potential for the control of the city. It never had more than a few prisoners and was not used much by the crown (Vincennes being preferred), until it was sure of its grip over the capital.

2 Johan van Oldenbarneveldt (1547–1619) was tried by a general synod representing foreign as well as Dutch Calvinists and executed. The ostensible issue was religious – for he espoused the cause of Arminianism for which he was attacked by the Orthodox Calvinists – but there was an underlying political issue between the States of Holland and the House of Orange.

3 Gondi, declared that she had 'the political capacity of queen Elizabeth [of England]'. Anne de Gonzague, Princesse Palatine (1616–84) was daughter of the duc de Nevers and Catherine de Lorraine. Her title came from her Bavarian husband.

4 The Benedictine order that took its name from Cluny was governed since its inception by an abbot-general and dominated by the mother house. The post being held *in commendam*, it was in effect in the pocket of a magnate. Practical responsibility for the order's affairs belonged to the grand prior; in practice however it was controlled by a small group of officials, self-selecting and conservative. Not surprisingly Cluny, like Citeaux, resisted the efforts to reform, first of Cardinal de la Rochefoucauld, as Bergin chronicles, then of Richelieu. Evidence for the weight of political and social factors can be seen in Anne's reluctant appointment of Conti to be *abbé–général.*

5 Charles-Amédée de Savoie, duc de Nemours, was early locked into the world of sedition by marriage with Elizabeth de Vendôme. Condé's principal lieutenant, as La Rochefoucauld described him, he was living in a dream world of

his own. His quarrels with his brother-in-law Beaufort helped to incapacitate the *frondeurs*.

6 Charles de Monchy, marquis d'Hocquincourt, was one of the most reliable of the '*condottieri*' generation of commanders, loyal to Mazarin not least because he saw no reason why the war should end: campaigns were a seasonal, dangerous but honourable ritual.

7 Jean Perrault was *président* in the *Chambre des Comptes*, a friend of Condé and, to emphasise the boldness of the advice, he had been imprisoned along with Condé.

8 Of whom Abraham de Fabert, who figures largely in Mazarin's correspondence and worked closely with him, was to be the most significant.

9 They were useful to Mazarin as recipients and agents of patronage, minor power-brokers in the ecclesiastical world – but have left little mark on the history of the Church.

10 Isaac Bartet was the more important of the two. Described by Gondi as 'a ridiculous little Basque' – perhaps because he was over-familiar with the grandees with whom he was required to deal, he was employed by Mazarin on some important missions, notably to Paris in November 1651 to negotiate the separation of Turenne from the princes' faction. For Millet was secured the position of under-governor to the duc d'Anjou: it was a useful listening post at court for the absent Mazarin. Relatively obscure *créatures* like these could do more valuable service at this crisis in Mazarin's fortunes than some more public figures.

11 Jacques Rousse was to be prominent in the 'ecclesiastical *fronde*', for which see pp. 207–08.

12 Claude Joly was uncle of Guy Joly, Gondi's secretary (see p. 351, n. 6.) Though on the cautious fringe of the *frondeurs*, he found himself in hot water after Gondi's escape from the château of Nantes – of which the chapter of Notre-Dame publicly approved.

13 Claude de Seyssel (1450–1520), bishop of Marseille, was author of *The Great Monarchy of France* (1519). He believed that there should be three restraints on the monarchy: religion, justice and established ordinances.

14 For La Porte's relationship with Anne, see also p. 358, n. 7.

15 Mme de Senécy had been dismissed in 1638 after Anne's recovery from childbirth: she had helped to persuade Louise de la Fayette to take the veil (see p. 335, n. 12). She was also suspected of encouraging Anne's hostility towards Richelieu. Anne reinstated her after her husband's death and made her also governess of the royal children. Marie de Hautefort had to combine duties as lady-in-waiting with attention to Louis XIII's needs (see p. 335, n. 11). In 1639 she too had been dismissed. Reinstated with Mme de Senécy she sought to persuade Anne to dismiss Mazarin. Anne wearied of her moral lectures and was persuaded by Mazarin to dismiss her. However she then married Schomberg, Mazarin's friend and became once more persona grata at court.

16 All foreigners, including naturalised Frenchmen, and cardinals, whether French or foreign, were to be excluded from royal councils. If the document had been drafted in the form of a 'grace' (like that of Alais to the Huguenots) it would have been harder for Louis subsequently to renounce.

21 MAZARIN RETURNS

1 Mazarin's nieces were invaluable political assets. What started as a typical negotiation for material advantage had become a matter of urgency for Mercoeur: he had lost his heart to Laura.

2 Champlâtreux was militia colonel of the quarter in which the palais de Justice is situated. The episode is typical of those in which Gondi is involved. His appetite for fame fed on sensations. The less his control of events or sense of direction, the greater his need to appeal to Parisian sentiment on behalf of 'the old Fronde'.

3 While the majority of commissions were so restricted, there were special authorisations. Foullé in the Limousin (see p. 169) had a *lettre de cachet* empowering him to carry out the functions of an *intendant des finances*. Where necessity ruled, names and titles mattered less than authorisation to act.

4 People fended for themselves, as had John Evelyn (see note 6) when travelling from Calais in the previous August. 'The Regiment of Picardy, consisting of about 1,400 horse and foot ... being come to town, I took horses for myself and marched under their protection to Boulogne. It was a miserable spectacle to see how these tattered soldiers pillaged the poor people of their sheep, poultry, corn, cattle, and whatever came their way: but they had such ill pay, that they were ready themselves to starve.' His would have been a familiar experience.

5 'Messieurs', said Louis, 'I have come to my *Parlement* to tell you that, following the law of my state, I wish henceforth to take upon myself its government and administration. I trust that, with God's grace, this will be with piety and justice. Monsieur the chancellor will explain my intentions in greater detail.' After Anne had responded with a gracious renunciation of her powers and knelt before him, the king continued: 'Madame, I thank you for the pains you have taken with my education and the administration of my kingdom. I beg you to continue to give me the benefits of your good counsel and desire that, after me, you should be the head of my Council.'

6 John Evelyn (1620–1706) was a Balliol man, cautious royalist, sound Anglican and, providing a major source for English history besides – for this period – a useful one for French history, indefatigable diarist for sixty-six years.

7 Thomas Hobbes (1588–1679) knew Europe as a regular tutor and companion for young Cavendishes. He was in Paris from 1640 to 1652. He was the friend of Gassendi and the respectful critic of Descartes – though he accepted the Frenchman's basic notion of the mechanistic character of nature. In 1651 he published his *Leviathan*, 'the most powerful piece of political philosophy which any Englishman had produced' (C. P. Hill). It was influenced by the Civil War which he observed from across the Channel. Were not his views also affected by the Fronde? The political society projected in *Leviathan* was controlled by expediency. The sanctions of religion and morality were cast aside. Hobbes returned home after *Leviathan* had made him obnoxious to the authorities in Paris.

8 This was the Condéan, Jacques de Saulx, comte de Tavannes, not to be confused with his uncle, the marquis de Tavannes, *lieutenant du roi* and Mazarin's *fidèle*.

9 Jean-Gaspard-Ferdinand, comte de Marsin, was commander of the French force in Catalonia. The failure of the French in that province illustrates the problem of maintaining the war effort during the Fronde.

10 The career of Denis Marin reveals the ever closer links between finance and administration. He seems to have moved easily between money broking

and commissions in the provinces, seeing there the conditions and exerting the powers which conditioned the return on his loans. Between 1640 and 1650, with his partner Bonneau, he contributed about fifty-seven million *livres*, a tenth of total loans to government.

11 Henri de Plessis Guénégaud, like Le Tellier, had been in office since 1643: besides five provinces, he was responsible for the city of Paris, the royal household, and the clergy. Never in the forefront, though invaluable in the areas of government that lay between peaks of decision-making and mere routines, he would hold the office till 1669. Mazarin deliberately brought le Tellier to the fore, needing his expertise in army administration and knowing that 'he would not aspire to be first in order, that he might more securely be second'.

12 Like team colours, the scarf was not merely an ornament. Soldiers in un-uniformed units needed to be able to identify friend from foe. Mazarinist green scarves were distinguishable from the king's white and the Condéans' straw colour. A contributor to Mazarin's force was the Elector of Brandenburg (who had the Rhineland territories of Cleves and Mark).

13 To raise money for the reward, in little over a month, despite Louis XIV's express instruction to Fouquet to intervene to stop the sale, the splendid library of 40,000 volumes, of which Naudé was the devoted custodian, had been dispersed in a hundred directions. A friend declared that 'the Goths and Vandals had never done anything as bad as this *Parlement* of Paris'. With pilfering, favouritism towards well-placed bibliophiles (Séguier was one of a number who made off with precious books) and inefficiency, the sale realised barely more than an average of a *livre* per volume. For Naudé and the library see pp. 377–8, n. 10.

14 The arguments are well marshalled by Anne's biographer, Ruth Kleinman. While some may incline to take more seriously the expressions of affection both explicit and suggested by the coded symbols they used, her reasoning and insights convince me. It is essential to view the relationship in the context provided by her past conduct and known principles and by his career, singularly free of emotional entanglements such as would surely have been reported of such a public figure. 'False as the devil', Vincent de Paul said when asked about rumours of a secret marriage: it may be assumed that he was referring to the rumours, not to Mazarin. One may also wonder if the young Louis XIV would have enjoyed the same relationship of trust with his minister and godfather if he had been given cause to wonder about Mazarin's relationship with his mother. The historian cannot close this file – but may allow common sense to suggest an answer to the question so persistently asked by twentieth-century students.

22 THE DEFEAT OF CONDÉ

1 Henri Chabon, duc de Rohan, an unimpressive sprig of the great warrior family, could have been dangerous to Mazarin if he had succeeded in mobilising the nobles of the Estates of Brittany and bringing them to reinforce his clients in Anjou. He was thwarted by La Meilleraye whose stewardship of the Mazarinist cause in Brittany shows him again to have been a main contributor to the defeat of the Fronde.

2 Henri Arnauld, one of the great Arnauld clan (for Antoine and Jacqueline see pp. 294–7) was an outstanding bishop, as Isabelle Bonnot's recent study has shown. Combining Jansenist principles with pastoral zeal, he provides an

example of what Jean Orcibal called 'le rôle capital des individus dans la réforme catholique'.

3 Denis de Heere was already an experienced *intendant*, having served at Bourges and Tours, the latter from 1642 to 1647 (see p. 346, n. 3). He returned to Tours in 1651 as *intendant de l'armée* and remained there, taking wider powers, till 1656. His experience in this large *généralité* shows the essential continuity in government through these years and provides a model, in the shape of one man's efforts, for absolutism in its critical phase.

4 For the story and significance of the *Ormée*, for which Sal Westrich (see bibliography) is the main authority, see pp. 203–04.

5 Wherever the court might be, and with it the executive, Paris remained the centre of government and its essential bureaucratic staff.

6 He declared that he was fighting to execute *Parlement*'s *arrêts* against Mazarin and his family and promised to lay down his arms once that had been achieved. Vallier probably reflected bourgeois opinion when he treated Condé's claim with scorn and that of a growing number when he put the alternative view: why should the queen (nominally the king) abandon the right to choose ministers, only to deliver the crown into the hands of the princes – and that when the Spanish were at the gates of Graveslines?

7 Gaston's daughter had gone to the city, with the comtesses de Fiesque and de Frontenac, clad, wrote Motteville, as Amazons. Refused admission at the main gates they were rowed around the city walls till they found a side port open and proceeded to the town square. The citizens were expecting Molé and legal authority; perforce they had to accept Mademoiselle and her dramatic version of the Fronde.

8 Mazarin had advised retreating to Bourges. It was not a happy precedent, Louis XIV would have heard of another 'king of Bourges', the unhappy Charles VII. Turenne's calmness and professional skill was invaluable at this critical juncture.

9 Continal frustration and high living had sapped Chavigny's health. He was now a man in a hurry. Some ascribed his sudden death, following a stroke, to Condé's contemptuous rejection when, in August, he suspected Chavigny of negotiating with Gaston.

10 Before Bléneau Turenne had looked at the flames that lit up the horizon and observed bleakly: 'M. le Prince has arrived'. His own troops were little better. Mazarin had at first tried to prevent Turenne campaigning in the vicinity of Paris for fear of the hostile reaction in the city.

11 For Charles's earlier involvement in French politics and his motivation see p. 31.

12 Jean-Baptiste Balthasar had a long tour of duty as *intendant* in Languedoc and then a spell with the army of Italy. He was now at Limoges. Bonney sees him as 'the supreme example of the secular politician' who would do anything for his masters. His words now could have been Mazarin's: 'civil divisions ought rather end in accommodation than in victory. It is preferable to persuade men by reason than by force'. To this limited extent the Fronde had gained something which would not be entirely lost.

13 Nor did he forget the wider scene. In January 1653 he would write to Le Tellier: 'I hardly know how to describe the inhumanity practised by the Prince [Condé] in the places he passes. His troops pillage and burn everything – and that, one knows, is not only by the license of war but by his express order'.

14 Charles le Prévôt was only a councillor in *Parlement*. He represents a trend.

Chéruel suggests that the bourgeois were now generally and keenly royalist. It is more likely that there were still deep divisions and serious doubts. It is why Condé's behaviour and that of his allies, in the next few weeks, was so crucial. On 30 July Nemours and Beaufort fought their notorious duel. Nemours' shot passed harmlessly through Beaufort's hair. Beaufort advanced and shot his brother-in-law dead at close range. Most condemned Beaufort and Condé grieved for the generous, honourable, if scatter-brained, Nemours: it did not cause him to moderate his behaviour.

15 Jacques Marigny was an unusual companion for Condé. Born Jacques Carpentier, son of an iron merchant, he found his niche in *frondeur* haunts as composer of *Mazarinades*, typically crude parodies and songs. After Mazarin's return Paris became too hot for him. Guy Joly describes his escape over rooftops clad only in shirt.

16 Disillusionment with Retz, even among the *dévôts*, is expressed by Arnauld d'Andilly: 'the *co-adjuteur* has all Mazarin's bad qualities and none of his good ones'.

23 UNFINISHED BUSINESS

1 Nothing apparently had happened to change Louis' mind since the previous October when he wrote to Mazarin: 'It is time to put a stop to all the afflictions which you have willingly endured for love of me'. The words that followed indicate precisely how Louis interpreted the Fronde and why Mazarin not merely survived – but returned in a position of greater strength: 'the authors of these present troubles have only included you among their grievances to cover, by this pretext, the design they have formed with the Spaniards to take up arms on their behalf and to set light to civil war in my realm.'

2 Catalonia had been lost when Marsin decided to join the cause of the princes and withdrew his army; likewise Dunkirk, also in 1651, when Harcourt moved east to enable Mazarinist forces to concentrate more effectively.

3 Though not by recent historians of the Fronde. In varying degrees Moote, Bonney, Hamscher and Golden have stressed the uncertainties of the first post-Fronde years, the tentative nature of the crown's measures to reassert authority and the caution necessitated by evidence of discontents in Paris and the provinces. 'Unfinished business' indeed.

4 Colonel Sexby would represent to most Frenchmen the unacceptable face of rebellion. He subsequently took his radicalism as far as involvement in Wildman's republican plot (1656–7), wrote the pamphlet *Killing No Murder* in which he justified assassination, was imprisoned, and, in 1658, died in the Tower.

5 Few enough by now. Hearing that 400 villages had been burned, Mazarin observed that 'he [Condé] will not be much loved in that country'.

6 Son of d'Epernon. For the importance of the family in Guienne, see pp. 150–51.

7 Charles II experienced the same difficulty after his restoration in 1660. Out of the grievances of the disappointed, particularly over the land settlement, grew embittered opposition in Parliament.

8 For the significance of the *sacre*, see p. 95.

9 Even by the standards set by himself, the story of Retz's escape, after several abortive efforts, ranks high. His scarlet cloak was so arranged as to represent him praying in the castle garden while he climbed by rope into the river that flowed beneath the walls. He was hauled out of the river, set on horseback,

escorted in a gallop out of the city, thereafter carried, since he damaged his shoulder in a fall, to the sea, but not to safety. He evaded efforts of his guards to re-capture him but the fishing boat which he chartered had to avoid pirates and survive storms before he made land in San Sebastian.

10 Fabio Chigi was Pope Alexander VII, from 1655 to 1667. When he became ill in 1659 he provided Mazarin with a brief, tantalising vision of another kind of career since the minister, widely praised for the Peace of the Pyrenees, was talked of as his successor. He recovered, Mazarin died, leaving a large sum to the Pope to revive the crusade against the Turks.

11 The career of this *illuminé* belongs to the frontier area between religious fervour, and the political field so temptingly opened up by the Fronde. Contemporary English history, in its Fifth Monarchists and Muggletonians, for example, offers interesting millenarian parallels. Typical manifestations are a sense of special destiny, a private vision and way to God, intolerance towards other ways, and concern for the needs of the poor. Addressing his message about the coming 'reign of glory' (which he had been selected by God to usher in) to the poor, 'the little ones' and calling for the re-distribution of wealth, Morin could only be an embarrassment in a diocese managed by Retz and dominated by more orthodox *dévôts*. He was imprisoned four times.

12 The reader may choose between two authoritative judgements. Doolin states that *Parlement* lost 'much of what had been gained in 1648–1649'. Moote points out that 'nothing was done at the *lit de justice* . . . to undo the reforms enacted four years earlier'. For the lasting significance of the October *lit* one has to look at subsequent events, for what they reveal of the collective psychology of *Parlement* and the mood of Mazarin and his king.

13 In 1713, at the climax of the ageing king's attempt to destroy Jansenism by enlisting the support of the Pope, whose predecessors he had previously defied, notably over the *régale* then using the very Gallican arguments which he now seemed to repudiate, he secured a bull defining Jansenist heresies.

14 Bellièvre, a grandson of a notable chancellor, *président* in the *Grande Chambre* had been acceptable to Mazarin because, unlike Novion, who was better qualified, he had not had connections with Condé. He had also had experience as a diplomat.

15 Séguier's letter to Mazarin of 23 August, dealing with the 'affront to royal authority' which he saw in *Parlement's arrêt* of 18 August (and no doubt a personal slight) warned of serious implications: it would 'elevate the *Parlement* above it [the council], making it the first company in the kingdom which can judge the faults of others . . .' In 1648 they claimed that edicts, taxes and tax-contracts which had not been verified in *Parlement* could not be carried out. So the king's affairs would be 'subject to their ambitions'. He also feared, hearing of letters from *Parlement* asking for similar decrees from other *parlements*, that the movement would spread to the provinces.

16 What was forming in Colbert's mind can be gauged by this extract from a letter he wrote to Mazarin in August 1659; 'I cannot stop myself telling Your Eminence something which you know even better than I, that the royal finances have great need of a severe and energetic extraordinary tribunal.'

17 James B. Wood, *The Nobility of the Election of Bayeux, 1463–1666* Princeton, 1980.

18 As the tone of Le Tellier's letters to the exiled Mazarin make clear. For example, in April 1651: 'It is certain that these Estates can be advantageous neither for His Royal Highness [Gaston] nor for Monsieur the Prince and that . . . they should not be refused, but rather eluded or deferred.'

19 A *cahier* was a formal statement of grievances and requests.

20 François de Saint-Aignan, duc de Beauvilliers, had been generally loyal during the Fronde – and enjoyed Louis's apparent favour during the early years of the personal reign; possibly Louis gave him court jobs so that he could keep an eye on him.

24 THE FRONDE CONSIDERED

1 Only in this limited sense can Doolin's view of the Fronde as a movement for constitutional rights be supported. The claims figure prominently in the rhetoric. According to *L'Avis d'Etat à la Reine* (1649): 'Richelieu has perverted and overturned the old forms of government and changed the precepts of legal monarchy to those of tyranny.' However the *frondeurs* failed to develop a convincing critique of *raison d'état*. Typical of many was Bouchu, *président* of the *parlement* of Burgundy and a leading *frondeur* there, who, in 1651, criticised the *intendants* but added: 'it is allowed to the prince himself to act on the basis of mere suspicion for he is the master'. Argument was reduced generally to one about personalities. Novion could 'recognise that Cardinal Richelieu has been responsible for great violations' but 'they have been tolerated because he is French and acts with prudence and responsibility'. There was recognition of a kind of security that had been created by authoritarian rule. Balzac was grateful to Louis XIII, 'thanks to whom I am dreaming in safety on the bank of the Charente'; he would not have felt safe there in 1652. So long as the state was conceived in moral and religious terms, those who abused its powers were likely to be condemned as if they were heretics or aliens. When Mazarin caused consternation in *Parlement* in February 1648 by asking how far it considered it had the right to go in opposition, he had raised the difficulty seen by Broussel: 'the very formulation [of the question] shakes the authority of the king and reduces the obedience of the people'. He also showed his ignorance of 'the special character of the state' and blundered into 'this sort of silence, religious and sacred' in which it was hidden. Gondi's words convey the sense of outrage of the original *frondeurs* – but also its evaporation with the gradual focusing of loyalties on the person of the king. Mazarin having survived with the favour of the crown, it became possible for the pragmatist to look to him for advancement and for the idealist to console himself with the thought that the Cardinal had learned – if not to be a Frenchman, at least about Frenchmen. Constitutional arguments were then wheeled off the stage like so many discarded props.

2 Blaise Pascal (1623–62), Auvergnat, the son of a *président* of the *cour des aides*, a mathematician and scientist of genius, whose work on atmospheric pressure, the equilibrium of fluids and the infinitesimal calculus was each of seminal importance. His theological and moral concerns, expressed characteristically, in the *Pensées*, were no less profound. His involvement with Port Royal ensured that the author of the *Lettres Provinciales* would lend a special distinction to the Jansenist controversy.

3 Mazarin's methods were no less effective in the provinces. The kind of dissension within provincial courts, as in the *parlement* of Aix, where the *premier président*, Henri de Forbin d'Oppède led a local revolt in 1649, was turned to the advantage of government when Mazarin first succeeded in splitting his opponents, then forged an alliance with Oppède which was sealed in 1657 when he became acting *intendant*, without formal commission. Always with Mazarin, it was the man and his potential influence, not the office, that

counted. With Oppède as his well placed agent, the riots of 1659 in Aix and Marseille would be crushed easily and followed by the kind of exemplary severity that did so much to establish Louis XIV's rule on unassailable foundations.

4 Vincent de Paul (1576–1660) was canonised in 1737, but he was already regarded with veneration during his lifetime. Among early experiences, his capture and imprisonment by Tunisian pirates and spells as *curé* in a poor district and chaplain to the royal galleys, helped to prepare him for his life's work, inspiring charitable works through organisations like the *Filles de Charité*, for which see p. 290.

5 For whom, see particularly p. 318, n. 4.

6 Built, in conformity with the edict, just outside and to the east of Paris, it was large enough to hold more than 3,000 and enjoyed the prestige that came with its many educated, even fashionable worshippers.

7 Grounded in the *mentalité* of a city of densely peopled streets, alleys and courts, with limited light and few gardens, this hysterical, orgiastic, murderous outbreak of 1572 remained a disturbing memory. Those who sought to enlist popular support for any cause might still think twice.

8 For the rising of these 'clog-makers' in the Sologne in 1658, and its ramifications, see p. 214.

9 For the Edict of Nantes and Grace of Alès, see pp. 220 and 320, n. 6.

10 Barthélémé Hervart (1606–76), *intendant des finances*, was a banker and munitioneer of German origin who was an invaluable ally and agent to Mazarin and stood sufficiently well with Colbert to ensure a place on the new *conseil royal des finances* in 1661 when others were being charged with corruption. For his loans and services to Mazarin see p. 368, n. 9.

11 The *Académie* was the protégé of Séguier, more appreciative than Mazarin of native French artists. It enjoyed royal incorporation from 1655. Its significance was increased under Colbert.

12 Testelin's commissions included the king. Aged ten, in 1648, he is shown on a throne, holding a crown of laurel in his right hand.

13 Jacobus Arminius (1559–1609) taught (cp. Calvin) that Christ died for all believers. If sinners repented and believed, they could become the elect of God. His liberal views were condemned by the Synod of Dort (see the trial of Oldenbarneveldt, p. 360, n. 2) but they gained ground at the expense of Calvinist orthodoxy.

14 Moise Amyraut (1596–1664) and his influential Saumur School would be criticised by Léonard, historian of French Protestantism, for softening the Huguenot position and facilitating conversions to Rome. Recognising the improving climate of the sixties and seventies for plans for reunion, the Catholic Orcibal, writing about the Revocation, takes broadly the same view.

15 Though not the view of Thomas Erastus (1524–83), the Swiss physician who denied the church the right to inflict excommunication and physical penalties, 'Erastian' had come by now to signify recognition of the superior sovereignty and jurisdiction of the state over the Church.

16 For the circumstances, see pp. 251–2.

17 The *trésoriers* had alleged that *maîtres des requêtes* had been sent out to make new levies without letters of authorisation. In issuing a directive to *élus* and other officials to ignore and refuse cooperation with the maîtres, the *trésoriers* had committed 'an outrage without example and worthy of punishment since it displays contempt for His Majesty's authority with the design of depriving his subjects of the alleviation which they ought to expect.' Here is a minister,

not only asserting the rights of the maîtres (in effect *intendants*) but at the same time seeking to recover the moral high ground conceded in the preceding constitutional struggles.

18 For which, see pp. 341–2.

19 Burgundy had been acquired in 1477 after the death of duke Charles the Bold. When Louis XI seized it, without waiting for the diplomatic process, he was bequeathing to his successors intractable conflict. Mary, Charles's outraged daughter brought to her marriage with the Habsburg emperor Maximilian, to be inherited by her descendants, emperors or kings of Spain, the sense of loss and injustice that was to fuel subsequent wars and affect the peoples concerned, inhabitants of 'the two Burgundies'.

20 Typically Verdun sur-le-Doubs, not remarkably affected by war or billeting; annual burials normally between 60 and 80; 1650, 120; 1652, 234. In the latter year there were 37 baptisms; 80 was the average.

21 Amsterdam, Leipzig and Danzig each experienced record grain prices.

22 The revolt of the Vivarais, one of several in the first ten years of Louis XIV's personal reign, pales into insignificance compared with the Breton revolt of 1675 – but it was serious, with some 4,000 villagers in arms for several months before they were put down. '*Vive le roi, Fy les élus!*' was their cry.

23 The process is precisely documented, with examples of ruthless and sometimes unscrupulous behaviour by those rich townspeople who stood to benefit, by Marc Venard for the Ile-de-France and G. Roupnel for the Dijonnais.

24 Not only women. Gastonde Renty, a leading member of the *Compagnie du Saint Sacrement*, died from exhaustion after climbing stairs to the fifth floor lodgings of the Paris poor. Naturally noblewomen were most prominent. But most of the recruits to Madame de Marillac's *Filles de Charité*, as Vincent de Paul had advised, were 'good village girls', who would be used to physical labour and would not be worried about lice or sickened by the stench of the poor. The example of *soeur* Marie Joseph may be taken to represent this heroic movement of charity. In 1652, after two years nursing on the battlefields, she came to Etampes and worked there till she died; she literally gave her life to the poor. Alongside such examples it may seem easy to detect some exhibitionism in rich *dévôts* who fluttered about the sickbeds. No doubt there were some whose motives were mixed. But there is much evidence for true charitable feeling and deeds. The ordinary people would have been the first to detect the false or superficial. When in 1651, the corpse of Marie de Lamoignon, wife of *président* of *Parlement*, was laid in the Paris church of Saint Leu et Saint Gilles, awaiting burial in a conventional grave, the poor, remembering the large amounts she had bestowed during her life, expressed their gratitude and wish to keep their benefactress among them by burying her on the spot while the family mourners were at dinner.

25 TOWARDS WESTPHALIA

1 A continuing flow of bullion was a vital element in the sustained war effort; it was considerably larger than official statistics reveal. It is arguable however that the illusory revival which made the Spanish think that they could benefit from continuing the war contributed to a worsening of the situation in the long term. In 1653 a bankruptcy was declared. Until there was peace there could be no genuine economic revival – and Spain's war with Portugal continued until 1668.

2 Breitenfeld, Lützen, Wittstock and Jankau: four Swedish victories – but none

were decisive. Mazarin's letters, particularly after 1653, whether from camp, where he spent much time with generals, often with the king, or from Paris, show a keen interest in strategy and commissariat. Commanders received clear briefs, the impression of an intelligent minister working with and trusting them, and information about enemy designs. In June 1653, for example, he wrote to Turenne, following 'advice received from a very reliable source': 'I believe that the main purpose of the enemy, in planning his deployment of troops, is to cause anxiety at several different points and force us to divide our forces.' After discussing various eventualities he added, in his own hand, 'we must keep our eyes constantly on Verdun'.

3 B. Priolo's chronicle was of sufficient interest to English readers to find an English translator, C. Wase; *The History of France under the Ministry of Cardinal Mazarin* (London, 1671).

4 Jean-Baptiste Budes, comte de Guébriant; he died afterwards of a badly treated wound.

5 Frederick Henry (1584–1647) was the third son of William of Orange, *stadholder* and captain-general of the United Provinces from 1625 until his death. Inheriting sympathy for France from his Huguenot mother Anne de Coligny and exploiting the diplomatic needs for Richelieu after the battle of Nördlingen, he found regular French subsidies a valuable aid to his designs on Spanish Flanders. In his diplomacy he assumed quasi-monarchical powers. However his declining health and influence, combined with the war-weariness of the Dutch, the insensitivity of the French ambassador d'Avaux (over the Catholic question) and Mazarin's rash attempt to make a territorial deal at the expense of Spain, had already jeopardised the French alliance by 1647. See also p. 240.

6 Daughter of Gustavus Adolphus, Christina (1626–89) inherited the throne in 1632 and came of age to rule in 1644. A lady of strong personality and independent mind, with a keener interest in philosophy (her critics would allege) than in practical aspects of government, she displayed a shrewd tactical sense in the manoeuvres which led to the resolution of the crisis of 1650, but tired of her position. Having decided to become Roman Catholic and being aware of the difficulties that this would cause in a Lutheran environment, she abdicated in 1654 and spent the rest of her life in Rome.

7 Lennart Torstensson (1603–51) had been trained by Gustavus Adolphus and was an expert in the handling of artillery: its mobility was the decisive factor at the battle of Jankau. His grimly effective style of military terrorism represents a logical development in a war in which statesmen were as much helpless spectators as they were manipulators of the *danse macabre*.

8 As Lionne saw: see also p. 240.

9 Godefroy, comte d'Estrades, was subsequently ambassador in London and involved in 'the Affair of the Ambassadors', in 1661, when the Spanish ambassador refused to give him precedence at the court of Whitehall. Louis XIV took up the case, secured an apology and, in the following year a formal concession by the Spanish of the right of French ambassadors to precedence at all courts. Marking, in honorific terms, a permanent change in the balance of power the incident would make a fitting, posthumous comment on Mazarin's diplomatic achievement.

10 The early career of Sébastien le Prestre de Vauban (1633–1707) witnesses the dilemmas posed by the Fronde to a young man. Of a minor noble Burgundian family, ambitious but honourable, he first served Condé (then governor of the province) and followed him into Spanish service. Taken prisoner in 1653

he was persuaded by Mazarin to enter the royal service. He was one of the engineers responsible for the capture of Stenay. Thereafter there was no wavering in his career as royal siege-master and military architect. He conducted fifty successful sieges and designed or improved one hundred and sixty fortresses, many of which can still be seen.

11 Giambattista Pamfili, elected Pope Innocent X (1644–55); his elevation marks the Papacy's return to its long-standing support of the Habsburgs. It was less of a diplomatic setback to France than it would have been if Innocent had been more resolute or consistent in his policies.

12 Urbain de Maillé, duc de Brézé (1597–1650) was Richelieu's brother-in-law, Condé's father in law, an effective commander and governor of Anjou. His was a case where Richelieu's unblushing nepotism had produced a satisfactory result.

13 He did not. Charles-Emmanuel II remained duke until his death in 1675. For the circumstances of his succession and Mazarin's role in Savoyard affairs, see p. 50.

14 For details of the revolt of Naples see also p. 112.

26 THE LONG HAUL

1 The Emperor Ferdinand III (1637–57) has yet to receive an adequate biography – and remains a shadowy, perhaps under-estimated figure. He brought a degree of realism after the intense fanaticism of his father. The treaty of Linz, for example (1645), confirmed Protestant rights in Hungary.

2 Münster was Catholic. The Swedes went to meet Imperial representatives at nearby Protestant Münster.

3 For John and his Portuguese claim, see p. 49.

4 The career of the valiant Ottovio Piccolomini, so indefatigable in the Habsburg cause, brings a kind of romance to the sordid chronicles of these wars. He had seven horses shot under him at Breitenfeld. 'Send for Piccolomini' was ever the Habsburg cry in times of trouble. His transference to the Flanders front illustrates the extent to which the Spanish had become a drag on the Austrian war effort. Fittingly he was host at the great banquet held in 1650 by the diplomats and generals to celebrate the completion of the Westphalia arrangements.

5 'A large, red-raced, rather stupid man, easily rattled, very haughty, too fond of wine and women' is Wedgwood's description of Johan Oxenstierna. A loud fanfare signalled his rising, dining and retiring. He would have liked the war to continue to sustain his own importance: that was to Mazarin's advantage.

6 Count Guzmàn de Peñaranda was a man of elegant manners but inclined to miss the point. Fortunately, at his side was Antoine Brun, civil servant, a supple humanist who understood how to negotiate.

7 For Servien in the domestic context, see pp. 271–2.

8 One of the reasons why Longueville later became a rebel, if only briefly, was perhaps that he felt that he had been treated simply as a figurehead: it is hard to see what else he could have been.

9 Maximilian, count von Trautmansdorff, was an abler man than any of the other grandees. But it is plain that, while it was necessary in this aristocratic age to have the highest representation at ceremonies, negotiation, time-consuming, requiring an eye for detail and willingness to bargain had to be the work of professionals: Salvius for Sweden, Brun for Spain, Servien for France, Volmar for the Empire. The Dutch did not conform to this pattern. Tensions

arose between their two emissaries, Adrian Pauw for Holland, Jan van Knuyt for Zeeland, representing respectively the party of peace and that of the House of Orange.

10 Frederick William had succeeded to an impoverished inheritance in 1640. In the pursuit of his political aims, notably sovereignty over East Prussia and the acquisition of West Pomerania, he proved to be an unreliable ally to France and – when it appeared to suit him, as during the Dutch war, an opponent.

11 It is expressed in his important essay in the collective work, *Mazarin*, ed. G. Montgrédien (Paris 1959). Dealing with the argument that Mazarin abandoned his concern for peace when he came to serve France, Schuman urges that it was precisely because Mazarin refused to pursue policies of aggression that the peace of Westphalia became possible.

12 A strong case is made out for this view in several of the essays in *Louis XIV and Europe*, ed. R. Hatton (1976), notably those of Hatton herself, G. Livet and G. Symcox. See also 'Louis XIV and Europe' in my *Making of Modern Europe* (Routledge, 1985).

13 Though, as a diplomatic asset, it was wasted rather than exploited, the cultural hegemony of France is suggested by the universal use, after 1714, of French as the diplomatic language, and confirmed by the almost slavish imitation of French institutions in Germany, and admiration for French writers generally in the Age of Enlightenment. 'Young people, wrote Leibnitz, 'come near to making Germany a tributary of French power.'

27 GERMAN APPROACHES

1 Isaac de Feuquières was instructed to inform Oxenstierna that Louis had no long-term designs on the area: he only wanted to set up 'barriers against eventualities in order to protect his friends'. In 1634 the Swedes were seen as a greater threat in the area than the Spanish.

2 Montbéliard, covering the southern approach to Burgundy, was placed under French protection in 1633.

3 Isaac Volmar (1582–1662) was a Swabian Protestant and Freiburg professor who became a baron as reward for his diplomatic services. The use made by Habsburg rulers of such jurists is significant. They contributed to the evolution of a distinctive Habsburg style of quasi-absolutist government, different from the French model, but sufficiently effective to pose a challenge to Bourbon influence in Europe before the end of the century.

4 The *réunions* gave their name to a phase of French policy, between the peace of Nijmegen, ending the Dutch War in 1678, and the truce of Ratisbon, confirming many of the gains made by this process of piecemeal annexation. Feudal law was exploited to justify claims to territories that were 'dependencies' of places indisputably French. The thinking of Louvois (son of le Tellier and his successor as war minister) was dominated by military requirements, a defensible frontier. The principles have a contrived look about them but they were subscribed to by the Austrians – before 1648 – and by the French diplomats at Münster. For more on this topic, see particularly G. Zeller, 'Louvois, Colbert de Croissy et les Réunions de Metz' in *Aspects de la Politique Française sous l'ancien régime* (1964).

5 However, in 1664, in accordance with the provisions of the League, the French sent a contingent of 4,000 troops, as large as that of the princes of the League – and they contributed usefully to the victory of St Gothard. The contrast between that response – when Louis was still operating within the framework

bequeathed by Mazarin – and that of 1683, entirely negative and opportunistic, is striking.

6 Leopold I was to be emperor till 1705. His important reign which was to see the decisive defeat of the Turks, the re-conquest of Hungary, the first major defeat of a French army (Eugene's and Marlborough's victory at Blenheim in 1704) and the recovery by Austria, at the expense of France, of her traditional influence in Germany, has received a fitting biography: J. P. Spielman, *Leopold I of Austria* (1977). His elder brother Ferdinand had already been designated heir as king of the Romans, before his death, in 1654, had diverted Leopold from the ecclesiastical role for which he had been prepared.

7 Johan-Philip von Schönborn, was arch-chancellor of the empire and took his responsibilities seriously. He was largely responsible for the election of Leopold to be emperor but only after Leopold had accepted a condition undertaking to abstain from participation in the Franco-Spanish war.

8 Henri Hauser, in *La Prépondérance espagnole (1559–1660)*, (1934) provides an invaluable, concise account of these and other diplomatic affairs.

28 THE ENGLISH ALLIANCE

1 Henri, marquis de la Ferté–Senneterre was governor of Lorraine from 1643–61 and a linch-pin in Mazarin's frontier strategy of entrusting sensitive governorships to trusted soldiers.

2 In the course of his campaign against the Irish 'rebels' in the late summer of 1649 Cromwell had stormed Drogheda and Wexford. Both successes were followed by the slaughter of their garrisons.

3 The son of James II, James Edward Stuart was 'the warming-pan baby' whose unexpected birth had been a factor in the crisis which led to the invasion of William of Orange and James's overthrow.

4 For the involvement of Louis and Mazarin in this important campaign, see p. 306.

5 In August Mazarin warned Anne not to let Beaufort (newly pardoned) have too much access to the king 'for he rules his father'. On another occasion, responding to her anxieties about Louis' safety in Turenne's camp, he had said that 'he would be as safe there as in the Louvre'. He held it important that 'the king should be present at councils of war where he will hear the generals discussing plans of campaign'.

6 Richard Cromwell retired in May 1659.

29 PEACE WITH SPAIN

1 Daughter of Philip IV and Louis XIV's aunt, Elisabeth of France whose marriage in 1615 marked the brief period of entente between the two countries, Maria Teresa (1638–83) was twenty-two but decidedly unsure about life. Patronising or plain scornful, the French found her unworldly to the point of childishness.

2 King in 1665, Charles 'the sufferer' would live a kind of life till 1700. His well-documented physical defects and painful self-consciousness would have him a figure of pity in a Spanish village. It was his fate to be born to the throne of a vast empire and to be incapable of producing an heir. His mind was not so slow that he did not suffer from the humiliation of knowing that his empire was discussed chiefly in terms of a foreign succession.

3 Maria Mancini (1639–1715) was the younger daughter of Mazarin's sister

NOTES

Girolama and Lorenzo Mancini (see pp. x and 325, n. 17). Her sister Olympe was married to the comte de Soissons (1657). For Maria, in 1661, was found a grand but eccentric husband, the prince of Colonna. A widow after 1689, she consoled herself by writing her memoirs. She blamed Mazarin for ruining her idyll.

4 A French caricature of 1659 shows a deaf pantomime clown crouching before the diminutive figure of the *Infanta*. Representing Spain, he is clearly in no position to pay his stipulated due. The dowry remained almost totally unpaid. Lands were therefore claimed in lieu. The law of devolution – that the child of a first marriage should inherit to the exclusion of the child of a second marriage (private, not public law of Brabant but convenient) provided a pretext. The campaign that began in May 1667 proved Spanish decline. The peace of Aix, a year later, was one that Mazarin would have approved, with its acquisition of a string of Flemish towns, notably Lille and Tournai, to be bastions of a new frontier. It was the finishing of the business of 1659.

5 Lionne saw to the insertion of a single word into article four of the marriage contract. It read: That on condition [*moyennant*] that the said sums are made over to His Most Christian Majesty . . . the said most serene *Infanta* will rest content with the said dowry and not therefore sue for any other of the rights'. *Moyennant* was crucial, turning a statement of intent into something more like a contract.

6 That Louis, advised by Lionne, was unlikely to be soft with regard to his queen's 'rights', could be guessed from the way in which he took the opportunity afforded by a dispute between the French and Spanish ambassadors at Whitehall (1662) to secure from Philip IV acceptance of the right of diplomatic precedence over the Spanish.

7 A simplified diary of his travels in three years, starting in August 1658, tells its own story: where the date is given it is that of his day (approximately) of arrival:

  1658 August: Calais – Graveslines – Vincennes
    September: Fontainebleau – Paris (19)
    October-November: Corbeil (25) – Sens – Auxerre
    December: Dijon (5) – Beaune (20) – Lyon (27)
  1659 January: Roanne (16) – Nevers (21) – Briare (23) – Paris (27)
    February-May: Paris or Vincennes
    June: Fontainebleau – Notre-Dame de Cléry (26) – Saint Dié – Amboise
    July: Poitiers – Châteauneuf – Monthieu – Libonn – Cadillac(15) – Bayonne (21) – St Jean de Luz (27)
    August-October – St Jean
    November: Dax (15) – Nogaret (22)
    December: Toulouse
  1660 January: Béziers (2) – Montpellier – Nimes (11) – Tarascon – Arles (18) – Aix
    February: Toulon (18) – Aix
    March: Marseilles (2) – Aix (6) – Toulon (10) – Arles (16) – Avignon (18) – Montpellier (31)
    April: Carcassonne (9) – Toulouse (15) – Auch (22)
    May: Bayonne (10) – St Jean de Luz
    June: Rocquefort de Marsan (25) – Bordeaux
    July: Lusignan (4) – Poitiers (5) – Fontainebleau (13)
    August: Paris (20)

374

30 ARBITER OF PEACE

1 Coming to the throne at the age of four, Charles XI (1660–97) endured a long regency before asserting himself forcefully in the critical situation created by war against the Danes. The victory of Lund (1676) sealed the relationship of trust between Charles and a group of young officers and ministers. He moved on to an assertion of absolutist principles which then became the basis of reform, centring on the recovery of crown lands, which postponed Sweden's eventual retreat from Germany.

2 The Polish officer Chmielnicki led the Ukrainians in a revolt against Polish landowner colonisation which threatened to reduce the steppe-Cossacks to the serf-status of Poland's peasants. Russian 'protection' of the rebels was not disinterested. In the ensuing war between Poland and Russia, Russia gained Kiev and Smolensk with huge tracts of land up to the Dnieper.

3 The transfer of sovereignty to the Elector, who had formally held East Prussia as a fief from Poland, opened the way to higher taxation, a larger army and, eventually the title of king of Prussia, conceded by the Emperor in 1701.

4 Catherine of Braganza (1638–1705) was the daughter of John IV of Portugal (see p. 49). She was married to Charles II in May 1662 and remained devoted to him despite their childlessness and his repeated infidelities.

5 Frederick Hermann, duke of Schomberg, transferred early to French service and enjoyed a distinguished career. Despite his Protestantism he was promoted *maréchal* in 1675. But in 1686, pushed to the margin by the revocation of the edict of Nantes, he came over to William III, and served at the Boyne, where the hopes of James II were dashed and where he fell in battle in 1690. For Louis XIV the loss of such soldiers, whom Mazarin had cultivated, represented the necessary price of religious conformity.

6 Philippe, duc d'Anjou, after the death of Gaston in 1660 duc d'Orléans (1640–1701) was married in April 1661 to Henrietta Maria, Charles II's sister, 'so lovable in herself she could not fail to please'. Vita Sackville-West called him 'the little prinking shrimp of a prince married to a rare girl he did not deserve'.

31 FOUQUET

1 Inevitably during these years of makeshift provision the line between the Cardinal's money and credit-worthiness, and the crown's, was hazy. In an important letter of May 1651 to Lionne, enumerating the occasions and amounts of his politic generosity, Mazarin cites money lent (in each case a substantial sum) to Venice, Charles II, German princes, rebel Neapolitans, Sweden's allies and for diplomatic presents in the Westphalia negotiations; also to the military building programme, to fortify Dunkirk and to provide campaign expenses. 'My bankers, Contarini, Serantoni, Cenami and Hervart have a great interest in publishing the above so that all France sees that it is useful money that they have disbursed and that they should not be considered as *partisans* who make no advance except for excessive interest'.

2 Fouquet was arrested after the king's visit to his new château of Vaux-le-Vicomte and an astonishingly lavish entertainment which probably only confirmed Louis' doubts about the *surintendant* who could command such resources for his personal use.

3 For the periodic use of the *chambre de justice* as a weapon of political and financial values, see p. 352, n. 13.

4 By 1667 the net yield of taxes had risen from thirty-one to sixty-three million *livres*.

5 Scrutiny, for example, of the way in which the revenues of Mazarin's duchy of the Nivernais were diverted to Mazarin's personal account might suggest that Colbert had served the Cardinal better than the king. He would argue that it came to the same thing.

6 For the upright Ormesson, the way in which his stance would affect his career, and his memoirs, see p. 350, n. 12.

7 The politically-minded *abbé* was of particular use to Mazarin as a liaison between Brühl and Paris during the minister's exile.

8 Dent has identified 116 people in Fouquet's *clientèle* during the fifties, two more than in Mazarin's. Most of the larger *clientèles* were those of financiers, led by Monnerot, with 69. Servien's was relatively small. For more on the *clientèle* and its vital place in the organisation of finance and government, see p. 278.

9 The reader may wish to refer, at this point, to the account of the workings of the financial machine on pp. 81ff.

10 Jacques Le Tillier was a reliable witness. One of Fouquet's key clients, Charmeil shows him to have been a particularly resourceful *intendant des finances* in the struggle, during the Fronde, to ensure a sufficient flow of money from the provinces.

11 For Bellièvre's role in the post-Fronde years see p. 210.

12 Louis Le Vau, appointed royal architect in 1656, was at Mazarin's service, re-building part of Vincennes, building the Salpetrière and new works at the Louvre. From there, the king's principal architect, he would design the king's new palace of Versailles. Christopher Wren, visiting Paris, declared the works at the Louvre to be 'the best school of architecture in Europe'. The landscapist André le Notre brought to perfection the *jardin d'intelligence*, the art of the garden as an extension of architecture. Besides the 15,000 acres of Versailles, his work can be seen at St Cloud, St Germain de Laye, Fontainebleau and – in England – St James's Park.

13 Lambert's magnificent house on the Ile-St-Louis, Servien's château at Meudon to give only two examples of many.

14 A financier involved in a *parti* or *traité*, a contract to collect indirect royal taxes. See also p. 341, n. 26. Like *traitant*, the word was used indiscriminately, generally pejoratively, to denote any financier engaged in state business.

15 Daniel Dessert (see Bibliography) sees the pursuit of profit as the central political motivation in Fouquet's and Mazarin's world. It could not be openly avowed. When the *chambre de justice* (see p. 352, n. 13) tried to unravel the skeins it found forgeries, tampering with accounts, blotted out names, but evidence enough for the implication of ministers, great men and women, *traitants, munitionnaires* and officials right down to the clerks who managed the business. The very greatest escaped identification. But the *chambre* cast its net wide. Of 176 identified by Dent as the primary financing elite, 87 were fined a total of 107,918,000 *livres*.

32 THE GREATEST PRIVATE FORTUNE

1 *Un généreux* was expected to be disinterested as well as open-handed – but someone had to pay for the means.

2 Johan de Witt was Pensionary of Holland, 1653–72; in its republican and federal constitution that meant power – but with restraints that called for

political skills of a high order. He displayed a stoical indifference to the trappings of power. Temple noted that he was usually seen about 'like the commonest burgher of the town'. It was more than the physical distance that separated Amsterdam and de Witt from Paris and Mazarin, with his treasure-laden *hôtel,* busy entourage and guard of musketeers.

3 Karl Liechtenstein (1569–1627) enjoyed spectacular preferment comparable to that of Wallenstein with marriage to a rich heiress, conversion to Catholicism and devoted service to three emperors.

4 Francisco, duke of Lerma (1553–1625) was *privado* of Philip III, in effect chief minister from 1598 to 1618. His career was marked by failure to capitalise on the benefits of a brief peace, the expulsion of the Moriscoes (1609) and his lucrative monopoly of crown patronage.

For the English and Swedish examples of the 'favourite' phenomenon, belonging to a period when the powers and responsibilities of the state began to out-strip the capacity of the monarch to handle its business, Buckingham and Oxenstierna, see p. 325, n. 12.

5 Born a peasant on the La Rochefoucauld estates, serving in succession La Rochefoucauld, Condé, Fouquet, Mazarin and the king, Jean Hérauld (before he took the name of Gourville), became a valet, then confidential agent, flourishing in the abnormal conditions of the Fronde; under Fouquet he made a fortune; under the scrutiny of Colbert he lost it; he returned from exile to find favour in royal circles; not only was he regarded as 'a character' but he was entrusted with confidential diplomatic missions. He wrote memoirs in old age (two vols, ed. L. Lécestre, 1894–5) which are as entertaining as any – if less reliable than most. See F. R. Freudmann, whose book's title, *L'Etonnant Gourville, 1625–1703* (1960) is justified by the story it tells.

6 Only nine out of nearly five hundred that have been attributed were French; even the three Poussins and two Claudes were essentially Italian in character. The collection represents the taste of his immediate circle and his friends in Rome: he tended to receive the pictures that his agents knew would please him.

7 Twenty-six canvases; but – to put the number in proportion – this prolific artist painted five hundred portraits before his death, in 1641, at the early age of forty-two.

8 He was a relative of Sublet de Noyers. The artists commissioned or persuaded to work in Paris included Mariani, Romanelli and Sassi; the greatest, Pietro da Cortona could not be persuaded.

9 Mazarin did not allow Le Brun the apartment in the Louvre vacated by the death of Simon Vouet.

10 For the sale of the library, see p. 363, n. 13. Gabriel Naudé (1600–53), humanist, voluminous author of largely forgotten works and 'a gourmand of books' was diverted from his medical studies (during which he became friend of Guy Patin – see p. 327, n. 10) by an offer to become personal librarian to de Mesmes. He went on to serve Mazarin and was largely responsible for what, by 1651, he could justly describe as 'the most beautiful, the best and the largest library which has ever been brought together in this world'. He thought it scandalous that 'the public is to be deprived of so great a treasure and that the noble intentions of His Eminence are being so ill repaid'. The scholars who were allowed daily into the great reading room, with its fifty Corinthian columns, in the Mazarin's palace would have agreed. Remarkable too was the recovery of this library, largely through return of books from recent 'purchasers' (many were simply taken) who wished now to

placate the minister; also from bulk purchases, like that of Naudé's own collection of ten thousand volumes. Everything to do with Mazarin was on the grandest scale. In this case he served the nation. He bequeathed the reconstituted library to his Collège des Quatre Nations on the rue de Conti. Its collections, augmented by books confiscated during the Revolution, now number about 400,000 volumes. For Naudé's interesting life at the centre of a group of Paris intellectuals, for his relations with Mazarin and in particular for the Cardinal's public spirited attitude (self-advertising his detractors would say) in opening his library to the scholarly public, see J. A. Clarke, *Gabriel Naudé* (1970).

11 For the Swiss guards and their special importance during the Fronde see p. 227.

12 For an authoritative analysis of Mazarin's wealth, see Daniel Dessert, 'Pouvoir et finance au XVIIe siècle: la fortune du cardinal Mazarin', *Revue d'Histoire moderne et contemporaine*, XXIII (June 1976). For the ecclesiastical property, see J. A. Bergin, 'Cardinal Mazarin and his Benefices', *French History*, vol. 1, March 1987. For the amassing of a fortune up till 1648 see Claude Dulong, *La Fortune de Mazarin* (1990). The account books of the Venetian Contarini, confiscated and eagerly scrutinised during the Fronde, show that he had deposited, by 1648, eight million *livres*.

13 For Colbert's early service to Mazarin and disservice to Fouquet see p. 157 and pp. 273–4.

14 For the *abbé*'s services, then, see p. 35.

15 Though far removed from the principles of the Council of Trent, this apparently scandalous appointment was not made solely for mercenary or family reasons: until its possession was confirmed by the treaty of Westphalia, along with Toul and Verdun, it was vital to keep Metz under direct royal control, as it could be through this episcopal puppet.

16 For La Rochefoucauld and his commission to reform the monasteries, see p. 76, n. 2.

17 Charles would eventually be Louis XIV's foreign minister; Nicolas would have several abbeys, then a bishopric; as in the case of Mazarin, and of Le Tellier, the success of one member of a family meant promotion for all.

33 THE GREAT AGE OF SOULS

1 H. Brémond's masterpiece is *A Literary History of Religious Thought in France*, trans. K. L. Montgomery, from the original work of 1916. The relevant volume here is *II The Coming of Mysticism* (1930).

2 J. Bergin's *Cardinal de la Rochefoucauld* (1987), is also an impressive study of the French Church during the long working life of François de la Rochefoucauld (1559–1645) when he was a central and influential figure, latterly as Papal commissioner for the reform of the religious orders. Nobleman, *dévôt*, administrator, reformer, single-minded in all he undertook, the Carlo Borromeo of the French Church, as some contemporaries saw him, this member of one of the greatest families in the land invites comparison with France's other cardinals, notably Richelieu and Mazarin: that may give an idea of the extremes to be found within the Church which was the Body of Christ, the nursery of aspiring statesmen, and the wealthiest and most powerful of corporations.

3 François de Salignac de la Mothe de Fénelon (1651–1715) was, besides Bossuet, the greatest of French churchmen in the age of Louis XIV. Like Bossuet

he was a high dignitary (archbishop of Cambrai) and a figure at court (tutor of the duc de Bourgogne, Louis' grandson): like the more orthodox Bossuet he was an accomplished writer. By sharp contrast with the famous court preacher, the writer of *Télémaque* was destined to be most famous as a subversive (in Louis' eyes), the supporter of the unorthodox mystic Mme Guyon, and critic of the king's policies. He ended his days in disfavour and exile from the court. For Sales and Bossuet, see pp. 325, n. 15 and 346–7, n. 9.

4 It was about 1630 that Ventadour, then *lieutenant-général* in Languedoc, decided to devote the rest of his life to his movement for Catholic action. By the time of the Fronde there were over fifty branches of the *Compagnie.*

5 Saint Teresa of Avila (1516–82) took her religious exercises to an extraordinary degree of asceticism, wrote much about her own experiences to inspire others, notably *The Way of Perfection*, and influenced numerous devotees of her mystical approach to God. By her death there were sixteen Spanish houses of her reformed Carmelite order. The first Carmelite convent in France was founded, under the auspices of Bérulle and Mme Acarie, in 1603.

6 The idea of the *hôpital*, a place where the aged, crippled, destitute and orphaned could find voluntary refuge, was taken over by the state in a way that reflected Colbert's utilitarian approach to social problems: in 1662, by royal edict, the institution was merged with older places of refuge and care to become part of a chain covering eventually the whole of France with some two thousand houses. For all the limitations and the inevitable dilution of the original Christian purpose of the founder, the *hôpitaux* represent the most impressive effort in pre-revolutionary Europe, far-ahead of provision in England, for example, to deal with the many-sided problems of destitution and disease.

7 See pp. 342–3, n. 1 for political aspects of the League.

8 *Tartuffe* a play about a religious confidence man, was censored, at the instigation of the *Compagnie*, in 1664.

9 The term *honnête homme* is almost impossible to define since, as used in the seventeenth century, it took its tone from the values of the writer or his particular circle. Retz, for example, would use it subjectively: so differently, and with quite different objectives, would Richelieu. The main virtue of the *honnête homme*, 'in a sense the only virtue' writes Adam, was urbanity. 'He might be seen to have a sensitive awareness of the requirements of good manners which caused him to shun extremes and cultivate the middle path. His rule was easy and unconstrained dignity. Honesty he prized to such an extent that he could see no difference between a good man and an *honnête homme*.' Antoine Adam has written widely about French literature and culture. His *Grandeur and Illusion: French Literature and Society (1600–1715)*, trans. H. Tint (1972), makes him accessible to English-speaking readers.

10 For Rousse in the context of the *Fronde*, see p. 207–08.

11 It is hard to say whether it was Saint-Cyran's religious extremism, the dangers of the spread of heresy ('If only Luther had been locked up at the outset it would have saved a lot of trouble'), the potentially dangerous links with *parlementaires* or the known relationship with the Spanish apologist Jansen, that most worried Richelieu. Together they amounted to a more than sufficient reason for taking action.

12 Jean-Jacques Olier (1608–57) figures largely in the work of H. Daniel Rops. *The Church in the Seventeenth Century*, trans. H. J. Buckingham (1963). 'History may declare that among the architects of clerical reform produced in the seventeenth century he stands out as the most thorough and most effective.'

13 Justly famous for his missionary work in Normandy.

14 For the council of Trent and its decrees, see also p. 316–17, n. 12.

15 For these towering figures see pp. 346, n. 6 and 367, n. 2 respectively.

16 It is clear from the evidence of the *carnets* that Mazarin was much exercised by the knowledge that Monsieur Vincent, representing the *dévôts*, but with the authority too of his reputation for disinterested saintliness, was urging his dismissal. With as much courage as naivete, Vincent would later write to Mazarin urging him to resign. Months later, in September 1652, he was writing 'Mazarin's only ambition is for the good of the king, the queen and the state': a significant change of mind.

17 For the Jesuits, see also pp. 5–6.

18 For Louis IX, see p. 326, n. 1.

19 'For Monsieur Vincent' and the *Filles de Charité* during the Fronde, see pp. 228 and 290.

20 The uncle of Paul de Gondi, for whom, and for the links, through him, between the Fronde and the *dévôts*, see p. 128.

21 Jeanne de Chantal was founder-member and chief inspiration, under the direction of Sales, of the order of the Visitandines (formed 1607–10). In her words, they were to be 'daughters of prayer'.

22 It was only with the regency that the council, previously summoned *ad hoc* when Louis XIII wanted advice about appointments, began to meet regularly. Although the council was dominated by his clerical opponents Mazarin benefited from the opportunity to display his credentials as Cardinal, his concern for sound appointments – all under the protection of the queen.

34 THE CHALLENGE OF PORT ROYAL

1 The move from the site in the damp valley of the Chevreuse, south of Versailles was made in 1625–6. In 1638 the deserted buildings were taken over by a group of male solitaries. They in turn moved out to the Grange on the hillside when a group of the nuns returned to their former house in 1648. For Saint-Cyran and Jansen, see p. 330, n. 31.

2 Jansenists had some of the highest contacts; they also had one of France's greatest painters. Famed for his natural and life-like portraits, that of Richelieu being among the most notable, Champaigne was involved from 1643 with Jansenism. Its influence was reflected in a new austerity of style. His portraits of prominent nuns show a typically sensitive response to his sitters. One of the most striking, *Ex Voto* (1662), depicts the miraculous cure of his daughter, then a nun at Port Royal.

3 Competing aims, notably concerning education, and concern about theological positions account for this rivalry which prefigured (and influenced) the more serious and harmful conflict between the Jansenists and Jesuits.

4 Robert Arnauld d'Andilly, oldest of Marc-Antoine Arnauld's ten surviving children (of twenty) had been the first to forge links with Saint-Cyran, in the 1620s. Intense, scrupulous, introspective, he retired to be one of the early solitaries in 1646 but maintained his contacts with *parlementaires* and, after 1648, some of the *frondeurs*. He was the author of two of the more high-minded *Mazarinades*. His son, Simon, marquis de Pomponne (1618–99) was destined for a great career, as Louis's foreign minister (1671–9). Besides his desire to show Jansenism in the best possible light, concern for the career of his brilliant son seems to have been one of Arnauld d'Andilly's motives behind his efforts to convert Mazarin to a favourable view of Port Royal.

5 Antoine Arnauld (1612–94) won admirers for his intelligence, probity and loyalty. Brémond, generally sympathetic to Jansenism, is one of them. R. A. Knox, in *Enthusiasm* (1950), though not uncritical of the Jesuits, sees in him the least attractive of Jansenist traits, the spirit of party, with secretive ways and insufficient charity.

6 Edmond Richer, then head of the Theological Faculty at the Sorbonne, had published a treatise (1611) in which he asserted the supreme importance of bishops: 'an essential part of the Church of which the Pope is an accessory'. This was too extreme for most – though he had a following in Paris among the more radical *curés*.

7 Notably by Richard Golden, *The Godly Rebellion: Parisian Curés and the Religious Fronde, 1652–1662* (1981).

8 Of Pierre Nicole (1625–95) and his followers Mme de Sévigné wrote: 'Never has the human heart been anatomised more thoroughly than by these gentlemen'. The *petites écoles* were less formal, and, as the name suggests, less ambitious than the Jesuit schools. Started with the prime aim of forming character they appealed mainly to Jansenist sympathisers. Nevertheless the Jesuits did their best to discredit them.

9 Pierre de Marca (1594–1662) had been commissioned by Richelieu to produce a report on relations between Rome and the Church in France. In *De Concordia Sacerdotii et Imperii* he had responded with a moderate but clear Gallican case. He stated that 'an ecclesiastical law does not become final and binding until it has received the consent of the nation [that is government]'. His book was placed on the Index. He submitted, and was rewarded with promotion: eventually he was to become archbishop of Paris. While his work continued to furnish arguments for opponents of Rome, he was now striving to establish credentials as an exponent of orthodoxy. It may be that this was a trimming of sails to respond to the change in the political wind. Mazarin was less sympathetic to Gallicanism (with its *parlementaire* associations) than Richelieu – and more sensitive to the wishes of Rome.

10 For Louis Cognet (see Bibliography), the traditional centres of opposition to royal absolutism, the *robe, parlements*, tended to gravitate towards Jansenism, even more because it was at this moment that the development of the system of *commis* was depriving the *robe* of its *raison d'être*. Judges might have a fellow feeling for Augustinian theologians: both groups looked to a golden past as the panacea for contemporary ills; both valued fidelity to tradition and respect for established rights.

11 Roger du Plessis, duc de Liancourt, had been a marked man before his association with Port Royal. In July 1652 he had received a *lettre de cachet* after giving hospitality to an assembly of noblemen.

12 The *Lettres*, like the *Pensées* (see note 14 below) can be read in the Penguin edition, translated and edited by A. J. Krailsheimer (1967). They were of instant interest to English readers: the first translation appeared in 1657.

13 The term came, to Voltaire and the *philosophes*, to signify a movement with an explicit purpose, to 'enlighten' minds and persuade rulers to promote reforms conceived in the light of reason.

14 The notes which Pascal jotted down in preparation for a reasoned defence of Christian belief. Their unfinished form conveys Pascal's insight into truths about God, man and the universe with a memorable force.

15 The emperor was K'hang-hi, the principal Jesuit Matteo Ricci. Arnauld used the affair to criticise the Jesuits. Now most Christians would praise them for their willingness to take seriously another culture and faith.

16 The *reducciones*, thirty settlements eventually, in the Paraña-Uruguay basin, were the best known of all the missions. The settlements were destined to fall victim to the anti-Jesuit campaign of the 'enlightened' Portuguese minister Pombal (the Jesuits were expelled from Portugal in 1759), to the benefit of some colonists, but a great loss to the native Indians.

17 The few nuns left at Port Royal (nineteen: in 1669 there had been seventy) refused to accept the papal bull *Vineam Domini* (1705), condemning their attitude of 'respectful silence' towards the question of attribution of the Five Propositions. Their two houses were suppressed and they were sent to other houses.

18 Louis' *Mémoires pour l'Instruction du Dauphin,* ed., C. Dreyss, 2 vols (Paris, 1860), are a revealing source for studying his views and priorities. He began with a resumé of the problems that faced him on accession.

19 Hardouin de Péréfixe was appointed master of studies to the young Louis XIV; under Mazarin's direction he coordinated the work of the several tutors (see p. 304–05). In 1664 he became archbishop of Paris.

20 Pope Clement IX contented himself with ambiguous statements of obedience from the Jansenists in order to put an end – a temporary one it was to prove – to the quarrel over the Five Propositions.

35 THE LAST YEAR

1 Mme de Beauvais was one of Anne's most trusted ladies-in-waiting. Among her unauthorised services, if contemporary reports are to be credited, was that of providing Louis XIV, then aged sixteen, with his first sexual experience.

2 Mme de la Fayette frequented salons, wrote novels (notably *La Princesse de Clèves,* 1667) and presented to an appreciative readership portraits and stories, historical and fictitious, of rare subtlety and the kind of insight associated with her friend Mme de Sévigné.

3 The traditional view concerning Louis XIV's enlargement of the original hunting seat at Versailles to house both his court and his government is that he was determined, after his experiences during the Fronde, to get away from Paris. Bluche stresses however the positive reasons for his decision: his love of fresh air, space and the pleasures of the countryside, especially the hunting and gardening which took him often to Saint-Germain while Versailles was being planned and built. It should be added that he had a horror of crowds; also that his reign saw royal sponsorship of building in the capital on a huge scale: the *Hôpital-Général,* the Invalides, the Gobelins, the enlarged Louvre, for example.

4 Mazarin cuts a poor figure in the dialogue that Fénelon imagined his having with Richelieu in his celebrated *Dialogues des Morts* (published at different times from 1700). The gist of the case against him, as it emerges in Richelieu's charges and Mazarin's own defence, was that the latter achieved his goals by stealth and subterfuge, that his chief aim was the abasement of the nobility, and his chosen instruments were the mean and mercenary. It is interesting mainly as an expression of the mood of the *fin de siècle,* of disillusion with militarist and mercantilist policies. As such it says more about Fénelon, the *dévot* and nobleman, naturally sympathetic to Mazarin's opponents, than it does about Mazarin. It helped however to strengthen 'the black legend' which has influenced views of Mazarin to this day.

5 For la Porte's attitude towards Mazarin, see also p. 183.

6 If this book were to be read to the accompaniment of the Baroque music of

the time, from that of Monteverdi to Rossi (see p. 326, n. 19), it might be beguiling, even distracting – but hardly inappropriate: Mazarin loved music, like Louis XIV, who followed him in this as in so much else; at work, or in rare moments of leisure, he was never far, if he could help it, from its soothing strains.

36 A CHRISTIAN DEATH

1 On the eve of the royal wedding, Anne found him on his couch. He bared his discoloured legs. 'See madame, these limbs have lost their peace in giving it to France'. For this and other episodes in Mazarin's last year, Loménie de Brienne, the attentive, increasingly compassionate secretary, is a prime source. For his position, see p. 354, n. 10.

2 As late as August 1660 he was writing to Gramont of 'his great longing to get better', and hopeful, despite being 'bled six times, purged fourteen or so times and given an infinite number of remedies', that 'your conversation will complete my recovery'.

3 Motteville would also note how calm, apparently unmoved Anne was in the days after Mazarin's death. That need not surprise us. Used to presenting a calm front, consoled by her faith, satisfied by the political outcome, Anne may also have felt relieved that so much suffering was over. 'She trusted that God would be merciful.'

4 As typically in the *Mémoires*: 'It is important that kings have long arms, but it is important that they also have foresight, and that they become aware of things long before they happen'.

5 Bissaro of the Theatine order introduced into France and specially favoured by Mazarin, had been his confessor since 1651. He wrote a secret account of the Cardinal's end.

6 According to Bissaro, Mazarin recommended to Louis M. Le Tellier, as having a perfect knowledge of domestic affairs, M. de Lionne the same for foreign affairs and M. Fouquet as having the greatest understanding and resources for the finances.

7 For pithiness and punch-lines the following may be chosen:

> *Ci-gît l'Eminence deuxième.*
> *Dieu nous gard' de la troisième.*

and

> *Enfin le cardinal a terminé son sort.*
> *Français, que dirons nous de ce grand personnage?*
> *Il a fait la paix, il est mort,*
> *Il ne pouvait pour nous rien faire davantage.*

8 Notably after the Revolution, when the building became the College of Unity (1791) and the seat of the Committee of Public Safety (1793) before being allotted to the Institute, established in 1801 in place of the five academies suppressed in 1793. The Chapel became a session chamber for the Académie française. The tomb of Mazarin, the work of Coysevox, Le Hongre and Tubi, completed in 1689, is now in the Louvre.

BIBLIOGRAPHICAL NOTE

Compiling this list, I have several kinds of reader in mind. One may wish to know my sources; another may seek guidance before embarking on his own, perhaps specialised study; another, student or general reader, may want to follow up a particular line of enquiry: details of government, for example, or an individual career. Where an English translation exists I have given it preference over the French original. Where an earlier work has been largely supplanted I may have omitted it – though not without respect for what was valuable in its day. The study of France during Mazarin's ministry – as indeed the whole century – has been enormously enriched during the last thirty years by the work of scholars on both sides of the Atlantic. I can hardly do justice to them. I can only acknowledge with gratitude research that has made my work possible.

What has always been available to Mazarin's biographer has been a large corpus of contemporary memoirs. Seventeenth-century journals are deliberately similar to historical narratives. They tend to describe the public lives of men or women who appear to have little or no private life, who write as observers of their own careers, or that of someone they have served as companion and confidant. Almost invariably the authors lack awareness of the inner self – or are reluctant to share it. Henri de Campion (see p. 337) is a rare exception when he confesses his feelings for his little daughter who filled his memory with 'her luminous and sorrowful presence'.

Some of the *mémoires* are printed in the collective work, Michaud et Poujoulat, *Nouvelle collection de Mémoires pour servir à l'histoire de France*, 2nd, 3rd series (Paris, 1838–9): among them I have drawn particularly on the *mémoires* of H. A. Loménie de Brienne, C. Joly, G. Joly, P. Lenet, P. La Porte, the marquis de Montglat, the duchesse de Montpensier, Mme de Motteville (for appraisal see p. 335, n. 13), the duchesse de Nemours, the duc de la Rochefoucauld, Omer Talon and the vicomte de Turenne. Other important *mémoires* include those of N. Goulas, ed. C. Constant, 3 vols (Paris, 1879–82); M. Molé (ed.) A. Champollion-Figeac, 4 vols (Paris, 1855–7). In a category of their own, the *mémoires* of Louis XIV, are available in an English translation P. Sonnino (ed.) (New York, 1970). In the attractive series, 'Le Temps retrouvé' (Mercure de France), are those of Marie and Hortense Mancini, G. Doscot (ed.) (Paris, 1965) and Henri de Campion, M. Fumaroli (ed.) (Paris, 1967). Similar in style, though entitled '*journal*' are those of O. L. d'Ormesson, P. A. Chéruel (ed.) 2 vols (Paris, 1860–1); J. Vallier, Vaissière de Courteault (ed.), 4 vols (Paris, 1902–18), and, providing a foreign view, Abraham de Wicquefort, *Chronique discontinue de la Fronde*, R. Mandrou (ed), Paris, 1978). *Sui generis*, commanding a place in the literary history of the time, are the *Mémoires* of Cardinal de Retz (see also p. 343, n. 9: M. Allen and E. Thomas (eds) (Paris,

1956). Entertaining and affording glimpses into the gossip-world, and therefore into the *mentalité* of *frondeurs*, are the *Historiettes* of Tallemant des Réaux G. Montgrédien (ed.), 8 vols (Paris, 1932–4).

Letters are another important source. Pride of place, among those printed, belongs to the nine volumes, *Lettres du Cardinal Mazarin pendant son ministère* (A. Chéruel (ed.), Paris, 1872–1906). For his relationship with Anne, see *Lettres du Cardinal Mazarin à le reine, à la princesse Palatine, etc., écrits pendant sa retraite hors de France entre 1651 et 1652*, J. A. D. Ravenel (ed.) (Paris, 1836). Relevant to Mazarin's later years are the letters in vol. 1, J.-B. Colbert, *Lettres, instructions et mémoires de Colbert*, P. Clément (ed.) Paris, (1861–73). Independent, sometimes caustic views are expressed in Guy Patin, *Lettres du temps de la Fronde*, A. Thérive (ed.) (Paris, 1921); see also his *Lettres à Charles Spon, médecin à Lyon*, J. H. Réveillé-Parise (ed.), vol. 3 (Paris, 1846). Valuable evidence concerning the condition of France is contained in *Lettres et mémoires addressés au chancelier Séguier, 1633–49*, R. Mousnier (ed.) (Paris, 1934).

The record of secondary works directly concerned with Mazarin's life, is a chequered one (see Preface, pp. xiii–xiv). A massively sound foundation was laid by P. A. Chéruel, *Histoire de France pendant la minorité de Louis XIV*, 4 vols (Paris, 1879). A magnificent work of scholarship, it is still indispensable. For our century, Karl Federn's *Mazarin* (Paris, 1934), trans. from the German of 1922, offered a more accessible account. Recently Mazarin studies have been dominated by two eminent scholars, Madeleine Laurain-Portemer, author of invaluable articles, and Georges Dethan, Chéruel's great-nephew: to both, my debt is immense. For the Italian dimension and for Mazarin's personal relationships, Dethan's *Mazarin et ses amis*, trans. S. Baron (Paris, 1968), *The Young Mazarin* (London, 1977) is invaluable; his attractive and compelling *Mazarin, un homme de paix à l'age baroque, 1602–61* (Paris, 1981), grew out of the earlier study: the emphasis is still however on relationships rather than on institutions and policies. P. Goubert's *Mazarin* (Paris, 1990), brings his deep knowledge of French society to enrich a compelling narrative: by contrast, that of P. Guth, *Mazarin* (Paris, 1972), though ample, verges at times on caricature.

Certain biographies of leading contemporaries of Mazarin deserve prominent mention. M. Carmona, *Richelieu: ambition et pouvoir* (Paris, 1983), is the best of French biographies of Mazarin's mentor; R. J. Knecht, *Richelieu* (London, 1991), concise but comprehensive, is the most recent of English studies. A. Lloyd Moote's *Louis XIII, the Just* (California, 1989) does full justice to that under-appreciated sovereign. Claude Dulong, *Anne d'Autriche* (Paris, 1980) established her as an important figure in her own right. Ruth Kleinman, *Anne of Austria* (Ohio, 1985), is a convincing study, sympathetic but judicious. G. Dethan, *La vie de Gaston d'Orléans* (Paris, 1992) and Simone Bertière, *La vie du Cardinal de Retz* (Paris, 1990), present balanced accounts of those flawed but important characters: the latter does not replace J. Salmon, *Cardinal de Retz* (London, 1969). The student of Condé still needs to go back to the duc d'Aumâle, *Histoire des princes de Condé pendant les XIVe et XVIIe siècles* vol. 5, (Paris, 1885). More recent, and slight, is G. Montgrédien, *Le grand Condé* (Paris, 1959). J. Béranger, *Turenne* (Paris, 1987), does justice to the general and the man. L. André, *Michel le Tellier et Louvois* (Paris, 1942), provides the best account of Mazarin's loyal *créature* and war minister. D. Dessert, *Fouquet* (Paris, 1987), brings unrivalled knowledge of the financial system to an evaluation of the minister. J. Meyer, *Colbert* (Paris, 1982), is solidly convincing. Two royal lives, J. B. Wolf, *Louis XIV* (New York, 1968) and François Bluche, *Louis XIV* (London, 1990), trans. Greengrass from the original *Louis XIV* (Paris, 1984), provide much detail about the king's youth and Mazarin's influence, on which the main authority remains G. Lacour-Gayet, *L'éducation politique de Louis Quatorze* (Paris, 1898).

Certain books may be singled out as contributing much towards understanding government and society in Mazarin's France. Articles on the constitution, *la patrie*, taxation and Gallicanism figure in *Comment les français voyaient la France au XVIIe siècle*, by Mousnier, Tapié, Meuvret and Martimort respectively, in a special number of *XVIIe siècle* (Paris, 1955): the names inspire confidence. For a succinct introduction to French history in this period, turn to R. Briggs, *Early Modern France, 1560–1715* (Oxford, 1987); for a more detailed account of the century, G. R. R. Treasure, *Seventeenth Century France*, 2nd edn (London, 1981); for a general view of society, P. Goubert, *Ancien Régime* (Paris, 1969, 1973); 2 vols; vol. 1 trans. A. Cox (London, 1973); for a comprehensive study of social mores, R. Mandrou, *Introduction to Modern France, 1500–1640*, trans. R. E. Hallmark, (London, 1975); the original, 1961, is significantly subtitled *essai de psychologie historique*. For a uniquely rich, at times eccentrically wide-ranging survey of France, with a geographer's perspectives, F. Braudel, *The Identity of France*, vol. 1 (1988) and vol. 2 (London, 1990), both trans. Sian Reynolds, from the original *L'Identité de France* (Paris, 1986). For government during the period of the cardinals first see David Parker, *The Making of French Absolutism* (London, 1983); for a well-documented view of institutional change and the role of the ministers, councils and intendants under the cardinals, R. J. Bonney, *Political Change under Richelieu and Mazarin, 1624–61* (Oxford, 1978); also his *Society and Government in France under Richelieu and Mazarin, 1624–61* (London, 1988), document-based, as is J. H. Shennan, *Government and Society in France, 1461–61* (London, 1961); for a convincing view of the far from absolute nature of 'absolute' royal government, the first half of Roger Mettam's *Power and Faction in Louis XIV's France* (Oxford, Blackwell, 1988); for what constituted 'the crisis' of the title, the editor's excellent introduction to the collection of articles in P. G. Coveney (ed.) *France in Crisis, 1620–75* (London, 1975); see also, Mousnier etc., in Articles section; for mechanisms and *mentalités*, R. F. Harding, *Anatomy of a Power Elite: the Provincial Governors of Early Modern France* (New Haven, 1978); J. P. Labatut, *Noblesse, pouvoir et société en France au XVIIe siècle* (Limoges, 1987): collected articles by a leading authority. For the context in which government was practised (networks of relationships where Mazarin proved a quick learner and adroit practitioner), following her seminal *Judicial Politics and Urban Revolt in Seventeenth Century France: the Parlement of Aix, 1629–59* (Princeton, 1978), Sharon Kettering, *Patrons, Brokers and Clients in Seventeenth Century France* (New York, 1986); for Mazarin's apprenticeship in politics, M. Laurain-Portemer, 'Monarchie et gouvernement: Mazarin et le modèle romaine' in *La France et l'Italie au temps de Mazarin* (Grenoble, 1986). For the heart of society and crucible of politics, Paris, see Orest Ranum, *Paris in the Age of Absolutism* (New York, 1968) and R. Mousnier, *Paris capitale au temps de Richelieu et Mazarin* (Paris, 1978). For financial aspects of the mid-century crisis, Julian Dent, *Crisis in Finance: Crown, Financiers and Society in Seventeenth Century France* (Newton Abbot, 1973); also J. B. Collins, *Fiscal Limits of Absolutism: Direct Taxation in Early Seventeenth Century France* (Berkeley, 1988). For the provinces, from a large field, W. Beik, *Absolutism and Society in Seventeenth Century France: state power and provincial aristocracy in Languedoc* (Cambridge, 1985); older, but a masterpiece, G. Roupnel, *La ville et la campagne au XVIIe siècle: étude sur les populations du pays Dijonnais* (Paris, 1922). For women in this century, Wendy Gibson, *Women in Seventeenth Century France* (London, 1989). For 'the condition of the people question' and for popular risings, (again, works are numerous, the choice difficult) Y. M. Bercé, *History of Peasant Revolts*, trans. A. Whitmore (New York, 1990), from

Histoire des Croquants (Paris, 1986), itself a condensation of the original 2 vol. work (Geneva, 1974).

Students of the Fronde long had to rely on the extended essay on constitutional aspects of P. R. Doolin, *The Fronde* (Harvard, 1935) and E. H. Kossman, *La Fronde* (Leiden, 1954). They are still valuable. P. G. Lorris, *La Fronde* (Paris, 1961) offered a brisk narrative. Lloyd Moote, *The Revolt of the Judges: the Parlement of Paris and the Fronde, 1647–52* (Princeton, 1971), broke new ground in a fine book which provides ample documentation for the view that the concerns of the magistrates should be taken seriously, that their resistance was significant for the future of a monarchy which needed to think more of cooperation than of coercion. Orest Ranum, *The Fronde, a French Revolution* (New York, 1993), provides a rich, stimulating account: Paris-orientated, though with a good treatment of Bordeaux, it neglects Normandy, for example and, more seriously, religious and constitutional aspects. A lucid synthesis, with a résumé of different viewpoints, is provided by H. Méthivier, *La Fronde* (Paris, 1984). For noble attitudes, see Arlette Jouanna, *Le devoir de révolte: la noblesse française et la gestation de l'état moderne, 1559–1661* (Paris, 1989). The most important provincial *fronde*, in Anjou, is dealt with in C. Tilly's wide-ranging *The Contentious French* (Harvard, 1986). Other important aspects of the Fronde are covered by references, for example, to the work of Golden and Hamscher, in my general list, and to Bonney, Mousnier, *et al.*, among the articles. There is an invaluable collective work, arising out of a conference, *La Fronde en questions* (Marseille, 1989), with contributions from nearly all leading specialists in the field. Finally, however Mazarin might have wished it otherwise, the *Mazarinades* come into the picture. Many have been brought together and analysed in H. Carrier, *Les Mazarinades* 2 vols (Geneva, 1992); see also M. N. Grand-Mesnil, *Mazarin, la Fronde et la presse* (Paris, 1967) and Christian Jouhaud, *La Fronde des mots* (Paris, 1985).

The study of propaganda leads the reader to the cultural milieu where there is again a wide choice. For Baroque Rome and Paris, see V. L. Tapié, *The Age of Grandeur* (London, 1960), trans. from *Baroque et classicisme* (Paris, 1957); for Catholicism, J. Delumeau, *Le catholicisme entre Luther et Voltaire* (Paris, 1971); also L. Châtellier, *The Europe of the Devout: the Catholic Reformation and the Formation of a New Society* (Cambridge, 1989); for controversies, E. Préclin et E. Jarry, *Les luttes politiques et doctrinales aux XVIIe et XVIIIe siècles* (Paris, 1955); for the Huguenots, G. A. Rothrock, *The Huguenots* (Chicago, 1979); for Jansenism, briefly but skilfully synthesised, L. Cognet, *Le Jansénisme* (Paris, 1961); more particularly, P. Jansen, *Le cardinal Mazarin et le mouvement janséniste* (Paris, 1967); for the world of ideas, A. Adam, *Grandeur and Illusion: French Literature and Society, 1600–1715*, trans. H. Tint (London, 1974); E. J. Kearns, *Ideas in Seventeenth Century France* (Manchester, 1979); R. Briggs, *Communities of Belief: Cultural and Social Tensions in Early Modern France* (Oxford, 1989); for popular culture, though specifically relating to the sixteenth century, Natalie Zemon Davies, *Society and Culture in Early Modern France* (Stanford, 1965); for musical aspects, D. Launay, *Fanfares, ballets et chansons; la musique dans le temps de la Fronde* (Paris, 1986). For books and Mazarin's library, J. A. Clarke, *Gabriel Naudé, 1600–53* (Connecticut, 1970).

SELECT BIBLIOGRAPHY

BOOKS

The following list includes other books which have proved useful for particular aspects: works on other states and statesmen of Mazarin's day, some others of general interest, some offering material of the highly specialised kind upon which other historians gratefully feed.

M. Baulant et J. Meuvret, *Prix des céreales extraits de la Mercuriale de Paris, 1520–1698*, 2 vols (Paris, 1962).

D. C. Baxter, *Servants of the Sword: French Intendants of the Army 1630–1670* (Urbana, 1976).

F. Bayard, *Le monde des financiers au XVIIe siècle* (Paris, 1988).

Y.-M. Bercé, *Fête et révolte: des mentalités populaires en France du XVIIe au XVIII siècle* (Paris, 1976).

J. A. Bergin, *Cardinal de la Rochefoucauld* (Yale, 1987).

J. A. Bergin and L. W. B. Brockliss, eds, *Richelieu and his Age* (Oxford, 1992).

D. Bitton, *The French Nobility in Crisis, 1560–1640* (Stanford, 1969).

J. M. G. Blakiston, *Reminiscing in the Seventeenth Century* (Winchester, 1985).

P. Blet, *Le clergé de France et la monarchie, étude sur les assemblées générales du Clergé entre 1615 et 1666*, 2 vols (Rome, 1659).

R. Bonney, *The King's Debts: Finance and Politics in France, 1589–1661* (Oxford, 1981) (see also his important article in *Richelieu and his Age, op. cit.*).

——, *The European Dynastic States, 1494–1660* (Oxford, 1991).

J. F. Bosher, ed., *French Government and Society 1500–1850* (London, 1973) with the editor's important essay, 'Chambres de Justice'.

L. W. B. Brockliss, *French Higher Education in the Seventeenth and Eighteenth Centuries: a Cultural History* (Oxford, 1987).

J.-P. Charmeil, *Les Trésoriers de France à l'époque de la Fronde* (Paris, 1964).

P. Chaunu, *La Civilisation de l'Europe classique* (Paris, 1960).

W. F. Church, *Constitutional Thought in Sixteenth-Century France* (New York, 1941).

C. M. Cipolla, ed., *The Fontana Economic History of Europe*, vol. 1 (London, 1974).

G. N. Clark, *The Seventeenth Century*, 2nd edn (Oxford, 1947).

——, *War and Society in the 17th Century* (Cambridge, 1958).

J.-M. Constant, *Les conjurateurs: le premier libéralisme politique sous Richelieu* (Paris, 1987).

J. P Cooper, ed., *The Decline of Spain and the Thirty Years War, 1609–48/59* (Cambridge, 1970).

A. Corvisier, *Armée et societé en Europe de 1494 à 1789* (Paris, 1976).

V. Cousin, *La jeunesse de Mazarin* (Paris 1865): a good source for the diplomatic history of the years 1629–31.

G. Couton, *Corneille et la fronde* (Paris, 1951).

E. Daniel-Rops, *L'Eglise des Temps Classiques* (Paris, 1958).

P. Deyon, *Etudes sur la société urbaine au XVIIe siècle: Amiens, capitale provinciale* (Paris, 1967).

A. G. Dickens, ed., *The Courts of Europe: Politics, Patronage and Royalty, 1400–1800* (London, 1977).

F. Dornic, *Louis Berryer, agent de Mazarin et de Colbert* (Caen, 1968).

G. Duby, *Histoire de la France rurale*, vol. 2 (Paris, 1975).

J. H. Elliott, *The Revolt of the Catalans* (Cambridge, 1963).

——, *The Count-duke Olivarez. Statesman in an Age of Decline* (Yale, 1986).

——, *Richelieu and Olivarez* (Cambridge, 1984).

A. Feillet, *La misère au temps de la Fronde et Vincent de Paul* (Paris, 1862).

M. Foisil, *La révolte des Nu-pieds et les révoltes normandes de 1639* (Paris, 1970).

R. Forster and Jack Green, eds, *Preconditions of Revolution in Early Modern Europe* (Baltimore, 1970).

F. Freudmann, *L'Etonnant Gourville (1625–1703)* (Paris, 1960).

M. Fumaroli, *L'Age d'eloquence* (Geneva, 1980).

P. Geyl, *The Netherlands in the Seventeenth Century*, 2 vols (London, 1961, 1963).

R. Golden, *The Godly Rebellion: Parisian curés and the Religious Fronde, 1652–62* (North Carolina, 1981).

G. P. Gooch, *Courts and Cabinets* (London, 1944): essays on Mme de Motteville, Anne of Austria and la Grande Mademoiselle.

P. Goubert, *The French Peasantry in the Seventeenth Century*, trans. I. Patterson (London, 1986).

A. Hamscher, *The Parlement of Paris after the Fronde, 1653–73* (Pittsburg, 1973).

S. Hanley, *The 'Lit de Justice' of the Kings of France: Constitutional Ideology in Legend—Ritual and Discourse* (Princeton, 1983).

E. Harth, *Ideology and Culture in Seventeenth Century France* (Ithaca, 1983).

R. Hatton, ed., *Louis XIV and Absolutism* (London, 1976).

H. Hauser, *La Prépondérance espagnole, 1559–1660* (Paris, 1934).

H. B. Hill ed., and trans., *The Political Testament of Cardinal Richelieu* (Madison, 1965).

M. P. Holt, ed., *Society and Institutions in Early Modern France* (Georgia, 1971).

J. Jacquart, *La crise rurale en Ile de France 1550–1670* (Paris, 1974).

R. F. Kierstead, ed., *State and Society in Seventeenth Century France* (New York, 1975). Note P. Deyon's important essay, 'Relations between the French Nobility and the Absolute Monarchy during the first half of the Seventeenth Century'.

P. Knachel, *England and the Fronde: The Impact of the English Civil War and Revolution in France* (Cornell, 1967).

C. Korr, *Cromwell and the New Model Foreign Policy: England's Policy Towards France* (Berkeley, 1975).

J. P. Labatut, *Les ducs et pairs de France au XVIIe siècle* (Paris, 1972).

E. le R. Ladurie, *The French Peasantry 1450–1660* (Aldershot, 1987).

M. Laurain-Portemer and R. A. Weigert, eds, *Mazarin, homme d'état et collectionneur* (Paris, 1961): exhibition catalogue of exceptional quality.

E. G. Léonard, *Le Protestant français* (Paris, 1955).

G. Livet, *L'Intendance d'Alsace sous Louis XIV, 1648–1715* (Paris, 1956).

P. Logie, *La Fronde en Normandie*, 3 vols (Paris, 1951–2).

A. D. Lublinskaya, *French Absolutism* (Cambridge, 1968).

J. Lynch, *Spain under the Habsburgs*, vol. 2: *Spain and America 1598–1700* (London, 1969).

J. R. Major, *Representative Government in Early Modern France* (Yale, 1980).

M. Marion, *Dictionnaire des institutions de la France aux XVIIe et XVIIIe siècles* 2nd edn (Paris, 1968).

J. Meuvret, *Le problème des subsistances à l'époque Louis XIV,* 3 vols (Paris, 1977).

John Miller, ed., *Absolutism in Seventeenth Century Europe* (London, 1990).

G. Montgrédien, ed., *Mazarin*, 'Génies et Réalités' series (Paris, 1959).

Mark Motley, *Becoming a French Aristocrat: the Education of the Court, 1580–1715* (Princeton, 1990).

R. Mousnier, *La vénalité des offices sous Henri IV et Louis XIII*, 2nd edn (Paris, 1971).

——, *La plume, la faucille et le marteau* (Paris, 1970) – collected essays.

——, *The Institutions of France under the Absolute Monarchy* (Chicago, 1979), trans. from vol. 1 of the original, 1974.

G. Pagés, *The Thirty Years War,* trans. D. Maland and J. Hooper from the original (Paris, 1939, London, 1970).

Geoffrey Parker, *The Thirty Years War* (London, 1985).

——, *The Army of Flanders and the Spanish Road, 1567–1659* (Cambridge, 1972).

R. Pillorget, *Les mouvements insurrectionales de Provence entre 1596 et 1715* (Paris, 1975).

R. Pintard, *Le libertinage érudit dans la première moitié du XVIIe siècle* (Paris, 1983).

B. Porchnev, *Les soulèvements populaires en France de 1623 à 1648* (Paris, 1963).

M. Prestwich, ed., *International Calvinism, 1514–1715* (Oxford, 1985): see E. Labrousse, 'Calvinism in France 1568–1695'.

O. Ranum, *Richelieu and the Councillors of Louis XIII* (Oxford, 1963).

——, *Artisans of Glory: Writers and Historical Thought in Seventeenth Century France* (North Carolina, 1980).

E. M. Rich, C. H. Wilson, eds, *The Cambridge Economic History of Europe*, vol. IV (Cambridge, 1967).

H. J. Rowen, *The King's State* (New Jersey, 1980).

J. C. Rule, ed., *Louis XIV and the Craft of Kingship* (Ohio, 1969).

V. Sackville-West, *Daughter of France: La Grande Mademoiselle* (London, 1959).

J. Sawyer, *Printed Poison: Pamphlet Propaganda, Faction Politics and the Public Sphere in Early Seventeenth Century France* (Los Angeles, 1991).

I. Scoloudi, ed., *The Huguenots in Britain and their French Background* (London, 1987): particularly for the essay by Menna Prestwich, 'The Huguenots under Richelieu and Mazarin, 1629–61. A golden age?'

J. H. Shennan, *The Parlement of Paris* (London, 1968).

Y. Singer Lecoq, *Le tribu Mazarin* (Paris, 1989).

H. M. Solomon, *Public Welfare, Science and Propaganda in Seventeenth Century France: the Innovations of Théophraste Renaudot* (Princeton, 1972).

R. A. Stradling, *Philip IV and the Government of Spain, 1621–65* (London, 1988).

——, *Europe and the Decline of Spain, 1580–1720* (London, 1981).

D. J. Sturdy, *The d'Aligres de la Rivière: Servants of the Bourbon State in the Seventeenth Century* (London, 1986).

A. Talon, *La Compagnie du Saint-Sacrement (1629–67): Spiritualité et Société* (Paris, 1990).

G. R. R. Treasure, *Richelieu* (London, 1972).

J. Villain, *Mazarin, homme d'argent* (Paris, 1956).

D. A. Watts, *Cardinal de Retz: Ambiguities of a Seventeenth-century Mind* (Oxford, 1980).

J. B. Wood, *The Nobility of the Election of Bayeux, 1463–1666: Continuity through Change* (Princeton, 1980).

P. Zagorin, *Rebels and Rulers, 1500–1660* (London, 1982).

G. Zeller, *Aspects de la politique française sous l'ancien régime* (Paris, 1964).

ARTICLES

The following are especially interesting and relevant.

B. Barbiche, 'La hiérarchie des dignités et des charges', *XVIIe siècle* 157 (1987), pp 359–70.

F. Bayard, 'Les financiers et la Fronde', *XVIIe siècle* 145 (1984), pp 255–62.

W. Beik, 'Urban factions and the Social order during the Minority of Louis XIV', *French Historical Studies* 15 (1987), pp 36–37.

J. Bergin, 'Cardinal Mazarin and his benefices', *French History* 1 (1987), pp 3–26.

P. Blet, 'Richelieu et les débuts de Mazarin', *Revue d'Histoire moderne et contemporaine* 6 (1959), pp 241–68.

R. Bonney, 'The French Civil War, 1649–53', *European Studies Review* 8 (1978), pp 71–100.

——, 'Cardinal Mazarin and the Great Nobility during the Fronde', *English Historical Review* 96 (1981), pp 818–33.

——, 'La fronde des officiers', *XVIIe siècle* 145 (1984), pp 323–39.

J. Bosher, 'Chambres de Justice in the French Monarchy', *French Government and Society, 1500–1800*, ed. J. Bosher (London, 1973), pp 19–40.

H. Carrier, 'Mécénat et politique: l'action de Mazarin jugé par les pamphleteers de la Fronde', in *L'age d'or du mécénat*, ed. R. Mousnier (Paris, 1985).

P. A. Chéruel, 'Les Carnets de Mazarin pendant la Fronde, Sept–Oct 1648', *Revue historique*, 20 (1887), pp 103–38.

J. Collins, 'Sur l'histoire fiscale du XVIIe siècle', *Annales* 34 (1979), pp 325–47.

J.-M. Constant, 'La troisième Fronde: les gentilshommes et les libertés nobiliaires', *XVIIe siècle* 145 (1984), pp 341–54.

M. Cubells, 'Le Parlement de Paris pendant la Fronde', *XVIIe siècle* 35 (1957), pp 170–98.

R. Darricault et M. Laurain-Portemer, 'La mort du cardinal Mazarin', *Annuaire bulletin de la Société de l'Histoire de France* (1960), pp 59–120.

R. Descimon and C. Jouhaud, 'La Fronde en mouvement', *XVIIe siècle* 145 (1984), pp 305–22.

R. Descimon et J. Nagle, 'Les barricades de la Fronde parisienne', *Annales* 45 (1990), pp 397–422.

D. Dessert, 'Finances et société au XVIIe siècle: à propos de la chambre de justice de 1661', *Annales* 29 (1974), pp 847–84.

G. Dethan, 'Madame de Motteville et Mazarin, ou le complèxe d'Oenone', Société d'Etude du XVIIe siècle, *Actes et Colloques* 22 (1979), pp 103–10.

——, 'Mazarin avant le ministère', *Revue historique* 227 (1962), pp 33–66.

P. Deyon, 'A propos des rapports entre la noblesse française et la monarchie absolue', *Revue historique* 231 (1964), pp 341–56.

R. Golden, 'The mentality of opposition: the Jansenism of the Parisian Curés during the Religious Fronde', *Catholic Historical Review* 64 (1978), pp 565–80.

P. Grillon, 'Mazarin, un homme de paix à l'age baroque', *Revue Histoire Diplomatique* (1982).

J. Jacquart, 'La Fronde des princes dans la région parisienne et ses conséquences materielles,' *Revue d'Histoire moderne et contemporaine* 7 (1960), pp 257–90.

C. Jones, 'The Organisation of Conspiracy and Revolt in the *Mémoires* of the Cardinal de Retz,' *European Studies Review* 11 (1981), pp 125–50.

C. Jouhaud, 'Ecriture et action du XVIIe siècle: sur un corpus de Mazarinades,' *Annales* 38 (1983), pp 42–64.

S. Kettering, 'Forum: Fidelity and Clientage: patronage and Politics during the Fronde', *French Historical Studies* 14 (1986), pp 409–41.

——, 'Patronage and Kinship in early modern France', *French Historical Studies* 16 (1989).

R. Kleinman, 'Changing Interpretations of the Edict of Nantes: the administrative aspect, 1643–61', *French Historical Studies* 10 (1978), pp 548–71.

——, 'Gratitude Revisited: the Declaration of Saint-Germain, 1652', *French Historical Studies* 5 (1968), pp 249–62.

H. Koetting, 'L'Ormée (1651–3): dynamique sociale dans la Fronde bordelaise', *XVIIe siècle* (1984), pp 377–9.

J. P. Labatut. 'Situation sociale du quartier du Marais pendant la Fronde', *XVIIe siècle* (1958), p 38.

M. Laurain-Portemer, 'Le Statut de Mazarin dans l'église: aperçus sur l'haut clergé dans la contre-réforme', *Bibliothèque de l'Ecole des Chartes* 127 (1969), pp 355–419 and 128 (1970), pp 5–80.

P. Lebvre, 'Aspects de la fidelité en France au XVIIe siècle: le case des agents du prince de Condé', *Revue historique* 201 (1973), pp 59–106.

J. Knecht, 'The Fronde', Historical Association, *Appreciations in History* (1975).

E. W. Marvick, 'Favourites in Early Modern Europe: A Recurring Psychopolitical Role', *Journal of Psychohistory* 10 (1983), pp 463–89.

A. Lloyd Moote, 'The French Crown versus its Judicial and Financial Offices', *Journal of Modern History* 34 (1962), pp 146–60.

——, 'The Parlementary Fronde and Seventeenth Century Robe Solidarity', *French Historical Studies* 2 (1962), pp 330–55.

R. Mousnier, 'Quelques raisons de la Fronde: les causes des journées révolutionnaires parisiennes de 1648', *XVIIe siècle* 2 (1949), pp 33–78.

——, 'Recherches sur les syndicats d'officiers pendant la Fronde', *XVIIe siècle* 42–3 (1959), pp 76–117.

D. Parker, 'Sovereignty, Absolutism and the Function of the Law in Seventeenth Century France', *Past and Present* 122 (1989), pp 36–74.

David Parrot, 'The Causes of the Franco-Spanish War of 1635–59', in J. Black, ed., *The Origins of War in Early Modern Europe* (Edinburgh, 1987).

——, 'Richelieu, les Grands and the Army', in Bergin and Brockliss eds, *Richelieu and His Age, op. cit.*

D. Roche, 'Aperçus sur la fortune et les revenues des princes de Condé à l'aube du XVIIe siècle', *Revue d'histoire moderne et contemporaine* 14 (1967), pp 217–43.

S. Vernes, 'Un Frondeur, le président Viole', *Revue d'histoire diplomatique* 65 (1951), pp 16–38.

INDEX

Abbeville, 73

Absolutism, 6, 47, 51, 73, 74, 88;
French compared to English, 97;
implications of, 352 n. 12; Mazarin
and, 92; and Roman law, 97, 347
n. 19; Séguier and, 88–90; system or
process of, 93 ff., 347 n. 19

Acarie, Mme Barbe Avrilot, mystic, 38,
285, 289; significance of, 329 n. 31

Admiralty, plan, 17, 18

Agen, 75

Aguesseau, Henri François d',
eighteenth-century chancellor, 114,
349 n. 13

Aglié, Philippe d', Savoyard minister,
and Christina of Savoy, 37;
significance of, 329 n. 2

agriculture, in France, 69, 72; see also
war, effects of

aides, 81, 103, 213; see also cour des aides

Aiguillon, Marie-Madeleine de
Vignerot du Pontcourlay, duchesse
d', 53, 56, 130, 179

Aix-en-Provence, 74, 141, 146, 149–50

Alais, Louis-Emmanuel de Valois,
comte d', governor of Provence, 30,
50, 142, 354 n. 16; and Aix, 149–50,
162, 175, 338 n. 23

Alais, or Alés, peace or 'Grace' of, 15,
65, 220, 325 n. 6

Alexander VII, Fabio Chigi, Pope, 207;
and Jansenism, 295, 299, 365 n. 10

Aligre, Etienne d', 89, 343 n. 3

Alsace: constitution of, 245–6; among
'Four Nations', 310; governorship
of 205; and peace of Westphalia, 241,
244, 245–7, 281

Amiens, 34, 47

Amsterdam, and finance, 236, 342 n. 2,
340 n. 21

Amyraut, Moise, Huguenot scholar,
222, 366 n. 13

Angers, 74, 75, 103; in the Fronde, 149,
151, 196

Angoumois, revolt in, 76

Anjou, Philippe duc d' (1660, duc
d'Orléans), married Henrietta
Maria of England, 375 n. 6

Anjou, province of, 196, 220

Annat, père François, Jesuit confessor,
289

Anne of Austria, queen, queen-mother
and regent: character and beliefs,
58, 90, 110, 114, 127, 137, 193, 252;
temper, 110, 112, 117, 127, 133, 177,
226, 288; Louis XIII's wife and
consort, 25, 53–4, 62, 89, 255, 323
n. 18, 344 n. 5; as regent, 58 ff., 66,
67, 103, 105, 109 ff., 117, 122–3,
152, 153, 166, 167–8, 177–8, 186,
188, 226, 302; methods and style of
government of, 110–14, 129–30, 180,
189, 200, 201; in *Mazarinades*,
181–2; and Mazarin, 25, 61, 63, 88,
90–2, 119, 127–8, 129, 154, 159, 166,
174, 176, 177, 180, 181–2, 183, 186,
187, 189–90, 192–3, 195, 199, 202,
255–62, 279, 288, 301–2, 307, 308,
309, 363 n. 14, 383 n. 3; and
Parlement, 110, 112, 113, 114, 117,
133, 158, 168, 178–9, 186, 193–4,
199; and *frondeurs*, 129–30, 137, 139,
142, 177; and Princes, 166, 178–80;
and Mme de Chevreuse, 62, 66,
154; and Louis XIV, 54, 62, 133, 180,
189, 198, 253; and Gondi, 200–1;